UNIVERSALS OF HUMAN LANGUAGE

VOLUME 2

Phonology

Universals of Human Language

Edited by Joseph H. Greenberg

Associate Editors:
Charles A. Ferguson & Edith A. Moravcsik

VOLUME 2

Phonology

Stanford University Press, Stanford, California
1978

173814

Stanford University Press
Stanford, California
©1978 by the Board of Trustees of the
Leland Stanford Junior University
Printed in the United States of America
ISBN 0-8047-0966-1
LC 77-89179

Several of the papers in this volume were published originally in *Working Papers on Language Universals,* published for limited distribution by the Language Universals Project at Stanford University in sixteen numbers, 1970-76, as indicated in the opening footnotes to the individual papers. Most have been modified to some extent for publication here. Number 7 in this volume, by Greenberg, is a slightly revised version of one originally published in Russian in the journal *Voprosy jazykoznanija* (1964, no. 4, pp. 41-65); an English-language version appeared subsequently in *Linguistics* (1965, no. 18, pp. 5-34).

Preface

The mainspring of the contemporary interest in language universals is the conviction that linguistics as a science must develop
broader goals than the description of the structures of the thous-
ands of individual languages which exist in the present or of which
we have records from the past. It must be broader even than a
body of generalizing theory concerning how such descriptions can
be carried out.

Theory of this latter type already existed by the early 1950's,
although many defects have since become apparent. As compared
with other human sciences of the time, it seemed to possess an
evident superiority in methodological sophistication and rigor.
Yet a thoughtful and alert observer could raise fundamental problems not evident to the practical purveyor who took for granted
the tacit premises of his science.

It fell to the lot of one of the present writers, as a participant
in the seminar on psycholinguistics sponsored by the Social Science
Research Council in the summer of 1951 at Bloomington, to give an
exposition of linguistics for the psychologists present. The task
was undertaken with a sense of pride in the accomplishments of
the linguistics of the period. One of the psychologists, Charles
Osgood, was suitably impressed. He commented, however, to
the effect that while linguistics had an admirable and well worked
out method, it was being applied merely to the description of individual languages. Could the linguists present tell him anything
about all languages? That would be of the highest interest to psychologists. To this the linguistics of the period had no real answer.

The stimulating quality of these remarks and of the other discussions that followed bore fruit in the work of the Social Science
Research Council, leading ultimately to the Dobbs Ferry conference on Language Universals in 1961. This meeting played an
essential part in inaugurating a period of renewed interest in this
topic.

While there were several papers at that conference which stated
tentative generalizations of universal scope regarding several
aspects of language, it was realized that to extend such studies
from these modest beginnings was an enormous task requiring
relevant data regarding numerous other aspects of language to be

drawn from adequately large samples of languages. Hence arose
the notion of a research project in which scholars would undertake
concrete research of this sort on a large variety of linguistic
topics.

This took shape at Stanford where the Project on Language
Universals was organized. It began its activities in October 1967
and brought them to an end in August 1976. During its entire nine-
year period it was directed by Charles A. Ferguson and Joseph H.
Greenberg, both professors at Stanford University, as principal
investigators. Its main source of financial support was the National
Science Foundation, which, over the years, contributed slightly
below $1,000,000. In addition to the two principal investigators,
the Project staff included altogether thirty-two part-time or full-
time linguists, some of whom held short-term visiting positions
not spanning more than a few months, while others were with the
Project up to several years. The names of these linguists are as
follows: Rebecca Agheyisi, Alan Bell, D.N.S. Bhat, Jean Braine,
Richard Carter, Eve Clark, Harold Clumeck, John Crothers,
Gilles Delisle, Talmy Givón, Victor Girard, Mary Ellen Greenlee,
Helga Harries-Delisle, Laurence Horn, Charles Jennings, Joan
Kahr, Dorothea Kaschube, Ian Maddieson, James Michael Moore,
Edith Moravcsik, Chris O'Sullivan, Andrew Rindsberg, Merritt
Ruhlen, Gerald Sanders, Philip Sedlak, Susan Steele, Leonard
Talmy, Russell Ultan, Marilyn Vihman, Krystyna Wachowicz,
Werner Winter, and Karl Zimmer. The staff also included Nicholas
Zirpolo on a short-term bibliographer appointment, and Dal
Dresser, Vicky Shu, and Vicki Fahrenholz as successive secretary-
bibliographers for the Project; budgetary questions were attended
to throughout by Jean Beeson. In addition to those mentioned here,
from time to time visiting scholars with outside funding collabor-
ated with the Project for varying periods. Among these was
Hansjakob Seiler.

The original goals of the Project were stated by Greenberg in
his introductory words to the first issue of Working Papers in
Language Universals (WPLU) in November 1969. They were to
formulate cross-linguistic and, if possible, universally valid
empirical generalizations about language structure; generalizations,
that is, which hold true for some significant universe of languages
and which at the same time are capable of being refuted by actual
language data. The fact that such generalizations cannot be verified without reliable cross-linguistic data justifies the other original objective of the Project, which was to collect data from various languages of the world and store them in precise and comparable form. These two objectives were seen as not in themselves

sufficient but nonetheless necessary parts of the long-range goal
of accounting for similarities and differences among human language
in terms of increasingly general laws overarching various apparently unrelated aspects of language structure.

The particular format chosen for the realization of these two
initially conceived goals of the Project was the following. At any
one time the staff consisted of the two directors, a secretary-
bibliographer, and three or four researchers. Although the selection of staff linguists reflected adherence to the basic goals of the
Project, once on the staff, linguists were free to follow their own
philosophies and methodologies regarding research on typology
and universals. The papers in WPLU indeed reflect the resulting
theoretical and methodological diversity. The choice of topics was
similarly left up to the individual investigator, subject in principle
to the veto of the directors -- a power, however, which was never
actually exercised. Middle-range projects were encouraged,
requiring not more and possibly less than half a year to complete.
The rich linguistic resources of the Stanford University library,
as well as Ferguson's and Greenberg's private libraries, provided
most of the basic data. For some studies linguistic informants
from Stanford and the surrounding area were also utilized. Frequent biweekly or weekly meetings of the Project, attended at
times by other linguists from Stanford and from neighboring universities and by scholars visiting the area, provided opportunities for
reporting on and criticizing ongoing or completed work. The working paper series of the Project ensured informal and rapid dissem-
ination of results to wider circles.

It is in accordance with this mode of organization that the Project progressed toward the realization of its two goals. As far as
data collection is concerned, almost every one of the sixty-eight
working papers that were published in the twenty issues of WPLU
presented data from a variety of languages in comparable terms.[1]
In addition to the actual data, efforts were also made to provide
guidelines for data collection. This was done by "check lists" or
sets of parameters related to specific aspects of language data and
of use both to linguistic fieldworkers and to cross-linguistic re-

---

[1]This includes all full-size working papers published in the series, whether written by Project members (54) or contributed by
linguists not associated with the Project (14). The number does not
include the survey papers and shorter notes contained in WPLU.

searchers. After several years of the operation of the Project,
attempts to archive data on phonetics and phonology, an area which
seemed particularly promising in this respect, took the shape of
an independent research endeavor, the Phonology Archiving Project. This group was also Stanford-based, had the same directors
as the Language Universals Project, and received funding from the
same source. A still ongoing enterprise, the Phonology Archiving
Project has to date computer-stored the phonetic segment inventory of about two hundred languages, as well as phonological rule
information on some of them.[2] Although tentative plans for a
similar large-scale computer archiving project with respect to
grammatical information were made, their realization is still a
matter for the future.

As far as the other aim is concerned, the establishment of
cross-linguistically valid generalizations about language structures,
we believe that substantial progress has been made, as the papers
in WPLU attest, making allowances for the inevitable future revisions and even the abandonment of certain generalizations in the
light of further investigation. It seems reasonable to conclude that
a substantial portion of this work will prove, in the long run, to have
contributed substantially to our understanding of human language.

As the Project's end drew nearer, it was felt that a publication
that is both more formal and also more widely available than the
WPLU series should stand as a summary of our activities.[3] Thus

---

[2] For access to this material, write to Phonology Archiving Project, Department of Linguistics, Stanford University, Stanford,
California 94305.

[3] Copies of issues 11-20 of WPLU nonetheless remain available
at $2.00 apiece. Write to Working Papers on Language Universals,
Department of Linguistics, Stanford University, Stanford, California 94305. A bibliographical list including all references cited in
WPLU papers (about 2,000) arranged according to languages (about
750) is also available from the same address (under the name
"Bibliography") for $1.00 a copy; and so are the proceedings of a
conference on nasals and nasalization held in 1974 at Stanford,
entitled Nasalfest, for $6.50 a copy. Xerox and microfiche copies
of individual papers contained in any of the twenty issues of WPLU
are also available from ERIC clearinghouse in Languages and Linguistics, Center for Applied Linguistics, 1611 North Kent Street,
Arlington, Virginia 22209.

the idea of the present book was conceived. The original intention of simply summarizing what we have done was then complemented by the desire to answer the very patent need in the present linguistic literature for a comprehensive statement on where exactly we are in our knowledge about cross-linguistically recurrent structural properties of language. The "we" in the latter part of this sentence is not confined to Project members. In the past few years endeavors to establish and test similar generalizations have been increasingly initiated by individual scholars and organized projects in other countries as well as in Western Europe and the Soviet Union. In addition, even those whose basic methodology and approach are quite different from that employed for the most part in the Project have taken note of its results and have felt the need of accounting for them by incorporating them within their own theoretical framework, or even modifying that framework to account for them.

In accordance with these aims, we have sought to make these volumes as comprehensive as possible, consistent with the current stage of research and the particular interests and competences of those scholars who were either active in or basically sympathetic with our enterprise.

These volumes consist of forty-six papers. Roughly corresponding to three fundamental aspects of language structure, the data-oriented papers have been grouped into three classes: those mostly pertaining to phonology, those mostly dealing with morphological and lexical properties of the word-unit, and those primarily involved with syntactic and related semantic problems. The second, third, and fourth volumes of the book each contain one of these three groups of papers. The first volume presents the general papers which discuss questions of the theory and methodology of typological and universals research. Each paper in the book is preceded by an abstract and followed by its own list of references. At the end of each volume is an author index and a language index specific to papers in that volume.

Of the forty-six studies included in the book, thirty-five appear here for the first time. These have been written in part by scholars who were either members of or associated with the Stanford Project on Language Universals, in part by scholars not formally associated with the Project who have been invited by the editors to deal with a specific topic. Among the latter are Elaine Andersen, Dwight Bolinger, Bruce Downing, Thomas Gamkrelidze, Brian

Head, Larry Hyman, Hans-Heinrich Lieb, Adam Makkai, Yakov
Malkiel, and Elizabeth Closs Traugott. The remaining thirteen
papers are original or revised versions of working papers that
were previously published informally. They were written by members of this group as part of their work for the Project.

In general, the arrangement is topical; it reflects the manner
in which research was actually carried out under the aegis of the
Project and of the typical product as seen in the Working Papers.
This approach has some advantages. In general, it selects areas
of research comprehensive enough not to be trivial and, on the
other hand, not so all-encompassing as to be impractical. It leads
to numerous concrete and testable generalizations. We are also
keenly aware of certain inevitable defects. Since, to begin with,
we did not provide a comprehensive a priori scheme and did not
impose particular topics on investigators, there are necessarily
major omissions. There is also the danger that a somewhat ad
hoc and piecemeal approach will lead to the neglect of topics that
do not easily fall within present classificatory rubrics, as reflected
in the overall organization of this work. For example, there is
much to be learned from the phenomenon of word accent as it
relates to morphological systems. However, this topic does not
easily fall within conventional classifications.

The other defect is more closely tied into the basically, but not
exclusively, inductive nature of this approach. Interconnections
based on the presence of similar general psychological or other principles, or of even more specific factual relevance, may be overlooked through compartmentalization. Still, as an initial strategy,
we believe it to be defensible in terms of its immediate fruitfulness.
This is, however, something for the linguistic community as a
whole to judge. Moreover, many of our investigations, it can be
claimed, have already involved at least an adumbration of more
comprehensive principles -- for example, of marking theory.

In behalf of the authors of the papers included in this work and
in our own behalf, we would like to express our deep gratitude to
all of those who made the appearance of the books possible. Thus,
we would first like to thank Vicky Shu for the competence and genuine care she brought to the editing and typing of the final camera-
ready version of the manuscript. We are furthermore grateful to
Stanford Press and to William Carver in particular for their
guidance in our endeavor to produce a book that is pleasing to the
eye. Our most sincere thanks should go to Stanford University,

especially to the Department of Linguistics and its current chair-
person, Clara Bush, for being such an understanding host to the
Language Universals Project in the past nine years, and to Deans
Halsey Royden and W. Bliss Carnochan, and Provost William
Miller for their generous financial support toward the preparation
of the manuscript in final form. Finally, we thank the National
Science Foundation for its continuing support of the work of the
project.

J.H.G.
C.A.F.
E.A.M.

Contents

Contributors

Alan Bell is Assistant Professor of Linguistics at the University of Colorado in Boulder. He was a member of the Stanford Project on Language Universals in 1968-70 and a visiting member in the summer of 1971.

D.N.S. Bhat is Reader at the Linguistic Department of the Deccan College Postgraduate and Research Institute. He was a visiting member of the Stanford Project on Language Universals in 1973-75.

Dwight Bolinger is Professor Emeritus of Romance Languages and Literatures, Harvard University. He has had no formal connection with the Stanford Project, but has been in close touch with the Project's work and participants.

John Crothers is a Research Associate in the Linguistics Department, Stanford University. Since 1972 he has been a member of the Stanford Phonology Archiving Project.

Charles A. Ferguson is Professor Linguistics at Stanford University. He was Co-Director of the Stanford Project on Language Universals and is Associate Editor of these volumes.

Thomas V. Gamkrelidze is Professor of Structural and Comparative Linguistics at the University of Tbilisi. In the spring of 1975 he was a visiting member of the Stanford Project on Language Universals.

Joseph H. Greenberg is Professor of Linguistics and Anthropology at Stanford University. He was Co-Director of the Stanford Project on Language Universals and is the Editor of these volumes.

Larry M. Hyman is Associate Professor and Chairman of the Department of Linguistics at the University of Southern California.

Ian Maddieson is a Research Linguist at the University of California, Los Angeles. He was a Research Associate with the Stanford Project on Language Universals in the spring and summer of 1975.

Merritt Ruhlen is a Research Associate in the Department of
   Linguistics at Stanford University. He was a member of the
   Stanford Project on Language Universals from 1972 to 1976.

Russell Ultan is an American Council of Learned Societies postdoctoral fellow conducting research in Turku, Finland. His
   association with the Stanford Project on Language Universals,
   longer than that of any other Project member, spanned the
   years 1968-74.

Marilyn May Vihman has been a Research Associate on the
   Stanford Phonology Archiving Project since 1971.

UNIVERSALS OF HUMAN LANGUAGE

VOLUME 2

Phonology

Introduction

JOSEPH H. GREENBERG

The present volume, the first of three concerned with substantive areas of research on language universals, consists of 13 papers dealing with phonology. Like the other volumes, it does not set for itself the virtually unattainable goal of exhaustiveness, either in topical coverage or in the reporting of the concrete generalizations thus far proposed. It is to be hoped, however, that it succeeds reasonably well in the more modest goal of reflecting the current state of universals research in phonology, as well in its emphases and achievements as in its omissions and difficulties.

Historically, and probably even now, phonology holds a special place in the attempt to arrive at empirically valid generalizations across languages. It can claim to be that subfield of linguistics with the largest body of specific and generally accepted results -- results that transcend differences among theoretical approaches. There is, of course, lively and even acrimonious discussion regarding fundamentals which, naturally enough, looms large in the consciousness of the specialist. Yet the generalizations based on broad typologically oriented surveys of the world's languages, first launched some half-century ago by the members of the Prague School, chiefly Trubetzkoy and Jakobson, and taken up in the United States by Hockett, produced concrete results that have largely stood the test of time. What is perhaps at least as surprising is that more recent work, while naturally enough both extending and rectifying these earlier conclusions, still largely rests on such fundamental concepts as distinctive features, marking hierarchy, and implicational universals, which we owe mainly to the Prague School.

For example, the generalizations stated by Postal in his discussion of 'naturalness' (1968, especially pp. 81-82) and those implicit in Chomsky and Halle's marking conventions (1968), do not differ in basic content from those of earlier work based on other theoretical orientations. The special position of phonology becomes more apparent when we consider that the basic concepts mentioned above appeared first in phonology and, although extended by many to other aspects of language, have continued to hold a more central and assured position in phonology than elsewhere.

For these reasons generalizations in phonology give an impression both of precocious achievement and of coherent progress when compared, for example, to syntax.

However, the justifiable euphoria flowing from the foregoing
considerations should be tempered by the realization that the very
real successes alluded to were largely attained by a narrowing of
basic focus to what might be called the phonological system in its
most restricted sense, the synchronic structure of the segmental
inventory of languages. Although much still remains to be accom-
plished within this well-established framework, the areas of phonology that lie outside of it and that have by comparison been much
less intensively explored, offer the greatest opportunities for future
progress. Signs are not lacking that this broadening of content is
to some extent under way, as is evidenced by the present collection. Such developments not only are significant in regard to their
content, but they also raise important theoretical problems since
in some respects the theoretical concepts developed in synchronic
segmental studies require significant modification and might even,
in some instances, have to be abandoned as simply not appropriate
(e.g. as regards intonation).

There are three main directions in which to look for a broadened
basis for phonological generalization. These are the diachronic or,
more inclusively stated, the processual dimension of phonological
systems, the syntagmatic plane of sound sequencing, and the relation between phonology and the grammatical and semantic aspects
of language.

Turning to the papers with the preceding discussion in mind, we
note that, indeed, the concept of feature and, to nearly the same
extent, the concept of feature hierarchy or markedness, play prominent roles. Many of the papers have the name of some feature in
the title (e.g. Bhat on palatalization, Gamkrelidze on stops and
fricatives, Ruhlen on nasal vowels, Crothers on vowels), and,
even when they do not, features generally provide the underlying
framework for the analysis. This is true for example of Ultan's
papers on metathesis and size-sound symbolism and Ferguson's
study of phonological process which is concerned chiefly with stops
and fricatives. This gives a degree of theoretical unity to this
volume not present to the same extent in the other volumes of the
work.

It may be pointed out that in the present collection, what has
proven to be the most useful delimitation of studies devoted to
particular features, are not in general the single features most
current in contemporary theory. Thus no one evidently finds it
useful to survey languages in terms of such features as coronal,
or even vocalic; topics have rather been staked out in terms of

more traditional features, all of them no doubt definable in present day theory but only as particular feature combinations, e.g. vowels defined as segments that are +vocalic, -consonantal. The one exception, apparently, is the feature specification +nasal , which in any event happens to coincide with a traditional feature.

The analysis in terms of features, proceeding under certain very common limitations, does not encounter insuperable difficulties in regard to diachronic change. Provided we confine ourselves to the segmental system, we can handle the dynamic situation by couching our description in terms of changes in feature specifications.

The diachronic study of word accent and sentence intonation, particularly the latter, is, in any case, fraught with difficulties because such changes are not reflected in orthographies nor, even in the rare instances where such changes obtruded on the consciousness of earlier observers, were they equipped with a conceptual apparatus adequate for their description. This difficulty, of course, has still not been completely overcome.

The integration of diachronic and synchronic approaches is an outstanding recent trend. One of its manifestations is the quasi-monographic study of a single feature from a combined standpoint. Examples of this in the present volume are Bell's paper on syllabic consonants, Ruhlen's on nasal vowels and Bhat's on palatalization. The last of these is of special interest from this point of view, since it leads to the conclusion, largely on the basis of differences in the type of change involved, that palatalization is a term that has been employed for several distinguishable phenomena with differing synchronic correlates. For such single-feature synchronic-diachronic studies, the reader is referred to Ferguson's pioneering study of nasality (Ferguson 1963), many of the papers in a volume devoted to the study of nasals, particularly that of Hyman (Hyman 1975), as well as to my own studies of voiceless vowels and of glottalic consonants (Greenberg 1969, 1970).

Several of the papers that do not take the form of the single feature study involve a similar interweaving of the synchronic and diachronic viewpoints, notably Ferguson's paper on phonological processes and Ultan's on metathesis. In work not included in the present volume, Gamkrelidze has, by a set of hypotheses similar to those advanced independently by other Indo-Europeanists, applied some of the conclusions advanced in his paper on stops and fricatives to propose a new and challenging theory regarding the phonetic nature of the various stop series of Proto-Indo-European.

But, Ferguson's paper on processes in this volume reminds us, diachrony can be subsumed under a broader notion of process -- including, along with still other phenomena, synchronic processual derivations, language acquisition, and the pathological disintegration of language. Taken in this wider context, generative phonology, with some of its historical roots in the item-process model of American structuralism (cf. Hockett 1954), has prepared the ground for a diachronic approach through its development of a synchronic processual model of phonology.

While conceding the fruitfulness of processual considerations in the broadest sense, I would consider that the diachronic approach proper has superior explanatory power. This claim can be illustrated by the well-known example of the Classical Greek alternations of the type nom. sg. thriks, gen. sg. trikhos 'hair', where synchronically there is metathesis of h, which Ultan (this volume) qualifies as "apparent metathesis". The metathesis is only "apparent" because it results from a sequence of two processes, neither of them metathetic: the conditional loss of aspiration in clusters of aspirated stop + s and the regressive dissimilation to zero of aspiration, i.e. *thrikhs > thriks, *thrikhos > trikhos. Incidentally, I would consider the much discussed and, on the face of it, unusual metathesis of word final CV to VC in Rotuman also to be the merely apparent result of two successive changes of well-attested types, namely anticipation of the vowel quality of the final syllable (of which umlaut is just one type) in that of the penult, and subsequent loss of the final, now redundant vowel (e.g. *hosa 'flower' *hoasa > hoas.

A number of the papers illustrate the second of the areas of expanding interest mentioned earlier, that from the axis of simultaneity to the axis of succession. Examples in point are Maddieson's paper on tone, Bell's on syllabic consonants, mine on consonant clusters, Hyman's on the word, Vihman's on consonant harmony in children's language and Bolinger's on intonation. The theoretical framework of tone and marking hierarchy retains its usefulness here also in some instances. It is even possible, in regard to segment sequences, to formulate a master processual principle, namely, the tendency of marked features to spread in the chain, a principle by now so familiar that Maddieson employs it as one of his definitional criteria of markedness, rather than as an empirical universal about marked features.

As a consequence of the prevalence of such processes of spread and, at the same time, because the boundaries of grammatically

significant units can constitute barriers to the diffusion, there arise
phenomena such as vowel and nasal harmony, characterizing especially the word as a unit and describable in terms of the feature
that has spread. It is at this point, however, that such syntagmatic
units as the syllable, morpheme, word and sentence begin to demand
theoretical attention by phonologists. Indeed, even on the most restricted segmental level, the American and Prague Schools of
structuralism required either open or tacit reference to the word,
i.e. to word boundary in statements of allophonic conditioning and
likewise cryptic reference to the syllable, if only by resorting to
syllabicity as a kind of segmental property (cf. Volume III in this
book).

In this matter there have been two opposed theoretical tendencies. One may be called reductionist, by which is meant the attempt to deprive units other than the single segment composed of
segmental features, of independent status. This can be done either
by defining them as merely special kinds of sequences of segments
or as special kinds of phonemes. Examples of the former are
definitions of the syllable as specified sequences of vowels and
consonant phonemes, or of intonations as sequences of pitch phonemes. An instance of the latter is the introduction of junctural
phonemes to account for morpheme or word boundaries. American
structuralist theory in particular tended toward this type of reduc-
tionism. The opposite point of view was most strongly represented
by the British prosodic school, which posited such entities as prosodies of the syllable and the word and sought, at the same time, to
reduce unisegmental properties (the so-called phonematic units) to
a minimum.

It is in this area of sound sequencing and the phonological properties of the syllable, morpheme and word that most remains to be
done. My own study of consonant sequences in the present volume
does not include word medial sequences. Consonant-vowel sequences
and diphthongs have not been studied systematically in terms of
broad cross-linguistic samples. The accentual properties of the
word have been the subject of several recent studies (Greenberg
and Kashube 1976; Hyman, to appear). In regard to harmonic
properties, the most conspicuous one, vowel harmony, has an extensive literature including the cross-linguistic study of Ultan
(1973). Other harmonic properties, e.g. nasality, have been less
studied, and we lack any overall treatment of harmonic properties
as such. Which features participate and why are just these features, and not others, susceptible to harmonization (cf. Ferguson
1975:184-185) ?

The existence of an opposite property of grammatically defined
units, which might be called disharmonic, has largely been overlooked in theoretical discussion and has been studied in only a few
individual cases. By a disharmonic property is meant the existence of a rule by which certain feature values cannot occur more
than once in a particular unit. An example is the "incompatibility"
rules of Semitic, and indeed of most of Afroasiatic, as well as the
similar phenomena uncovered by Uhlenbeck in Javanese (Uhlenbeck
1949, Greenberg 1950). The basic rule in Semitic, omitting certain
important qualifications, is that no triconsonantal verb root morpheme, except for the special case of identity of the second and
third consonant, may have two consonants with the same place of
articulation. For example, a root *s-b-m would be excluded because the second and third consonants are both labials. Incidentally, these rules are not stated in terms of either syllabic structure or the word. For example t and d can cooccur in the same
word, and even be in the same syllable in t-adxulu 'she enters' in
which t- indicates a feminine third person singular subject.

Outside of syllabic structure of the word (e.g. Bell 1971), this
whole area of what Hockett called canonical form, in particular
that of the morpheme, awaits systematic cross-linguistic study,
both synchronically and diachronically.

The relation of particular sound types to the expression of semantic structure is treated by Ultan in his paper on diminutive
symbolism. Partly because of the doctrine of the arbitrariness of
the linguistic sign and partly because this area has been treated at
times in a highly speculative manner, the whole area of sound symbolism has tended to suffer from a certain lack of linguistic respect-
ability. However, the reality of symbolism, at least as a statistical
phenomenon, based on cross-linguistic research and on psycholinguistic experimentation can hardly be doubted (e.g. Fonágy 1963,
Jakobson 1960). It is, I believe, more extensive than usually realized. For example, one may suggest a correlation between words
for 'lip' and 'mouth' and the existence of labial consonants, and
between 'nose' and nasal consonants. Again, in verbs for certain
bodily actions an onomatopoetic tendency is evident, e.g. 'to blow',
'to spit', 'to sneeze'.

One further advantage of phonology is that because of its relatively restricted and transparent subject matter, it serves to bring
certain issues of explanatory theory into particularly sharp focus.
It is no accident that limitations of purely formal accounts were
noted by Chomsky and Halle in relation to phonology in their now

famous Chapter 9 of <u>Sound</u> <u>Pattern</u> <u>of</u> <u>English</u>. The attempt at
functional explanation in Crothers's paper on vowel systems shows
how attention to physiological and perceptual factors must figure
as part of any truly explanatory theory. The study of phonological
universals, in fact, helps to restore the close relationship between
phonetics and phonology that was to a certain extent weakened during
the period of structuralism. Moreover, it is a two-way street: not
only do already established phonetic facts help us to account for
phonological generalizations but, as noted by Ruhlen, "The search
for phonetic explanation is triggered by phonological observation."

It is our hope that this collection of phonological papers will
contribute not only to the further testing and expansion of empirical
results, but also to the encouraging of research into areas that have
been up to now relatively neglected.

BIBLIOGRAPHY

Bell, Alan. 1971. Some patterns of occurrence and formation of
syllable structures. Working Papers on Language Universals
6. 23-137. Stanford University, Committee on Linguistics.

Chomsky, Noam and Morris Halle. 1968. The sound pattern of
English. New York: Harper and Row.

Ferguson, Charles A. 1963. Some assumptions about nasals: a
sample study in phonological universals. Universals of language, ed. by Joseph H. Greenberg, 53-60. 2nd ed. Cambridge: MIT Press.

_____. 1975. Universal tendencies and natural nasality.
Nasálfest: papers from a symposium on nasals and nasalization,
ed. by C. A. Ferguson, L.M. Hyman, and J.J. Ohala, 175-196.
Stanford University, Department of Linguistics.

Fonágy, Ivan. 1963. Die Metaphern in der Phonetik; ein Beitrag
zur Entwicklungsgeschichte des wissenschaftlichen Denkens.
The Hague: Mouton.

Greenberg, Joseph H. 1951. The patterning of the root morpheme
in Semitic. Word 6. 162-181.

Greenberg, Joseph H. 1969. Some methods of dynamic comparison
in linguistics. Substance and structure of language, ed. by J.
Puhvel, 147-203.

_____. 1970. Some generalizations concerning glottalic con-
sonants, especially implosives. WPLU 2. 1-38.

_____ and Dorothea Kaschube. 1976. Word prosodic systems:
a preliminary report. WPLU 20. 1-18.

Hockett, Charles F. 1954. Two modes of grammatical description. Word 10. 210-231.

Hyman, Larry M. 1975. Nasal states and nasal processes.
Nasálfest: papers from a symposium on nasals and nasalization, ed. by C.A. Ferguson, L.M. Hyman, and J.J. Ohala,
249-264. Stanford University, Department of Linguistics.

_____. Forthcoming. On the nature of linguistic stress. To
appear.

Jakobson, Roman. 1960. Why "mama" and "papa"? Perspectives
in psychological theory, ed. by B. Kaplan and S. Warner, 124-
134. New York: John Wiley and Sons.

Postal, Paul M. 1968. Aspects of phonological theory. New York:
Harper and Row.

Uhlenbeck, E.M. 1949. The structure of the Javanese morpheme.
Lingua 2: 239-70.

Ultan, Russell. 1973. Some reflections in vowel harmony.
WPLU 12: 37-67.

On the Correlation
of Stops and Fricatives
in a Phonological System

THOMAS V. GAMKRELIDZE

ABSTRACT

Bundles of distinctive features (phonemes) are classified as
more or less strongly marked, depending on their commonness in
the languages of the world. In the voice correlation, /g ɣ / are
marked, /b v/ unmarked in the voiced series. In the voiceless
series, /p f/ are marked, /k x/ unmarked. Among the dental
fricatives, /θ ð/ are more strongly marked than /s z/. The
existence of /p g/ implies redundancy of /f ɣ/ and inversely.

CONTENTS

1. Hierarchic Relation of Markedness between Phonemic Units

1.1   During the last decade in linguistic theory interest in the
traditional problem of the marking of linguistic categories has increased in connection with the elaboration of problems of linguistic
typology and linguistic universals.

The concept of the presence of marked (feature-bearing, "merkmaltragend") and unmarked (lacking a feature, "merkmallos")
categories in a language system arose in the Prague School, in the
works of N. Trubetzkoy and R. Jakobson. [1] As is well known, in
Trubetzkoy's Principles of Phonology (1939) the concept of the
marking of phonological oppositions, connected with the problem
of neutralization and the archiphoneme, already plays an essential
role.

However, in the subsequent period of intensive development in
descriptive linguistics, some withdrawal from working out problems of marking, due to taxonomic restrictions, is to be observed.
Only in recent years has particular attention been given to the traditional problems of the marking of linguistic categories and the
ascertainment of the hierarchical correlations of elements in a
system.

In this respect the recent works of R. Jakobson played a decisive
part; in them the traditional problem of marking undergoes substantial development and reformulation, being treated as a universal hierarchical relation between linguistic categories.

1.2   The problem of the marking of linguistic categories holds
a special place in the linguistics of universals, in J. Greenberg's
theory.

The relation of marking is connected by Greenberg with the
frequency indices of linguistic units. The unmarked member of
the relation, which is functionally more normal and widespread,
has a greater frequency of occurrence in a text compared to the
marked member, which is a more complex and textually more
restricted unit. In positions of internally conditioned neutralization the unmarked member of a phonological opposition appears.

---

[1] On the terms 'marked' and 'unmarked' as correlates of the
RUSSIAN terms 'priznakovyj' and 'bespriznakovyj' see Jakobson
1971c.

Thomas V. Gamkrelidze

Linked with these characteristics of the unmarked member of
a phonological opposition are its capacity for wider distribution
compared to the corresponding marked member, the appearance
of the unmarked member in a greater number of phonological environments, and its wider subphonemic variability. [2]

Thus, for example, on material from a large number of languages with various sorts of systems, we can determine that unglottalized consonants have a substantially greater frequency of
occurrence than the corresponding glottalized consonants, which
are opposed to the unglottalized consonants as the marked members
of an opposition to the unmarked members. The feature of glottalization is, in the present case, the marked feature. Aspiration is
also a marked feature, opposing the aspirated phonemes to the unaspirated phonemes as the marked members of the opposition to
the unmarked members, which are characterized by a greater
relative frequency of occurrence.

On the basis of the statistical data we can maintain that glottalization is a stronger feature of marking than aspiration, and the
normal hierarchy of increasing markedness of a phoneme is represented in the sequence: unaspirated -- aspirated -- glottalized
(Greenberg 1966a: 17ff).

In a system of vowels the nasal vowels are opposed to the oral
vowels, which have a greater frequency of occurrence (unmarked)
as opposed to the former (marked). The same ratio holds for the
long vowels (marked members) in opposition to the short vowels
(unmarked members of the opposition).

In general we can maintain that the number of phonemes of a
marked category never exceeds the number of phonemes of the
unmarked category (cf. the situation noted by C. Ferguson, that
the number of nasal vowels can never exceed the number of non-
nasal vowels; Ferguson 1963). We can formulate this as an implicational statement: the presence in a language of a marked
category presupposes the existence in it of the corresponding unmarked category (cf. the assertion that in all languages with nasal
vowels there are also oral vowels, where the marked feature appears as the implicans and the unmarked feature as the implicatum). [3]

---

[2] See Greenberg 1966a. The factor of frequency of occurrence
as a characteristic of the marking relation has been previously
mentioned by Trubetzkoy and Jakobson; see Jakobson 1941: 366ff.

[3] Greenberg 1966a, 1966b. Concerning implicational rules in
phonology see Jakobson 1939. See also Jakobson 1963 and 1971.

1.3   The distribution of empty slots (gaps) in a paradigmatic
system is also connected with the statistical characteristics of the
marked members of oppositions, which are distinguished by a narrower textual frequency compared to the unmarked members. The
empty slots (gaps) appear in place of marked members of oppositions, as cells, as it were, which would be filled by marked members of a relation; these marked members have a frequency of zero
(see Hockett 1955:142ff.).

In the series of glottalized consonants (marked),[4] as opposed
to the unglottalized consonants (unmarked), the labial glottalized
phoneme /p'/ is distinguished by the least frequency of occurrence
in a text; in a number of languages in which a series of glottalized
stops is represented, /p'/ is absent, creating an empty slot (gap)
in the system (e.g. in a number of CAUCASIAN languages, in many
African and AMERINDIAN languages, etc.). In the present case
the empty slot reflects a general linguistic regularity: the greatest
marking is that of the glottalized labial phoneme /p'/, the frequency
of which drops to zero in a number of systems (Greenberg 1970).

Analogous correlations in the system may be established for
the series of pharyngealized stops as well. The pharyngealized
stops ṗ ṭ ḳ are opposed to non-pharyngealized (pure) stops as the
marked members of an opposition to the unmarked. Incidentally,
the labial member represents the weakest link in the pharyngealized
series, forming in many languages with pharyngealized stops a gap
in the system (cf. e.g. the system of SEMITIC languages with the
emphatic consonants ṭ and q, the labial *ṗ being absent). It is
worth noting in this connection that in the opinion of some scholars
the SEMITIC emphatic (pharyngealized) consonants derive from
corresponding glottalized counterparts (see Cantineau 1952, Martinet
1953).

The proposal that the marking relation is of a conditioned character, determined by the context, the environment in which the given
feature appears, acquires special significance in Greenberg's theory.
Thus, for example, the feature of voicing is a marked feature in
nonresonant consonants (i.e. in the environment of the features
making up these phonemes), while in the resonants it is an unmarked
feature. In the case of the resonants the marked feature is [-voiced],
i.e. voicelessness (Greenberg 1966a:24).

---

[4] On 'series' (séries) and 'groups' (ordres) in a paradigmatic
system, see Martinet 1955:69ff.

1.4   The principle of the conditioned nature of the marking relation advanced by Greenberg becomes one of the fundamental principles in working out problems of marking in the theory of transformational-generative grammar (Chomsky and Halle 1968: 402ff., Postal 1968). A certain distinctive feature [F] does not assume the value [mF] (i. e. marked) or [uF] (i. e. unmarked) invariably, independently of the conditions of the given feature's functioning, but in accordance with the character of the environment, the context in which it appears in a 'vertical' (simultaneous) and/or 'horizontal' (linear) sequence.[5] Therefore each of the values + and − of a certain feature [F] can be specified as m̲ or u̲, depending on the environment. Thus, for instance, in an example of the conditioned character of the marking relation cited by Greenberg, the feature 'voicing' with the value +, i. e. [+voiced], is defined as [mF] (i. e. 'marked') in the nonresonant consonants, while in the resonants the feature [+voiced] is an unmarked feature [uF] (in the case of the resonants the feature of voicing with the value −, i. e. 'voicelessness,' is 'marked;' cf. the presence of voiceless resonant phonemes in a number of language systems). Analogously, the feature of labialization (flatness) [+F] is the marked feature [mF] for front vowels, but the same feature of labialization (flatness) [+F] is unmarked [uF] for back vowels. (See Cairns 1969:865, Postal 1968:80ff.)

In other words, because of the conditioned character of the marking relation, a one-to-one correspondence can not be established between the values m, u and +, − of a certain feature, as was the case in the traditional interpretation of the marking relation, which assumed the presence of a certain feature in the 'marked' member of an opposition (feature-bearing, i. e. a feature with the value +) and its absence in the 'unmarked' member (lacking a feature, i. e. a feature with the value −). It is here that a difference of principle is to be observed between the present conception of the marking relation and its conception in the Prague Linguistic School. (See Chomsky and Halle 1968:404ff., also Shapiro 1972.)

2. Marking Conventions in the System of Occlusive Phonemes

2.1   Basing her work on Greenberg's conception of the marking relation, and taking into account the statistical characteristics of phonemes and the distribution of empty slots in a system,

---

[5] On 'vertical' and 'horizontal' sequences of features, constituting the 'environment' of a given feature, see Gamkrelidze 1968.

I. Melikishvili establishes a number of regularities pertaining to the correlations of nonresonant consonants in a paradigmatic system, and determines for them a rather general and universal hierarchical dependence with respect to marking. (See Melikishvili 1970, 1972.)

In particular, the following hierarchical correlations between phonemic units of various series and groups (points of articulation) are established.

In systems with an opposition of stops on the feature voicing/ voicelessness the voiced labial phoneme /b/ is functionally a stronger unit than the voiced velar stop /g/. This correlation is determined on the basis of the greater relative textual frequency of the phoneme /b/ compared to the velar /g/ in various language systems with an opposition of stops on the feature voicing/voicelessness. In other words, the feature of labiality, in the condition of simultaneous combination with the feature of voicing, is unmarked, as opposed to the feature of velarity, which is a marked feature in combination with voicing.

In the voiceless stops (both simple and glottalized), on the other hand, the velar stop /k/ (and correspondingly /k^h/ and /k'/), which is the unmarked member of the opposition, has a greater functional load than the labial stop /p/ (and correspondingly /p^h/ and /p'/), which is the marked, functionally weaker member. In the labial group the frequency of the voiced phoneme is greater than the frequency of the voiceless one, while in the velar group the frequency of the voiceless phoneme is greater than the frequency of the voiced one.

Thus, velarity combined with voicelessness and labiality combined with voicing form the optimal combinations /k/ and /b/, but uniting voicelessness with labiality and voicing with velarity creates the functionally weak units /p/ and /g/.

Gaps (empty slots) in paradigmatic systems are distributed in accordance with the established functional correlations of feature marking. Systems with gaps in the class of plosives, opposed on the feature voicing/voicelessness, have basically the following forms (Fig. 1):[6]

---

[6] The LIFU language is occasionally cited to illustrate a gap in the system in place of the labial /b/, which at first sight contradicts the established regularity concerning the unmarked nature of the

```
(a)  b  –      (b)  b  p      (c)  b  –
     d  t           d  t           d  t
     g  k           –  k           –  k
```

Figure 1

2.2   The dental group is opposed to the labial and velar groups
as that group which has the greatest general frequency of occurrence; it is thereby characterized as unmarked with respect to the
two other groups. However, the possibility of such systems as (2),
with gaps in place of the voiced stops of both the velar and dental
groups, [7] shows the greater marking of the voiced dental stop in
comparison to the voiced labial, and its lesser marking compared
to the velar (Fig. 2).

```
     b  p  p'
     –  t  t'
     –  k  k'
```

Figure 2

From the standpoint of combinations with the feature voicing/
voicelessness, the features for point of articulation form a definite

---

(ftnt. 6 cont.)
labial member in the series of voiced phonemes as opposed to the
velar member (cf. Martinet 1955: 103). The alleged gap in the
place of the phoneme /b/ is assumed from the fact that /b/ occurs
in LIFU words borrowed from EUROPEAN and neighboring MELAN-
ESIAN or POLYNESIAN languages, whereas the phonemes /d/ and
/g/, as well as the voiceless /ptk/ occur in the native forms of
LIFU (cf. Lenormand 1952). However, such an assumption of a gap
of /b/ in diachrony may not reflect the real state of affairs, for the
series of voiced stops in LIFU must have originated from phonemes
of a different nature; the series in question may be traceable to the
unvoiced series with a regular absence of the labial member that
appeared later during the transition of unvoiced series to the corresponding voiced. (In this connection it would be interesting to
investigate the correspondences of the voiced stops /d g/ in LIFU
to consonants of related MELANESIAN languages.)

[7] A system of this sort is represented, for example, in the
AMERINDIAN languages: in SIRIONÓ see Priest 1968, in TZO-
TZIL and ALAKALUF see Milewski 1967:13, 41, in AMUZGO see
Longacre 1965:46, in QUECHUA, TZELTAL, HUASTECO and in
other languages of the MAYAN group see Jackson 1972:109ff.

hierarchical series. Voicing is best combined with labiality, and
voicelessness with velarity, while dentality occupies an intermediate position. We can represent this correlation in the following
figure (with arrows indicating the direction of increase of the functional load of the feature; Fig. 3) (Melikishvili 1972 : 23):

$$\uparrow\begin{matrix} b & p \\ d & t \\ g & k \end{matrix}\downarrow$$

Figure 3

2.3   In the class of voiceless stops the degree of marking is
increased by the addition of the secondary features of aspiration
and glottalization; furthermore, the feature of glottalization is a
more marked feature than the feature of aspiration, so that the
hierarchical sequence on the feature of marking in the class of
voiceless stops has the following form: voiceless simple -- aspirated -- glottalized.

Thus, the glottalized labial /p'/ is the marked member of the
opposition with respect to the aspirated /p^h/, while the aspirated
/p^h/ is marked with respect to the simple voiceless phoneme /p/.

Gaps in paradigmatic systems appear in accordance with these
correlations. The following systems, with empty slots in the groups
of voiceless stops, are possible (Fig. 4):

(a) b   p^h –   (b) b   –   –
    d   t^h t'   d   t^h t'
    g   k^h k'   g   k^h k'

Figure 4

But less probable are systems of the type (c), i.e. systems with
glottalized labial /p'/ and a gap in place of the aspirated /p^h/[8]
(Fig. 4a):

(c) b   –   p'
    d   t^h t'
    g   k^h k'

Figure 4a

---

[8] The system of a dialect of BORANA belongs to such an extremely
rare type (cf. Andrzejewski 1957:354-74). See also Sasse 1973:2ff.

2.4   The same sorts of correlations between different series
in the class of voiceless stops can also be ascertained in systems
without an opposition of stops on the feature voicing/voicelessness.
The gaps in such systems are distributed in accordance with the
degree of marking of the members of the labial group (Fig. 5).

(a) p -   (b) p -   -   (c) p -   p'   (d) -   -   p'
    t t'   t t^h t'   t t^h t'   t t^h t'
    k k'   k k^h k'   k k^h k'   k k^h k'

Figure 5

There are systems of types Fig. 5 (a)[9] and (b),[10] but less probable
are systems of type Fig. 5 (c). Even less probable are Fig. 5 (d)
systems with glottalized labial /p'/ and gaps in place of the aspirated and/or simple voiceless labial phonemes. The glottalized
labial phoneme is functionally a weaker member than the voiceless
aspirate, the latter being weaker than the simple voiceless phoneme.

But united with the feature of velarity the feature of glottalization can also create a functionally stronger unit than aspiration can.
In many systems the glottalized velar phoneme /k'/ has a greater
relative frequency of occurrence than the corresponding aspirated
or simple voiceless velar /k/; it is thereby the unmarked member
of the opposition with respect to the unglottalized voiceless velar
phoneme.[11]

2.5   The regularities established for the velar group of stops
can be extended a fortiori to the postvelar (uvular) group. The
weakest element (most marked member), in functional terms, in
the group of voiced phonemes is the postvelar (uvular) phoneme
/G/, which creates a gap in a number of systems in which there
is a phonemic postvelar (uvular) group. The postvelar phoneme

---

[9] Cf., for example, the TONKAWA language (Hoijer 1933-38).

[10] Cf., for example, NAVAHO (Sapir and Hoijer 1967, also Hoijer
1966) and HUPA (Woodward 1964). The unmarked series of voiceless stops, in contrast to the marked aspirated and glottalized series, is represented with the LATIN symbols for voiced b, d, g
in the descriptions cited above.

[11] Melikishvili 1972: 17; see also Greenberg 1970.

/G/ is at the same time the marked member with respect to the velar /g/; there are no systems with a voiced postvelar stop /G/ and a gap in the velar group in place of the voiced /g/.

The systems of stops in a number of CAUCASIAN languages are a typical example of paradigmatic systems of this sort, with a gap in place of the voiced postvelar stop /G/ (see Deeters 1963: 19ff.). Compare, for example, the system of the SVAN and OLD GEORGIAN languages (Fig. 6):

$$
\begin{array}{ccc}
b & p^h & p' \\
d & t^h & t' \\
g & k^h & k' \\
- & q^h & q'
\end{array}
$$

Figure 6

In the group of voiceless postvelar stops the glottalized velar stop /q'/ is the functionally strongest member; its frequency is greater than that of the corresponding aspirated phoneme /q^h/ (cf. the functional load of the glottalized velar phoneme /k'/). The loss, in a number of cases (e.g. in MODERN GEORGIAN), of the marked unglottalized member of the opposition, and the appearance of a gap in the paradigmatic system in its place, must be explained by such a correlation between unglottalized and glottalized postvelar phonemes.

3. An Interpretation of the Relationship of Markedness

3.1   The concept of markedness, which arose in phonology as a characteristic of the presence of a feature in a certain member of an opposition in contrast to its absence, assumed that the members of an opposition were whole phonemic units in privative opposition to one another (Trubetzkoy 1939: 82ff.). The transference of the oppositional function of marking from phonemes to separate distinctive features of phonemes, and the recognition of the contextually conditioned nature of the marking relation extended its sphere of application and changed the original conception of this hierarchical relation as an opposition between feature-bearing and non-feature-bearing units.

3.2   In its present-day conception the marking relation must be interpreted as the 'normalness,' the 'naturalness' of a certain unit of a system, present in all or in a majority of language systems, in contrast to a phonetically less normal and natural, and therefore less widespread unit, which has definite restrictions in the system.[12] The degree of 'normalness' and 'naturalness' of the units of a system under consideration also determines the hierarchical relation of marking between them. The phonetically more normal, natural, and widespread (functionally strong) elements of a system are characterized as 'unmarked,' in contrast to the 'marked' elements, which are the less normal and widespread (functionally weaker) elements in the system.[13]

Naturally the statistical characteristics of the oppositional members of the marking relation are also linked with such an interpretation of the function of marking. We should expect that the more normal and natural member of the relation (the unmarked unit) will have a greater frequency of occurrence than the less normal and natural member of the relation (the marked unit).

The calculation of indices of frequency, the counting of textual frequencies of phonemes in determinining the marked or unmarked character of correlated phonemic units, is founded in principle on such an assumption.

However, the logically relevant link is not that between the degree of marking of the phonemic units and their relative textual frequency, but rather the link between their marking and their frequency in the system, the extent to which they are encountered in the lexicon, which gives a basis for determining the functional load and thereby the degree of marking of the given phonemic units.

The textual frequency of phonemic units purports to be only an indirect reflection of the frequency of their occurrence in the system (lexicon) to which the degree of markedness of the given units seems to be directly related. However, inasmuch as a single-

---

[12] On the concept of 'naturalness' in a system, cf. Fromkin 1970, also Postal 1968:53ff.

[13] Under such an interpretation the investigation of the marking relation between oppositional phonemic units leads to defining the basic, primary phonological oppositions and determining the minimal phonemic inventory of a language, complicated by later secondary phonological features, i.e., the problems investigated by Jakobson on the basis of a study of child language and aphasia; see Jakobson 1941.

valued correspondence can be empirically established between the
textual frequency of phonemic units and their frequency in vocabulary (the frequency ratio 'more-less' within the opposed pairs in
the text coincides with their correlation in the system) the count
of the textual frequencies of phonemes may serve as a kind of
heuristic procedure for determining their relative frequencies in
the system (lexicon), which give a logical basis for determining
the degree of marking of a phoneme in relation to the other phonemic units of the system. [14]

3.3   But with respect to which elements of the phonological
system is the hierarchical dependence of marking determined;
which units function in phonology as the oppositional members of
the marking relation; separate distinctive features, or entire
bundles, simultaneous combinations of these features?   (See
McCawley 1968: 556.)

It is assumed that the condition of marking affects not phonemic
units as a whole, but separate distinctive features of phonemes,
which constitute a hierarchical relation of marking in the environment of other features.   It is further emphasized that a definite
marking value is not assigned to a concrete distinctive feature invariably, independent of the conditions of its functioning in simultaneous combination with other distinctive features, but conditionally,
contextually, depending on the character of the other distinctive
features which the given feature is combined with in a phoneme or
phonemic sequence.   One and the same feature can take the value
of either a marked or an unmarked member depending on the concrete environment of distinctive features making up the content of
the phoneme.

---

[14] In this sense the category of marking on the level of phonology
is distinct in principle from the marking relation in grammar (semantics), which is manifested in the textual frequency of the corresponding units; the parallelism (isomorphism) in the character
of the marking relation on different linguistic levels (in phonology,
grammar, semantics) is thereby, as it were, broken.   This parallelism was brought to light by Jakobson (1931), and analyzed
in detail by Greenberg, who also notes the difference between these
categories on different linguistic levels (Greenberg 1970: 56ff.).
The distinction can also extend to the factors underlying the marking
relation in phonology and grammar (semantics).   On the phonological
level the marking relation is a function of psycho-physical factors
governing the combinability of distinctive features (see below).

Indeed, the marked feature of labialization (flatness) in nonlow front vowels, i. e. in the environment of the features [+syllabic, −nonsyllabic, −low, −grave], [15] automatically determines the value of all these features to be 'markedness,' i. e. the feature [+syllabic] in combination with the features [−nonsyllabic, +labialized, −low, −grave] will be characterized as 'marked;' the feature [−grave] in the environment of the features [+syllabic, −nonsyllabic, +labialized, −low] will be defined as 'marked,' and so on for each feature of the given environment.

Perfectly analogous to this, the nonmarkedness of the feature of labialization (flatness) in nonlow back vowels, i. e. in the environment of the features [+syllabic, −nonsyllabic, −low, +grave], automatically determines the value of all these features to be 'nonmarkedness,' i. e. the feature [+syllabic] in combination with the features [−nonsyllabic, +labialized, −low, +grave] will be defined as 'unmarked,' the feature [+grave] in the environment of the features [+syllabic, −nonsyllabic, +labialized, −low] will be defined as 'unmarked,' and so on for each feature of the given environment.

3.4   The monovalence of all the distinctive features of a certain bundle, of a certain combination of features, with respect to marking must be interpreted to mean that the category of markedness affects not the separate distinctive feature appearing in a certain simultaneous environment of features, but is rather a function of the entire given group of features as a whole, affects the whole given bundle of features. It is not the separate distinctive

---

[15] The system of distinctive features used in the present investigation is somewhat different from the traditional system proposed by Jakobson and his colleagues (see Jakobson, Fant, and Halle 1962), and modified by Chomsky and Halle (1968: 293ff.). In particular, in place of the features [± vocalic] and [±consonantal], which are tautological regarding the definition of vocalic and consonantal phonemes, it seems expedient to introduce the features [±syllabic] and [±nonsyllabic], which give the specific character of sound segments in accordance with their ability to form syllabic peaks, i. e. to appear as a syllable-forming (central)∼nonsyllabic-forming (marginal) element in a sequence of sounds. Accordingly, the vowels will be characterized by the features [+syllabic, −nonsyllabic], the consonants by the features [−syllabic, +nonsyllabic], and the sonorant phonemes (resonants/sonants), which appear as syllable-forming or nonsyllable-forming elements depending on the environment, will be defined as [+syllabic, +nonsyllabic] (cf. Lehmann 1952, Chomsky and Halle 1968: 354).

feature that is marked or unmarked, but the entire aggregate of features as a whole.

Accordingly, instead of designating the marking values of separate distinctive features [mF] and [uF] we should introduce the designation of the marking of an entire aggregate, an entire bundle of distinctive features, i. e. (Fig. 7):

$$
m \begin{bmatrix} \alpha F_1 \\ \alpha F_2 \\ \alpha F_3 \\ \vdots \\ \alpha F_k \end{bmatrix} \quad \text{and} \quad u \begin{bmatrix} \alpha F_1 \\ \alpha F_2 \\ \alpha F_3 \\ \vdots \\ \alpha F_\ell \end{bmatrix} \text{, where } \alpha = + \text{ or } -
$$

Figure 7

Specifically, the correlations of labial and velar stops examined above must not be interpreted as the markedness of velarity in the condition of simultaneous combination with voicing, in opposition to the nonmarkedness of the feature of labialization, or as the markedness of labialization in the condition of simultaneous combination with voicelessness, but as the markedness of the simultaneous combination of features [voiced, stop (interrupted), velar] in contrast to the unmarked combination of features [voiced, stop (interrupted), labial], and as the markedness of the simultaneous combination of features [voiceless, stop (interrupted), labial], in contrast to the unmarked combination of features [voiceless, stop (interrupted), velar].[16] Thereby the marking relation is transferred

---

[16]These combinations of features, when united with other distinctive features, make up the complete bundles of features that characterize the corresponding marked and unmarked labial and velar occlusive phonemes /g b k p/:

$$
m \begin{bmatrix} \text{-syllabic} \\ \text{+nonsyllabic} \\ \text{+interrupted} \\ \text{+voiced} \\ \text{velar} \end{bmatrix} \sim u \begin{bmatrix} \text{-syllabic} \\ \text{+nonsyllabic} \\ \text{+interrupted} \\ \text{+voiced} \\ \text{labial} \end{bmatrix} \quad m \begin{bmatrix} \text{-syllabic} \\ \text{+nonsyllabic} \\ \text{+interrupted} \\ \text{-voiced} \\ \text{labial} \end{bmatrix} \sim u \begin{bmatrix} \text{-syllabic} \\ \text{+nonsyllabic} \\ \text{+interrupted} \\ \text{-voiced} \\ \text{velar} \end{bmatrix}
$$

Consequently, m → u, where [velar] → [labial] in the presence of the feature [+voiced]; u → m, where [velar] → [labial] in the presence of the feature [-voiced]. The features 'velar' and 'labial' can be represented in terms of binary acoustic features as the feature combinations [compact, grave] and [diffuse, grave] respectively.

from the separate distinctive feature to the simultaneous combination of features, to the whole bundle of distinctive features making
up the content of the phoneme.

It is easy to see that such a conception of the marking relation,
in which hierarchical dependency is not attributed to separate distinctive features but to combinations of features as a whole, comes
close to its traditional conception in the Trubetzkoy-Jakobson
theory, in which markedness/nonmarkedness is determined for
whole phonemic units viewed as bundles of distinctive features.
However, interpreting the marking relation as the presence or
absence of a certain feature in a phoneme remains different in
principle from interpreting it as a hierarchical relation determining the degree of normalness, naturalness, and frequency of occurrence of concrete combinations of distinctive features. [17]

3.5   In such a conception marking must be viewed as the
capacity of certain distinctive features for uniting into simultaneous bundles, for combining with one another on the axis of simultaneity and forming various phonemic units. The different capacities
of features for combining with each other into simultaneous combinations, into 'vertical' sequences, also creates various types of
combinations of features in the system, characterized by different
degrees of marking; that is, there are combinations of features
which are normal, natural, have a high frequency of occurrence in
the system (unmarked), and there are the less normal, less natural
combinations of features, which have a lower frequency of occurrence (marked). Both whole phonemic bundles, and subphonemic
combinations making up only a certain part of the phonemic unit,
can be combinations of distinctive features of the sort that a marking relation is established with respect to.

Depending on the different capacities of distinctive features for
combining with one another in a simultaneous bundle, it is possible
to provide a complete gradational scale of the marking of simultaneous ('vertical') combinations of features. The opposite extreme

---

[17] Therefore the marking relation can be extended to all kinds
of phonological oppositions, affecting not only privative oppositions,
but also gradual and equipollent oppositions (following Trubetzkoy's
logical classification). Thereby the terms 'marked' and 'unmarked'
diverge from their original etymological meanings 'merkmaltragend'
and 'merkmallos,' assuming the new meanings of 'nonnormal' and
'normal' feature combinations.

values on this sort of marking scale are: (a) the obligatory combinability of distinctive features on the axis of simultaneity, i. e.
maximally unmarked combinations (for example, combinations of
features such as [+syllabic, –nonsyllabic], [–syllabic, +nonsyllabic]
or [stop, dental], etc. , which are represented in any phonological
system, being component parts of the phonemes which enter into
the minimal phonemic inventory of a language); and (b) incombinability, mutual incompatibility of features which potentially form
maximally marked combinations (for example, the features [glottal-
ized] and [voiced] or the features [nasalized] and [fricative], which
cannot combine together into simultaneous bundles.

All the possible simultaneous combinations of distinctive features, with their various degrees of marking, are distributed between these extreme values of marking, with greater or lesser
approximation to the extreme values, reflecting the various capacities of the distinctive features for combining with one another in
simultaneous bundles.

3. 6   Such a marking scale for combinations of distinctive features should, in principle, have a sufficiently high degree of universality, insofar as it reflects a property common in human
language: the capacity of certain phonetic, acoustico-articulatory
properties for combining more or less freely with one another to
form synchronous articulatory complexes. Certain phonetic features, because of their acoustico-articulatory properties, combine
with one another on the axis of simultaneity more easily than others.

Marked bundles of features, in contrast to unmarked bundles,
reflect the limited capacity of certain features for entering into
simultaneous combinations with one another, their lesser inclina-
tion toward mutual combinability. Therefore such bundles are less
normal, less natural combinations of features, distributed closer
to the maximal marking value on the scale of markedness. [18]

---

[18]Underlying these sorts of restrictions imposed on the mutual
combinability of certain phonetic features are the particular properties of the human articulatory apparatus, on the one hand, and
the perceptual possibilities of vocal communication, on the other.
    Taking into account these psycho-physical characteristics of
speech, we can determine which combinations of phonetic features
are most optimal in the acoustico-articulatory and perceptual respects (which would correspond to unmarked combinations on the

It is natural to expect that such bundles (and accordingly the phonemes they represent) will have a lesser degree of realization in languages than bundles of features which, because of their acoustic and articulatory properties, combine with one another easily, representing natural, normal combinations of features. The first group of feature bundles (and accordingly the phonemes they represent) constitutes functionally weak units in the system, which have both a lower frequency of occurrence and distributional restrictions, and, in a number of systems, are completely absent, creating empty slots (gaps) in the paradigm; the second group of bundles, the more normal and natural, and, in this sense, the 'unmarked' group, constitutes the functionally strong units of the system, which have a greater distributional freedom and a higher frequency of occurrence -- some of them, in fact, with a frequency of occurrence equal to one (the maximally unmarked combinations of features). Thus, for example, the features [+syllabic, −nonsyllabic, +labialized, −low, +grave] combine with one another into a simultaneous bundle, creating the unmarked group of labialized back vowels, more easily than the features [+syllabic, −nonsyllabic, +labialized, −low, −grave], which characterize the marked group of nonlow labialized front vowels. On the other hand, the features [+syllabic, −nonsyllabic, −labialized, −low, +grave] are less inclined to combine together to create the group of nonlabialized back vowel phonemes, than the features [+syllabic, −nonsyllabic,

---

(ftnt. 18 cont.)
phonological level) and which combinations are nonoptimal in these respects, whose production and perception require great effort (the phonologically marked combinations) (see Greenberg 1966a, Greenberg and Jenkins 1964: 177, Postal 1968: 170ff.). Thus, for example, we can explain the very high marking of 'nasalized fricatives' by the incompatibility of the features 'nasality' and 'friction' in a single articulatory complex, by the physical impossibility of producing a sharp nasalized fricative, since, when the soft palate is lowered to open the nasal resonator, the pressure in the oral cavity behind the constriction proves to be insufficient to produce turbulence. In the same way, the incombinability of the features 'voicing' and 'glottalization' is explained by the particular articulatory properties of glottalized and voiced sounds. A glottalized consonant is articulated with a compression or a complete closure of the glottis, while voicing presupposes an articulation of the sound under the conditions of an open glottis and an accompanying vibration of the vocal cords (see Chomsky and Halle 1948: 300ff., Cairns 1969: 868ff.).

–labialized, –low, –grave] , which characterize the nonlabialized front vowels. [19]

Analogously, the features [–syllabic, +nonsyllabic, +voiced, stop, velar] (for the marked voiced velar stop /g/) combine together with greater difficulty than the features [–syllabic, +nonsyllabic, +voiced, stop, labial] (for the unmarked phoneme /b/). The combination of features [–syllabic, +nonsyllabic, +voiced, stop, dental] holds an intermediate position in this respect.

The features [–syllabic, +nonsyllabic, –voiced, stop, velar] (the unmarked phoneme /k/) combine together more easily than the features [–syllabic, +nonsyllabic, –voiced, stop, labial] (the marked phoneme /p/). [20] Combining these features in a simultaneous articulatory complex becomes yet more complicated when

---

[19]This general tendency, i. e. the absence of labialization in the nonlow front vowels, and, on the other hand, the presence of labialization in the nonlow back vowels, is explained by the particular perceptual properties of vowel sounds. The combinations of greatest contrast, and in this sense the optimal combinations for the perception of the vowels, are created by uniting the tonality features 'peripherality' (gravity) and flatness, with identical values. i. e. [+grave, +flat] (the labialized back vowels) or [–grave, –flat] (the nonlabialized front vowels) (see Cairns 1969:879ff.). It is noteworthy that nonlabialized back vowels and labialized front vowels are characterized as 'abnormal' in the phonetic literature, i. e. as less natural compared to labialized back vowels and non-labialized front vowels (see Pike 1961:9).

[20]These characteristics of the occlusive phonemes should be explained by their acoustico-articulatory properties. The most compact consonants (velars and postvelars), located at a point of articulation close to the glottis, do not combine easily with an accompanying vibration of the vocal cords as different from the most diffuse consonants (the labials), located at the point of articulation farthest from the glottis. The dental occlusives, which are articulated farther from the glottis compared to the velars, but closer compared to the labials, occupy an intermediate position.

On the other hand, inertness of the vocal cords (voicelessness) is the most optimal state for the articulation of the most compact consonants (the velars) and the least favorable property for the articulation of the most diffuse consonants (the labials).

one adds to this combination the feature of aspiration or (to a greater degree yet) the feature of glottalization, which respectively form the marked phoneme /pʰ/ or the marked phoneme /pʼ/, the latter distinguished among the stops for the greatest degree of marking (see above).

Thus, certain distinctive features combine together in simultaneous bundles more easily than other features, whose combinations on the axis of simultaneity create articulatorily and perceptually more complex (and therefore less optimal) formations, with a limited distribution in the system.

3.7   Since in the class of sibilant (strident) spirants and affricates (phonemes of the types s – š, z – ž, c – č, ʒ– ǯ) the voiceless (unmarked) phonemes are opposed to the corresponding voiced (marked) phonemes (the frequency of voiceless phonemes, as a rule, exceeds that of the voiced ones; gaps in a system are usually observed in place of the voiced sibilant spirant and affricate phonemes), whereas in the class of stops, along with the numerous systems which reflect the correlation of voiceless and voiced as an opposition of unmarked phonemes to marked phonemes, there are also systems with the reverse correlation (i.e. the voiced stops are unmarked, the voiceless stops marked; the CAUCASIAN languages in particular, and also an INDO-EUROPEAN language of the CAUCASIAN region -- OSSETIAN -- belong to the class of such systems; Melikishvili 1972:9ff.), we can maintain that in the general case the feature 'voicing' is more inclined to combine in a simultaneous bundle with the feature of 'occlusion' ('interruptedness') than with the feature of 'affrication' or 'friction' ('continuantness') united to the feature 'stridency.'[21]

3.8   One of the fundamental problems of contemporary typological phonology is to set up these kinds of universal models of the combinabilities of distinctive features into simultaneous bundles, into vertical sequences, along with determining their oppositional function of marking in a system. This permits us to ascertain the universally valid hierarchical dependence between correlated

---

[21]Apparently the momentary opening of the articulatory organs (abrupt offset) characteristic of the stops creates more favorable conditions for an accompanying laryngeal articulation (vibration of the vocal cords) than the sort of opening of an occlusion or incomplete closure of the organs that create the complex obstacles with a powerful air turbulence that are characteristic of the articulation of the sharp fricatives and affricates.

units of a phonological system and to distinguish the basic nucleus
of phonemic oppositions, the deep phonological structures themselves, which constitute the foundation of the phonological system
of human language, invariant with respect to both concrete phonemic
systems in synchrony and the possible transformations of these
systems in diachrony.

4.   Markedness in the Class of Fricative Phonemes and the
     Interrelationship of Occlusives and Fricatives

4.1   In this sense the question of the correlations of occlusive
and fricative phonemes in a phonological system is of particular
interest.

Labial /w/v -- f/ and velar fricatives /ɣ-- x/ opposed on the
feature of voicing/voicelessness are correlated with one another in
a relation of marking analogous to that of the corresponding occlusive phonemes.

In the labial group the unmarked member of the opposition is
the voiced fricative phoneme /w-v/[22] in contrast to the marked
voiceless member /f/,[23] while in the velar group the voiceless
fricative /x/ functions as the unmarked unit in contrast to the
marked voiced fricative /ɣ/, i.e. f → w/v and ɣ → x (where the
arrow points from the marked member of the opposition to the
unmarked member).

---

[22]The bilabial spirant [w], [β], and the labiodental spirant [v]
both represent the voiced labial fricative phoneme. In many systems
these phonetic segments appear as variants of a single voiced labial
fricative phoneme; in others they can be opposed to one another as
independent phonemic units. When this happens, the voiced labial
fricative /w/, together with the palatal fricative /y/, usually belongs
to the class of resonant phonemes, the so-called 'semivowels.'
Thanks to its dual acoustico-articulatory features the voiced labial
fricative phoneme /w/ is correlated with both the class of sonorants
and the class of non-resonant consonants, thereby forming a bila-
teral dependency (see Pulgram 1959). In the present case we are
interested in the correlations of the labial fricative /w/ with the
remaining fricative phonemes of the labial and velar groups.

[23]The voiceless labial fricative phoneme /f/ is usually realized
in a language as the labio-dental spirant [f] or the bilabial [φ].

In the series of voiced phonemes the labial fricative /w-v/ is opposed to the velar fricative /ɣ/ as the unmarked member of the opposition to the marked: ɣ→w/v; in the series of voiceless fricatives the velar fricative /x/ is the unmarked member of the opposition, in contrast to the marked member, the labial fricative /f/: f → x.

The hierarchical dependence of marking among the members of the articulatory groups and series of fricative phonemes can be represented in combined form in a rectangle of dependences, with arrows pointing from the marked member of the opposition to the unmarked member (Fig. 8):

Figure 8

4.2   Such universally valid correlations of marking between fricative phonemes of the labial and velar groups are determined on the basis of the statistical characteristics of these phonemes in various language systems and the distribution of the empty slots (gaps) in a paradigmatic system.

Systems with labial and velar fricatives opposed on the feature voicing/voicelessness have fundamentally the following forms (Fig. 9):

(a) w-v   f   (b) w-v   –   (c) w-v   f   (d) w-v   –

     ɣ   x   ɣ   x   –   x   –   x

Figure 9

The systems in Fig. 8 (b)–(d), with gaps in place of the marked members in the labial and velar groups (i. e. [w/v   –] and [–   x] are extremely widespread types, attested in numerous languages of the most various structures (see Pierce 1957: 36ff.), while systems with the reverse correlation of fricatives in the labial group (i. e. [–   f]) are not encountered at all, and in the velar group (i. e. [ɣ   –]) they are a rare exception.[24]

---

[24] Cf. the isolated cases of language systems with the velar fricative /ɣ/ that lack its voiceless correlate /x/ (e. g. TIBETAN, Rerikh 1961; BAMBARA, Toporova 1966; LOMA, Hockett 1955: 113).

The statistical characteristics of the voiced and voiceless fricatives in the labial and velar groups are also distributed in accordance with these correlations (see Table 1). In languages with very
different systems, the relative frequency of the voiced fricative
/w-v/, as a rule, exceeds that of the corresponding voiceless fricative /f/ in the labial series, while in the velar series the voiceless
fricative /x/ statistically predominates over the corresponding
voiced fricative /ɣ/. At the same time $P_{(w-v)} > P_{(ɣ)}$ and $P_{(x)} > P_{(f)}$,
i. e. in the voiced series of fricatives the labial phoneme is statistically predominant over the labial. [25] At the same time the unmarked member of the opposition generally has a greater distributional freedom than the corresponding marked member.

In terms of implicational rules these correlations can be formulated in the following statements: the presence of the voiceless
labial fricative phoneme /f/ in a system presupposes the simultaneous presence of the voiced labial fricative phoneme /w-v/:f →w/v;
and the presence of the voiced velar fricative phoneme /ɣ/ in a
system presupposes the simultaneous presence of the voiceless
velar fricative /x/: ɣ →x.

4.3   On the level of the combinabilities of distinctive features,
we can characterize the correlations of fricative phonemes examined
above as follows: the combination of features [-syllabic, +nonsyllabic,
-voiced, fricative, velar] is unmarked in contrast to the marked
combinations [-syllabic, +nonsyllabic, -voiced, fricative, labial]
and [-syllabic, +nonsyllabic, +voiced, fricative, velar].

Consequently, the features [-voiced, fricative, labial] do not
combine together as well as the features [-voiced, fricative, velar],
while replacing the feature 'voicelessness' with the feature 'voicing,'
i. e. [-voiced] → [+voiced], the reverse correlation arises: the
features [+voiced, fricative, labial] combine together in a simultaneous bundle more readily than the features [+voiced, fricative,
velar]. Thereby a complete correspondence is established with
respect to marking in the subclasses of occlusive and fricative

---

[25] Language systems with deviations from such statistical correlations of fricative phonemes are extremely rare. Among such
systems are in particular, GERMAN: /v/ = 3.88, /f/ = 3.94, /x/ =
5.32; SPANISH: /w/ = 2.18, /f/ = 0.90, /x/ = 0.64; and SAMOAN:
/v/ = 1.4, /f/ = 3.68 (see Delattre 1965:93ff., Schnitzer 1967:58-
72, Sigurd 1968:1ff.).

phonemes.[26] The functionally strong (unmarked) members in a
vertical correlation (i. e. in the series, cf. the phonemes /w-v/
and /x/ respectively in the oppositional pairs [w/v --ɣ] and [f-- x])
prove to be the functionally strong (unmarked) units in a horizontal
correlation too (i. e. in the groups, cf. the phonemes /w-v/ and /x/
respectively in the oppositional pairs [w/v -- f] and [ɣ-- x]) (Fig. 10):

Stops   Fricatives

Figure 10

4.4   The correlations between the subclasses of stop and
(nonsibilant) fricative phonemes in a paradigmatic system are not
limited solely to the identical direction of marking in the oppositional members of the labial and velar groups.

More important in this respect is the connection between these
subclasses of nonresonant consonantal phonemes that is manifested
in the functional dependence of the fricatives on the corresponding
stops, in the conditioning of the functioning of the fricative subclass
by the subclass of stop phonemes.[27]

In particular, an analysis of the gaps (empty slots) in the paradigmatic system among the occlusive and fricative phonemes permits

---

[26] Apparently the same rules of combinability for the sonority
features compact/diffuse and the feature of laryngeal articulation
hold for the fricatives as well as for the occlusives. The articulation of the most compact fricatives is combined less easily with
vibrations of the vocal cords than the articulation of the less diffuse fricatives, while the inert state of the vocal cords, which
causes the voicelessness of a consonant, is an optimal condition
for the articulation of the compact fricatives and a less suitable
condition for the articulation of the diffuse fricatives.

[27] On the general dependence of the fricative phonemes on the
stops, in the sense of the priority of the stops in a phonological
system, which precedes the appearance of the fricatives when the
child acquires the language, see Jakobson 1941: 320.

us to assume a definite interconnection between the absence of the
functionally weak, marked members in the subsystem of stops (i. e.
the absence of the voiceless labial stop[28] or the voiced velar stop)
and the presence, the functioning in the system of the corresponding
fricative phonemes (i. e. of the voiceless labial phoneme /f/ or the
voiced velar phoneme /ɣ/ respectively). Namely, the absence of
the voiceless stop /p/ from the labial group presupposes the presence of the corresponding voiceless fricative /f/ in the system;
and the absence of the voiced stop /g/ from the velar group presupposes the presence of the corresponding voiced fricative /ɣ/ in the
system: i. e. p̄ → f and ḡ → ɣ.

Thus, if the marked combination of features [–syllabic, +non-
syllabic, –voiced, stop, labial] has a frequency of zero in a system
(i. e. if there is a gap in place of the voiceless labial stop phoneme(s)
in a paradigmatic system in which the labial group of stops is generally represented),[29] then the marked combination of features

---

[28] Under the "absence of the voiceless labial stop" is understood
here not a gap in place of one of the voiceless labial phonemes while the
other voiceless labial members are present (e. g. the glottalized phoneme is absent from the labial group while the voiceless aspirate
remains, cf. system 4. a above, languages of the type of the
DAGHESTANIAN languages, cf. Gudava 1964, or the glottalized
and aspirated phonemes are absent while the simple voiceless
labial remains, cf. system 5. b above, languages of the type of
NAVAHO); instead, the voiceless stops are completely absent in
the labial group, i. e. systems of types 1. a, 1. c, and 4. b, with
gaps in place of all the voiceless members of the labial group,
are intended.

[29] The labial and velar groups of occlusives are represented in
the phonological systems of an overwhelming majority of the languages of the world. Consonantal systems with a missing labial
or velar group are a rare exception. For example, the absence
of the velar group of occlusives is observed in some SLOVENIAN
dialects (see Trubetzkoy 1939: 142). A system with a missing labial
group of occlusives is encountered in a number of AMERINDIAN
languages belonging to the IROQUOIAN group and the NADENE
family. The latter includes TLINGIT, which lacks a labial group
of stops and nasals (see Milewski 1967: 20, Pinnow 1966: 42). However, as has been observed by Jakobson (1941: 357ff.), the absence
of a labial group of occlusives is possibly a secondary phenomenon,
explained by ritual mutilation of the lips, also observed in a number
of Central African tribes.

[-syllabic, +nonsyllabic, +voiced, fricative, labial] has a frequency exceeding zero (i. e. the voiceless labial fricative phoneme /f/ is present in the system). If the marked combination of features [-syllabic, +nonsyllabic, +voiced, stop, velar] has a frequency of zero in a system (i. e. if there is a gap in place of the voiced velar stop in a paradigmatic system in which the velar group of stops is generally represented), then the marked combination of features [-syllabic, +nonsyllabic, +voiced, fricative, velar] has a frequency exceeding zero (i. e. the voiced velar fricative phoneme /ɣ/ is present in the system). [30]

But the presence of the voiceless labial /f/ in a system implies, as was noted above, the presence of the corresponding unmarked voiced /w-v/, and the presence of the voiced velar fricative /ɣ/ in a system implies the presence of the corresponding unmarked voiceless phoneme /x/. Consequently, if the functionally weak, marked members in the labial and velar groups of the subsystem of stops are absent, thereby creating empty slots in the paradigmatic system, these gaps would be filled, as it were, by the corresponding fricative phonemes, i. e. by the fricative phonemes of the velar and labial groups. Thus, the fricative phonemes /f/ and /ɣ/ (and the implied or unmarked members, /w - v/ and /x/ respectively) are a substitute for the corresponding marked stops /p/ and /g/, compensating, as it were, for their absence and thereby establishing a 'balance' in a paradigmatic system with an opposition of phonemes on the feature voicing / voicelessness.

4.5   Paradigmatic systems with gaps in place of the marked stops 'filled in' by the corresponding fricative phonemes have fundamentally the following forms (Fig. 11):

(a)		(b) w/v	f	(c) w/v	f	(d) w/v		f
b	p	b	–	b	–	b	–	–
d	t	d	t	d	t	d	t	t'
–	k	g	k	–	k	g	k	k'
ɣ	x			ɣ	x			

Figure 11

---

[30]In other words, in occlusive phonemes characterized by a frequency of zero in the system, replacing the feature [stop] with the feature [fricative] ([stop] → [fricative] or [+interrupted] → [-interrupted]) converts these bundles of features into combinations with a frequency exceeding zero.

DUTCH, BELORUSSIAN, UKRAINIAN, CZECH, SLOVAK, the
SOUTHERN GREAT RUSSIAN dialects (Bernshtejn 1961:292ff.),[31]
KET (Kreinovič 1968:453ff.),[32] CHUAN (Moskaljev 1971), and
TUVIN (Iskhakov and Pal'mbakh 1961: 50ff.) are examples of lan-
guage systems of type (a); YORUBA (Toporova 1966 : 219ff.),
BERBER (Zavadskij 1967), BORA (Matteson 1972:31ff.),EGYPTIAN
ARABIC, YEMENI ARABIC, CENTRAL ASIAN dialects of ARABIC
(Sharbatov 1966, Tsereteli 1956:XII-XIII), ETHIOPIC (GEEZ) are
examples of the system of type (b); system (c) is represented in
VIETNAMESE (Gordina and Bystrov 1970:192ff.) and CLASSICAL
ARABIC; and system (d) is characteristic of HAUSA (where the
implosives /'b/ and /'d/ are also present) (Jushmanov 1937:7ff.).

4.6   We can assume that the tendency toward such a 'balance'
in a paradigmatic system is evoked by a general tendency to symmetrically fill[33] the three basic articulatory regions, the labial,
dental, and velar (pre-/postvelar) regions, with sounds of consonantal articulation, stops or fricatives.[34]

---

[31] In some of these languages the phoneme /ɣ/ is realized as a
voiceless pharyngeal spirant. Naturally, in such languages the
pharyngeals do not constitute a special phonemic group (cf. Kučera
1962).

[32] An analogous correlation is also observed in KET with respect
to the postvelar (uvular) group, where the missing voiced occlusive
phoneme is replaced in the system by the corresponding fricative
phoneme.

[33] On symmetry in a paradigmatic system, cf. Hockett 1955:140ff.

[34] Consonants articulated in these regions make up the three
basic articulatory groups represented in almost all the languages of
the world: the labial, dental (apical), and velar (dorsal) groups (the
consonants p, t, and k are included in the minimal phonemic inventory of language, cf. Milewski 1967:15ff., Chomsky and Halle
1968:414). Consonantal sounds produced at these points of articulation can be regarded as 'the most natural,' in the sense that their
appearance results in the most simple and natural manner from the
activity of the mobile parts in the oral cavity (see Trubetzkoy 1939).
     The 'velar region' covers the prevelar point of articulation as
well as the postvelar (uvular) point and the velar region in the strict
sense. In a number of language systems the nonvocoid sounds produced at these points of articulation are phonologically opposed units;
in other systems these same sounds are subphonemic variants of a
single consonantal phoneme which covers an undifferentiated velar
region and can thus be characterized as 'velar' or 'guttural' (dorsal),

The absence of a functionally weak occlusive member of a system (a voiceless labial or voiced velar stop) is compensated by the presence of the corresponding fricative member, which fills the gap in articulation corresponding to the voiceless or voiced element in the labial or velar articulatory region.

We can assert that, if one ignores the feature occlusion/friction (interrupted/noninterrupted), each 'pigeonhole' of the voiced and voiceless series of the labial, dental and velar groups is filled with a corresponding phoneme, and that in a paradigmatic system with an opposition of nonresonant consonantal phonemes on the feature voicing/voicelessness there are no gaps (empty slots). [35]

(ftnt. 34 cont.)
and acoustically as 'compact and grave (peripheral)' (see Jakobson, Fant, and Halle 1962: 173ff. in the RUSSIAN edition, Trubetzkoy 1939).

[35] This sort of dependency between a marked occlusive and a corresponding fricative phoneme is not observed in a number of language systems, which constitute by their nature an exception to the established rule. Thus, for example, in the paradigmatic systems of some AMERINDIAN languages with a gap in place of the voiced velar occlusive /g/, the corresponding substitute, in the form of the fricative /ɣ/, is not found (cf. the system of ITONAMA, Liccardi and Grimes 1968:6-7; QUILEUTE, Andrade 1933-38: 151ff. It is characteristic that in the majority of languages cited the class of fricatives is extremely restricted.).
Some SOUTHEAST ASIAN languages also constitute an exception in this respect, in particular THAI, KHMER and LAOTIAN (cf. Glazova 1970:283-303).
From an analysis of the exceptions with respect to the interdependency of occlusive and fricative phonemes we can conclude that these exceptions chiefly concern the velar group of stops and fricatives. Systems with similar exceptions with respect to the labial group are extremely rare and limited to a small number of AMERINDIAN languages (cf. Wheeler 1972:93ff.). This property of the labial group, which distinguishes it from the velar group, is very likely one of the manifestations of the priority of the labial group (along with the dental group) in comparison to the velar group (cf. Jakobson 1941). From this standpoint a defective group of velar occlusives without the corresponding substitutes in the form of fricative phonemes is, in a number of language systems, a reflection of an original linguistic state, with the basic oppositions of consonants restricted to the labial and dental regions. These systems can be thought of as being in the process of filling the gaps in the velar group with the missing members in the form of the voiced occlusive or the corresponding fricative phonemes (cf. the appearance of the consonants /g/ and /ɣ/ in some THAI dialects; see Moskaljev 1970:260ff.).

4.7 When the marked stops /p/ and /g/ are present in a system, i.e. the frequency of the combinations of features [-syllabic, +nonsyllabic, -voiced, stop, labial] and [-syllabic, +nonsyllabic, -voiced, stop, velar] exceeds zero, the presence of their substitutes in the system, in the form of the corresponding fricative phonemes /f/ and /ɣ/, is facultative. In the system such fricative phonemes represent redundant consonantal elements of the labial and velar groups (labial and velar points of articulation).

There are 'redundant' systems in which both the marked stops and their substitutes, in the form of marked fricative phonemes of the labial and/or velar groups, are present.[36] In such systems with the 'redundant' pairs [p -- f] and [g -- ɣ] one of the members of these pairs (and only one) can become lost in the process of diachronic phonemic transformation. However, at least one of the members of these pairs must be present in the system, because of the tendency to symmetrically fill the three basic articulatory regions with consonantal phonemes of the voiced and voiceless categories.[37]

---

[36] In particular, many IRANIAN and TURKIC languages, with completely filled groups of both the occlusive and fricative phonemes, are typical examples of such 'redundant' systems. The reconstructed COMMON SEMITIC phonological system, with a voiced velar stop /*g/ alongside a velar group of fricatives /*ɣ, *x/, is also 'redundant' (cf. Moscati 1959:25ff.).

[37] The development of the COMMON SEMITIC phonemes /*g/ and /*ɣ/ in the historical SEMITIC languages can serve as an example of a diachronic process of this sort. The fricative phoneme /*ɣ/, which gave the laryngeal phoneme /'/ as a reflex in EAST SEMITIC (AKKADIAN), merged with the pharyngeal /ʕ/ in HEBREW, SYRIAN, and ETHIOPIAN, thereby conditioning the preservation of the voiced velar occlusive phoneme /g/ in these languages. In contrast to this, the change of COMMON SEMITIC velar /*g/ to the affricate /ǰ/ in CLASSICAL SOUTH SEMITIC (ARABIC) contributes to the preservation of the velar fricative /ɣ/ in this language, compensating, as it were, for the absence of the voiced occlusive in the velar group.

In its turn the COMMON SEMITIC /*p/ changes to the labial fricative phoneme /f/ in ARABIC and ETHIOPIAN; as a result there appears a gap in the series of voiceless stops, which is filled by the fricative phoneme that had appeared. An analogous development with respect to the voiced velar stop /g/, forming a gap in the system of stops when it changes into its substitute, the corresponding

The complete or partial absence of fricative phonemes in various paradigmatic systems, whose labial and velar groups are filled with 'primary' elements in the form of occlusive phonemes, is also explained by this sort of dependence of the labial and velar fricatives on the functioning of the corresponding voiced and voiceless stops in the system. [38]

4.8. The weak functional role of the interdental fricatives [ð---θ] in the paradigmatic system is explained by an analogous dependence. Since the dental group of stops [d --- t] is distinguished for the greatest frequency of occurrence, being the most stable of the groups of stops (see Manczak 1959, Guiraud 1959: 100 ff.), the group of mellow fricatives corresponding to it is functionally the weakest among the fricative groups. As a consequence of the fact that there are no systems missing the dental group of stops (see Trubetzkoy 1939, Jakobson 1944), the (inter)dental group of fricatives [ð---θ], their substitutes, is always facultative, redundant

---

(ftnt. 37 cont.)
fricative phoneme, can be observed in the example of transformations in many phonological systems (cf. the development of the phoneme /g/ in BELORUSSIAN, UKRAINIAN, CZECH, SLOVAK, the SOUTHERN GREAT RUSSIAN dialects, etc.).

On the other hand, the development in some RUSSIAN dialects of the spirant /f/, which is replaced with the unmarked sequence [xv] (cf. xvunt and xunt 'pound, ' grax 'count,' torx 'peat'), or the merger of the velar fricative phoneme /x/ with the labial /f/ in EARLY MODERN ENGLISH can serve as typical examples of the transformation of a 'redundant' fricative phoneme (see Panov 1966: 115, Pilch 1964:136). The latter case is a rarer phenomenon in language, the merger of an unmarked phonemic unit with a marked one. The change of a marked phonemic unit in a system into an unmarked one, i.e. its merger with the latter, as a result of which an empty slot could appear in the system, is more normal and natural (cf. Postal 1968:170).

[38] Thus, for example, the labial and velar fricatives are completely absent in a majority of AUSTRALIAN languages (see Capell 1967:85ff.). In some systems the labial group of fricatives is absent and the velar group present (cf., for example, YAKUT, Ubrjatova 1966:403ff.; BAKAIRI, Wheatley 1967:81) or, on the other hand, the velar group of fricatives is absent and the labial group is present (ENGLISH, FRENCH, ALBANIAN, INDIAN languages, etc.).

in the system. This should also explain the restricted distribution
of the (inter)dental spirants in the languages of the world, compared
to that of the labial and velar fricatives.

4.9   Thus, the (nonsibilant) fricative phonemes of the labial,
dental, and velar groups, i. e. [w/v --- f], [ǯ---θ], and [γ---x] respectively, are correlated with the occlusive phonemes of the corresponding groups (the labials [b ---p], the dentals [d---t], and the
velars [g---k]) as their substitutes, filling the gaps in the paradigmatic system when the functionally weak members in the class of
stops are absent. Thereby the occlusive and the nonsibilant fricative phonemes constitute a definite interdependent subsystem, opposed to the subsystem of the sibilant spirants and the affricates
and to the subsystem of the resonant consonants within the general
paradigmatic system of a language.

A definite hierarchical order among the various types of phonological oppositions is revealed in this interdependence, testifying
to the existence of a certain strict stratification of phonological
values in a linguistic system, the basic features of which were revealed earlier by Jakobson (see Jakobson 1939); we must assume
that diachronic phonemic changes in a system, seeming at first
glance to be processes uncoordinated and unconnected with one
another, can be comprehended as interdependent, mutually conditioned transformations, governed by such a hierarchy of phonological values.

APPENDIX : Relative Frequencies of Fricatives[1]

Languages:	Phonemes:			
	/w-v/	/f/	/x/	/ɣ/
ABKHAZ	1.3	0.3	1.77	0.16
ADYGHE	0.45	0.1	2.89	1.41
AZERBAIJANI	1.66	0.13	0.94	0.69
ARABIC[2]	2.38	1.23	0.26	0.09
ARABIC (Central Asian)	0.99	0.95	0.64	0.54
GILYAN[3]	0.38	0.26	1.31	0.29
OSSETIAN	2.05	1.72	3.53	0.2
PERSIAN	1.74	0.6	1.63	0.28
TAJIK	1.69	1.07	1.46	0.26
UDIN[4]	0.45	0.1	2.82	1.41
AKHVAKH[5]	4.74	--	1.9	0.31
GEORGIAN	4.17	--	2.65	0.79
SVAN[6]	3.5	--	4.89	0.98
MUNJAN[7]	1.67	0.63	0.95	--
POLISH	5.96	0.25	1.44	--
RUSSIAN[8]	2.75	0.29	0.68	--
ASSYRIAN[9]	2.57	--	4.58	--
PIRO[10]	1.42	--	0.39	--
ALBANIAN[11]	0.83	0.49	--	--
ENGLISH[12]	1.88	1.3	--	--
HUNGARIAN[13]	2.06	0.12	--	--
TURKISH	1.34	0.55	--	--
FRENCH	2.15	1.11	--	--
HINDI[14]	1.78	0.18	--	--
SWEDISH[15]	2.6	1.8		

---

[1] The relative frequencies of fricatives (in percentages) in a text 10,000 to 30,000 phonemes long (depending on the language) are given in the table. The calculations of the textual frequencies of the fricatives is based on the assumption of the uniformity of random samples relative to the statistical distribution of phonemes in increasing or decreasing frequency (cf. Segal, 1972:169ff.).

[2] Tsereteli 1956:51-60.

[3] Rastorgueva 1971:268-73.

[4] Dzhejranashvili 1971:139-72.

[5] Magomedbekova 1967:151-55.

[6] Shanidze 1939:13-17.

[7] Grjunberg 1972:74-82.

[8] Cf. Kučera and Monroe 1968:33.

[9] Tsereteli 1965:14-26.

[10] Cf. Matteson 1963.

[11] Cf. Shirokov 1964:53ff.

[12] Cf. also Sigurd 1968.

[13] Cf. Vértes 1953:125ff.

[14] Konsovskij 1968:167-81.

[15] Sigurd 1968.

BIBLIOGRAPHY

Andrade, N. Y. 1933-38. Quileute. Handbook of American Indian languages, 3, ed. by Franz Boas.

Andrzejewski, B. W. 1957. Some preliminary observations on the Borana dialect of Galla. Bulletin of the School of Oriental and African Studies, 19. 2. 354-74.

Bernshtejn, S. B. 1961. Ocherk sravnitel'noj grammatiki slovjanskih jazykov. Moscow.

Broadbent, S. M. and H. Pitkin. 1964. A comparison of Miwok and Wintun. Studies in California Linguistics. Berkeley and Los Ageles: University of California, 19-53.

Cairns, C. E. 1969. Markedness, neutralization and universal redundancy rules. Language 45.

Callaghan, C. A. 1964. Phonemic borrowing in Lake Miwok. Studies in California Linguistics. Berkeley and Los Angeles: University of California, 46-53.

Cantineau, J. 1952. Le consonantisme du sémitique. Semitica IV. 290-294.

Capell, A. 1967. Sound systems in Australia. Phonetica 16.

Chomsky, Noam and M. Halle. 1968. The sound pattern of English. New York: Harper and Row.

Deeters, G. 1963. Die kaukasischen Sprachen. Handbuch der Orientalistik 7. Leiden-Köln: B. Spuler.

Dzhejranashvili, J. 1971. Udinskij jazyk. Tbilisi.

Ferguson, Charles A. 1963. Assumptions about nasals; a sample study in phonological universals. Universals of language, ed. by J. H. Greenberg, 42ff.

Fromkin, V. 1970. The concept of "naturalness" in a universal phonetic theory. Glossa 4. 29-45.

Gamkrelidze, T. V. 1968. Dezaffrikatizatsija v svanskom. Pravila perepisyvanija v diakhronicheskoj fonologii. Tibilisi.

Glazova, M. G. 1970. K opisaniju fonologicheskikh sistem nekotorykh jazykov jugovostochnoj Azii. Jazyki jugovostochnoj Azii. Moscow.

42   Thomas V. Gamkrelidze

Gordina, M. V. and Bystrov, I. S. 1970. O foneticheskom stroje nekotorikh tsentral'nykh govorov v' etnamskogo jazyka. Jazyki Jugo - vostochnoj Azii. Moscow

Greenberg, Joseph H. 1966a. Language universals. Current Trends in Linguistics, ed. by Thomas A. Sebeok, 61ff. The Hague — Paris: Mouton. (A slightly revised and amplified edition of this work appeared as Language universals (1966) with special reference to feature hierarchies. The Hague — Paris: Mouton. Citations in the paper are from this edition.)

_____. 1966b. Synchronic and diachronic universals in phonology. Language 42. 508-17.

_____. 1970. Some generalizations concerning glottalic consonants, especially implosives. Working Papers on Language Universals 2; also International Jou.:nal of American Linguistics 36. 2.

_____. (ed.) 1963. Universals of language. Cambridge, Mass.: M. I. T. Press.

_____ and J. Jenkins. 1964. Studies in the psychological correlates of the sound system of American English. Word 20.

Grjunberg, A. A. 1972. Mundzhanskij jazyk. Jazyki vostochnogo Gindukusha. Leningrad.

Gudava. T. Z. 1964. Konsonantizm andijskh jazykov. Tbilisi.

Guiraud, P. 1959. Problèmes et méthodes de la statistique linguistique. Bordrecht: Reidel.

Hockett, C. F. 1955. A manual of phonology. Baltimore.

Hoijer, H. 1933-38. Tonkawa: an Indian language of Texas. Handbook of American Indian Languages, ed. by Franz Boas (3rd ed.). New York.

_____. 1966. Hare phonology: an historical study. Language 42. 499-507.

Iskhakov, F. G. and Pal'mbakh, A. A. 1961. Grammatika tuvinskogo jazyka. Fonetika i morfologija. Moscow.

Jackson, F. L. 1972. Proto-Mayan. Comparative studies in Amerindian languages, ed. by E. Matteson et al. The Hague: Mouton.

Jakobson, Roman. 1931. Zur Struktur des russischen Verbums. Selected writings II, 1971: 3-15.

_____. 1939. Les lois phoniques du langage enfantin et leur place dans la phonologie générale. Selected writings I, 1971:357ff.

Jakobson, Roman. 1941. Kindersprache, Aphasie und allgemeine Lautgesetze. Selected writings I, 1971:317-40.

_____. 1963. Implications of language universals for linguistics. Universals of Language, ed. by J.H. Greenberg, 208ff.

_____. 1971a. Signe zéro. Selected writings II, 1971:211-19.

_____. 1971b. Pattern in linguistics. Selected writings II, 1971:223ff.

_____. 1971c. Krugovorot lingvisticheskikh terminov. Selected writings I, 1971:734ff.

_____, G. Fant and M. Halle. 1962. Preliminaries to speech analysis (Russian edition), Novoje v linguistike II. Moscow.

Jushmanov, N.V. 1937. Stroj jazyka khausa. Leningrad.

Konsovskij, A.I. 1968. Nekotoryje predvaritel'nyje dannyje o chastotnosti grafem i fonem sovremennogo literaturnogo jazyka khindi. Jazyki Indii, Pakistana, Nepala i Tsejtona. Moscow.

Krejnovič, Je. A. 1968. Ketskij jazyk. Jazyki narodov SSSR, 5. Moscow.

Kučera, H. 1962. The phonology of Czech. 'S-Gravenhage.

_____ and G. Monroe. 1968. A comparative quantitative phonology of Russian, Czech, and German. New York.

Lehmann, W.P. 1952. Proto-Indo-European phonology. Austin: University of Texas.

Lenormand, H. 1952. The phonemes of Lifu (Loyalty Islands): the shaping of a pattern. Word 8.3. 252ff.

Liccardi, M. and J. Grimes. 1968. Itonama intonation and phonemes. Linguistics 38.

Longacre, R. 1965. On linguistic affinities of Amuzgo. International Journal of American Linguistics 32.

Magomedbekova, Z.M. 1967. Akhvakhskij jazyk. Tbilisi.

44   Thomas V. Gamkrelidze

Manczak, W. 1959. Frequence d'emploi des occlusives labiales, dentales et velaires. BSLP 208-14.

Martinet, A. 1953. Remarque sur le consonantisme sémitique. BLSP 49.68-70.

_____. 1955. Economie des changements phonétiques; traité de phonétique diachronique. Berne.

Matteson, E. 1963. The Piro (Arawakan) language. Berkeley and Los Angeles: University of California Press.

_____. 1972. Toward Proto-Amerindian. Comparative Studies in Amerindian languages, ed. by E. Matteson. The Hague -- Paris: Mouton.

McCawley, J.D. 1968. Review of Current Trends in Linguistics, III: Theoretical Foundations. Language 44.

Melikishvili, I. 1970. The conditions of markedness for the features voicing, voicelessness, labiality, and velarity. Matsne 5. 137-58. Tbilisi. (in Georgian)

_____. 1972. Otnoshenije markirovannosti v fonologii (uslovija markirovannosti v klasse shumnykh fonem). Tbilisi: Avtoreferat dissertatsii na soiskanije uchenoj stepeni kandidata filologicheskikh nauk.

Milewski, T. 1967. Typological studies on the American Indian languages. Kraków.

Moscati, S. 1959. Lezioni di linguistica Semitica. Rome.

Moskaljev, A.A. 1970. Predvaritel'nyje zamechanija po fonologii govora tjan'ba. Jazyki Jugo-vostochnoj Azii. Moscow.

_____. 1971. Grammatika jazyka chzhuan. Moscow.

Oswalt, R.S. 1964. A comparative study of two Pomo languages. Studies in Californian linguistics. Berkeley and Los Angeles: University of California, 49-162.

Panov, A.V. 1966. Russkij jazyk. Jazyki Narodov SSSR, I. Moscow.

Pierce, J. E. 1957. A statistical study of consonants in New World languages I. Introduction. International Journal of American Linguistics 23.

Pike, K. L. 1961. Phonetics: a critical analysis of phonetic theory and a technic for the practical description of sounds. Ann Arbor: University of Michigan Press.

Pilch, H. 1964. Phonemtheorie I. Bibliotheca Phonetica I. Basel -- New York.

Pinnow, H. -J. Grundzüge einer historischen Lautlehre des Tlingit. Wiesbaden.

Postal, Paul. 1968. Aspects of phonological theory. New York: Harper and Row.

Priest, P. 1968. Phonemes of the Sirionó language. Linguistics 4.

Pulgram, E. 1959. Introduction to the spectography of speech. 'S-Gravenhage.

Rastorgueva, V.S. (ed.) 1971. Giljanskij jazyk. Moscow.

Rerikh, Ju. N. 1961. Tibetskij Jazyk. Moscow.

Sapir, E. and H. Hoijer. 1967. The phonology and morphology of the Navaho language. University of California Publications 50. Berkeley and Los Angeles: University of California Press.

Sasse, H. Y. 1973. Elemente der Galla-Grammatik (Borana-Dialekt). Universität München.

Schnitzer, R.D. 1967. A statistical study of the structure of the Spanish syllable. Linguistics 37. 58-72.

Segal, D.M. 1972. Osnovy fonologicheskoj statistiki. Na materiale pol' skogo jazyka. Moscow.

Shanidze, A. G. 1939. Svanskije prozaicheskije teksty. Tbilisi.

Shapiro, M. 1972. Explorations into markedness. Language 48. 345ff.

Sharbatov, G. Sh. 1966. Sootnoshenije arabskogo jazyka i sovremennykh arabskikh dialektov. Moscow.

Shipley, W.F. 1964. Maidu grammar. Barkeley and Los Angeles:
University of California Press.

Shirokov, O.S. 1964. O sootnoshenii fonologicheskoj sistemy i
chastotnosti fonem. Voprosy Jazykoznanija 1.

Sigurd, B. 1968. Rank-frequency distribution for phonemes.
Phonetica 18.

Toporova, I.N. 1966. Materialy k opisaniju fonologicheskikh
sistem jazykov Mande i gvinejskoj gruppy v svjazi s problemami
tipologii. Jazyki Afriki. Moscow.

Trubetzkoy, N. 1939. Principles of phonology. (Citations are
from the Russian edition. Moscow, 1960.)

Tsereteli, G.V. 1956. Arabskije dialekty Srednej Azii I. Tbilisi.

Tsereteli, K.G. 1965. Materialy po aramejskoj dialektologii I.

Ubrjatova, Je.N. 1966. Jakutskij jazyk. Jazyki Narodov SSSR
II.. 403ff.

Vértes, E. 1953. Phonetischer Aufbau der ungarischen Sprache.
Acta Linguistica Academiae Scientiarum Hungaricae III. 1-2.

Wheatley, J. 1967. Bakairi verb structure. Linguistics 47. 81.

Wheeler, A. 1972. Proto-Chibchan. Studies in Amerindian
languages, ed. by E. Matteson et al. The Hague -- Paris:
Mouton.

Woodward, M.F. 1964. Hupa phonemics. Studies in Californian
Linguistics. Berkeley and Los Angeles: University of California
Press, 199-216.

Zavadskij, J.N. 1967. Berberskij jazyk. Moscow.

A General Study
of Palatalization

D. N. S. BHAT

ABSTRACT

A cross-linguistic study of palatalization has revealed that there
are at least three distinct processes, namely tongue-fronting, tongue-
raising, and spirantization which, occurring either individually or
in different combination, produce the effects that are generally denoted by the cover term, palatalization. The environments in which
these processes occur are also distinct: for example, an unstressed
front vowel (or a palatal semivowel) is very effective in producing
tongue-raising (or apical palatalization), whereas a stressed front
vowel is more effective than an unstressed one in producing tongue-
fronting (or velar palatalization). A detailed study of the above
three processes, the environments that induce them, and the effects
they have on consonants and vowels are presented in this paper.

Reprinted from Working Papers on Language Universals 14,
April 1974, 17-58.

48   D.N.S. Bhat

CONTENTS

1. Introduction

We have examined for this paper about 120 instances of palatalization occurring in languages and dialects belonging to different languages families. These were generally instances of assimilation of different consonants brought about by a neighboring front vowel or a palatal semivowel. They also included, though less frequently, cases of assimilation of a consonant to a neighboring palatal consonant, unconditioned palatalization, and also some of the changes that symbolized diminutive formation, or rapidity of speech.

In view of this varied use of the term palatalization in linguistics, it is somewhat difficult to provide a definition that would take care of all the instances that are generally included under it. However, one can specify two different conditions in such a way that the presence of at least one of them would automatically bring a change under the above cover term. The conditions are: 1) the environment that induces the change must be a "palatalizing environment" (i.e. it must be a front vowel, a palatal semivowel, or a palatal or palatalized consonant), and 2) the sound that results from the change must be palatal or must have a secondary palatal articulation. In cases such as the RUSSIAN second velar palatalization (Shevelov 1964), for example, only the first condition is present, whereas in a dental palatalization occurring before a high back vowel (see 2.3 below), only the second condition is present. In most of the instances that are included under the term palatalization, however, both the above conditions would be present.

1.1 Constituents of palatalization

Palatalization has been considered to be a single diachronic (or morphophonemic) process by linguists, and it is represented by a single palatalization process in the traditional terminology. Even though the generative terminology represents it by a two-fold process, namely 1) the change of the velars to a $\begin{bmatrix} +high \\ -back \end{bmatrix}$ position, and 2) of the dentals and labials to a [+high] position, this distinction in the effect of palatalization on velars and non-velars is considered to be "structurally motivated" (i.e. the dentals and labials are considered to be [-back] by definition) (Chomsky and Halle 1968), and hence no importance is given to the distinction in a general study of palatalization. Thus, linguists such as Jakobson et al. (1963), Allen (1957), Chen (1971, 1973), Lightner (1965), Campbell (1974) and others have treated palatalization as a single diachronic process while making generalizations regarding its occurrence, spread or disappearance in various languages.

This is rather unfortunate because, as is shown below, raising
(or changing to [+high]) and fronting (or changing to [-back]) could
be differentiated from one another not only from the point of view
of the consonants that are affected by the change, but also from the
point of view of the environments that have actually induced the
change in a given language. The two also could occur independently
of one another, as for example in the RUSSIAN second velar palatalization, where fronting occurs independently of raising (k, g, x
to c, z, s before ay and oy), and in the dental palatalization where
raising occurs independently (i. e. to the exclusion) of fronting.

There are in fact three different diachronic processes, namely
tongue-fronting, tongue-raising, and spirantization which could
occur either alone or in different combinations to produce the
instances that have been denoted by the cover term, palatalization.
One could differentiate these processes 1) by the environments that
induce them, 2) by the consonants that are affected by them, and
3) by the languages or dialects that have actually undergone these
changes. For example, tongue-fronting is effective on velars, and
is induced by a following front vowel occurring preferably in a
stressed syllable. Tongue-raising, on the other hand, is effective
on apical and labial consonants, and is induced by a following semivowel or high vowel (especially front). The third process, namely
spirantization, could affect the velars and apicals, and also the
palatals, but rarely the labials. All the three may occur in a language either jointly or in different combinations, or even individually
to the exclusion of others.

2. Differentiating the Three Processes

One could easily give an articulatory basis for differentiating
between the three underlying processes, namely fronting, raising
and spirantization. Acoustically, the tongue-fronting is said to
represent a raise in the frequency of the second formant, whereas
the tongue-raising is said to represent the lowering of the frequency
of the first formant (Jones 1959). Both have the effect of increasing
the gap between the first and the second formants. The third process, namely spirantization, represents the addition of stridency
to the consonant under consideration.

We have used the term spirantization in this paper to represent
the process by which stridency or friction is added to a consonant
in a given environment. This is somewhat different from the sense
in which it is generally used in historical linguistics. In the latter
usage, it represents the "weakening" of sounds, such as the change

of stops to affricates or fricatives in the intervocalic position. Other effects of this weakening in the intervocalic position are said to be the change of apical stops and trills to flaps, of fricatives to approximants, and of flaps and laterals to semivowels or even to their complete loss. It is evident that the addition of stridency (or "spirantization" in its narrow sense) is only one of the processes that constitute this intervocalic weakening.

Secondly, the addition of stridency may take place as the effect of an opposite tendency as well, namely "strengthening." This would depend, of course, upon the environment in which the process is actually taking place. For example, when a word-initial or word-final consonant is affricated or changed from an approximant to a fricative, one cannot consider it as a case of weakening. Similarly, as has been pointed out below (2.2), the occurrence of spirantization in the palatalizing environment also cannot be considered as a case of weakening. Evidently, the cover processes such as weakening and strengthening need a more detailed study. What is clear at the moment is that spirantization is only one of the constituent processes that occur under both these tendencies.

In the following two sections, we propose to put forth phonological arguments for considering the three constituent processes, namely fronting, raising and spirantization, as independent entities. These arguments would be based on distributional limitations of the relevant sounds, their allophonic or morphophonemic alterations, and their dialectal relationships. All these represent, in one way or the other, the diachronic developments of these sounds. We present the reasons for separating the first two processes (namely fronting and raising) from one another in the first section, and for separating the third (spirantization) from the rest in the second section.

2.1 Fronting and raising as distinct processes

The evidence for considering tongue-fronting and tongue-raising as two distinct processes is quite strong. Apicals are affected mainly by the latter tendency, and as a result of that change, a wider surface of the tongue is made available for the articulation of these consonants. That is, instead of the tip of the tongue, blade is used as the articulator, and hence the apicals are changed into laminals. The velars, on the other hand, may be affected by fronting only, or by fronting and raising. The latter is found in cases in which the velars have been changed into fore-tongue consonants. There is also an appreciable differentiation in the environments used for inducing these changes. As could be seen from the following

three sub-sections, the processes are separated from one another
by differences existing in the effective environments, such as semivowel vs. vowel (2.1.1), high vowel vs. front vowel (2.1.2), and
unstressed vowel vs. stressed vowel (2.1.3).

2.1.1 Semivowel vs. front vowel A following front vowel is the
strongest environment that induces the fronting (and hence the palatalization) of a velar consonant, whereas a following yod (palatal
semivowel) is an even stronger environment for raising (and hence
palatalizing) an apical consonant. In a given language, for example,
a following yod may affect an apical consonant, but may fail to affect
a velar consonant; or it may need additional support from a preceding or following front vowel to affect the latter. The palatalization of an apical, on the other hand, may take place compulsorily
before a following yod, but only optionally before a following front
vowel. The following are some of the instances that support these
contentions.

a. Yod not affecting a velar consonant

1. In some ZOQUIAN languages, a contiguous y palatalizes an
    alveolar consonant to an alveopalatal one, but not a velar
    consonant (Wonderly 1949).

2. In NUPE, s, z are palatalized to š, ž before front vowels
    and also before y, whereas the velars are fronted before
    front vowels only (Smith 1967).

3. In CILUBA of Congo, a following y palatalizes t, s, l and
    n only (Spaandonck 1964).

4. In EASTERN OJIBWA, apicals, but not the velars, were
    palatalized by a following y (Bloomfield 1956).

5. In KASHMIRI, palatalization of n, l, r is especially seen
    before y (Kelkar and Trisal 1964).

6. In ROMANIAN, t, d, s are palatalized before final i (> i̧)
    and k, g before i (> zero), e (Ruhlen 1972).

7. In MODERN ENGLISH, t, d, s, z are palatalized before y
    but not the velars (Jespersen 1912).

8. In INDO-ARYAN, dentals (including r) are assimilated to
    palatals while occurring in clusters with y, whereas the
    velars remained unchanged (Katre 1942).

9. In the SEMITIC languages of Ethiopia, velars were palatalized by i, e and also y (Ullendorff 1955).

b. Yod needing additional support to affect the velars

1. In KARACAY (TURKIC), k is palatalized by a following y
   only when occurring after a front vowel; but t is palatalized
   by it even otherwise (Hebert 1962).

2. In MIDDLE CHINESE, medial yod occurring before i, e
   palatalized a preceding velar or h, but the yod occurring
   before other vowels did not; whereas the dental stops were
   palatalized by a medial yod before any vowel (Pulleyblank 1962).

c. Front vowels not affecting the apicals

1. In LATIN, t and d were palatalized by a following y only,
   whereas k and g were affected by a following front vowel
   as well (Martinet 1949).

2. In COMMON SLAVIC, the dental palatalization occurred
   before y only, whereas the velar palatalization occurred
   before front vowels as well (Shevelov 1964).

3. In HAKKA (CHINESE), t was palatalized before yod (or
   before a palatalized s or h), whereas k was palatalized
   before front vowels as well (Henne 1968).

d. Front vowels optionally affecting the apicals

1. In MODERN GREEK, velars were palatalized before i, e
   and y in all dialects; dentals, on the other hand, were
   affected mainly by y, and less so by i or e; y had the
   strongest palatalizing effect on the dentals. For example,
   the sibilants s and z were palatalized only before y in
   Epirus, Peloponnese and Cyprus. In the Epirot dialects,
   however, they were also palatalized by a following i, provided that the vowel was further followed by a velar obstruent
   (Newton 1972).

2. In SENECA, s was palatalized before y, and optionally between t and i (Chafe 1960).

3. In JAPANESE, t was palatalized before y only, but dialectally before i too (Bloch 1950).

2.1.2 <u>High vowel vs. front vowel</u>   Tongue height of the following
vowel (or semivowel) is crucial for the palatalization of an apical
consonant, whereas the frontness of the tongue rather than its height
is more crucial for the palatalization of a velar consonant. In cases
where a mid-front vowel is more effectively advanced than a high-
front vowel, velar palatalization has been reported to have taken
place before a mid-front vowel, while failing to do so (or occurring
only optionally) before a high-front vowel. Similarly, the palatalization of an apical may take place before a high-back vowel, but at
the same time it may fail to take place before a high- or mid-front
vowel.

a. <u>Stronger effect of a mid-front vowel on velars</u>

1. In UZBEK of Tashkent, initial k is palatalized before a
   stressed e, but not before i. The vowel i in this dialect is
   described as open and "considerably back" (Wurm 1947).

2. In EASTERN ARMENIAN, consonants in the initial and
   stressed syllables are accompanied by a palatal offglide,
   which is most marked in velars when followed by e (Allen
   1950).

3. In WESTERN OSSETIC, palatalization is more readily perceived before e than before i. Phonetically e is said to be
   longer than i in this dialect (Henderson 1949).

4. In GREEK, vowel e has a greater palatalizing effect on velars
   as compared with i. Palatalization before i is in fact considered as exceptional: k^w is palatalized before i and e,
   but g^w and k^{hw} are palatalized only before e (Allen 1957).

5. In FANTI, velars are palatalized before both i and e, but
   the alveolars only before i (Welmers 1946).

b. <u>Apical palatalization before a high-back vowel or a back semi-</u>
<u>vowel</u>

1. In PAPAGO, t, d, s, n are palatalized before i, e and u
   (Miller 1967).

2. In TEPEHUAN, d is palatalized before i, e and u (Miller 1967).

3. In BASQUE, s is strongly palatalized while adjacent to u
   (Lochak 1960).

4. In PROTO-IRANIAN, s is palatalized by a preceding i and u (Andersen 1968).

5. In SENTANI, d is palatalized by a neighboring i, y, u and w (Cowan 1965).

6. In TSWANA, it appears from the examples given by Cole (1955) that the palatalization has produced prepalatal affricates and fricatives when they occurred with labialization (w), but only alveolar affricates and fricatives otherwise.

In addition, it may be noted here that the non-distinctive assimilation of a consonant to the tongue-position of a following vowel has been observed very frequently in the case of the velars, but rather rarely for the apicals.

2.1.3 Unstressed vowel vs. stressed vowel   It would be clear from the instances given below that the tongue-fronting is induced more effectively by a following stressed front vowel, whereas the tongue-raising is effected more commonly by a following unstressed vowel. This generalization is further supported by the instances given under 2.1.1 above, in which a following yod is shown to have a stronger palatalizing effect on apicals; because, in a number of languages, the yod is derived from an earlier unstressed vowel.

a. Velar palatalization before a stressed vowel

1. In UZBEK of Tashkent, initial k is palatalized before a stressed e (Wurm 1947).

2. In EASTERN ARMENIAN, consonants (most markedly the velars) are accompanied by a palatal offglide in the initial and stressed syllables (Allen 1950).

3. In SINDHI, velars have a fronted allophone in syllables under primary stress with a high front vowel (Bordie 1958).

4. In COMMON SAMOYED, URALIC k becomes č in stressed position, before an unrounded front vowel (Collinder 1960).

5. In SIRIONO, g is palatalized before a strongly stressed high front vowel; and k is palatalized before a strongly stressed low central vowel a (the latter does not occur -- as is apparent from the vocabulary -- before a stressed high-front or mid-front vowel) (Firestone 1965).

b. Apical palatalization before an unstressed vowel

1. In CHOCO, č and ǰ are highly palatalized before unstressed
i in a vowel cluster (Loewen 1963).

2. In KAVINEÑO, the palatalization caused by i and occasionally
e in unstressed position appears to affect only the apical sounds
c, t, n and r (Girard 1971).

3. In the NIMBORAN language, t, d, n and s are lamino-domal
before an unaccented i, when followed by another vowel
(Anceaux 1965).

4. In the northern dialects of GREEK, l and n are palatalized
before an unstressed i which is later deleted (Newton 1972).

5. In WESTERN POPOLOCA, the palatalization of t and n before e is optional in a stressed CV syllable (Williams and
Pike 1968).

2.2 Spirantization as distinct from fronting and raising

Since spirantization can occur independently of fronting and raising
(see below for the supporting instances), it will have to be considered
as a distinct process, forming one of the constituents of the cover
process, namely palatalization. Its occurrence in the intervocalic
position has been generally considered as a case of assimilation of
a consonant to the more open neighboring vowel(s). That is, it is
treated as a case of "opening." However, the occurrence of spirantization in the palatalizing environment is basically an opposite process, namely non-opening. The semivowel y and the trill r are
also affected by it before front vowels, and in these instances it is
hard to explain spirantization as a case of opening. Similarly, the
change of stops to affricates in the palatalizing environment is in
fact a change from abrupt release to a delayed release. Articulatorily, one could explain this change as a case of assimilation.
That is, when followed by a fore-tongue vowel, it would be "easier"
to produce a fore-tongue consonant with a delayed release rather
than with an abrupt release. The distinctiveness of spirantization
could be supported by the instances of change or alternation grouped
under the following three sub-sections: 2.2.1 occurring alone,
2.2.2 occurring either with fronting or with raising, and 2.2.3
fronting and raising occurring without spirantization.

2.2.1 Spirantization occurring alone

a. The semivowel y, which by definition is a fronted and raised sound, generally shows only spirantization as the effect of the palatalizing environment. The following instances may be noted.

1. In CARIB, palatalization adds friction to y (Hoff 1968).

2. In NUPE, y has an audible oral friction before front vowels (Smith 1967).

3. In SELEPET, y becomes z^y initially before front vowels (McElhanon 1970).

4. In WEST GERMANIC, the semivowel tends to become a palatal spirant especially in the medial position after e and i (Priebsch and Collinson 1966).

5. In FANTI, y is ž before i and e (Welmers 1946).

6. In AWA, y is a voiced alveopalatal grooved fricative before i (Loving 1966).

7. In the LOWER GRAND VALLEY DANI, y becomes ž before i, u (Bromley 1961).

b. Another consonant that is generally affected by spirantization alone in the palatalizing environment is the apical trill.

1. In POLISH, palatalized r is ž (Shevelov 1964).

2. In CZECH, r becomes ř in contact with front vowels, and this ř sometimes interchanges with ž (Cowan 1959).

3. In BASQUE, there is a strong tendency towards the fricative articulation of the so-called "soft" r, notably between vowels, and there is agreement between BASQUE r and CAUCASIC affricates (Cowan 1959).

4. In CARIB, r is an alveolar flap which, when palatalized, is changed into a laminal ungrooved fricative in co-articulation with d (Hoff 1968).

5. In ALBANIAN, r tends to become rather fricative, especially initially and in the vicinity of i, when unvoiced (Lowman 1932).

6. In TSWANA, r becomes s when palatalized (which further

changes to tsh when nasalized), and s̆w when labialized (Cole 1955).

c. The apical stops also have been reported in some languages to show only spirantization as the effect of palatalization.

1. In WEST SLAVIC, t and d became dental affricates before y (Chomsky and Halle 1968).

2. In FANTE (AKAN), t and d became ts and dz before palatal vowels (Schachter and Fromkin 1968).

3. In FINNIC, URALIC initial t became s before i (Collinder 1960).

4. In ROMANIAN, d became z (through dz) initially before i or i̯e and intervocally before i (Mendeloff 1969).

5. In CHEYENNE, the conditioning factor for the affrication of t to ts historically has been the occurrence before a front vowel (Davis 1962).

6. In EFIK, t is slightly affricated intervocalically, especially when the vowels i and u follow (Ward 1933).

d. The correlation between spirantization and the palatalizing environment could be seen in the following instances as well.

1. In KARAKTSAN (GREEK), palatalized y is a palatal semivowel with less friction before back vowels (Bidwell 1964).

2. In OGONI, c and j have an affricated release mainly before front vowels (Brosnaham 1964).

3. In SIRIONO, h is a velar fricative before front vowels, and a voiceless vocoid (with cavity friction) before other vowels (Firestone 1965).

4. In EFIK, h has more velar friction when occurring with the close vowels i or u (Ward 1933).

5. In PIRO, w is an unrounded or slightly rounded fricative before front vowels (Matteson 1963).

2.2.2 <u>Spirantization occurring with either fronting or raising</u>

a. Velars are generally affected by all the three tendencies in the palatalizing environment; they are fronted, raised, and also spirantized, as when k is changed to t̃s. However, there are instances in which velars have been affected by the first and the last (fronting and spirantization) or only by the first. Similarly, the approximant h could be affected by these two tendencies only, to the exclusion of tongue-raising.

1. In SLAVIC, k, g, x became c, z, s respectively before ay and oy, with the exception that in WEST SLAVIC x became š (Chomsky and Halle 1968).

2. In most of the GREEK dialects of Lesbos, k is changed into ts before front vowels (Newton 1971).

3. In SPANISH, k becomes s (through ts) before front vowels (Harris 1969).

4. In PAPAGO, h has a stronger apperceptual effect before i; it was often recorded as a prepalatal x in this position (Mason 1950).

5. In IFUGAO, h is s after the front vowels i and e (Newell 1956).

The change of k to ts has been regarded by some linguists (see Newton 1972) as a case of depalatalization, i.e. a change of k > t̃s > ts. Such an assumption would be unnecessary if palatalization is analyzed as made up of three distinct constituent processes.

b. The occurrence of spirantization with raising only is quite common, and is seen in the case of apicals and labials (t > t̃s or p > t̃s).

2.2.3 Fronting and raising occurring without spirantization
The occurrence of fronting and raising without the accompaniment of spirantization is specifically seen in the case of palatalized nasals. Apical nasals are only raised, whereas none of them have been reported to show spirantization as the additional effect of palatalization.

Both velar and apical stops, when palatalized, generally become spirantized as well. But, there do exist instances in which the latter change has failed to take place.

1. Thus in SOUTH SLAVIC, a dental stop, when palatalized,

does not become an affricate, but only a palato-alveolar
stop (Chomsky and Halle 1968).

2. In ACOMA, dental stops are realized as palatal stops before
front vowels (Miller and Davis 1963).

3. In MODERN GREEK, the fronted k', g', x', ɣ' (before i, e,
y) are generally non-strident; in many insular dialects,
however, k' and x' further change to č and š; in CRETAN,
ɣ' changes to ž (Newton 1972).

4. The most common tendency of slightly fronting (but not spirantizing) the velar stops in the palatalizing environment
could also be given as an illustration of the above point.

It would be clear from the foregoing, we believe, that the study
of palatalization in a language would fail to take care of all the relevant factors so long as it does not study the occurrence of the three
underlying processes, namely fronting, raising and spirantization
individually and in different combinations.

3. The Palatalizing Environment

As we have already seen above, the palatalizing effect of a given
environment would depend upon the consonant that is actually being
changed (that is, whether it is a labial, apical, or velar consonant).
Generalizations made by earlier linguists (Chen 1971, Neeld 1973)
regarding these environments have turned out to be erroneous mainly
because they had overlooked these correlations that exist between
the palatalizing environments on the one hand, and the consonants
that are being affected by them on the other.

3.1 A following front vowel or yod

The most prominent environment that could induce palatalization
in a consonant is a following front vowel (especially the high- and
mid-front unrounded vowels i and e), and a following palatal semivowel (yod). These are reported to be effective in palatalizing a
preceding consonant in almost all the languages examined by us.
A following yod is more effective on apicals, whereas a following
vowel, especially stressed, is more effective on velars (see Sec.
2.1 for details).

Velars may also be palatalized by a following low front vowel,
as for example, in ENGLISH (before ae, æ also) and in FRENCH

(dialectally before a also). In RUSSIAN, all consonants were palatalized before æ (Fairbanks 1965). Similarly, the apicals may be
palatalized by a following high back vowel or semivowel as seen in
PAPAGO, TEPEHUAN, BASQUE, and others (see 2.1.2 above).

3.2 Effects of rounding

a. Rounding of a following vowel as such, apparently, has no
effect on its palatalizing capacity. The following instances may be
noted in this context.

1. In WESTERNMOST VOTIC, t was palatalized before i as
   well as before ü (Collinder 1960).

2. In NORWEGIAN, initial k and g were changed to š and j
   before i, ei and ü (Popperwell 1963).

3. In the AKRU dialect of KURDISH, k was palatalized before
   both rounded and unrounded front vowels (Mackenzie 1961).

4. In MANDARIN, velar and dental palatalizations had taken
   place before both rounded and unrounded high-front vowels.

b. However, the change of g to z in FRENCH has apparently
failed to take place before front rounded vowels (Neeld 1973). The
reason for this failure of a rounded front vowel to palatalize a preceding velar may not be its rounding as suggested by Neeld, but its
insufficient fronting (unless, of course, one is able to show that
lip-rounding has a centralizing effect on front vowels); that is, at
the time of palatalization, the vowel (derived from an earlier back
vowel) might not have been fronted enough in FRENCH to effect
fronting on a preceding velar consonant. Similar instances of derived front vowels failing to effect palatalization (mainly because
of the palatalization process occurring diachronically earlier than
the fronting or raising of the vowel) have been noted.

1. In ENGLISH, the velar palatalization did not take place before
   the vowel i derived through umlaut from u (Penzl 1947).

2. In the OHUHU dialect of IGBO, the vowel i derived from an
   earlier e or a either by reduplication or vowel assimilation
   was incapable of palatalizing the apical sibilants (Green and
   Igwe 1966).

c. Rounding, on the other hand, has been reported in some instances to have actually induced tongue-raising on apical consonants.

1. In TSWANA, bilabials become apicals when palatalized,
   which are further changed to palatals when labialized (Cole
   1955).

2. In COCOPA (YUMAN), c becomes š before a bilabial sound
   (Wares 1968).

3.3 A preceding front vowel

There are only a limited number of instances in which a front
vowel (or a high back vowel) is reported to have palatalized a following consonant. These fall into two different sets.

a. Firstly, there are instances in which a language that has
undergone extensive palatalization has some limited environments
in which the front vowel also palatalizes a following consonant.

1. Thus, in COMMON SLAVIC velars were palatalized after
   an oral or nasalized i, unless followed by a consonant or an
   u-type vowel (Shevelov 1964).

2. In IRISH, palatalization under the influence of a preceding
   vowel is rare, occurring mainly in the case of IE r (Lewis
   and Pedersen 1937).

3. In ENGLISH, k has become č finally after i, ī and also medially after i if the consonant is not followed by a velar
   vowel (Penzl 1947).

b. Secondly, there are instances in which palatalization appears
to have taken place exclusively as a progressive change. Such a
change is restricted to a fricative (or affricate) in the following
instances.

1. In PAME, an apical affricate or fricative is palatalized after
   i (Gibson 1956).

2. In HAVYAKA (KANNADA), the causative suffix su is šu
   after verbs ending in i, e, or y (Bhat 1971).

3. In AVESTA, IE s was changed to š after i, u (also after k,
   r (Andersen 1968).

4. In CENTRAL BAVARIAN, x is changed to an alveopalatal
   spirant after front vowels (Kufner 1960). A similar change
   has occurred in STANDARD GERMAN.

5. In SENTANI, h is changed to s after y and i (Cowan 1965).

6. In CROW, k is palatalized after i, i:, e and e:, provided the former is directly preceded by š or č (Kaschube 1967).

c. There are two instances in which no such restriction is apparent. They need further study.

1. In PAME, an alveolar stop or nasal is also palatalized by a preceding i (see 1. above); however, the consonant gets a y-offglide in these instances, and hence the change could as well be considered as regressive (i.e. as an effect of the offglide).

2. In ESEʔEXA, k^w becomes k^y after i (Girard 1971). Compare this change with the one recorded for other TAKANAN languages such as TAKANA in which k^w was palatalized before i or e.

3.4 A neighboring palatal consonant

Changes caused by a neighboring palatal consonant (excepting y) are not generally considered as instances of palatalization. Such changes, however, are quite common, especially in the case of nasals which, as part of their general tendency to get assimilated to the point of articulation of the following stop or affricate, also become palatals when occurring before a palatal stop or affricate. Similar changes are observed in the case of liquids as in BENGALI (Ferguson and Chowdhury 1960), MANTJILTJARA (Marsh 1969), HAUSA and others, and in the case of sibilants before palatalized sonants in OLD CHURCH SLAVONIC, and before palatalized velars and dental stops in COMMON SLAVIC (Shevelov 1964).

A more interesting aspect of the palatal consonants, reported for some languages, is their ability to extend their palatalizing influence across the intervening vowel, or even to affect all the apical consonants occurring in the word. The change appears to be generally regressive in nature, and has been called "palatal harmony" by some linguists. The following instances may be noted.

1. In PENGO, root-initial t becomes č when the root terminates in č or j (Burrow and Bhattacharya 1970).

2. In SOUTHERN PAIUTE, any two of the segments s, š, c and č agree in point of articulation within a word, and separated by a vowel (Lovins 1972).

3. In CHUMASH, if a word-final sibilant is a blade consonant, then all preceding sibilants will appear as blade sibilants, and if it is apical, all will appear as apicals. There are only a few exceptions to this rule (Beeler 1970).

4. In CHIRICAHUA APACHE, an s consonant (s, z, ẓ, c, or c̣) preceding an š consonant (č, ž, ẓ̌, č̣, č̣) in a prefinal or stem syllable of the same word assimilates to the corresponding š consonant, and vice versa. In both cases, the assimilation is optional. The frequency of its occurrence is determined by 1) the distance of the two consonants from one another, and 2) by the rapidity of speech (Hoijer 1946).

5. In MOROCCAN ARABIC, no morpheme containing s or z ever contains also š and ž anywhere within its bounds, nor does s or z ever occur in morphemes with š or ž (Harris 1944).

6. In HARARI, not orly the consonants in direct contact with e, i, or ya is palatalized, but also any other dental or sibilant of the root, and quite often, two or three consonants are palatalized at the same time (Tucker and Bryan 1966).

7. In NORTHWESTERN KARAITE, the consonants of a word are either all sharp (palatalized) or all plain (Lightner 1965).

8. In HIGI, palatalization may extend its influence over more than one syllable; the effect of palatalization occurring in neighboring syllables is cumulative (Mohrlang 1972).

9. In NAVAHO, there is a limitation of distinction among the phonemes z, c, c', s, z and j, č, č', š, ž; no word occurs which contains some phoneme of the first set and also some phoneme of the second set. The assimilation is conditioned by the consonant occurring in the last morph of the word (Harris 1945).

3.5 Diminutive meaning, rapidity of speech and speaker distinction

a. Palatalization is used to express diminutive meaning in some languages. In RUSSIAN and BELORUSSIAN, for example, such a usage has been reported especially in the case of substantives ending in l, n and r, which, according to Shevelov (1964) is an extension of an earlier diminutive suffix. In the native INDIAN languages of America, the above correlation between palatalization and diminutive

meaning has apparently originated in a limited number of languages,
but has later on spread areally to other neighboring languages as
well (Nichols 1971). Because of this spread, it is difficult at the
moment to give any historical explanations to the development of
this correlation. It may be noted, however, that a similar correlation exists between front vowels and diminutives which, as a
symbolic correlation, has probably a universal validity. One may
note, however, that the reverse change, namely depalatalization,
has been used by some AMERICAN INDIAN languages to denote
diminutive meaning (Nichols 1971).

b. Secondly, the rapidity of speech has a marked effect on the
occurrence and also spread of palatalization across the syllables
in a stretch of speech. The following are some of the instances
that show this correlation.

1. In EASTERN ARMENIAN, the presence or absence of palatalization in medial unstressed syllables is largely dependent
on the speed and care of utterances (Allen 1950).

2. In CAYUVAVA, h becomes š before i, e in rapid speech
(Key 1961).

3. In HIGI, increasing the rate of speech tends to increase both
the degree and distance of influence of palatalization. In extremely quick speech, palatalization may extend its influence
over two or three syllables in both directions (Mohrlang 1972).

4. In BINI, palatalization is said to occur as a fast speech phenomena (Neeld 1973).

5. In CHIRICAHUA APACHE, one of the factors that determine
the occurrence of palatal harmony is the rapidity of speech
(Hoijer 1946).

It may be possible to specify articulatory features as "rough"
and "fine" such that the rapidity of speech would tend to strengthen
(or newly introduce) the former, whereas it may weaken or delete
the latter. Palatalization would belong to the "rough" class, as it
generally gets strengthened and even newly introduced into a stretch
of speech as the rapidity of speed increases. A feature like retroflexion, on the other hand, would belong to the "fine" class, as it
generally gets weakened, or even lost completely in rapid speech
(see Bhat 1973). We may perhaps generalize that the rapidity of
speech has a levelling effect on speech.

c. There is also probably a correlation between palatalization
and female speech, as shown by the following two instances.

1. In CHAM of Vietnam, t or men's speech correspond to t^y
of women's speech (Blood 1967).

2. In ANYULA, in an area of noun affixation, gi alternates with
dj -- the former exclusively used by male speakers and the
latter by female speakers (Kirton 1967).

A similar correlation also apparently exists between children's
speech and adults speech, and the presence or absence or palatalization.

3.6 Blocking environments

a. We have noted only two environments that could be specified
as capable of blocking palatalization. They are 1) an apical trill
or tap, and 2) a retroflexed consonant. Both these could prevent
the palatalization of a velar consonant; that is, they could block the
tongue fronting tendency of a given environment. The following
instances may be noted.

1. In SINDHI, velars are fronted before front vowels, if they
are not further followed by r or a retroflexed flap (Bordie
1958).

2. In TELUGU, k becomes č before front vowels, except when
it is directly followed by r (through metathesis) (Krishnamurti
1961).

3. In HIGI, palatalization could occur with all syllables except
those with r as the consonant onset (Mohrlang 1972).

4. In TAMIL and MALAYALAM, k became č before front vowels,
except when they were further followed by a retroflexed consonant (Krishnamurti 1961).

b. However, in the case of apical sibilants, r appears to induce
palatalization (raising) as seen in the following instances.

1. In AVESTA, s becomes š before r (Burrow 1955).

2. In COMMON SLAVIC, s becomes š after r (Martinet 1951).

c. There are a few additional environments that appear to block palatalization, as for example, a following uvular fricative in EASTERN ARMENIAN (Allen 1950), a following t or s in AKAN (Schachter and Fromkin 1968), or the occurrence in the initial position in AMHARIC (Bender et al.1976). Further study is necessary to make any generalizations regarding these instances.

4. The Effects of Palatalization on Consonants and Vowels

There are evidently two different ways in which palatalization could affect a consonant: 1) it could modify the primary articulation itself, or 2) it could add a secondary palatal articulation to the consonant, leaving the main articulation unaltered. Changes that produce the effects of the latter type are comparatively less frequent and are also probably areally restricted. (See Bhat 1973 for a discussion of "areal restriction.") However, when they do take place, they appear to affect almost all the consonants occurring in the language, thereby creating a two-fold distinction (variously designated as palatalized -- non-palatalized, sharp -- plain, or soft -- plain, or soft -- hard) in all its consonants. Changes that induce the effects of the former type, on the other hand, are generally less systematic in nature, and depending upon the underlying tendencies involved (fronting, raising or spirantization), they affect only a limited portion of the consonantal system. It is possible, however, for the effects of both these types to occur together in a language, as for example, the former with one set of consonants such as labials, and the latter with another set such as velars or apicals.

We are not in a position, at the moment, to make any definite statement regarding the development of palatalization as a secondary articulation (especially its areal spread, which appears to be quite restricted). The environments that induce it are most probably identical to those that produce tongue-raising. Instead of directly affecting the articulation of the consonants concerned, tongue-raising in this case functions as a simultaneous secondary articulation. Generally, the central part of the tongue is raised for producing this secondary effect. It is hence possible for any consonant that is not produced with the center of the tongue as its main articulator to have this secondary articulation added to it (DeArmond 1966).

The above two types of palatalization (i.e. those with the main articulation altered, and those with an added secondary articulation)

are evidently distinct from one another. However, because of the
different continuums of the following nature, it is rather difficult
to make a clear-cut distinction between them. Firstly, there is a
continuum of simultaneity: the palatal articulation may form an
on-glide to the consonant under consideration, or a simultaneous
secondary articulation, or an off-glide — it could fall anywhere
between these three, or form combinations of two or all the three
of them. Secondly, the center and the back of the tongue (or the
center and the blade) may form two distinct articulations, or one
long (distributed) articulator stretching from center to back, or
center to blade (Heffner 1950), and there may as well be intermediate stages. Thirdly, the relative strength of the two articulations
may vary in several ways -- the secondary articulation may be
stronger than the main articulation (or vice versa), and may even
replace the latter, and so on.

It is clear, however, that the generally held view that any type
of palatalization has to pass through a stage in which palatalization
forms a secondary articulation cannot be valid. Thus according to
Bloomfield (1933), "palatalization changes consonants at first to
varieties which the phonetician calls palatalized," and according to
Allen (1957), "the sequence of palatalization in its most extended
form is the general pattern ķ > ƫ > tš̓ > s." These postulations
cannot be correct because, firstly, the occurrence of a secondary
palatal articulation, as far as we could see in modern languages,
is restricted to a few areally connected languages, and secondly,
unlike the other type of change, it has an extensive effect on the
consonantal system as a whole.

A detailed study of the effects of palatalization, especially on the
main articulation of the sounds concerned, will be presented in the
following sections.

4.1 The labials

a. Among the labial consonants, the most susceptible to palatalization is the semivowel w, which in many languages is a labiovelar rather than a simple labial. There are two different directions
in which it may change under the influence of a palatalizing environment. Firstly, it may retain its lip-rounding, but may take on an
additional palatal secondary articulation (and may later on lose its
lip-rounding and merge with the palatal semivowel). Secondly, it
may get retracted from its bilabial position to a labio-dental position. This latter tendency (and also the second stage of the former
tendency) is evidently a case of assimilation to the unrounded nature

of the palatalizing environment, but it has been reported in some
languages as forming part of the palatalizing process.

The bilabial semivowel is reported to occur as a palatal semivowel with lip rounding before front vowels in FULA (Arnott 1970),
KURDISH (Mackenzie 1961), and AKAN (Schachter and Fromkin 1968);
it has merged with y before front vowels in HAUSA (Gregersen 1967),
TUNDRA YURAK (Collinder 1960), and WESTERN OSSETIC (Henderson 1949).

It has become a labio-dental before front vowels in KANNADA
(Bright 1958), TULU (Bhat 1967), WESTERN POPOLOCA (Williams
and Pike 1968), KONDA (Krishnamurti 1969), VIETNAMESE (before
y) (Thompson 1969), etc. This particular correlation is probably
more frequent than has been reported. The following additional
changes may be noted.

1. In WESTERN OSSETIC, palatalized w may optionally become
   v (Henderson 1949).

2. In RUNDI, palatalized b becomes v (Spaandonck 1964).

3. In CHONTAL, w is a labio-dental fricative before i or e
   (Keller 1959).

4. In PIRO, w is an unrounded or slightly rounded fricative
   before front vowels (Matteson 1963).

5. In MIDDLE CHINESE, labials split into bilabials and labio-
   dentals, the latter occurring before medial iu and open final
   iu (Cheng 1973).

6. In GAELIC (of Torr), palatalized labials have no tongue
   articulation as such, but the lips are tightly drawn; the
   non-palatalized labials, on the other hand, are velarized
   (Sommerfelt 1952).

b. Palatalization of other labial consonants has been noted in
JAPANESE (Bloch 1950), SLAVIC languages (Fairbanks 1965),
AMHARIC (Bender et al. forthcoming), IRISH (Lewis and Pedersen
1937), NUPE (Smith 1967), WESTERN OSSETIC (Henderson 1949),
CARIB (Hoff 1968), and a few other languages as well. It is not
clear, however, in some of these cases, whether the resultant
labial sound has a secondary palatal articulation added to it, or
whether it has merely a palatal off-glide or on-glide attached to it.

c. There are comparatively few instances in which the main articulation of a labial has been changed into palatal or apical by palatalization. The following instances may be noted.

1. In the town of Tres Pueblos, CHONTAL w is a palatalized fricativized dental stop before i and e (Keller 1959).

2. In TSWANA, p, ph, b, f, m, when palatalized, are changed into tšw, tšhw, jw, šw, and ny respectively (Cole 1955).

3. In ROMANIAN, p, b, m, f, v are palatalized dialectally to k', g', n', h', y' (or g') respectively (Rosetti 1968).

4. In FULA of Adamawa, implosive b may be replaced by ʔy before front vowels (see Greenberg 1970).

5. In LUMBAASABA, p becomes y before i and e except after w (Brown 1972).

d. This general tendency of not altering the main articulation of palatalized labials has an interesting effect on the distribution of these consonants in the following two languages.

1. In AKHA, only labials occur as palatalized (which are treated as clusters with y) (Katsura 1973).

2. In LISU, consonants that can occur in initial clusters with y are only labials, glottal stop, and h (Hope 1971).

e. Another interesting change that has affected the labials is the following; in all SLAVIC languages, the INDO-EUROPEAN labials, when palatalized before y, show forms with an l initially (ply, bly, mly, vly); in the medial position, some languages have l, but some (such as WEST SLAVIC, BULGARIAN and MACEDO-NIAN) do not; the latter have probably lost it at later stage (Fairbanks 1965).

4.2 The apicals

The effect of palatalization on apicals is generally to change them into laminal consonants. That is, the articulator is changed from apex to blade, so that a wider surface of the tongue is brought into contact with the alveolar ridge or the hard palate. We have considered this as a case of tongue-raising. The above change is generally accompanied by a retraction of the tongue from dental to

alveolar position, and from alveolar to prepalatal position. This
retraction is to a certain extent automatic, as it would result from
the use of the blade rather than the tip of the tongue as the articulator. It could also be considered as a case of anticipatory assimilation to the following palatalizing environment, which would have
a retracted tongue-position as compared to that of an alveolar or
dental consonant.

The consonants that are the most susceptible to palatalization
among the apicals are 1) the sibilants (or affricates that have a
sibilant release) and 2) the nasals. These, especially the first,
could be affected by a wider range of palatalizing environments (as
for example, by a following or preceding back vowel, a preceding
front vowel, or even a neighboring velar or labial consonant) than
the other apical or non-apical consonants. Sibilants and affricates
are also the most frequently affected apical consonants by palatal
harmony. There are instances in which these sounds have changed
from apicals to laminals (or vice versa) even unconditionally.

a. As has been pointed out above, the most common effect of
palatalization on apical stops is to change them into palatal affricates.
But as we have seen earlier, it could also change them into apical
affricates (see 2.2.1), or palatal stops (2.2.3). Trills are generally
spirantized (2.2.1) and the laterals may either become laminals or
may change into palatal semivowels, and in this latter case, they
may even get deleted.

1. In AMHARIC, l becomes y when palatalized (Bender et al.
   1976).

2. In ROMANIAN, initial l becomes y before i or ye; medially
   before i, l (derived from ll) disappears (Mendeloff 1969).

3. In VIETNAMESE, l occurring after front vowels is lost
   (Barker et al. 1970).

b. There are two additional effects that the palatalizing environment has on liquids. Firstly, it appears to change a continuant or
a trill into a flap, and secondly, a non-lateral into a lateral. These
are yet to be studied in greater detail. The following instances may
be noted.

1. In GANDA, l is a one-tap sound consistently after i, e (Cole
   1965).

2. In TSWANA, r is a flap before close vowels i, u and a lateral flap before front vowels (Cole 1955).

3. In IFUGAO, l is a dental lateral before central and back vowels, and a lateral flap before front vowels (Newell 1956).

4. In EAST CHEREMIS, r is a palatalized single dental-alveolar flap or a single palatal flap before y (Ristinen 1960).

5. In BANTU generally, the flapped consonant (medial or lateral) is commonly found in association with the forward vowels i and e (Doke 1954).

6. In SOTHO, l is flapped before the close vowels î and û (Doke 1954).

7. In BARIBA, the alveolar flap r has a slight lateral resonance before front vowels (Welmers 1952).

8. In USURUFA, r is an alveolar lateral flap after i, before i, e, a; elsewhere it is a vibrant flap (Bee 1965).

9. In the KARANGA cluster, r is a flapped lateral invariably before the vowel i, and sometimes before e (Doke 1954).

4.3 The palatals

Among the palatals, only the semivowel y appears to show any marked difference in the palatalizing environment. As pointed out above (2.2.1), the effect on y is mainly spirantization. As for the remaining palatal consonants, one could argue that the palatalizing environment has a conservative effect on them because in some languages such as MARATHI, NORTHERN KANNADA, TELUGU, KASHMIRI, etc. the palatal affricates have been changed into apical affricates in a non-palatalizing environment.

4.4 The velars

The effect of palatalization on velars is generally seen as tongue-fronting. The consonant may remain as prevelar if the change is slight, but may change into a palatal one (or even an apical-alveolar or dental one) if the change is more marked. Stops generally become affricates, but may continue to remain as stops as well. That is, the raising and spirantization may or may not co-occur with fronting in velar palatalizations (see 2.2 for details).

4.5 The vowels

Languages appear to vary from one another (or from one stage to the other) in giving prominence to their vocalic or consonantal systems. According to Sommerfelt (1922), for example, consonants were dependent upon their neighboring vowels in COMMON CELTIC; whereas in IRISH, the consonants formed the most important part of the phonological system, and the timbre of every vowel was modified by preceding and following consonants. If this hypothesis is valid, one can hold it responsible for the occurrence of the following two contradictory tendencies of palatalization in different languages.

Firstly, there are languages in which a front vowel or semivowel has induced palatalization on a <u>preceding</u> consonant, and as an extreme case of this tendency, the palatalized consonant has "absorbed" all the palatalness of the following vowel and has turned it into a non-palatal.

Secondly, there are also languages in which a palatal or a palatalized consonant has affected a <u>following</u> vowel by raising it or by fronting it, and once again as an extreme case of this tendency, the vowel has "absorbed" the palatalness in some cases, and has either turned the consonant into a non-palatal or has effected its deletion.

a. We have already examined the instances in which a front vowel or semivowel has palatalized a preceding consonant. The following instances are illustrative of the absorption or deletion of these environments by the consonants concerned.

1. In SPANISH, LATIN initial l was palatalized when occurring before i or e; the vowel i was absorbed in palatalization (Mendeloff 1969).

2. In ROMANIAN, k and g were palatalized before final i or e, of which i was later deleted (Ruhlen 1972).

3. In COMMON SLAVIC, the vowel ĕ became a after the hushing consonants and y; after palatalizing a preceding consonant, the palatal semivowel y got deleted (Shevelov 1964).

4. In AMHARIC, palatalization was accompanied by the change of i to ɨ and e to ə (Bender et al. 1976).

5. In NUPE, palatalization occurs before a which has an underlying æ (Hyman 1970).

6. BURUSHASKI, dentals are palatalized before the plural
   suffix o which was probably yo earlier (Lorimer 1935).

7. In PROTO-KERESAN, stems with an initial front vowel
   palatalize a preceding pronominal affix; some have an initial
   a, suggesting an earlier ia or a similar sequence (Miller
   and Davis 1963).

8. In LISU, velars, alveolars and palatals do not occur before
   y (Hope 1971); the first two evidently changed into palatals
   before y , and the semivowel was absorbed by them.

9. In spoken KANNADA, initial e has developed a non-phonemic
   y-glide; and dialectally this initial sequence ye- has changed
   further to ya-.

   b.   The palatalizing effects of a consonant on its neighboring
(mostly following) vowel could be seen in the following instances.

1. In COMMON SLAVIC, rounded vowels were delabialized
   and fronted after palatal and palatalized consonants (Shevelov
   1964).

2. In RUSSIAN, vowels following palatalized consonants are
   higher, fronter and tenser; between two palatalized consonants, the incidence of highness, frontness and tenseness is
   still stronger (Bidwell 1962).

3. In MARSHALLESE, vowels are fronted by palatalized consonants (Bender 1968).

4. In YAGUA, y may have three degrees of influence on the
   vowel nucleus -- strongest between two y's, less strong after
   y, and least strong before y (Powlison 1962).

5. In KOREAN, ɔ is considerably centralized (approaching ə)
   after y. For many words, y corresponds to ye or e dialectally (Martin 1951).

6. In HIGI, a slightly raised and fronted set of vowels tend to
   occur with the palatalized variants of consonants (Mohrlang
   1972).

7. In EAST SLAVIC, õ becomes ü after palatals, and u elsewhere (Fairbanks 1965).

8. In some DRAVIDIAN languages, the distinction between a and e is neutralized after the palatal nasal (Krishnamurti 1961).

9. In IRISH, non-final a becomes e after a palatal consonant in post-tonic syllables; final a, o also become e (Lewis and Pedersen 1937).

10. In NORTHERN CHINESE, a becomes ε before palatal endings (Hishimoto 1970).

11. In IRISH, stem-final a becomes i before a palatal consonant in post-tonic syllables (Lewis and Pedersen 1937).

c. Absorption or deletion of the consonantal environment by a following vowel could be illustrated with the following instances.

1. In spoken HAUSA, there is a tendency with less strong pala-talized consonants to shift all the y-coloration on to the vowel, thereby producing a sub-phoneme e in root syllables (Parsons 1970).

2. In UKRANIAN, after items ending in palatalized (and post-alveolar) consonants, initial o of a following element is replaced by e; concomitant with this change, an automatic replacement of the final palatalized consonant by its plain counterpart takes place before this e (Bidwell 1967-8).

3. In certain CENTRAL DRAVIDIAN languages, the vowel a is changed to e after an initial y, and the semivowel is deleted (Krishnamurti 1961).

4. In the northern dialects of GREEK, y is deleted intervocally when followed by a front vowel (Newton 1972).

d. Since the effects of both these cases of absorption (of vowels to consonants and vice versa) are identical on the distribution of the relevant segments, namely of restricting the occurrence of palatal consonants to non-palatalizing environment, it is difficult to separate the instances as belonging to one or the other of these two processes without knowing the exact history of those instances, as for example, through a comparison of these with other related languages that have not undergone the change. The following are some of the instances that have possibly resulted from one of these processes of absorption.

1. In AYUTLA MIXTEC, t^y, d^y and ñ do not occur before i
   and ĩ (Pankratz and Pike 1971).

2. In WESTERN POPOLOCA, ñ does not occur before i (Williams
   and Pike 1968).

3. In KAVINEÑO, palatalized consonants do not occur before i
   and e (Key 1968).

4. In SOUTHERN PAIUTE, the general tendency is for s and c
   to occur near front vowels and š and č near back vowels
   (Lovins 1972).

5. In KOREAN, y does not occur in syllables containing i (Martin
   1951).

6. In SRE, a palatal glide may not follow another palatal consonant, or a cluster whose initial member is a palatal consonant (Manley 1972).

7. In ACOMA, palatal stops do not occur before front vowels
   (Miller 1965).

8. In DAN, palatalized consonants never occur before high front
   vowels ĩ and i (Bearth and Zemp 1967).

9. In FOX, the affricates do not occur before y (Hockett 1956).

10. In numerous NORTH ESTONIAN dialects, phones before i,
    e, ae do not show the sharp-plain contrast; the degree of
    palatalization is often weak or optional (Zeps 1962).

11. In KARAKATSAN (GREEK), the palatalized and non-palatalized
    nasals and laterals occur in free variation before front vowels
    (Bidwell 1964).

    e. Since absorption is an extreme case of palatalization both in
the case of vowels and also of consonants, there are many instances
in which such a change (i.e. absorption) has not yet taken place, or
has altogether failed to take place. These instances appear to be
contradictory to the ones given earlier (in section d. above) in which
the absorption has completed its course. The occurrence of palatal
consonants is restricted to the palatalizing environment in these "non-
absorbed" instances, (see below for illustrations) where it is restricted
to the non-palatalizing environment in the "absorbed" instances. The

resultant instances are evidently contradictory to one another, but there is no contradiction as such in their underlying processes.

There are many instances in which the palatals are in complementary distribution with the non-palatals, the former occurring in a palatalizing environment and the latter elsewhere. In addition to these, there are also instances of the following type in which the two sets of consonants, though contrastive, still show a distributional limitation of the above nature.

1. In MBE, palatal consonants can occur only before the close vowels i, u and the diphthongs which all begin with a close vowel (Bamgboṣe 1967).

2. In TURKISH, the palatal stops and the lateral l occur before front vowels and a, while the velars and the lateral l occur before back vowels u, o and a (Swift 1963).

3. In MODERN ICELANDIC, only palatals (and not velars) can occur before i, e, ei and ai (Haugen 1958).

According to Sommerfelt (1922), palatalization has brought about, by "reaction," the velarization of non-palatalized consonants in IRISH. In the GAELIC dialect of Torr also, palatalized labials are said to have no tongue articulation as such, but the non-palatalized labials, on the other hand, are said to be velarized (Sommerfelt 1952). It is possible that the puzzling case of PERSIAN palatalization represents an opposite tendency: that is, of palatalization occurring by reaction to velarization or pharyngealization. Today, the velars k and g occur as palatalized in PERSIAN in environments other than before back vowels (i.e. before front vowels, before consonants, and also in the final position). One can postulate that the velars were pharyngealized before back vowels to start with, and the non-pharyngealized variants, by "reaction," were later on palatalized, and this latter change has brought about the modern distribution of palatalized velars in PERSIAN.

BIBLIOGRAPHY

Allen, W.S. 1950. Notes on the phonetics of an Eastern Armenian speaker. Transactions of the Philological Society (1950), 180-206.

Allen, W.S. 1957. Some problems of palatalization in Greek. Lingua 7.2. 113-133.

Anceaux, J.C. 1965. The Nimboran language. 's Gravenhage.

Andersen, H. 1973. Abductive and deductive change. Language 49.4. 765-793.

_____. 1968. IE *s after i, u, r, k in Baltic and Slavic. Acta Linguistica Hafniensia 11.2. 171-190.

Ariste, P. 1968. A grammar of the Votic language. Indiana University Uralic and Altaic Series 68.

Arnott, D.W. 1970. The nominal and verbal systems of Fula (Combe dialect). Oxford University Press.

Bamgboṣe, A. 1967. Notes on the phonology of Mbe. Journal of West African Languages [JWAL] 4.1. 5-12.

Barker, M.A. and M.E. Barker. 1970. Proto-Vietnamuong (Anna-moung) final consonants. Lingua 24.3. 268-285.

Bartholomew, D. 1960. Some revisions of Proto-Otomi consonants. International Journal of American Linguistics [IJAL] 26.4. 317-329.

Bearth, T. and H. Zemp. 1967. The phonology of Dan (Santa). Journal of African Languages 6.1. 9-29.

Bee, D. 1965. Usarufa distinctive features and phonemes. Papers in New Guinea Linguistics 4. 39-68.

Beeler, M.S. 1970. Sibilant harmony in Chumash. IJAL 36.1. 14-17.

Bender, B.W. 1968. Marshallese phonology. Oceanic Linguistics 7.1. 16-35.

_____, G. Francescato and Z. Salzmann. 1952. Friulian phonology. Word 8.3. 216-223.

Bender, M.L., J.D. Bowen, R.L. Cooper and C.A. Ferguson. 1976. Language in Ethiopia. London: Oxford University Press.

Berry, J. 1955. Some notes on the phonology of the Nzema and

Ahanta dialects. Bulletin of the School of Oriental and African
Studies 17.1.160-165.

Bhat, D.N.S. 1965. Studies in Tulu. Bulletin of the Deccan
College 25.

_____. 1971. Outline grammar of Havyaka. Poona.

_____. 1973. Retroflexion: an areal feature. Working Papers
on Language Universals [WPLU] 13. 27-67. Stanford University.

Bidwell, C.E. 1962. An alternative phonemic analysis of Russian.
Slavic and East European Journal 6.2.125-130.

_____. 1964. On Karakatsan phonology. Word, Special Pub-
lication no. 5.

_____. 1966. The language of the Backa Ruthenians. The Slavic
and East European Journal 10.1. 32-45.

_____. 1967-8. Outline of Ukranian morphology. International
studies program, University of Pittsburgh.

Bloch, B. 1950. Studies in Colloquial Japanese IV: phonemics.
Language 26.1. 86-125.

Blood, D.L. 1957. Phonological units in Cham. Anthropological
Linguistics 9. 8. 15-32.

Bloomfield, L. 1933. Language. New York.

_____. 1956. Eastern Ojibwa. Ann Arbor.

Bluhme, H. 1971. The phonetic system of Russian consonants.
Orbis 20.1.102-107.

Bondarko, L.V. and L.R. Zinder. 1968. Distinctive features of
phonemes and their physical characteristics. Zeitschrift für
Phonetik, Sprachwissenschaft und Kommunikationsforschung
21.1.2. 74-76.

Bordie, J.G. 1958. A descriptive Sindhi phonology. Doctoral
dissertation, University of Texas.

Borgstrom, C. Hj. 1941. The dialects of Sky and Ross-Shire.
Norwegian University Press.

Bright, William. 1958. An outline of colloquial Kannada. Poona.

Bromley, H. M. 1961. The phonology of Lower Grand Valley Dani. 'sGravenhage.

Brosnahan, L. F. 1964. Outline of the phonology of Gokana dialect of Ogoni. JWAL 1.1. 43-48.

Brown, G. 1972. Phonological rules and dialect variation: a study of the phonology of Lumbasaaba. Cambridge.

Burrow, T. 1955. The Sanskrit language. London.

_____ and S. Bhattacharya. 1970. Pengo. Oxford University Press.

Campbell, L. 1974a. Phonological features: problems and proposals. Language 50.1. 52-65.

_____. 1974b. Quichean palatalized velars. IJAL 40.2. 132-34.

Chafe, W. L. 1970. Seneca morphology: introduction. IJAL 26.1. 11-22.

Chen, M. 1971. Metarules and universal constraints on phonological theory. Project on Linguistic Analysis, University of California, Berkeley, 13. MC1-MC56.

Cheng, T. M. 1973. The phonology of Taishan. Journal of Chinese Linguistics 1.2. 256-322.

Chomsky, N. and M. Halle. 1968. The pattern of English. New York.

Cohen, D. 1969. Why the Slavic "second palatalization" comes first. Papers from the fifth regional meeting of the Chicago Linguistic Society. Chicago. 306-313.

Cole, D. T. 1955. Introduction to Tswana grammar. London.

_____. 1967. Some features of Ganda linguistic structure. Johannesburg.

Collinder, B. 1960. Comparative grammar of the Uralic languages. Stockholm.

Cowan, H.K.J. 1959. Phonostatistical diagnosis of loan words. Studia Linguistica 13.1-28.

_____. 1965. Grammar of the Sentani language. 'sGravenhage.

Daniloff, R.G. and R.E. Hammarberg. 1973. On defining coarticulation. Journal of Phonetics 1.3.239-248.

Darden, B.J. 1970. The fronting of vowels after palatals in Slavic. Papers from the sixth regional meeting of the Chicago Linguistic Society. Chicago. 459-470.

Dasgupta, P. 1972. Coronality, Old-Indo-Aryan palatals and ṇatva. Indian Linguistics 33.2. 99-122.

Davis, I. 1962. Phonological function in Cheyenne. IJAL 28.1. 36-42.

De Armond, R.C. 1966. "Palatal" and "palatalized" redefined. The Canadian Journal of Linguistics 11.2.109-113.

Dixon, R.M.W. 1970. Proto-Australian laminals. Oceanic Linguistics 9.2. 79-103.

Doke, C.M. 1954. The Southern Bantu languages. Oxford University Press.

Drage, C.L. 1967. Factors in the regressive palatalization of consonants in Russian. Zeitschrift für Phonetik, Sprachwissenschaft und Kommunikationsforschung 20.1.2. 119-142; 3.181-206.

Dunatov, R. 1963. Palatalization and palatal — a definition. Slavic and East European Journal 7.4. 401-404.

Dunstan, E. 1964. Towards a phonology of Ngwe. JWAL 1.1.39-42.

Echeverria, M.S. and H. Contreras. 1965. Araucanian phonemics. IJAL 31.2.133-135.

Edel, M.M. 1944. The Tillamook language. IJAL 10.1.1-57.

Emeneau, M.B. 1956. India as a linguistic area. Language 32.1. 3-16.

Fairbanks, G.H. 1965. Historical phonology of Russian. Poona.

Fast, P.W. 1953. Amuesha (Arawak) phonemes. IJAL 19.3.191-194.

Ferguson, C.A. and M. Chowdhury. 1960. The phonology of Bengali. Language 36.1. 22-59.

Ferrell, J. 1970. Cokane and the palatalizations of velars in East Slavic. The Slavic and East European Journal 14.4. 411-422.

Firestone, H.L. 1965. Description and classification of Siriono. Mouton.

Franklin, K.J. 1968. The dialects of Kewa. Pacific Linguistics, Series B., Monograph no. 10, Canberra.

Fromkin, V.A. 1970. The concept of naturalness in a universal phonetic theory. Glossa 4.1. 29-45.

Fudge, E.C. 1967. The nature of phonological primes. Journal of Linguistics 3.1. 1-36.

Gamkrelidze, T.V. 1967. Kartvelian and Indo-European: a typological comparison of reconstructed linguistic systems. To Honor R. Jakobson, Vol. I. 707-717.

Gibson, L.F. 1956. Pame (Otomi) phonemics and morphophonemics. IJAL 22.4. 242-265.

Girard, V. 1971. Proto-Takanan phonology. University of California Publications in Linguistics [UCPL] 70. Berkeley and Los Angeles.

Green, M.M. and G.E. Igwe. 1966. A descriptive grammar of Igbo. Oxrod University Press.

Greenberg, J.H. 1941. Some problems of Hausa phonology. Language 17.4. 316-323.

_____. 1963. Vowel harmony in African languages. Actes du Second Colloque International de Linguistique Negro-Africaine, Dakar. 33-38.

_____. 1970. Some generalizations concerning glottalic consonants, especially implosives. WPLU 2. 1-37. Also in IJAL 36. 123-145.

Gregersen, E.A. 1967. The palatal consonants in Hausa. Journal of African Languages [JAL] 6.2. 170-184.

Grimes, J.L. 1969. The palatalized velar stop in Proto-Quichean. IJAL 35.1. 20-24.

Gulya, J. 1966. Eastern Ostyak Chrestomathy. Indiana University Uralic and Altaic Series 51.

Guma, S.M. 1971. An outline structure of southern Sotho. Pietermaristzburg.

Halle, M. 1959. The sound pattern of Russian. Mouton.

Halpern, A.M. 1946. Yuma. Linguistic Structures of Native America, ed. by C. Osgood. Viking Fund Publications in Anthropology 6. 249-288.

Harms, R.T. 1962. Estonian grammar. Indiana University Uralic and Altaic Series 12.

Harris, J.W. 1969. Spanish phonology. Massachusetts Institute of Technology.

Harris, Z.H. 1944. Simultaneous components in phonology. Language 20. 181-205.

_____. 1945. Navaho phonology and Hoijer's analysis. IJAL 11.4. 239-246.

Hashimoto, M.J. 1970. Internal evidence for Ancient Chinese palatal endings. Language 46.2. 336-365.

Hattori, S. 1967. The principle of assimilation in phonemics. Word 23.1.2.3. 257-264.

Haugen, E. 1958. The phonemes of modern Icelandic. Language 34.1. 55-88.

Hebert, R.J. 1962. Karacay phonology. Indiana University Uralic and Altaic Series 13.

Heffner, R.M.S. 1950. General phonetics. Madison.

Henderson, E.J.A. 1949. A phonetic study of western Ossetic. Bulletin of the School of Oriental and African Studies 13.1. 36-79.

Henne, H. 1965. Sathewkok Hakka phonology. Norsk Tidsskrift for Sprogvidenskab 20. 109-161.

Hockett, C.F. 1956. Central Algonquian t and c. IJAL 22.3. 202-203.

Hodge, C.T. 1946. Serbo-Croatian phonemes. Language 22.2. 112-120.

Hoff, B.J. 1961. Dorsal phonemes with special reference to Carib. Lingua 10.4. 403-419.

_____. 1968. The Carib language. Hague.

Hoijer, H. 1946. Chiricahua Apache. Linguistic Structures of Native America, ed. by C. Osgood. Viking Fund Publications in Anthropology 6. 55-84.

Hope, E.R. 1971. Problems of phone assignment in the description of Thailand Lisu phonology. Papers in South East Asian Linguistics 2. 53-77.

Hughes, J.P. 1962. The science of language. New York.

Ivic, P. 1965. Roman Jakobson and the growth of phonology. Linguistics 18. 35-78.

Jackson, K.H. 1967. A historical phonology of Breton. Dublin.

Jakobson, R., C.G.M. Fant, and M. Halle. 1963. Preliminaries to speech analysis. Massachusetts Institute of Technology.

Jespersen, O. 1912. English phonetics. Copenhagen.

Jones, L.G. 1959. The contextual variants of the Russian vowels. In Halle 1959, 154-167.

Kaschube, D.V. 1967. Structural elements of the language of the Crow Indians of Montana. University of Colorado Press.

Katre, S.M. 1942. The formation of Konkani. Poona.

Katsura, M. 1973. Phonemes of the Alu dialect of Akha. Papers in South East Asian Linguistics 3. 35-54.

Kelkar, A.R. and P.N. Trisal. 1964. Kashmiri word phonology: a first sketch. Anthropological Linguistics 6.1. 13-22.

Keller, K.C. 1959. The phonemes of Chontal (Mayan). IJAL 25.1. 44-53.

Key, H. 1961. Phonotactics of Cayuvava. IJAL 27.2. 143-150.

Key, M.R. 1968. Comparative Tacana phonology. Mouton.

Kirton, J.F. 1967. Anyula phonology. Papers in Australian Linguistics 1. 15-28.

Klagstad, H.L., Jr. 1958. A phonemic analysis of some Bulgarian dialects. American Contribution to the Fourth International Congress of Slavists. Mouton. 157-166.

Krishnamurti, Bh. 1961. Telegu verbal bases. UCPL 24.

Kučera, H. 1958. Inquiry into co-existent phonemic systems in Slavic languages. American Contribution to the Fourth International Congress of Slavists. Mouton. 169-188.

_____. 1963. Mechanical phonemic transcription and phoneme frequency count of Czech. International Journal of Slavic Linguistics and Poetics 6. 36-50.

Kufner, H.L. 1960. History of central Bavarian obstruents. Word 16.1. 11-27.

Ladefoged, P. 1964. A phonetic study of West African languages. Cambridge.

_____. 1971. Preliminaries to linguistic phonetics. Chicago.

Lako, G. 1968. Proto-Finno-Ugric sources of the Hungarian phonetic stock. Mouton.

Leonard, C.S., Jr. 1969. A reconstruction of Proto-Lucanian. Orbis 18.2. 439-484.

Leslau, W. 1959. Sidamo features in the south Ethiopic phonology. Journal of American Oriental Society 79.1. 1-7.

Lewis, H. and H. Pedersen. 1937. A concise comparative Celtic grammar. Göttingen.

Lightner, J.M. 1965. On the description of vowel and consonant harmony. Word 21.2.244-250.

Lochak, D. 1960. Basque phonemics. Anthropological Linguistics 2.3.12-31.

Loewen, J.A. 1963. Choco II: phonological problems. IJAL 29.4.357-371.

Lorimer, D.L.R. 1935. The Burushaski language, I. Oslo.

Loving, R.E. 1966. Awa phonemes, tonemes and tonally differentiated allomorphs. Papers in New Guinea Linguistics 5. 23-32.

Lovins, J.B. 1972. Southern Paiute s and c. IJAL 38.2.136-141.

Lowman, G.S. 1932. The phonetics of Albanian. Language 8. 271-291.

Mackenzie, D.N. 1961. Kurdish dialect studies, I. London.

Manley, T.M. 1972. Outline of Sre structure. Hawaii.

Mann, S.E. 1963. Armenian and Indo-European (Historical phonology). London.

Marsh, J. 1969. Mantijiltjara phonology. Oceanic Linguistics 8.2.131-152.

Martin, S.E. 1951. Korean phonemics. Language 27.4. 519-533.

Martinet, A. 1949. Occlusives and affricates with reference to some problems of Romance phonology. Word 5.2. 116-122.

_____. 1951. Concerning some Slavic and Aryan reflexes of IE s. Word 7.2. 91-95.

Mason, S.A. 1950. The language of the Papago of Arizona. Philadelphia.

Mathews, W.K. 1956. Phonology of the palatal plosives in East-European languages. Archivum Linguisticum 8.1. 51-65.

Matteson, E. 1963. Piro (Arawakan) language. UCPL 42.

McDavid, Jr. 1949. /r/ and /y/ in the South. Studies in Linguistics 7.1. 18-20.

McElhanon, K.A. 1970. Selepet phonology. Pacific Linguistics, Series B, no. 14. Canberra.

Meinhof, C. 1932. Bantu phonology. Tr. by N.J. Van Warmelo. Berlin.

Mendeloff, H. 1969. A manual of comparative Romance linguistics. Washington.

Miller, W.R. 1965. Acoma grammar and texts. University of California Publications in Linguistics 40.

_____. 1967. Uto-Aztecan cognate sets. UCPL 48.

_____ and I. Davis. 1963. Proto-Keresan phonology. IJAL 29.4. 310-330.

Mohrlang, R. 1972. Higi phonology. Studies in Nigerian Linguistics 2.

Naro, N.J. 1971. Directionality and assimilation. Linguistic Inquiry 2.1. 57-67.

Neeld, R.L. 1973. Remarks on palatalization. Working Papers in Linguistics 14. 37-49. Ohio State University.

Newell, L.E. 1956. Phonology of the Guhang Ifugao dialect. Philippine Journal of Science 85. 523-39.

Newman, P. 1970. Historical sound laws in Hausa and Dera. JWAL 7.1. 39-51.

_____ and R. Ma. 1966. Comparative Chadic: phonology and lexicon. JAL 5.3. 218-251.

Newton, B.E. 1963. Patterns of sound change in Greek. Lingua 12.2. 151-164.

_____. 1971. Modern Greek post-consonantal yod. Lingua 26. 2. 132-170.

_____. 1972. The generative interpretation of dialect: a study of Modern Greek phonology. Cambridge University Press.

Nichols, J. 1971. Diminutive consonant symbolism in Western North America. Language 47.4 826-848.

Oblensky, S., K.Y. Panah, and F.K. Nouri. 1963. Persian basic course. Washington.

Ohala, J.J. 1971. The role of physiological and acoustic models in explaining the direction of sound change. Project on Linguistic Analysis 15. 25-40.

Painter, C. 1970. Gonja, a phonological and grammatical study. Mouton.

Pankratz, L. and E.V. Pike. 1972. Phonology and morphophonemics of Ayutla Mixtec. IJAL 38.

Parker, G.J. 1969. Ayacucho Quechua grammar and dictionary. Mouton.

Parsons, F.W. 1970. Is Hausa really a Chadic language? Some problems of comparative philology. African Language Studies 11. 272-88.

Penzl, H. 1947. The phonetic split of Germanic k in Old English. Language 23. 1. 34-42.

Popperwell, R.G. 1963. The pronunciation of Norwegian. Cambridge.

Posti, L. 1953. From pre-Finnic to late Proto-Finnic. Finnisch-Ugrische Forschungen 31.1.2. 1-91.

Powlison, P.S. 1962. Palatalization portmanteaus in Yagua (Peba-Yaguan). Word 18.3. 280-299.

Priebsch, R. and W.E. Collinson. 1966. The Germanic language. London.

Pulleyblank, E.G. 1962. The consonant system of Old Chinese. Asia Major 9. 58-144, 206-265.

Purnell, Jr., H.C. 1965. Phonology of a Yao dialect spoken in the province of Chiengrai, Thailand. Hartford Studies in Linguistics, no. 15.

Rabin, C. 1963. The origin of the subdivisions of Semitic. Hebrew and Semitic Studies, ed. by D.W. Thomas and W.D. McHardy, 104-105. Oxford University Press.

Ramanujan, A.K. and C. Masica. 1969. Toward a phonological typology of the Indian linguistic area. Current Trends in Linguistics, ed. by T.A. Sebeok, vol. 5, 543-577.

Raun, A. 1971. Essays in Finno-Ugric and Finnic linguistics. Indiana University Uralic and Altaic Series 107.

Ray, P.S. 1964. Outline of Lhasa Tibetan structure. Indian Linguistics 25. 247-261.

Reichard, G.A. 1958. A comparison of five Salish languages, I. IJAL 24.4. 293-300.

Ristinen, E.K. 1960. An East Cheremis phonology. Bloomington.

Robins, R.H. 1964. Some typological observations on Sundanese morphology. Lingua 15. 435-450.

Rosetti, Al. 1968. Istoria Limbii Romane. Bucharest.

Ruhlen, M. 1972. Synchronic palatalization in Romanian. Revue Romains de Linguistique 17.6. 565-569.

Samuels, M.L. 1972. Linguistic evolution. Cambridge.

Schachter, P. and V. Fromkin. 1968. A phonology of Akan: Akuapem, Asante, Fante. Working Papers in Phonetics 9. University of California, Los Angeles.

Schane, S.A. 1971. The phoneme revisited. Language 47.3. 503-521.

Schebeck, B. 1965. The structure of Kabardian. La Linguistique 1. 113-119.

Schmalstieg, W.R. 1960. Baltic ei and depalatalization. Lingua 9.3. 258-266.

_____. 1964. Palatalization and palatal -- a sharp compact
acute definition. Slavic and East European Journal 8.2. 182-183.

Sherzer, J. 1973. Areal linguistics in North America. Current
Trends in Linguistics, ed. by T.A. Sebeok, vol. 10. 749-795.

Shevelov, G.Y. 1964. A prehistory of Slavic. Heidelberg.

Skinner, L.E. 1962. Usila Chinantec syllabic structure. IJAL
28.4. 251-255.

Smith, N.V. 1967. The phonology of Nupe. JAL 6.2. 153-169.

Sommerfelt, A. 1922. The dialect of Torr Co. Donegal. Christiania.

_____. 1925. Studies in cyfeiliog Welsh. Oslo.

_____. 1952. The structure of the consonant system of the
Gaelic of Torr. Eriu, vol. 16, 205-211.

Spandonck, M.V. 1964. Palatalization: a phonological process in
Bushɔ́ɔ́ŋ. JAL 3.2. 191-201.

Spence, N.C.W. 1965. The palatalization of k, g and a in Gallo-
Romance. Archivum Linguisticum 17.1. 20-37.

Stankiewicz, E. 1958. Towards a phonemic typology of the Slavic
languages. American Contribution to the fourth International
Congress of Slavists. Mouton. 301-316.

Swadesh, M. 1960. The Oto-Manguean hypothesis and Macro-
Mixtecan. IJAL 26.2. 79-111.

Swift, L.B. 1963. A reference grammar of Modern Turkish.
Mouton.

Taylor, D. 1960. On the history of Island Carib consonantism.
IJAL 26.2. 146-154.

Thompson, L.C. 1959. Saigon phonemics. Language 35.4. 456-476.

Trager,G.L. 1934. The phonemes of Russian. Language 10.4.
334-344.

Tucker, A.N. 1940. The Eastern Sudanic languages. Oxford
University Press.

_____. 1964. Kalenjin phonetics. In honor of Daniel Jones, ed. by Abercrombie et al. Longmans.

_____ and M.A. Bryan. 1966. The non-Bantu languages of North-Eastern Africa. Oxford University Press.

Ullendorff, E. 1955. The Semitic languages of Ethiopia. London.

Ultan, R. 1970. Size-sound symbolism. WPLU 3. S1-S 31.

Upson, B.W. and R.E. Longacre. 1965. Proto-Chatino phonology. IJAL 31.4. 312-322.

Van Der Tuuk, H.M. 1864. A grammar of Toba Batak, tr. by Scott Kimball, 1971.

Voegelin, C.F., F.M. Voegelin and K.L. Hale. 1962. Typological and comparative grammar of Uto-Aztecan, I: phonology. IJAL Memoir 17.

Von Essen, D. 1964. An acoustic explanation of the sound shift 1 > u and 1 > i. In Honor of Daniel Jones, ed. by Abercrombie et al., 53-58. Longmans.

Wang, W.S.-Y. 1969. The phonetic and tonal structure of residue. Competing change as a cause of residue. Language 45.1.9-25.

Ward, I.C. 1933. The phonetic and tonal structure of Efik. London.

Wares, A.C. 1968. A comparative study of Yuman consonantism. Mouton.

Welmers, W.E. 1944. A descriptive grammar of Fanti. Baltimore.

_____. 1952. Notes on the structure of Bariba. Language 28. 82-88.

Williams, A.F. and E.V. Pike. 1968. The phonology of Western Popoloca. Lingua 20.1. 368-380.

Wonderly, W.L. 1949. Some Zoquean phonemic and morphophonemic correspondences. IJAL 15.1.1-11.

Wurm, S. 1947. The Uzbek dialect of Qizil Qujas. Bulletin of the School of Oriental and African Studies 12.1. 86-105.

Zachariasen, U. 1970.   The palatalizing of g and k in Faroese.
    Orbis 19.1. 89-93.

Zeps, U.L. 1962.   Latvian and Finnic linguistic convergences.
    Indiana University Uralic and Altaic Series 9.

Typology and Universals
of Vowel Systems

JOHN CROTHERS

ABSTRACT

Following previous typologies I divide vowel systems into sub-systems based primarily on length and nasalization, and take the number and arrangement of vowel qualities in the short oral vowel system of a language as the main classificatory parameter. For a given number of such vowels, the types of arrangements found in the languages examined were subject to severe restrictions which can be expressed in a series of universal rules. These rules, in turn, can be largely explained by a modified version of Liljencrants and Lindblom's model of dispersion of vowels in the vowel space.

CONTENTS

1. Introduction[1]

This paper presents a new typology of vowel systems based on
an areally and genetically representative sample of languages developed by the Stanford Phonology Archiving Project. The representative nature of the sample makes it possible to determine with
more confidence than before which types of system are more natural
and which are marginal or deviant, and to set up a number of universal or near universal rules about such systems. The rules go
beyond earlier proposed universals about vowel systems (Trubetzkoy,
Jacobson, Hockett, Chomsky and Halle, Sedlak) in a number of respects. Further, a detailed comparison between the typology (and
universals) arrived at empirically and the theoretical typology generated by Liljencrants and Lindblom's model of dispersion of vowels
in the vowel space shows that with some revisions the model predicts
most universals of vowel quality systems. I consider this to be
evidence in favor of a 'functional' approach to language universals.

1.1 The sample

This study is made possible by the materials collected by the
Stanford Phonology Archiving Project, of which I am a member.
At the time of writing the Archive contained phonetic-phonemic
descriptions of 209 languages, the vowel systems of which I took
as the basis of my typology.[2] The sample is areally and genetically
balanced to the extent permitted by available descriptions of languages and current understanding of genetic relationships. The data
on each language is drawn from one or more published descriptions.
All symbols are translated into a standard set (see Appendix I for
the full set of vowel symbols used). The principles of the phonemic
analysis are briefly discussed in Sec. 1.4. In general the analysis
of the vowel system of a language presented in this paper corresponds
to the analysis in the Phonology Archive. However, in reviewing
the material I have made some changes in the phonemic analyses
in cases where I felt a change would bring the analyses more into
line with the principles stated in Sec. 1.4. This generally involved
elimination of marginal phonemes. In most cases the source grammar for each language in the Archive has been read by at least two

---

[1] I am very grateful to Alan Bell, Lynn Friedman and John Ohala
for their comments on an earlier draft of this paper. I would also
like to acknowledge the help of all the members of the Stanford Phonology Archiving Project in gathering and organizing the data on
which this paper is based.

[2] See Vihman 1976 for a detailed description.

people on the staff, the second checking the analysis for consistency.
I have also checked many details in preparing this paper. Doubtless,
mistakes of fact and interpretation remain; still, the sample offers
a large body of data that has been subjected to a fairly careful and
consistent analysis.

1. 2 Vowel quality

Vowels can be defined as syllabic sounds produced without closure
in the middle of the oral tract (Fant 1973:176ff). The quality of vowels with normal voicing is determined by the supraglottal resonators,
and can be classified acoustically in terms of their resonant frequencies. Oral vowels, produced with closed velum, are often classified
according to the center frequency of the first two resonances (formants; F_1 for first formant, F_2 for second formant, etc.). The third
formant is probably of some significance for high front vowels, and
also for vowels of opposite rounding and backness and the 'r-colored'
vowels. One approach (Liljencrants and Lindblom 1972, Fant 1973:
186ff) is to classify vowels by F_1 and a weighted average of F_2 and
F_3. Nasal vowels differ from oral vowels (in theory at least) by
the addition of nasal formants, by a broadening of the bandwidth of
all formants, by a reduction of their amplitude, and by an upward
shift of the first oral formant. (See Ohala 1975:294, also Wright
1975, calling the last point into question.)

It appears that there is only a partial correlation between the
positions of the articulating organs and the acoustic quality of a
vowel (Lehiste 1973). According to Lindblom and Sundberg, who
constructed a detailed model of vowel production, the shape of the
oral resonating cavity is controlled by the position of the lips, the
height of the jaw, the amount of constriction of the tongue and the
point at which it occurs (palatal, velar, pharyngeal), and the height
of the larynx. They make the following correlations between artic-
ulators and the vowel formants. 1) Tongue constriction in the palatal or velar region gives a relatively lower F_1, while pharyngeal
constriction produces a high F_1. 2) Palatal vowels have a relatively
high F_2; velar vowels have a low F_2, and pharyngeal vowels fall in
between. 3) Retraction of the tongue constriction raises F_1 somewhat and lowers F_2 considerably. 4) Opening the jaw raises F_1;
it also lowers F_2 for a palatal vowel and raises it for a velar vowel.
The traditional articulatory parameters 'open' and 'close' can be
interpreted as referring to the jaw opening normally (but not necessarily) used in the production of a particular vowel. 5) Increased
tongue constriction raises F_2 for a palatal vowel, decreases F_2 for
a velar vowel or a pharyngeal one. 6) Lip rounding lowers all

formants, primarily F_3 for palatal vowels, F_2 for velar vowels.
7) Lowering of the larynx lowers all formants. Correlations 1-6
are illustrated in the following diagrams; Fig. 1 representing an
outline of the acoustic space, Figs. 2-4 the main articulatory
parameters.

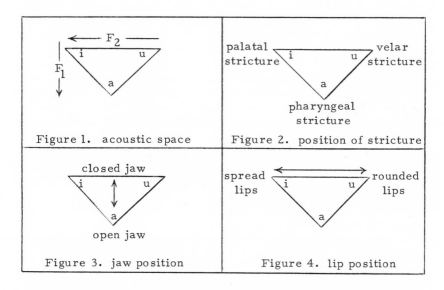

Figure 1. acoustic space

Figure 2. position of stricture

Figure 3. jaw position

Figure 4. lip position

Descriptive linguists generally use articulatory parameters,
the position of the lips and the tongue, to identify vowel quality.
Since tongue position is not observable without special equipment,
its specification is just a conventional label, not necessarily accurate, which linguists associate with a particular sound and the kin-
esthetic experience of producing that sound. The easiest way to
bring outdated linguistic terminology into line with modern phonetics
is to interpret the articulatory descriptions as specifying acoustic
qualities. In the process of translation, however, certain articulatory labels, such as lip rounding or central tongue position, lose
the independence they appear to have if interpreted literally. The
vowel [a], frequently referred to as central, is so only in acoustic
terms (F_2 neither high nor low). Articulatorily, the traditional
term is wrong, since there is considerable retraction of the tongue,
making [a] actually further 'back' than [u] in articulation. The
acoustic reinterpretation of the terminology actually saves it from
an error. Lip rounding, although articulatorily independent of
tongue position, acoustically only modifies qualities determined
by tongue position. Palatal vowels are generally unrounded because

this leads to a higher F_2 and F_3, which are high for palatal vowels;
velar vowels are generally rounded because this causes a lower F_2,
which is already low for them. In other words, rounding reinforces
the 'backness' of the velar vowels, and unrounding (spreading) reinforces the 'frontness' of the palatal vowels (cf. Fant 1973: 186ff).
Rounded palatal vowels and unrounded velar vowels fall acoustically
between 'front' and 'back.' It appears that rounded palatal vowels
are closer to the unrounded palatals, and unrounded velar vowels
closer to the rounded velars in the acoustic space. To this extent
the traditional terminology 'front rounded' and 'back unrounded' can
be taken as valid acoustically, but it must be remembered that both
types are acoustically centralized with respect to their maximally
'front' and 'back' counterparts, and that rounding is not an independent perceptual dimension which can be separated from the front-
back dimension.

The effects of an expanded pharynx, produced by lowering of the
larynx and advancement of the tongue root, can also be described
in terms of the first two formants, although the acoustic and articulatory facts are still not entirely clear. Lindau's in-depth study
of several African languages with vowel harmony shows that for
several KWA languages pharyngeal expansion (also called 'tongue
root advancement,' e.g. by Stewart) is the feature distinguishing
the two harmonic sets of vowels, and that the set with expanded
pharynx are acoustically considerably higher (lower F_1) than the
other set. (Due apparently to concomitant adjustments of the front
and body of the tongue, there is no corresponding lowering of F_2.)
It is not yet known whether vowels produced with expanded pharynx
exhibit anything like the 'singing formant,' ('covered voice') which
is also due to pharyngeal expansion (Sundberg). Lindau also found
that in two NILOTIC languages with vowel harmony superficially
quite similar to that found in West Africa, pharyngeal expansion
did not play a role.

A traditional vowel chart, such as the IPA, can be roughly interpreted as an acoustic chart, with the articulatory terms read as
acoustic ones. Thus 'high' means 'low F_1,' 'front unrounded' means
'high F_2,' etc. as shown in Fig. 5.

In determining the vowel systems of the sample languages I interpreted vowel tenseness in two different ways. When associated with
a difference between long and short vowels, I subsumed it under the
length feature. For example, languages which distinguish between
long /i·/ and short /I/ (e.g. GERMAN, ENGLISH) have been interpreted as having a primary length distinction rather than a distinction

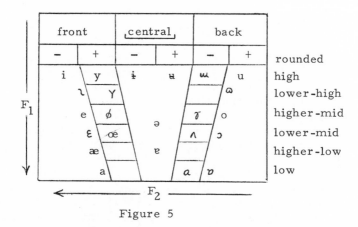

Figure 5

between two vowel qualities. On the other hand, in a language like PANJABI (Gill and Gleason 1963) there is said to be no appreciable length distinction between /i/ and /I/, so the difference is inter-preted as one of vowel quality. Acoustically, lax vowels are more central than their tense counterparts. (See American ENGLISH formant data in Peterson and Barney 1952. /I/ and /U/ are both lower and more central than /i/ and /u/, in addition to being shorter, in ENGLISH.) In general one is probably justified in interpreting lax vowels as central with respect to tense counterparts. However, in the descriptive literature [I] and [U] are frequently treated as being simply lower than [i] and [u]. In the few cases in the language sample where this raised questions about the relative position of phonemically distinct vowels of the same length, I have treated /I/ and /U/ as being both lower and more central than /i/ and /u/.

I have not included retroflex ('r-colored') vowels in the present survey. The relevant acoustic parameter is lowering of F_3 and F_4 (see Lindau 1975: 21), which involves another dimension of vowel quality. Since retroflexion of vowels is not common as an independ-ent, contrastive feature, its omission does not greatly affect the typological picture.

1.3 Types of vowel systems

The general basis for the typology of vowel systems laid down by Trubetzkoy and Hockett seems to me to be valid. In particular, different subsystems of vowels can be separated from each other on the basis of features other than the shape of the oral resonator, giving three separate subsystems: normal length oral vowels,

long oral vowels (or, in a few cases, overly short vowels), and
nasal vowels. Long nasal vowels may of course be found in
languages with both long oral vowels and nasal vowels, but their
inclusion does not seem to add much to a typological survey. Differences in voice quality may also occur, e.g. normal versus
creaky or breathy voice, but when this does occur, it can often be
interpreted in conjunction with the consonantal or tonal system of
a language. VIETNAMESE, for example, has both creaky and
b reathy voice in addition to normal voicing, but both are associated with specific tonal configurations. There are a few cases
of languages with vowel subsystems differing in voice quality, but
they are too rare to be of typological importance. The basic vowel
quality system of a language is the arrangement of qualities of
normal length oral vowels. Languages may have anywhere from
three to about twelve distinct vowel qualities in the basic system.
The arrangement is determined to a large extent simply by the
number of vowels; for a given number of vowel qualities, only one
or two arrangements occur with any frequency in the world's languages. This makes it a natural basis for vowel system typology.
(See Sedlak 1969, Liljencrants and Lindblom 1972. Also, Jakobson
(1968) and Chomsky and Halle (1968) use number of vowels at least
as a basis for discussion.)

For the purpose of further distinctions I have found it most useful to distinguish between 'peripheral' and 'interior' vowels, the
former including the extreme palatal (front unrounded), the extreme
velar (back rounded), and the low vowels, the latter including all
acoustically more 'central' vowels, i.e. back unrounded, front
rounded, and non-low central or centralized vowels. See Fig. 6.

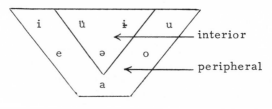

Figure 6

The number of interior vowels supplies a second typological parameter. Types of vowel systems can be identified by a pair of numbers,
x : y, where 'x' is the total number of vowels and 'y' the number of
interior vowels. The standard five vowel system /i e a u o/, having
no interior vowels, is 5 : 0; the four vowel systems /i e a u/ and

/i i a u/ are symbolized 4:0 and 4:1 respectively. This is sufficient to characterize all of the relatively common systems and a
number of less common ones as well. Further refinements, where
needed, are based on the arrangement of the peripheral or interior
vowels. First, on the basis of the most common systems (e.g. 5:0),
certain arrangements of peripheral vowels can be established as
normal. Other arrangements, differing from these in having a gap
at any position, are termed 'defective.' This is symbolized by an
asterisk preceding the number of vowels in the system (*x:y). If
two different defective systems are found with the same number x:y,
a single asterisk is used for one, a double asterisk for the other.
Thus *5:1 and **5:1 represent two different five vowel systems,
each with one interior vowel, but with different gaps in the peripheral system. Since such systems are not common, there seems to
be little point in incorporating into the notation the precise nature
of the gap. Several differences of arrangement are found in languages with two or more interior vowels. The commonest type is
a vertical arrangement, as in FRENCH, GERMAN and VIETNAM-
ESE, with /ü ö ɜ/, /ü ö/, and /ɨ ə/ respectively, which is left unmarked in the notation: 11:3, 7:2, and 10:2 respectively for these
languages. If there is a distinction between front rounded and back
unrounded, as in TURKISH, with /ü ö ɨ/, this is noted by an apostrophe after the second number, x:y' (for TURKISH 8:3'). A double
apostrophe indicates systems with centralized /IU/ in contrast with
/i u/, as in PANJABI, 10:3". The notation is summarized in Fig. 7.

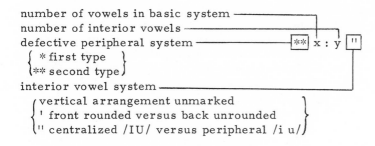

```
number of vowels in basic system ─────────────┐
number of interior vowels ──────────────────┐ │
defective peripheral system ──────────────┤**│x : y│"│
⎰ * first type  ⎱                          └──┘    └─┘
⎱** second type ⎰
interior vowel system ─────────────────────────────┘
⎰ vertical arrangement unmarked                    ⎱
⎰ ' front rounded versus back unrounded            ⎰
⎱ " centralized /IU/ versus peripheral /i u/       ⎰
```

Figure 7

The systems of Trubetzkoy and Hockett for classifying vowel
quality systems, based on the number of height and backness distinctions, are needlessly complex for typological purposes, since
these parameters are roughly determined by the total number of
vowels in a system. Trubetzkoy's distinction between linear, triangular, and quadrangular systems does not seem to be especially

useful. Linear systems either do not exist at all, or if they do, are
subject to a variety of problems of interpretation (see discussion
of two vowel systems below, Sec. 2.4). The distinction between
triangular and quadrangular systems is based simply on whether
there is one (triangular) or two (quadrangular) low vowels. Actually,
due to the shape of the vowel space, all systems are roughly triangular in phonetic terms, and the overwhelming majority are triangular by Trubetzkoy's criterion.

1. 4 Phonemic analysis

The vowel system of each language in the sample is analyzed
along the lines of classical phonemic method. This is not the place
for a general discussion of the pros and cons of phonemic analysis.
The following remarks are offered only as a general guide to my
interpretation of the phoneme, and its relevance to typology. The
basic principle of phonemics is contrast: two sounds are in contrast
if they can occur in the same environment and are not generally in
free variation. This principle, modified to allow for partial overlap
of phonemes, is probably sufficient in the majority of cases to decide whether the difference between two sounds is phonemic or not.
But as various critics of the phoneme have pointed out (see Chomsky
1964), this principle, if rigorously applied, may in some cases lead
to the establishment of more phonemes than linguists would generally
like. Criticisms of this type can be largely met, in my opinion, by
adding to phonemic theory a distinction between marginal and full
phonemes, the former including all phonemes with a severe distributional restriction in terms of phonological environment, or morphological or lexical function. Marginal phonemes may include
phonemes in unassimilated loans, phonemes that occur in limited
contexts as the result of morphophonemic fusion, sounds that generally have non-contrastive distribution but, due to a sound change
or some special morphological pattern (e.g. reduplication), occur
contrastively in a limited environment. In short, I think one should
recognize that phonological systems, being always in a state of
change, may at any time contain sound differences that are neither
fully phonemic nor fully non-phonemic. I have tried to restrict the
vowel systems here to the more fully phonemic vowels. In all likelihood the results would not be very different if more marginally phonemic vowels were included.

One difference between the approach used here and some other
approaches to phonemic analysis is that here primary emphasis is
placed on the phonetic manifestation of phonemes. Each phoneme

is characterized by a phonetic unit, its major realization (primary member). For example, if the only high front vowel in a language is phonetically [I], the phoneme is called /I/, not /i/. The rationale for this is simply that if one is interested in what sorts of phonetic means languages employ to make distinctions, it is important not to normalize the data prematurely, and thus build preconceived ideas into the results. Of course, for typological purposes considerable normalization is necessary, but I have done this at the last minute, as it were, in the assignment of particular phonemic systems to a general type. For example, all of the three vowel systems in the sample are grouped into a single type: /i a u/. The phonetic manifestations vary considerably, particularly in the case of /u/. (All these manifestations are listed in Appendix III.) However, the decision to treat the different phonetic units, [u U ɯ o], as being typologically /u/ was only made at the point when I was considering all of the three vowel systems, to determine how many basically different patterns of arrangement they exhibited. In the phoneme inventories of each language, the high back vowel is characterized phonetically.

Another point on which my type of analysis may differ from that of others is the phonemic status of neutral vowels, that is vowels (most often [ə]) which are phonetically different from the other phonemes of a language, but do not contrast with them, the neutral vowels being restricted to unstressed position. I have tried to exclude such vowels from the phoneme inventories, although it is not always easy to determine from phonological descriptions whether a symbol /ə/ represents an independent phoneme or a neutral vowel.

There are both practical and theoretical reasons for basing phonological typology on the classical phoneme, thus interpreted. On the practical level, the majority of modern language descriptions have a phonemic basis. On the theoretical level, phonemic analysis answers a basic phonological question: what phonetic features are employed distinctively in a language? The abstract systematic phonemes of generative phonology do not provide an answer to this question since they do not express phonetic features in a direct way. For example, there is no way to tell from Chomsky and Halle's systematic vowel phonemes of ENGLISH what phonetic properties are actually used to distinguish one vowel phoneme from another. Indeed, it is not possible to tell, without detailed comparison of the effects of all the complex rules on all of the vowels, which of the systematic vowel phonemes contrast with each other at the surface level.

2. Survey of Vowel Systems by Type

2.1 General

The types of basic vowel quality systems found in the sample are indicated in Table 1. (See Appendix III for a full listing of languages by type, including phonetic specification of each vowel.) Table 2 gives the approximate vowel qualities found in the more common systems. The number of vowels in the basic system of the sample languages ranges from three to twelve. The more common types, in descending order of frequency, are 5:0, 6:1, 3:0, 4:0 plus 4:1, 7:2, 7:0, 9:2 and 6:0. (See Fig. 8. The reason for grouping 4:0 and 4:1 together is explained in Sec. 2.3.) These types account for over 80% of the sample languages, and no other type represents more than 3% of the total; all these others can be regarded as marginal types, essentially deformations of the more common types. The predominance of type 5:0 is well known. A further fact which can be observed in earlier surveys (e.g. Sedlak), though it does not seem to have been commented on, is that the more frequent types cluster around the 5:0 system (Figs. 8 and 9). Well over 80% of the sample languages have from three to seven vowels, and the only relatively common system outside this range is 9:2. The 5:0 system thus represents an optimum system in a special sense, as the high point in the frequency distribution of types. It can be taken as a single, very rough norm or archetype for language in general.

Table 1. Basic vowel system types

Type	No. of languages	Type	No. of languages	Type	No. of languages
?2:0	1	6:0	7	9:2	7
3:0	23	*6:0	1	9:2"	3
4:0	13	**6:0	1	*9:2	1
4:1	9	6:1	29	9:3'	4
5:0	55	*6:2'	2	10:2	2
*5:0	1	7:0	11	10:3'	1
*5:1	5	*7:1	3	10:3"	1
**5:1	1	7:2	14	?10:3"	1
***5:1	1	8:1	2	11:3	1
*5:2	1	?8:1	2	?12:3	1
		8:2	2		
		8:3'	3		

?indicates considerable uncertainty about the analysis.

Table 2. Common vowel system types

3:0	i	a	u					
4:0	i	ɛ	a	u				
4:1	i	ɨ	a	u				
5:0	i	ɛ	a	u	ɔ			
*5:1	i	ɛ	ɨ	a	o			
6:0	i	e	ɛ	u	o	ɔ		
6:1	i	ɛ	ɨ	a	u	ɔ		
7:0	i	e	ɛ	a	u	o	ɔ	
7:2	i	e	ɨ	ə	a	u	o	
9:2	i	e	ɛ	ɨ	ə	a	u	o	ɔ

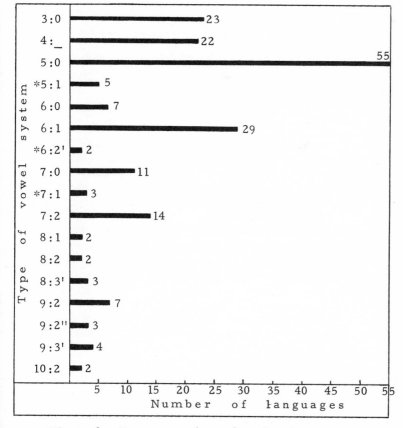

Figure 8. Frequency of vowel system types
(Types represented by only one language are omitted. Types
4:0 and 4:1 are grouped together as 4:_.)

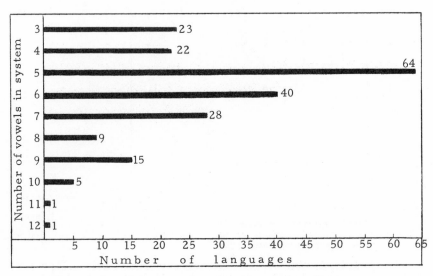

Figure 9. Frequency by size of vowel system

2.2 Peripheral vowels

The number of peripheral vowels ranges from three to eight in
the sample languages (one questionable case of nine). For a given
number of peripheral vowels there is only one common type of
arrangement. There are 17 languages which I consider defective
types, one of the common types with a vowel missing at some point
(generally /e/, /u/ or /o/, never /i/). The general reason for this
kind of patterning seems to be that the vowel space has 'corners,'
namely /i/ and /u/, where the vowels stay relatively fixed, forcing
the remaining vowels into a narrow range of positions. Fully 3/4
of the sample languages have a peripheral system with one of the
'triangular' patterns 3:0, 5:0 or 7:0 (see Table 3). The 4:0 peripheral system does not occur with any interior vowels because
systems that could be interpreted this way (*5:1, *6:2) are more
naturally interpreted as defective versions of the peripheral 5:0
system (see Sec. 2.4 on four vowel systems).

2.3 Interior vowels

Languages with more than one interior vowel make up only about
1/4 of the sample. As noted earlier, these have been divided into
three types, those with a vertical arrangement (unmarked notation),
those with front rounded and back unrounded vowels ('), and those

with centralized /I U/ (''). As can be seen from Table 4, only the
vertical arrangement is common. Generally speaking, the interior
column has back unrounded vowels, /ɨ ə/; front rounded vowels are
found chiefly in Europe and north Asia (see Crothers 1975). Only
two cases of three height distinctions in the interior vowels are
found in the sample, FRENCH and PACOH, and the latter is uncertain.

Table 3. Peripheral vowel systems (questionable types omitted)

type of peripheral vowel system	found in basic system	no. of languages	defective peripheral system	no. of languages	total
3:0 /i a u/	3:0	23			32
	4:1	9			
4:0 /iɛ a u/	4:0	13			13
5:0 /iɛauɔ/	5:0	55	*5:1	5	101
	6:1	29	**5:1	2	
	7:2	14	*6:2'	2	(+10 def.)
	8:3	3	*5:2	1	
6:0 /i e æ u oɒ/	6:0	7	*5:0	1	13
	8:2	2			
	9:3	4			(+1 def.)
7:0 /i e ɛ a u o ɔ/	7:0	11	*6:0	2	26
	8:1	2	*7:1	3	
	9:2	7			(+5 def.)
	9:2''	3			
	10:3'	1			
	10:3''	2			
8:0 /i e ɛ æ a u o ɔ/	10:2	2	*9:2	1	3
	11:3	1			(+1 def.)

Table 4. Interior vowel systems (questionable types included)

no. of interior vowels and type	found in basic vowel systems	no. of languages	total
0	3:0	23	112
	4:0	13	
	5:0	55	
	6:0	7	
	7:0	11	
	*5:0	1	
	*6:0	2	

(continued next page)

Table 4 cont.

no. of interior vowels and type	found in basic vowel systems	no. of languages	total
1	4:1	9	52
	*5:1	5	
	**5:1	2	
	6:1	29	
	7:1	3	
	8:1	4	
2	*5:2	1	29
	7:2	14	
	8:2	2	
	9:2	7	
	10:2	2	
	*9:2	1	
3	11:3	1	
	?12:3	1	
2'	*6:2'	2	10
3'	8:3'	3	
	9:3'	4	
	10:3'	1	
2''	9:2''	3	5
3''	10:3''	2	

2.4 Comments on types of systems

2.4.1 Two vowels   The sample contains one language with a
two vowel system, KABARDIAN, with /ɨ ə/. In my opinion this is
not a clear case, because, according to Kuipers, there is a normal
set of five long vowels of the type 5:0.   He analyzes these as phonemic diphthongs of one of the two short vowels plus /y/, /w/ or
/h/; phonetically, however, they are simple vowels.   Further, the
long vowels have about the same duration as short vowels in other
(European) languages, while the two short vowels are extremely
short.   In fact /ɨ/ seems to be little more than a transitional sound
between consonants, and is regularly lost under certain conditions.
For these reasons I think it would be preferable to regard the five
'long' vowels as forming the basic vowel system of KABARDIAN,
treating the two short vowels as a reduced or 'overshort' system.
This is not to deny that KABARDIAN has a peculiar vowel system;

the peculiarity, however, lies in the high frequency of the reduced
vowels, and not in the structure of the basic vowel quality system.
A similar reinterpretation can probably be made of other linear
vowel systems mentioned by Trubetzkoy. In any case, this type
of phenomenon has been found only in a few CAUCASIAN languages,
and, though interesting as an extreme, has little bearing on the
general picture of vowel system typology.

2.4.2 <u>Three vowels</u>   I have assigned all three vowel systems
in the sample to the same type, in spite of a number of differences
in phonetic quality of the phonemes, because in all cases the three
vowels stand in the same relative relationship and occupy the same
regions of the vowel space. Of the three vowel types, /i a u/, the
last ranges most widely, from [o] through [U] and [u] to [ɯ], the
last being found in two languages, JAQARU and NUNGGUBUYU. Together with ALAWA (4:0) and possibly ONEIDA, these are the only
languages in the sample which do not have lip rounding as a phonetic
feature of the vowel system. Unfortunately, one cannot tell from
the descriptions whether the 'unrounded' quality of the vowels in
question is an acoustic quality or is just based on observation of
the lips. This question is relevant, since, as anyone can tell for
himself, it is possible to produce vowels of 'back rounded' perceptual quality with little or no lip rounding. Whatever the phonetic
details, however, they will not prevent the classification of these
languages to the basic 3:0 type (4:0 for ALAWA), because the general character of the phoneme oppositions remains the same: roughly
high front /i/ versus roughly high back /u/ versus roughly low
central /a/. These oppositions are <u>not</u> simply relative; they involve specific areas of the vowel space; it is just that in a three
vowel system the areas are larger and more vague than in a more
complex system. In other words, a hypothetical three vowel system
/i ü ɛ/ does not fall within the basic 3:0 type, because although the
relative position of the vowels in the system is correct (front versus
back, high versus low), they are bunched up much too closely in one
part of the vowel space. No such system has ever been reported.

The vowels of three vowel systems often show considerable subphonemic variation. For example, in GREENLANDIC ESKIMO,
/i/ includes [i], [e] and [ə], /u/ includes [ü], [u], [o] and [ɔ], and
/a/ includes [æ] and [ɑ] (Thalbitzer 1904).

2.4.3 <u>Four vowels</u>   By my system of classification there are
two types of four vowel systems, 4:0 (/i ɛ a u/) and 4:1 (i ɨ a u/),
which probably should be regarded as subtypes of a single type,
which might be characterized as /i ə a u/. The peculiarity of four

vowel systems is that in addition to the vowels of the basic 3:0
system, they have a fourth vowel which may range anywhere from
mid or even low front, through mid central, up to high central.
The reason for this, according to my revised model of the vowel
space (see Sec. 4.3), is that four vowels do not pack very efficiently
into the vowel space, and this leaves room for the fourth or central
vowel to move into different positions. As in three vowel systems,
there is considerable variation, especially in the position of the
back vowel, and the general statements made with regard to the
specific phonetic character of vowels in a three vowel system apply
here too. The types of vowel systems reported in the literature
all fall within the range of 4:0 or 4:1, with the exception of the system /i a u o/, not found in the sample, but reported by Hockett for
CEBUANO BISAYAN, and by Sedlak for KALINGA and CROW.
(Note: the interpretation of the CROW vowel system remains in
doubt; there is an [e] of uncertain status, and /o/ appears to be
infrequent (Kaschube 1954). In KALINGA, in spite of some apparent minimal pairs for /u/ and /o/, the two vowels are mostly in
free variation (Gieser 1958). In any case, this type of system, if
it exists, is a very marginal one.)

2.4.4 <u>Five vowels</u> The system 5:0 is the only five vowel system
that occurs with any frequency. The degree of deviation from the
typical vowel positions is considerably smaller than that found in
three and four vowel systems. The system *5:1, found in five languages in the sample, resembles the 6:1 system with one of the back
vowels removed. (It might also be interpreted as a 5:0 system with
/u/ fronted to /ɨ/.) Trubetzkoy reports such a system with /ü/ as
the interior vowel in TABARASSAN and KYURI; all the languages
in the sample have a back unrounded vowel. The peculiar system
/i ɨ a u ɔ/, which looks like 6:1 with /ɛ/ removed, is found in PA-
PAGO. (Note: comparative evidence indicates that the system
derives from a normal 5:0 with /ɛ/ becoming /ɨ/ (Voegelin, Voegelin
and Hale 1962). The Voegelins' and Hale's interpretation, that the PA-
PAGO system represents PROTO-UTO AZTECAN, and that /ɨ/,
found only in the SHOSHONEAN branch of UTO AZTECAN, developed into /ɛ/ in the AZTEC and SONORAN branches, strikes me as
implausible on typological grounds, and also because /ɛ/ is the more
common modern reflex.) The EVENKI system /i æ ə u ʌ/ is clearly
a defective 6:1, since the long vowel system has /E·/ in addition to
/æ·/. SENECA, with /i e æ a ʌ/(also in the long vowels) resembles
6:0 with /u/ missing, an isolated type.

MANDARIN CHINESE, with /i ü ë a u/ (5:2) is another isolated
type. (Hockett adds a retroflex vowel /r/, which I am regarding

as part of the consonant system.) This is closer to the 6:1 system
than to any other common type, and it is notable that /ĕ/ has allophones [ɛ] and [o]. Still, by any phonemic analysis these are variants of /ĕ/. A similar system, with interior vowels /ɨ ə/ is reported
for MANOBO, in a very brief article (Meiklejohn 1961). Sedlak has
reported a 5:2' system (with /ü ɨ/) for CHACOBO, but this must be
due to a mistaken transcription; the system is 4:1, without /ü/.

2.4.5 Six vowels The most frequent six vowel system in the
sample is 6:1, the second most frequent of all vowel systems,
while the type 6:0 is represented by seven languages. Other six
vowel systems may be considered typologically unimportant. Until
recently (cf. Ruhlen, to appear), the typological importance of the
6:1 system does not seem to have been recognized. The interior
vowel of the system is generally a central unrounded vowel (/ɨ/ or
/ə/) while the remainder of the system consists of the vowels of
5:0. One language in the sample, the WU dialect of CHINESE, has
/ü/ as the interior vowel, a type mentioned by Sedlak for BASQUE,
and by Trubetzkoy for UKRANIAN. TAKI-TAKI, cited by Hockett
and Sedlak, has /ü/, but only rarely, and exclusively in DUTCH
words (see Hall 1948 for TAKI-TAKI). Medieval GREEK is supposed
to have had /ü/, but of course there is no way of knowing the actual
phonetic character of this vowel.

The 6:0 system is the only type of any frequency that could be
regarded as a clear representative of Trubetzkoy's quadrangular
type, but it is not frequent enough to figure prominently in a typology. In addition to the languages in the sample, 6:0 has been found
by Hockett in DARGWA, MENOMINI and UKRANIAN; by Sedlak in
BATS, GALLA and ZAPOTEC; and by Trubetzkoy in UZBEK,
without major deviations from the pattern described here.

Two languages, CHUVASH and HOPI, which can be classed as
*6:2', are peculiar in having only one back rounded vowel, and in
distinguishing a front rounded from a back unrounded vowel. In
the interior vowel area the closest thing to this would be the 8:3',
9:3' or 10:3' systems (eight languages altogether) which have both
front rounded and back unrounded. CHUVASH in particular seems
to represent an extreme typological deviation in having so few peripheral vowels for the arrangement of interior vowels.

There are two defective 6:0 systems, ENGLISH (RP) with /I E
æ ǽ U ɒ / (*6:0) (Note: the long and short vowel systems are
separated), which looks most like a 7:0 system with /o/ removed,
and EWE, with /i ɛ a u o ɔ/(**6:0), again resembling 7:0, with /e/

removed. (Note: in fact some dialects do have /e/, but in the
dialect described, it has merged with /ɛ/ (see Stahlke 1971)).

2.4.6 Seven vowels Both 7:0 and 7:2 are not uncommon systems. Liljencrants and Lindblom find 7:0 to be the most common
seven vowel system in the literature, and Ruhlen (to appear) also
finds 7:0 to be relatively common (by implication more common
than 7:2). I find that 7:0 and 7:2 are about equally common. This
is due to my grouping together two subtypes, those with front
rounded and those with back unrounded interior vowels, into the
7:2 system. This grouping has been used before (e.g. by Hockett)
and is well motivated acoustically.

The system *7:1 is found in three sample languages and resembles 6:1 with an extra front vowel /e/, or 8:2 with an interior vowel
removed. Sedlak finds this system in TAMIL and LIFU. (He also
mentions SINHALESE, with the interior vowel /ə/, interpreted in
this survey as 6:0. See footnote 19.) Hockett and Trubetzkoy mention BULGARIAN dialects and VOTYAK. In any case it is not very
common compared to 7:0 and 7:2.

2.4.7 Eight vowels None of the eight vowel systems is common
enough to be important typologically. The 8:1 type resembles 7:1,
and 8:2 resembles the more common 7:2 and 9:2. The 8:3' system
is the smallest found with three interior vowels. No languages with
8:0 were found in the sample, though this type has been reported by
Trubetzkoy and Hockett for POLISH dialects. Other systems reported in the literature can be classed with 8:1, 8:2 or 8:3', but
there are not many beyond the nine languages in the sample.

2.4.8 Nine vowels 9:2 is the only common type with more than
seven vowels, with a vertical arrangement of the two interior vowels.
All seven languages in the sample with this system have back unrounded vowels. Such systems seem to be found chiefly in Central
America and Southeast Asia. Another subtype with front rounded
vowels is mentioned in the literature for several GERMANIC and
URALIC languages (e.g. ESTONIAN, NORWEGIAN, ICELANDIC).
In the present sample several similar systems are found, but not
the 9:2 system.

The reasons for treating /I U/ of the 9:2" system as interior
vowels are given in Sec. 1.2. The only other system that resembles
it is the 10:3" system.

The *9:2 system of SOMALI is peculiar in having four front
vowels and only two back (rounded) vowels. This is due to a skewed

vowel harmony system of the basic African type: there are four pairs of vowels which differ roughly on a back to front axis, e/ɛ, æ/ə, ʌ/ɔ, Ʊ/U, except that for the first pair the difference is exclusively one of height, to judge from the rather explicit phonetic characterization by Armstrong. (Note: these vowels alternate in suffixes. /i/ does not occur in suffixes, but as a stem vowel short /i/ generally takes back harmonic suffix forms, and long /i·/ takes front harmonic forms.)

The 9:3' system, like 8:3', has a backness distinction in the interior vowels, and this type of arrangement bears comparison with the 9:2" system, in which /I/ and /U/ show a backness contrast. It is notable that many of the languages with this kind of contrast in the interior vowels have vowel harmony, either the African pharyngeal (or height or tenseness) type, or the palatal type of URALIC, ALTAIC and early GERMANIC. The 9:3' system, like 8:3', occurs chiefly in languages with palatal vowel harmony. All three languages in the sample with 8:3' have palatal harmony, and two of those with 9:3' do (AZERBAIJANI and OSTYAK). The third, NORWEGIAN, of course historically had a form of palatal harmony in palatal umlaut. The 9:2" and 9:2 systems form a kind of areal and typological counterpart of 8:3' and 9:3'. The latter are found in northern Eurasia, along with cases of 9:2 which have front rounded vowels (see Crothers 1975); remaining cases of 9:2 (with back unrounded vowels) are found in Southeast Asia and Central America, while 9:2" is restricted to Africa. Considering that languages with more than seven vowels altogether make up only about 15% of the sample, one might lump them all into a general type of 'large vowel system,' with different areas of the world specializing in slightly different techniques for developing the extra vowels.

2.4.9 <u>Ten or more vowels</u> Languages with more than nine basic vowel qualities are quite uncommon. (There are only seven in the sample, and the typological summary by Liljencrants and Lindblom has only a few.) The types found closely resemble the different types of nine vowel system in the arrangement of the interior vowels, with the exception of FRENCH (11:3), with three distinct vowel heights in the interior vowels. (PACOH (?12:3) may have such a system with back unrounded vowels, but the data is suspect.) A few cases are cited by Liljencrants and Lindblom: NORWEGIAN dialects and MARATHI. I do not regard VIETNAMESE (cited by Sedlak 1969) as a case of this type because, although it has /Ï ë ʌ /, it does not have a clear /a/ which would be below /ʌ/ in the vowel space. Instead, it has a somewhat retracted /æ̇/, which seems to be opposed to /ʌ/ more as front to back. Thus /æ̇/ and

/ʌ/ seem to be functioning as the low vowels in the system, leaving only two interior vowels, /Ï ë/.

3. Universals of Vowel Systems

3.1 <u>The vowel hierarchy</u>   On the basis of the observed types of vowel systems, it is possible to set up a hierarchy of vowels based on implicational statements of the form: 'if a language has a vowel phoneme of type z, it also has one of type w.' (See Greenberg <u>et al</u>. 1966.) This hierarchy is represented in Fig. 10. The arrows can be read with the following meaning: 'beginning with the system /i a u/ construct a larger vowel system by adding the vowel at the head of the arrow.' The vowel symbols have both a relative and an approximate absolute value. In the relative sense each symbol must be interpreted in relation to all the other symbols that precede it in the hierarchy. The symbol /e/ must be interpreted with reference to /ɛ/, which precedes it; /e/ thus means a specifically higher mid vowel in contrast with /ɛ/, whereas the latter symbol, though it typically stands for a lower mid vowel, may also stand for a mid or even higher mid vowel in a system without a higher vowel between it and /i/. The symbols also have an absolute value in the sense that they usually stand for the phonetic value indicated, and other values stand in a cluster around this point in the vowel space. A strict definition of hierarchical rank, corresponding to the notion of implicational hierarchy, is that a vowel x on the chart has a higher rank than a vowel y if y can only be reached by passing through x. Due to branches in the chart, many pairs of vowels have no rank with respect to each other, by this definition. Thus /ɨ/, even though it occurs high on the chart, has no hierarchical

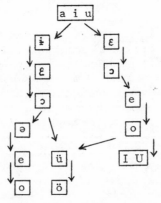

Figure 10

rank relative to /e/, which stands much lower. In other words the existence of /e/ in a language does not imply the existence of /ɨ/. However, it is possible to define a weaker sort of rank, (call it 'precedence') by which /ɨ/ 'has precedence over' /e/. We can say that x̲ has precedence over y̲ if x̲ can be reached on the chart in fewer steps than y̲. This simply means that x̲ may occur in smaller vowel systems than y̲. The implicational universals on which the chart is based are given as universals 1-7 below. (See Appendix I for a restatement of universals.)

1. All languages have /i a u/.

The closest one comes to finding counterexamples to this statement are the following cases. a) Three languages in the sample have only one back vowel, which is unrounded (JAQARU, NUNGGU-BUYU, ALAWA). As noted earlier (Sec. 2.4), I take [ɯ] in these cases to be reasonably close to [u], given the range of variation found in three and four vowel systems. b) There are a number of languages in which the only back rounded vowel is [o] or lower; with 3:0, ALABAMAN and AMUESHA; with 4:0, NAVAHO, ONEIDA, HUPA, MAZATEC, CAMPA; with 4:1, ADZERA, SQUAMISH, AMA-HUACA, CHACOBO; with *5:0, SENECA; with *5:1, NEZ PERCE, OCAINA. In all of these cases we find an /ɨ/ or /o/ bordering on the /u/ area; often one of these phonemes has [u] as an allophone or free variant. In the case of three and four vowel systems, it seems to me that this [o] is reasonably close to [u], given typical variation in such systems, and can be interpreted as /u/. In the case of the five vowel systems, there is clearly a gap at the /u/ position, since there is in each case a mid front vowel paired with a mid back rounded vowel, but no high back rounded vowel paired with the high front vowel. We thus have three languages which are clear exceptions to the rule (SENECA, NEZ PERCE, OCAINA), and another eleven cases that may be regarded as borderline, or, including the cases mentioned under a), a total of fourteen borderline cases (1.5% clear exceptions, 7% borderline).

The typology of vowel systems does not allow a ranking of /i a u/, there being no systems of a smaller type, so that a ranking must be established by other criteria, such as frequency or neutralization. The frequency counts by Greenberg (1966) clearly indicate a consistent pattern a > i > u, which corresponds to the hierarchy set up by Jakobson. On the typological level one might take the fact that /u/ comes closest to being an exception to the universality of /i a u/ as a reason to rank it lower than the other two.

2. All languages with four or more vowels have /ɨ/ or /ɛ/.

All of the 185 languages in the sample which are subject to this rule obey it. The system /i a u o/, not found in the sample, but cited in the literature (see Sec. 2.4), is an exception.

3. Languages with five or more vowels have /ɛ/. They generally also have /ɔ/.

Of 163 sample languages subject to this rule, one, PAPAGO, with **5:1, violates the first part. Nine languages violate the second part, the five languages with *5:1, one with *5:2, one with *5:0, and two with *6:2'. (The chart of the vowel hierarchy is constructed to reflect only the first part of this rule, i.e. it allows for the *5:1 system without /ɔ/.)

4. Languages with six or more vowels have /ɔ/ and also either /ɨ/ or /e/, generally the former.

Of 108 languages in the sample subject to this rule, two (both languages with *6:2') are exceptions to the first part. One language, EWE (*6:0) lacks both /ɨ/ and /e/.

5. Languages with seven or more vowels have /e/ and /o/, or /ɨ/ and /ə/ (/ü/ and /ö/ may represent the types /ɨ/ and /ə/).

Of 68 sample languages subject to this rule, there are four exceptions, the three languages with *7:1, and ALBANIAN (7:2) which has /ü/ and /ə/. All four have two of the six vowels mentioned in the rule, but not in the proper pairing.

6. Languages with eight or more vowels have /e/.

Of 40 sample languages subject to this rule, three, with 8:3', are exceptions.

7. Languages with nine or more vowels generally have /o/.

There are enough exceptions to this rule to make it a 'tendency' rather than a 'near universal.' Of 22 sample languages subject to it, five are exceptions, four with 9:3' and one with *9:2. In addition to the vowels mentioned in rule 5, languages with nine or more vowels may also have /I U/. The situation is summed up in Table 5.

3.2 Normal vowel system

My remaining generalizations are quantitative, concerning the number of vowel contrasts in a system or in different parts of a

Table 5

Rule	applies to —— languages	no. of exceptions	% exceptions
1	204	3	1.5%
2	185	0	0%
3a*	163	1	1%
3b	163	10	8%
4a	108	2	2%
4b	108	3	3%
5	68	4	6%
6	40	3	8%
7	22	5	23%

*The letters a and b indicate the narrower and wider inter-
pretations of the rules, respectively.

system. The dominant fact, with respect to quantity, is the general
preference for the 5:0 system (Sec. 2.1) restated as follows:

8. A contrast between five basic vowel qualities is the norm for
   human language, and in general the most common systems
   are those that have close to this number of basic vowels.

3.3 Height and backness

9. The number of height distinctions in a system is typically
   equal to or greater than the number of backness distinctions.

(The 'backness' dimension is here understood to include both
backness and rounding. For example /ü/ is further 'back' than /i/
(see Sec. 1.2).) The interpretation of this rule depends on whether
the opposition of /a/ to /ɛ/ and /ɔ/ is taken as a height opposition.
In terms of the acoustic space both height and backness are involved.
I have interpreted it as a height distinction, which of course biases
the data in favor of more height distinctions. Thus, the 5:0 system
is interpreted as having more height than backness distinctions.
Clearly, however, to regard the opposition /ɛ/-/a/-/ɔ/as strictly
a backness opposition would be even more unrealistic acoustically.
It has to be understood that this rule can be interpreted only in a
very rough way. There are 18 languages in the sample that are
exceptions (see Table 6), although for the languages with 4:1 there
is a tendency for the central /ɨ/ or the back /u/ to be mid rather
than high, so that in these cases the violation is marginal (seven
languages). (Note: the 4:1 system, if interpreted as having three
degrees of backness and two degrees of height, violates Chomsky
and Halle's rule (1968: 410, rule no. 9) to the effect that an interior

vowel (front rounded or back unrounded) is more marked than a
mid vowel. If interpreted as a universal implication, the marking
convention thus has a number of exceptions, although it is still true
as a general tendency, and in fact is just a special case of my more
general rule 9.) (Note: the 6:1 system is a borderline case, since
it <u>may</u> be interpreted as having only two degrees of height, but
<u>must</u> be interpreted as having three degrees of backness, as illus-
trated:

$$i \quad ɨ \quad u$$
$$\widehat{e} \, \binom{a}{a} \, \widehat{o}$$

The two height interpretation is rejected here for the reason given
above in connection with the role of /a/ in the 5:0 system.)

Table 6. Number of height and backness contrasts

height = backness		height > backness		height < backness	
type	no. of languages	type	no. of languages	type	no. of languages
3:0	23	5:0	55	4:1	9
4:0	13	*5:0	1	*6:2'	2
*5:1	5	6:0	7	8:3'	3
**5:1	2	*6:0	2	9:3	4
*5:2	1	7:0	11	total	18
6:1	29	7:1	3		
7:2	13	8:1	4		
10:3	3	8:2	2		
total	89	9:2	7		
		9:2"	3		
		*9:2	1		
		10:2	2		
		11:3	1		
		total	99		

Another approach to this rule is to find the average number
of vowels, based on the whole sample, found on the horizontal
and vertical dimensions of the vowel space. I considered the
distance from /i/ to /u/, from /i/ to /a/, and from /u/ to /a/, and
found the following average number of vowels: /i-u/ 2.5, /i-a/3.1,
/u-a/ 2.9. If these figures are taken as defining a triangular
'vowel space,' it has a 'height,' a distance from /a/ to /ɨ/ of
about 2.7, just a little larger than the backness dimension of
2.5.

Still another measure of the horizontal and vertical dimensions
can be found in the maximum number of contrasts, four in both
cases. Hockett also finds four contrasting degrees to be the maximum. Trubetzkoy says that five heights are quite rare, but finds
six in GWEABO; this, however, involves the problematic feature
of pharyngeal expansion. Moulton reports cases of five heights.
It seems at least that four heights cannot be regarded as an absolute maximum, while there are no reported cases of languages with
more than four backness distinctions. Also there are more sample
languages with the maximum number of heights than with the maximum degrees of backness, 35 with four heights, 14 with four degrees
of backness, so that one might say that the limit on heights comes
closer to being exceeded than that on backness.

The relation between height and backness and the minimum and
maximum number of distinctions in each has been commented on in
typological studies and work on feature systems. Trubetzkoy (and
apparently Jakobson) based the notion of the primacy of height over
backness on the existence of linear vowel systems. (All languages
have height distinctions, not all have backness distinctions, an implicational universal: backness implies height.) However, since
linear systems and the associated universal are at best problematic,
the relation between the two dimensions has to be established by
other means.

There seems to be general agreement that the minimum number
of height distinctions is two, and that the maximim number of distinction is four for both height and backness, with the exceptions
for height mentioned above. The present results confirm this. An
apparently different view is expressed in the feature systems of
Jakobson, Fant and Halle (1951), and of Chomsky and Halle (1968),
which allow for a maximum of three height distinctions. However,
in both systems the feature of tenseness is available for further
distinctions (cf. the treatment of the FRENCH e/ε distinction by
Jakobson, Fant and Halle 1951: 37), and in principle could generate
three additional vowel 'heights,' so that despite initial appearances
these feature systems do not go beyond what Trubetzkoy claimed
in Principles of Phonology. Still, it is notable that not many languages have more than three height distinctions, and that if one is
willing to live with the classification of /ε a ɔ/ as equally 'low'
vowels, distinguished by backness and rounding only (e.g. in the
7:0 and 9:2 systems), the three height system can be made to work
for the overwhelming majority of languages. There are only four
languages in the present sample for which this would not work,
SOMALI (*9:2), IAI and VIETNAMESE (10:2), and FRENCH (11:3).

As for the 'backness' dimension, general agreement on the maximum of four degrees conceals some problems in the interpretation of the features of backness and rounding. Trubetzkoy realized that the two articulatory features were interrelated, and subsumed them under the notion of 'timbre,' with front unrounded and back rounded as the 'extreme' degrees of the feature; but at the same time he remained reluctant to use a single feature, and in fact made a major point of determining for particular vowel systems whether backness or rounding was a distinctive feature. It has become a kind of tradition in phonology to notice the relationship of backness and rounding,but to continue to use two features, no doubt chiefly for articulatory reasons. When this is done in a feature system, some kind of separate statement is necessary to establish the connection between the two features. Chomsky and Halle, for example, have a marking convention (1968: 405, no. XI) saying that front rounded and back unrounded are more marked than front unrounded or back rounded, though of course the convention does not express why this is so (see Sec. 1.2). Use of two binary features, backness and rounding, is sufficient to characterize the different degrees of backness in nearly all languages. A problem, found only in NORWEGIAN in the sample, occurs when both the interior vowels of a set of four high vowels are rounded, i.e. a set like /i ü u̇ u/. The corresponding problem in SWEDISH has been much discussed (see Fant 1973: 192-201). The general problem is that /u̇/ cannot be either back rounded or front rounded unless some other feature distinguishes it from /ü/ or /u/. While Fant's suggestion of an additional 'classificatory' feature labial has found approval elsewhere (see Anderson 1975: 299), Fant also adds that "perception of a vowel probably operates with a direct identification of its approximate place in a multidimensional parameter space," rather than by "a strict decomposition in terms of phonological features." The features, I might add, are made up by linguists for the sake of an ideal of classificatory neatness. In the vowel space /u̇/ is simply a central vowel, between /ü/ and /u/, and would be most simply and accurately characterized as having a third degree of backness out of the possible four. The fact that this position in the vowel space is achieved by different articulatory means than the more usual unrounding of a back vowel is of course interesting, but does not affect universals or typology.

A related problem for feature systems is the interpretation of the vowels /I U/ in the systems 9:2" and 10:3". Doubtless these would be classified by the tenseness or pharyngeal expansion feature, but the problem remains that the contrast between these vowels and /i u/ is one of vowel quality, i.e. a difference in acoustic height

and backness. Surely, the relative rarity of such systems and
their complementary distribution with vowel systems containing
front rounded or back unrounded vowels has to be explained in
terms of the place of these vowels in the vowel space. The atom-
istic feature approach, in separating tenseness (or pharyngeal expansion) from the general vowel quality features, fails to express
a significant fact about vowel system typology.

3.4 Interior vowels

The relation of the interior vowels to the front and back vowels
has often been commented on. Trubetzkoy says that an interior
vowel column must have a high vowel. This is only trivially true
in that the /ɨ/ of systems 4:1, 6:1, 7:1, etc. is often more like /ə/,
mid rather than high. (Note: in languages with only /ɨ/ in the
interior vowel system, it is phonetically mid in about half the instances, five languages (out of nine) with 4:1, three (of five) with
*5:1, 12 (of 29) with 6:1, and two (of three) with 7:1.) Since this
kind of system (or one with /ö/ but not /ü/) is the main kind of
evidence one would look for to test the validity of the proposed
rule, it will hardly do to reclassify these counterexamples as having an 'indeterminate' vowel /ə/, as Trubetzkoy does. Hockett
states a similar rule: that there are not more backness distinctions
at the lower positions than at the higher ones, but he notes that there
are some exceptions. I find, in addition to these cases with one
interior vowel /ə/, CHEREMIS (8:3') and KOREAN (9:3') with two
mid interior vowels and only one high one.

A weaker version of these rules, stated as 10., seems to be
generally valid:

10. Languages with two or more interior vowels always have
     a high one.

There are 31 such languages in the sample and one exception, HOPI,
with /ö/ and /ĕ/ (type *6:2).

Another of Trubetzkoy's rules is restated here as 11.

11. The number of vowels in a column of interior vowels cannot
     exceed the number in the front or back columns (low vowels
     excluded).

There are 39 languages in the sample with a height contrast in the
interior vowels; one, MANDARIN CHINESE (*5:2), with /i ü ĕ a u/

is an exception to the rule. MANOBO, with a similar arrangement
(see Sec. 2.4 on the *5:2 system) is the only other exception cited
in the literature.

The relation of interior vowels to front and back vowels can also
be stated separately. Sedlak, for example, says that a front rounded
vowel of a given height implies both a front unrounded vowel and a
back rounded vowel at the same height. This is always true in the
present sample (the rule applies to 21 languages, including two with
'central' rounded vowels). He also says that a back unrounded vowel
of a given height implies a front unrounded vowel of the same height.
MANDARIN CHINESE is an exception to this rule, as are the five
languages with 4:1 which have /ə/ as the interior vowel. There
remain 65 languages with back unrounded vowels for which the rule
holds true. A corresponding rule, not stated by Sedlak, is that a
non-low back unrounded vowel of a given height generally implies
a back rounded vowel of the same height. (This rule, of course,
cannot be generalized to the low vowels, since it would fail completely for /a/.) There are some exceptions, MANDARIN CHINESE
again, six languages with 4:1 in which the /ɨ/ and /u/ differ substantially in height, and all five languages with *5:1 (a total of 11),
leaving another 59 languages for which the rule holds true.

3.5 Front and back vowels

12. The number of height distinctions in front vowels is equal
     to or greater than the number in back vowels.

This rule presents no real interpretation problems, since /a/
can be either included in both front or back series, or excluded
from both. In the 6:0 system, where /a/ contrasts with a low front
vowel, I have counted it in the back series. On the other hand, in
the 4:0 system, /a/ is typically lower than /ɛ/, and I have taken it
to be low central, while the latter is front (lower-mid). As can be
seen from Table 7, the great majority of languages (all common
types except 4:0) show equal numbers of height distinctions in front
and back vowels. There is thus a general tendency toward symmetry in this sense, though other factors contribute to overall symmetry. Systems with two or more interior vowels generally show
symmetry there. In the vertical arrangement of interior vowels,
they generally all have the same degree of backness (front rounded
or back unrounded), though there are some exceptions: ALBANIAN
(7:2), MANDARIN (*5:2). However, all eight languages with the
_:3' interior vowel system (i.e. three interior vowels including
both front rounded and back unrounded) are asymmetrical. It is

difficult to say to what degree a property of overall symmetry is to be found in vowel systems (cf. Chomsky and Halle's rule (10), 1968: 410).

Table 7. Height contrasts in front and back vowels

front = back		front = back		front > back		front < back	
type	no. of languages	type	no. of languages	type	no. of languages	type	no. of languages
3:0	23	8:3'	3	4:0	13	**5:1	1
4:1	9	9:2	7	*5:0	1	**6:0	1
5:0	55	9:2''	3	*5:1	5		
**5:1	1	9:3'	4	*6:0	1		
*5:2	1	10:2	2				
6:0	7	10:3'	1	*6:2'	2		
6:1	29	10:3''	2	*7:1	3		
7:0	11	11:3	1	*8:2	2		
7:2	14			*9:2	1		
8:1	4	total	177	total	28	total	2

3.6 Correlations between the basic vowel system and the systems of long and nasalized vowels

3.6.1 Long vowels   Nearly half (45%) of the sample languages have contrasting long and short vowels. In most cases (70%) the vowels of the two systems are equal in number and arrangement, either identical in quality or showing minor differences. In another 19% the long vowel system is larger than the short vowel system, while 8% have more short than long vowels. By far the most commonly reported difference of quality between long and short vowels of corresponding positions is centralization (laxing) of the short high vowels, i.e. short /I U/ versus long /i· u·/, reported in 20% (19 languages) of the languages with long vowels. (It seems likely that the real proportion would be higher, and that this detail is simply overlooked in many phonemic descriptions.) However, in another 5% (five languages) one or both of the long high vowels is lower than the corresponding short vowel. In seven languages the short /a/ is reported to be more centralized than the long /a·/. Other quality differences are not common enough to make generalization worthwhile.

13.   There is a tendency for high and low vowels of a short vowel system to be more central than the corresponding long vowels.

3.4.2 <u>Nasal vowels</u>   As for the nasal vowel systems, the well
known universal stated as 14. (cf. Ferguson 1966, Ruhlen 1975) is
confirmed by the sample.

14.   The number of vowels in a nasal vowel system is equal to
      or smaller than the number in the oral vowel system.

The sample has 50 languages (24%) with nasal vowel systems, which
compare with the basic systems as shown in Table 8.

Table 8

	$V = \tilde{V}$	$V > \tilde{V}$	$V < \tilde{V}$
No. of languages	22	28	0

The one apparent exception to the rule, OJIBWA, is not a real one
since, although the short vowel system is 3:0 and the nasal vowel
system 4:0, the long vowel system is also 4:0, and the nasal vowels
are actually long. (There is, in addition, a system of short nasal
vowels, only marginally contrastive and not counted as part of the
phonemic system, of the type 3:0.) So actually, the nasal vowel
system is identical in structure, if not contrastive function, to the
oral vowel system. As for the 28 languages in which the nasal system is smaller than the oral, the following tendency, in agreement
with previous work (Ruhlen 1975), is found:

15.   If a nasal vowel system is smaller than the corresponding
      basic vowel system, it is most often a mid vowel (front,
      back, or both) that is missing from the nasal system.

This is shown in Table 9. The numbers do not add up because
some languages fall into two categories.

Table 9.   Relation of nasalized systems to larger basic systems

	No. of languages
1. mid vowel missing (includes 2)	20
2. front and back mid vowels missing	(12)
3. high vowel missing (includes 5)	5
4. low vowel missing (includes 5)	5
5. high and low vowel missing	3
6. ?	1

4. Vowel Dispersion: An Explanatory Model

Vowel system typology and the associated universals can be explained, in large part, by the principle that the vowel phonemes of a language tend to disperse evenly in the available phonetic space. Using a characterization of the vowel space in terms of the first three formants, and a measure of dispersion, Liljencrants and Lindblom were able to construct theoretical vowel systems that corresponded closely to a substantial number of actual vowel systems, though there were some discrepancies, especially in the interior vowels of larger systems.

I have made some revisions in the model which lead to a better fit; in this section I present my revised model and examine the extent to which it predicts actual vowel system typology. Lindblom, in a recent paper, has incorporated several revisions into the original model which correspond roughly to the ones I have made, though mine are mathematically cruder. As far as I can see my results are similar to, but not the same as Lindblom's. Since his new model has not been presented in detail, and since my own beginning point was the original L&L model, in what follows I compare my revised model chiefly with the original.

4.1 The L&L model   The vowel space is defined as a two dimensional space in which one dimension is F_1 and the second is a weighted average of F_2 and F_3. To disperse vowels in this space L&L set up a computer program to maximize the sum of the distances between all pairs of vowels in the space, with each vowel defined as a point in the space. For a given number of vowel points, the configuration giving the maximum sum of distances between vowels is the optimal arrangement. This model generates vowel systems which are close matches for the empirical systems 3:0, 4:0, 5:0 and 6:1 (i.e. over half the sample languages). For larger systems the model is defective in producing too many interior high vowels. The seven and eight vowel systems have four degrees of backness in the high vowels, with no interior mid vowels. The nine, ten, eleven and twelve vowel systems have five degrees of backness in the high vowels, and an interior mid vowel appears first in the eleven vowel system. Only a few systems in the sample approach this arrangement of interior vowels, three languages with 9:2" (interior vowels /I U/) and CHUVASH (*6:2') with /ü ɨ/. The general defects of the model seem to be a tendency to push all vowel points to the perimeter of the space, and too much space between /i/ and /u/.

4.2 <u>Optimal vowel system</u> A further point which L&L did not
try to account for is the optimal size for vowel quality systems
(five vowels), which must, in some sense not yet defined, depend
on a balance between the maximization of perceptual distance between vowels and maximization of the information content of the
speech signal, the former favoring fewer vowels further apart,
the latter more vowels. Theoretically, this optimal size should
be predictable from such factors as the limits on the human ability
to distinguish vowels, the average amount of noise in the speech
situation, the average information content of spoken communica-
tions, the relative contribution of consonants and vowels to the
total information content, and so on. Since a number of these factors seem difficult to quantify, much less to relate to each other
in a principled way, we have to be content for the moment simply
to observe that the preference for five vowel systems is a fact.

4.3 <u>Revised model</u> In my revision of the L&L model I define
the vowels as (equal) circular areas rather than as points, and the
optimal arrangement is that which allows the maximum diameter
for a given number of vowels in the vowel space. (One can imagine
that a number of vowel circles are set into the vowel space, and
are allowed to grow until they bump into each other or the sides of
the vowel space. Actually, I kept the vowels as circles of a constant diameter, and the vowel space was 'shrunk' around them
until the smallest possible vowel space was achieved. All that is
needed for this is a set of checkers and a set of graduated outlines
of the vowel space. The checkers are pushed around until a smallest vowel space is found, and one generally becomes apparent quite
rapidly.) If the center of each vowel circle is considered its locus
in the vowel space, then each vowel can be thought of as a point
which 'repels' its nearest neighbors and the perimeter of the vowel
space (if it is adjacent) to an equal degree, but exerts no repulsive
force on vowels further away in the system. This seemed to me
to be a plausible technique for dispersing the vowels, and I thought
it might reduce the number of vowels on the perimeter of the space.

The relative dimensions of the perceptual vowel space are a
problem because it is not known how the acoustic signal is modified
perceptually. I think there is some basis for reducing the F_2 dimension in the perceptual space (distance from /i/ to /u/) to about
half the scale it has in the acoustic space, i.e. to half the scale of
the F_1 dimension (distance from /a/ to /ɨ/). Flanagan has found
that it takes a considerably greater change in F_2 than in F_1 to make
a perceptible difference in vowel quality. (While Flanagan's figures
for different vowels vary considerably, the average change in F_1

needed to get 80% judgments of a change in vowel quality was about 30 hz, while the change in F_2 needed to get similar judgments averaged about 75 hz.)

Lindblom, in coming to grips with this problem, has made a similar, though more complex, change in the model, reducing the contribution of F_2 (and higher formants) to the perceptual space in proportion to how low F_1 is. High vowels /i u/ with low F_1 suffer the greatest reduction in the theoretical perceptual salience of higher formants; i.e. the distance between /i/ and /u/ is considerably reduced. As an empirical basis for this change Lindblom cites data on DUTCH vowels, showing that confusions between vowels are correlated strongly with differences in F_1, but weakly with distance in an F_1-F_2-F_3 acoustic space.

This change of scale makes the theoretical model of the vowel space correspond much more closely than a strictly acoustic scale to the empirically determined average dimensions of vowel systems. As observed earlier (Sec. 3.2), the horizontal distance /i-u/ is empirically more or less equal to the vertical distance /a-ɨ/, whereas in the original L&L model the former is about twice the latter. It would be nice to be able to say that this change in scale is directly motivated by our understanding of vowel perception. However, as it stands we only have a few general indications, just cited, that F_1 is more important perceptually than higher formants. The proper weighting remains to be determined.

In Fig. 11 the vowel systems predicted by the revised model are compared with the predictions of the original model. An advantage of the revised model is that it allows construction of 'reasonably good' non-optimal systems, some of which are offered for comparison in Fig. 11. The general criterion I adopted for such systems was that the diameter of the vowels should be larger than in the next larger optimal system. For example, the alternate seven vowel system is better (the vowels have a larger diameter) than what one would obtain by simply removing a suitable vowel from the optimal eight vowel system.

No. of vowels	L&L's model	Revised model
3	i u a	i u a

Figure 11.
(continued next page)

John Crothers

No. of vowels	L&L's model	Revised model
4	i u / ɛ a	i u / ɛ/ɜ a
5	i u / ɛ ɑ / a	i u̇/u / ɛ ɔ / a
6	i ɨ u / ɛ ɔ / a	i ɨ/ə u / ɛ ɔ / a
(alternate)		i u̇/u / e/ö o / ae a
	i ü ɨ u / ɛ ɔ / a	i ɨ/ï u / e o / ae
(alternate)		i u̇/u / e/ö u/o / ɛ ɔ / a
8	i ü ɨ u / ɛ ɔ / ae a	i ɨ u/o / e ə / ae ɔ / a
9	i ü u̇ ɨ u / ɛ ɔ / ae a	i ɨ u / e ə o / ɛ ɔ / a
10	i ü u̇ ɨ u / e ɛ ɔ/ɒ / a ɑ	i ɨ u / e/ö ə o / ɛ ɔ / ae a
11	i ü u̇ ɨ u / e ə ɛ ɔ / a ɑ	i ü/u̇ ɨ/u / e/ö ə o / e/ɛ ɜ̇ ɔ / ae a

No. of vowels   L & L's model   Revised model

12

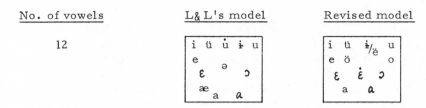

Figure 11

4.4 Comparison of predicted and actual systems

Three vowels   The predictions of the two models are the same and agree with actual types.

Four vowels   The revised model allows the fourth vowel to range anywhere from /ɛ/ through /ə/ to nearly /ɨ/. This allows for both the 4:0 and 4:1 systems, whereas the original model only generates 4:0. An additional contribution of the revised model is that it shows the four vowel system to be inefficient -- the vowel diameter in this system is only slightly larger than in the 5:0 system, but much smaller than in the 3:0 system. To put it another way, if you remove a vowel, say /ɔ/, from the 5:0 system, it is very difficult to reposition the remaining four vowels so that they will make use of the extra space; most of it just goes to waste. This may explain why four vowel systems are less common than the 3:0 or 6:1 systems, even though they are close to the optimal number of vowels.

Five vowels Both predictions are similar, and correspond closely to the 5:0 type. The revised model shows a slight shift of /u/ toward /u̇/. Two languages in the sample show this (JAPA-NESE and GARO), but it is not a general trend.

Six vowels   Both models predict the common 6:1 system. An alternate system is reasonably close to the less common 6:0 type.

Seven vowels Both models fail to generate either of the common seven vowel systems, 7:2 and 7:0. However, the revised model comes a good deal closer, in generating the intermediate 7:1 system (found in three languages in the sample), while L & L's model generates a relatively unnatural system with both /ü/ and /ɨ/. (AL-BANIAN, with 7:2, comes closest to this.) An alternate system is fairly close to 7:0. The empirical 7:2 system can be obtained from the predicted eight vowel system by removing a low vowel.

<u>Eight vowels</u> There are no common eight vowel systems. The revised model seems to be reasonably close, in predicting 8:2, since 8:1, 8:2 and 8:3' are all attested. There are no cases of 8:2' with both /ü/ and /ɨ/, as predicted by the original model.

<u>Nine vowels</u> The revised model offers a good match for the common 9:2 system. The original model is badly off here in predicting three interior high vowels /ü ʉ ɨ/. The 9:2'' system comes closest to the original model, but is still not a good match, there being only two interior high vowels.

<u>Ten, eleven and twelve vowels</u> There are too few actual systems of these sizes to make detailed comparison worthwhile. The original model again predicts too many high interior vowels, while the revised model generates a more nearly vertical arrangement of the interior vowels, which is closer to the actual systems. Both actual systems 10:2 and 11:3 are predicted by the revised model.

The general success of the revised model in predicting actual vowel system types can be judged in the following table, in which I give the types and numbers of actual vowel systems which are 1) good matches for the predicted systems, 2) obtainable by removing one vowel from the optimal system of the next larger size, and 3) obtainable by removing two vowels from an optimal system. (In most cases the vowels to be removed are interior vowels, mid vowels, or low vowels; in a few cases /u/, but never /i/). For comparison the number of good matches for the original model is also given, showing that the improvement is found in the larger vowel systems.

Table 10.a Relation of predicted to actual vowel systems

good match		remove one V from predicted system		remove two V from predicted system	
type	no. of languages	type	no. of languages	type	no. of languages
3:0	23	6:0	7	*5:2	1
4:0	13	7:0	11		
4:1	9	7:2	14	*6:2'	2
5:0	55	*5:1	5	8:3'	3
6:1	29	**5:1	2	9:2''	3
7:1	3	8:1	2	9:3'	4
8:2	2	*5:0	1	10:3''	1
9:2	7	*6:0	1		
10:2	2	**6:0	1		
11:3	1	*9:2	1		
		10:3	1		
total	144 (70%)	total	46 (23%)		14 (7%)

Table 10.b   L&L model related to empirical vowel systems

type	3:0	4:0	5:0	6:1	total
no. of languages giving good match	23	13	55	29	120 (58%)

4.5 Comparison with random hypothesis. While it seems obvious that in some sense the L&L model (and the revised version) predict possible vowel systems, in order to actually demonstrate this it is necessary to show that the systems predicted differ in some clear way from what would be predicted by a more random arrangement of vowels. This can be done by an example of possible random arrangements of a certain number of vowels. Let us imagine the vowel space divided into 16 compartments representing vowels qualities known to be distinct in some of the world's languages (see Fig. 12).

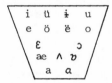

Figure 12

We then consider possible five vowel systems containing any combination of five of the 16 vowels. If the number of such systems which is reasonably close to a 5:0 system, when compared with the total number of combinations, comes anywhere near the actual percentage which the 5:0 system represents of all actual five vowel systems (86%), then obviously we can dispense with the vowel dispersion theory, and explain vowel system typology as due to random arrangements of perceptibly different vowels. Given the 16 vowels, the total possible number of five vowel systems is $16!/11! \, 5! = 4,368$. Interpreted somewhat loosely, matches for the 5:0 system could be obtained by the following combinations:

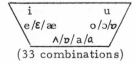

(33 combinations)

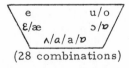

(28 combinations)

The total of 61 vowel systems represents just 1% of all possible combinations. Another 300 or so possible combinations come reasonably close to some other attested five vowel system (*5:1, etc.), which still adds up to less than 10% of the possible random

combinations. In other words, 10% of the random possibilities
account for 100% of attested five vowel systems. Clearly, the random hypothesis is untenable in anything like this form.

4.6 Limits to predictability

The extent to which vowel quality systems are predictable must
not be overemphasized. What we find is not absolute predictability,
but clustering of types around general norms. The success of the
model lies in the fact that it separates these norms (the predicted
vowel systems) on a principled basis from other conceivable arrangements which are abnormal or altogether unattested. An analogy might be the kinds of predictions made by theoretical models
of weather systems. It is possible for such models to simulate
real weather conditions, beginning with factors such as the size of
the earth, rate of rotation, amount and distribution of solar radia-
tion at different seasons, distribution of continents and oceans,
density of the atmosphere, rates of water evaporation, etc. It
would be unreasonable to judge a model a failure if it failed to predict the skiing conditions in Sun Valley in January, 1980. It would
probably be quite a success just to predict the average annual snow-
fall within a few feet. In fact, a model might be judged a success
if it just showed snow falling in the right parts of the world at the
right times of year.

Randomness is found in several different aspects of vowel system
typology. First, the number of basic vowel qualities in languages
ranges from three to about twelve. Even if we take note of the fact
that the most frequently utilized vowels in any language are likely
to be those that are typologically the most common, i.e. short, non-
nasal /i e a u o/ (Greenberg 1966), this still represents a considerable
degree of randomness in vowel system typology. Second, the exact
phonetic value of the vowel phonemes of any particular type of system varies from one language to the next. For example, the theoretical model predicts /ɛ/ and /ɔ/ as the mid vowels of a 5:0 system.
Of 55 actual systems, 13 are explicitly described as having 'higher
mid' /e/ and /o/, rather than /ɛ/ and /ɔ/. Variability of about this
degree is built into the whole classification of vowel systems I have
presented, and has to be kept in mind when the predictions of the
model are judged. Another instance is the assignment of /ɨ/ and
/ü/ to the same general position. The model makes no distinction
between these two vowels in the predicted systems 6:1, 7:1, 8:2,
9:2, 10:2 and 11:3, so this remains a random element. Third, all
of the systems which can only be obtained by altering a predicted
system (30% of the sample of course represent a degree of randomness
for the model. Finally, it must be remembered that a set of

complicating factors has been ignored. Vowel quality may play an
auxiliary role in distinguishing short oral vowels from other vowel
types, such as long vowels, nasal vowels and diphthongs. Languages which have similar basic vowel quality systems may differ
considerably in the employment of vowel quality in any of the other
functions.

4.7 Prediction of universals

Since the dispersion model generates the major empirical vowel
system types, and since universal rules are derived from typology,
it obviously follows that many of the empirical universals are in
fact predicted by the model. This is my justification for saying
that the universals do not have any kind of independent status, but
are simply instances of much more general principles, namely
those built into the dispersion model. This can be seen in detail
in the vowel hierarchy based on vowel systems generated by the
model (see Fig.13). This ordering of vowel types corresponds pretty
closely to the empirically based orderings presented in Fig. 10.

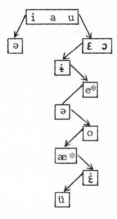

Figure 13. Vowel hierarchy predicted by model
(*These two vowels could be interchanged.)

To put it another way, most universals which concern the quality
of the vowels in a system of a given size are predicted by the model,
the seven vowel systems being an exception. On the other hand,
universals concerning the number of vowels in a basic system are
not predicted. The situation is summarized in the following table
(Table 11).

Table 11. Comparison of actual universals with predictions of model

Universal*	Prediction
1. All languages have /i a u/.	-Three vowel minimum not predicted. -Predicted for languages with three or more vowels.
2. Four V include /ɨ/ or /ɛ/.	-Predicted.
3. Five V include /ɛ/, generally also /ɔ/.	-Both /ɛ/ and /ɔ/ predicted, but not ranked.
4. Six V include /ɔ/, also /ɨ/ or /e/.	-Predicted. Model prefers /ɨ/ as sixth V.
5. Seven V include /e o/ or /ɨ ə/.	-Model predicts /e ɨ/, which is wrong, but at least involves two of the correct V.
6. Eight V include /e/.	-Predicted (for seven V).
7. Nine V include /o/.	-Predicted (but note high number of actual exceptions).
8. Five V is optimal number.	-Not predicted.
9. Height distinctions equal or exceed backness distinctions.	-Not predicted. (This feature is built into the model on the basis of typological evidence. There is some experimental basis (Sec. 4.3).)
10. Interior height distinctions do not exceed front or back height distinctions.	-Predicted.
11. Two interior V include one high V.	-Predicted.
12. Height distinctions in front V equal or exceed those in back V.	-Predicted.

*See Appendix II for a restatement of universals. Those dealing with the relation of the basic vowel system to other systems are not included in this chart.

4.8 Functional nature of the universals

The model of vowel systems presented above is a functional one in the sense that it relates phonological structure to factors operating

in the ordinary use of language. Stated simply, the idea is that
since the linguistic function of sounds is to distinguish different
meaningful elements, one would expect the dominant types of phonological system to be those which make the most efficient use of
the human sound production and perception abilities. Of course a
general notion like 'efficient use' cannot be appealed to in the abstract; it has to be exemplified by close study of the production
and perception of human speech sounds. The L&L model of the
vowel space and the achievements of modern phonetics which stand
behind it clearly show how this notion can be given a concrete meaning. The notion of 'dominant type of sound system' has to be established by collection of a sufficiently large and representative group
of accurate linguistic descriptions. I have tried to show, in this
paper, how a data base such as the Stanford Phonology Archive can
be used for this purpose. The fact that a number of the generalizations arrived at here concerning vowel systems were known or sus-
pected before, on the basis of other data collections, encourages
me to believe that large collections of this sort of descriptive data
will tend to converge on the same range of types or norms, in spite
of a number of methodological and theoretical uncertainties.

    The functional approach differs in several respects, two of which
I discuss briefly here, from the major current phonological theory,
generative phonology. First, the functional approach includes highly
explicit phonetic models, in this case a model of the vowel space.
In contrast generative phonologists have sought to reduce phonetic
description to feature systems, with a relatively limited number
of features and distinctions within each feature (only two at the
'classificatory' level). While features, when properly defined,
have the virtue of characterizing the kinds of contrasts or types
of rules that typically occur in languages, the justification for a
particular system of features and the system of relations between
features (marking conventions, etc.) is not readily apparent in the
features themselves. For example, the features [high, low, back,
round], interpreted as binary features, are obviously largely sufficient for characterizing the kinds of vowel contrasts that occur
in the world's languages; similarly, the marking convention to the
effect that mid vowels are less complex than front rounded or back
unrounded vowels reflects a well established typological fact. But
the generative model, in stopping with the mere statement of these
facts, however elegantly expressed, fails to explain why these features or this marking convention, rather than different features or
an opposite marking convention, should be the ones which are actually true or appropriate for human language. It is only by moving
on to an explicit phonetic model that we can justify either. In this
sense a functional model achieves a type of explanation which lies

beyond the range of the formal descriptive devices of generative phonology.

A second difference concerns the character and assumed basis of phonological universals. Most phonologists would agree that phonetics plays a prominent role in phonological universals. The careful attention given by Chomsky and Halle to the phonetic basis of distinctive features gives evidence of this. However, in the generative literature, primary emphasis in the search for phonological universals has been given to definition of the right classificatory feature system and development of the proper formal devices for description of phonological processes. The assumption behind this appears to be that the organization of phonological information in the human mind is highly formal, that the phonological structure of a language constitutes a highly complex formal organization imposed on the raw phonetic materials. If this assumption is true, then of course special attention must be given to this formal level, and the phonologist can expect to learn something important about phonological universals simply by investigating the interaction of formal devices in linguistic discriptions. The functionalist approach, in contrast, emphasizes the centrality of phonetics and the single functional principle of perceptual contrast. From this point of view, what is important in the phonological organization of individual languages is just that this organization constitutes a set of limitations on the contrastive role of the phonetic materials. To put it another way, the generativist assumes complex, innate phonological structure in addition to innate phonetic capacities, while the functionalist does not. Which of these viewpoints will prove most revealing in accounting for the entirety of phonological universals remains to be seen. However, in the limited area of vowel systems, a functional model is quite successful, and this confirms, for this area, the assumption that explicit phonetic models and the concept of perceptual contrast give a sufficient basis for explaining phonological systems.

APPENDIX I
Universals restated

1. All languages have /i a u/.
2. All languages with four or more vowels have /ɨ/ or /ɛ/.
3. Languages with five or more vowels have /ɛ/. They generally also have /ɔ/.
4. Languages with six or more vowels have /ɔ/ and also either /ɨ/ or /e/, generally the former.

5. Languages with seven or more vowels have /e o/ or /ɨ ə/.
    (The types /ɨ ə/ may be represented by /ü ö/.)
6. Languages with eight or more vowels have /e/.
7. Languages with nine or more vowels generally have /o/.
8. A contrast between five basic vowel qualities is the norm for
    human language, and in general, the most common systems
    are those with close to this number of basic vowels.
9. The number of height distinctions in a system is typically equal
    to or greater than the number of backness distinctions.
10. Languages with two or more interior vowels always have a high
    one.
11. The number of vowels in a column of interior vowels cannot
    exceed the number in the front or back columns.
12. The number of height distinctions in front vowels is equal to or
    greater than the number in back vowels.
13. There is a tendency for high and low vowels of a short vowel
    system to be more central than the corresponding long vowels.
14. The number of vowels in a nasal vowel system is equal to or
    less than the number in the corresponding oral vowel system.
15. If a nasal vowel system is smaller than the corresponding basic
    vowel system, it is most often a mid vowel that is missing from
    the nasal system.

APPENDIX II

Vowel categories used by Stanford Phonology Archive

Front		Central		Back		
i	ü	ɨ	u̇	ɯ	u	High
I	U	ɨ̵	U̇	Ï	U	Lower-high
e	ö	ė	ȯ	ĕ	o	Higher-mid
E	Ö	ə	Ȯ	Ë	O	Mid
ɛ	ɜ	ɛ̇		ʌ	ɔ	Lower-mid
ae		aė			ʌ	Higher-low
ä		a	ȧ	ɑ	ɶ	Low

unrounded   rounded

Length is indicated in Appendix III by a raised dot (·), nasalization by a tilde (~). The symbol (>) for 'retraction' is used in <u>ad hoc</u>
ways explained in the notes. It should be remembered that this
chart merely represents a convenient set of categories for labelling
the kinds of things that descriptive linguists say about vowels, and
is not meant to present a phonetic or phonological theory of vowels.

APPENDIX III
List of sample languages by basic vowel system type

(Notes at the end of the list)

? 2:0   KABARDIAN[1]   ɨ ɛ̇ // i· E· a· u· O·

3:0   ALABAMAN   I a o // e· a· o·
      ALASKAN ESKIMO   i a u // i· a· u·
      ALEUT   i a u
      AMUESHA   e a o // e· a· o·
      DIEGUEÑO[2]   I a U // e· a· o·
      GADSUP   i ɛ̇ u // e· ä· o·
      GREENLANDIC ESKIMO   i a u // I· a· U·
      HAIDA[3]   i a U
      JAQARU   i a ɯ // i· a· ɯ·
      KAROK   i a U // i· e· a· U· o·
      LAK[4]   i a u // i· a· u·
      MANTJILTJARA   i a u // i· a· u·
      MOROCCAN ARABIC   i æ u
      NUNGGUBUYU   I ǣ ɯ // a·
      NYANGUMATA   I a U // i· a· u·
      OJIBWA[5]   I a U // i· ɛ· a· o· // ĩ· ɛ̃· ã· õ·
      PUGET SOUND SALISH   I a U
      QUECHUA[6]   I a U
      SHILHA   i a u
      TAGALOG[7]   I ə U (e o) // i· a· u· (e·o·)
      TELEFOL   I ɛ̇ U // i· ɛ· a· u· o·
      TOTONAC   i a u // i· a· u·
      WESTERN DESERT
         LANGUAGE   i a U // i· a· u·

4:0   ALAWA[8]   i E a ɯ
      CAMPA   i e a o
      CAYAPA   i ɛ U ɑ
      CHAMORRO[9]   i æ u ɑ
      HUPA   I E a O // E· a· O·
      MALAGASY   i E a U
      MAZATEC   i ɛ a o // ĩ ɛ̃ ã õ
      MOXO   i ɛ a u
      NAVAHO   I ɛ a ɔ // i· ɛ· a· o· // ĩ ɛ̃ ã ɔ̃
      NOOTKA   I ɛ ə U // i· æ· a· u· ɔ·
      ONEIDA   i E a O // i· E· a· O· // ə̃ ũ
      PAEZ   i ɛ a u // ĩ ɛ̃ ã ũ
      WICHITA   i ɛ u ɑ // e· ɛ· o· ɑ·

4:1 ADZERA   i a ɯ o//i· a· o·
     AMAHUACA   I a ɯ o// Ĩ ã ɯ̃ õ
     CHACOBO   i a ɨ O
     JIVARO   i a ɯ u//ĩ ã ɯ̃ ũ
     KWAKIUTL   i a ə u// i· a· u·
     MARGI   i a ə u
     PASHTO   i a ə u// E· O· a·
     SQUAMISH   e a ʌ o
     WAPISHANA   i a ɨ u//i· a· ɨ· u·//ĩ ã ɨ̃ ũ

5:0 AWIYA[10]   i E a u O
     ATAYAL   i ɛ a u ɔ//i· u·
     AROSI   i ɛ a u ɔ//i· ɛ· a· u· ɔ·
     ASMAT[11]   i e a u ɔ
     AUYANA   i e ə u O
     AINU   i ɛ a u ɔ
     BATAK   i ɛ a u o
     BASQUE   I E a u O
     BULGARIAN[12]   i ɛ u ɔ ɑ
     BURUSHASKI   i E a u O//i· E· a· u· O·
     CANTONESE (TAISHAN)[13] i æ a u ɔ
     DAKOTA   i e a u o//ĩ ã ũ
     DIDO[14]   i E u o ɑ //E· ɑ·
     EGYPTIAN ARABIC[15] I E ä U O (ɑ)//i E ä u O (ɑ·)
     FULANI   I e æ̇ U o//i· ɛ· a· u· ɔ·
     GBARI   i e a u o
     GEORGIAN   I E ä U O
     GARO   i E a u̇ o
     HAKKA   i ɛ a u ɔ
     HAUSA   I E ə U O//i· E· a· u· O·
     HAWAIIAN   i E a u O//i· E· a· u· O·
     JAPANESE   i ɛ a u̇ o//i· ɛ· a· u· ɔ·
     KUNIMAIPA   i e a u U
     KUNJEN   I ɛ a U O
     KALIAI   i E a u O//i· E· a· u· O·
     KHASI[16]   I ɛ a U ɔ//i· ɛ· a· u· ɔ·
     KHARIA   i e a u o//ĩ ɛ̃ ã ũ õ
     KOTA   i E a u O
     LAKKIA   i ɛ a u ɔ//ĩ ɛ̃ ã ũ ɔ̃
     LUVALE   i e a u o//i· e· a· u· o·
     LUISEÑO   I E a U O//I E a U o
     MIXTEC   i e a u o//ĩ ã ũ õ
     MAUNG   i ɛ a u o
     MAORI   i ɛ u ɔ ɑ //i· E· u· o· ɑ·

5:0	MUNDARI	I E a U O
	MALTESE ARABIC	i ɛ a u O//i· E· a· u· O·
	BEEMBE	i ɛ a u ɔ//i· ɛ· a· u· ɔ·//ĩ ɛ̃ ã ũ ɔ̃
	NAMA[17]	i e ä u o //ĩ ã ũ õ
	NASIOI	i ɛ a u o //i·ɛ·a· u· o·
	NUBIAN	i E a u O//i· E· a· u· O·
	POMO	I ɛ a U ɔ//I· ɛ· a· U· ɔ·
	RUSSIAN	i ɛ ä u O
	RYUKYUAN	i E a u O//i· E· a· u· O·
	SPANISH	i E a u O
	SWAHILI	i E a u O
	TELUGU	I e ə U o//i· e· æ· a· u· o·
	TEWA[18]	i E a u O//i· e· ä· u· o·//ĩ ɛ̃ ãũ
	TZELTAL	I E a U O
	WIK MUNKAN	i ɛ a U ʌ//i· ɛ· a· U· ʌ·
	WALAMO	i E a u O // i· E· a· u· o·
	WOLIO	i e a u o//?i· e· a· u· o·
	ZAN	i E a u O
	ZOQUE	i ɛ a u O//Ẽ̃
	ZULU	i ɛ å u ɔ //i· ɛ· å· u· ɔ·
	ZUNI	i ɛ a u ɔ // i· ɛ· a· u· ɔ·
*5:0	SENECA	i e æ a O//i· e· æ· a· O·//ɛ̃ ɔ̃
*5:1	ISLAND CARIB	i E a Ë u//ĩ Ẽ ã Ẽ̈ ũ
	MARANUNGKU	i æ a ə U
	NEZ PERCE	I æ a Ï ɔ//i· æ· a· ɯ· ɔ·
	OCAINA	i ɛ a ɯ O//ĩ ã ɯ̃ Õ
	TOLOWA	i E a ə u//i· E· a·u·//ĩ ã ũ
**5:1	EVENKI	i æ ə u O//i· E· æ· ə u· O·
***5:1	PAPAGO	i a ɨ u o//i· a· ɨ· u· o·
*5:2	MANDARIN	i ü a ë u
6:0	CHIPEWYAN	i e ɛ a u o//i· ɛ· a· u·//ĩ ɛ̃ ã ũ
	LITHUANIAN	i ɛ æ U ɔ a //i· e· æ· u· ɔ· a·
	PERSIAN	i e ä u o a
	SELEPET	i ɛ a u o ʌ
	SINHALESE[19]	I E ä a U O//i· e· æ· a· u· o·
	SONGHAI[20]	i e ɛ a u o//i· E· a· u· o·
	YUCHI	i e æ u o ʌ//ĩ Ẽ ã Ũ Õ
*6:0	ENGLISH (RP)	I E æ ȧ U ɒ//i· ə· u· O· a·

6:0   EWE²¹   i ɛ a u o ɔ // i· ɛ· a· u· o· ɔ· (e·) // ĩ ɛ̃ ã ũ õ ɔ̃

6:1   ANGAS   e ɛ I> a u o // i· ɨ· a·
     ARAUCANIAN   i ɛ a ɯ u ɔ
     BARASANO   i ɛ a ɨ u o // ĩ ɛ̃ ã ɨ̃ ũ õ
     BODO   i E a ə u ɔ
     CARIB   i E ǽ ɯ u O // i· E· ǽ· ɯ· u· O·
     CHONTAL   i E a ə u O
     CHUKCHI   i E a ə u O
     DAGBANI²²   i ɛ a ə u ɔ // i· e· a· u· o·
     DELAWARE²³   i ɛ a ə u ɔ // i· æ· a· u· ɔ· // ĩ· æ̃· ã· ə̃· ũ· ɔ̃·
     GILYAK²⁴   i E a ɨ u O
     GOAJIRO²⁵   i ɛ a ə u ɔ // i· ɛ· a· ə· u· ɔ· // ĩ ɛ̃ ã ũ õ ə̃
     GUARANI   i E a ɨ u O // ĩ Ẽ ã ɨ̃ ũ Õ
     IRAQW   i ɛ a ə U ɔ // i· e· u· o· a·
     ITONAMA   i e a ɨ u o
     KANURI   i E ä ɨ u O
     KET²⁶   i ɛ ä ɨ u ɔ // i· ɛ· ä· i· u· ɔ·
     KURUX   i E a ə u O // i· E· a· ə· u· O·// ĩ Ẽ ã ũ Õ
     MAIDU   i E a ɨ u O
     MALAY   i e a ə u o
     MALAYALAM   I e a ɨ U ɔ // i· e· a· u· o·
     PICURIS   i e ə u o α // ĩ ẽ ə̃ ũ õ ã
     POLISH   i ɛ ɨ u ɔ α // ɛ̃ ɔ̃
     SA'BAN   i ɛ a ɨ u ɔ
     SIRIONO²⁷   i e a i> u o // ĩ ẽ ã i>̃ ũ õ
     TARASCAN²⁸   i ɛ a ɨ u o
     TICUNA   i E a ɨ u O // ĩ ã ɨ̃ ũ Õ
     WU   i E ü a u O // ĩ æ̃ Õ
     YUKAGHIR²⁹   I ɛ ä ə u O // ʔi· a· u· o·
     YURAK³⁰   i E Ë u O α // ʔa·

6:2' HOPI   i ɛ ö a ë o // i· ä· ö· a· ë· o·
     CHUVASH   i E ü ɯ u α

7:0   BENGALI   i E æ a u o ɔ // ĩ Ẽ æ̃ ã ũ õ
     BURMESE³¹   i e ɛ a u o ɔ // ĩ æ̃ Ũ
     GA   i e ɛ ä u o ɔ // ẽ ɛ̃ ã ũ ɔ̃
     GBEYA³²   i e ɛ a u o ɔ // ĩ æ̃ ã ũ ɔ̃
     ITALIAN   i e ɛ a u o ɔ
     KPELLE   i I ɛ a u U ɔ // i· I· ɛ· a· u· U· ɔ· // ĩ ẽ ɛ̃ ã ũ õ ɔ̃
     NENGONE   i e ɛ a u o ɔ // i· e· ɛ· a· u· o· ɔ·
     PORTUGUESE   i e ɛ a u o ɔ // ĩ ẽ ɛ̃ ũ õ
     SEDANG³³   i e æ a u o ɔ // ĩ ã õ ɔ̃

(7:0)   TUNICA   i e ɛ a u o ɔ
        YAO   i e æ a u o ɔ//a·

*7:1   SENTANI   i e ɛ ä ə u ɔ
        WASHKUK   i e ɛ a ɨ u O
        WOLOF[34]   i e ɛ a ə u ɔ// i· e· ɛ· u· o· ɔ· a·

7:2   ALBANIAN   i E ü ə u O ɑ
        AMHARIC   i e a ɨ ə u o
        BRETON[35]   i E ä ü Ö u O// i· ɛ· ü· ö· u· o· ɑ· // ã·
        DAFLA   i ɛ ɯ ʌ u ɔ a// i· ɛ· ɯ· ʌ· u· ɔ· a·
        GERMAN[36]   I ɛ Ü ɔ̈ æ U ɔ// i· e· ü· ö· a· u· o·
        HUNGARIAN   i ɛ ü ö u o ɑ// i· e· ü· ö· a· u· o·
        KOHO[37]   i ɛ a ɯ ë u ɑ// i· e· ɛ· a· ɯ· ë· u· o· ɑ·
        KOMI   i E a ɨ ə u O
        MONGOLIAN   i e ü Ó U ɔ a // I· e· ü· Ó· ɔ· a·
        NAGA   i E a ɯ ə u O
        RAWANG   i E a ɨ ə u O// i· E· a· ɨ· ə· u· O·
        SUNDANESE[38]   i ɛ a ɨ ə u o
        RUMANIAN   i e a ɨ ə u o
        YAY[39]   i ɛ a ɯ ə u O// a

8:1   EWONDO   i e ɛ a ė u o ɔ// i· e· ɛ· a· ė· u· o· ɔ·
        JAVANESE   i e ɛ a ə u o ɔ

?8:1   APINAYE[40]   i e ɛ a ɯ u o ɔ// ĩ Ɛ̃ ã ɯ̃ ũ õ
        MIANKA   i e ɛ a ŏ u o ɔ// ĩ ẽ ã õ ũ õ

8:2   ICELANDIC   i e ɛ ö ɔ̈ u o ɑ
        TIBETAN   i ɛ æ ü ö a u o// i· ɛ· æ· ü· ö· a· u· ɔ· //
                        ?ĩ· Ɛ̃· ã· ũ· ũ̈· õ·

8:3'   CHEREMIS   i ɛ ü Ö ə ʌ u ɔ
        KIRGHIZ   I ɛ ü ŏ a ɨ U o// I· ɛ· ü· ö· ɨ· U· o·
        TURKISH   i ɛ ü ɔ̈ a ɯ u O

9:2   CHAM   i e ɛ a ɨ ə u o ɔ
        KAREN   i e ɛ a ɨ ė u o ɔ
        LAHU   i e E a ɨ e u o ɔ
        LAO   i e ɛ a ɯ Ë u ɔ ɑ// i· e· ɛ· a· ɯ· Ë· u· O· ɔ· ɑ·
        MAZAHUA   i e ɛ a ə ʌ u o ɔ // ĩ ẽ ã ə̃ ũ õ
        NUNG   i e ɛ ė ɨ ė u o o// æ· a· ɑ·
        OTOMI   i e æ a ɨ ə u o ɔ// ĩ æ̃ ã ũ

9:2''   AKAN[41]   i I e ɛ a u U o ɔ// ĩ Ĩ ã Ũ ũ
        GREBO[42]   i e e⟩ ɛ a u o o⟩ ɔ// ĩ ẽ Ɛ̃ ã ũ õ õ̃
        LUO[43]   i I E ɛ a u U O ɔ

*9:2	SOMALI	I e ɛ æ Ʊ Ó ə U ɔ//I· e· ɛ· æ· Ʊ· Ó· a· U· ɔ·
9:3'	AZERBAIJANI	i ɛ ä ü ö ɯ U o ɑ
	KOREAN	i e æ ö a ɯ ë u o//i· e· æ· ɯ· ë· u· o·
	NORWEGIAN	I E æ Ü ʒ a ü u n//i· e· æ· ü· Ö· a· u· u·O·
	OSTYAK	i E ä ü Ö ɯ u O ɑ
10:2	IAI	i e ɛ æ ü ʒ a u o ɔ//i· e·ɛ· æ· ü· ʒ· a· u· o· ɔ·
	VIETNAMESE	I e ɛ æ̈ ï ë ʌ U o ɔ// ä·
10:3'	AKHA	i e ɛ ö a ɯ ə u o ɔ
10:3"	PANJABI	i I E æ a ə u U Oɑ//ĩ Ĩ Ẽ æ̃ã ə̃ũ Ũ Õ ɑ̃
?10:3"	LOGBARA	i I e ɛ a ɛ́ u U o ɔ//
		i· I· e· ɛ· a· ɛ́· u· U· o· ɔ·
11:3	FRENCH	i e ɛ ä ü ö ʒ u o ɔ ɑ // æ̃ ʒ̃ õ ɑ̃
?12:3	PACOH	i eˆ e ɛ ɨ ə ˆ ə a u oˆ o ɔ//
		i· eˆ· e· ɛ· ɨ· ə ˆ· ə a· u· oˆ· o· ɔ·

Notes:

1 The short vowels of KABARDIAN seem to form a reduced system. See Sec. 2.4 on two vowel systems.

2 I have analyzed DIEGUEÑO /ə/ as a neutral vowel.

3 The HAIDA vowel system presented here is not certain.

4 LAK has three 'guttural' (gortanye) vowels. Possibly they are pharyngealized (cf. DIDO (5:0)). Depending on the details, this could be a six vowel system.

5 OJIBWA long nasal vowels occur as independent phonemes word finally. Short nasalized vowels are the result of loss of /n/ before /s/.

6 /E O/ occur in SPANISH loans.

7 TAGALOG /e o/ occur in ENGLISH and SPANISH loans. Apparently, there is still some instability.

8 ALAWA probably derives from a 3:0 system, but has developed a new contrast, /ɛ/, though it is not an especially common vowel.

9 CHAMORRO /e o/ have been set aside as SPANISH loans. /æ/ has a somewhat marginal status; it is chiefly derived from /a/ after /i/ in a preceding syllable, but there is a certain amount of contrast.

10 AWIYA has a /ə/, but it seems to be a transitional sound in consonant clusters.

11 The grammar says that /ə/ is an independent phoneme, but I can find it only in unaccented position in the examples given.

12 A neutral vowel /ə/ occurs unstressed in BULGARIAN.

13 Other CANTONESE dialects have quite different vowel systems.

14 DIDO has a full set (5) of pharyngealized vowels. There seems to be a question as to whether they can be interpreted as allophonic variants adjacent to pharyngealized consonants. If not, this is a ten vowel system.

15 According to the grammar, there is a marginal contrast between /ä/ and /ɒ/, which are chiefly in complementary distribution. This is difficult to evaluate.

16 The grammar treats /i/, which contrasts with /I/ as /ii/, though, apparently, it is not as long as the other long vowels. I treat /i/ as long. Phonemic status of long vowels uncertain.

17 NAMA has an [ə] which seems to be in complementary distribution with [i].

18 TEWA also has /æ/, which is at best marginal (three instances reported).

19 SINHALESE has a /ə/ that may be marginally contrastive.

20 The contrast of /e/ and /ɛ/ is hard to evaluate. They may contrast only finally.

21 Stahlke (1971) calls /ɛ/ and /ɔ/ 'retracted.'

22 DAGBANI /ə/ does not occur in open syllables and is partially in complementary distribution with /i/, but there seems to be a certain amount of contrast.

23 It is not clear that DELAWARE /ə/ is phonemic.

24 GILYAK has four unstable long vowels deriving from vowel followed by velar spirant before consonant.

25 While /ə̃/ is rare, /ə̃i/ is very common.

26 The grammar gives a ten vowel system for KET. But /e o/ seem clearly to be initial allophones of /ɛ ɔ/. The three central unrounded vowels given in the grammar as distinct phonemes are very hard to judge. I have tentatively grouped them into a single phoneme /ɨ/, though there is no clear evidence for this.

27 The symbol /i / represents "a voiced, high, close, front unrounded vowel with friction and back tongue rounding or grooving ...not the same as the back unrounded vocoid found in other TUPI-GUARANI languages."

28 The vowel /ɨ/ is described as 'retroflexed,' and occurs only after sibilants, sometimes being replaced by a long sibilant. The distribution seems suspicious, but there are minimal pairs with most of the other vowels. The situation is difficult to evaluate; in any case the system borders on being 5:0.

29 The /ə/ of YUKAGHIR is described as slightly retracted from the position of /ɛ/ and weakly labialized. Only four long vowels are exemplified.

30 The grammar lists both /i/ and /ɯ/, but from the discussion it appears that they must be in complementary distribution, with /i/ after palatalized consonants, /ɯ/ elsewhere.

31 BURMESE has, in addition, four nasalized diphthongs.

32 /ɛ ɔ/ are harmonic pairs of /e o/, probably 'retracted.'

33 According to the grammar, all the oral vowels of SEDANG have creaky voiced counterparts which are distinctive. There are supposed to be six nasal vowels, but only four are exemplified.

34 WOLOF /ə/ has also been described as /ö/.

35 BRETON /ə/ seems to be a neutral vowel.

36 In some types of GERMAN, /ɛ·/ is marginally distinctive.

37 The long vowels always have falling pitch. /ě/ and /ɶ/ merge in one dialect.

38 Nasal consonants cause extensive nasalization of vowels, which can be considered nondistinctive, except for one very marginal environment.

39 YAY /ə/ is rare in closed syllables.

40 The grammar gives three back unrounded vowels, /ɯ ě ʌ/, but the examples do not establish a contrast.

41 The vowels /I ɛ a U ɔ/ form a harmonically 'retracted' set.

42 GREBO /e› o›/ are 'retracted' or 'muffled.'

43 LUO has extensive vowel harmony. The vowels can be divided into tense and lax, or advanced and retracted sets.

APPENDIX IV
Language references

Abbreviated references are given here for all languages in the sample. Most can be found in their full form in the Bibliography to Working Papers on Language Universals (Fahrenholz 1976). References for all other languages referred to in this paper can also be found there. References not to be found there are marked a code letter, (R) indicating that the full reference is in Ruhlen 1975a; (B) indicating that it is given below under "Bibliography." A complete bibliography for the sample languages can also be obtained on request from the Stanford Phonology Archiving Project, Department of Linguistics, Stanford University, Stanford, California 94305.

ADZERA Holzknecht 1973

AINU Simeon 1969 (R)

AKAN (FANTI) Welmers 1946 (R)

AKHA Katsura 1973

ALABAMAN Rand 1968

ALASKAN ESKIMO Mattina 1970 (R)

ALAWA Sharpe 1972

ALBANIAN Newmark 1957

ALEUT Menovshchikov 1968 (R)

AMAHUACA Osborn 1948

AMHARIC Leslau 1968

AMUESHA Fast 1953

ANGAS Burquest 1971
APINAYE Burgess and Ham 1968
ARAUCANIAN Echeverria and
   Contreras 1965
AROSI Capell 1971
ASMAT Voorhoeve 1965
ATAYAL Egerod 1966 (R)
AUYANA (USARUFA) Bee 1965
AWIYA (AGAW) Hetzron 1969 (B)
AZERBAIJANI Householder 1965
BARASANO Stolte and Stolte 1971
BASQUE N'diaye 1970
BATAK (TOBA BATAK) Tuuk 1971
BEEMBE (BEMBA) Jacquot 1962
BENGALI Ferguson and
   Chowdhury 1960
BODO (BORO) Bhat 1968 (B)
BRETON Ternes 1970
BULGARIAN Aronson 1968 (R),
   Klagstad 1958 (B)
BURMESE Okell 1969
BURUSHASKI Morgenstierne 1945
CAMPA Dirks 1953
CANTONESE (TAISHAN) Cheng
   1973 (R)
CARIB Peasgood 1972 (R),
   Hoff 1968
CAYAPA Lindskoog and Brend
   1962
CHACOBO Prost 1967
CHAM Blood 1967
CHAMORRO Topping 1973
CHEREMIS Ristinen 1960
CHINESE Chao 1968; Cheng
   1973 (B); Dow 1972 (B)
CHIPEWYAN Li 1946
CHONTAL Keller 1959
CHUKCHI Skorik 1968 (R)
CHUVASH Andreev 1966 (R)
DAFLA Ray 1967 (R)
DAGBANI Wilson and Bendor-
   Samuel 1969 (R)
DAKOTA Boas and Deloria
   1939 (B)
DELAWARE Voegelin 1946

DIDO Bokarev 1967 (R)
DIEGUEÑO Langdon 1970
EGYPTIAN ARABIC Mitchell 1962
ENGLISH O'Connor 1973 (R)
EVENKI Konstantinova 1968 (R)
EWE Berry 1951, Stahlke 1971
EWONDO Abega 1970 (R)
FRENCH Sten 1963
FULANI Stennes 1967
GÃ Berry (no date)
GADSUP Frantz 1966
GARO Burling 1961
GBARI (GWARI) Hyman and
   Magaji 1970
GBEYA Samarin 1966
GEORGIAN Robins and Waterson
   1952; Vogt 1938, 1958, 1971
GERMAN Moulton 1962
GILYAK Panfilov 1968
GOAJIRO Holmer 1949
GREBO Innes 1966
GREENLANDIC Rischel 1974 (B);
   Thalbitzer 1904
GUARANI Gregores and Suarez
   1967; Lunt 1973; Uldall 1956
HAIDA Sapir 1923
HAKKA (CHINESE) Hashimoto 1973
HAUSA Greenberg 1941; Kraft
   and Kraft 1973 (R)
HAWAIIAN Pukui and Elbert
   1965 (B)
HOPI Whorf 1946
HUNGARIAN Hall 1944 (B)
HUPA Golla 1970 (B); Woodward
   1964
IAI Tryon 1968
ICELANDIC Malone 1952
IRAQW Whiteley 1958
ISLAND CARIB Taylor 1955
ITALIAN Agard and DiPietro 1969
ITONAMA Liccardi and Grimes
   1968
JAPANESE Bloch 1950; Jorden
   1963
JAQARU Hardman 1966

JAVANESE Horne 1961
JIVARO Beasley and Pike 1957 (R)
KABARDIAN Kuipers 1960
KALIAI Counts 1969 (R)
KANURI Lukas 1937
KAREN Jones 1961
KAROK Bright 1957
KET Krejnovich 1968 (R)
KHARIA Biligiri 1965
KHASI Rabel 1961
KIRGHIZ Hebert and Poppe 1963
KOHO (SRE) Manley 1972
KOMI Lytkin 1966
KOREAN Cho 1967; Martin 1951
KOTA Emeneau 1944
KPELLE Welmers 1962
KUNIMAIPA Pence 1966
KUNJEN Sommer 1969
KURUX Pfeiffer 1972 (R)
KWAKIUTL Boas 1947
LAHU Matisoff 1973 (R)
LAK Murkelinskij 1967 (R)
LAKKIA Haudricourt 1967 (R)
LAO Roffe 1946 (R)
LITHUANIAN Ambrazas 1966 (R)
LOGBARA Crazzolara 1960
LUISEÑO Bright 1965; Kroeber and Grace 1960; Malecot 1963
LUO Gregersen and Alstrup 1961
LUVALE Horton 1949
MAIDU Shipley 1956, 1964
MALAGASY Dahl 1952 (R)
MALAY Verguin 1967
MALAYALAM Sreedhar 1972 (B)
MALTESE ARABIC Borg 1973
MANTJILTJARA Marsh 1969
MAORI Biggs 1961
MARANUNGKU Tryon 1970
MARGI Hoffman 1963
MAUNG Capell and Hinch 1970 (R)
MAZAHUA Spotts 1953
MAZATEC Pike and Pike 1947
MIANKA Prost 1964 (B)
MIXTEC Hunter and Pike 1969

MONGOLIAN Hangin 1968
MOROCCAN ARABIC Abdel-Massin 1973 (B); Harrell 1962, 1965
MOXO (IGNACIANO) Ott and Ott 1967
MUNDARI Gumperz 1957
NAGA Bhat 1969 (R)
NAMA (HOTTENTOT) Beach 1938
NASIOI Hurd 1966 (R)
NAVAHO Sapir and Hoijer 1967
NENGONE Tryon 1967
NEZ PERCE Aoki 1966, 1970
NOOTKA Sapir and Swadesh 1955 (R)
NORWEGIAN Vanvik 1972
NUBIAN Bell 1971
NUNG Freiberger 1964 (R)
NUNGGUBUYU Hughes and Leeding 1971 (R)
NYANGUMATA O'Grady 1964
OCAINA Agnew and Pike 1957
OJIBWA Bloomfield 1956
ONEIDA Lounsbury 1953
OSTYAK Gulya 1966
OTOMI Blight and Pike 1976 (R)
PACOH Watson 1964
PAEZ Gerdel 1973
PANJABI Gill and Gleason 1963
PAPAGO Hale 1959 (B); Saxton 1963
PASHTO Shafeev 1964
PERSIAN Obolensky, Panah and Nouri 1963
PICURIS Trager 1971
POLISH Wierzchowska 1965
POMO Moshinsky 1974 (B)
PORTUGUESE Head 1964 (R)
PUGET SOUND SALISH Snyder 1968 (R)
QUECHUA Bills 1969; Lastra 1968
RAWANG Morse 1963
RUMANIAN Agard 1958
RUSSIAN Jones and Ward 1969
RYUKYUAN Martin 1970 (R)

148 John Crothers

SA'BAN Clayre 1973
SEDANG Smith 1968
SELEPET McElhanon 1970
SENECA Chafe 1967
SENTANI Cowan 1965
SHILHA Applegate 1958
SINHALESE Coates and
  de Silva 1960
SIRIONO Priest 1968
SOMALI Armstrong 1964
SONGHAI Prost 1956 (B)
SPANISH Navarro 1961
SQUAMISH Kuipers 1967
SUNDANESE Anderson 1972;
  Robins 1953, 1957; Van Syoc
  1959
SWAHILI Polome 1967
TAGALOG Schachter and Otanes
  1972
TARASCAN Foster 1969 (R)
TELEFOL Healy 1964
TELUGU Lisker 1963
TEWA Hoijer and Dozier 1949
TIBETAN Chang and Shefts 1964
  Roerich and Dhuntshok 1957 (B)
TICUNA Anderson 1959 (B)
TOLOWA Bright 1964
TOTONAC Aschmann 1946

TUNICA Haas 1940
TURKISH Lees 1961; Swift 1963
TZELTAL Kaufman 1971
VIETNAMESE Thompson 1965
WALAMO Tucker and Bryan
  1966 (R)
WAPISHANA Tracy 1972
WASHKUK Kooyers, Kooyers and
  Bee 1971 (R)
WESTERN DESERT Douglas
  1955 (B)
WICHITA Garvin 1950
WIK MUNKAN Sayers and
  Godfrey 1964 (B)
WOLIO Anceaux 1952
WOLOF Manessy and Sauvageot
  1963; Sauvageot 1965; Ward 1939 (B)
WU (CHINESE) Chao 1970 (R)
YAO Purnell 1965
YAY Gedney 1965
YUCHI Ballard 1975 (B);
  Crawford 1973
YUKAGHIR Krejnovich 1968 (R)
YURAK Decsy 1966
ZAN Kizirin 1967 (R)
ZOQUE Wonderly 1951
ZULU Doke 1961
ZUNI Newman 1965

BIBLIOGRAPHY

Abdel-Massih, E.T. 1973. An introduction to Moroccan Arabic.
  Ann Arbor: Center for Near Eastern and North African Studies,
  University of Michigan.

Anderson, L. 1959. Ticuna vowels with special regard to the
  system of five tonemes. Publicacoes de Museu Nacional, Serie
  Linguistica Especial 1.

Anderson, S. 1975. The organization of phonology. New York:
  Academic Press.

Armstrong, L.E. 1934. The phonetic structure of Somali. Mitteil-
  ungen des Seminars für Orientalischen Sprachen 37. 116-61.

Ballard W.L. 1975. Aspects of Yuchi morphonology. Studies in
  Southeastern Indian languages, ed. by J.M. Crawford, 164-187.

Bhat, D.N.S. 1968. Boro vocabulary. Poona: Deccan College.

Blight, R.C. and E.V. Pike. 1976. The phonology of Tenango Otomi. International Journal of American Linguistics [IJAL] 42. 51-57.

Boas, F. and E. Deloria. 1939. Dakota grammar. Memoirs of the National Academy of Sciences, Vol. xxiii, second memoir.

Bright, W. 1965. Luiseño phonemics. IJAL 31.4. 342-345.

Cheng, C.C. 1973. A synchronic phonology of Mandarin Chinese. Monographs on Linguistic Analysis 4. The Hague: Mouton.

Chomsky, N. 1964. Current issues in linguistic theory. The structure of language, ed. by Fodor and Katz, 50-118.

_____ and M. Halle. 1968. The sound pattern of English. Harper.

Crothers, J. 1975. Areal features and natural phonology: the case of front rounded vowels. Proceedings of the Second Annual Conference of the Berkeley Linguistic Society, 124-136.

Douglas, W.H. 1955. Phonology of the Australian Aboriginal language spoken at Ooldea, South Australia. Oceania 25. 216-229.

Dow, F.D.M. 1972. An outline of Mandarin phonetics. Oriental Monograph Series 10. Canberra: Australian National University Faculty of Asian Studies.

Fahrenholz, V. 1976. Bibliography to Working Papers on Language Universals. Supp. to WPLU 20. Stanford Dept. of Linguistics.

Fant, G. 1973. Speech sounds and features. Cambridge, Mass.: M.I.T. Press.

Ferguson, C.A. 1966. Assumptions about nasals. Universals of language, ed. by J.H. Greenberg. Cambridge, Mass.: M.I.T. Press, 2nd ed.

Flanagan, J.L. 1955. A difference limen for vowel formant frequency. Readings in acoustic phonetics, ed. by Lehiste, 288-292.

Gieser, C. Richard. 1958. The phonemes of Kalinga. Studies in Philippine Linguistics, Oceania Linguistic Monographs 3. 13-28.

Gill, H.S. and H.A. Gleason. 1963. A reference grammar of Panjabi. Hartford.

Golla, V.K. 1970. Hupa grammar. Doctoral dissertation, University of California, Berkeley.

Greenberg, J. 1966. Language universals, with special reference to feature hierarchies. The Hague: Mouton.

_____, C. Osgood and J. Jenkins. 1966. Memorandum concerning language universals. Language universals, ed. by J.H. Greenberg. Cambridge, Mass.: M.I.T. Press.

Hale, K. 1959. A Papago grammar. Doctoral dissertation, Indiana University.

Hall, Robert A. Jr. 1944. Hungarian grammar. Language Monograph 21, LSA. Reprinted by Kraus Reprint Co.

_____. 1948. The linguistic structure of Taki-Taki. Language 24.1. 92-116.

Hockett, C.F. 1955. A manual of phonology. IJAL Memoir 11.

Jakobson, R. 1968. (tr. by Keiler) Child language, aphasia, and phonological universals. The Hague: Mouton.

_____, G. Fant and M. Halle. 1951. Preliminaries to speech analysis. Cambridge, Mass.: M.I.T. Press.

Kaschube, Dorothea. 1954. Examples of tone in Crow. IJAL 20.1. 34-37.

Klagstad, H. Jr. 1958. The phonemic system of colloquial standard Bulgarian. The Slavic and East European Journal 16. 42-54.

Kuipers, A.H. 1965. Phoneme and morpheme in Kabardian. The Hague.

Ladefoged, P. 1964. A phonetic study of West African languages. Cambridge University Press.

_____. 1971. Preliminaries to linguistic phonetics. University of Chicago Press.

Lehiste, I. (ed.) 1967. Readings in acoustic phonetics. Cambridge, Mass.: M.I.T. Press

_____. 1973. Review of Sweet and Russell. IJAL 39. 2. 123-126.

Liljencrants, J. and B. Lindblom. 1972. Numerical simulation of vowel quality systems: the role of perceptual contrast. Language 48. 4. 839-862.

Lindau, M. 1975. Features for vowels. UCLA Working Papers in Phonetics 30.

Lindblom, B. 1975. Experiments in sound structure. Paper read at the Eighth International Congress of Phonetic Sciences, Leeds.

_____ and J. Sundberg. 1971. Acoustical consequences of lip, tongue, jaw and larynx movement. Journal of the Acoustical Society of America 50. 1166-1179.

Meiklejohn, P. and K. Meiklejohn. 1961. Accentuation in Sarangani Manobo. Oceania Linguistic Monographs 3. 1-5.

Moshinsky, J. 1974. A grammar of Southeastern Pomo. University of California Publication in Linguistics 72.

Ohala, J. 1975. Phonetic explanations for nasal sound patterns. Nasálfest, ed. by Ferguson, Hyman and Ohala, 289-316. Papers from a symposium on nasals and nasalization, Berkeley, Nov. 23-24, 1974.

Peterson, G. E. and H. L. Barney. 1952. Control methods used in a study of the vowels. In Lehiste 1967: 118-127.

Prost, R. P. A. 1956. La langue songay et ses dialectes. Mémoires de l'Institut Français d'Afrique Noire 47. Dakar.

_____. 1964. Contribution à l'étude des langues voltaïques. Mémoires de l'Institut Français d'Afrique Noire 70. Dakar.

Pukui, M. and S. H. Elbert. 1965. Hawaiian-English dictionary. Honolulu: University of Hawaii Press.

Rischel, J. 1974. Topics in West Greenlandic phonology. Copenhagen: Akademisk Forlag.

Roerich, G. N. and T. L. Dhunsthok. 1957. Textbook of Colloquial Tibetan, dialect of Central Tibet. Government of West Bengal, Education Department, Education Bureau.

Ruhlen, M. 1975a. Guide to the languages of the world. Stanford University Press.

John Crothers

Ruhlen, M. 1975b. Patterning of nasal vowels. Nasálfest, ed. by
    Ferguson, Hyman and Ohala, 333-352. Stanford Univ. Press.

Ruhlen, M. (to appear) The geographical and genetic distribution
    of linguistic features. Linguistic studies presented to Joseph
    H. Greenberg on the occasion of his 60th birthday, ed. by A.
    Juilland. Saratoga, Calif.: Anma Libri.

Sayers, B. and M. Godfrey. 1964. Outline description of the alpha-
    bet and grammar of a dialect of Wik-Munkan, spoken at Coen,
    North Queensland. Occasional Papers in Aboriginal Studies 2.
    Canberra: Australian Institute of Aboriginal Studies.

Sedlak, P. 1969. Typological considerations of vowel quality sys-
    tems. WPLU 1. 1-40.

Sreedhar, M.V. 1972. Phonology of the Cochin dialect of Malaya-
    lam. International Journal of Dravidian Linguistics 1. 100-125.

Stahlke, Herbert. 1971. Topics in Ewe phonology. Doctoral dis-
    sertation, University of California, Los Angeles.

Stewart, J.M. 1967. Tongue root position in Akan vowel harmony.
    Phonetica 16. 185-204.

Sundberg, J. 1977. The acoustics of the singing voice. Scientific
    American 236.3. 82-91.

Thalbitzer, W. 1904. A phonetical study of the Eskimo language.
    Meddeledser om Grønland 31.

Trubetzkoy, N.S. 1969. (tr. Baltaxe) Principles of phonology.
    University of California Press.

Vihman, M. (ed.) 1976. A reference manual and user's guide for
    the Stanford Phonology Archive, Part I. Stanford University

Voegelin, C.F., F.M. Voegelin and K.L. Hale. 1962. Typological
    and comparative grammar of Uto-Aztecan: I. IJAL Memoir 17.

Ward, I.C. 1939. A short phonetic study of Wolof (Jolof) as spoken
    in Senegal. Africa 12. 320-324.

Wright, J. 1975. Effects of vowel nasalization on the perception of
    vowel height. Nasálfest, ed. by Ferguson, Hyman and Ohala, 373-
    387. Sympos. on nasalization, Berkeley, Nov. 23-24, 1974.

Syllabic Consonants

ALAN BELL

ABSTRACT

Some synchronic and diachronic generalizations about syllabic consonants are presented, based on a comparison of 85 languages. The main process of their formation, which is loss of a vowel and concomitant shift of syllabicity to an adjacent consonant, occurs fairly commonly in favored environments. It apparently does not generalize easily to wider contexts, however, so that in most languages the syllabicity of consonants is predictable at a relatively low phonological level. A wide variety of consonants, both resonants and obstruents, may function as syllable peaks. Resonants are preferred to obstruents as syllabics, although in some languages the only syllabic consonants are obstruents. Contrary to predictions by most scales of sonority, nasal syllabics are preferred to liquid ones. Detailed diachronic examination of nasal syllabics shows that m and ŋ are dominant, although the synchronic pattern of occurrence of nasal syllabics is not conclusive in this regard. The preference largely derives from the diachronic generalization that when syllabic nasals are formed, mu, um, ŋu, and uŋ are the first nasal-vowel combinations to be affected. Among obstruents, fricatives dominate stops as syllabics; six languages possessing syllabic stops were found, all possessing syllabic fricatives also.

A preliminary version of this paper appeared in Working Papers on Language Universals 4, November 1970. The investigation was supported by NIMH Fellowship 1-F1-MH-40, 650-01 (CUAN) and the Stanford Universals Project, NSF Grant GS 1880. I am grateful to the project members, especially J.H. Greenberg and Edith Moravcsik, and to W. S-Y. Wang for their help.

CONTENTS

1. Introduction

Vowels function as syllable peaks in all languages. In some languages consonants are also syllabic, as has long been known. The syllabics ṛ and ḷ were recognized by the Indian grammarians, although their phonetic nature was not clearly expounded (Allen 1963). In an early phonetics handbook Brücke (1876:105)[1] mentions syllabic ṛ and ḷ as sounds of SANSKRIT, emphasizing that "Ich bin... der Ansicht, dass r an und für sich und ohne Beihilfe eines Vokals silbenbildend auftreten kann..." The emphasis shortly became unnecessary. By the time of the works of Sievers (1876) and Sweet (1877), and Brugmann's (1876) article on INDOEUROPEAN *m̥ and *n̥, resonants were established as reputable syllabics.

Our knowledge of the nature of syllabic consonants has advanced haltingly since then. A reluctance to recognize that obstruents, too, may be syllabic has never been overcome.[2] And even though it has been widely recognized that the role of syllabic consonants is pivotal in any theory of the syllable, this does not seem to have stiumulated much advance in our empirical knowledge of their nature.[3]

The present study is a typological comparison of 85 languages possessing syllabic consonants. These languages were a part of a larger sample of 182, chosen primarily to represent the major language families and language areas of the world, and secondarily to include those with syllabic consonants.[4] It describes what consonantal sounds occur as syllable peaks and what contexts they

---

[1] The first edition of 1856 was unavailable to me.

[2] For example, Chomsky and Halle (1968:354), exclude the possibility 'by definition,' perhaps following Trubetzkoy (1949:198). Yet Trubetzkoy admitted that the syllabic sibilants of CHINESE caused 'difficulties,' Grammont (1933) earlier stated as a matter of fact that obstruents may be syllabic, citing MOROCCAN ARABIC syllabic fricatives, and Sievers (1893:272) had remarked that "Naturally sounds other than liquids and nasals can also become syllabic ..."

[3] The futile controversy between Hála (1964) and Rosetti (1962) is a wonderful example.

[4] A full description of the coverage of the total language sample is given in Bell 1970:97-111.

occur in, noting regularities of their occurrence. I have indicated
the linguistic significance of some of the synchronic regularities
by describing the diachronic processes behind them, in greatest
detail for syllabic nasals (4.2.2).[5]

2. Methodological Assumptions

The level of comparison is that of phonetic representation,
largely because descriptions of different theoretical bases are
most easily rendered comparable at this level.

At this level, I assume that all segments are marked as +syl-
labic or –syllabic. A syllabic consonant is a segment of a phonetic
representation which is +syllabic and not a vowel, i.e. either
– sonorant or +consonantal.[6]

Roughly speaking, a phonetic segment is +syllabic when it functions phonetically as a syllable peak from the point of view of the
native speaker.

Theoretical assumptions that differ widely from these are sometimes used in linguistic descriptions, making absolute comparability of my data probably unattainable. I used the following rules of
thumb to improve comparability as much as possible.

A description was accepted if there was no reason to believe that
the investigator was using criteria incompatible with those above.
This included a few phonemic descriptions lacking phonetic detail
in which the phonemic segments were interpreted as if they were
phonetic. The use of the label 'chest pulse' was not taken to indicate incompatibility. Although the theory behind it is now discre-
dited, there is no reason to suppose that in descriptive practice
it was anything but a neutral label corresponding to 'syllabic.'

The clearest cases of incompatibility were those where syllabicity was explicitly defined in terms of some other parameter.

---

[5] For the importance of the diachronic plane in typological comparison, see Greenberg 1966: 97-111.

[6] I take the +sonorant sounds to include vocoids (vowels and
glides but not the laryngeals [h, ɦ, ʔ]) and resonants (liquids and
nasals), and +consonantal sounds to include resonants and obstruents.

Relative duration, which has been used as a criterion traditionally in JAPANESE and also in ARABELA was not accepted as a criterion for syllabicity by itself. Syllabics based on the equation 'sonority peak equals syllable peak' were rejected unless other evidence was given. Similarly, 'tone-bearing' segments were not considered to necessarily be syllabic. (This usage of 'syllabic' has a certain tradition in African linguistics.)

The greatest difficulty was in connection with the concept of 'segment of phonetic representation' and the representation of transitional elements. Some investigators apparently feel that a consonant cannot be syllabic if even the slightest vocalic transition or release accompanies it.[7] Some cases appear to be indeterminate, i.e. a decision to assign syllabicity to a consonant or an associated vocalic transition would be arbitrary. These cases aside, my position is that the consonant should be specified as syllabic unless there is independent evidence that the associated vocalic element is a segment. The problem is most acute with syllabic obstruents and I return to it below (5.2).

Syllabic consonants are not indicated in some languages because in the researcher's view they are phonetic phenomena of no particular importance. This does not affect the analysis of the characteristics of syllabic consonants where they do occur. An exhaustive sample is impossible in any case. It may prejudice generalizations about conditions under which syllabic consonants do not occur.

3. General Characteristics of Syllabic Consonants

The three basic types of syllabics are vowels, resonants and obstruents. The archetypical syllabic is a vowel. Most languages have no other kind, and all languages possess them. Among consonants, obstruents are more disfavored than resonants. The relative preference of the three main types of syllabics is nicely expressed in terms of the major class features 'sonorant' and 'consonantal.' Sonorant syllabics are preferred to nonsonorant ones (i.e. obstruents are disfavored); nonconsonantal are preferred to consonantal sonorant syllabics (i.e. vowels are favored over nasals and liquids).[8]

---

[7] Alonso (1930) and Malécot (1960) for example.

[8] Laryngeals, assumed to be [-sonorant, -consonantal], do not fit so neatly, since they are the least favored syllabics (5.1, 5.2).

This hierarchy is supported by the occurrence of syllabics in the languages of the sample, which are classified according to the types of their syllabics in Figure 1.

	Syllabic resonants	
	+	−
Syllabic +	24	10
obstruents −	47	97

Figure 1.   Summary of the classification of languages according to their possession of syllabic types.[9]

For 47 languages, the only syllabic consonants were resonants. There are 34 languages with syllabic obstruents, of which ten have no syllabic resonants.

This means that there is no implicational relationship between the occurrence of syllabic resonants and obstruents comparable to the one between vowels and syllabic consonants.   That is, we

---

[9]Languages possessing both syllabic resonants and syllabic obstruents: ARABIC ARABIC, EGYPTIAN ARABIC, FRENCH, HAKKA CHINESE, HSIANG CHINESE (Changsha), JAPANESE (Standard), KABARDIAN, KAN CHINESE, KORYAK, KWAKIUTL, LENDU, LUGANDA, MANDARIN CHINESE, MOROCCAN ARABIC, NAVAHO, PIRO, RUSSIAN, SHILHA, SOMALI, SPANISH (Mexican), TODA, WU CHINESE (Suchou), WU CHINESE (Wenchou), ZUALA BERBER. Languages possessing only syllabic resonants: ABAZA, AKAN, AKHA, AMHARIC, AMUZGO, CANTONESE, CHAM, CZECH, DAN, ENGLISH, HAUSA, HOTTENTOT (Korana), HOTTENTOT (Nama), IDOMA, IJO, IRISH, KHASI, KHMER, KHMU, LIVONIAN, MAMBILA, MARGI, MBE, MINNAN CHINESE (Amoy), MINNAN CHINESE (Gaoxiong), NORWEGIAN (Standard), NORWEGIAN (Trondheim), PACOH, PALAUNG, PALESTINIAN ARABIC, PAME, QUIOTEPEC CHINANTEC, RUMANIAN (Istrian), RUMANIAN (Standard), MAJINGAY SARA, NGAMBAY SARA, SIRIONO, SPANISH (New Mexico), SQUAMISH, SUSU, SWAHILI, TSWANA, USILA CHINANTEC, WALAPAI, YAKUR, YAO, YORUBA.   Languages possessing only syllabic obstruents: ACOMA, AHI, CHIPAYA, GARO, HSIANG CHINESE (Hankow), LAHU, NYI, SIERRA NAHUAT, SINHALESE, WICHITA.   Unclassifiable: AGUACATEC, JAPANESE (Kyuushuu), KOLAMI, MINPEI CHINESE (Fuchou).

cannot say that languages possessing syllabic obstruents necessarily possess syllabic resonants. Even so, I do not reject the hierarchy vowel-resonant-obstruent for syllabics, but surmise that the preference for resonants over obstruents is the outcome of a complex of diachronic processes. [10]

It is possible that a finer hierarchy for syllabicity in terms of a scale of sonority or aperture, perhaps language-specific to some degree, might also be established. A comparable or larger sample of more detailed language descriptions would probably be necessary. Examination of preference for syllabicity in the environment #__ [-son] and [-son]__# in the present sample did not support a finer hierarchy. It is also clear that a statement such as "segments become syllabic when they are surrounded by units ... which are not more sonorant than they are" (Houlihan 1973) is too strong. The counterexamples are far more numerous than those she mentions.

3. 1 It is fairly common to find that the syllabic consonants of a language occur only in grammatical particles and affixes, as in NAVAHO and GAOXIONG (Taiwan) CHINESE, or largely in such elements, as in SWAHILI. Syllabic consonants also commonly occur without restriction to syntactic categories, as in CZECH and EGYPTIAN ARABIC. In our sample, 20 systems of syllabic consonants occurred only in grammatical particles and affixes, 17 largely in such elements, and 34 largely independently. Twenty-one systems could not be classified. [11]

---

[10] The clean separation between vowels and syllabic consonants derives from the dominance of two processes in determining their occurrence: vowel loss, which is never unconditioned, and creation of syllabic consonants, which is usually conditioned by prior presence of a vowel. See 3. 5.

[11] The totals in this classification and in those following (with respect to word boundaries, Section 3. 2; with respect to stress, Section 3. 3; with respect to margins, Section 3. 4) do not agree with each other or with the total number of languages in the sample with syllabic consonants (85). The reason is that I have not counted every language as a unit, since some languages have a number of systems which behave differently. For example, in CZECH m̩ does not occur in stressed position, but r̩ and l̩ do; thus CZECH would be counted twice in the classification according to occurrence under stress but only once in this classification according to occurrence in grammatical particles.

The following generalization appears to hold for our sample although the frequent lack of information concerning the effect of constituent structure in the descriptions makes it possible that counter-examples were missed.

1. If in a given language a syllabic consonant occurs in the phonological context X in root morphemes, then it occurs also in other morphemes, given that they contain the context X.

This preference is certainly connected with the preference for syllabic consonants to arise in unstressed position. Evidently it is but one factor which for many reasons may be dominated by others. Further, it may not be specific to syllabic consonants. In view of their usual formation by vowel loss (Section 3.5), it may reflect a more general tendency for the phonetic substance of particles and affixes to diminish more readily than that of other constituents.

3.2   Phrase, word, and morpheme boundaries play a significant role in the development of syllabic consonants. In our data the effect of word boundary is clearest, owing partly to the greater attention it usually receives in phonological descriptions. Twenty-four languages have systems of syllabic consonants which appear only word-medially. Initially and medially, there are 11; finally and medially, 10; in all three positions, 8. There were no systems in initial and final positions only. Systems for which the classification is inappropriate (for example most CHINESE languages) numbered 15 and there were 14 unclassifiable systems.

The preference for constituent-initial position can sometimes be seen in morphophonemic alternations. Compare LUGANDA phrase-initial /m̩.pa/ 'Give me!' to /ku.mpà/ 'to give me' and /n̩.va/ 'relish' to /saagalà nva/ 'I don't like relish' (Tucker 1962: 140). A similar alternation, but with a different pattern of syllabification is seen in YAKUR (Bendor-Samuel 1969): /ɛ̀to/ 'house' /n̩wɛ̌nɛ̌/ 'book,' /ɛ̀toŋ.wɛ̀nɛ̀/ 'school.' But in TSWANA, which like LUGANDA has initial syllabic nasal prefixes, the syllabicity of the nasal is normally retained even when it follows another prefix. Although I see no reason why it should not be possible under the right circumstances for the opposite pattern to occur (nonsyllabic in initial position alternating with syllabic in medial position) I have found no examples. A parallel alternation in final position is claimed by Vanvik (1966) for TRONDISK NORWEGIAN, e.g. ['baːʎ] 'ball,' ['baːʎn̩] 'the ball;' ['saːl] 'saddle,' ['saːln̩] 'the saddle.' The claim is disputed by Sivertsen (1968); see note 29.

The preference of syllabic consonants for occurring in initial and final position is evidently the result of a complex diachronic picture. It is probably related to the preferences they have for occurring without margins and in particles and affixes. A syllabic with an initial margin obviously cannot be word-initial. In contrast, note that word-initial position is not a favorite one for vowels; in some languages, all words begin with a consonant; no language has been reported to begin all words with a vowel. [12] A more general tendency may also be involved here, namely for certain processes to initiate at constituent boundaries and spread to other environments. (This could only be one of the contributing factors, not a dominant one, since syllabic consonants sometimes arise first in medial position, e.g. in TSWANA and RUSSIAN. See 3.5).

3.3   Syllabic consonants tend to occur in unstressed positions.[13] In our sample, 33 systems of syllabic consonants occurred only unstressed, 12 systems occurred under stress (and usually also unstressed), and 42 systems occurred in languages without stress accentual systems or whose stress distribution was not known. Since syncope, which probably does not occur in stressed syllables unless it has occurred in unstressed ones, is the usual path to syllabic consonants, this tendency is not surprising.

On the other hand, stressed syllabic consonants are by no means rare, as in ENGLISH, CZECH, and KORYAK. There may even be cases where consonants are syllabic only under stress. KWAKIUTL m, n, l are so described by Boas (1947), although his account of syllabicity in that language is hardly limpid. A more firmly established example is TSWANA, whose class 9 prefixes take the form of syllabic nasals only when they occur in stressed position. A similar alternation is found in SWAHILI, except that there is still some free variation between syllabic and nonsyllabic nasals in

---

[12] Although some of the KUNJEN languages of Australia come close (Sommer 1969, Dixon 1970).

[13] This is not quite the same as saying that they tend to be unstressed. A tendency to be unstressed is a more appropriate description of voiceless vowels, which, when they occur in stressed position, often act to shift the stress to an adjacent syllable, Greenberg (1969). Syllabic consonants may sometimes act this way, too, as perhaps in WICHITA, where syllabic ș is not counted in the placement of alternating secondary stress (David Rood, personal communication).

unstressed position. These systems are consistent with a historical process which weakened the unstressed syllabic nasals, leaving
the stressed ones as remnants.

This suggests that the role of stress in the processes that create
and destroy syllabic consonants will figure importantly in the explanation of the distribution of syllabic consonants with respect to
stress. This role can be expressed by the diachronic generalizations 2. and 3.

2. If in a given language, syllabic consonants are created by
syncope in stressed syllables, then they have been created by
syncope in unstressed syllables.

3. If in a given language, stressed syllabic consonants become
nonsyllabic or are lost, then nonstressed syllabic consonants
have become nonsyllabic or have been lost.

I discovered no particular restriction of the distribution of syllabic consonants with respect to tonal elements.

A contrast in length in syllabic consonants occurs but rarely,
even at the phonetic level. In TSWANA, penultimate accent is
manifested by length of the syllabic, whether vowel or syllabic
resonant. MOROCCAN ARABIC [tl̩t] 'three' contrasts with [tl̩·to]
'they multiplied by three' (Harrell 1962a). SANSKRIT r̩ and r̩̄,
though the latter is very limited in occurrence, is perhaps a more
familiar example (Whitney 1960). And the SLOVAK contrast exemplified by tlstý 'thick' vs. tl̄k 'pestle,' cited by Andersen 1972,
occurs also for r̩ in SLOVAK, SLOVENIAN, and SERBOCROATIAN.

3.4   Syllabic consonants exhibit a strong preference for occurring in syllables without margins or with margins markedly simpler
than those found in syllables with vocalic nuclei. In the sample, 46
systems of syllabic consonants occurred only as simple nuclei, 30
systems occurred in syllables with at most an initial marginal segment, 8 systems with at most a final segment, and but three with
more complex margins.[14] Three systems could not be classified.
In every case, the maximum final and initial margin is less than or

---

[14] The three cases with more than one marginal segment are
ENGLISH (e.g. bannisters, candles), CZECH (e.g. smrt 'death'),
and KWAKIUTL (e.g. /saʔgwn̩s/ glossed by Boas (1947) as 'meat
comes visiting').

equal to the maximum for syllables with vocalic nuclei. Generalization 4. is thus proposed. [15]

4. If a language contains syllables with vowel nuclei of the
form $C^m V C^n$ and syllables with consonantal nuclei of the form
$C^{m'} \underset{\text{\tiny ,}}{C} C^{n'}$, then $m' \leq m$, and $n' \leq n$.

The stronger conclusion that the margins of consonantal nuclei are
fewer than those of vowel nuclei $(m' + n' < m + n)$ does not hold. [16]

The processual implications of 4. are twofold: first, no process
of formation of syllable consonants increases the marginal segments
of a syllable, and second, no process of margin formation acts preferentially upon syllables with consonantal nuclei, nor any of margin
reduction upon those with vowel nuclei. [17]

These restrictions are eminently reasonable. Where syncope is
involved, as it usually is, the first restriction will always be met

---

[15] The notation X^n means a string of X's of any length less than
or equal to n, including zero.

[16] The stronger condition might be expected as a consequence of
a plausible condition on the origin of margins. If a syllabic consonant and its margin(s) derive always by syncope from a single
syllable, then the resulting syllable will naturally have one less
marginal segment. A counterexample to the synchronic condition
is IDOMA, which has syllables of the type CV and V plus C̩l syllables, apparently formed from CVlV words, perhaps with an intermediate geminate stage: C̩l.V < C̩l.lV < CVl.lV < CV.lV. Another
potential counterexample is illustrated by AKHA. Nasal codas in
AKHA have been lost, those in -Vn producing the nasalized vowel
ɔ̃, those in -Vm producing syllabic m̩. AKHA just misses being a
counterexample because it still possesses a final glottal stop after
vowels. Notice that neither example invalidates the diachronic conjecture.

[17] The actual situation is slightly more complex, since the possibility of a language's most complex syllables all developing consonantal syllabics (or else all but some, which then undergo reduction
of their margins) must also be excluded. For example, a language
with syllables CCVC, CVC, CV presumably will not undergo processes to produce CCC̩, CC̩, C̩, CVC, CV.

even when the consonant becoming syllabic is not a margin of the
lost vowel; in other words, even an unusual change like CV.CCV >
CÇ.CV would not increase the margin size. In the usual case, the
syllabic consonant was formerly a marginal segment of the syllable,
so that the resulting syllable necessarily has one less marginal
segment. Processes not involving syncope (see 3.5 below for
examples) all involve shift of a vowel from -consonantal to +con-
sonantal, and hence do not affect the marginal complexity of the
syllable.

Generalization 4. and its processual implications suggests that
in a given language, syllables with consonantal nuclei should have
roughly one less marginal segment than those with vowel nuclei.
The synchronic distribution shows a greater preference for single
margins (either initial or final) than this. Casual inspection of
particular cases confirms that maximum margins of syllabic consonants are frequently more than one segment less than the maximum margins of vocalic nuclei. Some examples are CHIPAYA-
C^3VC^3 vs. ÇC^1; RUSSIAN - C^5VC^4 vs. Ç; LUGANDA - C^2VC^1
vs. Ç; and so on. Generalization 4. is probably as strong a statement about the limits of marginal complexity for languages in general as we can make, but the processual implications derived from
it are not nearly stringent enough. The formation of syllabic consonants from syllables of CVC and greater complexity is disfavored.[18]

I shall not attempt to unravel the numerous processes and circumstances that are undoubtedly involved in this interesting phenomenon. Certain contributing factors are, however, immediately
indicated. In initial and final position, where syllabic consonants
are frequently formed from grammatical particles and affixes, it
is to be expected that frequently the substance of these elements
will already be reduced compared to other formatives. Syllabic
consonants developed from certain favored sources, e.g. C'V.C'
(see 3.5 below), necessarily have simple margins. The preference
for unstressed vowel loss may also be relevant, given the correlation between stress and closed syllables (Greenberg and Kaschube
1976, Hyman 1975).

_____

[18]The alternative is that the processes of margin accretion and
simplification act preferentially, vowel nuclei favoring accretion
and consonantal nuclei favoring simplification. This is possible,
but it is unsupported by any case of change or alternation that I
know of.

3.5   In this section and the next, I focus on the general nature
of changes characteristic of syllabic consonants and the ways in
which the changes are peculiar to them. Some details of the processes are discussed in 4.2.2 and in Bell 1972, but most must
be left for the future.

The syllabicity of syllabic consonants never arises spontaneously
from a marginal consonant, as far as I can ascertain. The source
of the syllabicity is always a vowel. By far the commonest process
of origin is syllabic syncope, that is, loss of a vowel and shift of
syllabicity to one of its margins. Note that the transfer and loss
of a feature is like assimilation of marked features (as in VN > ṼN >
Ṽ), but the process is distinguished by the peculiarity that syllabicity
is apparently never transferred as long as the vowel retains its segmental status (i.e. a change such as muaba > m̩waba would not occur).
Of course, in syncope, a vowel's syllabicity may well die with it as
live on in its margin. The formation of clusters is a competing
process.

Two main types of syncope can be distinguished: reduced-vowel
syncope, in which the process of vowel loss initiates with lax, central vowels, and high-vowel syncope, in which loss first occurs
with high vowels. The first type is often associated with progressive shortening, unstressed position, and open syllables; the second
is sometimes accompanied by devoicing (Greenberg 1969). The
distinction is relevant to the explanation of certain regularities of
syllabic nasals (See 4.2.2 below and Bell 1972), appears to be
pertinent to the development of syllabic liquids (Section 4.1), and
syllabic obstruents (Section 5), and probably has wider application.

I am tempted to posit that the characteristics of syllabic consonants are explainable in terms of two factors: the circumstances
that lead to vowel loss and those which lead to retention of its
syllabicity in a consonant. This approach may be a fruitful tactic,
but the two factors are not actually independent. The development
of medial syllabic l̩ in TSWANA is a striking illustration. In
certain dialects /e/, /ɛ/, /o/ are elided in the context /l_l/, giving -l̩l-, as in /molelo/ > /mol̩lô/ 'fire.' On the face of it, this
is odd, for it is the high vowels /i/, /u/ that one would expect to
be lost. As it happens, [l] has become an alveolar flap [ɾ] before
i and u. Since flaps, for obvious reasons, are highly disfavored
syllabics, the conclusion is that the circumstances that favor the
consonant's retention of syllabicity are intertwined with those that
favor vowel loss.

One favored source for syllabic consonants is C_1VC_2 where C_1 and C_2 are identical or at least homorganic. Consider NORWE-GIAN <u>landene</u> [lan:.n̩.nə] 'the countries,' <u>kattene</u> [kat.n̩.nə] 'the cats,' but <u>krabene</u> [krab.bə.nə] 'the crabs' and <u>skjeggene</u> [ʃeg.gə.nə] 'the beards,' and <u>komme med meg</u> '(to) come with me' [kom.m̩.me.mɛj] or even [kom.m̩.m̩.mɛj];[19] FRENCH <u>elle me</u> <u>maltraite</u> [ɛlm̩maltʁɛt], <u>elle se souvenait</u> [ɛls̩suvne], etc.;[20] TSWANA /moḽlo/ cited above; identical continuants in 'literary' RUSSIAN, e.g. <u>slivovyi</u> [slíɣvəj] 'plum' (adj.) (Avanesov 1968); NREBELE (a dialect of ZULU) m̩.mX < mu + ɓX.

These are all examples where the syllabic consonants arise only in this context. This process should be distinguished from assimilation of syllabic consonants to adjacent consonants, which leads to the same outcome. These contexts of course favor vowel loss independently of the survival of syllabicity, as has been noted by Heffner (1950: 200) among others.

No preference for CV or VC syllables as sources for syllabic consonants has been found. The syllabic consonants of ENGLISH have come from both sources. Among CHINESE languages, several have syllabic ŋ from ŋV, but in MINNAN CHINESE of Amoy, which has the highest lexical frequency of ŋ, it is derived from CVŋ̩.

The other source of syllabic consonants may be roughly described as the assimilation of consonantality by a vowel. For obvious articulatory reasons, this probably occurs only with high vowels. Examples are sibilant + z̩ < sibilant + i in many CHINESE languages, kŋ̩ < kū in YORUBA (Siertsema 1957-58) and DAN, and a few JAPANESE words such as <u>umasa</u> [m̩masa] 'sweetness.'[21]

---

[19]Citations are from Popperwell 1963, except for <u>komme med meg</u>, personal observation.

[20]Personal observation. Reduction of the particles <u>le, me, ne, se</u>, and possibly <u>je</u> and <u>re-</u> to a syllabic consonant before identical consonants is common in ordinary spoken FRENCH, although not noted in standard descriptions of pronunciation (e.g. Fouché 1959) or even in most discussions of schwa-deletion (e.g. Pulgram 1950-61).

[21] The latter example might be derived from an intermediate form [um.masa]. An analogous morphophonemic alternation occurs in IDOMA, where a stem vowel assimilates to an infixed syllabic m̩: kwu_u + m̩ ⟶ kwu.m̩.u ⟶ kwu.m̩.m̩.

One conceivable source for syllabic consonants is the spontaneous rise of syllabicity in a member of a cluster. It is common for
syllables to develop through epenthetic vowels; why not without
them? For example, a priori it does not appear unreasonable that
an initial nt- should become ṇt-. Nevertheless, this process, if
it occurs, is at least highly disfavored.[22] The possible examples
I have been able to find are doubtful.

CZECH syllabic r̥, l̥, m̥ are thought to derive in at least some
cases from nonsyllabic r, l, m. Thus Komárek (1958) postulates
krve > kr̥ve, vedl > vedl̥, bratr > bratr̥, sedm > sedm̥, etc. There
is no reason to doubt that the resonants were nonsyllabic at one
time, at least in some dialects or styles, since this is in accord
both with metrical evidence from isosyllabic poetry and with the
loss of the resonants in some forms such as modl > mod, vyvedl >
wiwed. The development of medial syllabics such as krve > kr̥ve
is perhaps an analogical neutralization on the model of previously
existing syllabic resonants in this context, e.g. pr̥vé. There are
at least two other ways that the syllabics could have developed.
The actual sequence may have been first development of an epenthetic vowel, followed by syllabic syncope. Dobson (1968) argues
that this is the sequence of development of syllabic resonants in
words such as elm in some ENGLISH dialects. In CZECH itself,
words in final -n such as bázn went through the first stage, e.g.
bázn > bázen, but did not develop syllabic ṇ thereafter. The other
possibility is that syllabic and nonsyllabic forms coexisted in neighboring dialects, and the postulated temporal sequence reflects
either different dialects or else dialect borrowing.

The other possible instances in the sample are MAMBILA, a Benue-
Congo language, and NEW MEXICO SPANISH, where a non-vowel
source for syllabic consonants is weakly suggested by synchronic
distribution and by variation, respectively.

Some conjectures concerning the origins of syllabic consonants
are summarized in the following processual generalizations:

5. The source of syllabicity in syllabic consonants is always a
vowel, either directly, when a vowel changes into a consonant
(consonantalization), or else indirectly, when a vowel is lost

---

[22] Andersen (1972) has now postulated the spontaneous formation
of syllabic consonants (e.g. as a diachronic stage in SP. estar <
LAT. stāre) as a "hypothesis to be validated."

and its syllabicity is transferred to a consonant (syllabic syncope).

6. Only high vowels undergo consonantalization. [23]

7. A consonant may become syllabic only if it is an adjacent margin of a syncopated vowel. [24]

3. 6   The usual fate of a syllabic consonant is loss of syllabicity. Syllabicity may be lost, but the syllable retained by means of an epenthetic vowel. This process is the reverse of syllabic syncope. Or the syllable may be lost as well, the consonant joining the margin of an adjacent syllable.

One source of vowel-consonant metathesis is syllabic syncope followed by epenthesis. The development of the HAUSA first person singular prefix ni- is an example. The usual form is [n̩], but variants in [in] also occur. All three are found in the expression glossed 'I shall go': [zá·nì só·] ~ [zá· ?n̩ zó·] ~ [zá· ?ìn zó] (Hodge 1947).

The degree to which syllabic consonants can tolerate modification without loss of syllabicity is an open question. Assimilation of nasals in point of articulation is common, and homorganic systems in which a syllabic nasal has become l̩ can occur, for example in SHAKA, a BANTU language: ŋri 'tree,' miri 'trees,' l̩lo 'gravestone,' milo 'gravestones.' More drastic mutations without loss of syllabicity are not common, if our material is any guide. The most drastic change is perhaps the realization of the homorganic syllable N̩ as h̃ before h in AKAN (Welmers 1946), which looks like a step farther down the path begun in PIRO where the assimilated sequence ỹ.x- is found. A few cases of devoicing of syllabic resonants have also been reported. In WALAPAI there is a voicing variation L̩ ~ l̩ parallel to vowels, but m̩ has no voiceless variant. In restricted environments N̩ occurs in PAME.

---

[23] So the present data indicates. It is possible that the process may spread to low vowels, in which case 6. would have to be restated in implicational form.

[24] IDOMA l̩ may be a counterexample. See note 16.

3.7   Some further inferences about their processes of origin
and mutation can be made from observations about the stability of
syllabic consonants. As we have seen, syllabic consonants are
not particularly rare. The impression that they are secondary
phenomena comes rather from the restricted environments in
which they occur, and the related fact that their syllabicity is
usually predictable at a relatively low level of the phonology. In
our sample, there are only 12 languages in which the syllabicity
of consonants is not predictable from the segmental context, and
in many of these it is doubtless predictable given the constituent
structure. [25]

We may draw two general conclusions. First, the processes of
development of syllabic consonants are likely to take place given
a suitable environment, but unlike some phonetic changes, they
are not easily generalizable to wider contexts. Second, the processes of loss of syllabicity are likely to take place before further
processes can destroy the environment conditioning syllabicity
(or before widespread generalization), and/or the syllabicity of
a consonant depends so intimately upon its context that destruction
of the context leads to loss of syllabicity.

4. Syllabic Resonants

Syllabic nasals are greatly favored over liquids in the languages
of our sample. In the classification shown in Figure 2, there is
only one language with syllabic liquids only, but 35 with syllabic
nasals only.

Nasal resonants

		+	−
	+	28	1
Non-nasal			
resonants	−	35	X

Figure 2. Classification of languages possessing syllabic
resonants according to nasality. [26]

---

[25] In KORYAK alone has the formation of syllabic consonants
been so extensive that their syllabicity might best be specified in
the lexicon. A close look at the morphology might show lexical
specification unnessary even here.

[26] The language possessing only syllabic liquids is LENDU.
Languages possessing both syllabic liquids and syllabic nasals are:

This preference conflicts with the relative sonority of nasals
and liquids. Liquids are ranked above nasals in three major scales
of sonority: Jespersen's (1904) 'sonority,' Grammont's (1933)
'aperture,' and Fletcher's (1929) 'phonetic power.'

The conflict between our results and traditional rankings of
sonority does not necessarily discredit the latter. The notion of
a sonority hierarchy is a useful principle in certain applications.
For example, in his analysis of consonant sequences, Greenberg
(1965) found that in tautosyllabic sequences of voiced liquids and
nasals the preferred order is for the liquids to be next to the vocalic peak, which is consonant with an ordering of decreasing
sonority toward syllable margins.[27] It simply does not appear to
be relevant to the processes of origin and loss of syllabic resonants.

(ftnt. 26 cont.)
AKAN, AMUZGO, CZECH, EGYPTIAN ARABIC, ENGLISH, FRENCH,
HOTTENTOT (Korana), IDOMA, IRISH, KABARDIAN, KHASI,
KHMER, KHMU, KORYAK, KWAKIUTL, MANDARIN CHINESE,
MOROCCAN ARABIC, NORWEGIAN (Standard), NORWEGIAN
(Trondheim), PIRO, RUMANIAN (Istrian), RUMANIAN (Standard),
SHILHA, SPANISH (New Mexico), SQUAMISH, TSWANA, WALAPAI,
WU CHINESE (Suchou). Languages possessing only syllabic nasals
are: AKHA, AMHARIC, CANTONESE, CHAM, DAN, HAKKA CHI-
NESE, HAUSA, HOTTENTOT (Nama), HSIANG CHINESE (Changsha),
IJO, JAPANESE (Standard), KAN CHINESE, LIVONIAN, LUGANDA,
MAJINGAY SARA, MAMBILA, MARGI, MBE, MINNAN CHINESE
(Amoy), MINNAN CHINESE (Gaoxiong), MINPEI CHINESE (Fuchou),
NAVAHO, NGAMBAY SARA, PACOH, PAME, QUIOTEPEC CHI-
NANTEC, SIRIONO, SPANISH (Mexican), SUSU, SWAHILI, USILA
CHINANTEC, WU CHINESE (Wenchou), YAKUR, YAO, YORUBA.
Nine languages could not be classified: ABAZA, ARABIAN ARABIC,
JAPANESE (Kyuushuu), PALAUNG, PALESTINIAN ARABIC, RUS-
SIAN, SOMALI, TODA, ZUALA BERBER.

[27] In a similar vein, Wells (1965) and Bailey (1967) have remarked
that ENGLISH r̩, l̩ are freer in distribution than n̩. Hála (1961)
and Dobson (1968) have claimed that liquids have the greater tendency to be syllabic when a liquid and a nasal are juxtaposed. This
latter tendency is not universal, however. IDOMA l̩ occurs following most consonants, but not after m; instead of ml̩, the combination m̩l is found (Abraham 1951:191b).

The processual picture behind the synchronic distribution of syllabic nasals and liquids is evidently complex. If language could be shown to have only syllabic liquids because there were no nasals in the environment of the process of origin, then we could postulate a general implicational principle of nasal-liquid dominance in the creation of syllabic resonants. Unfortunately, syllabic ṛ in LEN-DU appears to arise in contexts containing nasals as well as liquids but has no syllabic nasals. RUSSIAN may also be a counterinstance. [28] Furthermore, the development of SANSKRIT, with only syllabic liquids, from PROTO-INDOEUROPEAN, presumably with both syllabic liquids and nasals, shows that syllabic liquids can be preferentially retained. The following observation may prove to be useful in an eventual explanation of the preference for syllabic nasals. Among the languages with only syllabic nasals, very few are subject to vowel reduction; of those with syllabic liquids, all but a handful do have some form of vowel reduction. The formation of syllabic liquids may be strongly disfavored where nonreduced vowel syncope is the process of origin, but not disfavored under reduced-vowel syncope.

4.1   The term 'liquid' covers a wide variety of speech sounds, which may be conveniently divided into laterals and nonlaterals (r-sounds). Nonlaterals may be trills, flaps, or approximates, with primary constriction ranging from dental to uvular. They may also be palatalized or velarized. I distinguish four kinds of lateral approximants: 'clear,' palatalized, velarized or 'dark,' and retroflex. The first three are in fact regions along a continuum of vocalic coloring Lateral flaps also occur.

In our sample of languages, flaps do not occur as syllabics, except reportedly in PIRO; Matteson (1965) omits any phonetic description of the segments she labels syllabic, which include [w̩], [y̩].

Among the r-sounds, the denti-alveolar trill is most common, occurring in 12 of the 14 languages whose syllabic ṛ's were described in detail. The other two instances were alveolar approximants. A syllabic uvular approximant occurs in the Bergen dialect of NORWEGIAN instead of the usual alveolar trill, and SHILHA has a velarized trill that may be syllabic.

---

[28] Avanesov (1968) says that 'non-plosive' consonants become syllabic, but gives no examples for nasals, although they would appear to occur in the appropriate context, e.g. momentálno.

All four types of laterals occur as syllabics in the data, although the single instance of a syllabic retroflex lateral is disputed.[29]

A syllabic glottalized lateral also occurs in KWAKIUTL.

There are a few hints that dark laterals are favored as syllabics. Vanvik (1966) states that the syllabic l̩ of TRONDHEIM NORWE-GIAN is more velarized than the nonsyllabic l. Bailey (1969) has described carefully the extreme velarization of the stressed syllabic l̩ in SOUTHERN STATES ENGLISH. From the account of Avanesov (1968) it appears that only the 'hard' l of RUSSIAN becomes syllabic, and not the palatalized ones. Although there is at least one clear case of a palatal ʎ occuring as the only syllabic lateral of a language,[30] there is no instance of a language possessing a darker and a lighter l and only the light l becoming syllabic or of a syllabic l̩ being a lighter variant of a nonsyllabic l.

4.2   If we had to guess, what order of preference would we assign to the types of syllabic nasals? For nonsyllabic nasals the hierarchy is clearly n → m → ŋ (Ferguson 1966). On the other hand, m and ŋ have been regarded as having the greater inherent sonority (Fletcher 1929, Dobson 1968). As we shall see, the hierarchy in the major process of origin is (m, ŋ) → n, consistent with the sonority ranking.

For all practical purposes, we can limit ourselves to the three nasal types m, n, ŋ. The palatal nasal ɲ is clearly highly disfavored as a syllabic.[31] It occurs independently in a single language of our sample, TRONDHEIM NORWEGIAN.[32] All other

---

[29] Vanvik (1966) cites syllabic l̩ and ʎ̩ in the context /XV:_+n, as in [jaːl̩n] 'the earl' and [baːʎɲ] 'the ball' for the NORWEGIAN of Trondheim. Sivertsen (1968) demurred, claiming that the rhythm of such words seemed to her to be the same as in [fuːtn̩] 'the foot,' etc. Both Vanvik and Sivertsen are native speakers of the dialect.

[30] RING CO. IRISH has ʎ̩; the original unpalatalized lateral has become ɣ^w.

[31] Hála (1961) remarks upon this, attributing it to ɲ's extreme lack of inherent sonority.

[32] There are two instances of syllabic ŋ in CHINESE languages which may reflect the processes ɲi > ɲ̩ > ŋ̩ (WU CHINESE of Wenchou) and ɲy > ɲ̩ > ŋ̩ (HAKKA). (The only final nasal in WENCHOU WU is -ŋ ; HAKKA has -m, -n, -ŋ.)

instances are by assimilation to an adjacent palatal segment. As
with nonsyllabic homorganic nasals, assimilation to a palatal does
not always take place. Further evidence for ɲ's disfavor comes
from WALAPAI, whose final suffixes -m and -l become syllabic
in the environment /C_, but the remaining suffix -ɲ does not.

Syllabic labiodental ɱ̩ and labiovelar m͡ŋ also occur by assimilation in MBE and doubtless elsewhere. Retroflex ɳ̩ occurs as
a syllabic in TRONDHEIM NORWEGIAN, but nowhere else in our
sample. Its general rarity may be the reason for this. Glottalized
syllabic m̩ˀ, n̩ˀ occur in KWAKIUTL. A voiceless syllabic N̩ is
reported in PAME.

The following instances of syllabic nasal fricatives or approximants have been reported: ʋ̃ , a nasalized labiodental approximant
in KELE which is possibly syllabic; ɣ̃ , a syllabic velar fricative
occurring allophonically before x in PIRO; and ᵐʙ̩̃, a syllabic pre-
nasalized and velarized bilabial trill occurring in a single lexical
item in AMUZGO. Henceforth in this section we use m, n, ŋ as
cover symbols for labial apicolaminal, and dorsal nasal stops.

4.2.1   The distribution of types of inventories of syllabic nasals
is given in Figure 3.

Inventory of syllabic nasals			Number of language-systems
m̩			12
	n̩		5
		ŋ̩	5
m̩	n̩		12
m̩		ŋ̩	4
	n̩	ŋ̩	1
m̩	n̩	ŋ̩	7
homorganic			21
			67

Figure 3.   Classification of systems of syllabic nasals
according to their inventories. [33]

---

[33] Language-systems, not languages are tabulated, since 10 languages contain two systems of syllabic nasals differing in origin
and environment. For example, LUGANDA has a system of prefixed homorganic syllabic nasals word-initially, plus a more

The most common inventory is a homorganic system, in which articulation of the nasals is predictable from the segmental context. Among the nonhomorganic inventories, m̩ seems to be preferred. It occurs as the only syllabic nasal in 12 cases to 5 cases for n̩. In combination with ŋ it occurs four times to n's once. The preference for n̩ over ŋ̍ is slight, considering the markedness of ŋ among non-syllabic nasals. It is reasonable to suspect that in the process from nonsyllabic to syllabic, n is disfavored.

Even though the size of our sample is fairly large, I would not wish to draw any firm conclusion from the preferences suggested by the synchronic distribution. The importance of such synchronic regularities is that they may indicate that there is a significant generalization to be found. In other words, they pose a problem. To resolve it we must move to the diachronic plane and seek what generalizations apply to the processes that create and shape syllabic nasal systems.

(ftnt. 33 cont.)

recently developed syllabic m̩ word-finally. It is thus listed in both categories below.

Languages possessing systems with m̩ only are AKHA, AMUZGO, CZECH, JAPANESE (Standard), LUGANDA, MAJINGAY SARA, MANDARIN CHINESE, MINNAN CHINESE (Amoy), MINNAN CHINESE (Gaoxiong), QUIOTEPEC CHINANTEC, SWAHILI, USILA CHINANTEC. Languages with n̩ only are HSIANG CHINESE (Changsha), IRISH, LIVONIAN, NAVAHO, NORWEGIAN (Trondheim). Languages with ŋ̍ only are DAN, MINNAN CHINESE (Amoy), TSWANA, WU CHINESE (Wenchou), YORUBA. Languages with m̩, n̩ only are AKAN, EGYPTIAN ARABIC, ENGLISH, FRENCH, HOTTENTOT (Korana), HOTTENTOT (Nama), KABARDIAN, KWAKIUTL, NORWEGIAN (Standard), SPANISH (New Mexico), SQUAMISH, YAO. Languages with m̩, ŋ̍ , only are CANTONESE, HAKKA CHINESE, IDOMA, MINPEI CHINESE. The language with n̩, ŋ̍ only is KAN CHINESE. Languages with m̩, n̩, ŋ̍ are CHAM, KHASI, KORYAK, MARGI, NGAMBAY SARA, SWAHILI, WALAPAI. Languages with homorganic systems are AKAN, AMUZGO, DAN, HAUSA, IDOMA, IJO, KHMU, LUGANDA, MAMBILA, MBE, PACOH, PAME, PIRO, RUMANIAN (Istrian), RUMANIAN (Standard), SIRIONÓ, SPANISH (New Mexico), SUSU, TSWANA, YAKUR, YORUBA. Six languages could not be classified: AMHARIC, KHMER, MOROCCAN ARABIC, SHILHA, SPANISH (Mexican), WU CHINESE (Suchou).

4.2.2   The obvious way for a language to develop one kind of
syllabic nasal is for it to have just that nasal in the context of syncope. The context may even be a single particle, or a small set
of them. (It must also resist assimilation, a point I take up below.)
NAVAHO, whose only syllabic nasal is n̦, is an example. Syllabic
n̦ occurs only in affixes. The segment m is rare in NAVAHO, and
occurs only in stems. Our sample contains numerous cases of
this kind. All twelve languages with just syllabic m̦ and n̦ had
only m and n in the context of syncope. There were 11 other instances of restricted sources among the systems lacking one or
more nasal types.[34]

----

[34] MAJINGAY SARA has syllabic m̦ only for the 1st p. sg. subject prefix; there is a 3rd p. sg. pronoun ni which is restricted to
'indirect style.' MANDARIN CHINESE m̦ is found only in familiar
forms of the plural personal pronouns. In HSIANG CHINESE (Changsha) n̦ 'you' (sg.) is the only formative with a syllabic n̦; syllabic
ŋ̦ has a more general development. Syllabic nasals in RING CO.
IRISH occur as variants finally after homorganic consonants by loss
of preceding reduced vowel ə. A tabulation of the final sequences
of the form $-C_1 \partial C_2 \#$ from the many citations given by Breatnach
(1947) shows that final -m is rare in this context, and is not found
at all after a labial consonant. Indeed, no words in $-C_1 \partial C_2$ were
found where C_1 and C_2 were labial. Eric Hamp (personal communication) has pointed out that indigeneous final m in IRISH would
have to have come earlier from medial clusters, most likely *-mm-
or *-sm-. LIVONIAN n develops from loss of word-final vowels
in the context /Cn_#, and no other nasals occur in this position.
NAVAHO has been discussed. Syllabic n, ɲ, ŋ̦ in TRONDHEIM NOR-
WEGIAN occur in post-stressed final position from the particles
-en 'def. sg.' han '3rd p.m. sg.,' and final -Cen where C is alveolar
or palatal. Unstressed final -CVm, C labial, is rare in NORWEGIAN,
occurring only in a few loans such as 'minimum, 'album, which, like
'maraton, 'kanon, do not reduce, and in the compound prepositions
framom, oppom. Syllabic m̦ in STANDARD NORWEGIAN occurs
mainly in combinations of infinitive -med 'with,' as in komme med
[komm̦e:]. In the Trondheim dialect, the final -e of infinitives
has everywhere been lost, hence the pronunciation [kom.me:].
TSWANA final ŋ̦ is the realization of several suffixes. CANTON-
ESE m̦ and MINPEI CHINESE (Fuchou) ŋ̦ are negative particles.
IDOMA final m̦ is the 1st p. sg. object suffix; the only other object
suffix with a nasal is -anu '3rd p. sg.' Final ŋ̦, however, is one
of the negative particles, which also include no, ni. KAN CHINESE
n̦ is the 2nd p. sg. pronoun, cognate with HSIANG CHINESE n̦.

Alan Bell

Inventory of syllabic nasals	Number of language-systems	
	I[a]	II[b]
m̩	11	12
n̩	0	5
ŋ̩	7	5
m̩ n̩	0	12
m̩ ŋ̩	1	4
n̩ ŋ̩	0	1

[a]Systems whose inventories are not explainable by the prior distribution of nonsyllabic nasals.

[b]Total classification, repeated from Figure 3.

Figure 4. Classification of systems of syllabic nasals with incomplete inventories of nasal types.

The distribution of the incomplete inventory types is strikingly transformed by removal of the cases whose inventory reflected the pattern of occurrence of nonsyllabic nasals (Figure 4). The increase in ŋ inventories is at the expense of the m̩, ŋ and n̩, ŋ inventories in which only syllabic m̩ or n̩ had a restricted source. See note 34. There definitely appears to be some factor or factors in the processes of origin or mutation of syllabic nasals that favors m̩ and ŋ over n̩.

A minor process or origin of syllabic consonants, the assimilation of a vowel to the consonantality of an adjacent consonant, occurs in our sample only for m and ŋ. This accounts for JAPANESE m̩ and for YORUBA and DAN ŋ̩.

While it is most common for syncope to be accompanied or followed by assimilation of the nasal to a neighboring consonant, systems of one or two articulation types must necessarily avoid this process. This suggests the hypothesis that m is more resistant to assimilation than n. The hypothesis is supported by four languages, out of those which contain all three nasal types, in which m is the only syllabic nasal appearing in a heterorganic context.[35] Further

---

[35] CHAM, NGAMBAY SARA, SWAHILI and TSWANA. The SWAHILI and TSWANA initial syllabic nasal systems could be regarded

support was found in a preliminary survey of heterorganic clusters of stops and nasals (Bell 1970). To the extent that the results are generalizable to syllabic nasal systems, they indicate that n will assimilate more readily than m in word-initial systems, but that there is no preference in word-final systems. This generalization helps explain the pattern found in the four languages above with only heterorganic ṃ, for they are all word-initial systems. It does not happen to be a major factor in the predominance in this sample of inventory types with just syllabic ṃ, for only one of them (MAJINGAY SARA) is a word-initial system.

Another possibility is that syllabic ṃ and ŋ resist loss more than syllabic ṇ. If this is the case, its effect in the languages of our sample is slight. CZECH is the only language where this process may be applicable. MODERN CZECH has only syllabic ṃ. When it was originally formed by loss of the final jer, syllabic ṇ may also have been formed. If it was, soon afterward it mutated to -en, whereas the comparable development -ṃ > -um only began recently and is still in progress (see 3.5 above).

The remaining possibility that might account for the observed synchronic distribution of syllabic nasals is that ṃ and ŋ are favored in the main process of development by syncope. One important way that they are favored is connected with the apparent readiness with which they develop from original combinations with high, back, rounded vowels. Thus AKHA ṃ comes from um and am, AMUZGO ṃ from om (i e o a vowel system), HOTTENTOT ṃ from mu (and other sources too; but syllables of the form mu are missing entirely), final ṃ in LUGANDA from mu, medial ṃ in SWAHILI from mu, and in various CHINESE languages ŋ from ŋu.

The frequent development of m from mu in our data suggests a general statement of the sort "if any nasal-vowel sequence becomes a syllabic nasal, then mu becomes m (or a homorganic syllabic nasal)." This can be briefly symbolized by "NV > Ṇ $\implies$ mu > Ṇ."

(ftnt. 35 cont.)
as composed of two morphologically separate ones, a completely homorganic prefix (the 'class 9' prefix) and prefixes in ṃ (the 'class 1' and 'class 3' prefixes). There is also one language, KHASI, where ṇ is the only syllabic nasal appearing in heterorganic contexts. Of approximately 20 prefixes of the form CṆ-, just two, pṇ- 'causative' and mṇ- 'ago,' do not assimilate to the following consonant.

Certain qualifications need to be kept in mind. The statement per-
tains only to syncope of nonreduced vowels. It is also presumed
to apply to a set of nasal-vowel sequences in a given environment.

Even so qualified, the statement is clearly incomplete. Consider
a simple system in which the nine combinations of m, n, ŋ with the
three vowels u, i, a occur. It predicts the order of development
for the pairs of sequences if one is mu (8 pairs). But there are 28
other pairs of nasal + vowel sequences that it says nothing about.
In other words, the statement "NV > Ṇ ⟹ mu > Ṇ" tells us where
the change initiates in systems containing mu, but does not indicate
direction of spread. Further, for systems lacking the sequence
mu the statement is empty -- neither point of initiation nor spread
is predicted.

With these considerations in mind, I propose the following generalizations.

8.   In all languages, if in a given context nasal-vowel (NV)
sequences occur, and u represents the highest back rounded
vowel appearing in these sequences, then:
A.   NV > Ṇ ⟹ mu > Ṇ or ŋu > Ṇ, and
B. NV_{low} > Ṇ ⟹ NV_{nonlow} > Ṇ,
and similarly for contexts containing vowel-nasal sequences.

Some idea of the predictive power of 8. can be gained by applying
it to the nine-sequence system used earlier. In that system,
statement A establishes 14 preferences and B establishes 18
(of which A also covers 6), for a total of 26 out of a possible 36.
In that same system, 8. establishes a partial ordering, namely
(mu, ŋu) ⟹ (mi, nu, ni, ŋi) ⟹ (ma, na, ŋa).[36]

Now let us return to. our data and see how it supports 8. The
examples of AKHA, AMUZGO, HOTTENTOT, LUGANDA, and
SWAHILI already cited are clearly covered. A number of other
instances are not so obvious.

Syllabic m̩ occurs in both QUIOTEPEC and USILA CHINANTEC,
but is accorded a different phonemic identity in the descriptions.

---

[36]I take diachronic implicational statements such as 8. to apply
to the initiation of a change. Thus ŋa > Ṇ does not necessarily
imply ŋi > Ṇ (nor a mutation of mi, ni, nu) unless mu and ŋu are
lacking.

Robbins (1961a) phonemicizes m̩ as /mɨ/ in QUIOTEPEC CHINAN-
TEC ; mɨ, mö, and mü do not occur phonetically, although both mu
and mo occur. In USILA CHINANTEC, Skinner (1962) phonemicizes
m̩ as /ũ/; all vowels but /u/ occur nasalized. From the comparative study of OTOMANGEAN by Rensch (1966) it seems likely that
m̩ has a common origin in the two languages, since he gives at
least four cognate sets containing QUIOTEPEC and USILA m̩, for
instance 'rain' OJITLAN hmĩ, USILA ohũ, QUIOTEPEC hmɨ̃ ti,
PALANTLA hmi, LALANA hmĩh. Although PROTO-OTOMANGEAN
*u remained in PROTO-CHINANTECAN, there does not appear to
have been a PROTO-OTOMANGEAN *mu that remained in CHINAN-
TECAN. However, there may have been another source: "In environments where PCh *u occurs following most consonants, *ɨ,
whether an oral or a nasalized reflex, occurs following labial consonants. For example, POM *in > PCh *u following most consonants in PCh but > *ɨ following labials" (Rensch 1966:311).
Rensch indicates that QCh and UCh m̩ are reflexes of *mi. Another
explanation is possible. POM *in etc. could have developed to PCh
*u everywhere, including after labials. In some dialects mu > m̩,
which was retained in QCh and UCh, and otherwise *u > ɨ/ labial__.
This explanation requires the assumption of two competing changes
at the time the CHINANTECAN languages split, and is thus perhaps
somewhat less likely than the orderly development Rensch assumes.
If he is correct, it is the only example in our sample of m̩ developing initially by non-reduced vowel syncope from an unrounded vowel.
Even so, 8. would hold, if I am right that CHINANTECAN had no
*mu from PROTO-OTOMANGEAN.

Syllabic m̩ occurs in so few lexical items in the CHINESE languages that its development, though conforming in general to 8.,
is not very revealing. Syllabic m̩ occurs only in single lexical
items in CANTONESE, HAKKA, MANDARIN, and WU (Suchou),
and in four items in AMOY.[37] I do not know the origin of m̩ in
CANTONESE and HAKKA. In MANDARIN it is a reduction of
[mən], and in WU its source is probably mu. Of the AMOY items,
the source of one, glossed 'not,' is not apparent. Two vary with
mui and one varies with mau. The Zihui gives no instance of mu
in AMOY, and only one of mo.

---

[37]According to the dialect dictionary Hanyu Fangyin Zihui. The
statements of origin for CHINESE languages that follow are also
based on the dictionary, except MANDARIN, for which Chao (1968)
is the source. For the limitations of the Zihui see Lyovin (1969).

Syllabic ŋ, however, is much more common in the CHINESE
languages. WU, KAN, HAKKA, and CANTONESE have syllabic
ŋ derived from ŋu. HAKKA also has ŋ probably from ŋy (once),
and WENCHOU WU ŋ from sequences of ŋ with lower back vowels
and (once) from a high front vowel. All this is in accord with 8.
The relationship between m̩ and ŋ̩ is of interest here. Since these
languages have developed syllabic ŋ but not m̩ (KAN, WENCHOU
WU), or else have developed m̩ only in isolated instances (CAN-
TONESE, HAKKA, MANDARIN, SUCHOU WU), this argues for a
preference of ŋ̩ over m̩ in our processual hierarchy. However,
the evidence is not compelling, and I have preferred not to postulate a preference. In CANTONESE and SUCHOU WU, mu does not
occur. The vowel that is the source of syllabic ŋ̩ is lowered to o
after m in SUCHOU WU, and to ou in CANTONESE.[38] In HAKKA,
KAN, and WENCHOU WU, mu does occur. But WENCHOU WU
has only a single instance, the usual development being mo; HAKKA
has but two instances of mu; and KAN, in which mu is more usual,
has only a single word, 'five,' in syllabic ŋ̩ .

AMOY CHINESE is quite different from the other dialects in that
syllabic ŋ̩ has developed from syllables of the form CVn. The
historical picture is not entirely clear, but the main source appears
to be from original syllables in -aŋ which were raised to -ɔŋ.
Syllables corresponding to MANDARIN -uŋ are also -ɔŋ, but
these do not develop syllabic nasals. Syllabic ŋ̩ also appears to
have developed from -un in some cases, either through -uŋ or n̩.
The vowel+ nasal sequences now remaining in AMOY are -im, -am,
-in, -un, -an, -Iŋ, -ɔŋ, -aŋ.

Among NIGER-CONGO languages, the AKAN suffixes -mu, -mi,
-nu become syllabic in rapid speech; suffixes -ma and -na of the
same class do not. (There is also a suffix -ni that does not become
syllabic, but it may not have the same constituent structure.)
TSWANA prefixes mo- are syllabic m̩ before some labial stems;
the original form of the prefixes was *mu- and there are no mu-
prefixes in TSWANA today. YORUBA first person singular pronouns mó, má are homorganic syllabic N̩ before a class of preverbs.
Again, there are no mu forms in this context. The source of the

---

[38]The high vowel is retained in CANTONESE, HAKKA, and KAN
closed syllables, so that muk, mun, etc. occur. As already noted
in 3.4 above, complex syllables are apparently disfavored as sources
of syllabic consonants. Syllabic nasals do not develop from initial
nasals in closed syllables in the CHINESE languages.

IDOMA negative suffix -ŋ is unknown, but the occurrence of other negative suffixes -ni, -no̱ suggests that it might have come from the sequence -nV > -n̩ > ŋ.

A natural conjecture is that ni might be a favored source for n̩, analogous to mu and ŋu for m̩ and ŋ. There is some slight evidence for this. The principal source for HAUSA n̩ is the first person singular pronoun ni. The KAN and HSIANG CHINESE second person singular pronoun is n̩, derived from ni. NAVAHO prefixes ni- and na- reduce to n̩ before consonant-initial stems. Unfortunately, none of these cases offer a situation in which ni can be compared with nu, mi, or ŋi as a source of syllabic nasals.

The only such case in the sample occurs in TSWANA. Some TSWANA verbs in final -n take the causative suffix -isa, and are realized as -n̩tsha: <u>-bôna</u> 'see,' <u>-bôntsha</u> 'show.' Most verbs in final -n take the causative suffix -ya: <u>-fêna</u> 'succumb,' <u>-fênya</u> 'conquer.' These sometimes receive a second causative in -isa: <u>-fêntsha</u> 'cause to conquer.'[39] Verbs in final -m do not undergo this process: <u>huma</u> 'become rich,' <u>humisa</u> 'enrich.'

A parallel development occurs in NEW MEXICO SPANISH, where before the stressed diminutive -ita, syllabic m̩ and n̩ are formed from stems in final -m and -n: <u>bonita</u> bon̩ta, <u>lomita</u> lom̩ta.

Although the processual hierarchies of 8. are well-supported by our data, the picture of the development of syllabic nasals by non-reduced vowel syncope is incomplete in several respects, as I have pointed out. The best hope for filling in these details is to compare the outcomes of situations in which the critical sequences occur in the same context. This approach is exemplified in Bell 1972 by the comparison of the outcomes of BANTU noun-class prefixes mu-, mi-, and ma-.

Basically four diachronic factors in combination determine the synchronic distribution of syllabic nasal types. They are 1) the sources available for processes of origin; 2) the processes of origin; 3) processes of mutation; and 4) processes of loss. In each of these we have explored preferences for the nasal types, and it is possible,

---

[39]Nasals before consonants are syllabic in TSWANA. The penultimate syllable is long in TSWANA words, so that the syllabic nasals in these formations may be said to be accented. Orthographic <u>ny</u> represents [ɲ].

I think, to understand the observed synchronic distribution in a
general way from the preferences we have discovered in each of
the factors. However, our results are not yet a predictive model,
even in incomplete form, but rather the components for such a
model. It is still necessary to integrate the processual factors
and evaluate their relative importance, to the extent that this is
possible. The Markovian process-state models of syllable structure in Bell 1971 illustrate this approach in greater detail.

5. Syllabic Obstruents

Continuants are preferred over noncontinuants among syllabic
obstruents, as the classification of Figure 5 shows. I thus propose
the obvious generalization:

9. If a language contains syllabic stops or affricates, it contains syllabic fricatives.

		Syllabic noncontinuants	
		+	−
Syllabic	+	6	24
continuants	−	0	X

Figure 5.   Classification of languages with syllabic obstruents
according to the feature continuant. [40]

5.1   Fricatives at virtually all articulation points are attested
as syllabic: labiodental, alveolar, palatoalveolar, retroflex, palatal, velar, and pharyngeal, plus lateral and rounded fricatives.
One type is dominant. In every language (except KORYAK, discussed below) one of the fricatives is an alveolar or palatoalveolar
sibilant.

---

[40]Languages with syllabic continuants and noncontinuants: ARA-
BIAN and EGYPTIAN ARABIC, KORYAK, KWAKIUTL, LUGANDA,
SHILHA. Languages with only syllabic continuants: ACOMA, AHI,
CHIPAYA, FRENCH, HAKKA CHINESE, HSIANG CHINESE (Chang-
sha), HSIANG CHINESE (Hankow), GARO, JAPANESE (Kyuushuu),
JAPANESE (Standard), KAN CHINESE, LAHU, LENDU, MANDARIN
CHINESE, NAVAHO, NYI, PIRO, RUSSIAN, SIERRA NAHUAT, SIN-
HALESE, SPANISH (Mexican), WICHITA, WU CHINESE (Suchou),
WU CHINESE (Wenchou). Five languages could not be classified:
KABARDIAN, MOROCCAN ARABIC, SOMALI, TODA, ZUALA BER-
BER.

10. If a language possesses syllabic obstruents, it possesses syllabic ş or š̢, given that it has nonsyllabic s or š.

The last clause is added to provide for rare cases like KORYAK, which has no s but whose fricatives (β, v, y, ɣ, ʕ) may all be syllabic.

I assume that laryngeal aspirates belong to a system of syllabic fricatives if they become syllabic. The present sample contains no examples, but COLUMBIAN SALISH is reported to contain syllabic h̢ in those contexts where other syllabic fricatives occur. Thus the generalization:

11. If a language possesses a syllabic laryngeal h then it possesses syllabic fricatives. [41]

See 5.2 below for a similar statement regarding glottal stops.

It is remarkable that from our small sample of languages, three distinct types of systems of syllabic obstruents emerge: sibilant, fricative, and reduction systems.

Sibilant systems occur mainly in SINO-TIBETAN languages, which make up a large part of our sample (seven CHINESE languages and the LOLO-BURMISH languages AHI, LAHU, and NYI). Syllabic fricatives in these languages are coronal, strident, and voiced -- in other words, z-like sounds. In some cases there are contrasts between rounded and unrounded, or between retroflex and nonretroflex varieties. Their distribution is limited, occurring only after coronal fricatives and affricates. [42] The process of origin does not appear to be syncope, as with other systems of syllabic obstruents. It is rather an assimilation of a high vowel to the consonantality of the preceding sibilant, as attested by the syllabic

---

[41] This is only roughly correct. For example, AKAN h̢ noted in 3.6 casts doubt that all syllabic laryngeals must be part of a syllabic fricative system. Our meager data does not warrant more detailed conjecture, and the general idea that syllabic laryngeals are subordinate to other syllabic consonants is sound.

[42] In the languages of our sample. Spread to other environments is possible, since Egerod (1967) notes briefly three CHINESE dialects in which they appear elsewhere: NW MANDARIN of Wenshui (after p, m, t) (1967:103) and two WU dialects in SE Anwei (after n) (1967:110).

retaining the vowel's voicing and frequently its rounding. The only non-SINO-TIBETAN language with syllabics of this type is LENDU, a CENTRAL SUDANIC language.

Fricative systems contain only syllabic fricatives. Coronal fricatives predominate, but MEXICAN SPANISH and KYUUSHUU JAPANESE have syllabic f̩, and STANDARD JAPANESE syllabic f̩ and ç̩. The only instance of a voiced syllabic fricative in systems of this type is NAVAHO z̩, but except for MEXICAN SPANISH the other languages (ACOMA, CHIPAYA, GARO, SIERRA NAHUATL, WICHITA and those just cited) do not have voiced nonsyllabic fricatives. The source of this type of syllabic system is high-vowel syncope in all cases, except possibly CHIPAYA, for which I have no information. In ACOMA and JAPANESE the syncope is the final stage of vowel devoicing. This may be the general process for the whole class, in view of its preference for unvoiced fricatives (Greenberg 1969).

Reduction systems are those in which potentially all obstruents become syllabic. All the languages with syllabic stops belong to this type, as well as RUSSIAN and PIRO, which have only syllabic fricatives. The process of development for this type is reduced vowel syncope in all cases except perhaps LUGANDA. [43] Syllabic obstruents in such systems show no preference for voicing, reflecting whatever inventory of nonsyllabic obstruents the language possessed.

5.2   Up to now I have simply asserted the existence of syllabic stops, on the basis of the claims of half a dozen language descriptions. Some linguists may doubt their existence or even phonetic

---

[43]In LUGANDA when geminate consonants occur word-initially in the imperative form of the verb and in certain nouns, the first member is syllabic. The origin of gemination (initially and elsewhere) in LUGANDA is connected with a preceding PROTO-BANTU *i̯. For example, to LUGANDA -mma 'refuse' there corresponds NKORE -ima and KIKUYU -ima (Meeussen 1955). The vowel *i̯ was presumably very close and tense, but whatever its phonetic nature, it has produced consonantal mutations in many BANTU languages. Thus the gemination is understandable in a way, but the details of the loss of *i̯ or about its intermediate reflexes and the transfer of syllabicity are quite mysterious. They will remain so, in all likelihood, since the development of geminates is unique to LUGANDA among BANTU languages.

realizability. They are certainly realizable. An unreleased voiced stop, for example, can be uttered in isolation. Sivertsen (1960) reports just this kind of syllabic stop as occasional in COCKNEY ENGLISH in the word probably [probblei]. A more general distribution is found in LUGANDA, where all voiced stops may be syllabic in initial position.

Unvoiced stops are a more difficult problem. To be audible before another obstruent, they must be released. In languages which have been described as possessing syllables without vowels, such as BELLA COOLA, we always find that phonetically there is a release or transitional vocoid present. The question that must be asked is how such syllables should be specified in phonetic representation.

In some cases, the proper solution will be to accord the transition element the status of a segment. It will then bear the specification +syllabic. This is probably not a universally available solution.

The best evidence for this comes from SHILHA, a BERBER language, and KORYAK, a PALEOSIBERIAN language. In SHILHA, Applegate (1958) has reported that initial stops can form a syllable under certain circumstances. This is supported by the domain of tenseness, which in SHILHA is harmonic over the syllable. Thus [tfah:] 'apples' is monosyllabic and the initial t and f are tense; [tdu:] 'she went' is disyllabic and only the d is tense. (The symbol ':' stands for tenseness.) Applegate investigated the acoustic nature of the releases of such syllable-forming stops. He found that their formant frequencies corresponded to those found in word-final nonsyllabic stop releases -- in other words, the acoustic character of the release was inherent in the stop itself.

One might argue that such releases should still be segments in phonetic representation, standing for a vowel target that is unrealized because of the brevity of the segment. I would not deny that this may sometimes be the proper solution. However, it does not fit the attested facts for KORYAK. Kreinovič (1958) reported that the Koryaks deny there are vowels in certain syllables. He found that these syllables in fact contained a very short (three to four vibrations) vocalic element, as we would expect, but found it impossible to induce speakers to prolong this element. The conclusion is that the phonetic representation of KORYAK indeed contains syllables composed only of unvoiced stops. Parenthetically, it is worth noting that these syllables may take primary and secondary stress.

The crucial and fascinating question is how to specify the syllabicity of stops in such syllables. The choice is directly connected to what view we take of the essential nature of the syllable: if it is an obligatory nucleus to which marginal segments may be attached, then the stop is surely +syllabic; if on the other hand the essence of the syllable is that it consists of a mutually adherent group of segments with an optional nucleus, the specification −syllabic remains possible. Both must be considered seriously, and to my knowledge the presently available data do not indicate which is to be preferred. [44]

The choice would have a definitional effect on the limits of the segments that may be syllabic. If unvoiced stops constituting a syllable are +syllabic, then all segment classes may be syllabic; otherwise, only voiced stops may be syllabic. In either case, the following generalization would apply:

12. If a language possess voiceless syllabic stops, then it possesses voiced syllabic stops.

---

[44] The notion of syllables without nuclei calls to mind two earlier concepts of the syllable, the 'point vocalique' of de Saussure (1960: 87) and Grammont (1933: 102) and Hockett's (1955: 57) 'onset-type' syllable.

For de Saussure and Grammont the syllable consists of a sequence of rising segments ('à tension croissante') and falling segments ('à tension decroissante'). Between the last rising segment and the first falling segment lies the 'point vocalique.' This is the beginning of the peak vowel, if the syllable contains one, but the notion of a vowel or syllabic as an essential constituent of the syllable is denied. This is equivalent to eliminating 'syllabic' as a phonetic feature, and using instead some feature corresponding roughly to the distinction between initial and final margin.

Hockett's notion of onset-type syllable is not based on a general theory of the syllable, but on an ad hoc typology of syllable types, in which is included the so-called 'duration syllable' exemplified by JAPANESE. In certain languages like BELLA COOLA, Hockett says, all syllables contain at least an onset, and may also have a peak or coda. Thus the onset is nuclear, and peak and coda are satellites.

This statement is supported directly by LUGANDA, in which voiced stops may be syllabic, but not voiceless ones. [45]

The laryngeal noncontinuant, or glottal stop, is attested as syllabic in our sample only in KORYAK, where it behaves parallel to the other stops. Its presence in EGYPTIAN ARABIC may perhaps be inferred from the account of Harrell (1956), but he cites no examples. Like syllabic ḥ with fricatives, I conjecture that it occurs only in conjunction with a system of syllabic obstruents which includes stops:

13. If a language possesses the syllabic laryngeal ?, then it possesses syllabic obstruent stops.

6. Languages Cited

The languages used in the investigation, followed by the sources consulted, are listed alphabetically below.

ABAZA	Allen 1956
ACOMA	Miller 1965
AGUACATEC	McArthur and McArthur 1956
AHI	Miller 1969
AKAN	Schachter and Fromkin 1968,
	Welmers 1946
AKHA	Burling 1967
AMHARIC	Cohen 1936
AMUZGO	Bauernschmidt 1965
EASTERN ARABIAN ARABIC	Johnstone 1967a, 1967b
BELLA COOLA	Hockett 1955
CANTONESE	Cheng 1968
CHAM	Blood 1967
CHIPAYA	Olsen 1967
COLUMBIAN SALISH	M. Dale Kinkade (personal com.)

---

[45] At the phonetic level. At some higher level of the phonology, voiceless stops would probably also constitute syllables. The initial segments of the geminates (see end of 3.5) bear low tone, which, even if not phonetically realized, affects the tonal realization of the following syllables.

The generalization may not hold for a language without non-syllabic voiced stops. If so, a further condition would have to be added to 12.

CZECH	Komárek 1958, Kučera 1961
DAN	Bearth and Zemp 1967
EGYPTIAN ARABIC	Harrell 1956
ENGLISH	Bailey 1967, 1968, Bailey and Milner 1967, Dobson 1968
ENGLISH (Cockney)	Sivertsen 1960
ENGLISH (RP)	Jones 1959, Wells 1965
ENGLISH (Southern States)	Bailey 1969
FRENCH	Fouche 1959, Pulgram 1960/61, personal observation
HAKKA CHINESE	Henne 1965
HAUSA	Hodge 1947, Greenberg 1941
HOTTENTOT (Korana)	Beach 1938
HOTTENTOT (Nama)	Beach 1938
HSIANG CHINESE (Changsha)	Egerod 1967, Hànyǔ fāngyīn zìhùi
HSIANG CHINESE (Hankow)	Egerod 1967, Hànyǔ fāngyīn zìhùi
IDOMA	Abraham 1951
IJO	Williamson 1965
IRISH (Ring County)	Breatnach 1947
JAPANESE (Standard)	Bloch 1950, Martin 1952, 1959
JAPANESE (Southern Kyuushuu)	Wenck 1954
KABARDIAN	Kuipers 1960
KAN CHINESE	Egerod 1967, Hànyǔ fāngyīn zìhùi
KELE	Guthrie 1953
KHASI	Henderson 1965, Pinnow 1959, Rabel 1961
KHMER	Henderson 1952, Jacob 1960, 1966 Noss 1966
KHMU	Smalley 1961
KIKUYU	Barlow 1960
KOLAMI	Emeneau 1955
KORYAK	Kreinovič 1958
KWAKIUTL	Boas 1947
LAHU	Burling 1967, Matisoff 1969
LALANA CHINANTEC	Rensch 1966
LENDU	Tucker 1940
LIVONIAN	Marilyn Vihman (personal com.)
LUGANDA	Cole 1967, Meeussen 1955, Tucker 1962
MAMBILA	Perrin and Hill 1969
MANDARIN CHINESE	Chao 1948, 1968, Hockett 1947
MARGI	Hoffman 1963, Ladefoged 1968
MBE	Bamgboṣe 1967
MINNAN CHINESE (Amoy)	Egerod 1967, Hànyǔ fāngyīn zìhùi
MINNAN CHINESE (Gaoxiong)	Tung 1968

MINPEI CHINESE (Fuchou)   Egerod 1967, Hànyǔ fāngyīn zìhùi
MOROCCAN ARABIC   Harrell 1962a, 1962b, 1965
NAVAHO   Sapir and Hoijer 1967
NKORE   Meeussen 1955
NORWEGIAN (Bergen)   Personal observation
NORWEGIAN (Standard)   Christiansen 1928, 1930,
                               Naes 1930, Popperwell 1963
NORWEGIAN (Trondheim)   Sivertsen 1968, Vanvik 1966
NREBELE   Ziervogel 1948
NYI   Miller 1969
OJITLAN CHINANTEC   Rensch 1966
PACOH   Watson 1964
PALANTLA CHINANTEC   Rensch 1966
PALAUNG   Shorto 1960
NORTH PALESTINIAN ARABIC   Blanc 1963
PAME   Gibson 1956
PEKING CHINESE   Hànyǔ fāngyīn zìhùi
PIRO   Matteson 1965, Matteson and
                               Pike 1958
QUIOTEPEC CHINANTEC   Robbins 1961a, 1961b
RUMANIAN (Istrian)   Petrovici 1964
RUMANIAN (Standard)   Avram 1962, Rosetti 1964
RUSSIAN   Avanesov 1956, 1968, Isačenko
                               1947, Shapiro 1968
SANSKRIT   Allen 1953, Whitney 1960
SARA (Majingay)   Bouquiaux 1963, Hallaire and
                               Robinne 1955-59
SARA (Ngambay)   Vandame 1963
SHAKA   Müller 1947
SHILHA   Applegate 1958
SIERRA NAHUAT   Key and Key 1953
SINHALESE   Coates and de Silva 1960,
                               de Silva 1959
SIRIONÓ   Firestone 1965
SOMALI   Armstrong 1934, Pia 1965
SPANISH (Mexican)   Alonso 1930, Canellada and
                               Zamora Vicente 1960, Malmberg
                               1964
SPANISH (New Mexican)   Espinosa 1925
SQUAMISH   Kuipers 1967
SUSU   Houis 1963, Sangster and Faber 1968
SWAHILI   Polomé 1967
TODA   Emeneau 1957
TSWANA   Cole 1955
USILA CHINANTEC   Skinner 1962

WALAPAI	Redden 1966
WICHITA	Rood 1971, personal communication
WU CHINESE (Suchou)	Egerod 1967, Hǎnyǔ fāngyīn zìhui
WU CHINESE (Wenchou)	Hànyǔ fāngyīn zìhùi
YAKUR	Bendor-Samuel 1969
YAO	Purnell 1965
YORUBA	Bamgboṣe 1966, Siertsema 1957-58
ZUALA BERBER	Mitchell 1957

BIBLIOGRAPHY

Abraham, R.C. 1951. The Idoma language: Idoma wordlists, Idoma chrestomathy, Idoma proverbs. Lagos, Nigeria: Idoma Native Administration.

Allen, W. Sidney. 1953. Phonetics in ancient India. London: Oxford University Press.

_____. 1956. Structure and system in the Abaza verbal complex. Transactions of the Philological Society, 127-76.

Alonso, Amado. 1930. Problemas de dialectología hispanoamericana VIII. Consonantes silábicas. Biblioteca de dialectología hispano-americana 1.431-9.

Andersen, Henning. 1972. Diphthongization. Language 48. 11-50.

Applegate, Joseph R. 1958. Outline of the structure of Shilha. New York: American Council of Learned Societies.

Armstrong, Lilias E. 1934. The phonetic structure of Somali. Berlin. Republished 1964. Ridgewood, N.J.: Gregg Press.

Avanesov, R.I. 1956. Fonetika sovremennogo russkogo literaturnogo jazyka. Moscow: University of Moscow.

_____. 1968. Russkoe literaturnoe proiznoshenie. 4th ed. Moscow: Izdatel'stvo Prosveščenie.

Avram, Andrei. 1962. Interpretarea fonologică a lui [î] initial în limba romînă. Fonetica și Dialectologie 4. 7-23.

Bailey, Charles-James N. 1967. Problems in syllabification. Ditto.

Bailey, Charles-James N. 1968. Dialectical differences in the
    syllabification of nonnasal sonorants in American English. Gen-
    eral Linguistics 8. 79-91.

_____. 1969. Introduction to Southern States phonetics, IV:
    the obstruents. University of Hawaii Working Papers in Lin-
    guistics 5. 135-84.

Bamgboṣe, Ayo. 1966. A grammar of Yoruba. West African Lan-
    guage Monographs 5. Cambridge: Cambridge Univ. Press.

_____. 1967. Notes on the phonology of Mbe. J. of West African
    Languages 4. 5-11.

Barlow, A. Ruffell. 1960. Studies in Kikuyu grammar and idiom.
    Edinburgh: Blackwood.

Bauernschmidt, Amy. 1965. Amuzgo syllable dynamics.   Lan-
    guage 41. 471-83.

Beach, D.M. 1938. The phonetics of the Hottentot language. Cam-
    bridge: W. Heffner.

Bearth, Thomas and Hugo Zemp. 1967. The phonology of Dan
    (Santa). J. of African Languages 6. 9-29.

Bell, Alan. 1970. Heterorganic combinations of stop and nasal
    consonants. Syllabic consonants. Appendix. Working Papers
    on Language Universals 4. B32-B37. Stanford University,
    Committee on Linguistics.

_____. 1971. Some patterns of occurrence and formation of
    syllable structures. Working Papers on Language Universals
    6. 23-137. Stanford University, Committee on Linguistics.

_____. 1972. The development of syllabic nasals in the Bantu
    noun class prefixes mu-, mi-, and ma-. Anthropological Lin-
    guistics 14. 29-45.

Bendor-Samuel, J.T. 1969. Yakur syllable patterns. Word 25.16-23.

Blanc, Haim. 1953. Studies in North Palestinian Arabic. Jeru-
    salem: Israel Oriental Society.

Bloch, Bernard. 1950. Studies in colloquial Japanese IV, pho-
    nemics. Language 26. 86-125.

Blood, David L. 1967. Phonological units in Cham. Anthropological Linguistics 9. 8. 15-32.

Boas, Franz. 1947. Kwakiutl grammar, with a glossary of suffixes.
Transactions of the American Philosophical Society 37. 3. Philadelphia: American Philosophical Society.

Bouquiaux, L. 1963. A propos de la phonologie du sara. J. of
African Languages 3. 260-72.

Breatnach, Ristead B. 1947. The Irish of Ring Co. Waterford:
a phonetic study. Dublin: Dublin Institute for Advanced Studies.

Brücke, Ernst. 1876. Grundzüge der Physiologie und Systematik
der Sprachlaute. 2nd ed. Vienna: C. Gerold's Sohn.

Brugmann, Karl. 1876. Nasalis sonans in der indogermanischen
Grundsprache. Curtius Studien 9. 287-338. Reprinted in
A reader in nineteenth-century historical Indoeuropean linguis-
tics, ed. by W. P. Lehmann, 190-96. Bloomington: Indiana
Univ. Press.

Burling, Robbins. 1967. Proto Lolo-Burmese. IJAL 33. 2, part II.

Canellada, M. J. and A. Zamora Vicente. 1960. Vocales caducas
en el español mexicano. Nueva revista de filología hispanica 14.
222-41.

Chao, Yuen Ren. 1948. Mandarin primer, an intensive course in
spoken Chinese. Cambridge, Mass.: Harvard Univ. Press.

_____. 1968. A grammar of spoken Chinese. Berkeley and
Los Angeles: University of California Press.

Cheng, Teresa. 1968. The phonological system of Cantonese.
Project on Linguistic Analysis, 2nd Series 5. C1-C85. Berkeley:
Phonology Laboratory, University of California.

Chomsky, N. and M. Halle. 1968. The sound pattern of English.
New York, Evanston, and London.

Christiansen, H. 1928. Silbendegeneration und -generation im
Norwegischen. Norsk Tideskrift for Sprogvidenskap 2. 306-17.

_____. 1930. Über die Spannung in silbenbildenden Konsonanten
im Norwegischen. Norsk Tideskrift for Sprogvidenskap 4. 71-5.

Coates, William A. and M. W. S. de Silva. 1960. The segmental phonemes of Sinhalese. University of Ceylon Review 18. 163-75.

Cohen, Marcel. 1936. Traité de langue amharique. Paris: Institut d'Ethnologie.

Cole, D. T. 1955. Introduction to Tswana grammar. N. Y.:Longmans.

_____. 1967. Some features of Ganda linguistic structure. Johannesburg: Witwatersrand University Press. (African Studies 24. 3-54, 71-116, 199-240.)

Dixon, R. M. W. 1970. Olgolo syllable structure and what they are doing about it. Linguistic Inquiry 1. 273-276.

Dobson, E. J. 1968. English pronunciation 1500-1700, II, phonology. 2nd ed. Oxford: Clarendon Press.

Egerod, Søren. 1967. Dialectology. Current trends in linguistics, II, Linguistics in East Asia and South East Aisa, ed. by Thomas A. Sebeok, 91-129. The Hague: Mouton.

Elson, Benjamin and Comas. 1961. A Wm. Cameron Townsend en el vig-ésimoquinto aniversario del Instituto Lingüístico de Verano. Mexico.

Emeneau, Murray B. 1957. Toda, a Dravidian language. Trans-actions of the Philological Society, 15-66.

Espinosa, A. M. 1925. Syllabic consonants in New Mexican Spanish. Language 1. 109-18.

Ferguson, Charles A. 1966. Assumptions about nasals: a sample study in phonological universals. Universals of language, ed. by Joseph H. Greenberg, 53-60. 2nd ed. Cambridge: MIT Press.

Firestone, Homer L. 1965. Description and classification of Siriono, a Tupí-Guaraní language. Janua linguarum, ser. prac-tica 16. The Hague: Mouton.

Fletcher, Harvey. 1929. Speech and learning. N. Y.: Van Nostrand.

Fouché, Pierre. 1956. Traité de prononciation français. Paris: Klincksieck.

Gibson, Lorna F. 1956. Pame (Otomi) phonemics and morpho-phonemics. IJAL 22. 242-65.

Grammont, Maurice. 1933. Traité de phonetique. 8th ed. Paris: Delagrave.

Greenberg, Joseph H. 1941. Some problems in Hausa phonology. Language 17. 316-23.

_____. 1965. Some generalizations concerning initial and final consonant sequences. Linguistics 18. 5-34.

_____. 1966. Language universals. Current trends in linguistics III, ed. by T.A. Sebeok, 61-112. The Hague.

_____. 1969. Some methods of dynamic comparison in linguistics. Substance and structure of language, ed. by Jaan Puhvel, 147-203. Berkeley and Los Angeles: University of California Press.

_____ and Dorothea Kaschube. 1976. Word prosodic systems: a preliminary report. Working Papers on Language Universals 20. 1-18. Stanford University, Department of Linguistics.

Guthrie, M. 1953. The Bantu languages of western equatorial Africa. London: Oxford University Press.

Hála, Bohuslav. 1961. La syllabe, sa nature, son origine, ses transformations. Orbis 10. 69-143.

Hallaire, J. and J. Robinne. 1955-59. Dictionnaire sara-français. Koumra-Fourrière. Mimeo.

Hànyǔ fāngyīn zìhuì. 1962. Peking: Wénzì gǎigé chūbǎnshè.

Harrell, Richard S. 1956. The phonology of colloquial Egyptian Arabic. Ph.D. dissertation, Harvard University. (Manuscript version.)

_____. 1962a. Consonant, vowel and syllable in Moroccan Arabic. Proceedings of the Fourth International Congress of Phonetic Sciences, Helsinki, 1961, 643-7. The Hague: Mouton.

_____. 1962b. A short reference grammar of Moroccan Arabic. Washington: Georgetown University Press.

_____. 1965. A basic course in Moroccan Arabic. Washington: Georgetown University Press.

Heffner, R-M. S. 1950. General phonetics. Madison: University of Wisconsin Press.

Henderson, Eugenie J. A. 1952. The main features of Cambodian pronunciation. Bulletin of the School of Oriental and African Studies 12. 149-74.

_____. 1965. Final -k in Khasi: a secondary phonological pattern. Lingua 14. 459-66.

Henne, Henry. 1965. Sathewkok Hakka phonology. Norsk Tide-skrift for Sprogvidenskap 20. 109-61.

Hockett, Charles F. 1947. Peiping phonology. Journal of the American Oriental Society 67. 253-67.

_____. 1955. A manual of phonology. IJAL Memoir 11.

Hodge, Carleton T. 1947. An outline of Hausa grammar. Lan-guage dissertation 41. (Supplement to Language 23.4.)

Hoffmann, Carl. 1963. A grammar of the Margi language. London: Oxford University Press.

Houlihan, Kathleen. 1973. On a universal rule for syllabic seg-ments. Minnesota Working Papers in Linguistics and Philosophy of Language 1. 53-61.

Houis, Maurice. 1963. Etude descriptive de la langue susu. Memoir de l'Institut Français de l'Afrique Noir 67. Dakar.

Hyman, Larry. 1975. On the nature of linguistic stress. Studies on stress and accent, ed. by L. Hyman, 37-82. Los Angeles: University of Southern California.

Isačenko, A. V. 1947. Fonetika spisovnej Ruštiny. Bratislava: Slovenská akadémia vied a umení.

Jacob, Judith M. 1960. The structure of the word in Old Khmer. Bulletin of the School of Oriental and African Studies 23. 351-68.

_____. 1966. Some features of Khmer versification. In memory of J. R. Firth, ed. by C. E. Bazell et al., 227-47. London: Longmans.

Jespersen, Otto. 1904. Lehrbuch der Phonetik. Leipzig: B. G. Teubner.

Johnstone, T.M. 1967a. Eastern Arabic dialect studies. London: Oxford University Press.

Johnstone, T.M. 1967b. Aspects of syllabication in the spoken Arabic of 'Anaiza. Bulletin of the School of Oriental and African Studies 30. 1-16.

Jones, Daniel. 1959. The use of syllabic and non-syllabic l and n in derivatives of words ending in syllabic l and n. Zeitschrift für Phonetik, Sprachwissenschaft und Kommunikations-forschung 12. 136-44.

Key, Harold and Mary Key. 1953. The phonemes of Sierra Nahuat. IJAL 19. 53-6.

Komárek, Miroslav. 1958. Historická mluvnice Česká. Prague: Státní Pedagogické Nakladatelství.

Kreinovič, E.A. 1958. Opyt issledovanija struktury sloga v korjakskom jazke. Doklady i soobščenija instituto jazykoznanija. Akad. nauk SSSR 11. 151-67.

Kučera, Henry. 1961. The phonology of Czech. The Hague: Mouton.

Kuipers, Aert H. 1960. Phoneme and morpheme in Kabardian. The Hague: Mouton.

_____. 1967. The Squamish language, grammar, texts, dictionary. The Hague: Mouton.

Ladefoged, Peter. 1968. A phonetic study of West African languages. 2nd ed. Cambridge: Cambridge Univ. Press.

Lyovin, Anatole. 1968. Review of Hànyŭ fāngyīn zìhuì. Language 45. 687-97.

Malécot, André. 1960. Nasal syllabics in American English. Studia Linguistica 14. 47-56.

Malmberg, Bertil. 1964. Note sur la structure syllabique de l'espagnol mexicain. Zeitschrift für Phonetik, Sprachwissenschaft und Kommunikationsforschung 17. 251-5.

Martin, Samuel E. 1952. Morphophonemics of Standard Colloquial Japanese. Language dissertation 47. (Supplement to Language 28. 3.)

Martin, Samuel E. 1959. Review of Japanische Phonetik, by von Günther Wenck. Language 35. 270-82.

Matisoff, James A. 1969. Review of Proto Lolo-Burmese by Robbins Burling. Language 44. 879-97.

Matteson, Esther. 1965. The Piro (Arawakan) language. UCPL 42. Berkeley and Los Angeles: University of California Press.

_____ and Kenneth L. Pike. 1958. Non-phonemic transition vocoids in Piro (Arawak). Miscellanea Phonetica 3. 11-30.

McArthur, Harry and Lucille McArthur. 1956. Aguacatec (Mayan) phonemes within the stress group. IJAL 22. 72-6.

Meeussen, A. E. 1955. Les phonèmes du ganda et du bantou commun. Africa 25. 170-80.

Miller, Roy Andrew. 1969. The Tibeto-Burman languages of South Asia. Current trends in linguistics, V, Linguistics in South Asia, ed. by Thomas A. Sebeok, 431-49. New York: Humanities Press.

Miller, Wick R. 1965. Acoma grammar and texts. UCPL 40. Berkeley and Los Angeles: University of California Press.

Mitchell, T. F. 1957. Long consonants in phonology and phonetics. Studies in linguistics, 182-205. Oxford: Philological Society.

Müller, Emil. 1947. Wörterbuch der Djaga-Sprache (Madjame-Mundart). Hamburg: Eckardt and Messtorff.

Naes, Olav. 1965. Norsk grammatik, elementaere strukturer og syntaks. 2nd ed. Oslo: Fabritius and Sønners.

Noss, Richard B. 1966. The treatment of */R/ in two modern Khmer dialects. Studies in comparative Austroasiatic linguistics, ed. by Norman H. Zide, 88-95. (Indo-Iranian Monographs 5.) The Hague: Mouton.

Olsen, Ronald D. 1967. The syllable in Chipaya. IJAL 33. 300-04.

Perrin, Mona J. and Margaret V. Hill. 1969. Mambila (parler d'Atta) description phonologique. Université fédérale du Cameroun, Section de linguistique appliquée.

Alan Bell

Petrovici, Emile. 1964. Résistance du système phonologique à une forte influence phonétique étrangère -- à propos des sonants "syllabiques" istro-roumaines r̩, n̩ et m̩. Zeitschrift für Phonetik, Sprachwissenschaft und Kommunikationsforschung 17. 281-5.

Pia, John Joseph. 1965. Somali sounds and inflections. Ph.D. dissertation, Indiana University.

Pinnow, Heinz-Jurgen. 1959. Versuch einer historischen Lautlehre der Kharia-Sprache. Wiesbaden: O. Harrassowitz.

Polomé, Edgar C. 1967. Swahili language handbook. Washington, D.C.: Center for Applied Linguistics.

Popperwell, R.G. 1963. The pronunciation of Norwegian. Cambridge and Oslo: Cambridge Univ. Press and Oslo Univ. Press.

Pulgram, Ernst. 1960-61. French /ə/: statics and dynamics of linguistic subcodes. Lingua 10. 305-25.

Purnell, Herbert, Jr. 1965. Phonology of a Yao dialect. Hartford Studies in Linguistics 15. Hartford: Hartford Seminary Foundation.

Rabel, Lili. 1961. Khasi, a language of Assam. Baton Rouge: Louisana State Univ. Press.

Redden, James E. 1966. Walapai I: phonology. IJAL 32. 1-16.

Rensch, Calvin R. 1966. Proto-Otomangean phonology. Ph.D. dissertation, University of Pennsylvania.

_____ and Carolyn M. Rensch. 1966. The Lalana Chinantec syllable. Summa anthropologica en homenaje a Robert J. Weitlaner, ed. by Antonio Pompa y Pompa, 455-63. Mexico.

Robbins, Frank E. 1961a. Quiotepec Chinantec syllable patterning. IJAL 27. 237-50.

_____. 1961b. Palabras nasales sin vocales foneticas en el chinanteco de Quiotepec. In Elson and Comas, 653-6.

Rood, David S. 1971. Wichita: an unusual phonology system. Colorado Research in Linguistics 1. R1-R24.

Rosetti, A. 1962. La syllable phonologique. Proceedings of the
Fourth International Congress of Phonetic Sciences, Helsinki,
1961, 490-9. The Hague: Mouton.

_____. 1964. Remarques sur les voyelles roumaines ă et î.
Zeitschrift für Phonetik, Sprachwissenschaft und Kommunikationsforschung 17. 293-5.

Sangster, Linda and Emmanuel Faber. 1968. Susu basic course.
Final report, Project 6-2320, U.S. Department of Health,
Education and Welfare.

Sapir, Edward and Harry Hoijer. 1967. The phonology and morphology of the Navaho language. UCPL 50. Berkeley and Los
Angeles: University of California Press.

de Saussure, Ferdinand. 1960. Cours de linguistique générale.
3rd edition. Paris: Payot.

Schachter, Paul and Victoria Fromkin. 1968. A phonology of
Akan: Akuapem, Asanti, and Fante. Working Papers in Phonetics 9. Los Angeles: UCLA Phonetics Laboratory.

Shapiro, Michael. 1968. Russian phonetic variants and phono-
stylistics. UCPL 49. Berkeley and Los Angeles: University
of California Press.

Shorto, H. L. 1960. Word and syllable patterns in Palaung.
Bulletin of the School of Oriental and African Studies 23. 552-3.

Siertsema, B. 1957-8. Problems of phonemic interpretation, I,
Nasalized sounds in Yoruba. Lingua 7. 356-66.

Sievers, Edward. 1876. Grundzüge der Lautphysiologie. Leipzig:
Breitkopf and Hartel.

_____. 1893. Grundzüge der Phonetik. 4th ed. Leipzig: Breit-
kopf and Hartel.

de Silva, M. W. S. 1959. Syllable structure in spoken Sinhalese: a
prosodic statement. University of Ceylon Review 17. 106-16.

Sivertsen, Eva. 1960. Cockney phonology. Oslo: Oslo University
Press.

Sivertsen, Eva. 1968. Review of A phonetic-phonemic analysis of the dialect of Trondheim, by Arne Vanvik. Norsk Tideskrift for Sprogvidenskap 22. 136-44.

Skinner, Leo E. 1962. Usila Chinantec syllable structure. IJAL 28. 251-5.

Smalley, William A. 1961. Outline of Khmu? structure. New Haven: American Oriental Society.

Sommer, Bruce. 1969. Kunjen phonology: synchronic and dia-chronic. Pacific Linguistics. Series B-Monographs 11. Canberra: Australian National University.

Sweet, Henry. 1877. A handbook of phonetics. Oxford: Clarendon Press.

Trubetzkoy, N. 1949. Principes de phonologie. Paris.

Tucker, A.N. 1940. The eastern Sudanic languages, I. London: Dawsons.

_____. 1962. The syllable in Luganda: a prosodic approach. J. of African Languages 1. 122-66.

Tung, Chao-hui. 1968. The phonological system of Gaoxiong, a Min dialect of Chinese. Project on Linguistic Analysis, 2nd series 5. T1-T77. Berkeley: Phonology Laboratory, Univ. of California.

Vandame, Charles. 1963. Le Ngambay-Moundou: phonologie, grammaire, et textes. Memoir de l'Institut Francais de l'Afrique Noir 69. Dakar.

Vanvik, Arne. 1966. A phonetic-phonemic analysis of the dialect of Trondheim. Oslo: Oslo Univ. Press.

Watson, Richard. 1964. Pacoh phonemes. Mon-Khmer Studies I, ed. by John E. Banker et al., 135-48. Saigon: Linguistic Circle of Saigon and the Summer Institute of Linguistics.

Wells, J.C. 1965. The phonological status of syllabic consonants in English RP. Phonetica 13. 110-13.

Welmers, William Everett. 1946. A descriptive grammar of Fanti. Language dissertation 39. (Supplement to Language 22.3.)

Wenck, von Günther. 1954. Japanische Phonetik, I. Wiesbaden: O. Harrassowitz.

Whitney, W.D. 1960. Sanskrit grammar. 2nd ed. Cambridge, Mass.: Harvard University Press.

Williamson, Kay. 1965. A grammar of the Kolokuma dialect of Ijo. West African Language Monograph Series 2. London: Cambridge University Press.

Ziervogel, D. 1948. Notes on the noun classes of Swati and Nrebele. African Studies 7. 59-70.

Nasal Vowels

MERRITT RUHLEN

ABSTRACT

This paper is an investigation of nasal vowels from both a synchronic and diachronic perspective. We will attempt to determine
what constitutes a natural system of nasal vowels, as well as what
universal phonological processes lead to these natural synchronic
states. Section 1 sketches the geographical and genetic distribution
of languages with nasal vowels. Section 2 discusses the definitional
properties of nasal vowels, and section 3 reviews previous studies
of the topic. Section 4 and 5 deal, respectively, with synchronic
and diachronic aspects of vowel nasalization. Finally, in section
6 several avenues for further research are proposed.

A preliminary version of this paper was published in Working
Papers on Language Universals, 12, 1973.

Merritt Ruhlen

CONTENTS

1. Geographical and Genetic Distribution of Nasal Vowels

Unlike nasal consonants (NC's), which are found in practically every human language, nasal vowels (NV's) enjoy a more limited distribution. Not only are they found more frequently in certain areas of the world, but, in addition, they are more common in some language families than others. The present study is based on a language sample of roughly 700 languages, of which approximately 150 possess NV's (cf. Ruhlen 1975a for the phonological segments of these languages and a list of sources used; the languages with NV's are given in the Appendix to this paper).

In geographical terms NV's are extremely common in the western half of Sub-Saharan African, northern India, central Mexico, and South America. They are somewhat less widespread in Europe, the Caucasus, southeast Asia (including China), and North America. NV's are apparently quite rare in north and east Africa, north Asia, Australia, and Oceania. The genetic affiliation of languages with NV's is shown in the table on the following page.

2. Some Preliminary Definitions

What is a nasal vowel? From a physiological point of view one might be tempted to define a NV as a vowel produced with the velum at least partially lowered so that air may escape through both the mouth and the nose. However, linguists have long recognized that the mere physical presence of nasality is not in itself sufficient to define what have traditionally been called NV's. For example, it is well known that vowels adjacent to NC's are often at least partially nasalized, so that ENGLISH man is phonetically [mæ̃n]. The fact that the vowel of man is phonetically nasalized has not, in general, prevented linguists from considering it an 'oral' vowel, phonemically, for the simple reason that such nasalization is phonetically conditioned by the surrounding segments. Thus linguists have insisted that the nasalization of a NV must be in some sense inherent (intrinsic, phonemic, underlying, non-contingent, etc.) in the vowel, and not phonetically conditioned. The term NV has consequently been reserved for vowels that (I) show marked nasalization and (II) contrast phonetically with the corresponding oral vowel (OV). The vowel [æ̃] of man is not a NV according to these criteria because condition II is not satisfied. There is no form *[mæn] in ENGLISH which contrasts with [mæ̃n]. More strongly, ENGLISH phonological structure does not allow phonetic forms such as *[mæn] since such forms would violate an obligatory phonetic rule which nasalizes all oral vowels in a certain phonetic context.

The Genetic Affiliation of Languages with Nasal Vowels

FAMILY	Languages with NV's	Languages in Sample
AFRO-ASIATIC	0	29
NIGER-KORDOFANIAN	27	51
NILO-SAHARAN	1	25
KHOISAN	4	4
INDO-EUROPEAN	19	73
CAUCASIAN	14	37
URALIC	0	23
ALTAIC	1	39
PALEOSIBERIAN	0	8
DRAVIDIAN	2	10
SINO-TIBETAN	3	18
AUSTRO-ASIATIC	6	17
INDO-PACIFIC	3	51
AUSTRALIAN	0	24
AUSTRO-TAI	2	67
ESKIMO-ALEUT	0	5
NA-DENE	8	12
MACRO-ALGONQUIAN	2	13
SALISH	0	10
WAKASHAN	0	2
MACRO-SIOUAN	8	12
PENUTIAN	0	43
HOKAN	1	19
AZTEC-TANOAN	3	15
OTO-MANGUEAN	13	14
MACRO-CHIBCHAN	6	10
GE-PANO-CARIB	9	24
ANDEAN-EQUATORIAL	23	39
Language Isolates	0	12
TOTAL	155	706

This, however, raises the question of how allophonic nasalization such as is found in ENGLISH man is to be specified in a grammar. If the articulatory accommodation between an oral vowel and a following NC resulted in the same strength of nasalization in all languages, then the problem could be disposed of quite simply by positing a single universal rule which would specify the degree to which vowels are nasalized when preceding (or following) NC's. This does not appear to be the case, however, with respect to rules of accommodation between vowels and velar stops. Ladefoged (1971b: 55) points out that "in FRENCH the influence of the vowel on a following velar stop in words such as pique and pâque seems to be far greater than the influence of the vowel on the following stop in ENGLISH words such as peak and pock. We do not know if this is entirely due to differences in the targets of the vowels in FRENCH and ENGLISH; or whether, in addition to differences in targets, there are also differences in the conjoining rules. My present guess is that conjoining rules are not entirely language independent."

Recently Clumeck 1975 has found evidence that the 'conjoining rules' for oral vowels and NC's cannot be universally specified since languages differ in the degree of allophonic nasalization in both nasal and non-nasal environments. In PORTUGUESE and HINDI any NC appreciably nasalizes a preceding vowel, while in FRENCH and AMOY such allophonic nasalization is far less pronounced (cf. Clumeck 1975: 141). We might then specify allophonic nasalization in one of two ways. Either we postulate a set of universal conjoining rules, and then further specify how individual languages differ from the predictions of these universal rules, or else we simply posit language specific conjoining rules. The latter approach is somewhat unattractive in that it ignores the fact that there is certainly some natural accommodation between segments that is a direct consequence of the physiology of the vocal tract. The former hypothesis, however, poses the problem of how one is to determine just what this 'natural accommodation' is, and why languages differ from it in one direction or another. Clearly the specification of allophonic nasalization is a complex question that merits further investigation.

PORTUGUESE, unlike ENGLISH, is traditionally considered to have NV's. On the basis of such minimal pairs as:

(1) [vi] 'I saw'

(2) [vĩ] 'I came'

many linguists have argued that the nasalization of the vowel in (2)
is an intrinsic property of that vowel, and serves to distinguish (2)
from (1). According to this view speakers differentiate (1) and (2)
by the presence or absence of nasalization in the vowel.

Many European structuralists (cf. also Trager 1944), and more
recently generative grammarians, have argued that conditions I
and II are themselves not sufficient to establish the intrinsic nature
of vowel nasalization. On the basis of such minimal pairs as
FRENCH:

(3) [bo] 'beautiful' (m. sg.)

(4) [bõ] 'good' (m. sg.)

they argue that in spite of the surface contrast between [o] and [õ],
the feature [+nasal] is not an inherent property of the vowel in (4),
but is rather conditioned, not by phonetic structure, but by the
morphophonemic structure of FRENCH. Thus in order to show
that [bõ] 'good' (m. sg.) and [bɔn] 'good' (f. sg.) represent a single
lexical item, both surface forms are derived from the same underlying representation: /bon-/

PHONOLOGICAL LEVEL	/bon/	/bon+ ə/
Vowel Nasalization	bõn	
n̠ Deletion	bõ	
Schwa Deletion		bon
Vowel Lowering		bɔn
PHONETIC LEVEL	[bõ]	[bɔn]

Under this more restricted view the feature of nasality is considered
to be intrinsic only if it cannot be independently motivated from eithe
phonetic or morphophonemic structure. In ENGLISH man the nasali
of the vowel is phonetically conditioned; in FRENCH bon it is morphophonemically conditioned; in PORTUGUESE vim it is presumabl
unconditioned.

On the basis of the above discussion we may define three kinds
of NV's:

Definition 1: A phonetic NV is a vowel which is phonetically
                  nasalized.

Definition 2: A phonemic NV is a vowel which (I) is phonetically
                  nasalized, and (II) where the feature [+nasal] is not
                  predictable in terms of phonetic structure.

<u>Definition 3</u> :   A <u>phonological</u> NV is a vowel which (I) is phoneti-
cally nasalized, and (II) where the feature [+nasal]
is not predictable in terms of either (a) phonetic or
(b) grammatical structure.

Whatever other merits the above taxonomy may have, it is in-
dispensable in interpreting the available literature, where a failure
to distinguish different kinds of NV's has often led to misunder-
standing, and in many cases sterile debate. It is, for example,
futile to attempt to determine the date at which NV's arose in a
given language if one does not specify what type of NV's (phonetic,
phonemic, or phonological) he has in mind. All too often such
terminological questions have taken the guise of substantive discussion. For the most part, however, NV is used in the literature
to designate phonemic NV's, which in many, but by no means all,
cases are also phonological NV's.

Finally it should be noted that there is not necessarily a direct
correlation between the strength of nasalization and the type of NV,
though we might expect that, in general, phonological and phonemic
NV's would show greater nasality than phonetic NV's (this is surely
true of FRENCH). Nevertheless, Jackson (1967: 42) indicates that
in the LÉONAIS dialect of BRETON allophonic nasality may at
times be as strong as phonemic nasality, and Ferguson and
Chowdhury (1960: 37) report that in BENGALI "it sometimes happens that the nasal quality of a phonemically oral vowel next to a
nasal consonant is more striking phonetically than the nasal quality
of a phonemically nasal vowel." In POLISH the strength of nasality
in (phonological) NV's is at times so slight that some linguists have
argued that such vowels are in fact not nasalized at all (cf. Zagórska-
Brooks 1968). Surely a thorough cross-language comparison of the
strength of nasality in NV's would show even more overlapping than
occurs in the specific languages cited above.

3. Previous Studies

One of the earliest attempts to specify universals relating to
vowel nasalization is Issatschenko 1937. While his main thesis
(that oral vowel systems 'control' NV systems in the sense that if
the oral vowels form a triangular (quadrangular, etc.) pattern,
then the NV's must also constitute a similar pattern) appears today
somewhat dubious, we may still credit him with explicitly recognizing that the relationship between oral vowels and NV's in a given
language is far from arbitrary. This relationship is usually, if not
always, quite intimate, from a synchronic as well as from a diachronic

perspective. Issatschenko was certainly on firm ground when he
wrote that "on peut affirmer d'une manière générale que les sys-
tèmes des voyelles nasales sont plus pauvres que ceux des voyelles
orales." (270) (cf. Ferguson's universal 11 below). Nevertheless,
Issatschenko posited a number of other universals which we now
know to be incorrect: e.g. (1) No language may possess only one
NV. (2) Denasalization never affects a single vowel, but rather
must affect the whole class of NV's simultaneously. (3) NV's are
always a proper subset of the oral vowels. (4) No language opposes
long and short NV's.

A more recent investigation of universals, with respect to
both NV's and NC's, is found in Ferguson 1963. In that article
Ferguson proposed fifteen universals, five of which deal directly
with NV's:

10. No language has NV's unless it also has one or more
    P[rimary] N[asal] C[onsonant]'s.

11. In a given language the number of NV's is never greater
    than the number of nonnasal vowel phonemes.

12. In a given language the frequency of occurrence of NV's
    is always less than that of nonnasal vowels.

13. When in a given language there is extensive neutralization
    of NV's with oral vowels, this occurs next to nasal con-
    sonants.

14. NV's, apart from borrowing and analogical formations,
    always result from the loss of a PNC.

Several observations may be made concerning these five universals. First of all, as Ferguson notes, universal 10 is really
a corollary of his first universal:

1. Every language has at least one PNC in its inventory.

Ferguson mentions three languages as exceptions to this universal.
More recently Thompson and Thompson 1972 have discussed these
nasalless languages, indicating that each belongs to a different
language family. The authors also cite other nasalless languages
not referred to by Ferguson.

In addition to the languages discussed by Thompson and Thompson,
which lack NC's phonetically, several linguists have recently

proposed that some African languages lack NC's phonologically, though not phonetically. Thus, Schachter and Fromkin 1968, Hyman 1972, and Rouget 1972 all claim that the phonetic NC's of certain KWA languages derive from underlying voiced stops which become nasal when followed by a NV:

/bã/ $\longrightarrow$ [mã]

If indeed NC's do derive from underlying voiced stops in this way (which I doubt), then these KWA languages would constitute counterexamples not only to universal 1, but also to universal 10. Universals 1 and 10 thus appear to represent the normal state of affairs in the vast majority of the world's languages, but here and there exceptions to the rule may crop up.

Greenberg 1966 points out that universals 11 and 12 are in fact deducible from Ferguson's last universal about NV's (i.e. 14). While universals 10-13 represent constraints on synchronic states, universal 14 is diachronic in nature, specifying how NV's may arise. Assuming the validity of universal 14, Greenberg argues that universals 11 and 12 are then simply consequences of the historic origin of NV's. If NV's do indeed develop from earlier sequences of oral vowel + nasal consonant, it follows that the number of NV's cannot exceed the number of oral vowels (universal 11), and furthermore, the frequency of occurrence of oral vowels + N was surely less than the frequency of oral vowels not followed by N (universal 12). This should not be taken to mean that the frequency of each NV is always less than that of its oral partner; as Greenberg notes, subsequent merger of NV's may increase the frequency of a NV to the point where it surpasses that of the corresponding oral vowel. Valdman 1959 reports that this is the case for several pairs in FRENCH, and Andrews 1949 claims that in TEMOAYAN OTOMI /ũ/ is much more frequent than /u/. Greenberg explains this phenomenon in terms of two additional universals:

(5) A merger of oral vowels always presupposes the merger of the corresponding nasal vowels if they exist.

(6) If nasal and oral vowels merge unconditionally, the phonetic result is always an oral vowel.

As we will see in section 4 below, numerous languages show a distinction in the oral vowel system which is lacking in the NV system.

Several recent studies on NV's, which arrive at conclusions
similar to those developed in this paper, should be mentioned.
Among the most important are Lightner 1970, Schourup 1973, and
the work of Matthew Chen; a recent anthology on nasals and nasalization (Ferguson, Hyman, and Ohala 1975) provides a wealth of
information on NV's.

4. Synchronic Aspects of Vowel Nasalization

The principal task for synchronic studies of vowel nasalization
has traditionally been to determine when the feature [+nasal] is
inherent in a vowel, and when it is not. This is not to say that
other lines of research are devoid of interest, but simply that
past work has by and large relegated questions other than the
'inherentness' of vowel nasality to the periphery. Clearly, the
function that nasality may fulfill in a grammar is also an important question, but one which has received nowhere near the same
amount of attention.

One obvious difference in the use of NV's by various languages
is that in some languages NV's play a morphological role, while
in other languages they merely serve to distinguish morphologically unrelated lexical items. For instance, Jackson 1967 reports
that in the TRÉGORROIS dialect of BRETON vowel nasality dif-
ferentiates the first singular form of verbs from the second singular:

> [pərĩ] 'when I shall do'
> [pəri] 'when thou wilt do'

In BENGALI the presence of nasality may be used to show deference:

> [tar] 'his'
> [tãr] 'his' (honorific)

CHATINO also offers cases of nasality functioning as a morph:

> [mbilyi] 'your comadre'   [lsu] 'your beard'   [suwe] 'your chin'
> [mbilyĩ] 'my comadre'   [lsũ] 'my beard'   [suwẽ] 'my chin'

M. Ohala 1972 gives the following examples from HINDI-URDU:

> [hɛ] 'is'   [čoli:] 'she went'
> [hɛ̃] 'are'   [čolĩ:] 'they went'

Nevertheless, in many languages nasality fulfills a purely lexical function.

Vowel nasality may also have semantic and sociolinguistic import. According to Pandit 1972, the use of vowel nasalization in GUJARATI marks the speaker as a member of the higher classes. Ferguson (1975: 187) hypothesizes that nasality frequently has three semantic values: (1) hesitation/assent, (2) negation, and (3) deference relations.

In some languages [+nasal], originally a feature of individual segments, has become a feature of entire morphemes. Firthian linguists were probably the first to recognize the 'prosodic' nature of nasality in certain languages. Robins 1953, 1957 presented such an analysis for SUNDANESE (cf. also Anderson 1972), and Bendor-Samuel 1960 discussed a similar phenomenon in TERENA. More recent treatments along this line include Kaye 1971 on DESANO, and Lunt 1973 on GUARANI. Lunt (1973: 138) makes the interesting suggestion that Continental PORTUGUESE may now be in the process of extending the feature of nasality from segments to syllables and morphemes.

Let us now return to the problem of determining when nasality is inherent in a vowel, and when it is derived. Prestructural linguists were criticized for simply indicating nasality where it was physically present, and for not attempting to distinguish those cases where nasality was functional from cases where it was redundant. With the advent of structural phonemics, most linguists came to believe that the feature of nasality could be used in two fundamentally different ways. On the one hand, it could serve to distinguish one form from another. When used in this way, it was said to be phonemic. On the other hand, in some languages nasality would be physically present in the speech signal without having the power to differentiate forms. Such nasalization was allophonic. Thus structural linguists posed for the first time the problem of determining when vowel nasality is inherent (i.e. phonemic), and when it is not. It must be acknowledged, however, that there was no single structuralist answer to this question. European structuralists generally permitted the use of criteria which were rejected in the United States. One fundamental dispute between the two groups concerned the admissibility of non-phonetic factors in dealing with phonological phenomena. Most Americans insisted that phonology be kept independent of the rest of the grammar (Pike is a notable exception), while Europeans usually opposed any such separation of levels.

With the rise of transformational grammar, many American
linguists came to reject the doctrine of separation of levels as
unjustified. By denying this doctrine it was possible to reinter-
pret the nasality of certain NV's as being conditioned rather than
inherent. Where previously nasality had been considered inherent
unless it was phonetically conditioned, generative phonologists
relaxed this restriction somewhat (as their European colleagues
had already done long before). They argued that the feature of
nasality was inherent only if it was neither phonetically conditioned,
nor grammatically conditioned. The result of this was that in a
NV such as is found in FRENCH bon [bõ] 'good,' the feature
[+nasal], which had earlier been considered inherent, was now
held to be conditioned, not by phonetic structure, but by morphophonemic structure, because this form is paradigmatically related
to the feminine form bonne [bɔn] 'good.'

In their euphoria over having made predictable features which
earlier linguists had considered unpredictable, certain scholars
went so far as to declare that "the nasal contrast is not known to
occur with vowels at the phonemic level. In the systematic phonemic analyses of languages with nasal vowels (such as FRENCH,
IGBO), the interpretation of these as vowel plus nasal consonant
has consistently proved superior to the unit nasal vowel solution."
(Harms 1968: 36) Using FRENCH as an example, the argument
that vowel nasality is never inherent runs as follows (cf. Schane
1968a: 45-50, and fn. 37, p. 142). Since a phonological description
of FRENCH must, in any event, contain the segments /a/ and /n/
on the phonological level, and since [ã] clearly derives from /an/
in plan [plã] 'flat' (because of the inflectionally related form plane
[plan] 'flat'), a phonological description will be 'simpler' if one
uses the rule which derives [ã] from /an/ in plan to derive all
instances of [ã]. In this way NV's may be entirely eliminated
from the lexicon.

An obvious defect in this approach, however, is that it assumes
a priori that one of the goals of a phonological description is the
elimination of certain kinds of segments at the phonological level.
(The early transformational bias for economy in the lexicon over
economy in the phonological rules is well known; it seems likely
that this bias was a legacy of the structuralist period.) But such
an assumption is no more justified than the a priori structuralist
assumption that phonology and grammar are independent.

Furthermore, the elimination of all NV's from the lexicon
leads to problems which have not been satisfactorily resolved.

For example, since [ã] derives from /an/ in <u>plan,</u> but from /ɛn/ in <u>prendre</u> [prãdrə] 'to take' (cf. <u>prennent</u> [prɛn] 'they take' (subj.)), what does <u>en</u> [ã] 'in' derive from, /an/ or /ɛn/? Is there any way to make the choice of either /an/ or /ɛn/ non-arbitrary?

One suggested solution to this problem is to let markedness considerations determine the underlying form in cases of structural ambiguity. Thus Schane 1968b proposes that [ã] in <u>en</u> derive from /an/, not /ɛn/, because <u>a</u> is less marked then <u>ɛ</u>. While markedness does provide us with an answer, there has so far been very little empirical support to demonstrate that it is the <u>right</u> answer. In fact, Vennemann 1972 discusses several examples where the use of Schane's markedness principle leads to intuitively incorrect analyses.

A different, and to my mind more realistic, remedy to the problem of structural ambiguity is the Alternation Condition advocated in Kiparsky 1968, whose effect on NV's would be to make the feature [+nasal] inherent in those vowels which do not alternate morphophonemically with an oral vowel + nasal consonant. Thus <u>en</u> [ã] would derive directly from phonological /ã/.

However, in a number of languages (e.g. FRENCH, PORTUGUESE, HINDI-URDU), certain phonological rules apparently presuppose a /VN/ analysis for NV's which show no morphophonemic alternation. For instance, the phonological rule of FRENCH which is responsible for voicing -s- in <u>résister</u> [reziste] 'to resist' (cf. <u>persister</u> [pɛrsiste] 'to persist,' where <u>s</u> remains voiceless), presupposes a phonological analysis for <u>insister</u> [ãesiste] 'to insist' where -s- is not intervocalic, as it is phonetically (cf. Schane 1968a: 48). Were /ãe/ underlying in this verb, then the intervocalic -s- voicing rule would have to be complicated by distinguishing NV's from oral vowels in order to prevent the derivation of *[ãeziste] from phonological /ãe+sis+te/. The problem, then, is one of deciding whether NV's only <u>act</u> like closed syllables (in which case the <u>s</u> voicing rule will have to be complicated as indicated above), or whether NV's <u>are</u>, in fact, closed syllables at some point in the derivation (in which case the <u>s</u> voicing rule may retain its full generality).

In PORTUGUESE, syllables with NV's act like closed syllables with respect to several rules of the grammar (cf. Morais-Barbosa 1962):

(a) PORTUGUESE has two r̠ phonemes: alveolar r̠ and uvular
(or velar) R̠, which contrast only intervocalically: [muru] 'wall'
vs. [muRu] 'punch.' Elsewhere they are in complementary distribution, r̠ occurring only after a tautosyllabic consonant (e.g.
prato 'plate') or at the end of a syllable or word (e.g. Carlos, mar
'sea'), and R̠ word initially (e.g. rei 'king') or after a heterosyllabic
consonant (e.g. guelras 'gills'). However, in the context Ṽ__V,
we find only R̠, never r̠: genro [ʒẽRu] 'son-in-law;' honra [õRə]
'honor.' We can explain the presence of only R̠ if we assume that
[ʒẽRu] derives from /ʒenRu/, [õRə] from /onRə/, etc.

(b) /b, d, g/ each have two allophones in (Continental) PORTU-
GUESE: [β, ð, ɣ] intervocalically, and [b, d, g] elsewhere. Now
in words such as rombo 'blunt,' senda 'path,' and vingar 'to
avenge' we always find [b, d, g]. Thus /b, d, g/ are realized after
NV's exactly as if they were following a consonant.

(c) PORTUGUESE frequently merges two adjacent vowels: cidade
antiga [sidadantiɣə] 'old city.' However, a NV + OV never contract:
lã azul [lə̃əzuɬ] 'blue wool.' Again it would seem that [ə̃] should
be analyzed as /ən/.

However, if we do represent NV's in PORTUGUESE on the
phonological level as a sequence of oral vowel + NC, we are faced
with the problem of determining what the NC is. There are actually two problems here. The first is to determine how to represent the homorganic nasal in words like campo 'field,' senda,
vingar. Transformational studies have generally shied away from
the use of the archiphoneme N on the phonological level, but is the
choice of /n/ (dictated by markedness considerations) really better?

The second problem is to decide what the underlying NC is when
phonetically there is no NC at all. Here there are two cases:
(1) the NV precedes a continuant: [ʒẽRu], [kə̃furə] 'camphor,'
[gõzu] 'hinge;' (2) the NV is word final: [bẽ] 'good,' [fĩ] 'end,'
[bõ] 'good.' In three recent generative studies of PORTUGUESE
phonology (Saciuk 1970, St. Clair 1971, Brasington 1971) the inde-
terminacy of the NC which nasalizes vowels has simply been ignored.

Narang and Becker 1971 present arguments for HINDI-URDU
similar to those outlined above for FRENCH and PORTUGUESE;
however, M. Ohala 1972 disputes their analysis. In cases such
as these it is difficult to prove that what is being described truly
belongs in a synchronic grammar, and is not simply a fossilized

reflection of the past. In the FRENCH case, for instance, it is surely not obvious that the s̲ voicing rule is a part of a speaker's mental competence (cf. Love and Harris 1974 for a similar criticism).

In conclusion, we might observe that the general trend over the past several decades has been to eliminate [+nasal] as an inherent feature of vowels. It was first eliminated everywhere it was phonetically predictable. Next it was eliminated wherever it was either phonetically or grammatically conditioned (with the term 'grammar' being understood in its broadest sense). If, after eliminating all grammatically conditioned NV's from the lexicon, there are still indications that the feature [+nasal] should be derived in yet other forms (as the FRENCH, PORTUGUESE, and HINDI-URDU examples cited above purport to show), it would seem rather doubtful that further language specific considerations would be of much use. Rather it will be necessary to discover universal principles (supported by psycholinguistic, as opposed to strictly structural or methodological arguments) if we are to further restrict those cases where the feature of nasality is considered an inherent property of vowels. If past history is any indication, then the ebb and flow of abstract and concrete analyses may be with us for some time to come.

Although the question of when vowel nasality is inherent has dominated 'theoretical' literature (i. e. those studies dealing with the significance of specific data for linguistic theory), the 'practical' description of large numbers of languages has been carried out, by and large, on a common-sense basis. Linguists and laymen alike can apparently recognize a NV when they see one, whether or not they are aware of the latest theoretical developments. While I do not wish to disparage theoretical studies, I think it is a mistake to disregard descriptive statements simply because they do not make any theoretical breakthroughs. In looking at large amounts of admittedly superficial data one is often struck by patterns and generalizations that even the most exhaustive study of a single language may not reveal. What I would like to do now is to compare the systems of NV's of the 150 languages in the sample in an attempt to determine what constitutes a natural system of NV's. Much of what follows is a revision and an abridgement of Ruhlen 1975b.

Let us begin by looking at the phonological patterns of the oral and nasal vowels in FRENCH:

```
i   y       u
e   ø    ə   o                    õ
ɛ   œ        ɔ          (æ̃)
         a           æ̃   ã
```

Considered in isolation it is not immediately apparent how natural
the FRENCH NV system is. In order to answer this question, as
well as to develop a general notion of what constitutes a natural
system of NV's, let us examine the following two parameters of
the NV systems in our sample: (I) the number of NV's vs. the
number of OV's and (II) the relative position of the NV's vs. the
position of the OV's. With respect to (I) we observe that, in
FRENCH, there are far fewer NV's than OV's. With respect to
(II) we note that two of the FRENCH NV's occupy a position in
phonological space different from that of any OV (i.e. æ̃, ã), and
that FRENCH has no high NV's. Taken together these three factors
underscore the differential patterning between OV's and NV's in
FRENCH.

    For 83 of the 155 languages which comprise our sample the
number of phonemic NV's is equal to the number of OV's. These
languages are preceded by an asterisk in the Appendix. (One language, OJIBWA, has three short OV's, but four long OV's and
four long NV's. In all other cases the number of short NV's equals
the number of short OV's; long NV's, which occur in many languages (e.g. DAN, NEPALI, BAGVALI, KURUX, NAVAJO, SENECA,
MIXTEC, AUCA, AYORE), have not been taken into account. GREBO
has seven OV's and seven NV's; in addition, it has two 'muffled'
vowels which are always oral.) It seems that languages which exhibit prosodic nasalization are especially likely to have an equal
number of OV's and NV's. This may explain why so many South
American languages, where nasalization often has a prosodic character, have an equal number of OV's and NV's. For 77 of the 83
languages with an equal number of OV's and NV's both the number
and position of the NV's are reported to be identical. (More precisely, for 77 of the 83 languages no differences are reported between the height of OV's and NV's; grammars seldom specify,
however, that the height of OV's and NV's is, in fact, identical.)
The remaining 72 languages have fewer NV's than OV's; these
are the languages with no mark next to them in the Appendix.

    Let us now focus attention on those 72 languages which have
fewer NV's than OV's. For expository purposes I will discuss
this situation in terms of nasal vowel loss (e.g. a language has mid
OV's, but no mid NV's), and nasal vowel reduction (e.g. a language

has both higher-mid and lower-mid OV's [e, ɛ, o, ɔ], but only
lower-mid NV's [ɛ̃, ɔ̃], though I will argue later that these two
situations are really two aspects of the same phenomenon.

Nineteen of the 73 languages lack high NV's (front, back, or
both), but have high OV's: EBRIE, SANGO, NGWE, SARA, POL-
ISH, FRENCH (Parisian), FRENCH (Canadian), BRETON, BALUCHI,
INGUSH, TAMIL, WU, YUCHI, SENECA, DHEGIHA, AMUZGO,
CHINANTEC (Usila), OTOMI (Mezquital), SIRIONO;

e.g. EBRIE: i   u
                 e   o   ẽ   õ
                 ɛ   ɔ
                      a   ã

Thirty-three of the 73 languages lack mid NV's (front, back, or
both), but possess mid OV's: NUPE, YORUBA, FANTE, BAULE,
GBEYA, SANGO, KUNG, HOTTENTOT (Korana), HOTTENTOT
(Nama), BRETON, BALUCHI, NEPALI, BAGVALI, BOTLIX, BOT-
LIX (Godoberi), CHAMALAL, KARATA, XINALUG, WU, DOGRIB,
CHIPEWYAN (Fort Chipewyan), GALICE, CHASTA COSTA, ONEIDA,
BILOXI, DAKOTA (Teton), DAKOTA (Assiniboine), DHEGIHA, TEWA,
MIXTEC (Ayutla), MIXTEC (Molinos), OTOMI (Temoayan), OCAINA;

e.g. DAKOTA: i   u   ĩ   ũ
               e   o
                    a   ã

Only four languages lack both high and mid NV's (front, back,
or both), but have high and mid OV's: BRETON, BALUCHI, WU,
DHEGIHA;

e.g. BRETON: i   y   u   WU: i   y   u   ĩ
               e   ø   ə   o   (ẽ)   e   o   õ
                       a   ã   a   æ̃

Turning now to nasal vowel reduction we find that just two of the
73 languages distinguish high and lower-high OV's (front or back),
but possess only high NV's: BASILA, BALUCHI;

e.g. BALUCHI: i   u   (ĩ)   (ũ)
                 ɪ   ɷ
                 e   ə   o   ẽ   õ
                      a   ã

For mid vowels, however, reduction in vowel height distinctions is quite common; 28 of the 73 languages have two mid OV's (front, back, or both), but only one mid NV (front, back, or both): DAN, LOKO, BASILA, BINI, GA, IJO (Kalabiri), IJO (Nembe), EBRIE, YORUBA, YORUBA (Itsekiri), DOWAYAYO, GBEYA, NGWE, SARA, FRENCH (Parisian), FRENCH (Canadian), HAITIAN CREOLE, POR-TUGUESE (Lisbon), PORTUGUESE (Rio), MARATHI, CHIPEWYAN (Fort Chipewyan), BILOXI, TEWA, OTOMI (Mezquital), MAZAHUA, APINAYE, CAYAPO, YARURO;

e.g. MAZAHUA: i   u   ĩ   ũ
                 e   ə   o   ẽ   ə̃   õ
                 ɛ   ɐ   ɔ
                      a   ã

Not infrequently a system of NV's will have a 'gap' in either the high or mid series. That is, a language may have the mid vowel phonemes: /e, o, ẽ/, but no */õ/. Of the eight languages with a gap in the high NV's, for four the gap is in the back (SARA, DHEGIHA, CHINANTEC (Usila), SIRIONO), for two it is in the front (TAMIL, SANGO), while two languages have gaps in both the front and back series (NGWE, WU);

e.g. SIRIONO: i   ɨ   u   ĩ   ɨ̃
                 e   o   ẽ   õ
                      a   ã

Nineteen languages show a gap in the mid series, eight in the back and eleven in the front. Back: BALUCHI, NEPALI, BOTLIX, CHAMALAL, DOGRIB, CHIPEWYAN (Fort Chipewyan), TEWA, MIXTEC (Ayutla). Front: YORUBA, KUNG, HOTTENTOT (Korana), HOTTENTOT (Nama), POLISH, XINALUG, WU, BILOXI, MIXTEC (Molinos), DHEGIHA, OCAINA;

e.g. HOTTENTOT (Nama):   i   u   ĩ   ũ
                         e   ə   o   õ
                         ae   ãe

It is commonly noted in the literature that in languages with phonemic vowel length, long high vowels (ī, ū) tend to be higher than short high vowels (ɩ, ᴏ), while long low vowels (ā) tend to be lower than short low vowels (ə). The correct generalization is of course that long vowels tend to be peripheral, while short vowels tend to be somewhat centralized. Systems of NV's also manifest differential patterning. In six languages the height of the high NV's

and high OV's is reported to differ. In three cases the NV is
higher than the OV (i.e. IRISH, KIOWA APACHE, BILOXI); in
three cases the NV is lower than the OV: IJO (Kolokuma), HOT-
TENTOT (Korana), YUCHI;

e.g. HOTTENTOT (Korana):   i   u   ɩ̃   ɑ̃
                             e (ə) o   ɔ̃
                             æ   æ̃

While our data do not establish any particular pattern for high NV's,
I believe this may be due more to the difficulty of interpreting
language descriptions (which are all too often underspecified from
the phonetic point of view) rather than to the linguistic facts themselves. My hunch is that high NV's tend to be lower than high OV's.
In this regard we should note Chen's (1975: 111) observation for
CHINESE dialects: "The finals /iN, uN/ contain very lax vowels,
roughly [ɪ, ʊ], as opposed to the oral finals /i, u/ which approximate the values of their corresponding cardinal vowels [i, u] ...
Phonemic high NV's also show some degree of laxing."

In ten languages the height of the mid NV's and mid OV's differs.
In all ten cases the NV is lower than the OV: KUMAUNI, CHIPE-
WYAN (Slave), SIONA, YORUBA (Itsekiri), SANGO, POLISH,
FRENCH (Parisian), YUCHI, SENECA, OTOMI (Mezquital);

e.g. CHIPEWYAN (Slave):   i   u   ĩ   ũ
                            e   o   ɛ̃   ɔ̃
                                a   ã

Bhat (1975: 28-30) argues that nasalization tends to raise mid
vowels; it may be necessary, therefore, to distinguish the raising
effect of allophonic nasalization from the lowering tendency of
phonemic nasalization.

In five languages the height of a low NV and a low OV differs.
In four cases the NV is higher: NUPE, HAITIAN CREOLE, POR-
TUGUESE (Lisbon), PORTUGUESE (Rio). In one case (EYAK) the
NV is (reported to be) lower;

e.g. PORTUGUESE: i   u   ĩ   ũ
                     e   o   ẽ   õ
                     ɛ (ɐ) ɔ   ɛ̃
                         a

Bhat (1975: 27-8) cites numerous examples of low vowels being

raised by nasalization. Furthermore, due to the ambiguity of the
language description, it is not even clear that EYAK is a valid
counterexample to this tendency.

In summary, the results of our cross-linguistic comparison
show that in roughly half of the languages (83) the number of NV's
is reported to be the same as the number of OV's. The other half
of the languages (72) have fewer NV's than OV's. In languages
with fewer NV's than OV's this reduction usually manifests itself
either in the reduction of mid vowel height distinctions (28 cases),
or in the loss of the mid vowels (33 cases). Slightly less often
(19 cases) the reduced NV system, as in FRENCH, lacks high
NV's. In investigating gaps in the system neither high nor mid
vowels show any tendency for gaps to fall in either the front or
back series; this line of research thus provides no support for the
claim that nasalization is favored in conjunction with either front
or back vowels. While information on positional differences between NV's and OV's is quite sparse (and often difficult to interpret) I would hypothesize that high and mid NV's tend to be somewhat
lower than their oral equivalents, whereas low NV's tend to be
higher than their oral partners (cf. Wright 1975).

Let us now return to the question of what constitutes a natural
system of NV's. One of the most natural systems contains an equal
number of OV's and NV's. Furthermore, although OV's and NV's
are often described as having the same absolute vowel height, we
may hypothesize that where positional differences do exist there
is a universal tendency for high and mid NV's to be lower than
their oral partners, while low NV's tend to be higher than their
corresponding OV's. Like short vowels, then, NV's tend to be
centralized with respect to the OV's, though this does not imply,
of course, that they are centralized for the same physiological
reason.

A NV system which is only slightly less natural than the preceding is one in which vowel height distinctions are reduced, either
by the merger of the higher-mid and lower-mid phonemes in a single
mid series, or by the loss of the mid series altogether.

Less natural than either of the preceding systems, but still relatively natural, is a NV system which lacks one or both high NV's.
All other systems of NV's I consider to be more or less 'unnatural.'
We may define an unnatural system as one which has not evolved
solely through the action of universal phonetic tendencies which
operate across languages. For example, the evolution of the

modern FRENCH system (which I consider unnatural) involved at
least three phonetic changes which do not represent the effect of
universal phonetic tendencies: (1) the mergers $\tilde{\text{ɪ}}$, $\tilde{\text{ɛ}}$ > $\tilde{\text{æ}}$; $\tilde{\text{y}}$, $\tilde{\text{œ}}$ > $\tilde{\text{œ}}$;
(2) the unconditioned lowering of $\tilde{\text{u}}$ to $\tilde{\text{o}}$; and (3) the unconditioned
velarization of the low NV: $\tilde{\underline{\text{a}}}$ > $\tilde{\underline{\text{a}}}$. Other unnatural NV systems
are found in IROQUOIAN languages;

e.g. ONEIDA: i   ũ

                       e   o   ɜ̃

                              a

It would be interesting to know how such systems as these arose.

5. The Origin and Development of Nasal Vowels

    In the preceding section I defined a series of natural systems of
NV's. But since synchrony and diachrony are intimately related,
let us now inquire into the diachronic origin of synchronic naturalness.

    The process of vowel nasalization may be considered universal
in a very loose sense. Were it to take place without interference
from the rest of grammatical structure, it would tend to pass
through the stages outlined here. However, since there are always
many diverse pressures bearing on a language at any given point
in time, and since different pressures may push the structure of
the language in different directions, only rarely, if ever, do we
find NV's developing with no aberrations from the 'normal' course
of development. That is to say, the universal process of vowel
nasalization usually interacts with other (universal) processes to
produce sound patterns which are in part language specific.

    In general, we may break the process of vowel nasalization into
three phases:

    1. NASALIZATION
    2. NASAL CONSONANT DELETION
    3. DENASALIZATION

The first phase of the nasalization process begins when a vowel
preceding a NC comes to be pronounced with the velum lowered.
(Occasionally the NC precedes the vowel: cf. PORTUGUESE [mĩ]
'me' < LATIN mihi; Hyman 1972 postulates such 'perseverative'
nasalization in the KWA languages of Africa, and Chen 1975 mentions a similar phenomenon in the SOUTH MIN dialects of CHINESE.)

Typically, the vowel is low (i.e. a̲), and the NC is tautosyllabic.
(Chen (1975 : 97-9) presents evidence from the CHINESE dialects
that vowel nasalization occurs first before front NC's, and only
later before back NC's; in other words, m̲ is more likely to nasalize a vowel than n̲, and n̲, more likely than ŋ̲.) The naturalness
of this phonological process derives from two factors. First, the
velum is simply lowered a bit early through anticipation of the
following NC. Secondly, the degree of velic opening is normally
greater in low vowels than in high vowels (cf. Ladefoged 1971a:
34) so that nasalization thereby has a natural inroad on low vowels.
What happens, then, is not that formerly pure oral vowels are
nasalized, but rather the earlier slight nasalization now becomes
accentuated. Once the nasalization of the low vowel(s) is well
established (perhaps to the extent that it must be specified by a
language specific phonological rule), the environment for nasalization is progressively simplified, spreading first to the mid
vowels and finally to the high vowels. Some linguists have con-
tended that nasalization tends to affect front vowels before it affects
back vowels; other linguists have posited the reverse direction of
spread. The evidence is not overwhelming at present for either
position, though I suspect nasality is favored more with front vowels
(cf. Ohala 1975: 300-1). We may represent the nasalization process as follows:

(7)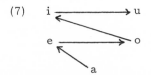

At this stage all of the vowels will be phonetically nasalized when
preceding a NC.

The development of NV's in FRENCH followed the above chronology rather closely (cf. Pope 1934: 166-82). a̲ was the first
vowel nasalized, probably as early as the tenth century. During
the eleventh century e̲ also begins to show nasalization. Finally,
the three high vowels, i̲, y̲, and u̲, were nasalized starting in the
thirteenth century. Chen (1971, 1973a) posits a similar chronology
for CHINESE dialects, and Jackson 1967 reports that in BRETON
phonemic vowel nasality arose first with a̲. I have been unable to
determine the order in which vowels were nasalized in PORTUGUESE
and the INDIC languages. The POLISH NV's ([ɛ̃] and [ɔ̃]) derive,
indirectly, from the PROTO-SLAVIC NV's ę̲ and ǫ̲. Historical
data are of course lacking for most African and Amerindian languages.

It may be the case that the chronology for vowel nasalization presented in (7) is also valid for child language acquisition. Bloch (1913: 51-2) indicates that the four FRENCH NV's appeared in the speech of his daughter in the following order: æ̃, ã, õ, œ̃.

During the second phase of vowel nasalization the NC's gradually merge and are finally lost in certain environments, often with compensatory lengthening of the NV. (This does not imply that the attrition of NC's invariably leaves behind a NV. Whether or not nasality survives in the vowel may well be a function of the strength of allophonic nasalization before the NC's were lost. In a language with slight allophonic nasalization, such as SWEDISH, NC's might disappear leaving behind purely oral vowels; in a language like American ENGLISH, with its heavy allophonic nasalization, the loss of NC's would stand a much greater chance of leaving behind phonemic NV's) Following Chen 1973a, we may hypothesize that syllable final NC's merge front to back.

(8)

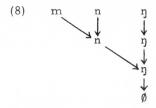

In addition to the support from CHINESE that Chen adduces for (8), FRENCH also appears to have followed the same path. First, m and n merged to n in OLD FRENCH; next ɲ was dentalized. Finally, all syllable final NC's became velar. Even today the FRENCH spoken in the south of France is characterized by a slight velar NC so that what is pronounced [tã] in Parisian FRENCH is often [tãᵑ] in the Midi. Similarly, in PROVENÇAL the only syllable final nasal is [ŋ] (cf. Coustenoble 1945). Furthermore, in certain American SPANISH dialects word final n has been velarized; e.g. bien [bjen] 'good' > [bjeŋ]. Finally, Needham and Davis 1946 report that word final NV's in CUICATECO often show a velar offglide [ᵑ]. There are, nevertheless, cases where word final NC's merge to n, rather than ŋ; neutralization to n must therefore be considered a possible, though perhaps less common, alternative to ŋ.

Of course not all NC's merge and are deleted; at least two factors seem to play a role here:

1. The position of the NC in the word.
2. The nature of the following segment (if any).

With respect to 1 it appears that preconsonantal NC's are lost
first; second, word final NC's are deleted when followed by a consonant; and third, the remaining word final NC's are lost. Lastly,
intervocalic NC's may disappear (as in PORTUGUESE), but such
consonants are probably retained more often than not because their
deletion creates a more complex syllable structure (i.e. C$\tilde{V}$V),
whereas the loss of NC's in other environments leads to open syllable structure (i.e. CVNCV > C$\tilde{V}$CV), which I assume is the least
marked.

With regard to 2 the evidence is somewhat conflicting. It would
be natural to assume that NC's would be lost first before fricatives,
and only later before stops and affricates. Were this the case, we
could say that the non-continuant nature of the NC was being assimilated to the continuant nature of the following fricative. The effect
of this assimilation would be the deletion of the nasals. Later the
environment for nasal loss could be generalized to include non-
continuant consonants as well. Putative support for the above
chronology might come from POLISH and PORTUGUESE, where
NC's following NV's have been lost only when followed by continuants. When followed by non-continuants there is a NC homorganic
with the non-continuant. In the ROMANCE languages LATIN ns
is often reduced to s (e.g. LATIN mensa 'table' > RUMANIAN
masă, FRENCH moise, SPANISH, PORTUGUESE mesa), though
it is not clear that the preceding vowel ever was nasalized. In
INDIC NC's were generally lost before continuants, with lengthening and nasalization of the preceding vowel (what the SANSKRIT
grammarians call 'anunasika'), but were retained in the form of
a homorganic NC before non-continuants ('anusvara'). Furthermore, INDIC languages suggest that homorganic NC's are lost
first before voiceless stops, and only later, if at all, before voiced
stops (with respect to HINDI, cf. M. Ohala 1972: 181-4). Some
varieties of American ENGLISH support this chronology: [kæt]
can't, but [kænd] canned, and Ingram (1974: 58) mentions an interesting pattern in the child's acquisition of nasal + stop clusters:
"there is a distinction between nasals occurring with voiced stops
and those occurring with voiceless ones ... the nasal is deleted
when the stop is voiceless, whereas the nasal is retained and the
stop deleted when the stop is voiced." On the other hand, Malécot
1960 points out that in certain dialects of American ENGLISH NC's
are not lost before fricatives (e.g. *[dɛ̃s] dense), but may be before
stops (e.g. [kæt] can't).

A related problem lies in determining whether the slight NC in groups such as $\tilde{V}^N$ [C, -continuant] represents (1) a trace of what is phonologically a full NC, or (2) a kind of transitional nasal glide, which has no underlying status, and which appears simply through articulatory convenience. For example, in PORTUGUESE we might ask what native speakers 'hear' when a word like [kɐ̃ᵐpu] 'field' is pronounced. According to Morais-Barbosa (1962: 703), educated people say this word has five sounds, while illiterates report only four. Hammarström (in Morais-Barbosa (1962: 709) claims that he frequently finds it difficult to persuade PORTUGUESE speakers that they do in fact pronounce an [ᵐ] in [kɐ̃ᵐpu]. The evidence is, therefore, conflicting as to whether [ᵐ] in [kɐ̃ᵐpu] derives from rule 9 or 10:

(9) $N \rightarrow {}^N / \tilde{V}\_\_$ [C, -continuant]

(10) $\emptyset \rightarrow {}^N / \tilde{V}\_\_$ [C, -continuant]

The choice of (9) or (10) depends of course on whether the proper phonological representation is /kəmpu/ or /kə̃pu/ (cf. Brito 1975).

After the deletion of NC's in various contexts, vowel nasality is no longer allophonic, but becomes <u>phonemic</u> in that surface contrasts between an oral vowel and its nasal partner are now possible. Such NV's may or may not be <u>phonological</u>, depending on whether or not the nasality of the vowel can be motivated in terms of morphophonemic structure, or other general principles.

The third and final phase of vowel nasalization is denasalization, which occurs in two parts. First, vowel nasality is lost where it has remained allophonic. Secondly, nasality may be lost even where it has attained the status of an underlying feature.

During the first part of phase three, NV's are denasalized if, and only if, they are still followed by NC's. It is this kind of denasalization which, in FRENCH, produced [bonə] from earlier [bõnə]. The order in which vowels are denasalized has been hypothesized (cf. Chen 1973b, 1975) to be the reverse of that in which they were nasalized:

(11)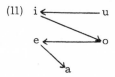

Somewhat paradoxically Chen (1975:108) reports that pattern (11) is rather rare among the CHINESE dialects where 'the earlier a NV enters the language, the earlier it tends to disappear." Chen proposes that pattern (11) and the 'first in, first out' principle are complementary, with the later taking precedence over the former. In any event, it seems to me that denasalization from high to low has, for the moment at least, less support than nasalization from low to high.

Denasalization in FRENCH before intervocalic NC's, a process which took place from the fifteenth to seventeenth centuries (cf. Pope 1934:170-2), did not follow precisely the path indicated in (11). Rather the first vowels denasalized, in the fifteenth century, were ĩ and ɛ̃, followed in the sixteenth century by first ỹ and later ã. õ was the last vowel to be denasalized, toward the end of the seventeenth century.

Finally, phonological NV's may themselves be denasalized. That is, nasality as an inherent feature of vowels is eliminated from the lexicon. Chen 1971, 1973a provides support from CHINESE dialects for the notion that NV's are denasalized in the reverse order from that in which they were nasalized. As reported in Jackson 1967, BRETON dialects also offer supporting evidence for this hypothesis. In the TREGORROIS dialect ũ has been denasalized, but the other NV's remain (i.e. ĩ, ỹ, ɛ̃, õ, ã). In the VANNETAIS and LÉONAIS dialects all of the high NV's have been lost, but the mid and low NV's have not yet been affected. In the ILE DE GROIX dialect, however, only the low NV ã is preserved. Pandit 1972 indicates that in GUJARATI diphthongs the first NV to be denasalized was the high NV ĩ, and Sardesai 1930 notes the early denasalization of the high NV ĩ in MARATHI. F. Trager 1971 found only a single instance of [ũ] in TIWA, and consequently suggested that the sound change ũ > u is currently taking place.

Wierzchowska and Wierzchowska 1969 point out that, in POLISH, denasalization may at times be conditioned by semantic factors. Thus, the [ɔ] in mąz [mɔʃ] 'a man' remains nasalized in mąz stanu 'statesman,' but is frequently denasalized in a context like mąz pani X 'the husband of Mrs. X.' Similarly, wąz is denasalized to [vɔws] when it means 'rubber pipe,' but retains nasality when its meaning is 'snake.'

There is of course no fundamental mystery as to why NV's should ultimately disappear. NV's are certainly phonologically (and phonetically) more complex than oral vowels, and consequently their loss means that marked segments revert to their normal unmarked state.

Since nasalization precedes from low vowels to high vowels, and denasalization (apparently) reverses this pattern, running from high to low, were the vowel nasalization process the only factor affecting synchronic states of NV's we should expect to find systems of NV's where all the NV's are bunched together in the lower portion of phonological space, as they are, more or less, in FRENCH. However, as we saw in section 4, while such systems are found here and there, they are by no means predominant. This implies that other diachronic factors, which interfere with the vowel nasalization process, must be sought.

One such factor appears to be a preference for systems in which all the vowels participate in the nasality contrast. Since over half of all languages in our sample have an equal number of NV's and OV's, it would seem that such systems are the most stable. Just as the voice contrast in stops tends to occur in all positions (bilabial, alveolar, and velar), so too does the nasal contrast with vowels tend to occur with all the vowel phonemes (whence the frequent factoring out of a nasal prosody by many linguists).

A second important factor influencing systems of NV's is, as Greenberg 1966 emphasized, that of merger. It is well known that vowel height distinctions are in many languages reduced (i.e. 'neutralized') before NC's. In other words, allophonic nasalization (coming from contiguous NC's) reduces vowel height distinctions. There is no reason to believe that phonemic nasalization (i.e. nasalization which is not phonetically conditioned) does not have this same effect. That is, nasality, whether allophonic or phonemic, tends to suppress vowel height distinctions. This principle explains the predominance of systems of NV's where vowel height distinctions in the mid range have either been compressed or eliminated, as we saw in section 4. Furthermore, the process of merger is clearly constrained by the principle of maximum differentiation, which requires that vowels (both oral and nasal) be kept maximally apart in phonological space.

Another factor which is often cited as an influence on the evolution of NV's is their supposed predilection for lowering. Except for the well known FRENCH case, however, there is very little data to support lowering as a universal tendency manifested by NV's in geographically and genetically diverse languages. It seems likely

that those linguists who have postulated lowering as a universal
property of NV's have been overly influenced by FRENCH. Be-
lieving FRENCH to possess a natural system of NV's, such linguists assumed it must have arrived at this natural state through
a series of natural evolutionary processes, one of which was taken
to be lowering. We saw in section 4, however, that the FRENCH
system is in fact unnatural (cf. also Hockett (1955: 90) for a similar assessment), and I would like to suggest that part of its unna-
turalness is due precisely to the lowered high NV's. Rather than
constituting a universal tendency, lowering is an idiosyncratic
characteristic of FRENCH, and serves to distinguish it, in part,
from the many natural systems of NV's we have examined.

A final factor which may interfere with the normal development
of NV's is the labialization, and subsequent raising, of low NV's.
Not infrequently certain NV's develop a w offglide (PORTUGUESE
and POLISH are two examples). If we then assume that a nasal
diphthong such as [ãw] might naturally evolve first to [ə̃w], then
[ũw], and finally [ũ], a number of disparate facts may be explained.
First of all, such an evolution seems indicated in the case of PROTO-
ATHAPASKAN */an/, which has evolved in DOGRIB to /ũ/ (with /ã/
being practically eliminated) (cf. Hoijer 1966: 507). Ferguson (personal communication) informs me that PERSIAN also offers examples of original ã being raised to ũ, so that the capital of Iran,
while still written Tehran, is often pronounced with the NV [ũ]
in the final syllable. Andrews 1949 observes that in TEMOAYAN
OTOMI ũ is much more frequent than its oral partner u, and it
seems at least plausible that such a situation might be a result of
the labialization process described here. Perhaps also it is this
process which accounts for the strange configuration of NV's in
ONEIDA, where the sole NV's are ũ and ə̃, neither of which has
an oral partner. In GUJARATI we find original *akam has evolved
to [ũ] in the modern language, and the earlier endings -āmi and
-āma have merged to [ũ] (though original -āni, with a dental rather
than labial NC, remained low: [ã]). A final example comes from
USILA CHINANTEC. According to Skinner 1962, the NV /ũ/ is
realized phonetically as a bilabial syllabic nasal [m̩]. If [m̩] is not
phonemicized as /ũ/, then oral /u/ has no nasal counterpart. Furthermore, Skinner claims that [m̩] occurs precisely where one
would expect [ũ]. All of these facts, then, would seem to indicate
a connection between labiality and nasality which may result in deviations from the normal nasalization process.

While the normal source of NV's is unquestionably from the
loss of a NC, NV's may on occasion arise through analogy,

borrowing, and spontaneous nasalization. Heffner (1964: 112-4)
provides a clear example of NV's arising through analogy. He reports that in some GERMAN dialects the pronunciation of Sohn
'son' has shifted from [zõ:n] to [zõ:]. After this change Floh
'flea' came to be pronounced [flõ:] on analogy with Sohn, so that
in Goethe we find the two words rhyming.

With respect to borrowing one may cite Goddard's (1971: 140)
hypothesis that "the phonological and areal limitations on the nasalization in the ABNAKI languages suggest that this innovation
was primary in the southern NE languages and diffused northward
secondarily ... The spread of an areal feature of vowel nasalization from IROQUOIAN to ALGONQUIAN languages seems indicated." In addition, Chatterji 1970 hypothesizes that certain
'spontaneously' nasalized vowels in BENGALI may in fact have
been borrowed from neighboring speech communities.

A final source of NV's is through spontaneous nasalization.
Grierson 1922 cites examples of spontaneous nasalization in the
INDIC languages, and Thalbitzer 1904 discusses similar phenomena in GREENLANDIC. More recently Ferguson (1963: 59) mentions that "in IROQUOIAN ... one of the NV's posited for the
protolanguage seems, on considerations of internal reconstruction,
to have derived from earlier /a/+ /i/ or sequences like /awa/."

Apart from analogy, borrowing, and spontaneous nasalization,
there is one other origin for NV's which has recently been proposed in the literature, and which does not involve NC's. Hetzron
1969, Matisoff 1970, 1975, and J. Ohala 1971a, 1972, 1975 all cite
cases of NV's arising through contact with glottal or pharyngeal
consonants. According to Matisoff 1970, "TIBETAN ḥ represented some sort of prenasalization of the following consonant, "
(41) and in some modern TIBETAN dialects " orthographic ḥ- has
allegedly acquired a nasal articulation in all cases." (41) Matisoff
also states that "the relationship between zero initial, ?, and
nasalization is an intimate one all over Southeast Asia. In Central
THAI, for example, many speakers nasalize words beginning with
?-, h-, or a nasal and having the vowel -a." (42) Finally, Matisoff
notes that "certain varieties of British ENGLISH offer us more
exotic, but quite parallel examples: [hã:f] 'half, ' [hã:t] 'heart, '
[ã:e] 'hour'." He concludes that 'nasality and glottality are interrelated in such a variety of ways that it is imperative to search
for an explanation in terms of universal articulatory fact." (42)

J. Ohala (1972: 1167-8) makes the following comments: "Velar
height for vowels varies directly with the 'height' of the vowel

(in the absence of any neighboring nasal consonant). Thus the so-
called low 'oral' vowels may have an opening of the velo-pharyn-
geal port. Glottal consonants such as [ʔ] and [h], however, seem
to require neither raised nor lowered velum but instead allow the
velar elevation to be determined by neighboring consonants and
vowels ... It is clear that the combination of glottal consonant
plus low vowel is particularly vulnerable to nasalization."

It is noteworthy that most of the alleged examples of spontaneous
nasalization in the environment of glottals involve low vowels, which
we have already observed are particularly susceptible to nasalization. In fact, J. Ohala (1975: 299) claims that for the low 'oral'
vowels of ENGLISH (e.g. in bad, bod, bawd) "a little bit of nasalization is not just tolerated..., it is required." The question thus
arises as to whether it is the glottal environment or simply the
lowness of the vowel (or both?) which has provoked the spontaneous
nasalization. Is there really a connection between glottality and
nasality? And if so, how do we explain this mysterious correlation? The answer seems to be that there is indeed a connection,
and Matisoff (1975: 272) gives the following explanation: "Vowel
nasalization frequently occurs in the environment of laryngeals
because (1) a nasal-oral coupling has negligeable acoustic/percep-
tual effect on laryngeals; (2) there is no aerodynamic requirement
for velar closure in the articulation of laryngeals; and (3) in the
case of [h], the open glottis exerts a positive acoustic effect on the
vowel similar to that exerted by a lowered velum."

6. Prospects for Future Research

In the preceding sections I have attempted to investigate NV's
from several different perspectives. In this section I would like
to briefly sketch three lines of research which future investigation
might take.

One area of study, which has hitherto been largely neglected,
is the acquisition of NV's by children. Studies of how children
acquire NV phonemes (hopefully in a number of different languages)
would be a welcome addition to the literature. Such studies should,
as a bare minimum, investigate the order in which NV's are learned,
both in relation to themselves and to the other speech sounds, especially the oral vowels. It would also be interesting to know whether
NV's are learned tel quel, or whether they first pass through a stage
when they are followed by a NC.

A second area in which more evidence is needed is the diachronic
development of NV's. While excellent recent studies on FRENCH

(Rochet, to appear) and CHINESE (Chen 1975) augur well for the future, historical studies of the rise and evolution of NV's are at present quite rare. Obviously for many languages with NV's historical documentation is lacking, and in these cases one is restricted to the comparative method and internal reconstruction. However, for PORTUGUESE, POLISH, and the INDIC languages historical documentation is available, and consequently diachronically slanted studies of the development of NV's in these languages is feasible.

A third possibility for future research would be a cross-linguistic study of phonological rules dealing with NV's. FRENCH has several rules involving the alternation of NV's with oral vowels followed by NC's in morphologically related forms. While not all languages with NV's have such rules, a careful survey of the available literature should turn up a sufficient sample for a useful cross-linguistic study. In this way one could approach the problem of what constitutes a natural phonological rule of nasality.

APPENDIX

List of all languages possessing nasal vowels

NIGER-CONGO
Dan
*Malinka
*Kpelle
Loko
Basila
Bini
*Urhobo
*Ewe
Ga
Ijo (Kalabiri)
Ijo (Kolokuma)
Ijo (Nembe)
*Kru
*Grebo
Ebrie
Nupe
Yoruba
Yoruba (Itsekiri)
Fante
Baule
Dowayayo

Gbeya
*Ngbandi
Sango
*Zande
Ngwe
*Bembe

NILO-SAHARAN
Sara

KHOISAN
Kung
Hottentot (Korana)
Hottentot (Nama)
*!Kɔ̃

INDO-EUROPEAN
Polish
*Saramaccan
French (Parisian)
French (Canadian)
Haitian Creole

Portuguese (Lisbon)
Portuguese (Rio)
*Irish
Breton
Baluchi
*Gujarati
*Punjabi
Hindi
*Urdu
*Bengali
*Oriya
Marathi
*Kumauni
Nepali

CAUCASIAN
*Axvax
Bagvali
Bezhita
*Bezhita (Gunzib)
Botlix
Botlix (Godoberi)

APPENDIX (continued)

CAUCASIAN (cont.)
  Chamalal
  Karata
  *Tindi
  *Xvarshi
  *Lezghian
  Xinalug
  Bats
  Ingush

ALTAIC
  *Nanaj

DRAVIDIAN
  Kurux
  Tamil

SINO-TIBETAN
  Wu
  *Taiwanese
  *Tibetan

AUSTRO-ASIATIC
  *Korku
  *Santali
  *Kharia
  *Juang
  *Sedang
  *Car

INDO-PACIFIC
  *Awji
  *Sko
  *Morwap

AUSTRO-TAI
  *Lakkia
  *Nenema

NA-DENE
  *Eyak
  Dogrib

Chipewyan
  (Fort Chipewyan)
*Chipewyan (Slave)
Galice
Chasta Costa
*Navajo
*Kiowa Apache

MACRO-ALGONQUIAN
*Ojibwa
*Hitchiti

MACRO-SIOUAN
Yuchi
Catawba
Seneca
Oneida
Biloxi
Dakota (Teton)
Dakota (Assiniboine)
Dhegiha

HOKAN
*Seri

AZTEC-TANOAN
*Kiowa
Tewa
*Tiwa

OTO-MANGUEAN
Amuzgo
*Chinantec (Sochiapan)
Chinantec (Usila)
Mixtec (Ayutla)
*Mixtec (Jamiltepec)
Mixtec (Molinos)
Trique
*Pame
Otomi (Mezquital)
Otomi (Temoayan)
Mazahua
*Mazatec
Chatino

MACRO-CHIBCHAN
*Warao
*Waica
*Colorado
*Waunana
*Epera
*Paez

GE-PANO-CARIB
*Yagua
Ocaina
*Bacairi
Apinaye
Cayapo
*Chavante
*Cashibo
*Cashinawa
*Amahuaca

ANDEAN-EQUATORIAL
*Auca
*Cayuvava
*Island Carib
*Yucuna
*Arawak
*Motilon
*Wapishana
*Guarani
Siriono
*Kawaib
*Guahibo
*Ayore
*Tucuna
*Guanano
*Tucano
*Cubeo
*Barasano
*Secoya
*Siona
*Jivaro (Aguaruna)
*Jivaro (Huambisa)
*Cofan
Yaruro

*The number of nasal and oral vowels are equal.

BIBLIOGRAPHY

Akamatsu, Tsutomu. 1967. Quelques statistiques sur la fréquence d'utilisation des voyelles nasales françaises. La linguistique 1. 75-80.

Anderson, Stephen R. 1972. On nasalization in Sundanese. Linguistic Inquiry 3. 253-68.

Andrews, Henrietta. 1949. Phonemes and morphophonemes of Temoayan Otomi. IJAL 15. 213-22.

Bendor-Samuel, John T. 1960. Segmentation in the phonological analysis of Terena. Word 16. 348-55.

Bhat, D.N.S. 1975. Two studies on nasalization. Nasálfest, ed. by Ferguson, Hyman, and Ohala, 27-48.

Bloch, Oscar. 1913. Notes sur le langage d'un enfant. Mémoires de la Société de Linguistique de Paris 18. 37-59.

Brasington, R.W.P. 1971. Noun pluralization in Brazilian Portuguese. Journal of Linguistics 7. 151-77.

Charbonneau, René. 1971. Étude sur les voyelles nasales du français canadien. Paris.

Chatterji, Suniti Kumar. 1970. The origin and development of the Bengali language. vol. 1, London.

Chen, Matthew. 1971. Metarules and universal constraints in phonological theory. Project on Linguistic Analysis (Berkeley) 13.

_____. 1973a. Cross-dialectal comparison: a case study and some theoretical considerations. Journal of Chinese Linguistics 1. 38-63.

_____. 1973b. On the formal expression of natural rules in phonology. Journal of Linguistics 9. 223-49.

_____. 1975. An areal study of nasalization in Chinese. Nasálfest, ed. by Ferguson, Hyman, and Ohala, 81-123.

Clumeck, Harold. 1975. A cross-linguistic investigation of vowel nasalization: an instrumental study. Nasálfest, ed. by Ferguson, Hyman, and Ohala, 133-51.

Coustenoble, Hélène N. 1945. La phonétique du provençal moderne. Hertford.

Décaux, Étienne. 1965. Notes sur les voyelles nasales et le (ŋ) polonais. Studia z filologii polskiej i słowianskiej 5. 269-73.

Dukiewicz, Leokadia. 1968. The acoustic-phonetic correlates of ą, ę, in present-day Polish. Speech Analysis and Synthesis 1, ed. by Jassem, 53-68.

Durand, Marguérite. 1953. De la formation des voyelles nasales. Studia Linguistica 7. 33-53.

Ferguson, Charles A. 1963. Assumptions about nasals: a sample study in phonological universals. Universals of language, ed. by Greenberg, 53-60. Cambridge, Mass.

_____. 1975. Universal tendencies and 'normal' nasality. Nasálfest, ed. by Ferguson, Hyman, and Ohala, 175-96.

_____, and Munier Chowdhury. 1960. The phonemes of Bengali. Language 36. 22-59.

_____, Larry M. Hyman, and John J. Ohala. 1975. Nasálfest: Papers from a symposium on nasals and nasalization. Stanford.

Foley, James. 1975. Nasalization as universal phonological process. Nasálfest, ed. by Ferguson, Hyman, and Ohala, 197-212.

Goddard, Ives. 1971. More on the nasalization of PA *aˑ in Eastern Algonquian. IJAL 37. 139-45.

Greenberg, Joseph H. 1966. Synchronic and diachronic universals in phonology. Language 42. 508-18.

Grierson, G. A. 1922. Spontaneous nasalization in the Indo-Aryan languages. Journal of the Royal Asiatic Society, 381-8.

Haden, Earnest F. and Edward A. Bell, Jr. 1964. Nasal vowel phonemes in French. Lingua 13. 62-9.

Harms, Robert T. 1968. Introduction to phonological theory. Englewood Cliffs, New Jersey.

Heffner, R. -M. S. 1964. General phonetics. Madison, Wisc.

Hetzron, Robert. 1969. Two notes on Semitic laryngeals in East Gurage. Phonetica 19. 69- 81.

Hockett, Charles F. 1955. A manual of phonology. IJAL, Memoir 11.

Hoijer, Harry. 1966. Hare phonology: an historical study. Language 42. 499-507.

House, Arthur and Kenneth N. Stevens. 1956. Analog studies of the nasalization of vowels. Journal of Speech and Hearing Disorders 21. 218-32.

Hyman, Larry M. 1972. Nasals and nasalization in Kwa. Studies in African Linguistics 3. 167-205.

_____. 1975. Nasal states and nasal processes. Nasálfest, ed. by Ferguson, Hyman, and Ohala, 249-64.

Ingram, David. 1974. Phonological rules in young children. Journal of Child Language 1. 49-64.

Issatschenko, A. 1937. A propos des voyelles nasales. Bulletin de la Société de Linguistique de Paris 38. 267-79.

Jackson, Kenneth Hurlstone. 1967. A historical phonology of Breton. Dublin.

Kaye, Jonathan D. 1971. Nasal harmony in Desano. Linguistic Inquiry 2. 37-56.

Kiparsky, Paul. 1968. How abstract is phonology? Unpublished MS.

Lacerda, Armando de, and Brian F. Head. 1963. Analise de sons nasais e sons nasalizados do portugues. Revista do Laboratorio de Fonetica Experimental da Faculdade de Letras da Universidade de Coimbra 6.

Ladefoged, Peter. 1971a. Preliminaries to linguistic phonetics. Chicago.

_____. 1971b. The limits of phonology. Form and substance, ed. by Hammerich, Jakobson, and Zwirner, 47-56. Copenhagen.

Lightner, Theodore. 1970. Why and how does vowel nasalization take place? Papers in Linguistics 2. 179-226.

Love, Nigel and Roy Harris. 1974. A note on French nasal vowels. Linguistics 126. 63-8.

Lunt, Horace G. 1973. Remarks on nasality: the case of Guaraní. A Festschrift for Morris Halle, ed. by Anderson and Kiparsky, 131-9.

Madonia, Giovanna. 1969. Les diphthongues décroissantes et les voyelles nasales du portugais. La linguistique 3. 129-32.

Malécot, André. 1960. Vowel nasality as a distinctive feature of American English. Language 36. 222-9.

Martinet, André. 1965. Les voyelles nasales du français. La linguistique 1. 117-22.

Matisoff, James A. 1970. Glottal dissimilation and the Lahu high-rising tone: a tonogenetic case-study. Journal of the American Oriental Society 90. 13-44.

_____. 1975. Rhinoglottophilia: the mysterious connection between nasality and glottality. Nasálfest, ed. by Ferguson, Hyman, and Ohala, 265-87.

McMillan, James B. 1939. Vowel nasality as a sandhi-form of the morphemes -nt and -ing in Southern American. American Speech 14. 120-3.

Morais-Barbosa, Jorge. 1962. Les voyelles nasales portugaises: interprétation phonologique. Proceedings of the Fourth International Congress of Phonetic Sciences (Helsinki, 1961), 691-708. The Hague.

Narang, G.C. and Donald A. Becker. 1971. Aspiration and nasalization in the generative phonology of Hindi-Urdu. Language 47.646-67.

Needham, Doris and Marjorie Davis. 1946. Cuicateco phonology. IJAL 12. 139-46.

Ohala, John J. 1971a. Monitoring soft palate movements in speech. Project on Linguistic Analysis (Berkeley) 13.

_____. 1971b. The role of physiological and acoustic models in exploring the direction of sound change. Project on Linguistic Analysis (Berkeley) 15. 25-40.

_____. 1972. Physical models in phonology. Proceedings of the Seventh International Congress of Phonetic Sciences (Montreal, 1971), 1166-71. The Hague.

Ohala, John J. 1975. Phonetic explanations for nasal sound patterns.
Nasálfest, ed. by Ferguson, Hyman, and Ohala, 289-316.

Ohala, Manjari. 1972. Topics in Hindi-Urdu phonology. UCLA
dissertation.

_____. 1975. Nasals and nasalization in Hindi. Nasálfest,
ed. by Ferguson, Hyman, and Ohala, 317-332.

Pandit, P.B. 1972. Parameters of speech variation in an Indian
community. India as a socio-linguistic area, ed. by Pandit.
Poona.

Pope, Mildred K. 1934. From Latin to Modern French. Manchester.

Posner, Rebecca. 1971. On synchronic and diachronic rules:
French nasalization. Lingua 27. 184-97.

Robins, R.H. 1953. The phonology of nasalized verbal forms in
Sundanese. Bulletin of the School of Oriental and African Studies
15. 138-45. Reprinted in Readings in Linguistics II, ed. by
Hamp, Householder, and Austerlitz, 322-8. Chicago, 1966.

_____. 1957. Vowel nasality in Sundanese: a phonological
and grammatical study. Studies in linguistic analysis. Oxford.

Rochet, Bernard. to appear. The history and evolution of the
French nasal vowels. Revision of a University of Alberta dissertation.

Rouget, Gilbert. 1972. La nasalisation des voyelles et le système
des consonnes en gun. Langues et techniques nature et société,
ed. by Thomas and Bernot, I. 209-19.

Ruhlen, Merritt. 1973. Nasal vowels. Working Papers on Language Universals 12. 1-36

_____. 1974. Some comments on vowel nasalization in French.
Journal of Linguistics 10. 271-5.

_____. 1975a. A guide to the languages of the world. Stanford.

_____. 1975b. Patterning of nasal vowels. Nasálfest, ed. by
Ferguson, Hyman, and Ohala, 333-51.

Saciuk, Bohdan. 1970. Some basic rules of Portuguese phonology. Studies presented to Robert B. Lees by his students, ed. by Sadock and Vanek, 197-222. Edmonton.

Sardesai, V.N. 1930. Some problems in the nasalization of Marathi. Journal of the Royal Asiatic Society, 537-65.

Schachter, Paul and Victoria Fromkin. 1968. A phonology of Akan: Akuapem, Asante, Fante. Working Papers in Phonetics 9. University of California, Los Angeles.

Schane, Sanford A. 1968a. French phonology and morphology. Cambridge, Mass.

_____. 1968b. On the non-uniqueness of phonological representations. Language 44. 709-16.

_____. 1971. The phoneme revisited. Language 47. 503-21.

Schourup, Lawrence. 1972. Characteristics of vowel nasalization. Papers in Linguistics 5. 530-48.

_____. 1973. A cross-linguistic study of vowel nasalization Working Papers in Linguistics 15. 190-221. Ohio State University.

Sherzer, Joel. 1972. Vowel nasalization in Eastern Algonquian: an areal-typological perspective on linguistic universals. IJAL 38. 267-8.

Skinner, Leo E. 1962. Usila Chinantec syllable structure. IJAL 28. 251-5.

Stahlke, Herbert. 1971. On the status of the nasalized vowels in Kwa. Papers in African Linguistics, ed. by Kim and Stahlke, 239-47.

St. Clair, Robert N. 1971. The Portuguese plural formation. Linguistics 68. 90-102.

Straka, Georges. 1955. Remarques sur les voyelles nasales, leur origine et leur évolution en français. Revue de linguistique romane 19. 245- 74.

Thalbitzer, William. 1904. A phonetical study of the Eskimo language. Meddelelser om Grønland 31.

Thompson, Laurence C. and M. Terry Thompson. 1972. Language universals, nasals, and the northwest coast. Studies in linguistics in honor of George Trager, ed. by Smith, 441-56. The Hague.

Trager, Felicia Harben. 1971. The phonology of Picuris. IJAL 37. 29-33.

Trager, George L. 1944. The verb morphology of spoken French. Language 20. 131-41.

Valdman, Albert. 1959. Les bases statistiques de l'antériorité articulatoire du françias. Le français moderne 27. 102-10.

Vennemann, Theo. 1972. Phonological uniqueness in natural generative grammar. Glossa 6. 105-16.

Wierzchowska, Bożena and Josef Wierzchowska. 1969. Nasal phonemes and their realization in Polish. Study of Sounds 14. 397-406.

Wright, James. 1975. Effects of vowel nasalization on the perception of vowel height. Nasálfest, ed. by Ferguson, Hyman, and Ohala, 373-87.

Zagórska-Brooks, Maria. 1968. Nasal vowels in contemporary standard Polish. The Hague.

Some Generalizations Concerning Initial and Final Consonant Clusters

JOSEPH H. GREENBERG

ABSTRACT

Based on a sample of 104 languages, 40 universals regarding initial and final clusters are formulated. These fall into five main groups: 1) the marked status of clusters as such; 2) preferred types of assimilation; 3) preferred types of dissimilation; 4) preferences based on the relation to the peak of the syllable; 5) preferences for certain consonantal types over others not dependent on factors involved in groups 2), 3) and 4).

This article is a somewhat revised version of one originally published in Russian in Voprosy Jazykoznanija (1964) 4. 41-65. An English version appeared subsequently in Linguistics 18. 5-34 (1965). It was subsequently utilized and commented on in Charles E. Cairns, Markedness, neutralization and universal redundancy rules, Language 45.4. 863-85 (1969); Doris L. Pertz, Sensitivity to phonological universals in children and adults, doctoral dissertation, Columbia University (1973), and Doris L. Pertz and Thomas G. Bever, Sensitivity to phonological universals in children and adolescents, Working Papers on Language Universals 13. 69-90 (December 1973).

I am particularly indebted to Doris L. Pertz for critical comments. The only substantial change incorporated into this version is owing to her. Former universal 34, asserting the existence of at least one initial cluster of liquid + nasal implies at least one of liquid + obstruent has been withdrawn through lack of sufficient empirical evidence, and subsequent universals have been renumbered.

The original study was supported by the National Institute of Health (M8 0739-01) and by a grant in aid of my personal research from the Behavioral Sciences division of the Ford Foundation. This assistance is gratefully acknowledged.

In the present study, which is of a preliminary nature, a number of generalizations are proposed regarding initial and final consonant sequences, based on a sample of approximately one hundred languages. All assertions made here are to be understood as not claiming any validity beyond this sample. It is, of course, reasonable to conclude that, although exceptions are to be expected with further investigation, they should be few in number and that, therefore, at least a statistical validity for the statements made here can be claimed.

Most previous study of consonant clusters has been related more or less directly to the question of the possible functional definition of phonemes in terms of their behavior in combinations. Almost the only attempt to generalize about the characteristics of consonant clusters is to be found in an article of Trnka, which was subject to a critique by Trubetskoĭ.[1] The most important suggestion of Trnka in relation to the present paper is that "...phonemes differentiated by a mark of correlation never combine in the same morpheme ..." As indicated by Trubetskoĭ, this is not true as a completely general statement since, for example, nasal and voiced homorganic stop is not only a permitted but even a favored combination. It does, however, hold for some features under certain conditions. The generalizations 11, 12, and 13 below are specific cases of this principle. Trnka also pointed out the incompatibility of combinations of two different kinds of sibilants, reflected in generalization 16 of the present paper. A further point in Trnka's discussion which has proven useful is his appreciation of morpheme boundaries as allowing combinations forbidden internally in the morpheme. This factor is involved in the statement of a number of the universals presented here.

The only other suggestion which has proven useful for this study is that of Hjelmslev in regard to resolvability, that is, the principle that longer consonant sequences in general contain as partial sequences shorter ones which are likewise occurrent.[2] This point is incorporated in generalization 2.

---

[1] B. Trnka, General Laws of Phoneme Combinations, Travaux du Cercle Linguistique de Prague 4. 75-61 (1931) and N. Trubetskoĭ, Principes de phonologie (Paris, 1949), 264-8. It is indicative of how little has been done in this area that no universals of consonant combinations figure in the general table of universals to be found in B. Uspenskiĭ's review of Universals of language (Cambridge, 1962) in Voprosy Jazykoznanija 5. 121-9 (1963).

[2] L. Hjelmslev, On the principles of phonematics, Proceedings of the Second International Congress of Phonetic Sciences (1936), 49-54.

The language employed in the present study are listed in the appended bibliography with a numerical designation for convenience of reference in the text of the article and with the chief sources employed for each language. Where I consider the material to be significantly defective in completeness or in phonetic information, this has likewise been indicated. It is clear that even incomplete information can yield relevant evidence for some generalizations, while being insufficient for others. Thus, a generalization that a lateral is never followed by a vibrant ("r" sound) can be refuted by a single valid example from a description which is seriously incomplete, while being insufficient to refute a generalization of other types, e.g. that every language which has an initial obstruent followed by a nasal also has some combination of initial obstruent followed by a liquid. In such a case we might find /kn/ among the clusters reported but no examples such as /kr/ because of the insufficiency of the material.

The exclusion of medial clusters was dictated chiefly by practical considerations. The number of such combinations is often very large. Further, many of the sources utilized in the present study contain statements regarding initial and final clusters only. The study of medial clusters also raises some theoretical problems not present in the case of initial and final clusters. For example, in languages with syllabic initial and final single consonants or clusters, except for possible word-sandhi phenomena, the medial clusters produced at word boundaries are in general predictable from initial and final combinations. Such clusters should evidently be distinguished from those which are word-internal and which may or may not be present in languages independently of the question as to whether word-boundary clusters exist. Again, morpheme boundary and morpheme internal clusters should be distinguished among word internal clusters. For these reasons a study of medial clusters would be much more elaborate and difficult to undertake from existing data.

Preliminary to setting forth specific results, it will be necessary to consider a few problems of theoretical method. These are only briefly discussed, insofar as they affect the procedure employed in the present study. The very phrase consonant cluster raises definitional problems which have to be decided in order to compare consistently data from different languages. A first question, then, concerns the definition of consonant. In accordance with the usual notion, consonant is understood here in terms of function in the syllable, i.e. as a margin rather than peak. This will mean, however, that the syllabic and non-syllabic allophones of the same

phoneme, e.g. [u], [w] in some languages, will have only the latter
allophones reckoned as consonants. Strictly speaking, if there are
both consonant and vowel allophones of the same phoneme, then
this distinction is an irrelevant feature for the phoneme concerned
at the same time that it is a central question in the present study.
It is clear that this same basic consideration arises at other points.
Consider, for example, the generalization stated below as number
5. This asserts that the presence of final heterorganic nasal obstruent combinations in any language implies the existence of
homorganic combinations. Now many languages have final combinations which are phonetically [ŋk] or [ŋg] where [ŋ] is to be
considered as a member of an /n/ phoneme containing [n] and [ŋ]
among its variants. A naive reading of a phonemic transcription
/nk/ would lead to its classification as a heterorganic combination.
Strictly speaking, however, since in this case the difference between dental-alveolar and velar position is a non-distinctive feature,
we have no right to classify it as either heterorganic or homorganic
on a phonemic basis. Yet a classification of the sounds on a phonetic
basis allows us to compare languages and draw general conclusions.[3]
Further, it is evidently the same tendency operating in different
languages which leads to this particular allophonic distribution of
[n] and [ŋ] in one language while in another which contains distinct
/n/ and /ŋ/ phonemes, it leads to a preference for sequences like
/nd/ and /ŋg/ while it disfavors /ng/ and /ŋd/.

Since allophonic information is, for the reasons just adduced,
essential to the present study, statements of phonemic combinations in the literature had to be supplemented by phonetic descriptions in the same or other works. For this reason also, data from
languages of the past were not included in the sample of 104, although
in certain instances such languages were taken into consideration
when the absence of phonetic detail did not seriously affect a particular hypothesis.

The other part of the phrase 'consonant cluster' also raises difficulties. It is well known that for certain classes of sounds, the
decision as to whether we have a cluster or succession of phonemes

---

[3] What is said here is in close agreement with the view of E.
Fischer-Jørgensen that "...the tendencies to free combinations or
to definite restrictions between different parts of the syllable seem
to be more easily formulated when the parts of the syllable are
defined on a phonetic basis." (On the definition of phoneme categories on a distributional basis, Acta Linguistica 7. 8-39 (1952)).

as against a single phoneme has not produced a usable unarbitrary
criterion which meets with general consent. Thus, in languages
with the phonemic contrast of unaspirated and aspirated consonants,
the alternative solution as a single phoneme, e.g. /p̓/ or a cluster
/ph/ depends on considerations of symmetry or "pattern" in the
sound system in general which often leads to individually different
solutions even for the same language. It seems unavoidable, for
purposes of valid comparison among languages, that one must make
a decision in such matters which, even though it may be arbitrary,
will be consistently applied. In general the sequences at issue are
well characterized in N. Trubetskoĭ's classic work on phonology
as "produced by a single articulatory movement or by means of a
progressive dissociation of an articulatory complex."[4] In the
former of these cases, that of the affricates, I have considered
the articulation to be a cluster of stop + fricative. The latter have
all been considered single consonants. These include aspirated,
glottalized, labialized, palatalized, velarized, and pharyngealized
sounds. The sequence nasal + homorganic voiced stop, treated as
a single phoneme in some languages by some analysts, e.g. FIJIAN,
is here always treated as a cluster.

A further problem of definition arises regarding the terms
'initial' and 'final.' In principle, initial and final in the utterance
is intended. Most studies are in terms of word initial and final
which generally comes to the same thing as utterance initial and
final. Where there are word sandhi rules, however, only the
utterance initial or final forms are considered in the formulation
of generalizations. Where word boundaries occur between members of a consonantal sequence which is actually or potentially utterance initial or final, the entire sequence is viewed as a valid
cluster. Thus, RUSSIAN v dome, 'in the house,' is considered
as having an initial consonant cluster [vd].

A particularly vexing question concerns the treatment of clusters
in borrowed words. The line between forms recent enough to be
considered borrowings and those which can be considered fully
assimilated into the language is difficult to draw. Moreover, some
of the studies utilized distinguished borrowed from native clusters,
while others did not. As far as possible this distinction was made
in compiling the material from the original sources where given,
from etymological dictionaries, or from my own knowledge. However, since such data were not obtained from all of the languages,

---

[4] N. Trubetskoĭ 1949: 58.

it is to be understood that, as a general rule, borrowed are included
along with indigenous clusters in the statements of the present article. While the exclusion of combinations in borrowed forms would
change the typological assignment of certain languages in the tables
below, in no case would such a change have been sufficient to in-
validate a hypothesis.

A further question concerns the distinction between clusters which
appear only with contained morpheme boundaries and those which do
not. Again an attempt was made to record this distinction as far as
possible, but in some instances the information at my disposal was
not sufficient to resolve this question. In several instances where
the relevant evidence was sufficient, the existence of morpheme
boundaries figures in the statement of generalizations.

Finally, there is the question as to what particular variety of a
language is intended, or even which speech tempo since, in many
instances, particular consonant sequences which occur in slower
and careful speech are contracted or assimilated in more rapid or
more colloquial instances. In general, I have treated so-called
"standard" languages simply because they have usually been more
carefully described from the phonetic point of view. In general,
the source cited in the bibliography will give sufficient indication
of the particular variety of a language which is being considered.
For HINDI the RANKHANDI dialect was used and for KAREN,
SGAW. On the question of speech styles, I have in general utilized
the lento forms as against the allegro, but I have recorded data
concerning such variation where they were present. It is plausible
to consider that allegro forms give important insight into the identification of "difficult" and less-favored sequences and into the
direction of historical change. However, their systematic treatment has been left for further investigation.

In general it proved useful to distinguish between initial and final
clusters as separate systems with distinct though often similar
properties. In the sample of 104 languages there were found to be
90 initial systems and 62 final systems. Although the possibilities
of certain connections are not to be excluded, in general initial and
final systems seem to function independently and it was not possible
to formulate any generalizations connecting them.

The first set of hypotheses concern properties of initial and
final systems which correlate with the length of the sequences.

1. For initial and final systems, if x is the number of sequences
    of length m and y is the number of sequences of length n and

$\underline{m} > \underline{n}$, and $\underline{p}$ is the number of consonant phonemes, then
$$\frac{x}{p^m} \leq \frac{y}{p^n}.$$

In other other words the propertion of the logically possible combination utilized decreases or remains the same with increasing length of the sequences. This may be illustrated for ENGLISH initial clusters as follows: the number of consonant phonemes are 22. All of these except /ž/ and /ŋ/ occur as single phonemes. The logically possible sequences of length 2 are $22^2 = 484$. Of these 28 occur. For length 3 the logically possible number of combinations is $22^3 = 10,648$. Of these only 8 occur. No sequences of length greater than 3 are found. Hence,

$$\frac{20}{22}\,(L{=}1) > \frac{28}{484}\,(L{=}2) > \frac{8}{10,648}\,(L{=}3) > 0\,(L{=}4) = 0\,(L{=}5) \text{ etc.}$$

It will be noted that the absolute number of combinations of length 2, i.e. 28, is greater than those of length 3, i.e. 8, etc. However, in the limiting case $L{=}1$, in this as in many other instances the number of combinations of length 2 is greater than length 1. We can therefore make the following statement regarding absolute length:

2. For initial and final systems, if $\underline{x}$ is the number of sequences of length $\underline{m}$ and $\underline{y}$ is the number of sequences of length $\underline{n}$, and $\underline{m} > \underline{n}$ and $\underline{n} \geq 2$, then $\underline{x} \leq \underline{y}$.

The statement in the "Memorandum concerning language universals," in Universals of language that "If syllables containing sequences of $\underline{n}$ consonants in a language are to be found as syllabic types, then sequences of $\underline{n}-1$ consonants are also to be found in the corresponding position (prevocalic or postvocalic) except that CV $\longrightarrow$ V does not hold," can be deduced as a corollary from either 1 or 2 above, insofar as it refers to word initial and final as a special case of syllabic initial and final.[5] Further, 1 and 2 make no assertion concerning $L{=}0$ since in this case there is no question of combinations.

In general the validity of 1 and 2, to which no exception was found in the 104 languages of the sample, provides objective evidence of the "difficulty" of clusters. This would seem to correlate with the diachronic tendency towards their simplification, since any simplification automatically reduces the number, both absolutely and

---

[5]Universals of language, ed. by J.H. Greenberg (Cambridge 1963), p. 263.

proportionally, of sequences of the length subject to reduction and increases the number of shorter sequences.

The next statement refers to the property of resolvability which was first suggested by Hjelmslev. A sequence is here said to be completely resolvable if every continuous subsequence also occurs. For example, if in a language initial <u>fstr</u> occurs then if <u>fs</u>, <u>st</u>, <u>tr</u>, <u>fst</u> and <u>str</u> all occur, it is completely resolvable. If some of these occur but not otherwise, it is partially resolvable, and if none occurs, it is non-resolvable.

    3. Every initial or final sequence of length m contains at least one continuous subsequence of length $m - 1$.

In the overwhelming majority of instances sequences are completely resolvable. In the weaker form asserted here there are still a very small number of unresolvable sequences in the material collected. These were from CHATINO, PAME, and COEUR D'ALENE and totalled 10 in all. Thus this assertion has only statistical validity but far beyond chance within any reasonable confidence limit. That this is not a chance phenomenon in the individual languages can be illustrated from initial clusters in ENGLISH. Here all 8 clusters of length 3 (<u>skw</u>, <u>skr</u>, <u>skl</u>, <u>skj</u>, <u>spl</u>, <u>spj</u>, <u>spr</u> and <u>str</u>) are completely resolvable. Now the only initial clusters of length 3 that can be formed from those of length 2 that conform to the requirement of complete resolvability are the following: <u>spl</u>, <u>spr</u>, <u>spj</u>, <u>str</u>, <u>stw</u>, <u>skl</u>, <u>skr</u>, <u>skj</u>, <u>skw</u>, <u>sfl</u>, <u>sfr</u>, <u>sfj</u>. That 8 clusters chosen at random out of $20^3 = 8,000$ logically possible combinations should all fall within a set of 12 is, of course, highly significant statistically. This generalization could be restated as follows: For every initial and final system and for every length, the number of completely resolvable sequences is greater than the number of those which are not completely resolvable. This statement has no exceptions in the present material.

The reason for the phenomenon of resolvability is, at least partly, that longer sequences are formed from shorter sequences by morphological or syntactic combination. The latter occurs, for example, in initial consonant sequences in the SLAVIC languages where prepositions consisting of a single consonant are found. From this it should follow, as a general result, that the longer a sequence the more likely it is to contain one or more morpheme or word boundary. Unfortunately, it was only possible to classify the sequences in this regard for a few languages. Two classes of sequences were distinguished, those which occurred exclusively with a contained morpheme or word boundary and those which occurred in at least some cases without such an internal boundary. The following generalization is therefore merely a probable conjecture which was verified in the few cases presented below.

4. In all initial and final systems, if there are sequences of length $\underline{m}$ and $\underline{n}$ and $\underline{m} > \underline{n}$, then the proportion of sequences of length $\underline{m}$ which only occur with internal morpheme boundaries is equal to or greater than the proportion of such sequences which occur of length $\underline{n}$. Since every word boundary will also be a morpheme boundary, it is sufficient to state the above generalization in terms of morpheme boundaries.

Among the cases investigated were Cœur d'Alene and Dutch. In Cœur d'Alene initial clusters the ratios were as follows:

$$\frac{0}{42} \, (L = 1) < \frac{83}{88} \, (L = 2) < \frac{42}{42} \, (L = 3) = \frac{2}{2} \, (L = 4).$$

The final ratios were:

$$\frac{0}{42} \, (L = 1) < \frac{62}{77} \, (L = 2) < \frac{11}{12} \, (L = 3) < \frac{1}{1} \, (L = 4).$$

Dutch initials do not have morpheme boundaries. Hence the results will of course be 0 $(L = 1) = 0 \, (L = 2) = 0 \, (L = 3)$. For finals we have:

$$\frac{0}{11} \, (L = 1) < \frac{2}{38} \, (L = 2) < \frac{20}{32} \, (L = 3) < \frac{10}{11} \, (L = 4) < \frac{2}{2} \, (L = 5).$$

We now turn to hypotheses of a more specific nature. These may be classified from two points of view, logical and material. Logically, we have an implication if, whenever a system has a particular property ϕ it also has some other, ψ. The majority of the hypotheses stated here are of this nature. If properties ϕ and ψ mutually imply each other, they are equivalent. Every language with property ϕ has ψ and vice versa. Another logical type consists of assertions regarding the intersection of all systems. Such properties may be considered basic in that they apply to all systems even those with the fewest combinations. If a particular logically possible type of combination does not occur in any system it belongs to the complement of the class union of all the systems. In this case even the most extensive system does not possess the particular property.

From the material or phonetic point of view hypotheses always have to do with the favoring of certain types of consonants or consonant sequences over other consonants or consonant sequences. Such hypotheses may be classified as contextual, ordinal and absolute. By contextual will be meant the tendency for one class of consonants to be favored over another in a particular context. Insofar as the context itself shares similarities with the class of consonants in question it is assimilatory, insofar as it differs it is dissimilatory. It is evident that these names which are properly applied to diachronic processes are appropriate here insofar as the operation of these types of change will tend to produce the given contextual properties in sequences described synchronically. By an ordinal hypothesis will be meant one which concerns the favoring of particular classes of consonants not only by context but also by reference to order. Such hypotheses are usually related to the structure of the syllable and to the tendency of certain classes of sounds to be peripheral (e.g. stops) and of others to be central (e.g. liquids, semivowels) in reference to the central vocalic nucleus. Finally, by an absolute hypothesis is meant one which concerns an overall tendency to favor one class of sounds as against another independently of context or orientation in the syllable. Thus, there is a tendency to favor unvoiced over voiced combinations, of un-glottalized as against glottalized, and of sibilants as against other spirants. In general we consider hypotheses here in conformity with the foregoing classification into assimilatory, dissimilatory, ordinal and absolute.

The first of our specific hypotheses has to do with the favoring of combinations which are homogeneous in respect to voicing over those which are heterogeneous.

5. There are no initial or final systems in which all obstruent combinations are heterogeneous in regard to voicing.

The force of this statement derives from the fact that there are languages in which all obstruent combinations are homogeneous in regard to voice, e.g. ENGLISH, POLISH.[6] An assertion of similar type cannot be made with regard to obstruent-sonant combinations because the sonant is most usually voiced whether in combination with a voiced or unvoiced obstruent.

---

[6]An exception outside of the sample is PALAYCHI KAREN all of whose (initial) obstruent clusters are unvoiced + voiced. A revised statement that in all languages with obstruent clusters, there are some with first member unvoiced would, as far as my knowledge goes, be without exception.

Another hypothesis of assimilation concerns the preference of nasals for the following voiced stop to be at the same point of articulation (homorganic combinations).

6. In final systems the existence of at least one sequence consisting of a nasal (voiced or unvoiced) followed by a heterorganic obstruent implies the existence of at least one sequence consisting of a nasal (voiced or unvoiced) followed by a homorganic obstruent.

As with other statements of the form $\phi \supset \psi$, the falsity of the opposite implication $\psi \supset \phi$ is tacitly asserted. If it were true, the universal would be stated in the form of an equivalence. As supporting evidence from the sample of 104 languages, we cite by number those which have both final heterorganic and homorganic sequences of nasal followed by obstruent and those which have homorganic sequences without heterorganic. In the implicitly asserted typology, then, one of the four logically possible types, the class of languages with heterorganic but without homorganic sequences of this kind is null.

Languages with final systems containing both heterorganic and homorganic combinations are, then, as follows: 1, 2, 3, 4, 7, 10, 13, 27, 28, 30, 33, 35, 36, 41, 42, 43, 48, 49, 61, 62, 64, 67, 72, 75, 76, 80, 81, 86, 87, 94, 101, 102, and 103. Languages with final systems containing homorganic without heterorganic combinations are: 5, 11, 15, 16, 23, 34, 44, 45, 46, 51, 66, 69, 70, 77, 82, 89, 93, 96, 97, 98. The data for 57 (KASHMIRI) were not sufficient to decide between these two possibilities. The remaining languages with final systems did not have any combinations of nasals and obstruents.

These results can be shown in the following table:

	Heterorganic	~Heterorganic
Homorganic	33	20
~ Homorganic	0	8

Table 1

A similar statement for initial systems holds in almost all cases, but a number of SLAVIC languages (e.g. RUSSIAN, POLISH, CZECH) are conspicuous exceptions in that they contain initial heterorganic combinations such as mg without having homorganic sequences. It should be noted that for purposes of the present hypothesis sequences of nasal followed by obstruent are included even when preceded or followed by one or more consonants. Thus, RUSSIAN /mgla/ counts as an instance of a heterorganic cluster.

We now consider hypotheses of dissimilation. The first group has to do with preference for combinations of stop and spirant as against stop + stop or spirant + spirant. The hypotheses presented here refers to sequences of length two only. In fact sequences of three or more stops or three or more fricatives are excessively rare and implicational universals analogous to the following could doubtless be formulated.

7. In initial systems the presence of at least one combination of stop + stop implies the presence of at least one combination of stop + fricative.

In fact languages with stop + stop almost always have both stop + fricative and fricative + stop combinations. Affricates are counted here as stop + fricative as explained in an earlier section. The following languages which have stop + stop combinations also have both stop + fricative and fricative + stop: 2, 10, 14, 16, 27, 28, 30, 31, 32, 34, 38, 41, 42, 44, 59, 61, 77, 79, 80, 81, 82, 93, and 102. Two languages, 47 and 87, have stop + stop and stop + fricative but do not have fricative + stop. Further details are given in Table 2.

	FS·SF	FS	SF	~(FS V SF)
SS	23	0	2	0
~ SS	35	3	20	7

Table 2

8. In final systems the presence of at least one combination of stop + stop implies the presence of at least one combination of fricative + stop. Here again most languages with stop + stop have both stop + fricative and fricative + stop. Languages with all three combinations are: 2, 3, 4, 7, 16, 27, 30, 33, 35, 36, 38, 41, 42, 43, 44, 48, 61, 62, 64, 67, 72, 77, 80, 81, 82, 86, 87, 94, 96, 101. Only one language, 98, had stop + stop and fricative + stop without stop + fricative. The details are shown in Table 3.

SS	FS·SF	FS	SF	~(FS V SF)
SS	30	0	3	0
~ SS	16	10	4	1

Table 3

The slight preference shown for initial stop + spirant and final spirant + stop in the above two statements, suggests a possible connection with syllabic structure in that the more open fricative is in each case closer to the vocalic center of the syllable.   .

Similar generalizations concerning initial and final fricative combinations are as follows:

9. In initial systems the existence of at least one fricative + fricative combination implies the presence of at least one stop + fricative combination or at least one fricative + stop combination.

In most cases both stop + fricative and fricative + stop combinations are found in languages with fricative + fricative. These are 1, 3, 10, 13, 14, 27, 28, 30, 33, 35, 36, 38, 39, 41, 42, 44, 48, 52, 61, 62, 63, 64, 75, 77, 80, 81, 82, 86, 93, 103, 104. Only one language has fricative + fricative without fricative + stop, 56. Two languages, 49 and 57, have fricative + fricative without stop + fricative. Further information is given in Table 4.

	FS·SF	FS	SF	~(FS∨SF)
FF	31	2	1	0
~FF	29	18	3	6

Table 4

10. In final systems the existence of at least one fricative + fricative combination implies the presence of at least one stop + fricative or at least one fricative + stop combination.

The languages with fricative + fricative combinations which have both fricative + stop and stop + fricative combinations are 3, 4, 7, 13, 18, 27, 30, 33, 35, 36, 41, 42, 43, 49, 61, 62, 64, 67, 75, 76, 77, 79 and 86. Two languages with final fricative + fricative lack the final stop + fricative combination, 34 and 98, and one language, 1, lacks fricative + stop. These and other results are summarized in Table 5.

	FS·SF	FS	SF	~(FS∨SF)
FF	23	2	1	0
~FF	22	3	9	2

Table 5

The general thesis of Trnka regarding the non-occurrence of
sequences which differ in only one feature holds in certain limited
cases, chiefly those involving differences in laryngeal adjustment
such as voicing, voicelessness and glottalization. In regard to the
contrast voiced vs. voiceless, sequences of voiced and unvoiced
nasals occur, the unvoiced often being phonemically interpreted as
/h/. There are legitimate though rare examples of sequences of
otherwise identical voiced and unvoiced fricatives. These are
initial /sz/, /fv/ and /ky/ in PALAYCHI KAREN, not in the present
sample, and final /vf/ in GILYAK. In regard to stops, initial /td/
was noted in BILAAN and KHASI. In both instances the absence of
detail in the accompanying phonetic description in the sources suggest the possibility of a svarabhakti vowel. The only example in
final systems is COEUR D'ALENE /dt/ in which, however, there
is a morphological boundary between the consonants. It is reasonable to expect that otherwise non-existent combinations will tend
to resist change when a morphological boundary is present through
the analogical presence of the other allomorphs which contain the
sounds in question. It will be seen later that the fact that in these
exceptions in initial systems the unvoiced precedes the voiced but
in final the voiced precedes the unvoiced is not accidental. Generalizations partly covering this same ground will be formulated
below.

The sequence of otherwise identical voiceless and glottalized
consonants is likewise extremely rare. The only example found in
the sample was initial /kk̓/ in KUTENAI involving a morpheme
boundary. Outside of the sample an instance in EYAK, but without
phonetic description, cited by Fang-Kuei Li, namely final /q̓q/ and
also involving a morpheme boundary was noted.[7] Finally, not a
single instance is found in the sample of a sequence of consonants
in which the only difference was between voicing in one and glottalization in the other. Thus not only such sequences as */p̓b/ do
not occur, but also */mm̓/ etc. are not found. Indeed, the general
tendency for glottalized sounds not to occur in clusters with voiced
leads to the formulation of a principle which partly overlaps the
preceding, namely, that no sequence of glottalized and voiced obstruents occur. The partial dependence of these two statements is
shown by the fact that a sequence */bp̓/ violates both. Their non-
identity is shown by the fact that */ll̓/ violates the first but not the
second, while */p̓g/ violates the second but not the first. None
of the statements in this paragraph are limited to sequences of two
consonants only. We have, then, the following generalizations:

---

[7] IJAL 22 (1956), p. 47.

11. An unvoiced stop in initial systems is never preceded
    immediately by a stop differing only by voicing, and in
    final systems is never immediately followed by such a stop.

12. In final systems a voiced stop is only followed immediately
    by a stop differing only in being unvoiced if there is a mor-
    pheme boundary between them.

13. No succession of consonants only differing in that one is
    unvoiced and the other is glottalized occurs in initial or
    final systems unless there is a morpheme boundary between
    them.

14. No combination of a voiced and glottalized obstruent is found
    in either initial or final systems.

Two further hypotheses concern the well-known tendencies of
liquid and sibilants not to occur together. While the final sequence
r̠l is fairly common, initial r̠l only occurs in MITLA ZAPOTEC
with morpheme boundary. No example of l̠r is found in the present
material. In regard to sibilants there is a strong tendency for different type sibilants, most commonly [s] and [š], not to combine.
Practically all examples occur with morpheme boundary. The only
example without morpheme boundary in clusters with only two members was SHILHA BERBER final /zž/. There was no case of final
hushing followed by hissing sibilant, e.g. */šs/ in final two-member
clusters. These generalizations can be stated as follows:

15. In initial and final systems a lateral is never followed im-
    mediately by an r̠-type sound. In initial system the sequence
    r̠ + lateral only occurs with morpheme boundary.

16. In final systems, clusters with two members never consist
    of a hushing followed by a hissing sibilant.

We next consider hypotheses of the ordinal type as defined earlier.
A first group concerns the tendency of liquids to follow obstruents in
initial systems and precede them in final systems. It is true that
the opposite order is sometimes found. In many such cases, particularly in final position in the word or in contact with voiceless
consonants, the liquid itself is voiceless. Even where this is not so,
statements of an implicational type can be made.

17. In initial systems the existence of at least one sequence
    containing a liquid, whether voiced or unvoiced, immediately
    followed by an obstruent implies the existence of at least

one sequence containing an obstruent immediately followed
by a liquid.

The following languages have liquid followed by obstruent and
also obstruent followed by liquid: 2, 10, 14, 20, 28, 30, 41, 59, 75,
77, 81, 103. The following have no obstruent liquid combinations
of any kind: 6, 21, 29, 31, 34, 47, 54, 58, 66, 71, 73, 79, 90, 99,
100. The remainder, representing the most common type, have
obstruent followed by liquid without liquid followed by obstruent.
These results are set forth in Table 6.

	OL	~OL
LO	12	0
~LO	65	15

Table 6

A comparable hypothesis is valid for final systems.

18. In final systems, the existence of at least one sequence
containing a stop immediately followed by a liquid implies
the presence of at least one sequence containing a liquid
followed by a stop.

The languages with both obstruent +liquid and liquid +obstruent
are: 2, 7, 15, 28, 38, 41, 43, 49, 67, 75, 76, 77, 80, 81, 97, 98
and 103. The largest group of languages has liquid + obstruent but
not obstruent +liquid. The remaining languages have no obstruent
liquid combinations at all. These are 5, 9, 23, 34, 44, 46, 58, 61,
79, 82, 83, 86, 89, 93, 99, 102 and 104. These data are summarized
in Table 7.

	LO	~LO
OL	18	0
~OL	27	17

Table 7

Semivowels, of course, show an equal or even greater tendency
than liquids to be adjacent to the peak of the syllable. There are
a very few cases in the present sample of sequences in which semivowels are separated from vowels by an intervening liquid or nasal,
e.g. initial wr and wl in PASHTO and CHATINO wn and yn. Voiceless semivowels occur with intervening consonants of various types.
However, there is no valid example of a voiced semivowel separated

from a syllabic peak by an obstruent. In CZECH at least in literary pronunciation, we have sequences such as /jde/ and /jsou/. However, CZECH j is described phonetically by Trávníček as fricative (třená) and possessing consonantal noise (souhláskový šelest) and by Kučera as "articulated with a moderate degree of lamino-palatal friction."[8] We have therefore the following statement:

19. Voiced semivowels are not followed by obstruents in initial systems or preceded by obstruents in final systems.

Although there are, as we have seen, instances of two voiced sonants adjacent to a vowel, such a sequence is never separated from the vowel by an obstruent. Nor are there sequences of three sonants in either initial or final systems. GILYAK phonemic final sequences such as xlŋ and nmŋ have phonetically short vowels between the consonants.[9] Hence we have this generalization.

20. Two successive voiced sonants are always followed by a vowel in initial systems and preceded by a vowel in final systems.

The strong tendency towards voicing assimilation was noted earlier. In a minority of instances sequences with both voiced and unvoiced members occur. An examination of these cases shows that in almost all such instances of combinations which are heterogeneous in voicing, the voiced single consonant or the voiced sequence of consonants is adjacent to the vowel. An overall count in the languages of the sample of the obstruent combinations with two members classified according to voicing was made. Where one of the consonants was partly voiced, i.e. voiced during part of the duration of the consonant and unvoiced during the remainder, the combination was not counted. Where there was free variation of two sequences which differed in voicing of one of the members, each variant was accorded half value. These cases were not numerous. Although the method is obviously a crude one and no significance should be attached to the exact figures, the results are of interest in the present connection as giving at least an approximate notion of the relative frequency of the different types. A total of 1030 two

---

[8] F. Trávníček, Mluvnice Spisovné Češtiny (Praha, 1951) I: 19 and H. Kučera, The phonology of Czech ('sGravenhage, 1961), p. 28.

[9] Personal communication, Robert Austerlitz.

member clusters were recorded for initial position and 683 for
final. The results are stated in Table 8 in percentages of the totals.

	Initial	Final
Unvoiced + Unvoiced	66.70	78.62
Voiced + Voiced	21.65	12.59
Unvoiced + Voiced	10.68	2.05
Voiced + Unvoiced	0.97	6.73

Table 8

For initial systems it holds in general, not for obstruent sequences
only, that an unvoiced consonant or succession of consonants preceding a vowel is not itself preceded by voiced segments. The exceptions were almost all instances of nasal + homorganic unvoiced
stop followed by a vowel, e.g. initial /nt/ and were noted for CHA-
TINO, CHRAU and PAME (OTOMI). The other instances of the
interruption of voicing in an initial sequence were from KHASI,
e.g. bt, dp, and BILAAN, e.g. bt, bs. There is also CZECH js,
in which as noted above, CZECH j was interpreted as a voiced
fricative. Since for KHASI and BILAAN few phonetic details were
forthcoming in the descriptions, it is quite possible that, as in
similar instances elsewhere, the initial stop /b/, /d/, etc. are
unvoiced lenes. The following statement is therefore made with
the awareness that the exceptions just noted may be valid.

21. Except for voiced nasal followed by homorganic unvoiced
    obstruent, an unvoiced consonant or sequence of unvoiced
    consonants in initial systems immediately preceding a
    vowel is not itself preceded by one or more voiced con-
    sonants.

In the three languages cited above as having voiced nasal followed
by unvoiced homorganic obstruents, the far more common combination of voiced nasal followed by voiced homorganic obstruent is likewise found. We have, therefore, the following implicational statement

22. In initial systems the presence of at least one sequence of
    voiced nasal + unvoiced homorganic obstruent implies the
    presence of at least one sequence of voiced nasal +voiced
    homorganic obstruent.

The symmetrical thesis for final systems corresponding to that
of 21 for initial systems, asserts that an unvoiced consonant or
sequence of unvoiced consonants immediately preceded by vowel

is not followed by a voiced consonant or sequence of voiced consonants. These two hypotheses taken together amount to the following.
There is a voiced center of the syllable consisting of the vowel and
possible successive preceding and following voiced consonants but
that voicing is normally confined to this nucleus, i.e. that voicing
is not interrupted and resumed within the same syllable. For final
systems again there are very few exceptions in the present material
and these often of doubtful validity. Exceptions include AMHARIC
final kd in a single word, CŒUR D'ALENE final tg^W, HUNGARIAN
šd described as rare by Vértes and not found in Hall, and a few
instances in ARABIC all involving pharyngeals. Corresponding to
the situation in initial systems there are cases of unvoiced obstruent
followed by voiced nasal, in this case not necessarily homorganic,
e.g. PAME tn, kŋ. There are no cases of voiceless liquids or
nasals being followed by voiced consonants. These results may be
summarized in the following statement:

23. In final systems, except for unvoiced obstruents followed
by a voiced nasal, an unvoiced consonant or sequence of
unvoiced consonants following a vowel is not followed by
one or more voiced consonants.

A set of ordinal hypotheses may also be formulated regarding
the tendency of liquids to be closer to the syllabic peak than nasals.
This can be stated in the common implicational form, with the
proviso that unvoiced liquids, as might be expected, do not share
with voiced liquids the property of being nearer to the syllabic peak
than nasals.

24. In initial systems the existence of at least one sequence
consisting of a voiced liquid followed by a nasal implies the
existence of at least one combination consisting of a nasal
followed by a liquid.

By 21, the second member of these combinations must also be
voiced, and by 20 this sequence must be followed by a vowel. Languages containing voiced liquid +nasal as well as nasal +liquid are
14, 30, 41, 59, 75, 77 and 81. Languages with nasal + liquid and
without voiced liquid +nasal are 16, 19, 25, 26, 37, 40, 43, 51, 55,
56, 57, 60, 72, 80, 82 and 84.   Language 2, 10 and 20 do not have
nasal + liquid and do have liquid + nasal but the liquid is voiceless.
MITLA ZAPOTEC (103) has /r̃N/ without any nasal + liquid combination. However, the distinction here is between lenis and fortis
rather than voice or voiceless and /r/ may be voiceless. Little
information on voice and voicelessness is given, hence this is

quite possibly not a real exception. Relevant information is given
in Table 9.

	N + L	~N + L
L + N	7	(1)
~ L + N	16	66

Table 9

The corresponding hypothesis for final systems can be put in
stronger form. Sequences of liquid + nasal are not only favored
over nasal + liquid but in general over all other combinations of
nasals and liquids, i. e. nasal + nasal and liquid + liquid.

25. In final systems, the existence of at least one sequence con-
    sisting of a nasal followed by a liquid, a nasal followed by
    a nasal or a liquid followed by a liquid implies the existence
    of at least one sequence consisting of a liquid followed by a
    nasal. Languages 4, 7, 13, 16, 27, 33, 36, 38, 41, 42, 43,
    49, 67, 72, 76, 77, 80, 86 and 98 have combinations of one
    or more of the types nasal + liquid, nasal + nasal and liquid
    + liquid along with liquid + nasal. Languages 3, 15, 18, 30,
    35, 44, 57, 64, 65, 75, 81. 82, 94 and 102 have liquid +
    nasal without having any combinations of the three other
    types. These data are set forth in Table 10.

	NL∨ NN∨ LL	~ (NL∨NN∨LL)
LN	19	14
~ LN	0	29

Table 10

The first set of hypotheses of the absolute type has to do with
the favoring of unvoiced obstruents over voiced obstruents. The
statistical predominance of unvoiced obstruent + unvoiced obstruent
over the other three types of voicing combinations in clusters with
two members was strikingly displayed in Table 8. A number of
non-statistical generalizations are also possible. Thus for initial
systems the following statement can be made.

26. In initial systems the existence of at least one combination
    consisting of two voiced obstruents implies the existence
    of at least one combination consisting of two unvoiced ob-
    struents. There is here a single exception, the SGAW

INITIAL AND FINAL CONSONANT SEQUENCES 263

dialect of KAREN (56) which has the voiced obstruent combination /bɣ/ but has no sequences with both members voiced. There are, however, combinations in which the first member is unvoiced and second is /ɣ/, for example /pɣ/ and /sɣ/. The languages with both voiced and unvoiced obstruent clusters are 1, 3, 10, 11, 13, 16, 18, 30, 36, 37, 40, 41, 42, 44, 49, 52, 59, 62, 63, 64, 67, 69, 75, 77, 80, 81, 82, 84, 86, 98 and 103. The remainder have only unvoiced obstruent clusters except 56 (KAREN) mentioned as an exception earlier and the following languages which have no clusters of obstruent + obstruent: 8, 9, 25, 29, 50, 57, 60, 74, 78, 90, 91, 95. These data are summarized in Table 11.

	Unvoiced +Unvoiced Obst. Obst.	~Unvoiced + Unvoiced Obst. Obst.
Voiced +Voiced Obst. Obst.	31	1
~ Voiced +Voiced Obst. Obst.	46	12

Table 11

It would be possible to eliminate KAREN as an exception by restating 26 so that the presence of voiced obstruent + voiced obstruent implied the presence of at least one combination with initial unvoiced obstruent.

The even more powerful tendency to the unvoicing of final obstruents is shown statistically in Table 8 as well as in Table 12 below in which the proportion of languages with only unvoiced obstruent combinations is greater than in initial position. Also there are no exceptions in final systems.

27. In final systems, the existence of at least one combination consisting of two voiced obstruents implies the existence of at least one combination consisting of two unvoiced obstruents.

Both voiced and unvoiced obstruent clusters are found in 3, 4, 7, 13, 36, 41, 44, 48, 64, 75, 76, 80, 82, 86, 98 and 103. All of the remaining languages have unvoiced obstruent clusters only, except 23, 28, 65, 88 and 89 which have no obstruent clusters at all. These data are presented in Table 12 below.

	Unvoiced + Unvoiced Obst. Obst.	~Unvoiced + Voiced Obst. Obst.
Voiced + Voiced Obst. Obst.	16	0
~Voiced + Voiced Obst. Obst.	41	5

Table 12

The dominance of unvoiced over voiced obstruent is shown not only in combination of obstruent with obstruent but also of obstruent with sonant. For initial systems the single case of OSAGE, reported by Wolff, in which one informant had initial [br-] in free variation with [bǝr-] and the other [bl-] in free variation with [bǝl-] and [bǝ𝄐-] but no other initial obstruent + liquid combination prevents the formulation of a single generalization covering all cases of initial obstruent + liquid. However, the following more limited statements have no exception in the present sample.

28. In initial systems the existence of at least one sequence of voiced obstruent + nasal implies the existence of at least one sequence of unvoiced obstruent + nasal.

29. In initial systems the existence of at least one sequence of voiced obstruent + semivowel implies the existence of at least one sequence of unvoiced obstruent + semivowel.

The distribution of languages in accordance with these two hypotheses is described immediately below in Table 13 and 14.

	Unvoiced + Nasal Obst.	~ Unvoiced + Nasal Obst.
Voiced + Nasal Obst.	24	0
~Voiced + Nasal Obst.	27	39

Table 13

	Unvoiced + Semivowel Obst.	~Unvoiced + Semivowel Obst.
Voiced + Semivowel Obst.	39	0
~Voiced + Semivowel Obst.	22	29

Table 14

For final systems a statement of unrestricted generality is
possible.

30. In final systems the existence of at least one combination
of sonant + voiced obstruent implies the existence of at
least one combination of sonant + unvoiced obstruent.
Details are given in Table 15.

	Sonant + Unvoiced Obst.	~Sonant + Unvoiced Obst.
Sonant + Voiced Obst.	24	0
~Sonant + Voiced Obst.	33	5

Table 5

Whereas, as has just been seen, voicelessness is dominant over
voice in obstruents, in sonants the situation is reversed. Unvoiced
nasals, liquids and semivowels, when they appear, are often allophonic variants which are then confined to voiceless environments.
Whereas, as has been seen, among obstruent sequences those in
which all members are unvoiced are the favorite type, sequences
of unvoiced sonants do not occur at all in the sample.

31. In initial and final systems an unvoiced sonant is never
immediately preceded or followed by another unvoiced
sonant.

Glottalized consonants, which may be in principle classified as
a third major group alongside of voiced and unvoiced consonants
since they involve a distinctive type of laryngeal adjustment, are
subordinate in relation to non-glottalized consonants. This is
shown by the fact that in languages with the glottalized and non-
glottalized consonants, if there are any clusters, there are always
some consisting exclusively of non-glottalized consonants but not
necessarily any containing one or more glottalized member. This
may be considered the limiting case of the following more general
rule.

32. If a language has at least one cluster containing n glottalized
consonants, it has at least one cluster with $\underline{n-1}$ glottalized
consonants.

This rule has been verified up to the maximum of three glottalized consonants with occurrence only in 41 (Georgian). Languages
with clusters containing two glottalized consonants and which, therefore, by 32, have clusters with single glottalized consonants as
well as clusters without any glottalized members are 27 and 102.
Language 2, 4, 23, 28, 53, 61, 73, 79, 87 and 92 have clusters
with a single glottalized member as well as those consisting exclusively on non-glottalized member. Languages 6, 24, 32, 50, 69,
71, 72, 100 have no glottalized combinations, although they have
glottalized phonemes.

By glottalized is meant here the common ejective type. The
number of languages with implosives, normally voiced, was too
small to draw any safe conclusions. However, it may be plausibly
conjectured that sequences of implosives with glottalized ejectives
do not occur, nor do sequences of implosives with voiced or unvoiced obstruents nor of different implosives with each other. All
sequences noted in the present sample were of implosives followed
by voiced liquid in initial systems.

Among basic sound types, a preference for obstruents over
nasals is shown, at least in the environment of liquids by the following group of four related hypotheses.

33. In initial systems the existence of at least one cluster
    consisting of nasal + liquid implies the existence of at
    least one cluster consisting of obstruent + liquid.

Languages with both nasal + liquid and obstruent + liquid combinations are 14, 16, 19, 25, 26, 30, 37, 40, 41, 43, 51, 55, 56, 57,
59, 60, 72, 75, 77, 80, 81, 82 and 84. The remainder, except for
these fifteen which do not have either type of combination (6, 21,
29, 31, 34, 47, 54, 58, 66, 71, 73, 79, 90, 99, 100) have obstruent
+ liquid while nasal + liquid clusters are lacking. These results
are summarized in Table 16.

	Obstruent + Liquid	Obstruent + Liquid
Nasal + Liquid	23	0
Nasal + Liquid	52	15

Table 16

34. In final systems the existence of at least one liquid + nasal
    cluster implies the existence of at least one liquid + obstruent
    cluster.

Languages with both liquid + nasal and liquid + obstruent are: 3, 4, 7, 13, 15, 16, 18, 27, 30, 33, 35, 36, 38, 41, 42, 43, 44, 48, 49, 57, 64, 65, 67, 72, 75, 76, 77, 80, 81, 82, 86, 94, 98 and 102. Those with liquid + obstruent and without liquid + nasal are: 1, 2, 10, 28, 51, 62, 69, 87, 88, 96, 97, 101 and 103. The remainder have neither type of combinations. The results are summarized in Table 17.

	Liquid + Obstruent	~Liquid + Obstruent
Liquid + Nasal	34	0
~Liquid + Nasal	13	15

Table 17

36. In final systems the existence of at least one nasal + liquid cluster implies the existence of at least one obstruent + liquid cluster.

Languages with both nasal + liquid and obstruent + liquid clusters are: 2, 7, 28, 38, 41, 43, 49, 76, 80 and 98. Those with obstruent + liquid and without nasal + liquid are: 27, 33, 67, 75, 77, 81 and 103. The remainder do not have either type of cluster. The results are shown in Table 18.

	Obstruent + Liquid	~Obstruent + Liquid
Nasal + Liquid	10	0
~Nasal + Liquid	7	45

Table 18

The dominance of obstruents over nasals is further shown by the following generalization.

36. In final systems the existence of at least one cluster consisting of nasal + nasal implies the existence of at least one cluster consisting of nasal + obstruent.

Nasal geminates are included in this statement. The languages with both nasal + nasal and nasal + obstruent are: 4, 7, 27, 41, 43, 64, 67, 72, 76, 77, 80 and 86. The remainder except for languages 9, 38, 58, 65, 79, 83, 99 and 104 which have neither type, have nasal + obstruent but do not have nasal + nasal. The results may be seen from Table 19.

	Nasal + Obstruent	~Nasal + Obstruent
Nasal + Nasal	12	0
~Nasal + Nasal	42	8

Table 19

A preference for liquids over nasals, at least in one environment, is shown in the following generalization:

37. In initial systems the existence of at least one cluster consisting of obstruent + nasal implies the existence of at least one cluster consisting of obstruent + liquid.

An exception is 31 (SANTEE DAKOTA) which has obstruent + nasal without having obstruent + liquid. However, it has no liquid consonants. Languages with both obstruent + nasal and obstruent + liquid are: 1, 2, 8, 10, 12, 13, 14, 16, 17, 20, 23, 26, 27, 28, 30, 32, 33, 35, 36, 38, 39, 41, 42, 43, 44, 48, 49, 51, 52, 59, 60, 61, 62, 63, 67, 69, 72, 75, 77, 80, 81, 82, 84, 86, 87, 92, 93, 98, 102 and 103. Languages 6, 21, 29, 34, 47, 54, 58, 66, 71, 73, 79, 90, 99 and 100 have neither combinations. The remainder, except for SANTEE have obstruent + liquid while obstruent + nasal combinations are lacking. The results are stated in Table 20.

	Obstruent + Liquid	~Obstruent + Liquid
Obstruent + Nasal	50	1
~Obstruent + Nasal	25	14

Table 20

The final hypotheses of the absolute type have to do with points of articulation. There is some evidence for the dominance of the dental-alveolar region over the labial and the palatal velar. This is most surprisingly shown in what may be called the law of the final dental-alveolar.

38. Every language with final clusters contains at least one cluster with a final obstruent in the dental-alveolar region.

Systems with very few final clusters are, of course, the strongest test of this hypothesis. Examples from ancient languages not found in the sample include CLASSICAL GREEK with the three final clusters ps, ks and ŋks and LATIN which has final clusters all of which end in s̲ or t̲. Within the sample are BALTI with only k̲s̲, r̲s̲, ŋ̲s̲ and k̲s̲ and MASAI with only r̲n̲, r̲t̲ and r̲d̲. From hypotheses 27 and 30 it follows that at least one of the final dental alveolar obstruents is unvoiced.

A corresponding statement for initial systems cannot be confined to obstruents since there are systems with initial nasal + obstruent combination only.

39. Every language with initial clusters contains at least one cluster with an initial consonant in the dental-alveolar region.

A strong confirming example is CHIRICAHUA APACHE which in addition to initial alveolar affricates has only s̲t̲ and s̲d̲̣.

A further piece of evidence is contained in the following hypothesis.

40. A language which has any affricates includes among them at least one in the dental-alveolar or alveopalatal region.

That is, languages like GERMAN with affricate such as p̲f̲ also have t̲s̲ (or t̲š̲, or their voiced or glottalized counterparts). Of the languages in the sample 3, 23, 28, 32, 42, 43, 48 and 61 have affricates of the alveolar or alveopalatal type as well as affricates at other points of articulation. Languages 8, 14, 15, 17, 19, 25, 29, 38, 39, 49, 50, 55, 56, 65, 70, 74, 78, 89, 90, 91 and 95 have no affricates. The remainder have dental-alveolar or alveopalatal affricates but no others. These results are tabulated in Table 21.

	Other Affricates	~Other Affricates
Dental and similar Affricates	8	0
~Dental and similar Affricates	75	21

Table 21

We may summarize at this point the chief conclusions concerning initial and final consonant clusters valid for the sample of 104 languages utilized in terms of objective preferences as revealed in the foregoing generalizations.

1. Shorter clusters are preferred over longer ones.
2. Clusters which are analyzable into subclusters which likewise occur are preferred over those which are unanalyzable.

3. In terms of assimilation, homorganic nasals + obstruents are preferred over heterorganic nasals + obstruents and obstruent combinations which are homogeneous in voicing are favored over those which are heterogeneous.
4. In terms of dissimilation, sequences which differ only in glottal adjustment are disfavored as are sequences of different kinds of sibilants or of different kinds of liquids.
5. In relation to the peak of the syllable, combinations are favored in which sonants are closer to the peak than obstruents and in which voiced consonants are closer to the peak than unvoiced.
6. In absolute terms unvoiced obstruents are preferred over voiced, voiced sonants are preferred over unvoiced, nonglottalized consonants are preferred over glottalized, liquids are preferred over nasals, and the dental-alveolar point of articulation is preferred over other positions.

At various points of the exposition allusion was made to the importance of other related topics. These remarks are here summarized and amplified. In general their importance is that they provide independent evidence for the conclusions based on initial and final clusters alone. They also tend to raise further related questions. It is clear that a more complete and valid set of generalizations and their explanation can not be carried out except in such a broader context.

Among the related topics are the study of medial clusters, of phonemic systems, of morphophonemic alternations, of canonical forms of morphemes and of diachronic sound change. The relevance of the first of these, medial clusters, is so obvious that it need only be mentioned as another part of the same general topic of consonant combinations. An example of the connection between the study of phonemic systems and that of clusters is the fact that, parallel to the favoring of obstruents over nasals in combinations is the fact that there are no languages without obstruents while there is a small number of languages without nasals. The study of morphophonemic alternations will show that certain "avoided" combinations are in general the subject of morphophonemic rules which provide replacements. For example, in MAYAN languages, which have the third person prefix with base form s- there is usually a rule by which stems with initial basic -š have a replacement form for the sequence sš. These alternations are, of course, the result of diachronic changes which are documented or inferred.

It is evident that facts of alternation as reflecting historical changes add a certain additional type of information which must be considered in any explanatory theory and may indeed aid in the solution. Thus, in the above example, a purely synchronic listing of the initial combinations shows only that s̠š̠ is absent. It is a further fact whether, where s̠š̠ is expected s̠ appears, š̠, or as is at least logically conceivable, some third sound or sound combination. From the cure we may perhaps receive some enlightenment regarding the disease.

The study of canonical form of morphemes also provides independent evidence on the same questions. Thus again, in the matter of sibilants, CHIRICAHUA APACHE allows no roots which have both s̠ and š̠. Such "distance phenomena" probably involve more complex psychological processes and may therefore differ somewhat from those involved in immediate sequences.

Thus, in SEMITIC, as a general rule several consonants with the same point of articulation are not found in the same root. Among the excluded combinations are the sequences of nasal and homorganic stop which are very common as direct sequences.

Finally, it may be pointed out that the generalizations presented here are only a portion of the conclusions that can be drawn either from this material or from other evidence. Thus, possible regularities concerning differential text frequency of different classes of combinations were not considered. Also systemic quantitative hypotheses were not considered as, for example, those regarding the relative size of class membership of phonemes immediately following or preceding particular phonemes or classes of phonemes. It is to be hoped that further investigations will test the hypotheses presented here as well as discover new ones.

LIST OF LANGUAGES

The letters after each entry indicate the following:
- I   Existence of Initial Clusters
- F   Existence of Final Clusters
- C   Information on clusters is seriously incomplete
- P   Phonetic information is incomplete or inadequate
- T   One of the sources contains a table or other form of statements concerning consonant clusters

1. AFRIKAANS (I, F, T)
   Meyer de Villiers, Afrikaanse Klankleer (Kapstaad, Amsterdam, 1958).

2. AGUACATEC (MAYAN) (I, T)
International Journal of American Linguistics [IJAL] 22. 72-6 (1956)

3. ALBANIAN (I, F, T)
Structural grammar of Albanian (Bloomington, 1957).

4. AMHARIC (F, P, C)
Armbruster, C.H. Initia Amharica, 2 vols. (Cambridge, 1908).

5. AMUESHA (ARAWAK) (I, F, T)
IJAL 19. 191-4 (1953); Miscellanea Phonetica 3. 15-21 (1958).

6. APACHE (I, T)
Linguistic Structures of Native America by Harry Hoijer and others [LSNA] (New York, 1946) 55-84.

7. ARABIC (EGYPTIAN) (F, T)
Harrell, R. The phonology of colloquial Egyptian Arabic (New York, 1957).

8. ARANTA (P, I, T)
Oceania 12. 255-302 (1942).

9. ARAPAHO (F, T)
IJAL 22. 49-56 (1956).

10. BALTI (TIBETAN) (I, F, P, C)
Read, A.F.C. Balti grammar (London, 1934).

11. BASQUE (I, F, P, C)
Lhande, P. Dictionnaire Basque-Française et Français-Basque (Paris, 1926-); Gavel, H. Eléments de phonétique basque (Bayonne, 1929).

12. BENGALI (I)
Language 36. 22-59 (1960); Wagner, Reinhard, Bengalische Texte in Urschrift und Umschrift (Berlin, 1930).

13. BERBER (SHILHA) (I, F, T)
Applegate, J. An outline of the structure of Shilha (New York 1958).

14. BILAAN (I, F, T)
Philippine Journal of Science 84. 311-22 (1955).

15. BRETON   (I, F, T)
    Sommerfelt, A.   Le breton parlé à Saint-Pol-Léon (Rennes,
    1921).

16. BULGARIAN (I, F, C)
    Minkov, M. Bălgaro-anglijski rečnik (Sofia, 1958); Stoikov,
    S. Uvod v bălgarskata fonetika (Sofia, 1955).

17. CAMBODIAN (I, T)
    Bulletin of the School of Oriental and African Studies [BSOAS]
    14. 149-74 (1952); Bulletin de la Société Linguistique de Paris
    [BSLP] 42. 112-31 (1942).

18. CATALAN (I, F, C)
    Badia Margarit, A. Gramática histórica catalana (Barcelona,
    1951); Falera, P. Diccionari de la llengua catalana (Barce-
    lona, 1954).

19. CHAM (I, P)
    Aymonier, E. and Cabaton A. Dictionnaire Čam-Français
    (Paris, 1906).

20. CHATINO (I, T)
    IJAL 20. 23-7 (1954).

21. CHINANTEC (QUIOTEPEC) (I, T)
    IJAL 27. 237-50 (1961).

22. CHINANTEC (USILA) (I, T)
    IJAL 28. 251-5 (1962).

23. CHONTAL (HOKAN) (I, F, T)
    IJAL 16. 35-39 (1950).

24. CHONTAL (MAYAN) (I, T)
    IJAL 25. 44-53 (1959).

25. CHRAU (I, C)
    BSLP 57. 171-91 (1962).

26. CHUKCHEE (I, P)
    Handbook of American Indian Languages [HAIL] II: 639-903
    (ed. by Franz Boas).

27. COEUR D'ALENE (I, F, T)
    HAIL III: 517-707.

28. COOS (I, F, P, C, T)
    HAIL II: 303-429.

29. CUICATEC (I, T)
    IJAL 12.139-146 (1946).

30. CZECH (I, F, C)
    Kucera, H. The Phonology of Czech ('s Gravenhage, 1961);
    Trávníček, F. Mluvnice spisovné čestiny vol. 1 (Praha, 1948).

31. DAKOTA (SANTEE) (I, P, T)
    HAIL I: 879-965.

32. DAKOTA (YANKTON) (I, T)
    IJAL 21.56-59.

33. DANISH (I, F, T)
    Martinet, A. La phonologie du mot en danois (Paris, 1937).

34. DELAWARE (I, F, T)
    LSNA 130-57.

35. DUTCH (I, F, T)
    Cohen, A. et al., Fonologie van het Nederlands en het
    Fries ('s Gravenhage, 1961).

36. ENGLISH (I, F, T)
    Bloomfield, L. Language (New York, 1933) 127-138.

37. EWE (I, P, C)
    Westermann, D. A study of the Ewe language (London,
    New York, 1960).

38. FRENCH (I, F, T)
    Nyrop, K. Manuel phonétique du français parlé (6th ed.,
    1951, Copenhagen); Lingua 5. 253-87 (1955-6).

39. FRISIAN (I, T)
    Same source as 35.

40. GÃ (I, C, P)
    Wilkie, B. Ga grammar, notes and exercises (Oxford, 1930).

41. GEORGIAN (I, F, P)
    Norsk Tidsskrift for Sprogvidenskap 18. 5-90; BSOAS 14.
    55-72.

42. GERMAN (I, F, T)
    Moulton, W.G. The sounds of English and German (Chicago, 1962).

43. GILYAK (I, F, P, T)
    Hattori, T. Versuch einer Phonologie des Südostgiljakischen Phonembestands, Journal of Hokkaido Gakugei University 13. 67-96 (1962).

44. GREEK (I, F, T)
    Koutsoudas, A. Verb morphology of Modern Greek (Bloomington, 1962).

45. HINDI (I, T)
    Language 34. 212-24 (1958).

46. HUAMBISA (F, T)
    Lingua Posnaniensis 6. 1-8 (1957).

47. HUICHOL (I, T)
    IJAL 11. 31-5 (1945).

48. HUNGARIAN (I, F, T)
    Acta Linguistica Academiae Scientarum Hungaricae 3. 125-57; 411-29 (1953); 4. 193-224 (1954); Hall, R. Hungarian grammar (Baltimore, 1944).

49. ICELANDIC (I, F, T)
    Kress, B. Die Laute des modernen Islandischen (Leipzig, 1937).

50. IOWAY-OTO (I, C, T)
    IJAL 13. 233-250 (1947).

51. IRISH (I, F, T)
    Ó Cuív, B. The Irish of West Muskerry, Co. Cork (Dublin, 1944).

52. ITALIAN (I, T)
    Hoare, A. An Italian dictionary (2nd ed. Cambridge, 1925); Hall, R. Descriptive Italian grammar (Ithaca, 1948).

53. IXCATEC (I, T)
    Miranda, M.T.F. de, Fonémica del Ixcateco (México, 1959).

54. JAPANESE (I, T)
    Language 26. 86-125 (1950).

55. JAVANESE (I, T)
    Uhlenbeck, De Structuur van het Javaanse Morpheem
    (Bandoeng, 1949).

56. KAREN (I, P, T)
    University of California Publications in Linguistics, vol. 25
    (1961).

57. KASHMIRI (I, F, P, C, T)
    Acta Orientalia 19. 79-99 (1943).

58. KERESAN (I, F, T)
    IJAL 12. 229-36 (1946).

59. KHASI (I, P, T)
    Rabel, L. Khasi, a language of Assam (Baton Rouge, 1961).

60. KORYAK (I, P, T)
    HAIL II: 639-903.

61. KUTENAI (I, F, T)
    IJAL 14. 37-42 (1948).

62. LATVIAN (I, F, C)
    Endzelin, J. and Hausenberg, Latviešu valodas vardnica
    (Chicago, 1956); Endzelin, J. Latviešu valodas gramatika
    (Riga, 1951).

63. LITHUANIAN (I, F, T)
    Otrebski, J. Gramatyka języka litewskiego (Warszawa,
    1958).

64. MARATHI (I, F, C)
    Kelkar, A.R.   The phonology and morphology of Marathi
    (Cornell dissertation, 1958).

65. MASAI (F, P, C)
    Tucker, A.N. and Tompo Ole Mpaayei, J., A Maasai gram-
    mar (London, 1955).

66. MAZATEC (I, T)
    IJAL 13. 78-91 (1947).

67. NORWEGIAN (I, F, T)
Norsk Tidsskrift for Sprogvidenskap 12. 5-29 (1942).

68. OSAGE (I, T)
IJAL 18. 63-8 (1952).

69. OSSETE (WESTERN) (I, F, C)
BSOAS 13. 36-79 (1951).

70. OSTYAK (F, T)
Steinitz, W. Ostjakische Grammatik und Chrestomathie
(2nd ed., Leipzig, 1950).

71. OTOMI (MAZAHUA) (I, T)
IJAL 19. 253-8 (1953).

72. OTOMI (PAME) (I, F, T)
IJAL 22. 242-65 (1956).

73. OTOMI (TEMOAYAN) (I, T)
IJAL 15. 213-22 (1949).

74. PALAUNG (I, T)
BSOAS 23. 544-57 (1960).

75. PASHTO (I, F, T)
Penzl, H. A grammar of Pashto (Washington, D.C.,
1955).

76. PERSIAN (F, T)
Nye, G.E. The phonemes of modern Persian (Michigan
dissertation, 1955).

77. POLISH
Benni, T. Fonetyka Opisowa, in Benni et al., Gramatyka
języka polskiego (Krakow, 1923); Bulas, K. and Whitfield,
F.J. The Kosciuszko foundation dictionary, vol. 2 (Mouton,
The Hague, 1961).

78. PORTUGUESE (I)
Boletim de Filologia 3. 1-30 (Lisboa, 1949).

79. QUILEUTE (I, F, T)
HAIL III. 149-292.

80. RUMANIAN (I, F, T)
Graur, A. and Rosetti, A. Esquisse d'une phonologie du
roumain, Bucarest, Universitatea, Facultatea de filosofie
și litere. Bull. Ling. 36. 5-29 (1938).

81. RUSSIAN (I, F, C)
Avanesov, R.I. Fonetika sovremennogo russkogo literaturnogo jazyka (Moscow, 1956).

82. SERBO-CROATIAN (I, F, T)
Language 22. 112-20 (1946).

83. SIERRA POPOLUCA (F, T)
IJAL 13. 13-17 (1947).

84. SINHALESE (I, C)
University of Ceylon Review 18. 163-75 (1960).

85. SPANISH (I, T)
Language 27. 248-53 (1951).

86. SWEDISH (I, F, T)
Studia Linguistica 9. 8-20 (1955).

87. TAKELMA (I, F, C, T)
HAIL II. 7-296.

88. TAOS (F, C)
LSNA 184-221.

89. TEMNE (F, T)
Wilson, W.A.A. An outline of the Temne language (London,
1961).

90. TERENA (I, T)
IJAL 12. 60-3 (1946).

91. THAI (I, T)
Abramson, A.S. The vowels and tones of Standard Thai
(Bloomington, 1962).

92. TOJOLABAL (MAYAN) (I, T)
IJAL 12. 34-43 (1946).

93. TOTONAC (I, F. T)
IJAL 12. 34-43 (1946).

94. TURKISH (F)
Sevortijan, E.V. Fonetika tureckogo literaturnogo jazyka
(Moscow, 1955); Turkce Sözlük (Ankara, 1955).

95. TWI
Schachter, P. Teaching English pronunciation to the Twi-
speaking student (Legon, 1962).

96. UZBEK (F, T)
Bidwell, Charles, A structural analysis of Uzbek (New York,
1955).

97. WAIGALI (I, F, P, C, T)
Norsk Tidsskrift for Sprogvidenskap 17. 146-324 (1954).

98. WELSH (I, F)
Jones, S. A Welsh phonetic reader (London, 1926);
Jones, T.G. and Gwynn, A. Geiradur gymraeg-saesneg a
saesneg-gymraeg (Cardiff, 1950).

99. WICHITA (I, F, T)
IJAL 16. 179-84 (1950).

100. WINNEBAGO (I, T)
Susman, A. The accentual system of Winnebago (New York,
1943).

101. YUMA (F, T)
LSNA 249-88.

102. YUROK (I, F, C)
University of California Publications in Linguistics 15 (1951).

103. ZAPOTEC (MITLA) (I, F, T)
Briggs, E. Mitla Zapotec grammar (Mexico, 1961).

104. ZOQUE (I, F, T)
IJAL 17. 105-23 (1951).

Consonant Harmony: Its Scope and Function in Child Language

MARILYN MAY VIHMAN

ABSTRACT

Consonant harmony (CH) is widespread in child phonology but
rare in the world's (adult) languages. This paper investigates CH
in child phonology in six languages by analyzing data from thirteen
children (ages 0;7-3;5). Every child shows some examples of CH,
but the nature and extent differ greatly, in part because of differences in phonological structure between languages and in part because of differences in individual strategies and paths of development
between children. Functions of CH in child phonology are: a) to
provide a source of substitutions for sounds the child cannot pronounce (most often liquids and s) and b) to allow focus on new
segments or extra syllables by reducing the overall complexity of
the word. The evidence suggests CH is not a universal innate
process which the child must overcome: it is rare in some children and when it is used, it often operates after the sounds involved
can be pronounced satisfactorily. CH in children seems analogous
to types of speech errors and patterns of alliteration in adults.

CONTENTS

1. Introduction

It has been suggested that "some form of consonant harmony appears to be universal [in child language]" (Smith 1973: 20), and indeed in the literature on child language examples abound of forms showing consonant assimilation in place or manner across vowels: see, for example, Lewis 1936, where over 100 examples of consonant harmony are cited from diary studies of three children, speaking ENGLISH, FRENCH, and GERMAN (pp. 297ff). Among recent detailed phonological studies of a single child, Menn 1971 and Smith 1973 both include rules of non-contiguous consonant assimilation that affect a large portion of the child's utterances. At the same time, it is common for theoretical interpretation of child language to attempt to relate children's rules to the rules of adult phonology, both synchronic and diachronic -- yet consonant harmony is conspicuous by its near absence from the adult languages of the world.

The present study was undertaken in an effort to establish whether or not consonant harmony is in fact universal in child phonology, how significant a rôle it can play for a given child, and what relation it bears to adult phonology. A second focus of the study is to investigate the degree to which the language being learned seems to affect the child's strategies, and the degree to which the differences one finds are ascribable to individual differences among children (cf. Macken 1976, Ferguson 1977).

2. Sources and Data

In order to make a meaningful evaluation of the relative importance of consonant harmony in a given child's speech, I required access to a complete set of data for the child for a given time period -- complete in the sense of all forms produced during regular visits (in the case of outside investigators reporting the data), or all forms recorded over the period in question (in the case of a diarist observer). To limit acceptable kinds of data to either of those cases would have been to eliminate several reports and thus severely cut down the already small number of children and languages covered. But to accept sample forms or illustrative examples would have been to preclude use of any quantitative analysis. Thus, the data described in Menn 1971 or those presented in Lewis 1936 could not be included because in their published form, they were fragmentary. Nor could I make any use of the more diffuse but unfortunately typical reference to various consonant harmony forms in a survey such as Kerek 1975, which fails to provide any indication of the child's age, size of total vocabulary, or other phonetic

or phonological characteristics of the data as a whole for any child.[1]
On the other hand, whenever a complete, apparently reliable data
source was brought to my attention, I made a point of including it.

The data sources used are characterized in Table 1. Six languages are represented, from five languages families or branches,
three of which are INDO-EUROPEAN, and all but one of which are
spoken in Europe. Though reports on child language acquisition in
Africa, Australia, etc. do occur in the literature, I was unable to
locate any with complete sets of data.[2]

Of the eight children growing up in America, all have been exposed to ENGLISH and all are to some extent bilingual. The degree
of influence from the non-dominant language may be roughly judged
from the percentage of words from that language out of the child's
total active (and spontaneous) lexicon — the range here being, for
ENGLISH as the second language, from 2% (for Linda) to 9% (for
Virve, who was attending an American day care center). Hildegard,
who was raised at home as a bilingual from the start, had 13% GER-
MAN words. The remaining children are all monolingual.[3]

Each language is represented by at least two child learners, with
the exception of CZECH, which may, however, be grouped with SLO-
VENIAN as far as general phonological structure is concerned.
ENGLISH and CHINESE were the target languages of three children
each. The work of nine primary investigators is represented by
these data.

As indicated on Table 1, all but two of the data sets are longitudinal. The exceptions are Chao's data on his granddaughter Canta,
which he collected over a period of one month and which thus represent a single (relatively advanced) stage in her acquisition of
MANDARIN, and Smith's data on his son Amahl, for whom only the
data reported for stage 1, the outset of Smith's study, were used here.

---

[1] I was unable to gain access to any of the sources of HUNGARIAN
data cited by Kerek.

[2] Apronti's article on DANGME phonology (1969), for example,
provides only a few sample forms.

[3] Though for Amahl's mother (INDIAN-)ENGLISH was the fourth
language, Amahl "was brought up monolingual" (Smith 1973: 8), and
refused to use HINDI even after a six-week trip to India.

Name of subject	Source and year[b]	Type of study[c]	Period covered	Age of child	Sex	Word total	% foreign(d) words
CHINESE							
Canta	Chao 1951	diary, 1 stage	1 month	2;4	F	311	5%
Didi[a]	Clumeck	visits	19 months	1;2 – 2;9	M	109	5%
Lolo[a]	Clumeck	visits	14 months	2;3 – 3;5	M	336	5%
ENGLISH							
Amahl	Smith 1973	diary, 1 stage	1 day	2;2	M	225	0%
Hildegard	Leopold 1939	diary	2 years	(0;10) – 2;0	F	322	13%
Jacob	Menn 1976a	visits	8 months	1;0 – 1;8	M	150	0%
ESTONIAN							
Linda	Vihman	visits	6 months	1;6 – 1;11	F	364	2%
Virve	Vihman	diary	2 years	(0;7) – 1;10	F	372	9%
CZECH							
Jiři	Pačesova 1968	diary?	2 years	(0;10) – 1;8	M	300	0%
SLOVENIAN							
Maja	Kolaric 1959	diary	2 years	(0;6) – 2;0	F	138	0%
Tomaž	Kolaric 1959	diary	2 years	(0;11) – 2;0	M	320	0%
SPANISH							
Jesus[a]	Macken	visits	10 months	1;9 – 2;3, 2;4 – 2;6	M	144	7%
Sofia[a]	Macken	visits	10 months	1;7 – 2;4	F	152	8%

Table 1. Data Sources and Subjects

(For notes see next page)

Of the longitudinal data sets, five are diary studies which begin
with the first words and include early onomatopoeia, exclamations
and the like (peep-peep, aha!, boom!), as well as variation in the
shapes of words over time. The remaining studies are based on
longitudinal naturalistic observation via regular visits over an' extended period of time.

The data collections vary in size from 109 forms (collected in
bi-weekly two- to four-hour visits over a period of 19 months from
a singularly non-talkative child, Didi) to 372 forms. Smith's corpus, as mentioned above, was restricted to the earliest stage which,
besides offering a sufficiently large number of forms to allow comparison with other children, was most uniform in that it appeared
to represent the complete lexicon recorded for the child at the outset of the study, whereas later stages reflect selection by the author
for the purpose of illustrating phonological development (see Smith
1973: 210). Pačesova's data were arbitrarily cut off at the 300-mark
(and at the date represented by that mark, in the case of words
whose form continued to evolve), to keep the size comparable to
the other collections. The total number of words in each lexicon
is indicated in Appendix 1.

(Notes for Table 1):
   (a) Name invented for mnemonic purposes for this study. The
SPANISH subjects appear as J and Si in Macken 1976. The nicknames Lolo and Didi are used in place of ENGLISH names to mark
these children as CHINESE speakers.

   (b) The year of publication is given here only for those data sets
which have been published in full. Harold Clumeck is preparing
his data on several CHINESE subjects for his forthcoming U.C.
Berkeley dissertation. Marlys Macken's data were collected as part
of the Stanford Child Phonology project: see Macken 1976. My own
data on Linda were described in Vihman 1971; my data on my daughter Virve were published in part in Vihman 1976.

   (c) All studies are longitudinal unless otherwise noted. "Visits"
means naturalistic observation conducted by a non-relative visiting
the child periodically, at home or elsewhere. Pačesova does not
specify her relationship to the subject of her investigation, but the
frequency of the forms recorded strongly suggests that this is a
(mother's?) diary.

   (d) The foreign words are ENGLISH and FRENCH for Canta,
GERMAN for Hildegard, and ENGLISH for the rest.

Only forms used spontaneously, with known adult models, were accepted for analysis: in just one case, Didi's, words classified as "repetitions" were included, though "imitations" were excluded as usual. "Repetition" is defined as words which the child used immediately after an adult, but with the child apparently focussing not on the shape of the word, but on the content of the communication (e.g. adult: "It's raining;" child (also looking out window): "Raining").

3. Method of Analysis

The purpose of the analysis is to arrive at a fair evaluation, for each child, of the degree of difficulty which consonantal contrast seems to represent for him, and the degree to which consonant harmony is used as a way out of the difficulty. As we shall see below, the function of consonant harmony seems to differ from one child to the next, as does the difficulty of producing contrasting consonant sequences. Still, percentages arrived at by applying uniformly defined categories to the various data sets give us a direct base of comparison, before we begin to inquire into the function of a particular process within a given child's phonological system.

Categories are defined for analysis here in such a way as to maximize the weight of consonant harmony and also, once words showing harmony are separated out, to give the child maximum credit for consonantal contrast (by disregarding substitutions and reorderings, as well as variants showing deletion, if two contrasting consonants appear in at least one child variant). The point of so defining the categories is to sharpen the focus on the two phenomena of interest, consonant harmony and consonant contrast, and also to reap as large a harvest of consonant harmony forms as possible, to provide data for a study of the kinds of assimilation that occur. The absolute rôle of consonant loss cannot be estimated from the figures given here, but its relative importance for any one child in comparison with the other children in the study is probably fairly assessed.

Four basic categories are distinguished for the purposes of this analysis. All the spontaneous words produced by the child have been scored for these categories, which I define as follows (examples from Amahl, on left, and Virve, on right, unless otherwise noted):

A. <u>Consonant harmony</u>: scored for a word if any child variant shows agreement in place and/or manner of articulation between two non-contiguous consonants which differ in that respect in the adult model. Examples:[4]

Full harmony   tiger → ġaigə   /tu.Pa/ 'into the room, to
                                               indoors' → pup:a
Partial harmony driving → waibin /su.Pi/ 'soup (obj.)' → fup:i

B. <u>Consonantal contrast</u>: scored for a word if no variant shows harmony, as defined above, and if there is at least one child variant showing two contrasting non-contiguous consonants -- which may be different consonants or in a different order than in the adult model. The adult model must also contain at least two contrasting consonants. Examples:

aeroplane → ɛ:bə'eịn   /parT/ 'duck' → pat:
back → bɛk   /plA.ster/ 'bandage' → 'pæ|sel
carpet → ġa:bi: /va.lmis/ 'ready' → masi

C. <u>Consonant deletion</u>: scored only where all variants of a word show loss of one or more consonants (or whole syllables), such that the child version does not show consonantal contrast, though the adult model does. Examples:

ball → ɓɔ: /sUr/ 'big' → su:
handle → ɛŋu   /va.Ni/ 'into the bath' → an:i
                        /üles/ 'up' → üọ̈s

D. <u>No contrast</u>: scored where the adult model contains no two non-contiguous true consonants contrasting in place or manner,

---

[4] The format used for examples here and throughout this paper is: adult word (in standard orthography or, for ESTONIAN, phonemic transcription) → child form (as found in the data source). The long or tense ESTONIAN segments are represented by uppercase letters in the phonemic transcription, while the accentual prosodic feature realized phonetically as further segmental or syllabic lengthening is indicated by a period following the syllabic nucleus, except in monosyllables, where the "extra length" is predictable (see Raun and Saareste 1965, Tauli 1973, E. Vihman 1974). Stress falls on the initial syllable in ESTONIAN, unless marked otherwise. In the phonetic transcription of children's forms, | indicates "temporal spacing (syllabic break accompanied by slight pause)," as in Vihman 1976; see Bush <u>et al</u>. 1973.

regardless of the shape of the child version. Examples:

elbow	/auh-auh/	'bow-wow'
eye	/auTo/	'car'
lorry	/o.tsa/	'(to an) end'
wee-wee	/kuKu/	'(don't) fall'

In addition to the four basic categories, a fifth was added for some children:

E. Pseudo-harmony: scored for a word when the child's regular consonant substitution rules result in a merger of the two consonants which contrast in the adult model, so that the child's form shows no contrast but nevertheless is not necessarily the product of a consonant assimilation rule. Examples:

flower → wæwə   Hildegard: kitty → diti
(cf. feet → wi:t)   (cf. kiek! 'peek-a-boo' → ti)

For the purpose of grouping words into these five categories, glides (yod, w) were taken to be consonants only when they occurred word-initially in the adult model. Medially, a glide in the adult model counted as a non-consonant. Where a child substituted a glide for an adult consonant in any position, the change was treated as a deletion, unless the glide was incorporated into a consonant harmony pattern (where it then counted as a consonant). Examples:

Amahl:
whistle → wibu   (A) (partial progressive labial harmony)
room → wum   (A) (partial regressive labial harmony)
watch → wɔt   (B) (glide...consonant = consonantal contrast)
new (→ nu:)   (D) (non-initial glide = non-consonant: no contrast in adult word)

Virve:
/jOkse/ 'run!' → jo.ksa   (B) (glide...consonant=consonantal contrast)
/ju.Tu/ 'a story (obj.)' → ut.u (C) (loss of initial glide = deletion)
/maja/ 'house' (→ maja) (D) (medial glide = non-consonant: no contrast in adult word)

Linda:
/jAna(-li.nt)/ 'ostrich' → ja.ja (A) (full progressive harmony)
/ru.Tu/ 'fast' → jut.u   (C) (consonant changes to glide: deletion)

The glottal fricative [h] constituted a class in itself for scoring purposes. In the adult model it was viewed as a consonant in all

positions (thus, adult EST. /maha/ 'down' has consonantal contrast,
whereas /maja/ 'house' does not); where a consonant was replaced
by [h] in the child version, however, [h] was treated as equivalent
to a glide, so that consonant-loss would be scored if the word had
at most one other consonant. Example:

Canta: bwu. shy 'is not' — bu.hy ~ bu   (C)

As indicated earlier, for purposes of categorization only contrast
in place and/or manner was considered relevant; contrast in voicing
or tenseness was disregarded -- as it tended to be disregarded by
the children, who sometimes established their own sub-phonemic
distribution rules for voicing (e.g. Amahl: cf. Smith 1973: 37; see
also Leopold 1947, who notes that "the distinction between voiced
and voiceless is ... one of those finer discriminations which were
not yet well achieved by the child" p. 197). Thus, ENGLISH teddy,
ESTONIAN /tæti/ 'aunt,' CZECH tady 'here' were all scored D.
Furthermore, where an adult form showed consonantal contrast
only by virtue of a consonant cluster which the child failed to reproduce (whether due to misperception, difficulty in production, or
some other unknowable source of error), the form was treated as
if it had no contrast in the adult model (D). Examples:

bump → b̥ʌp   /täht/ 'star' → tat:
church → də:t
tent → dɛt

On the other hand, where the adult cluster was preserved by the
child in a word of the shape $C_1 \ldots C_1 C_2$, $C_1 \ldots C_2 C_1$, etc., B was
scored. Examples:

Hildegard: kritze 'handbrush (family word)' → titsə
Jiři: kluk 'boy' → kluk
Linda: /kaks/ 'two' → kaks

Inflectional endings, often omitted by children at early stages of
language acquisition, were disregarded in scoring consonantal contrast. Just one child, Virve, made active use of consonant harmony
in acquiring inflections (see below, sec. 5.3.2). Derivation played
a significant rôle only in the case of the hypocoristic markers in
SLAVIC (see Sec. 4.1).

4. Results

In order to compare the importance of consonant harmony for
different children, as well as to assess the degree of difficulty

presented by consonantal contrast within a word, I first converted
the raw scores for the four (or five) categories for each child into
percentages, based on the total lexicon analyzed for that child. I
then rank-ordered the children separately for each category. Table
2 presents the figures thus arrived; the raw scores and percentages
are given in Appendix 1.

Table 2. Key: A = Harmony, B = Contrast, C = Deletion,
                D = No contrast, E = Pseudo-harmony (see Sec. 3)

Category A		Category B		Category C		Category D	
Amahl	32%	Tomaž	74%	Jacob	36%	Didi	50%
Virve	25%	Maja	72%	Hildegard	30%	Lolo	38%
Jesus	21%	Jiři	69%	Amahl	14%	Canta	34%
Sofia	18%	Linda	57%	Jesus	14%	Jacob	29%
Jiři	11%	Lolo	54%	Virve	12%	Hildegard	28%
Jacob	9%	Sofia	54%	Didi	12%	Linda	27%
Linda	9%	Canta	52%	Maja	9%	Sofia	25%
Canta	5%	Jesus	43%	Canta	7%	Virve	24%
Hildegard	5%	Virve	38%	Lolo	7%	Jesus	21%
Didi	3%	Didi	36%	Linda	7%	Tomaž	18%
Tomaž	3%	Hildegard	35%	Tomaž	4%	Maja	17%
Maja	1%	Amahl	33%	Sofia	3%	Jiři	17%
Lolo	1%	Jacob	25%	Jiři	3%	Amahl	16%
Mean	11%		49%		11%		26%
Median	9%		52%		9%		25%

Category E

Amahl	5%
Hildegard	3%
Canta	2%
Virve	1%

4.1 Language effects

Language effects are apparent in two sets of figures on Table 2.
Note, first, the clustering of all three CHINESE-speaking children
at the head of category D. This indicates that words lacking consonantal contrast in the adult model make up a larger part of the
lexicon of each of the CHINESE-speaking children than of the lexicon
of any of the other children. To verify that this preponderance of
adult model words lacking contrasting consonant sequences reflected
a peculiarity of the language these children were learning, I turned
to the Stanford Phonology Archive coding for (MANDARIN) CHINESE,
where I found the following definition of the syllable:

A syllable may begin with one or no consonant, followed by one or more glides, one vowel, and one or no ending (/yod, w, n, eng/).[5]

This definition may be compared with the following formulas encoded for ENGLISH:

$$(C)(C)(C) \, V \, (C)(C)(C)(C),[6]$$

for BULGARIAN (neither CZECH nor SLOVENIAN happen to be included in the Archive sample of 200 languages):

$$(C)(C)(C)(C) \, V \, (C)(C)(C),[7]$$

and for SPANISH:

$$(C)(C)(G) \, V \, (G)(C)(C).[8]$$

Though each of the CHINESE children had a large number of compound words in his lexicon, the monosyllabic word is also well-represented in each case.[9] From the syllable definition cited above it is clear that among monosyllabic words only those with final nasals present a possible consonantal contrast across the word.[10]

---

[5] For a description of the Archive, its language sample, contents and structure, see Vihman 1977. The primary source used for MANDARIN was Chao 1968.

[6] The Archive source was O'Connor 1973.

[7] Three consonant clusters are said to be very rare finally, while final two consonant clusters are only of the type liquid + consonant, in native words. The Archive source for the phonetic inventory was Klagstad 1958.

[8] G = glide; word-finally, only a singleton consonant may occur. The Archive source for the phonetic inventory was Navarro 1961.

[9] Compounds make up 41% of the CHINESE adult model words (i.e. excluding ENGLISH models) in Lolo's lexicon, for example.

[10] Harold Clumeck reports a tendency among the parents of his CHINESE subjects to omit final nasals, leaving heavily nasalized vowels. Indeed, out of 21 cases of consonant deletion in Lolo's vocabulary, 16 involved omission of a syllable-final nasal, where the omission may have had its source in the adult model. Since Lolo also had 37 monosyllabic words with final nasal intact, however (vs. 7 monosyllabic words with final nasal loss), we can come to no definite conclusion on this point.

Where languages other than CHINESE are being acquired, the percent of D words tends to correlate inversely with linguistic maturity, as evidenced by the results of analysis on earlier cross-sections of the data for three children — Jiři, Virve and Hildegard: see Table 3. At the point where the first fifty words had been acquired, D scores of 56%, 46% and 42% were registered, as compared to 17%, 24% and 28% for these same children at the end of their respective studies.[11]

Table 3. First Fifty Words

Categories:	A	B	C	D	E
Hildegard	10%	12%	30%	42%	6%
Jiři	--	36%	8%	56%	
Virve	16%	20%	18%	46%	

It should be noted that the CHINESE-speaking children happened to be, on average, older at the conclusion of their studies than the group of 13 children taken together (mean age of 2;10 vs. a group mean of 2;2 — or 2;0 for the ten non-Chinese children). It seems clear, then, that the phonological structure of adult MANDARIN must be responsible for the unusually large proportion of D words in the lexicon of all three Chinese children.

The second apparent language effect, though comparable to the first, is more difficult to interpret. I refer to the clustering of the three SLAVIC-language children at the head of category B, consonantal contrast. Here again, one might look to the phonological structure of the language being learned. Of the three SLAVIC languages coded in the Stanford Phonology Archive, for example, all have relatively large numbers of consonant phonemes (RUSSIAN, 32; POLISH, 34; BULGARIAN, 35), as compared with the other languages in our sample (ENGLISH, 26; MANDARIN, 24; SPANISH, 19; ESTONIAN, which is not coded in the Archive, is reported by Raun and Saareste 1965 as having 16 consonant phonemes). But Pačesova 1968 lists only 24 for CZECH, and even if SLOVENIAN were taken to include as large an inventory as those reported in

---

[11] These figures would seem to support the idea, repeatedly suggested recently by Ferguson and others (cf. Ferguson et al. 1973, Ferguson and Farwell 1975), that lexical selection on phonological grounds is one early strategy children use to keep the problems of word-production within manageable bounds.   See also Kiparsky and Menn 1975, Macken 1976, Menn 1976a and Vihman 1976.

the Archive, we would be left with the question of the relevance of
those figures. How would the presence in the language of a fairly
large number of different consonants, or even of formidable consonant clusters (up to five members in the child's vocabulary,
according to Pačesova, by the end of her study, when Jiři had
acquired 500 words and was just short of being two years old),
lead the child to develop early or unusually rapidly a facility for
producing consonantal contrasts?

To come to a fair understanding of this phenomenon, I analyzed
two further parameters for all the children. First, I counted the
number of consonant sequence types (e.g. p-t vs. p-k) in each
child's word productions to arrive at the type: token ratios presented in Table 4. Second, I checked word-length, or more precisely length of consonant-sequences (across vowels: consonant
clusters count here, as elsewhere in this study, as a single consonant) by calculating for each child the percent of all consonant-
sequence types represented by sequences of three or more consonants
(see Table 5).

Table 4. Ratio of types to tokens among consonant sequences

	Ratio : 1 to	No. of types	No. of tokens (= B words)
Maja	1.14	87	99
Jiři	1.16	178	206
Didi	1.22	32	39
Jacob	1.23	31	38
Sofia	1.30	64	83
Tomaž	1.39	171	238
Lolo	1.44	126	182
Linda	1.60	131	209
Virve	1.65	79	130
Jesus	1.82	34	62
Amahl	2.35	31	73
Canta	2.57	63	162
Hildegard	3.03	37	112
Mean	1.68		
Median	1.44		

From Table 4 we can see that two of the SLAVIC-language children, Jiři and Maja, still head the list; that is, they have the
most diverse array of consonant sequences proportionate to the
total number of B words reported for them. Tomaž, however, with

a type : token ratio of 1 : 1. 39, ranks near the median point of 1 : 1. 44
(though still well above the mean of 1 : 1. 68). On Table 5 the ranking
shifts further, with Maja falling to fifth place, while Tomaž falls
third from the bottom. This reflects the fact that both SLOVENIAN
children, but especially Tomaž, tended to drop syllables in their
word-productions, even while faithfully retaining a high number of
consonant sequences. It is worth remarking that Maja and Tomaž,
the only pair of siblings in our sample of 13 children, were only
one year apart in age; it is quite possible that Tomaž, who carried
the strategy of truncating words farther than his older sister, adopted
it from her, and in fact some of his words may have had one of
Maja's versions rather than the adults' as their starting point.
Since we do not know what Maja's phonology was like after age 2,
when the bulk of Tomaž's words appeared, there is no way to check
this point.

Table 5. Percent 3-(or more) consonant sequences relative to
total number of B-word types (see Table 4)*

Excluding diminutives
from SLAVIC lexicons

Canta	60%	Jiři	27%
Jiři	54%	Maja	2%
Virve	33%	Tomaž	1%
Sofia	25%	(other children as in	
Maja	23%	column on left)	
Jesus	21%		
Linda	20%		
Amahl	19%		
Hildegard	16%		
Lolo	15%		
Tomaž	14%		
Didi	10%		
Jacob	3%		
Mean	24%	Mean	18%
Median	20%	Median	19%

*Compounds and reduplications of B-roots are included here.

Jiři remains strikingly far ahead of the other children on the
consonant sequence or contrast measures on Tables 4 and 5. One
further factor needs to be considered, however. The word lists
for all the Slavic children reflected a well-known characteristic of
SLAVIC languages, namely, heavy use of diminutive or hypocoristic

affixes. If the relatively few long consonant sequences the Slovenian children produced are scanned for occurrence of these markers
(-cV, -kV, or -ek vs. -Vk or -ka for CZECH); they are found to
account for 90% of Maja's 3+ consonant words, and for 92% of
Tomaž's. For Jiři the figure is a more modest 44%. If we sub-
tract these diminutives from the long-consonant-sequence figures
and recalculate our percentages, Tomaž and Maja now fall to the
bottom of the list (with 1% and 2%, respectively), while Jiři now
ranks third with the much smaller figure of 27%

It is at least conceivable that the constant exposure to diminutive
markers whose addition frequently creates a consonantal contrast
played a rôle in advancing the capacity of these children to handle
consonant sequences. Of the adult models reported for Tomaž, 18%
are marked for diminutives, while fully 25% are marked on those
reported for Maja. It is often the case -- as the figures cited earlier
suggest -- that Maja and Tomaž include the diminutive ending in
their version of the word, while omitting one or more of the other
syllables (cf. Tomaž drevešček 'small tree' → [véško] at age 1;10,0,
balonček 'little balloon' → [lónčke] n. sg., at 1;10, 3, golobček
'little dove' → [lôpčka] at 2;0,7; Maja bombónčka 'candy' → [bónčka]
at 1;7,20; both children metuljček 'small butterfly' → [túlčək](Maja
at 1;7,24, Tomaž at 1;10,17 and 1;11,8). In Jiři's case the adult form
is only occasionally presented with a diminutive marker, though the
child forms abound in them. By the age of 1;8, when he had made
active use of 300 words, 122 or 41% of them included a hypocoristic.

Since Pačesova gives separate, dated entries for each word in
chronological order, we can easily trace the appearance of these
markers in the child's speech. By age 1;3, with 50 words, Jiři had
used no hypocoristic markers in his own speech, though at least
one of his words -- bebičko 'pain' (→ J. [bebe: ~ bibi:], etc.) -- apparently is not used without the marker in adult speech. By age 1;5,
with 100 words, 34% of his forms show a diminutive marker, the
earliest being bebičko, in the form [bibi:ško] (1;3,2). Of the first
50, 12 now have diminutive markers, with several appearing together
at 1;5,0 and 1;5,1 (máma 'mummy' → [mamišta], bába 'granny' →
[babišta ~ babiška]; kvítí 'flowers' → [kiťiški]; dítě 'child' →
[ďiťišto ~ ďiťiško]; čaj 'tea' → łaji:ček]).[12]

----

[12] Compare the relative infrequency of diminutive or hypocoristic
markers for the other children. In ESTONIAN there is a marker in
-u preceded by palatalization of the last stem consonant (or cluster,
if it is dental). This appears in five of Linda's words and five of
Virve's, or 1% of each child's lexicon; the marker more commonly

All three Slavic children present a profile of rapid development
where consonant sequences are concerned. We can only speculate
as to whether repeated exposure to the affectionate forms in -c-
and -k-, which the children soon begin producing themselves, facil-
itates progress in mastering the skills involved in the production
of consonantal sequences. If those skills are purely articulatory,
it is hard to see how the prevalence of a particular consonant or
pair of consonants will help. If the stumbling block is as much
mnemonic as articulatory, with consonant harmony playing the rôle
of simplifying the mnemonic problem involved for some children,
then the addition of a single morpheme, or a small number of phonologically related morphemes or morphemic variants, to a large
portion of the vocabulary should be a facilitating factor for the child.

4.2 Quantitative analysis

To return now to the general results presented in Table 2, we
can say that on average just over one-quarter of the child's lexicon
is accounted for by category D (or 22%, if the Chinese children are
excluded), while roughly half is accounted for by category B. Where
the child does not use a consonant sequence though the adult model
does, his version will fall in either category A or category C, which
account for equal share of the children's production, on average.
If over 5% use of either of these categories is taken to be significant,
we can say that seven (or over half) of the children made use of consonant harmony — which, however, was maximized by our method of
analysis (see Sec. 3); on the other hand, ten (or well over half) of
the children made significant use of consonant deletion — which was
minimized by our method of analysis.

(ftnt. 12 cont.)
used in adult speech, -Ke(ne) appears only in the words /væiKe/
'small' and /pisiKene/ 'tiny' among Virve's adult models (Virve
omits the marker in her version of the latter); Linda's lexicon
lacks the marker entirely. Among the ENGLISH-speaking children
the marker /-i/ (-ie, -y) makes an occasional appearance — once
for Amahl, three times for Jacob, five times for Hildegard, who
also has one GERMAN proper name bearing the marker -chen, for
a total of nearly 2% diminutives. Sofia has five words or 3% marked
by the diminutive -ito/-ita, while Jesus has none. Only in CHINESE
do we have significant use of a diminutive marker, -tzy in Chao's
orthography, -zi in the Pinyin orthography used by Clumeck. The
figures are Canta: 10%, Lolo: 7%, and Didi: 8%, but Didi disregards
the marker in his own production of seven out of nine words, substituting reduplication, which is also used in adult presentation.

We saw earlier that the results were skewed for the Chinese children, because the structure of their language was such that a disproportionate share of their words fell into the D category. Since that category is the only one primarily based on the adult forms regardless of the shape of the child's version, it seems reasonable at this point to eliminate the words falling in that category for each child and re-evaluate the rôle played by the other categories, based on percent of the remaining words. The results of that tabulation are given in Table 6. As far as the rank-position of individual children is concerned, notice that, as compared with Table 2, all three Chinese children now rank higher in the B category, with Lolo, the oldest of the 13 children at the end if his study, now ranking, along with Maja, second only to Tomaž. In the C category Didi has now moved up from sixth to third position. As far as A, consonant harmony, is concerned, there is no change in rank, nor are there any changes for the non-Chinese children.

Table 6

Category A		Category B		Category C		Category E	
Amahl	38%	Tomaž	91%	Jacob	50%	Amahl	6%
Virve	32%	Lolo	87%	Hildegard	41%	Hildegard	4%
Jesus	26%	Maja	87%	Didi	24%	Canta	2%
Sofia	23%	Jiři	83%	Amahl	17%	Virve	1%
Jiři	13%	Canta	79%	Jesus	17%		
Jacob	13%	Linda	78%	Virve	16%		
Linda	12%	Sofia	73%	Maja	11%		
Canta	7%	Didi	70%	Canta	11%		
Hildegard	7%	Jesus	56%	Lolo	11%		
Didi	6%	Virve	50%	Linda	10%		
Tomaž	3%	Hildegard	48%	Tomaž	5%		
Maja	2%	Amahl	39%	Sofia	4%		
Lolo	2%	Jacob	38%	Jiři	4%		
Mean	14%		68%		17%		
Median	12%		73%		11%		

As far as over-all percentages are concerned, the B category now accounts for well over half of the lexicon, on average (the median score is 73%, or nearly three-quarters consonant-sequence production). The rôle of A and C remains close, on average, though C now shows a larger average percentage. If we arbitrarily pick 10% as the limiting figure above which a category may be said to play a significant rôle in a child's production, we find that consonant

harmony is still significant for seven, consonant deletion for nine
out of the 13 children. Aside from the individual ranking of the
Chinese children, then, there is little change in the results after
elimination of category D.

On Table 7, the A-B-C profiles for all the children are displayed,
ordered by B rank. This set of graphs is based on the relative rank
frequencies given on Table 6, but the differing ranges reflected by
the actual percentage figures for the three categories (i.e. 53-point
range for B vs. 46-point for C and 36-point for A) have been translated here into a single six-point scale.

Table 7. A-B-C scores ordered by rank

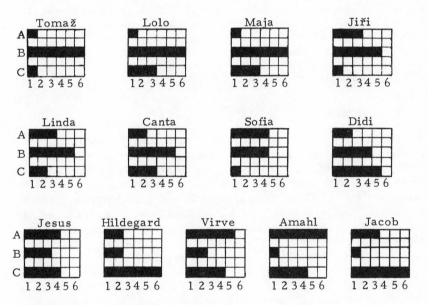

Looking at Table 7, we see that three children, the Slovenian
siblings and the oldest Chinese child, Lolo, scored 6 for category
B. Consonant harmony plays an insignificant rôle for all of them,
while consonant deletion is moderately important for Lolo and Maja
(recall, however, that Tomaž was inclined to truncate words; sophisticated in handling two-consonant sequences, he very rarely added
a third within the period studied).

Three children scored 5 on category B. Of these, two made
moderate use of consonant harmony, while only one made significant

use of consonant deletion. Among the three children scoring a
medium 3 or 4 on B, two make relatively heavy use of consonant
harmony, the other uses consonant deletion. And among the four
children with low scores of 1 or 2 on B, two score 5 or 6 on consonant harmony, two score 6 on consonant loss. Among these four,
only Hildegard, with a B score of 2, fails to make significant use
of the alternate, less-favored strategy as well (in her case, consonant harmony).

In short, as suggested by the close mean scores for A and C,
the children divide fairly evenly into those using harmony and those
preferring to omit troublesome consonants, with a predictably
heavier reliance on one or the other, or to some degree both, for
those children who score low on B. In a later section we will consider the function of consonant harmony and the issue of which
comes first: difficulty handling consonantal contrast, or a preference for a particular kind of phonological process.

5.   Consonant Harmony in the Children's Speech

5.1 Typology

When all the consonant harmony forms for all the children are
combined and categorized as to segments and gross articulatory
features involved, full or partial assimilation, and regressive or
progressive direction of assimilation, we arrive at the results
given in Table 8. The categories "full" and "partial" are not unam-
biguous. Change of k to t in the (discontinuous) environment of t,
for example, might be considered a change in place of articulation,
while change of l to v in the environment of m (Linda, three instances) yields incomplete agreement in place as well as in manner.
I count assimilations "full" where the surface result was two identical segments, "partial" where the two segments still differed in any
feature, even voice. Thus the first case cited above, k to t, would
be scored "full," while the l to v example counted as partial labial
assimilation. Since, as noted in Sec. 3, many children had subphonemic distribution rules for voicing, 1 combined the voiced and
voiceless pairs in tabulating the results. Those results are summarized more broadly in terms of percentages in Table 9, where
the figures for Amahl and Virve, who together account for 47% of
all the consonant harmony forms, are separated out from the rest.
It is apparent that since those two children had quite different kinds
of harmony, they fail to combine to skew the overall pattern in any
particular direction.

Table 8. Assimilating segments and features
in consonant harmony forms.*

I. Full assimilation

	Regressive	%	Progressive	%
p, b	16		14	
t, d, t', ɖ	29		16	
k, g	27		18	
STOP	72	50%	48	66%
f, v	4			
s, φ, š, ž	8		4	
FRICATIVE	12	8%	4	5%
m	12		4	
n	26		8	
NASAL	38	27%	12	16%
l	9		2	
yod, w	5		7	
LIQUID, GLIDE	14	10%	9	12%
h	1			
cluster	6			
TOTAL	143		73	

II. Partial assimilation

	Regressive	%	Progressive	%
labial, labiodental	30		15	
dental, palatal	21		3	
velar	22		15	
PLACE	73	74%	33	75%
stop, affricate	15		10	
nasal	10		1	
MANNER	25	26%	11	25%
TOTAL	98		44	

*The total here is not equivalent to the total number of A words
across all the children, because some words were counted as showing both directions of assimilation (e.g. Hildegard's grand(pa) →
[ŋæŋæ]; Virve's /pu.Tru/ 'porridge (obj)' → [p͡truːp͡tru]), while in other
cases both place and manner change were counted (e.g. l → d or
p = stop and dental or labial harmony).

Table 9. Consonant harmony types

	Virve		Amahl		Others		All	
Full, regressive	39	43%	22	31%	85	46%	146	42%
Full, progressive	14	16%	8	11%	49	26%	71	20%
Partial, regressive	23	26%	34	48%	29	16%	86	25%
Partial, progressive	14	16%	7	10%	23	12%	44	13%
Full	53	59%	30	42%	134	72%	217	63%
Partial	37	41%	41	58%	52	28%	130	37%
Regressive	62	69%	56	79%	114	61%	232	67%
Progressive	28	31%	15	21%	72	39%	115	33%
Total	90		71		186		347	

To illustrate the typology used, I cite in Appendix 2 all those
words which happen to show up in assimilated form in the vocabulary of more than one child in the study. The ENGLISH words are
of course part of the "foreign vocabulary" for Canta, Jesus and
Virve. In two cases I have compared the phonologically similar,
but not identical, forms of a word in two different languages (cf.
'soup,' 'tiger'). In just one case I have drawn, for comparison,
on a word that in fact appears in the harmony category for only one
child (Jacob). Amahl renders doggie as [ġɔgi:] only at stage 2, not
included in this study,[13] while Hildegard's [doti], superficially a
harmonized form, in fact has to be scored E, since she tends to
substitute dentals for syllable-initial velars in general (cf. cover->
[da], icecream -> [ati], kiss -> [diš], etc.).

By presenting words assimilated to a harmony pattern by more
than one child I hope to illustrate, in addition to the categories
used in typing the forms, the kind of consonantal sequence that
poses a problem or a challenge or temptation to the child, and, on
the other hand, the variety of patterns that can be applied to a single form. The word thank you, for example, was assimilated by
all four children who used it, with three different resultant patterns.

5.2 Function

Tables 8 and 9 are based entirely on the consonants used by the
child in his own productions. If we look as well at the consonants

---

[13]At stage 1, Amahl uses [wowo], which I score D, assuming it
derives from an adult wowwow. Smith unfortunately fails to specify
the actual shape of the likely adult source for such nursery words,
which tend to vary somewhat from family to family.

affected or replaced in the assimilation process, a pattern
emerges for most of the children who made significant use of consonant harmony (that is, those who scored 5% or more on Table 2),
which suggests the function of consonant harmony for the child in
question.

In Linda's data, for example, the consonant affected is typically
word-initial (25 out of 32 cases). If we compare the incidence of
the various manner-of-articulation types among word-initial consonants in each category, we arrive at the following results (A +C=
problem words, B +D = no problem for the child):[14]

	A	B	C	D	A+C	B+D
stop	7	127	5	23	21%	59%
s	5	11	1	7	11%	7%
v	-	18	-	1	-	7%
nasal	2	24	1	8	5%	13%
liquid	13	8	11	4	43%	5%
yod	5	10	1	3	11%	5%
h	-	8	5	2	9%	4%

It is obvious that liquids pose a problem for Linda (r was not produced at all during the period included in this study, while l is
changed to yod in nine words -- C category -- and assimilated in
nine). Similarly, s and yod tend to be assimilated, as shown by
their disproportionate incidence in category A. It seems clear
that Linda made use of consonant harmony, as well as consonant
deletion, to solve particular segmental problems.[15]

Canta, who scores only 5% harmony on Table 2, uses the process
almost exclusive to deal with l, which she does not produce at all.

---

[14] Of the initials on the seven A words in which a noninitial consonant was affected, five are k, one is p, one is yod.

[15] Linda's use of harmony is evaluated on the basis of a somewhat
more thorough analysis of the same data in Vihman 1971: "Linda is
operating with a tentative consonant assimilation rule which copies
the post-vocalic consonant initially just in case the initial consonant
is not a stop (oral or nasal). This 'rule' is optional at all stages,
and loses force steadily as the various consonantal articulations
are mastered. It thus constitutes, in effect, more of an operational
principle or strategy for dealing with difficult initial consonants
than a "productive rule" in the sense of adult grammars..." (p. 78).

Eight out of 14 cases of harmony affect l, assimilating it to n or
to a stop (l becomes d), while l is lost in 14 out of 22 cases of
consonant deletion. The remaining instances of l in the adult
models are assimilated to an adjacent, morpheme final n in the
child's corpus (five instances), deleted (four instances categorized
as B because there remain two contrasting consonants in the word),
or replaced by yod (six instances which fall into the B or D categories).[16]

The two SPANISH-speaking children, who rank third and fourth
in use of harmony after Amahl and Virve, both made use of the
process in dealing with long words (three syllables or longer). For
Sofia, 15 out of 26 consonant harmony words (or 57%) are at least
three-syllables long (some of these "words" are unanalyzed phrases,
such as ¿què es ésto? 'what is this ' or simply article plus noun:
la niña 'the girl'). Eleven of them (or 42%) have a three-consonant
structure (where a cluster counts as a consonant but non-initial glides
do not) in both adult and child form. Of the B words, in contrast,
only 22 out of 83 (or 25%) are three-syllables long or longer, and
14 (or 17%) have the three-consonant structure. Among the long
words or phrases, five show assimilation to a cluster:

> Fernando 'proper name' → tšəndando
> llorando 'crying' → ɲrdardno
> telefono 'telephone' → ɸweɸwʌno
> television 'television' → widsezo:n
> vestido 'sweater' → batsidzo

In five others, a fricative or liquid is assimilated to a stop:

> comiendo 'eating' → kabiendu
> la radio 'the radio → dadazo
> què es ésto 'what is this' → kiketo
> tenedor 'fork' → ɐbədʌɹ
> zapato 'shoe' → dəbata

Clearly Sofia is using (partial) harmony to help her deal with long
sequences of syllables, and she appears to favor the maximally
contrastive stop-vowel syllable structure.

Unlike Sofia, Jesus has only a slightly higher percentage of
three-consonant, three-syllable words among his A words than

16Because Chao deals only with the child's system, he fails to
mention Canta's treatment of adult l in his description of her phonology.

among his B words, whether we are counting those reduced to two
syllables in his version (9, or 29%, A words; 15, or 24%, B words),
or those which he successfully reproduces with at least three syllables (6, or 19%, A words; 8, or 13%, B words). Setting the six
long A words aside, however, on the assumption that these fall in
the harmony category because Jesus, like Sofia, is using assimilation as an aid in handling the long string of syllables, we find that
in the 25 remaining words, s is affected in eight and m or n in five.
Yet the nasals were among Jesus' earliest segments, according to
Macken 1976, though s had not yet been produced at the outset of
her study. In fact, the rôle of harmony in Jesus' phonological
system cannot be adequately described in terms of single segments
or total wordlength, but is related to the complete consonantal
structure of a word. At the beginning of Macken's study, "if two
consonants co-occurred in a word, they had to agree in place and
manner" (p. 42; compare Vihman 1976, where a similar condition
is described as operating during the period in which Virve's first
50 words were acquired). Later, for "words which have a final
nasal or a non-final fricative in the adult model, J's productions
showed a gradual increase in complexity in terms of the number,
type and order of syllables" (p. 47). "Fricatives in C_1VC_2V words,
where either C_1 ... or ... C_2 was a voiceless stop or nasal, underwent complete or partial assimilation" (p. 48). In general, Macken
notes that for Jesus, "the greater the similarity between two consonants, the fewer the restrictions on their co-occurrence in any
word" (p. 49).

Turning to Jiři, we find that k is the consonant affected in 30%
of the harmonized forms (11 out of 33 A words). Pačesova (1968)
notes that k at first tended to alternate with t, and that the majority of early occurrences of k were in interjections, where,
according to several sources she mentions, difficult sounds tend
to be mastered early. By the time 100 words had been acquired
(at 15 months), however, k had become the most commonly occurring consonant in Jiři's productions, yet where it co-occurs with
an alveolar, Jiři typically spreads either the alveolar or the velar
articulation across the word:

kolečko 'wheel' (dimin.) → tolešto (age 1;5,1)
tužka 'pencil' → tušta ~ kuška (1;5,1)
taška 'bag' → tašta (1;6,13), kašku (1;7,15)

A principle which Lewis formulated (1936) and supported with data
from three children appears to apply in this case: "Of the two
sounds in the adult word, the one which comes later in the child's

history is assimilated to the one that comes earlier, even if he
can pronounce both" (p. 183).

None of the instances of k̲ being assimilated to another consonant
occur earlier than 17 months. In fact, no consonant harmony forms
at all appear among Jiři's first fifty words (see Table 3), though
some of those words are produced in an assimilated form later.
For example (the number on the left indicates position in the acquisition order; the harmonized variants are underlined):

   35 balon 'ball' → baji ~ bali (1;2, 27), balo:n ~ balonek (1;5,1),
       babo:nek (1;7,19), baloŋki (1;8,0)

   47 na shledanou 'so long' → nosono (1;2, 30), naslono ~ naslenanou
       (1;5,1), nasledanou (1;7,13)

   86 ježek 'hedgehog' → jø:zø: (1;4, 30), jeďek ~ žežeček ~ žežek ~
       ješešek (1;5,1), žežeci (1;6,14), ježek, etc. (1;7,0)

   93 knoflik 'button' → noti:k, nofik (1;5, 0), oki:k ~ koki:kek
       (1; 5,1), kofi:k (1;6,12)

  164 gramofon 'gramophone' → mofo:n ~ mofo:nek (1;6,12), kakofo:n
       (1;7,19), gamofo:n ~ gagafo:n (1;8, 20)

In all but the first of these examples we see harmony being used
when a longer version of the word — a hypocoristic or a version
supplying syllables omitted earlier -- is first attempted. But no
such function can be claimed for harmony in such cases as

   90 žaba 'frog' → ba:ba ~ wa:ba (1;5,0)

  182 koupat 'to bathe' → po:pat ~ poupat (and poupala 'she bathed')
       (1;6, 20)

  259 čap 'stork' → pap (1;7, 20)

  270 sova 'owl' → fofa (1;7, 31)

Instead, we seem to see here the use of an optional rule of consonant
harmony as a kind of sound-play; perhaps the rôle of assimilation
in such cases is at least partially aesthetic, like the rôle of alliteration for adults in poetry or in formulaic phrases such as do or die,
to have and to hold, kith and kin, might and main, etc.

5.3 Extensive use of consonant harmony

As we have noted earlier, two of the children made such extensive use of consonant assimilation that their A forms account for
nearly half of the total harmony corpus. Each of these children
was observed by a parent who largely took notes on the spot, rather
than make tapes for subsequent transcription. On the other hand,
the data collection methods used in the Stanford Child Phonology
Project, from which the SPANISH data derive, were rigorous, with
two transcribers working first independently, then together, to arrive at as faithful a record of the children's speech as current technology and experience will allow (cf. Macken 1976). The gap on
Table 6 between the A figures for the two SPANISH-speaking subjects
-- 23% and 26% -- and the figures for Virve (32%) and Amahl (38%)
might be due in part to observer bias, since both Smith and I may
have tended to write down all the phonologically "interesting" forms
while disregarding some of the forms which were uninterestingly
close to their adult models. At the same time, one assumes that
there are also limitations inherent in an experimental situation such
as that used in the SPANISH studies, with a restricted range of stimuli and observers not intimately familiar with the children. In any
case the upper limits for the rôle of consonant harmony in a given
child's lexicon would simply have to be revised downward slightly.
Amahl and Virve are otherwise alike only in one respect -- namely,
in a preference for regressive harmony that exceeds the norm for
the other children (see Table 9).

5.3.1 Amahl

An exhaustive description of Amahl's phonology is to be found in
Smith 1973. Two consonant harmony rules account for the majority
of forms in our category A: Rule 19 (p. 20) assimilates alveolars
and palato-alveolars to the point of articulation of a following consonant -- optionally to a labial, obligatorily to a velar; Rule 17 (p.19)
assimilates non-nasal alveolars and palato-alveolars to the point of
articulation of a preceding velar and probably to a preceding labial
as well. Regressive assimilation (Rule 19) affects 36 or 71 A words,
while progressive assimilation (Rule 17) affects 11 words. Three
forms are affected by optional harmony Rule 5 (p. 15), which changes
continuants to nasals after a nasal plus vowel. Lastly, the rule affecting liquids and yod consists of three alternatives: realization
of any of these segments as /l/ if no consonant other than another
liquid or yod occurs in the adult word, or deletion intervocalically,
or realization as /d/. Four words fall under the first alternative

above at stage 1. Since an l̲ is present alongside r̲ or yod̲ in all
of these words, they are viewed here as products of assimilation:

lorry → lɔli (progressive)
troddler → lɔlə (regressive)
trolly → lɔli (regressive)
yellow → lɛlo (regressive)

An additional 16 words with initial liquid or yod̲ are viewed here as
assimilating to a following /d/ (from adult t̲, d̲, s̲, z̲, š̲) or /n/
(partial regressive assimilation).[17] Since we find š̲ → d̲ in shoe̲,
for example, and s̲ → d̲ in see̲ (stage 2), forms such as shirt̲ →
[dət], side̲ → [dait], etc. are categorized as E. But at stage 1
there are no examples of a single liquid or yod̲ with no other consonant in the environment, so that the context-free substitutes can
not be unambiguously determined (at stage 2 we already find alternation between /d/ and /r/ in Amahl's version of ray̲). It is possible
that we are over-estimating the extent of consonant harmony in
Amahl's lexicon by not placing the liquid and yod-initial words in E,
which would lower the absolute A score from 71 to 55 words (32%
to 22%) and raise the already high E score from 11 to 27 (5% to 11%),
or more than three times Hildegard's next-highest E score of 3%.

Amahl has in common with Hildegard a high type-to-token score
for consonant sequences (Table 4: Amahl 2.35 vs. Hildegard 3.03),
a sign of a small segment inventory. In fact Smith counts just eight
consonants for Amahl at stage 1 (p. 170), out of the 24 of adult ENG-
LISH (by Smith's reckoning). Hildegard, by comparison, had some
11 contrastive consonants by the end of Leopold's study, when she
was two years old, or a little younger than Amahl at stage 1. It
appears that where Hildegard made fairly massive use of consonant
deletion to make up for her difficulty with certain segments (30% C
words vs. 5% A words), Amahl preferred to use consonant harmony,
though he did delete consonants as well (14% C score).

It is interesting to note that of all 13 children Amahl makes the
least use of lexical selection to arrive at words with no contrasting
consonant sequences (16% D words) -- insofar as category D reflects
such selection. I pointed out earlier that, except for the special
case of CHINESE, relative use of D appears to be an index of linguistic maturity. On those grounds Jacob and Hildegard score at the

---

[17] One A word, lawnmower̲ (→ [mo:mə]), falls under none of
Smith's rules and is cited as an exception (p. 35).

opposite end of the scale from Amahl, who is also quite a bit older than the other ENGLISH-speaking children, for whom data was gathered and analyzed here from the first words to age 1;8 and 2;0, respectively. Recalling that Jiři developed a minor consonant-harmony strategy at around age 1;5, when he already had over 50 words in his lexicon, we can only speculate as to the earlier, un-recorded stages of Amahl's development. Smith mentions in pass-ing that 'sock' -- "which, by stage 1, was invariably [g̊ɔk]" (p. 29) -- was once pronounced [dɔk]; but he also guesses, on the basis of "a few 'remnant' forms," that the most general, regressive harmony rule (19) once applied to velars (in labial environment) as well as to alveolars and palato-alveolars.

5.3.2 Virve

Amahl's data reflect his lexicon at a single point in time. Virve's still larger array of assimilated forms represent a growing lexicon over a period of about seven months.[18] The kinds of assimilation we find recall Jesus' data, in the gradual relaxing of constraints on consonant combinations and on word-length, rather than Amahl's sweeping segment-substitution rules. The period of the first 50 words, ending at 1;4,12, is marked by two constraints of interest here: two syllables is the maximum word-length, and either place or manner is held constant across the consonants of a word, with a single exception (cf. piss, below). No liquids have yet been pro-duced, while v occurs once finally but is not produced syllable-initially.[19] s was among the earliest consonants to be used, and it remained stable. The nasals m and n appeared after the first twenty words. k was acquired slowly, with substitution by t for over half of this early period. Consonant harmony applies, option-ally, to stop-plus-nasal and stop-plus-s combinations during this period:

---

[18] Between the ages of 10 and 15 months, only 11 words were recorded. Except for one item, forms showing active use of con-sonant assimilation began to appear from 1;3,20 on, when about 30 words had been used spontaneously.

[19] The consonants occurring in native (adult) ESTONIAN words include three stops (p, t, k), two fricatives (v, s), two nasals (m, n), two liquids (l, r), the glide yod, h, and four palatalized dentals (t', s', n', l'). The stops are lax and partly voiced intervocalically and word-finally when short; the orthography marks them b, d, and g in such cases, but there is in fact no contrastive voicing.

/pIm/ 'milk' → mi:m ~ pim: (contrast /puM/ below)
/tantsi/ 'dance' → sa|si ~ ta|si

Where the initial consonant is k̲ or v̲, assimilation to a following
stop or s̲ is obligatory (or v̲ may be deleted).

Harmony	No Harmony
/kleiT/ 'dress' → tɛt·	/puM ~ pëM/ 'boom' → pim: ~ pi
/kIsu/ 'kitty' → (first) ti,	/maNi/ 'proper name' → man·i
(later) ši:š· ~ ši:s ~ ši·su ~	/parT/ 'duck' → pat· ~ pa:
ti·t'u	/piS/ 'pee' → p̥is
/veT/ 'water' → tɛt: ~ ɛt:	/teist/ 'other' → tis
/vO.ti/ '(to) bed' → po·t̥·	this → tis

In this early period active consonant assimilation can be seen to
come gradually into use, after several months of slow increase in
word-production constrained by limits on possible consonant (and
vowel) combinations (see Vihman 1976: 233ff). We know which consonants were difficult for Virve, based both on delay in attempting
adult words which include them (e.g. only two include a liquid by
1;4,12) and on the child's use of simple substitution (t̲ for k̲), deletion (cf. vett, above) or assimilation to handle them. Against this
background, we note the use of the following processes over the
period ending at 1;11:

1. **Liquids and v are assimilated or deleted** until 1;10. Medially,
these segments assimilate to word-initial stop or nasal, where no
other consonant follows:

/prAvo/ 'bravo' → papu (1;3)
/karu/ 'bear' → ka·u ~ kaɣu (1;5)
/kivi/ 'stone' → kiki ~ kip·i (1;4)
/ma.hla/ 'juice (obj.)' → mahma (1;5)
/priLit/ 'glasses' → pi·pi (1;5)

Where a stop or nasal follows, it is the preferred goal of assimilation:

/palun/ 'please' → panun (1;6)
/sUr auTo/ 'big car' → su·t·ot·o (1;6)

Where there is no stop or nasal in the immediate environment (i.e.
across a single syllabic nucleus), medial liquid or v̲ is deleted or
becomes a glide:

/elevan'T'/ 'elephant' → en· (1;4)
/hiLe/ 'proper name' → i· (1;8)
/orav/ 'squirrel' → oa (1;4)
/sü.Le/ 'into (your) arms, lap' → suija ~ süija (1;6)
/vælyas/ 'outside' → aijas (1;7)
/vEl/ 'more' → we· (1;5)
/üles/ 'up' → üös (1;7)

Where yod follows a medial liquid, the liquid is deleted:

/palju/ 'much, many' → paju (1;6)
/(vIna-)ma.rja/ 'grape (obj.)' → maj·a (1;5)

and word-final liquids are deleted as well, even after an initial stop:

/koer/ 'dog' → koa (1;4)
/pěL/ 'apron, bib' → pe (1;5)
(contrast /paL'/ 'ball' → pap· (1;4), paj (1;8))

Word-final v is retained in Virve's version only as part of the
cluster [hv] (which is perceptually very close to [f]): cf. /ahv/
'monkey' → [ahv] (1;3) and /hirv/ 'deer' → [ihv] (1;4).

Initial l and v assimilate to a medial nasal or stop just in case
the nasal or stop is part of a consonant cluster; otherwise l or v
is deleted (unless the word has more than two syllables: see below).
Where a tense stop follows the nasal, it serves as the goal of assimilation; where the stop is lax, the nasal serves.[20]

/laehme/ 'let's go' → mǽhme (1;10)
/lamP/ 'lamp' → pamp· (1;5)
/la.psi/ 'children' → pa|si ~ pat^{s}i (1;5)[21]

---

[20] The form /jænKu/ 'bunny' → [nae|nu] (1;5) fails to fit into
this formulation, which is in any case based on very few examples.
The same is apparently true of Amahl's tendency to delete the nasal
before a voiceless stop in a cluster, but retain the nasal and delete
the stop when the stop is voiced (Smith 1973: 166). For both children
the lax or voiced stop seems generally to be less "noticeable" (in
Priestly's terms), or lower on a strength hierarchy (in Macken's
terms), than the tense or voiceless stop.

[21] I derive Virve's version of /la.psi/ 'children (obj.)' and
/la.ntši/ 'lunch (obj.)' via the harmonized forms *[papsi] and *[nVnsi],
which seem to fit better into her system than the alternate metathesized mediating forms *[palsi] and *[nVl(t)si]. Reduction of the
resulting consonant cluster is to be expected in either case.

/linta/ 'proper name' —→ nin·a (1;4)
/la.ntši/ 'lunch (obj.)' —→ næ|si (1;10) (see footnote 21, above)
/van'Ka/ 'proper name' —→ pan'ka (1;10)

/læpi/ 'through' —→ æpi (1;8)
/lei.pa/ 'bread (obj.)' —→ ejpa (1;5)
/vA.Ta/ 'look!' —→ at:a (1;8)
/va.Ni/ 'into the bath' —→ an:i (1;4)
(But cf. /vana-ema/ 'grandmother' —→ manaema (1;9), /lume-
mEs/ 'snowman' —→ mumeme:s (1;10))

There are just two instances of harmony to a glide (note that w
does not occur in adult ESTONIAN):

/lěvi/ 'lion' —→ wijwi (1;6)
/væ.lja/ 'to outside' —→ jaija (1;4)

Initial r is always deleted.

2. <u>Labials assimilate dentals if the labial follows</u>, until 1;10. If
the dental follows, the consonant sequence is replicated as is (see
Table 10, A and B). There are five exceptions, as noted on the table:
/trapÉts/ and /pati/, /plIats/, /putel/, and /muna/, all but /trapÉts/
cases of unexpected assimilation (in the "wrong" direction in the
case of /muna/). One further special case is presented by the
word /puTru/ 'porridge,' which Virve somehow managed to assimilate in both directions, combining the labiality of the initial consonant with the stop/trill medial unit to produce a segment I noted
as ptr: [p̂trup̂tru] (1;5); by 1;6 the form was simply [put·u].

3. <u>Labials assimilate velars</u> until 1;8. <u>Peek-a-boo</u> is the sole
exception (see Table 10, C and D).

4. <u>Dentals assimilate velars</u> until 1;9. Two early exceptions
are /kOs/ and /ěi.kus/; at 1;9 Virve produced unassimilated forms
for /kæes/ and /kæet/, inflected variants of the word /kæsi/ 'hand,'
which is assimilated according to the rule, as is another inflected
variant of the same word, /kæ.Te/ (see Table 10, E). It seems
that here, as in the case of assimilation of liquids, syllable-initial
consonants exert the strongest pull.

The sequence k - n shows the expected dominance of regressive
over progressive assimilation at first, but at 1;8, when velars
begin to assimilate labials (/prüki/) and dentals (in the sequence
t - k), the direction of assimilation is reversed, and we find several instances of intervocalic and even word-final n —→ ŋ (which
occurs only pre-consonantally in adult ESTONIAN).

Table 10. Virve's treatment of consonant combinations

A. Labial followed by dental

	Harmony	No Harmony
p - t	/pati/ 'pillow' → papi ~ pai ~ pajpi (1;4) /pIIats/ 'pencil' → pi·p·i (1;5) /putel/ 'bottle' → pupa (1;5)	/parT/ 'duck' → pat· (1;4) /pO.ti/ 'to the store' → po:ti (1;5) /pĕter/ 'reindeer' → pĕtel (1;10)
p - s		/poiS/ 'boy' → pos'· (1;5) /aPelsin/ 'orange' → apəsi (1;5) /püksit/ 'pants' → pi|si (1;6)
p - n		/pirn/ 'pear' → pin· (1;5) it's a pin → səp·ĭn (1;5) /punane/ 'red' → punane (1;10)
m - t		/meT/ 'honey (obj.)' — mɛt· (1;5) /mesi/ 'honey' → mɛsi (1;5) /mO.si/ 'jam' → mo:si (1;5) /va.lmis/ 'ready' → masi (1;5) /mustat/ 'dirty (pl.)' → mus·at (1;9)
m - n	/muna/ 'egg' → nuna (1;5)	/maNi/ 'proper name' → man·i (1;3) /maNa/ 'farina' → manta (1;10)

B. Dental followed by labial

t - p	/tu.Pa/ 'into the room, to indoors' → pup:a (1;4) /tops/ 'cup' → pops (1;10) /tupa/ 'room' → pupa (1;10)	/traPÉts/ 'trapezoid' → tap·e·ts (1;7)
s - p	/su.Pi/ 'soup (obj.) → fup:i (1;7) /sEP/ 'soap' → fe:p (1;8)	/sApas/, /sApast/ 'boot' → sa:p, sa·p·at· (analogical) (1;10)
n - p	/napa/ 'navel' → papa (1;4)	
t - m	NO EXAMPLES	
s - m	/sEme/ 'seed' → fe·me ~ se·me (1;7) /sÖ.ma/ 'to eat' → fö:ma (1;7)	/spinaT/ 'spinach' → se·mæt (1;10)

Harmony	No Harmony

n -m /nImO.ti ~ nImoti/ 'this way;
    that's the way!'→ mi·mona (1;5)
    /minema/ 'to go → mimema (1;10)

C. Labial followed by velar

p-k <u>book</u> → pʊp· (1;4)   <u>peek(-a-boo)</u> → pík·(pù) (1;4)
    /prüki/ 'trash' → küki (1;8)   /pE.Kon/ 'bacon' → pe:kɔn (1;8)
                                        /paK/ 'package' → pak: (1;9)
                                        /piK/ 'tall' → pik: (1;8)

m-k /makama/ 'to sleep' → ma:ma (1;4) /miks/ 'why' → miks (1;9)
    /makap/ 'is sleeping' →   <u>Micky Mouse</u> → mík·imàus
     mamak (1;7)   (1;10)

D. Velar followed by labial

k-p /kærpes/ 'fly' → pæs (1;6)
    /ka.mPsun/ 'sweater' →
     pa|su (1;5)

k-m /kaM/ 'comb' → pam: (1;5)   /kolm/ 'three' → kom: (1;8)
    /krE.mi/ 'cream (obj.)' →   <u>come</u> → kam: (1;8)
     pe·mi ~ pi·mi (1;6)   /komPu/ 'candy' → komp·u (1;10)

E. Velar followed by dental

k-t /kleiT/ 'dress' → tɛt· (1;4)   /kæet/ 'hands' → kaeet (1;9)
    /kArT/ 'card' → ta:t (1;5)
    /ka.rTul/ 'potato' → ta|tu (1;5)
    /ka.tki/ 'broken' → ta|ti (1;4)
    /koT'/ 'bag' → tot: (1;5)
    /küTe/ 'heating' → tüt·e (1;7)
    /kä.Te/ 'into the hand' →
     tæt:e (1;9)

k-ts /klotsit/ 'blocks' → to|si (1;5)   (/kaks/ 'two' → kats (1;8))
                                      /kut's'uT/ 'puppy (obj.)' → kut's'ut·
                                       (1;9)

k-s /kIsu/ 'kitty' → ši:š ~ ši:su ~   /kOs/ 'together' → ko:s (1;7)
    ti·t'u (1;3); ti:su (1;6)   /ëi.kus/ 'right' → ëikus (1;8)
    /kA.sa/ '(take) along' →   /kuS/ 'where' → kus· (1;10)
     ta:sa (1;5)

Harmony   No Harmony

k-s /takasi/ '(go, take) back' --→   /karÁ.ži/ 'to the garage' --→
    tasisi (1;5)   ká:si (1;10)
    /kaesi/ 'hand' --→ taesi (1;9)   /kaees/'in the hand'--→ kaees (1;9)

k-st /kristi/ 'proper name' --→
    tsitsi (1;4); ti|si (1;9); kis·i (1;10)
    (cf. /kut's'u/ 'puppy' --→ tsutsu
    imitation, 1;4)

k-n /kilP-koN/'turtle' --→ti|ton: (1;5)   /ki.Ni/ 'closed' --→ kin·i (1;4)
    /kiNas/ 'glove' --→ tin·as (1;5)   <u>kleenex</u> --→ kí·neks (1;10)
    /aKen/ 'window' --→ atɛn (1;5);
    akɛŋ (1;10)
    /kana/ 'chicken' --→ kaŋa (1;8)
    /kena/ 'nice' --→ keŋa (1;8)
    /kaNap/ 'carries' --→ kaŋ.ak (1;9)
    /koN/ 'frog' --→ koŋ: (1;10)

F. Dental followed by velar

t-k /heat-ae.ka/ 'goodbye' --→   /tIK/ 'pond' --→ ti:k·(1;4)
    tata (1;5)   /tiku/ 'snail' --→ tiku (1;5)
    /tütruK/ 'girl' --→ kiuk (1;8)
    /teKi a.La/ 'to under the
    blanket' --→ kek·i al:a (1;9)
    /(kaks) tü.Ki/ '(two) pieces'
    --→ (kaks) kük:i (1;9)
    /teki/ 'did (it)' --→ keki (1;10)
    <u>thankyou</u> --→ kæ ŋku (1;10)

dž-g <u>jingle bells</u> --→ tintupeu (1;10)

s-k /soKit/ 'socks' --→ so|si (1;5);   /šoKolAt/ 'chocolate' --→ sɔk:
    sokit (1;7)   (1;10)

n-k /nuKut/ 'dools' --→ nu|nu (1;5);
    nuk·u (1;10)

Before 1;8 the sequence dental-velar results in assimilation to
the dental or, in two instances, in exceptional absence of harmony
(/tIK/, /tiku/). After 1;8 regressive assimilation obtains in all
cases of dental/velar stop combination, with the single exception
of <u>jingle-bells</u>, where we find [tintupeu] instead of the expected
*[kiŋkupeu].

Of the constraints obtaining in the early period, then, the manner
harmony requirement is applied only optionally already by 1;4, while
place harmony is still actively maintained for certain combinations
at 1;10. The word length constraint is relaxed in several stages.
Among the first fifty words, only two have an adult model longer
than two syllables -- /kìKeriKÍ/ and /paPakoi/ (see Table 11 for
the complete long word data). Those adult words which were typically presented in reduplicated form, such as /aLo-aLo/ 'hello-
hello (on the telephone),' bye-bye, or various animal sounds such
as /auh-auh/ 'bow-wow,' /kòKoKoKó/ 'cut-cut-cut-cut (of hens),'
were invariably reproduced without the reduplication: [ao], [paj],
[au], [kɔ](see Vihman 1976). At 1;4 Virve attempted five longer
adult words, reducing all to one or two syllables. At 1;5 the first
trisyllabic child forms appeared. Of the adult models with three
consonants as well as three syllables (counting clusters as single
consonants), Virve may have perceived, and in any case produced,
those with initial h or r, which she generally deleted, as having
only two (/heat-ae.ka/, /repane/), and the same was true of /aPel-
sin/ with its final nasal in unstressed syllable. It's a pin was an
ephemeral form, apparently a delayed imitation (used just once, but
in context) of an utterance remembered from the diaper-changing
routine at the day care center. The remaining forms, /panÁ.ni/,
/takasi/, /teist ri.nta/, and /nImoti/, pose different kinds of problems.

Table 11. Virve's long words

1;2   /kìKeriKÍ/ 'cock-a-doudle-doo' --→ tìtí:
1;3   /paPakoi/ 'parrot' --→ (pa)wawey; (1;4) pa
1;4   /panÁ.ni/ 'banana (obj.)' --→ pa·ni ~ ma·ni
      /kael-kirjaK/ 'giraffe (lit. spotty-neck)' --→ kak·i
      /elevan'T'/ 'elephant' --→ en·
      /makama/ '(to go) to sleep' --→ ma:ma
      peek-a-boo --→ pík(pu)
1;5   /aPelsin/ 'orange (fruit)' --→ ap·ǝ si (1;3 imitation: apwǝ)
      /panÁ. ni/ 'banana (obj.)' --→ pá·nini
      /eiTáha/ 'don't want' --→ ejtáha
      /heat-ae.ka/ 'goodbye' --→ tata
      /i.stuta/ '(to want) to sit' --→ it:uta
      it's a pin --→ sǝp· ín
      /nI mO.ti ~ nImoti/ 'this way, that's the way' --→ mi·mona
      /repane/ 'fox' --→ epa (cf. /hopu(ne)/ --→ ɔpu (1;3))
      /takasi/ '(to go, take) back' --→ tasisi
      /teist ri.nta/ '(to want to nurse) the other breast' --→ teisín·a
1;6   /leNuKiT/ 'airplane (obj.)' --→ nanunu
      /mAsiKas/ 'strawberry' --→ ma·sini

1;6 /porkantiT/ 'carrot (obj.)' —→ pɔnini
/rAmaTuT/ 'book (obj.)' —→ ma·nunu (cf. /rAmaT/ 'book'
—→ a· (1;5); also /rAmaTuT/ —→ ma·nut· (1;9), /rAmaTu peal/
'on the book' —→ ma·nu peaj (1;9))
/rosinat/ 'raisins' —→ o·sini
/virsiKuT/ 'peach (obj.)' (?) —→ is·uya (/sǔi.a/ may have
been intended)
1;7 /makus-toiT/ 'dessert (lit. sweet food)' —→ masusu
/mesilane/ 'bee' —→ mesini
/piKali/ 'full length, lying down' —→ pik·ak·aj
/viKerKAr/ 'rainbow' —→ vik·ak·ay
1;8 /mìne ǽera/ 'go away' —→ miáe·
/pitšama/ 'pajama' —→ pisama
1;9 all fall down —→ ɔ·fɔ·dáwn
/nU.tli su.Pi/ 'noodle soup (obj.)' —→ nu·dit sup:i
/pitu-kinkat/ 'party shoes' —→ pitutkiŋka
/tun't' (ae.ka)/ 'an hour('s time)' —→ tunti (kaeka)
Viviane —→ mimian
/jOnista/ 'draw' —→ nonini
/mëistaTus/ 'puzzle' —→ misusu
/mëistaTuse/ 'puzzle (total obj.)' —→ misuse
1;10 /ei óle/ 'is not' —→ ej óle
/karÁ.ši/ 'to the garage' —→ ká:si
/haeit pǔhi/ 'happy holidays' —→ haeit pǔhi
/intjÁ.nlane/ 'Indian' —→ éante
jingle bells —→ tintupeu
happy (birthday to you) —→ hæ̀p·i (tǒws:ei tǔu)
Mickey Mouse —→ mík·i màus
patty-cake —→ páelik·èyk
/punane/ 'red' —→ punane
/šoKolAt/ 'chocolate' —→ sɔk:
/unustas/ 'forgot' —→ unus
/Utiseit/ 'news' —→ u·tisi
/viTamÍnit/ 'vitamins' —→ mitan ~ mit·
/ǔle éla/ 'over the shoulder' —→ ǔléla

In /teist ri.nta/ we have place agreement across the consonants
in the adult form; Virve's version maintains all three syllables and
three consonants. In /nImoti/ the nasal dominance in the adult
model is extended in the child version, so that the long word is
further complicated by a place contrast, but not a manner contrast
(note that m - n was the earliest place contrast Virve used, in /ma-
Ni/, at 1;3, and compare /vana-ema/ 'grandmother' —→ mánaèma
(1;9)). For /panÁ.ni/ and /takasi/, with their combination of place
and manner contrasts, including the difficult dental/velar combination, Virve invented an idiosyncratic strategy reminiscent of the

bisyllabic word strategy described in Priestly 1977.[22] It involves maintaining the syllable count and overall syllabic structure of the adult word, while abandoning any attempt at segmental fidelity for all but one of the unstressed syllables.

In the following month we have five more instances of the tri-syllabic strategy (and no other new long words, except possibly /virsiKuT/). It is clear that nasals are (perceptually?) dominant here (see Table 11). The form [ma·sini] (← /mAsiKas/) is ano-malous; for a while it seemed that [-ni] was acquiring morpheme status as a marker of desirable foods, but no new items were added to the list. At 1;7 four new words, one the quadrisyllabic /mesilane/ (not a harmony form), were produced; at 1;9 two more words re-flecting the trisyllabic strategy, /jOnista/ and /mëistaTus/, completed the list, while as of 1;8 Virve produces more and more long words (several of them compounds) which fail to be adapted to the pattern: cf., for example, /pítšama/ and, at 1;10, /intjÁ.nlane/, /punane/, /Utiseit/.[23]

In reviewing the steps in Virve's progress from one- or two-syllable to longer words, I am inclined to doubt that she was in any sense "aware" that she was attacking a long -- or problematic, challenging -- word at 1;2 when she produced /kïKerikí/ (as [tití], but with a level/high-falling intonation taken from the adults' stereo-typed imitation of a cock's cry). By 1;4, on the other hand, she may well have perceived as long the few long words she attempted,

---

[22] Amahl's strategy for dealing with unstressed initial syllables (Smith 1973: 171ff) falls in the same category, though Amahl drew on ENGLISH derivational morphology rather than on the phonologi-cal context for a dummy syllabic shape.

[23] The number of multisyllabic ENGLISH compounds or bits of songs or games that Virve began using at this time, without shor-tening or applying any kind of harmony to them, is surprising. It could be argued that these set phrases, none of which can have had any "meaning" for Virve beyond the fact that they were frequently recited at the day care center (to which she had returned after a three-month absence, a few weeks earlier), were not filtered through her usual phonological system, but were repeated as closely as possible from some kind of aural store. The same kind of in-terest in, or talent for, mimicking wholly unintelligible foreign phrases was apparent much later when, for example, she could repeat at dinner a CANTONESE phrase, down to the tonal contour, that she had heard that day at lunch (she was nearly four at the time).

but she seems to have encoded as noise the syllable adjacent to a
liquid or velar when the word has more than two syllables, yielding
bisyllabic forms in the case of /kael-KirjaK/ and /makama/, a
monosyllable in the case of /elevan'T'/ (cf. also /karÁ.si/ at 1;10)[24]

By 1;5 we can see that the constraint on word-length has been
relaxed sufficiently to allow some trisyllabic forms to be produced,
presumably also reflecting improvements in perception and encoding
of underlying forms. Where the segments themselves present difficulties, independent of the length difficulty, the processing space
seems to be insufficient to allow full recording of all three syllables.
Instead, a rough sketch is made to serve, with an accurate syllable
count and some indication of vowel content. The form [pa·nini] (←--
/panÁ.ni/) may be based on Virve's own earlier output form [pa·ni],
with the addition of a reduplicated syllable as a kind of patchy re-
pair job to come closer to the trisyllabic adult model; in that case,
the choice of reduplicated vowel in [tasisi] (←- /takasi/) may have
been influenced by [pa·nini]. But it is equally likely that the contrast a̲-i̲ was encoded in both cases as the most striking aspect of
the total vocalic contour of either word.

The underlying forms for these words and those used in the following three months might be stated as in Ingram 1974: /takasi/ --→
[taSsi], /porkantiT/ --→ [poSni] (where S = syllable), together with a
rule: Reproduce S as identical to the unstressed syllable of the
underlying form: [taSsi] --→ [tasisi], [poSni] --→ [ponini].

The difficulties which led Virve to treat one of the unstressed
syllables in this cavalier fashion are similar to those Macken describes for Jesus ("the simultaneous realization of complex syllable
and consonant structures exceeded J's production abilities" p.56).
But it remains a moot question whether the source of the difficulty
lay in production, perception, or, as I am inclined to believe, encoding.

Some of Virve's consonant harmony forms persisted for a long
time after the period covered by this study, while new forms continued to appear even as her inventory of segments and syllable
shapes grew. The word /va.lmis/ 'ready,' for example, which
she used at 1;5 in the shape [mais], followed by [mas'] at 1;6 and

---

[24] Compare Linda's pattern of syllable loss: "In all cases in
which the second vowel is lost, that vowel is either preceded or
followed by /r/, the most difficult of consonants for Linda" (Vihman
1971: 71).

[masi] at 1;10, later developed the shape [malmis], which continued
to be used well into Virve's fourth year, when initial v̱ was otherwise well established.

Virve used one additional kind of consonant harmony as of 1;7,
when she began to include the final consonants which serve as inflectional markers. At 1;7 two nominative plural forms /-t/ show
harmony: /jænKut/ 'bunnies' --> [jǽeŋk·uk], /markit/ 'stamps' -->
[mǽeŋkik]. Only one such form appeared later (/soKit/ 'socks' -->
[sok·ik] at 1;9), but the marker for third person singular present
tense, /-p/, at first alternated between all three stops:

> 1;7 /tÖ.Tap/ 'works' --> tö·tat·
> /istup/ 'sits' --> it·ut·
> /kaNap/ 'carries' --> kaŋ·ak
> /makap/ 'sleeps' --> mamak, makak·
> /prOvip/ 'tries' --> po·pip

By 1;9 the marker was [t] for Virve unless the preceding consonant
was [k]:

> 1;9 /ai.Tap/ 'helps' --> ajt·at
> /aNap/ 'gives' --> an·at
> /hü.Pap/ 'jumps' --> hüp·at
> /kæip/ 'goes' --> kæjk
> /lóep/ 'reads' --> joet
> /næep/ 'sees' --> næet
> /pánep/ 'puts' --> pánet
> /sÖp/ 'eats' --> sö:t
> /tEp/ 'does, makes' --> te:t

At 1;10, when Virve produced her first third-person plural form,
she extended the harmony still further: /tÖ.Tavat/ 'they're working'
--> [tö·t·at·at]. By this time she was tending to mark the singular
with [t] even after [k]: cf. /kuKup/ falls' --> [kuk·ut] (1;10). Forms
in [p] finally began to appear at 1;11, regardless of medial consonant
-- e.g. /læhep/ 'goes,' /makap/ 'sleeps,' /mænkip/ 'plays.' It
should be mentioned that the second person marker is /-t/, so that
Virve may have interpreted the adult alternation between /-t/ and
/-p/ as phonological rather than semantic. She never produced a
nasal for the third-person, however, though the first person marker
/-n/ must also have presented a puzzle to her at this time.

6. Consonant Harmony in Adult Speech

We have seen that consonant harmony may serve different purposes for different children. Most narrowly, it can provide a source

of substitutes for a sound the child cannot produce (l for Canta,
r, l, and s for Linda, liquids for Virve, s for Amahl). In other
cases it may lower the number of uncontrolled variables, allowing
the child to focus on a new segment or an extra syllable (Jesus,
Sofia, Virve). As Lewis suggested, it is a sound acquired later
that will be assimilated to a sound acquired earlier in most of those
cases where the sound affected is well-established in the child's
system, as in the assimilation of k to t by both Jiři and Virve,
but the reverse also occurs, as when Jiři and Virve produce forms
showing assimilation of t to k.[25] Further, the assimilation of a
single consonant to a cluster (cf. Sofia, Virve) suggest that Priestly's
notion of the "most noticeable" sound may well describe the target
for some instances of consonant harmony. Clearly no simple notion
of "ease of articulation" will greatly advance our understanding of
the phenomenon.

Consonant harmony has been cited as one of a small number of
innate tendencies representing "universal characteristics of language," "which the child has to escape from in order to learn his
language" (Smith 1973: 206). There are in the present study two
kinds of evidence that seem to run counter to this way of thinking.
First, though consonant harmony is widespread among children and
is of considerable importance for some of them, it is not in fact
universal, unless the occasional occurrence of a harmonized form,
in the speech of children with less than 5% harmony in their lexicon,
can be taken as a sign of the child's struggle to escape from a "universal template" (Smith, ibid).

Secondly, consonant harmony is not necessarily applied to the
earliest forms a child produces, as was most obvious in Jiři's
case, described earlier. The two words exhibiting dental-velar
contrast in Virve's lexicon also seem to have been produced before
her rule of regressive assimilation in case of dental/velar stop
combinations had quite jelled. The velar stop was already being
assimilated to following dentals (though k did occur outside that
context), but no solution had yet been found for the opposite order.
The sequence t - k was generally avoided; /tIK/ and /tiku/ were

---

[25] Both Linda and Virve assimilated yod to l as soon as they
had begun to produce l. Thus, for Linda, /ja.lka/ 'onto the foot' →
[jal:ka] at 1;7, but [lal·ka] a month later (and still at 1;10); for
Virve, see footnote 29. These are further "exceptions that prove
the rule" for Lewis' principle. Lewis himself provides several
exceptions, but finds that the rule holds in 77% of the cases of
harmony that he recorded.

produced without assimilation, and /heat ae.ka/ 'goodbye,' lit.
'(have) a good time' was produced with dental assimilation. When,
at 1;8, Virve began to generalize her rule of regressive harmony
to cover the case of t̲ - k̲, several new words were produced. The
same point is made in Kiparsky and Menn 1975: "In the Daniel Menn
corpus, for example, the first twenty-nine words ... showed no consonant harmony, and then consonant harmony quite suddenly appeared,
as the cornerstone of the child's system of phonological rules."

The appearance of a particular kind of rule after the production
of forms which fail to conform to the rule, and which may be closer
to the adult model -- as in the case of /tIK/ and /tiku/ or, for Jesus,
tasa, which changed over time from [tata] to [tasa] to [sasa]: Macken
1976: 54; see also the example from Linda in footnote 25, and a further example, taken from a GERMAN-speaking child recorded at
the end of the last century, in Ferguson 1977: 29 -- is also evidence
against Stampe's hypothesis, that the rules a child uses represent
the natural unfolding of innate processes, automatically applied
from the onset of speech until the child has gained sufficient experience with the language spoken to him to know which ones to "limit
or suppress" (Stampe 1969:1973). As Lise Menn has pointed out
(1974), "it is not the case that ... the child initially has few phonemic contrasts because so many natural processes are operating.
...On the contrary, the evidence indicates that he speaks very
little at the beginning -- and hence displays few contrasts -- because
he does not hit on an orderly way of discarding enough information
for him to be able to handle the words" (p. 8). Consonant harmony
is a natural successor strategy to lexical selection, or avoidance
of words with difficult segments or segment combinations. Once
a child's vocabulary and commitment to verbal communication
reach a certain point, restriction of his active vocabulary to
certain phonological shapes is no longer a statisfactory strategy,
and recourse will now have to be had to substitution, deletion, or
assimilation. Like Menn, I believe the evidence shows that the
phonological processes a child uses are not "latent and ready to
spring into action" from the start, but have to be invented (Menn
1974; see also Ferguson 1977: 30).

Basic to Smith's and Stampe's theories is the analogy between
phonological processes used by children and those found in adult
language. Though consonant harmony was found here not to be a
universal of child phonology, it did in fact play a significant rôle
in the phonological system of several of the children. Yet no such
rule is found in the adult languages these children are learning to
speak -- CZECH, ENGLISH, ESTONIAN, SPANISH -- nor in most

of the adult languages of the world, where consonant harmony figures only very exceptionally.

In the present as yet incomplete inventory of rules stored in the Stanford Phonology Archive, three out of 88 languages (or 3%) include a rule that may be roughly characterized as a consonant harmony rule.[26] One rule of MOROCCAN ARABIC involves assimilation of an alveolar fricative to the palato-alveolar position when a palato-alveolar fricative occurs later in the word (Abdel-Massih 1973); two variable rules of NAVAHO involve the same classes of segments, in both progressive and regressive assimilation at a distance, with likelihood of the assimilation taking place, decreasing as the distance between the two consonants involved increases (Sapir and Hoijer 1967). Finally, an automatic morphophonemic rule of ALAWA partially assimilates a retroflex consonant to a palato-alveolar (the retroflex becomes alveolar) under certain conditions (Sharpe 1972).

It is interesting to note that of four adult rules of consonant harmony (out of 850 rules coded in the Archive — or 0.5%) three involve fricatives -- which account for only 8% of the cases of full regressive assimilation in the present study, 5% of the cases of full progressive assimilation. The low incidence of full assimilation to fricatives among these children is easily understood: for many of the children, fricatives are difficult segments which are typically deleted or replaced by another segment. That a disproportionate number of instances of consonant harmony in adult language should involve fricatives assimilating to one another in place of articulation might be viewed as also stemming from the fact

---

[26] A rule governing the occurrence of pharyngealized consonants in MOROCCAN ARABIC is sometimes characterized as consonant harmony, since it serves the same classificatory function for stems that is associated with rules of vowel harmony. But the vowels intervening between the pharyngealized consonants are also paryngealized in this case (cf. Abdel-Massih 1973:5), so that I would rather view this as a prosody -- like that affecting the occurrence of oral and nasal stops (and vowels) in GUARANÍ (Gregores and Suarez 1967) — than as consonant harmony in the sense I have been using it here. The spread of retroflexion in SANSKRIT, which changes an apical nasal to a retroflex, has also been termed a prosody (Allen 1953: 66). Whether the vowels intervening between the consonants involved were also "r-colored" is not known; this may be another example of true adult consonant harmony (i.e. assimilation at a distance).

that fricatives are difficult segments. Their articulation requires delicate articulatory adjustments, and the manner of articulation difficulty is perhaps compounded when two adjacent points of artic- ulation are to be distinguished in a single syntagmatic unit. It may be that s̠ - š̠ (and other combinations of the alveolar and palato- alveolar fricatives) represent, for adults, the same kind of difficulty that p̠ -t̠, t̠ -k̠, etc. apparently present for children.

The friction created in producing spirants can be considered a "mark," which renders a sound more complex and thus less favored (Greenberg 1966: 14; 1969: 476); within the marked series, of course, one expects to find less distinctions ("the number of phonemes with the marked feature is always less than or equal to the number with the unmarked feature but not greater," Greenberg 1966: 59), but this in itself will not explain why the subclass of sibilants, of all sets of neighboring sounds within a marked class, should stand out as the one subject to rules of non-contiguous consonant assimilation in adult language.

It has been observed that "in ENGLISH, voiceless fricatives tend to interact in tongue slips more frequently than plosives and other consonant-categories" (Laver 1973: 137). Laver hypothesized that "the more complex and delicate the adjustments for a particular class of sounds, the greater the likelihood of members of that class being mutually involved in tongue slips. One might expect that fric- atives need more precise muscular control than plosives..." (ibid.).

Some of the other regularities which have been found to charac- terize phonological slips of the tongue are reminiscent of our data on consonant harmony in children. For example, in an analysis of "phonemic speech errors in spontaneous DUTCH," Nooteboom (1973: 147) found that anticipation accounts for about 75% of the errors, perseveration for 20%, and transposition for only 5%. This may be compared with the incidence of regressive (or antic- ipatory) vs. progressive (or perseverative) harmony in our data (see Table 9), in which the former was clearly dominant, though not by as wide a margin as in Nooteboom's speech error data. I have not calculated the incidence of metathesis (or transposition) of consonants in the children's speech, but it certainly is no greater than 5% of any child's lexicon.

In his article on spoonerisms, or transpositions, Mackay (1973: 174ff) investigated the phonetic similarity of the consonants which interact in the corpus he analyzed (Meringer's GERMAN corpus, published at the end of the last century, which included 124 "involun- tary spoonerisms"). Mackay finds that the consonants interchanged

have the same value for "openness" (both stops, both fricatives,
or both sonorants) in 65% of the cases (vs. 36% chance similarity,
based on the frequency of these types in natural speech), and they
had the same value for nasality in 93% of the cases, vs. 65% chance.
Place of articulation, on the other hand, tended to differ, with labials and velars showing a tendency to interact in particular. The
analysis showed only 10% same place of articulation, vs. 26% chance.
In our consonant harmony data we are not, of course, looking at
spoonerisms or exchange of consonants, but we can consider both
the consonants involved in the assimilation, the affected consonant
and that which replaces it, to see how commonly manner vs. place
of articulation is held constant. Table 12 gives the results of that
analysis. It seems reasonable, first, to eliminate the cases involving liquids from the children's data, if we wish to compare the
data on assimilation in children with speech errors in adults, since
liquids are acquired late by most children and the inclusion of assimilatory substitutes for liquids biases the data in the direction of
manner of articulation change.

Table 12.   Relative proportion of types of consonant
change involved in assimilation

1. Place of articulation change, manner held constant

Eliminating liquids

Amahl	28%	36%
Virve	46%	59%
Other children	31%	40%
All children	35%	45%

2. Manner of articulation change, place held constant

Amahl	30%	27%
Virve	21%	17%
Other children	28%	19%
All children	27%	20%

3. Both place and manner change

Amahl	42%	36%
Virve	33%	24%
Other children	40%	41%
All children	39%	35%

Focussing on the results after the cases involving liquids have
been set aside, then, we see that the two consonants share manner
of articulation, but differ in place, in 45% of the cases; place of
articulation is shared, but not manner, in 20% of the cases; and
both change -- i.e. the two consonants involved are not notably
similar -- in 35% of the cases.[27]

Other characteristics of adult slips of the tongue cannot be compared with consonant harmony in children because of the more
primitive shapes on which the latter are based. For example, the
consonants that interfere with one another in slips of the tongue
overwhelmingly tend to share syllable position (98% of the cases
in Mackay's data (vs. 30% chance: p. 177), 100% in Nooteboom's
(p.149); see also Boomer and Laver's results in the same volume,
p. 126). But consonant clusters tend to be reduced to a single consonant in children's speech, so that syllable-final consonants are
relatively rare, and when clusters do occur, it is not syllable-
position but articulatory type that appears to determine the kind of
assimilation that will take place, if any (with liquids and lax or
voiced stops disfavored: see footnote 20 above). Virve's tendency
to assimilate (word- or syllable-initial) k to t before syllable-
initial but not syllable- (and word-) final t or s does provide one
parallel, however (see Sec. 5.3.2 above). Similarly, the tonic
syllable tends to be involved in adult slips, as do open-class words
in general, which typically dominate their "tone-groups" (see
Boomer and Laver p. 126; Nooteboom p. 150). But only the open
class words are normally used by children, at least in the earliest
stages of language acquisition, and unstressed syllables are often
omitted as well. These are, of course, further indications or consequences of the psychological or perceptual salience of stressed
words and syllables.

One crucial difference in kind between slips of the tongue and
the products of consonant harmony rules in children is their relative durability. Adults, aware of the gap between their production
and the word-shape they intended, frequently correct themselves,
and in any case would not be expected to produce the same slip
twice, even in subsequent uses of the exact same word or phrase
in which the slip appeared. The children, on the other hand, often
use a consonant harmony form for some months. It is obvious

---

[27]Liquids are affected in roughly one quarter of the cases in
each of our data-categories -- Amahl, Virve, and the other children
taken together (23%, 29%, and 22%, respectively).

from this fact alone that the children's use of consonant harmony processes is not due to undetected errors in the "neuro-linguistic program-planning" of an utterance (to use Laver's terminology: 1973:134), still less to a slip in the course of "myodynamic execution of the utterance" (ibid.); rather, these processes make up a part of the child's phonological organization — part of his system, in short.[28] Once the child has gained mastery over the difficult segments, segment sequences, and syllable-strings which the assimilated forms were created to avoid, these forms gradually disappear, as the child revises his entire system in the light of his new competence. The revision is not automatic nor instantly achieved, however; "new" and "old" forms typically co-exist for a time (see the discussion of "the lexical parameter in sound change" in Ferguson and Farwell 1975: 429ff).[29]

A second parallel between consonant harmony in children and in adult speech was mentioned in passing earlier, in connection with Jiři's use of harmony apparently for the mere pleasure of producing the forms in question. While it would be difficult or impossible to prove an aesthetic function for harmony in children, cases such as Jiři's or Virve's, in which the use of harmony long outlived other signs of phonetic immaturity or incompetence, seem to me to suggest such a function, at least secondarily. For adults, alliteration is very common in oral poetry, it is sometimes used in written

---

[28] It should be noted that slips of the tongue do occur in the speech of children as well: see the example in Vihman 1971: 84, footnote 7, where the child's efforts at self-correction provide clear evidence of a monitoring function at work.

[29] For example, at 1;9,13 Virve still had not begun producing l: /liL (oN) peal/ 'there's a flower on it' —→ [jij peaj]. By 1;10, 2 she was using l in several new words: /koala/ 'Koala bear,' /üle ĕla/ 'over the shoulder' (—→ [ülĕla]), /ei ole/ 'is not,' and in some old ones: /seLeka/ 'with this,' /kala/ 'fish,' but not in others: /laps/ 'child' still —→ [aps ~ japs]. At 1;10, 3 she produced the new harmonized form /lume-meM/ 'snowman' —→ [mumemem:], though the day before she had produced an initial (assimilated) l in /jae.Le/ 'again' —→ [læl:e], and on the following day she was able to use an initial and medial l in /li.Li/ 'flowers (obj.),' as well as to imitate the name /hiLe/ accurately, which she had been pronouncing [i:]. The verb 'to push' showed alternation (also at 1;10,4) between initial glide: /lü.Kap/ 'pushes' —→ [jük:ak] and l: /lüKaTa/ 'to push' —→ [lük·at·a].

verse, and it is a noticeable factor in formulaic expressions in
many languages (cf. the ENGLISH examples given earlier, and
such ESTONIAN expressions as võhivõõras 'total stranger,' in
which võhi-, like kith in kith and kin, is an archaism used in no
other such construction). In verse, "the most common type of
alliteration is that of initial sounds, especially of consonants or
consonant groups ... it is more prominent in the poetry of languages
with stress accent (especially where the accent regularly falls on
the first syllable, as in FINNISH, ESTHONIAN and CZECH) and in
verse which is meant to be spoken rather than sung or chanted..."
(Goldsmith 1965).

Goldsmith also notes that "in languages with tone systems or
quantitative structures [alliteration] is either completely absent
(as in CHINESE poetry, which is based on syllable count and tone
patterns), or used rarely and only for very special emphasis (as
in SANSKRIT ... and in JAPANESE...)" (ibid.). One cannot help
but be struck by the fact that two of the CHINESE children in our
sample made virtually no use of consonant harmony, while the third,
Canta, made very narrow and limited use of it. A larger sample
of children speaking a broader range of phonologically dissimilar
languages would have to be studied before we could decide whether
or not relative use of consonant harmony is in fact to some degree
dependent on the language a child is learning.

Goldsmith speculates that "alliteration was partly a mnemonic
aid to primitive oral recitation...," and adds, "the fondness for
alliterative formulas is still noticeable in a language like ENGLISH,
which uses them easily and habitually in and out of poetry" (ibid.).
In a detailed statistical study of Structural Alliteration in Finnish,
Leino found that "alliteration increases (or lack of alliteration di-
minishes) the average active life of a saying" (1970: 319). The psychological basis for our "fondness for alliterative formulas," as
well as for rhymes and assonance, has not, to my knowledge, been
explored. Goldsmith's suggestion that alliteration serves as a
mnemonic aid, supported by Leino's independent results, which
point in the same direction, seems intuitively satisfying, however.
Setting this notion beside Menn's hypothesis that consonant harmony
serves to increase "the redundancy of the articulatory instructions
necessary to produce the child's forms" (1974: 3; cf. also Menn 1976b),
we may expand on Menn's argument and suggest that the redundancy
of consonant harmony forms also in some sense simplifies the
child's mnemonic problems in recording and storing a rapidly
growing lexicon.

APPENDIX I

Raw scores and percentages for five categories*

	Total no. of words analyzed	A	B	C	D	E
CHINESE						
Canta	310	5% (14)	52% (162)	7% (22)	34% (107)	2% (5)
Didi	109	3% (3)	36% (39)	12% (13)	50% (54)	
Lolo	334	1% (4)	54% (182)	7% (22)	38% (126)	
ENGLISH						
Amahl	225	32% (71)	33% (74)	14% (32)	16% (37)	5% (11)
Hildegard	322	5% (16)	35% (112)	30% (96)	28% (89)	3% (9)
Jacob	150	9% (14)	25% (38)	36% (54)	29% (44)	
ESTONIAN						
Linda	364	9% (32)	57% (209)	7% (26)	27% (97)	1% (3)
Virve	372	25% (92)	38% (143)	12% (46)	24% (88)	
CZECH						
Jiři	300	11% (33)	69% (206)	3% (9)	17% (52)	
SLOVENIAN						
Maja	138	1% (2)	72% (99)	9% (13)	17% (24)	
Tomaž	320	3% (9)	74% (238)	4% (14)	18% (59)	
SPANISH						
Jesus	144	21% (31)	43% (62)	14% (20)	21% (31)	
Sofia	152	18% (26)	54% (83)	3% (5)	25% (38)	

*Figures in parentheses indicate the number of words analyzed as belonging to that category. All fractions of percentage points are rounded off to nearest whole number.

APPENDIX II

Examples of consonant harmony forms
(drawn from coincidental lexical overlap between children)

<u>Key</u>: children's names: A = Amahl, C = Canta, H = Hildegard, J = Jesus, Ja = Jacob, L = Linda, M = Maja, T = Tomaž, V = Virve; classification: F = full, P = partial; r = regressive, p = progressive

Language	Adult forms	Harmony forms		Classification
ENGLISH	book	Ja	bʌp	P, p (labial)
		V	pʊp.	P, p (labial)
	doggie	Ja	ʌdʌdi	F, p (d)
		(H	doti: scored E)	
		(A	g̣ɔgi: stage 2)	
	grandpa	H	ŋaeŋae	P, r (nasal);
				P, p (velar)
	guampa	C	pampa	F, r (p)
	spoon	Ja	pom	P, p (labial)
		J	pom	P, p (labial)
	thank you	Ja	gɛgu	F, r (g)
		A	g̣ɛgu	F, r (g)
		H	dada	F, p (d)
		V	kaeŋk·u	F, r (k)
	tiger	A	g̣aigə	F, r (g)
			(see SPANISH)	
ESTONIAN	/kiNas/ 'mitten'	V	tin·as	P, r (dental)
	/kintat/ 'mittens'	L	kiŋkat	F, p (k)
	/kleiT/ 'dress'	V	tɛt·	F, r (t)
		L	kik·	F, p (k)
	/lamP/ 'lamp'	V	pamp·	F, r (p)
		L	mamp·	F, r (m)
	/lint/ 'bird'	V	nint	F, r (n)
		L	nint	F, r (n)
	/napa/ 'navel'	V	papa	F, r (p)
		L	mapa	P, r (labial)
	/soKit/ 'socks'	V	sɔ|si·	F, p (s)
		L	kuk: i	F, r (k)
	/su.Pi/ 'soup (obj.)'	V	fup: i	P, r (labial)
			(see SPANISH)	
SLOVENIAN	bicikel 'bicycle'	M	bibi	F, p (b)
		T	bibi	F, p (b)
SPANISH	casa 'house'	J	kaka	F, p (k)
	casas 'houses'	S	kakəs	F, p (k)
	gato 'cat'	J	tata	F, r (t)
		S	kaka	F, p (k)
	jugo 'juice'	J	puwu	P, r (labial)
		S	ɸuwo	P, r (labial)
	sopa 'soup	J	pwopa	F, r (p)
			(see ESTON.)	

Language	Adult forms	Harmony forms	Classification
SPANISH (cont.)	tenedor 'fork'	J tədádə	F, r (d)
		S əbədáɹ	P, r (stop)
	tigre 'tiger'	J kíɣə	P, r (velar)
		(see ENGLISH)	

BIBLIOGRAPHY*

Abdel-Massih, Ernest T. 1973. An introduction to Moroccan Arabic. Center for Near Eastern and North African Studies, University of Michigan, Ann Arbor.

Allen, William Stannard. 1953. Phonetics in ancient India. London Oriental Series 1. London: Oxford University Press.

Apronti, E.O. 1969. The language of a two-year old Dangme. Paper presented at the Eighth West African Languages Congress.

Boomer, Donald S. and John D. M. Laver. 1973. Slips of the tongue. Speech errors as linguistic evidence, ed. by V.A. Fromkin. The Hague: Mouton. (Article first published in 1968.)

Bush, C.N., M.L. Edwards, J.M. Luckau, C.M. Stoel, M.A. Macken, J.D. Petersen. 1973. On specifying a system for transcribing consonants in child language, a working paper with examples from American English and Mexican Spanish. Child Language Project, Stanford University.

Chao, Yuen Ren. 1951. The Cantian idiolect: an analysis of the Chinese spoken by a twenty-eight-month-old child. Semitic and Oriental Studies ... to William Popper, ed. by W.J. Fisher, 27-44. Berkeley: University of California Press.

* _____. 1968. A grammar of spoken Chinese. Berkeley: University of California Press.

Ferguson, Charles A. 1977. Learning to pronounce: the earliest stages of phonological development in the child. Communicative and cognitive abilities -- early behavioral assessment, ed. by F.D. Minifie and L.I. Lloyd. Baltimore: University Park Press.

*An asterisk preceding a reference indicates that it is a Stanford Phonology Archive source and was not necessarily consulted by the author.

Ferguson, Charles A. and Carol B. Farwell. 1975. Words and sounds in early language acquisition: English initial consonants in the first fifty words. Language 51. 419-439.

Ferguson, Charles A., David B. Peizer and Thelma Weeks. 1973. Model and replica: phonological grammar of a child's first words. Lingua 31. 35-65.

Fromkin, Victoria A. (ed.) 1973. Speech errors as linguistic evidence. The Hague: Mouton.

Goldsmith, Ulrich K. 1965. Princeton encyclopedia of poetry and poetics, ed. by Alex Preminger. Princeton: Princeton Univ. Press.

Greenberg, Joseph H. 1966. Language universals. Janua Linguarum 59. The Hague: Mouton.

_____. 1969. Language universals: a research frontier. Science 1966. 473-478.

*Gregores, Emma and Jorge A. Suarez. 1967. A description of colloquial Guarani. Janua Linguarum, series practica, 27. The Hague: Mouton.

Ingram, David. 1974. Phonological rules in young children. Journal of Child Language 1. 49-64.

Kerek, Andrew. 1975. Phonological rules in the language of Hungarian children. Paper presented at the Proceedings of the 1975 Mid-America Linguistics Conference, Lawrence, Kansas.

Kiparsky, Paul and Lise Menn. 1975. On the acquisition of phonology. (To appear in Language learning and thought, ed. by J. Macnamara. New York: Academic Press.)

*Klagstad, Harold Jr. 1958. The phonemic system of colloquial standard Bulgarian. The Slavic and East European Journal 16. 42-54.

Kolaric, Rudolf. 1959. Slovenski otroški govor. Jahrbuch der Philosophischen Fakultät in Novi Sad, 4.

Laver, John D.M. 1973. The detection and correction of slips of the tongue. Speech errors as linguistic evidence, ed. by V.A. Fromkin. (Article first published in 1969.)

Leino, Pentti. 1970. Strukturaalinen alkusointu Suomessa (Structural alliteration in Finnish). Helsinki: Suomalaisen Kirjallisuuden Seura.

Leopold, Werner F. 1939. Speech development of a bilingual child, I: vocabulary growth in the first two years. Evanston, Ill.: Northwestern University Press.

_____. 1947. Speech development of a bilingual child, II: sound-learning in the first two years. Evanston, Ill.: Northwestern University Press.

Lewis, M.M. 1936. Infant speech; a study of the beginnings of language. New York: Harcourt, Brace and Co.

Mackay, Donald G. 1973. Spoonerisms: the structure of errors in the serial order of speech. Speech errors as linguistic evidence, ed. by V.A. Fromkin. (Article first appeared in 1970.)

Macken, Marlys A. 1976. Permitted complexity in phonological development: one child's acquisition of Spanish consonants. Papers and Reports on Child Language Development [PRCLD] 11. 28-60. Stanford University.

Menn, Lise. 1971. Phonotactic rules in beginning speech. Lingua 26. 225-251.

_____. 1974. A theoretical framework for child phonology. Paper read at the fiftieth annual summer meeting of the Linguistic Society of America.

_____. 1976a. Evidence for an interactionist-discovery theory of child phonology. PRCLD 12. 169-177.

_____. 1976b. Pattern, control, and contrast in beginning speech. Doctoral dissertation, University of Illinois, Urbana.

*Navarro, Tomas T. 1961. Manual de pronunciación española (Publicaciones de la Revista de Filologia Española 3). Madrid.

Nooteboom, S.G. 1973. The tongue slips into patterns. Speech errors as linguistic evidence, ed. by V.A. Fromkin. (Article first published in 1969).

*O'Connor, J.D. 1973. Phonetics. Middlesex: Penguin Books.

Pačesova, Jaroslava. 1968. The development of vocabulary in the child. Brno: Universita J.E. Pukyně.

Priestly, T.M.S. 1977. One idiosyncratic strategy in the acquisition of phonology. Journal of Child Language 4. 45-65.

Raun, Alo and Andrus Saareste. 1965. Introduction to Estonian linguistics. Ural-altaische Bibliothek 12. Wiesbaden: Otto Harrassowitz.

*Sapir, Edward and Harry Hoijer. 1967. The phonology and morphology of the Navaho language. University of California Publications in Linguistics [UCPL] 50. Berkeley: University of California.

*Sharpe, Margaret C. 1972. Alawa phonology and grammar. Australian Aboriginal Studies 37. Canberra: Australian Institute of Aboriginal Studies.

Smith, Neilson V. 1973. The acquisition of phonology: a case study. Cambridge: University Press.

Stampe, David. 1969. The acquisition of phonemic representation. Papers from the fifth regional meeting of the Chicago Linguistic Society.

_____. 1973. A dissertation on natural phonology. Doctoral dissertation, University of Chicago.

Tauli, Valter. 1973. Standard Estonian grammar, I. Acta Universitatis Upsaliensis: Studia Uralica et Altaica Upsaliensia 8. Uppsala.

Vihman, Eero. 1974. Estonian quantity re-viewed. Foundations of Language 11. 415-432.

Vihman, Marilyn M. 1971. On the acquisition of Estonian. PRCLD 3. 51-94.

_____. 1976. From pre-speech to speech: on early phonology. PRCLD 12. 230-243.

_____. 1977. A reference manual and user's guide for the Stanford Phonology Archive, Part I. Stanford University.

Universals of Tone

IAN MADDIESON

ABSTRACT

Three areas of phonological universals of tone are considered:
inventories of tone, tone rules, and interaction of tone with non-
tonal features. It is proposed that five is the maximum number of
phonemic tone levels that may contrast, and these five levels represent a phonetic scale. Languages with less than five levels use
a smaller portion of the scale, with their marked tones generally
drawn from the upper part. Contour tones do not occur unless at
least one level tone also occurs in the system, and bidirectional
contours only occur if simple contours also occur. These constraints on contours are related to parallel constraints on sequences
of level tones. Tonal assimilation and related processes of displacement and contraction are discussed, and some asymmetries
in their operation are explained by the usually marked status of
high tones. The unusually frequent occurrence of rules of tonal
polarity is pointed out. The final section comments on phonetic
and phonological relationships of tones with adjacent consonants
and with features of vowels.

The work reported in this paper was financed by grants from
the National Science Foundation to Stanford University for the
Language Universals Project and to the University of California
at Los Angeles for research on Linguistic Phonetics.

CONTENTS

1. Introduction

There are perhaps more difficulties in establishing phonological universals in the area of tone than in most of the other areas of phonology. This is because of the inherently relative nature of pitch contrasts which makes cross-language comparison of levels of pitch, intervals between pitch levels, degrees of pitch change, etc., unusually difficult to make in a non-arbitrary fashion. Additional difficulties result from problems in segmenting pitch sequences and the frequent interaction of tone with other phonological features. In addition, many of the available descriptions of tone languages are decidedly inadequate (grammars and phonological descriptions of tone languages even appear without any mention of tone at all).

Nevertheless, some picture of phonological universals of tone languages may be beginning to emerge. The suggestions below are partly my own and partly drawn from the developing literature on tone universals. They will be dealt with in three sections: a) inventories of tones and tone sequences, b) tone rules, c) interaction of tone and nontonal features.

2. Inventories of Tones and Tone Sequences

A conventional division is made between level tones and contour (or gliding) tones. K.L. Pike (1948) defines a level tone as "one in which, within the limits of perception, the pitch of a syllable does not rise or fall during its production." It is apparent that pitch fluctuates continuously in speech, however. A better definition would recognize a level tone as one for which a level pitch is an acceptable variant. This definition discounts the variations in pitch that arise from coarticulation with adjacent tones and segments, from superimposition of intonational patterns and from boundary phenomena. Predictable phonetic variations which result in a rising or falling pitch pattern are insufficient to show that the essential property of the tone is a pitch glide. On the other hand, a pitch glide which cannot be predicted naturally from factors such as coarticulation and intonation, is essentially a contour tone. A similar definition would proceed from the requirements of a speech synthesis program (compare the ideas in Ladefoged 1976). If an adequate synthesis of a tone can be made by specifying a single level, it may be considered a level tone. But a tone represented by a pitch glide which cannot be generated by rule from the environment (i.e. not by a default) requires specification of several points. Such a tone is a contour tone. In this section, level tones, sequences of level tones and contour tones will be discussed in that order.

2.1   Level tones

Although many different phonetically distinguishable levels of
pitch may be heard in speech, no known language makes a phonological contrast of more than five tone levels. Thus, statement 1.
describes a limit on tonal inventories.

1. A language may contrast up to five levels of tone, but no more.

Several languages have been described which do contrast as many
as five levels, DAN (Béarth and Zemp 1967), KPORO and ASHUKU
(Shimizu 1971) and NGAMAMBO (Asongwed and Hyman 1976) from
Africa; BLACK MIAO (data from F.K. Li, cited by Chang 1953
and Voegelin 1965; cf. also Wang 1967), TAHUA YAO (Chang 1953)
and some of the PUYI dialects (Sarawit 1973) from Asia, and
TRIQUE (Longacre 1952), TICUNA (L. Anderson 1959, D. Anderson
1962) and USILA CHINANTEC (Rensch 1968) from America among
them. Some of these languages, TRIQUE (Wang 1967) for example,
may be amenable to an alternative analysis in which one of the
levels is a predictable variant of another. This would place them
with four-level languages, such as the NIKKI dialect of BARIBA
(Welmers 1952), IGEDE (Bergman 1971), TOURA (Béarth 1971) and
FE'FE' BAMILEKE (Hyman 1972) from Africa, some varieties
of HAKKA CHINESE (Yang 1967) and TAISHAN CHINESE (Tung
1946), PO-AI (Li 1965) and YAY (Gedney 1965) from Asia, SOYAL-
TEPEC MIXTEC (E.V. Pike 1956), OJITLAN CHINANTEC (Rensch
1968) and CHATINO (Upson 1968) from America. Languages with
three tone levels are commonplace, while those with only two are
the most frequently encountered type of tone language.

A simple typology of tone systems with level tones may be constructed according to the number of contrastive levels in the system (cf. K.L. Pike 1948, Meeussen 1970). An unelaborated version
of this typology implicitly equates the high tone in, say, a system
with four tones with the high tone in a system of two tones. Pike
made such an equation explicit and proposed that the larger the
number of tone levels, the smaller the intervals that distinguished
them became (cf. Wang 1967). The figures in Table 1 suggest
that this is not so, although conclusive evidence could only be offered if stylistic and individual differences could be factored out.
Contrary to Pike's suggestion, it seems that 2. holds.

2. A larger number of tone levels occupy a larger pitch range
    than a smaller number.

Table 1. Pitch intervals between tones in languages with
          different numbers of level tones*

TWO LEVELS		THREE LEVELS					FOUR LEVELS
SISWATI	KIOWA	YORUBA I	THAI I	THAI II	TAIWANESE	YORUBA II	TOURA
							+50
		+26	+28	+32	+32	+52	+30
+18	+22	+16	+16	+16	+18	+27	+10
+0	+0	+0	+0	+0	+0	+0	+0

Difference in Hz between each tone and the lowest tone in the
system, showing that more levels tend to occupy a larger pitch
range.

*KIOWA (Siverts en 1956)   Average of two repetitions of a tonally
   minimal pair of words in identical environments utterance
   initially. Male speaker.
SISWATI (Goldstein 1976)   Average of peak F_0 in first syllable on
   two repetitions of eight words balanced for vowels and initial
   consonants, but contrasting tones. Female speaker.
THAI I (Erickson 1974)   Measured from diagrams giving average
   tones, one male subject selected (MJ). Central point of tone
   measured. No statement of number of tokens represented.
THAI II (Gandour and Maddieson 1976)   Central points of tones
   measured from diagrams representing about 80 tokens of each
   tone from one male speaker.
YORUBA I (Hombert 1976b) Central point of tones in second syllable
   of disyllabic nouns after mid tones measured from diagrams
   representing averages of ten tokens of each tone from one male
   speaker.
YORUBA II (Hombert 1976b) Central point of tones measured from
   diagrams representing averages of 35 monosyllabic words
   spoken in a frame by each of two male speakers.
TAIWANESE (Zee and Hombert 1976)   Published figures from
   fifteen tokens of each tone spoken in a frame from each of two
   male speakers.
TOURA (Béarth 1968)   Published averages given as the result of
   measuring 'several hundred' utterances from one male speaker.
   No details of frame employed or tokens measured.

This observation suggests that the equation of the highest tone in
one language with the highest tone in another language may often
be false. And if the equation is false, then generalizations about
high tones based on this equation will apply to a heterogeneous
class of objects. A different principle for equating tones across
languages is required, and from this a more elaborate typology
may be derived.

The five levels in a system with that number of contrasts may
be named and numbered as below:

Extra High   5
High   4
Central   3
Low   2
Extra Low   1

These five levels may be roughly equated with the five numbered
levels customarily used (since Chao 1930) to transcribe tones in
the literature on East Asian languages[1] and may be regarded as an
ordered series of potentially contrastive phonetic possibilities
similar to the ordered series of places of articulation (Ladefoged
1971) or degrees of glottal stricture (Gandour 1975). In this light,
tone languages may be considered to differ in respect of which of
the levels are selected for contrast as well as in the mere number
of levels involved. Thus, just as a language with three different
places of articulation for consonants might contrast, say, either
labial, dental and velar or labial, alveolar and velar, so a tone
language with three levels might employ Extra High, High and
Central (5, 4 and 3) or High, Central and Low (4, 3 and 2). Consequently, the problem of making equations between tones in different languages involves the determination of the location of the
tone levels in relation to the center and the extremes of a phonetic
dimension.

However, just as a language with three places of articulation
is more likely to employ either of the two sets of places given
above rather than, say, the set velar, uvular and pharyngeal, so

---

[1] Many such transcriptions are based on the 'false equation'
which equates the highest or lowest tones in different languages
and represents them with the same notation. However, in other
cases, particularly in dialect survey work and comparative studies,
it is often evident that a more phonetic principle has determined
transcription.

a tone language is more likely to employ certain sets of tones than others. The next paragraphs deal with limitations on the sets of tones used and on the relationships between the tones within the sets.

Many restrictions on the sets of tones used may be expressed in terms of markedness relations between tones. It is claimed that a non-arbitrary assignment of markedness is revealed by a convergence of several factors. Among the factors involved are text frequency and lexical frequency of tones in a language (a less frequent tone is marked); dominance in assimilatory processes (e.g. a tone which is not changed by assimilation is marked in relation to one which is); existence of neutralized tones (e.g. in a language where stress is a factor, tones in stressed syllables are marked in relation to their replacements in unstressed positions). There is also the question of the phonetic identity of the tones. An identifying acoustic property often found to occur concerns a glide in utterance-initial or word-initial positions — a lowering onglide to low pitch and a rising onglide to high pitch. Unmarked (i.e. Central) tones do not occur with this onglide. This characteristic allows a tone level to be placed on a phonetic continuum that does not depend on individual speaker variability.

Given recognized markedness relations based on the linguistic and phonetic factors reviewed above, 3. establishes limitations on the variety of such relationships.

3. Phonetically Central tones are unmarked, Extreme tones are highly marked.

In the first place, 3. defines some limits on the overall variability of possible tone systems. It also indicates which are more probable tone systems. For example, languages with two level tones might have either a marked high tone or a marked low tone, i.e. systems contrasting phonetic High and Central (4 and 3) or Central and Low (3 and 2) are both possible according to 3. and so are a number of other systems of two levels. However, a two level system in which the tones were placed at the extremes of the pitch range would be highly improbable (i.e. Extra High and Extra Low do not normally occur unless there are additional tones at levels in between). In systems with three or more level tones, 3. rules out a system in which a mid tone is the most highly marked tone and permits only systems in which either the highest or the lowest tone is the most highly marked tone or in which they are equally marked. Systems with three level tones in fact occur most frequently with an unmarked mid tone and marked high and low tones as in JUKUN

(Shimizu 1971), PANJABI (Bahl 1957) and STANDARD THAI (Gandour 1976). Other three level patterns known to occur include a system in which the low tone is the least marked (i.e. the system is made up of Extra High, High and Central Levels 5, 4 and 3). IDOMA (Armstrong 1972) and the related YALA (Armstrong 1968, Bunkowske 1972), and IXCATEC (Fernandez de Miranda 1959) have this kind of system. YORUBA (Maddieson 1972) has a system of Extra High, Central and Low (5, 3 and 2), as the high tone is marked in relation to the low and mid tones and the low tone is marked in relation to the mid tone.

Thus, it may be seen that languages with different relationships between like numbers of tone levels do exist. However, it is clear that there is an asymmetry among those systems that are possible, which may be expressed in 4.:

4. Systems in which high tones are marked are more frequent than systems in which low tones are marked.[2]

For example, while two level systems with a marked high and a marked low are both consistent with 3., those with the marked high tone are much more frequent (e.g. NAVAHO, Hoijer 1945; OCAINA, Agnew and Pike 1957; ACHOLI, Crazzolara 1938; ZULU, Cope 1959;

---

[2] If more systems occur with marked high tones, it follows that more high tones (tones above Central) occur in the languages of the world than low tones (tones below Central). In a survey of 737 descriptions of CHINESE tones, C.C. Cheng (1973) concludes that high tones are more frequent (over 61%) than low tones. Using the five-point scale of Chao (1930), he defines a tone with any digit above 3 as a high tone and all others as low tones. The vast majority of tones are transcribed with two digits (55, 31, 53, etc.). If all two-digit tones were equally frequent, then Cheng's method of counting would yield 64% of all tones as high tones. If all three-digit tones were equally frequent, then an even higher percentage of them would count as high tones. So Cheng's conclusion does not follow from the procedure he uses. Nonetheless, the claim does seem to be true: if an average is taken of the digits for each tone, more of them have an average above 3 than below 3. This 'average pitch' calculation is a more revealing procedure.

It may be that high tones are more frequently marked because an upward deflection of pitch is more naturally salient against an overall downward intonational contour than a downward deflection. Falling intonations seem the most frequent in speech.

P'U-MAN, Ferrell 1971 and numerous others). Those with a marked
low tone are rare, but appear to be found in at least HAUSA (Meyers
1976) and KORKU (Zide 1966), and perhaps MANDEKAN (Rowlands
1959, Courtenay 1974) and CILUBA (Burssens 1939). All the three
level systems noted in the previous paragraph include marked high
tones, while the highest level in four level systems is often the
most restricted in distribution. It is suggested that the principle
restrictions and asymmetries in systems of level tones are summarized in 3. and 4.

2.2 Sequences of level tones

The constraints 3. and 4. refer to the inventories of level tones
in a system. Restrictions may also be placed on combinations of
tones in sequence. We may conclude that 5. is the case.

5. Languages which permit a sequence of unlike tones on a word
   or morpheme also permit like tones on a word or morpheme.

Indeed, it may be suggested that, in some sense, sequences of like
tones are preferred to sequences of unlike tones. Thus, there are
languages like TOUHO and PAACI (Haudricourt 1968), PANJABI
(Bahl 1957) and BASSEIN PHO (Jones 1961) in which a word ordinarily shows the same tone throughout. Languages which permit sequences of unlike tones include at least one pattern with like tones,
although the permitted sequences are often less than the theoretical
maximum. For example, in disyllabic words in languages with
two level tones, BORO (Bhat 1968) permits only low-low (LL) and
low-high (LH) tone sequences; MARINAHUA (E. Pike and Scott 1962)
permits HH, LL and HL; MAHAS NUBIAN (Bell 1968) permits HH,
LL and LH; TUCANO[3] (West and Welch 1967) and WERI (Boxwell
1966) permit HH, HL and LH; the AUCHI dialect of OKPAMHERI
(Elugbe 1973) permits LL, HL and LH;[4] while languages such as
TRIPURI (Karapurkar 1972), HAUSA and ACHOLI permit all four
possible sequences.

---

[3] TUCANO is analyzed in the source as a language with three
level tones, but the mid tone is not reported for monosyllabic or
disyllabic words and can be predicted from an underlying sequence
of high and low tones in trisyllabic words. It is therefore regarded
as a language with only two level tones.

[4] There is one word reported with a high-high sequence. This
is ódzí "crab." In isolation this word is [ódzî], perhaps from
underlying high-high-low.

Apparent exceptions to 5. are AMAHUACA (Russell 1959), reported to permit only LH and HL, and MUINANE (Walton 1967) in
which only HL is reported for disyllables. In these and other
similar cases an alternation is generally found with level patterns.
A different choice of underlying forms would eliminate their exceptional status.

In some cases the restrictions on permitted tone sequences are
a rather fortuitous result of the morphemic sequences involved.
For example, in nouns of VCV format in YORUBA (Ward 1952) only
low or mid tone may appear on the first syllable, so the sequences
HL, HM and HH are excluded. However, in the closely related
IGALA (Fresco 1969) these three sequences are permitted, but the
first syllable may not be mid, so that ML, MM and MH are excluded. These restrictions result from the fact that the original
function of these initial syllables was as markers of noun classes
and that the morphological category of noun-class-prefix was
tonally noncontrastive, as it may still be seen to be in neighboring
EWE (Sprigge and Ford 1972).

In other instances more general phonological constraints in the
language control the limitations on permitted sequences. For
example, in MAHAS NUBIAN the absence of HL pattern on disyllables may be predicted from a rule that syllables after a marked
(high) tone are assimilated to the marked tone. Thus, in trisyl-
lables only LLL, LLH, LHH and HHH are possible. Note that
the unmarked status of L is confirmed by a neutralization process.
In nominal compounds tonal contrasts on words preceding the head
are removed and these words become low toned.

This MAHAS NUBIAN restriction may be stated in another way.
The disyllabic LH pattern and the trisyllabic LLH and LHH patterns each contain only one shift of tone level. In each case it is
a shift upwards from a low tone level to a high tone level. In the
non-occurring LHL pattern there are two shifts of tone level, one
upward and one downward. The language-specific restriction on
permitted sequences may thus be stated as a) a word may contain
no more than one shift of tone level and b) a shift of tone level may
only be upward. Other languages contain similar restrictions.
For example, in KORKU (Zide 1965) only a downward shift is permitted, and only one shift in a word is permitted. In KINGA
(Kähler-Meyer 1969) and HUAVE (K. L. Pike and Warkentin 1961)
a downward shift cannot be followed by an upward shift in the same
word. From examining numerous languages it is possible to make
the universal generalization 6. about restrictions of this kind.

6. A language which permits successive shifts of tone level in opposite directions within a word permits words with only one shift of tone level.

Thus, for example HLH or LHL does not occur without LH or HL. Discussion now turns to the question of tonal contours.

2.3 Tonal contours

Many languages -- especially languages of Asia — have been described as having tonal distinctions which are characterized not by the level of the tone alone but by a movement between levels. It has been much debated whether such 'contour tones' should be separated into component levels and regarded simply as the juxtaposition of level tones, or whether they should be regarded as indivisible units. This paper will not discuss this issue. The definition of a contour tone has been given above.

Linguistic descriptions that employ the contour tone concept do so because single syllables appear phonetically complex in regard to tone. There are two problems in using some of this literature for purposes of cross-language comparison. First, there may be a phonetic over-specification of tone shapes, and second, the attribution of non-pitch properties to broadened categories of 'tone' including syllabic length and properties of syllable-initial or syllable-final consonants (including even their very presence or absence). The relationship of such non-tonal properties to tone will be considered separately later. First, the generalization 7. concerning simplified tonal contours will be presented.

7. If a language has contour tones, it also has level tones.

Some languages have a number of level tones greater than the number of contour tones. Thus, by an analysis based on Donaldson (1963), the LAI CHAU dialect of WHITE TAI has a rising tone as well as three level tones. One variety of TAISHAN CHINESE (Tung 1946) has four level tones and one rising tone; a different variety (T.M. Cheng 1973) has three level tones and two falling tones. YAY (Gedney 1975) has four level tones, one rising tone and one falling tone. Languages reported to have two level tones and one contour tone are very frequent. Those with two levels and a falling tone include NORTH PAME (Gibson 1956) and SOUTH PAME (Manrique 1958), HAUSA and ZULU. HIGI (Mohrlang 1972) has two level tones and a rise. Elimelech (1974) reports a KRU dialect with two levels and a rising tone which rises above the level of the high tone. However, many languages have fewer level tones than contours or the same number of levels and contours. It does not therefore seem that contours are added to the inventory only when the available tone space has been exhaustively exploited for level tones. CENTRAL MONPA (Das Gupta 1968) is described as having only a high level and a rising tone; RIANG LANG (Luce 1965) as having a high level and a falling tone. Durand (1951) reports TAHITIAN as having a low level and a falling tone. TANKHUR NAGA (Bhat 1969) and TANGSI CHINESE (Kennedy 1953) have one level tone and a rise and a fall. SHEKKI CHINESE (Egerod 1956) and GADSUP (Frantz 1966) have two levels and a rise and a fall. MUONG (Barker 1966) has two levels, two rises and one fall, while the related NORTHERN VIETNAMESE has an additional rising tone. TEPETOTUTLA CHINANTEC (Westly 1971) has three levels, three rises and two falls. NGIE (Hombert 1976e) has three levels, one rise and two falls.

Apparent counterexamples to 7. may be due more to the linguist's preferences in the choice of descriptive labels. For example, KHAM TIBETAN (Ray 1965) is described as having only two tones -- a rise and a fall. Similarly, BORO (Bhat 1968) is described as having only two tones -- a high fall and a mid fall. Another analyst might regard both these cases as contrasts between level tones, with, in KHAM, a centralized origin for the tones and in BORO an intonational downward drift in pitch for citations. In other words, by the definition used here these may not be contour tones. It is probable that many descriptions that were included in C.C. Cheng's (1973) survey of tones in CHINESE dialects report tones as falling tones when they fall only because of intonational factors. The finding that falling tones outnumber level tones in CHINESE may be the result of this. Whatever the facts are for CHINESE, it is certainly not true for all languages that falling tones are more frequent than level tones.

The universal constraint 8. concerns the inter-relationship of differing contour tones.

8. A language with complex contours also has simple contours.[5]

---

[5] C.C. Cheng (1973) extracts two further implicational relationships between contour tones from his survey of CHINESE. These are: a) if a falling-rising tone occurs, then at least one of rising, level and/or falling tones must occur; b) if a rising-falling tone occurs in a dialect, then a rising tone must occur.

Complex contours are those which are bidirectional (even tri-
directional) in their movement. PEKINESE CHINESE (Chao 1948)
has a fall-rise tone but also a simple fall and a simple rise. Simmonds (1965) mentions three TAI dialects which have a rise-fall
tone, PHRAE and LUANG PRABANG having also two rising tones
and one falling tone, THAI NYO also having one rising tone and
three falling tones. TRIQUE (Longacre 1952) permits two fall-
rise glides, six different falling glides, and seven rising glides.

An apparent exception to 8. is one dialect of YENISEI (Werner
1972). This has a high tone and, in Werner's account, three rise-
fall tones. The high tone is described as slightly rising, but if it
is regarded as a rising tone so that 8. is not violated, then the language violates 7. by having no level tones. However, this language
has complex syllable-final phonation type contrasts between these
'tones.' Werner's description presents a very confusing picture,
and it is doubtful if this language is a genuine exception to either
of these two generalizations. The pitch phenomena are probably
predictable entirely from non-tonal properties of syllables.

Both 7. and 8. are interesting in relation to the generalizations
on sequences of level tones. They are essentially similar to the
constraints 5. and 6. Whereas 5. states that words with like tones
must occur if words with unlike tones occur, 7. states a similar
implication between level and contour tones on a single syllable.
Whereas 6. states that words with one shift of tone level must occur
if words with two (or more) shifts of tone level do, 8. states that
contours with a single direction of slope must occur if bidirectional
contours do. These four generalizations all state that more complex patterns do not occur unless simpler patterns are represented,
but there are specific similarities here between tonal patterns.
Such shared restrictions between contour and level tones imply
that it is correct to seek a unitary view of tone, whether as a
'suprasegmental' or a strictly segmental feature.

Two further restrictions on contour tones have been proposed.
These do not seem to be parallel to any restrictions on level tone
sequences. C.C. Cheng (1973) found that falling tones outnumber
rising tones and this finding has been widely repeated (e.g. in
Ohala 1973). Cheng's conclusion depends on the preponderance
of descriptions of MANDARIN dialects included in his survey.
In his gross tabulation of tones there are 335 more falling tones
than rising tones. In the MANDARIN dialects alone there were
348 more falling tones than rising tones. So, omitting MANDARIN,
rising tones would slightly outnumber falling tones. There are six

major genetic groups of CHINESE. The MIN and HAKKA-KAN
dialects surveyed by Cheng have more falling than rising tones,
like MANDARIN. But in WU and HSIANG dialects Cheng finds
more rising tones than falling tones, while in YÜEH (CANTONESE)
dialects the numbers are approximately equal. If each genetic
group is given equal weight, the excess of falling tones recedes
from prominence.

The fact that languages with more rising tones than falling tones
(including ones with one or more rising tones and no falling tones)
are common suggests that there is no sharp asymmetry between
the frequency of rising and falling tones, even though there probably are more languages which do have more falls than rises. The
similar absence of any marked prevalence of HL over LH in level
tone sequences suggests that any possible articulatory (Ohala 1973)
or perceptual (Hombert 1975) asymmetries favoring falling pitch
patterns do not play a major role in determining the constraints
on phonological inventories of tone. Falling pitch is, of course,
almost universally the unmarked intonational contour.

The second of these generalizations that has been discussed
widely is proposed partly on formal and partly on perceptual grounds
by Wang (1967) and concerns a limitation on the number and range
of tonal contours that may occur together in a language. Wang
suggests that no more than two falls or two rises may occur in a
language and each will occupy half of the available pitch range. In
terms of a five-point scale, this means tones 53, 31 and 35 are
all right, but *51, *15, etc. are out of order. The five-point scale,
taken literally, implies a theoretical maximum of ten falls and ten
rises. Such has never been reported in any language; however,
languages with more than two falls or more than two rises have
been reported. And that languages use tones more nearly covering
the whole voice range has been confirmed by a number of instrumental studies, including Dreher and Lee (1966) for PEKING CHI-
NESE, T.M. Cheng (1973) for TAISHAN CHINESE, Hombert (1976e)
for NGIE, Han (1969) for VIETNAMESE, and Abramson (1962) for
STANDARD THAI. Perceptual reasons would apparently favor
contours with wider pitch ranges (cf. Hombert 1975) in so far as
distinguishing them from level tones is concerned; but for distinction between contours with the same direction of movement, a
separation of the portions of the pitch range occupied is a major
factor (cf. Gandour and Harshman 1976; Gandour, to appear, b).
There is thus no simple advantage in perceptual salience to be
gained by having contours parallel in slope, for although distinguished by the range covered, they are closer to confusion with

each other in terms of the amount of pitch movement, and less distinct from level tones within the same portion of the pitch range. In short, the constraints suggested by Wang do not seem the right ones to explain the limits on numbers of contour tones, and the perceptual reasoning offered to support his contention is counter-balanced by other perceptual considerations.

So many varied systems which include contour tones seem permissible that an understanding of some probably complex trade-off between production and perception will be required before the limits on these systems can be understood. Some ideas of the trade-offs involved are discussed by Hombert (1976c).

3. Tone Rules

Only two general areas concerning the relationship of tones to adjacent tones will be dealt with here. These are assimilatory effects and polarity rules.

3.1 Assimilation

Complete assimilations between level tones are very common synchronic and diachronic tone rules. In such a case an underlying or historically prior tone is changed so that it assumes the same level as an adjacent tone. For example, in KIKUYU (Ford 1975) the initial low tone syllable of some nouns is raised to high tone when a high tone precedes. In IXCATEC (Fernandez de Miranda 1959) monosyllabic low tone words become high after a high tone. In TETELA (Jacobs 1962) disyllabic noun stems with a PROTO-BANTU HL pattern have changed to a new HH pattern. Above, it was suggested that MAHAS NUBIAN had undergone the effects of a similar historical change. In HAUSA (Meyers 1976, Wängler 1963) words with final LH are realized in sentence-final positions as LL. KORKU (Zide 1965) has apparently undergone a historical change which has left all tones low after the first low tone is encountered on the word.

The above examples illustrate perseverative assimilations. Anticipatory assimilations are also frequent. For example, in AUCHI (Elugbe 1973) the 'associative construction' is marked by a high tone between the two nouns involved. A disyllabic LL noun preceding this high tone becomes HH. In CHICHEWA (Trithart 1976) a historical change has produced HH from earlier LH nouns through an anticipatory raising of the low tone.

Hyman and Schuh (1974) suggest that anticipatory tone assimilations are "unnatural," chiefly on the grounds that they are more
rarely attested than perseverative assimilations. While it is probably true that there are more frequent perseverative tone assimilations in the West African languages from which Hyman and Schuh
drew their generalizations, anticipatory assimilations are certainly
not absent (even among West African languages, e.g. AUCHI). In
some language areas anticipatory assimilations even seem more
frequent. In the major groups of CHINESE apart from WU, such
assimilatory changes as occur seem predominently anticipatory.
For example, in CANTONESE (T.M. Cheng 1968) the high-mid
falling tone (53) becomes a high level tone when it precedes a high
level tone (or another high-mid fall). Equally, assimilatory changes
in the tone languages of the Americas often include anticipatory
changes. VILLA ALTA ZAPOTEC (E.V. Pike 1948) is reported to
have only anticipatory assimilations. MITLA ZAPOTEC (Briggs
1961) has both anticipatory and perseverative assimilations (HL and
LH become HH). Of two dialects of MIXTEC (Mak 1953), SAN ES-
TEBAN has both anticipatory and perseverative, SAN MIGUEL only
perseverative assimilations. There is thus no implicational relationship between the presence of anticipatory and perseverative
rules. Nor is there an overwhelming predominance of perseverative rules. Yet there does seem to be a certain excess of perseveration over anticipation. In an experiment designed to test if there
was a perceptual explanation for such an asymmetrical distribution
(Maddieson, to appear), it was found that there was a predisposition
to perceive an ambiguous case as one which included an anticipation
of the following pitch level rather than a perseveration. At the time
of writing, it remains unclear if any universal type of explanation
can account for the apparent asymmetry.

Hyman and Schuh also propose that it is more natural to encounter
assimilatory rules which have the effect of raising tones than rules
which have the effect of lowering tones. Such an observation is consistent with the observation 4. above that higher tones are more
often marked. When, in a given language, there is an asymmetry
of assimilatory rules with regard to their raising and lowering effect, then we may assume that it is the unmarked tones that undergo
assimilation and the marked tones to which they are assimilated.
Thus, in the unusual case of HAUSA, a two-level language with a
marked low tone, we find not only that low tone is less frequent in
lexical occurrence, but also that the principal assimilatory tone
rule is one that changes high tone to low (after low). In AUCHI,
where the low tone is the more frequent (unmarked) category, the
assimilatory rule discussed by Elugbe (1973) is one which raises

low tones to high (before high). The greater frequency of the AUCHI
type of rule can be predicted from the more general condition that
more systems have marked high tones.

It is important to note a negative finding. In no case has a rule
been found in which a contour tone is copied through an assimilatory
process.[6] For example, a rising tone never induces a similar rising tone on a following syllable. The assimilatory changes that result from contour tones concern only portions of the contour such
as the beginning or end points. In the CANTONESE case mentioned
earlier, the high-mid falling tone (53) becomes a high tone (55) when
another high-mid falling tone follows. The first falling tone assimilates to the beginning point of the following fall. In the MIAO dialect
of TA NAN SHAN (Miao Language Team 1962) a high-mid falling
tone (recorded as 43) lowers a following higher mid tone (44) to a
mid tone (33). The second tone assimilates to the end-point of the
preceding falling tone. These assimilatory effects must be distinguished from tone changes which cannot be described by any natural
phonological process (cf. the distinction drawn by Kao (1971) between
assimilated and changed tones in CANTONESE).

In some cases assimilatory processes work to spread the whole
of a tonal contour over an additional span. For example, in SHANG-
HAI (Eric Zee, personal communication) or TANGSI CHINESE
(Kennedy 1953) and other dialects of the WU group, the main tone
sandhi rule has the effect of incorporating a second syllable into
the domain of the tone of the preceding syllable. Thus, if the first
syllable has a falling tone, the combination has a falling contour
distributed over the two syllables, with the first part of the fall
achieved in the first syllable and the second part achieved in the
second syllable.

----

[6] There is evidence from other kinds of processes that contours
may be copied as a whole. It may be noted that in some cases a
reduplication of a syllable with a contour may also have the contour.
In LAHU (Matisoff 1973) reduplication is used for a variety of functions including making the reference of a noun indefinitely vague.
Reduplicated syllables are copied with contour tones. Similar
evidence comes from the study of speech errors, as well as word
games and secret languages. Errors concerning tones in STAND-
ARD THAI spoken by Southern Thai speakers (Gandour 1976b) often
include anticipation or perseveration of a contour. In the MIAO
secret language (Ai 1957) each syllable is made into two, and the
tone -- contour or level -- of the original syllable is repeated on
both new syllables.

Somewhat akin to rules of tonal assimilation are rules of tonal contraction and rules of tone displacement. In many environments in YORUBA (Maddieson 1972) two adjacent vowels contract to a single short vowel with the quality of one of the original vowels. The tone of the resulting vowel is not predictable from the quality or the order of the vowels, but can be predicted from the tone levels. If either vowel is high, the resulting vowel is high; failing that, if either vowel is low, the resulting vowel is low; only if both vowels are mid is the resulting vowel mid. In general, such contractions display an asymmetry that is predicted from the greater frequency of marked high tones, since high tones are usually dominant.

Displacement may be viewed as the consequence of a chain of assimilation rules, but may be better interpreted as a dislocation in relative timing of syllables and pitch patterns. Thus, if a sequence LH + LL is changed to give the output LHHH, we may talk of the low tones being assimilated to the preceding high. If the output is LLLH, then the high tone may be said to be displaced to the end of the string. The alternative view would say that each syllable is successively subject to assimilatory changes giving a derivation such as LHLL → LHHL → LLHL → LLHH → LLLH. Such a view requires assimilation of both high and low tones to be equally easy, contrary to the finding above in relation to 'true' assimilations, in which the origin of the assimilatory effect is left unchanged.

If tonal displacements are examined, they are found to be both perseverative and anticipatory. DJUKA (Huttar 1972) includes an anticipatory displacement in which LH words become HL before following low tones, i.e. LHL(L...) → HLL(L...). In LANGO (Maddieson, Shopen and Okello 1973) a noun with LH pattern in a compound with a following LL noun gives a pattern LLHL (i.e. LHLL → LLHL), a perseverative displacement. Tonal displacement rules seem to share with tone assimilation rules the same tendency for a slight preponderance of perseverative cases, though the number of cases on which this impression is based is smaller. It is clear, however, that tone displacement rules generally refer to location of isolated high tones -- a fact again related to the prevalence of systems with marked high tones.

3.2 Polarity

A striking phenomenon which emerges from a study of tone rules is the relatively greater frequency of rules of polarity than occurs with other phonological properties. In simple two-level systems, morphemes frequently occur with no underlying tone, rather their tone is determined by rule to be the opposite of an adjacent tone. In CILUBA (Burssens 1939) a singular imperative verb is formed with a suffixed /-a/ with tone opposite to the tone of the verb stem it follows. A distributive suffix in LONGUDA (Newman 1974) has tone polar to the last vowel of the preceding stem. Plural and second person singular subject pronouns have tone polar to the last tone in a preceding predicate in MARGI (Hoffmann 1963). A statement can thus be made which establishes a typological distinction of tonal properties from other phonological features.

9. Morphemes subject to a rule which assigns a tone opposite to an adjacent tone are much more frequently encountered than morphemes in which some other phonological property is governed by a rule of polarity.

It may be noted that a larger number of cases where a tone is polar to a preceding tone occurs. This may be connected with the fact that in tone assimilations, more cases where the preceding tone controls the assimilation occur. The tendency is for both effects to occur more often when the governing environment is to the left.

4. Interaction of Tone and Nontonal Features

4.1 Tone and consonants

In recent years there has been much discussion of the relationship between tones and features of adjacent consonants (e.g. Hyman 1973). Attention has particularly been focused on the way that small-scale phonetic differences following voiced and voiceless consonants may translate into a historical evolution of tonal distinctions. The statement in 10. is generally true at the phonetic level.

10. A descending pitch ramp follows a voiceless obstruent; a rising pitch ramp follows a voiced obstruent.

This seems to have two distinct consequences for historical phonology (cf. Maddieson 1976). In some cases the descending pitch ramp has caused lowered pitch reflexes after voiceless obstruents. These may be found in many TAI dialects (Sarawit 1973), NASU and LÜ-CH'ÜAN (Matisoff 1972) and some of the MIN CHINESE dialects (Norman 1973), as well as elsewhere. In other cases, the elevated level from which the descending ramp starts has caused raised pitch reflexes after voiceless obstruents. This has happened frequently

in the same language families as display the other historical development. Raised reflexes after historically voiceless obstruents
are probably more widely found than lowered reflexes, but the
predominance is not an overwhelming one.

Other laryngeal states of consonants such as aspiration and
glottalization frequently have restricted co-occurrence with tones
or can be shown to have been a factor in the historical development
of tone, but the effects are too heterogeneous and some of the historical scenarios too speculative to permit establishment of reliable general statements of the interaction of these properties with
tones. However, it should not be overlooked that the interaction
of tones and consonants is a mutual process. Hyman and Schuh
(1974) deny that tones may have effects on consonants. The linguistic literature does provide a larger number of reported cases
of consonants influencing tones (synchronically or diachronically),
but suggests that this may be something of an Asian areal phenomenon. Cases in which tones have effects on consonants are reported
from JINGPHO, PICURIS, NGOMBE, MIAO, MANDARIN and YÜEH
CHINESE, HAUSA and TANKHUR NAGA among others (Maddieson
1976).

4.2 Vowel quality and tone

A phonetic association of pitch level and vowel height has been
widely recognized. In general, 11. holds.

11. A low (open) vowel has a lower pitch than a high (close)
     vowel, other things being equal.

Unlike the phonetic interaction in 10. this association does not seem
to have phonological consequences. Cases of a claimed effect of
vowel height on tonal development are not generally persuasive. It
may be that the correlation in 11. serves simply as a cue to identification of vowel height (Hombert 1976a). Hombert suggests that,
although vowel height does not affect tones, tones may influence
vowel height. This is based on two instances (LAHU and FOOCHOW
CHINESE) for which other factors may well be responsible, as the
correlation of vowel height and tone is very imperfect (Maddieson
1975).

4.3 Vowel length and tone

From a survey of the literature, Gandour (to appear, a) finds
that the duration of a vowel (or syllable) is differentially affected
by the tone it bears. His conclusions are given in 12. and 13.

12. Vowels on low tones are longer than those on high tones, other things being equal.

13. Vowels on rising tones are longer than those on falling tones, other things being equal.

Although a clear counterexample to 12. is provided by TAIWAN CHINESE (Zee and Hombert 1976), Gandour shows that the tendencies in 12. and 13. are sufficiently strong to have governed a historical realignment of vowel length with tones in both NORTHERN and SOUTHERN THAI dialects. Long vowels have developed under rising and non-high level tones, short vowels under falling and high level tones.

In very many languages tone glides are confined to long vowels or syllables only. ZULU (Cope 1959), STANDARD THAI (Gandour 1976a) and ACOMA (Miller 1965) are among the many languages of which this is true. Such a correlation is often taken as evidence for a phonological analysis in which the glides are derived from sequences of dissimilar level tones on a geminate vowel or other sonorant sequence. The observations 12. and 13. suggest pairings in regard to length of low tones with rising tones and high tones with falling tones. Where this pairing does not obtain, additional support is gained for a view that the tone glides in the language in question derive from a source such as juxtaposed level tones.

4.4 Phonation type and tone

The class of tone languages includes some languages which also have contrasts of phonation type on the tone-bearing vowels or syllables. There is not necessarily any constraint on the co-occurrence of marked phonation types such as murmur or creak with tones. For example, Ladefoged (to appear) reports that MPI has six tones and on each tone has creaky voiced vowels in contrast with plain voiced vowels, and GURUNG (Hinton 1970) has breathy voiced vowels on both its tones.

Where a restriction does apply it is generally captured by 14.:

14. When a marked phonation type is restricted in distribution to certain tones, those tones are in the highest or lowest part of the scale used by the language concerned.[7]

---

[7] The generalization in 14. does not apply to syllable-final features which are more consonantal or consonant-derived than vocalic. Languages which conform to 14. may have adopted a phonation type contrast as an alternative to adding to the tone inventory.

Thus, KIOWA (Sivertsen 1956) has a contrast of plain and laryn-
gealized vowels, but only on low tone syllables, and BURMESE
(Burling 1967) has a contrast of plain and creaky voicing on high
tone. They both conform to 14., albeit somewhat vacuously, in
that the tone involved is either the highest or lowest (of two). In
systems with a larger number of tones, such as VIETNAMESE
(Han 1959), the restriction is more meaningful. And it is the low
tone in VIETNAMESE that may be 'constricted' (creaky).

BIBLIOGRAPHY

Abramson, Arthur S. 1962. Vowels and tones of Standard Thai:
acoustical measurements and experiments. Indiana University,
Bloomington.

Agnew, Arlene and Evelyn G. Pike. 1957. Phonemes of Ocaina
(Huitoto. International Journal of American Linguistics [IJAL]
23. 24-27.

Ai Ch'ing. 1957. A Miao secret language. Chung Kuo Yü Wen 59.
15. Translation in Purnell 1972: 235-236.

Anderson, Doris. 1962. Conversational Ticuna. Norman, Okla.:
Summer Institute of Linguistics.

Anderson, Lambert. 1959. Ticuna vowels; with special regard to
the system of five tonemes. Série Lingüistica Especial 1. 76-
119. Rio de Janeiro: Publiçãos do Museu Nacional.

Armstrong, Robert G. 1968. Yala (Ikom): a terraced-level language with three tones. Journal of West African Languages
[JWAL] 5. 49-58.

_____. 1972. Rules for Idoma morphophonology. Research
Notes, Department of Linguistics and Nigerian Languages,
University of Ibadan 5/2-3. 19-24.

Asongwed, Tah and Larry M. Hyman. 1976. Morphotonology of
the Ngamambo noun, in Hyman 1976: 23-56.

Bahl, Kalicharan. 1957. Tones in Punjabi. Indian Linguistics
17. 139-147.

Barker, Milton E. 1966. Vietnamese-Muong tone correspondences. Studies in Comparative Austroasiatic Linguistics (Indo-Iranian Monographs 5) 9-25. The Hague: Mouton.

Béarth, Thomas. 1968. Etude instrumentale des tons du toura. Cahiers Ferdinand de Saussure 24. 45-58.

_____ and Hugo Zemp. 1967. The phonology of Dan (Santa). Journal of African Languages [JAL] 6. 9-29.

Bell, Herman. 1968. The tone system of Mahas Nubian. JAL 7. 26-32.

Bendor-Samuel, John (ed.) 1974. Ten Nigerian tone systems. Studies in Nigerian Languages 4, Institute of Linguistics, Zaria and Center for the Study of Nigerian Languages, Kano.

Bergman, Richard. 1971. Vowel sandhi and word division in Igede. JWAL 8. 13-25.

Bhat, D.N.S. 1968. Boro vocabulary. Poona: Deccan College.

_____. Tankhur Naga vocabulary. Poona: Deccan College.

Boxwell, Helen and Maurice. 1966. Weri phonemes. Linguistic Circle of Canberra Publications, series A, 7. 77-93.

Briggs, Elinor. 1961. Mitla Zapotec grammar. Mexico City: Summer Institute of Linguistics.

Bunkowske, Eugene. 1972. Eliding boundaries in Ogoja Yala. Research notes, Department of Linguistics and Nigerian Languages, University of Ibadan 5/2-3. 59-71.

Burling, Robbins. 1967. Proto-Lolo-Burmese. Indiana University, Bloomington.

Burssens, Amaat. 1939. Tonologische Schets van het Tschiluba. Antwerp: De Sikkel.

Chang, Kun. 1953. On the tone system of the Miao-Yao languages. Language 29. 374-378.

Chao, Yuan-ren. 1930. A system of tone letters. Maître Phonétique 30. 24-27.

Chao, Yuan-ren. 1948. Mandarin primer. Cambridge: Harvard
    University Press.

Cheng, Teresa M. 1968. The phonological system of Cantonese.
    Project on Linguistic Analysis reports, 2nd series 5, C1-C77.

_____. 1973. The phonology of Taishan. Journal of Chinese
    Linguistics [JCL] 1. 256-322.

Cheng, Chin-Chuang. 1973. A quantitive study of Chinese tones.
    JCL 1. 93-110.

Cope, A.T. 1959. Zulu tonology. Afrika und Übersee 43. 190-200.

Courtenay, Karen. 1974. On the nature of the Bambara tone sys-
    tem. Studies in African Linguistics [SAL] 5. 303-323.

Crazzolara, J.P. 1938. A study of the Acooli language. London:
    Oxford University Press for International African Institute.

Das Gupta, K. 1968. An introduction to Central Monpa. Shillong:
    North-East Frontier Agency.

Donaldson, Jean. 1963. White Tai phonology. Hartford Seminary
    Foundation, Conn.

Dreher, J.J. and P.C. Lee. 1966. Instrumental investigation of
    single and paired Mandarin tonemes. Huntington Beach, Calif.:
    McDonnell-Douglas Advanced Research Laboratory.

Durand, Marguerite. 1951. Le système tonal du tahitien. Bulletin
    de la Société de Linguistique de Paris [BSLP] 47. 126-139.

Egerod, Søren. 1956. The Lungtu dialect. Copenhagen: Munks-
    gaard.

Elimelech, Baruch. 1974. On the reality of underlying contour
    tones. UCLA Working Papers on Phonetics 27. 74-83.

Elugbe, B.O. 1973. A comparative Edo phonology. Doctoral
    dissertation, University of Ibadan.

Erickson, Donna. 1974. Fundamental frequency contours of the
    tones of Standard Thai. Pasaa 4. 1-25.

Fernandez de Miranda, Maria. 1959. Fonemica del Ixcateco. Mexico City: Instituto Nacional de Anthropologia e Historia.

Ferrell, Raleigh. 1971. Le p'u-man, langue austro-asiatique. BSLP 66. 405-412.

Ford, Kevin C. 1975. The tones of nouns in Kikuyu. SAL 6. 49-64.

Frantz, Chester and Marjorie. 1966. Gadsup phoneme and toneme units. Linguistic Circle of Canberra Publications, series A, 7. 1-11.

Fresco, E.M. 1969. The tones of the Yoruba and Igala disyllabic noun prefix. JWAL 6. 31-34.

Gandour, Jack. 1975. The features of the larynx: n-ary or binary? Phonetica 32. 241-253.

_____. 1976a. On the representation of tone in Siamese. Studies in Tai linguistics, ed. by J.C. Harris and J.R. Chamberlain. Bangkok: Central Institute of English Language.

_____. 1976b. 'Counterfeit tones' in the speech of Southern Thai bidialectals. UCLA Working Papers in Phonetics 33. 3-19.

_____. (to appear, a) On the interaction between tone and vowel length: evidence from Thai dialects. Phonetica.

_____. (to appear, b) Tone perception. Tone: a linguistic survey, ed. by V.A. Fromkin. New York: Academic Press.

_____ and Richard Harshman. 1976. Cross language study of tone perception. Paper presented to the 51st annual meeting of the Linguistic Society of America, Philadelphia.

_____ and Ian Maddieson. 1976. Measuring larynx height in Standard Thai using the cricothyrometer. Phonetica 33. 241-267.

Gedney, William J. 1965. Yay, a Northern Tai language in North Vietnam. Lingua 14. 180-193.

Gibson, Lorna F. 1956. Pame (Otomi) phonemics and morphophonemics. IJAL 22. 242-265.

Goldstein, Louis. 1976. Perception of Siswati clicks. Unpublished paper, UCLA.

Han, Mieko S. 1969. Vietnamese tones. Acoustic Phonetic Research Laboratory, University of Southern California.

Haudricourt, Andre-Georges. 1968. La langue de Gomen et la langue de Touho en Nouvelle Caledonie. BSLP 63. 218-235.

Hinton, Bruce. 1970. Spectrographic confirmation of contrastive pitch and breathiness in Gurung. Occasional Papers of the Wolfenden Society on Tibeto-Burman Linguistics 3. 74-81.

Hoffmann, Carl. 1963. A grammar of the Margi language. London: Oxford University Press for the International African Institute.

Hoijer, Harry. 1945. Navaho phonology. University of New Mexico Publications in Anthropology 1. Albuquerque.

Hombert, Jean-Marie. 1975. The perception of contour tones. Proceedings of the first annual meeting, Berkeley Linguistic Society, 221-232.

_____. 1976a. Development of tones from vowel height. UCLA Working Papers in Phonetics 33. 55-66.

_____. 1976b. Perception of tones of bisyllabic nouns in Yoruba. SAL Supplement 6. 109-122.

_____. 1976c. Tone space and universals of tone systems. Paper presented at the 51st annual meeting of the Linguistic Society of America, Philadelphia.

_____. 1976d. Consonant types, vowel height and tone in Yoruba. UCLA Working Papers in Phonetics 33. 40-54.

_____. 1976e. Noun classes and tone in Ngie, in Hyman 1976: 1-21.

Huttar, George and Mary. 1972. Notes on Djuka phonology. Languages of the Guianas, ed. by J.E. Grimes, 1-11. Norman, Okla.: Summer Institute of Linguistics.

Hyman, Larry M. 1972. A phonological study of Fe?Fe? -Bamileke. SAL Supplement 4.

Hyman, Larry M. (ed.) 1973. Consonant types and tone. Southern California Occasional Papers in Linguistics 1. University of Southern California.

_____. (ed.) 1977. Studies in Bantu tonology. Southern California Occasional Papers in Linguistics 3. University of Southern California.

_____ and Russell G. Schuh. 1974. Universals of tone rules: evidence from West Africa. Linguistic Inquiry 5. 81-115.

Jacobs, John. 1962. Tetela-grammatica, Part 1: phonology. Ghent: Story-Scientia.

Jones, Robert B. 1961. Karen linguistic studies: description, comparison and texts. University of California Publication in Linguistics [UCPL] 25. Berkeley and Los Angeles: Univ. of California Press.

Kähler-Meyer, Emmi. 1969. Gibt es sprachhistorische Beziehungen der Töne im Kinga (Tanzania)? Ethnological and and linguistic studies in honour of N.J. van Warmelo, 1-12. Pretoria.

Kao, Diana L. 1971. The structure of the syllable in Cantonese (Janua Linguarum, series practica 78). The Hague: Mouton.

Karapurkar, Pushpa. 1972. Tripuri phonetic reader. Mysore: Central Institute of Indian Languages.

Kennedy, George A. 1953. Two tone patterns in Tangsic. Language 29. 213-225.

Ladefoged, Peter. 1971. Preliminaries to linguistic phonetics. University of Chicago Press.

_____. 1976. The phonetic specification of the languages of the world. UCLA Working Papers in Phonetics 31. 3-21.

_____. (to appear) Some notes on recent fieldwork. UCLA Working Papers in Phonetics 36.

Li, Fang-Kuei. 1965. The Tai and Kam-Sui languages. Lingua 14. 148-179.

Longacre, Robert. 1952. Five phonemic pitch levels in Trique. Acta Linguistica 7. 62-68.

Luce, G.H. 1965. Danaw: a dying Austroasiatic language. Lingua 14. 98-129.

Maddieson, Ian. 1972. Tone system typology and distinctive features. Proceedings of the Seventh International Congress of Phonetic Sciences, ed. by A. Rigault and R. Charbonneau, 958-961. The Hague: Mouton.

————. 1975. The intrinsic pitch of vowels and tones in Foochow. San Jose State Occasional Papers in Linguistics 1. 150-161.

————. 1976. A further note on tone and consonants. UCLA Working Papers in Phonetics 33. 131-159.

————. (to appear) Tone-spreading and perception. UCLA Working Papers in Phonetics 36.

————, Tim Shopen and Jenny Okello. 1973. Suprasegmentality, Lango tonology and paradigms. Paper presented to the Fourth African Linguistics Conference, New York.

Mak, Cornelia. 1953. A comparison of two Mixtec tonemic systems. IJAL 19. 85-100.

Manrique Castañeda, Leonardo. 1958. Sobre la clasificación del Otomi-Pame. Proceedings of the 33rd International Congress of Americanists, 551-559.

Matisoff, James. A. 1972. The Loloish tonal split revisited. Research Monograph 7, Center for South and Southeast Asia Studies, University of California, Berkeley.

————. 1973. The grammar of Lahu. UCPL 75.

Meeussen, A.E. 1970. Tone typologies for West African languages. African Language Studies 11. 266-271.

Meyers, Laura. 1976. Aspects of Hausa tone. UCLA Working Papers in Phonetics 32.

Miao Language Team. 1962. A brief description of the Miao language. Chung Kuo Yü Wen 111. 28-37. Translation in Purnell 1972. 1-26.

Miller, Wick R. 1965. Acoma grammar and texts. UCPL 40.

Mohrlang, Roger. 1972. Higi phonology. Studies in Nigerian Languages 2. Institute of Linguistics, Zaria and Center for the Study of Nigerian Languages, Abdullahi Bayero College, Kano.

Newman, John and Bonnie. 1974. Longuda, in Bendor-Samuel 1974: 109-116.

Norman, Jerry. 1973. Tonal development in Min. JCL 1. 222-238.

Ohala, John. 1973. The physiology of tone, in Hyman 1973: 1-14.

Pike, Eunice V. 1948. Problems in Zapotec tone analysis. IJAL 16. 161-170.

_____. 1956. Tonally differentiated allomorphs in Soyaltepec Mazatec. IJAL 22. 57-71.

_____ and Eugene Scott. 1962. The phonological hierarchy of Marinahua. Phonetics 8. 1-8.

Pike, Kenneth L. 1948. Tone languages. Ann Arbor: University of Michigan Press.

_____ and Milton Warkentin. 1961. Huave: a study in syntactic tone with low lexical functional load. A William Cameron Townsend en el 25 Anniversario del Instituto Linguistico de Verano, 627-642. Mexico City: Summer Institute of Linguistics.

Purnell, Herbert C. (ed.) 1972. Miao and Yao linguistic studies. (data paper No. 88.) Southeast Asia Program, Department of Asian Studies, Cornell University, Ithaca, New York.

Ray, Punya Sloka. 1965. Kham phonology. Journal of the American Oriental Society 85. 336-342.

Rensch, Calvin R. 1968. Proto-Chinantec phonology. Mexico City: Museo Nacional de Anthropologia.

Rowlands, E.C. 1959. A grammar of Gambian Mandinka. School of Oriental and African Studies, London University.

Russell, Robert and Delores. 1959. Syntactotonemics in Amahuaca (Pano). Série Lingüistica Especial No. 1. 128-167. Rio de Janeiro: Publicações do Museu Nacional.

Sarawit, Mary. 1973. The Proto-Tai vowel system. Doctoral dissertation, University of Michigan, Ann Arbor.

Shimizu, Kiyoshi. 1971. Comparative Jukunoid: an introductory survey. Doctoral dissertation, University of Ibadan.

Simmonds, E.H.S. 1965. Notes on some Tai dialects of Laos and neighbouring regions. Lingua 14. 133-147.

Sivertsen, Eva. 1956. Pitch problems in Kiowa. IJAL 22. 117-130.

Sprigge, R.G.S. and Kevin Ford. 1972. General tone rules for nouns and verbs in Ewe. Paper presented at the 10th West African Language Congress, Legon, Ghana.

Trithart, Lee. 1976. Desyllabified noun class prefixes and depressor consonants in Chichewa, in Hyman 1976: 259-286.

Tung, Yiu. 1946. The T'ai-shan dialect. Doctoral dissertation, Princeton University.

Upson, Jessamine. 1968. Chatino length and tone. Anthropological Linguistics 10. 1-7.

Voegelin, C.F. and F.M. 1965. Languages of the world: Sino-Tibetan Fascicle 3, Anthropological Linguistics 7/4.4.

Walton, James and Janice. 1967. Phonemes of Muinane, in Waterhouse 1967.

Wang, William S-Y. 1967. The phonological features of tone. IJAL 33. 93-105.

Wängler, Hans-Heinrich. 1963. Zur Tonologie des Hausa. Berlin: Akademie-Verlag.

Ward, Ida C. 1952. Introduction to the Yoruba language. Cambridge: Heffer.

Waterhouse, Viola (ed.) 1967. Phonemic systems of Columbian languages. Summer Institute of Linguistics Publication in Linguistics and Related Fields No. 14. Norman, Oklahoma: S.I.L., University of Oklahoma.

Welmers, William E. 1952. Notes on the structure of Bariba. Language 28. 82-103.

Werner, H. 1972. Die Tonität der gegenwartigen Jenisseischen
Dialekte. Zeitschrift für Phonetik, Sprachwissenschaft und
Kommunkationsforschung 25. 111-125.

West, Birdie and Betty Welch. 1967. Phonemic system of Tucano,
in Waterhouse 1967.

Westly, David O. 1971. The Tepetotutla Chinantec stressed syllable. IJAL 37. 160-163.

Zee, Eric and Jean-Marie Hombert. 1976. Duration and intensity
as correlates of F_0. Paper presented to the 92nd meeting of
the Acoustical Society of America, San Diego.

Zide, Norman H. 1966. Korku low tone and the Proto-Korku-
Kherwarian vowel system. Studies in Comparative Austro-
Asiatic Linguistics, Indo-Iranian Monographs 5. 214-229. The
Hague: Mouton.

A Typological View of Metathesis

RUSSELL ULTAN

ABSTRACT

Metathesis was examined as a more or less systematic process
that tends to preserve segments or features that would otherwise
be lost or changed through the effects of other processes, notably
reduction, assimilation, epenthesis, et al. It was also shown that
metathesis is recessive as opposed to most other competing processes. With one exception, a direct correlation between susceptibility
to metathesis and resonancy of the segment type was established.
Formal types and some of the major causes of metathesis were investigated: reduction, open syllable canon, analogy, phonological
constraints, anticipation, et al.

Reprinted from Working Papers of Language Universals 7,
December 1971, 1-44.

CONTENTS

1. Introduction

1.1 Status

In most treatises on general or diachronic linguistics as well as in many grammars, both historical and descriptive, the process referred to as metathesis[1] is given rather short shrift. Sievers (1901), for instance, groups metathesis with dissimilation and certain kinds of assimilation as "springende Lautwechsel" reserving the term "Lautwandel," with its implication of regular change, for the other, gradual types of sound change. For him, metathesis is largely limited to isolated instances without any discernable patterns, although he does admit the possibility that such phenomena may on occasion develop into systematic processes.[2] An extreme view -- all the more surprising at this late date -- is taken by Lehmann (1962:170): "Metathesis, like dissimilatory change, is apparently attested only as sporadic change." The opposing thesis, that metathesis may be more systematic in nature, is clearly demonstrated for SLAVIC and FRENCH by Martinet (1955: 327, 350-64). The ultimate stage of this line of thought is exemplified by Grammont's extensive treatment of the subject as a regular process (1950: 239-49, 339-57). His introductory remarks to the chapter on interversion (p. 239) are worth repeating:

"L'interversion est un phénomène qui consiste à placer deux phonèmes contigus dans un order plus commode. Par là on obtient une meilleure constitution des syllabes, on sauvegarde l'unité et l'harmonie du système phonique d'un parler en remplaçant les groupes insolites par des groupes usuels, on écarte les types imprononçables ou devenus imprononçables en leur substituant des types faciles, on evite des efforts articulatoires inutiles. C'est un phénomène intelligent, bien qu'il s'accomplisse d'une manière inconsciente. Il ne joue pas un grand rôle dans les langues, car la plus grosse part de leur vocabulaire est conforme à leur système phonique, puisque c'est elle qui le constitue; mais si quelque évolution phonétique amène une rencontre de phonèmes inaccoutumée, si des emprunts apportent une séquence inusitée, l'interversion, qui est déterminée

---

[1] More rarely dubbed transposition. Compare also GERMAN Umstellung, FRENCH interversion (contiguous) and métathèse (noncontiguous).

[2] Among others, see Passy 1890 and Wechssler 1900 for similar views on the subject.

par des principes d'ordre, de clarté, d'esthétique, intervient;
elle pourvoit à la bonne police du système et ramène à la norme
tout ce qui fait tache dans l'ensemble. Et naturellement, là où
elle apparait, elle accomplit son œuvre avec une régularité par-
faite. [emphasis mine]

To my knowledge, Grammont's is the only typological analysis and
classification of metathesis extant.

1.2 Purpose and scope

The purpose of the present paper is to reexamine the process of
metathesis in the context of additional cross-language data, primarily in terms of formal types, causes and effects, and interrelations between metathesis and certain other processes, notably:
umlaut, dissimilation, palatalization, aspiration, glottalization,
diphthongization, syncope and apocope, epenthesis and anaptyxis,
resyllabification, and others.

If metathesis is taken to include any transposition of linearly
ordered elements, we should consider a number of possible formal
types:

1. Inversion of syntactic constituents: He was here. vs. Was
    he here?

2. Transposition of syllables: TOBA (thieve's language): tema
    < mate 'dead.'

3. Transposition of sounds: irrevelant for irrelevant, or
    spoonerisms (transposition across word boundary of sounds
    occupying the same syllabic positions) like: a row of beery
    wenches for a row of weary benches.

4. Transposition of suprasegmental features: ímport (n.) vs.
    impórt (v.).

5. Transposition of phonological features: GREEK thríks (nom.
    sg.) vs. trikhós (gen. sg.) 'hair.'

In addition to these types, there are at least four parameters
which should be taken into account: voluntariness, systematicity,
permanence and motivation. There are involuntary metatheses
that occur only as nonce forms, such as spoonerisms and other
kinds of lapses, which may or may not be linguistically motivated.

Thus while the spoonerism cited above is not so motivated, Meringer and Mayer (1895: 82) note among others lapses like VIENNESE kšlaf for Sklave 'slave,' induced by analogy with the relatively higher frequency initial cluster kšl- (cf. g'schlafen, g'schliffen, etc.). Then there are systematic, permanent metatheses, found in various kinds of secret languages: argots, cants, jargons, etc. Compare, for example, PIG LATIN: opstay isthay arcay (stop this car) or Parisian butcher's argot: loe lušebɛm dü lwɛ̃ke (le boucher du coin). In the latter case, we have to do with a deliberately devised, socially motivated form of the base language, a quasi-artificial language, whereas in the former the metathesized forms are purely accidental and generally nonrecurrent. We also find voluntary, but usually nonsystematic, [3] not linguistically motivated (at least not directly so) and temporary, cases in the deliberate experimentation of young children or whimsical efforts of older speakers. It is essentially the remaining involuntary metatheses, which are the products of other phonological processes or are directly induced by phonological restrictions, now regularized, now irregularized by analogy or inhibited by other phonological developments, that are of immediate concern to us in the balance of this paper. These are all linguistically motivated, involuntary and permanent. They may be systematic ("regular") or nonsystematic ("sporadic").

This rough classification leads to a causal correlation which appears to be generally valid: voluntary metatheses imply non-phonological causes. The converse, that involuntary metatheses imply phonological causes, is not true. While many lapses appear to be relatable to phonological interference of one sort or another (see especially Meringer and Mayer 1895 and Meringer 1908), this does not seem to be generally so with spoonerisms. Also, metathesis may be brought on by purely grammatical factors, such as the analogical influence of the suffix -cla in VULGAR LATIN coacla < cloaca, or by lexicosemantic interference, as in GERMAN spucken 'to spit' < 18th century FRENCH escupir (or *escouper) contaminated by speien 'to spit.'

The foregoing discussion may be summarized in chart form (LM= linguistically motivated, Inv = involuntary, Per = permanent, Sys= systematic). The basically binary system of rating the various

---

[3] However, not necessarily so. Grammont (1950: 349) cites the case of a small French child (no age given) who invariably metathesized p...k: capè for paquet, coupè for bouquet, etc. In any event this does not appear to be an instance of deliberate experimentation.

categories is to be taken as a rough indication of prevalent tendencies rather than an absolute statement of the possibilities. Thus
for example, while most metatheses induced by phonological analogy appear to be fundamentally systematic (e.g. r...l>l...r in
OLD SPANISH due in part to the influence of a pattern of regressive dissimilation: r...r > l...r, as in peligro 'danger' < periglo,
milagro < miraglo, palabra < parabla), some are not or at least
cannot be shown to be so from the available evidence.

Sources and Pragmatic Types of Metathesis

	LM	Inv	Per	Sys
Phonologically induced	+	+	+	+
Analogically induced: phonological	+	+	+	+
grammatical	+	+	+	±
lexicosemantic	+	+	+	−
Secret language	−	−	+	+
Lapses	±	+	−	−
Child language experiment	−	−	−	−
Whimsy	−	−	−	−

   Returning now to the five formal types of metathesis cited above,
we omit from further consideration the inversion of syntactic constituents (1), since this type has no direct bearing on the phonology
of metathesis, and the transposition of syllables (2) which, while
superficially involving phonological units, is generally not phonologically induced. For the same reason, spoonerisms will not be
dealt with. While type 4, transposition of suprasegmental features,
may be relevant, lack of sufficient examples at present prevents us
from including it.

   Thus the scope of the investigation is limited to transpositions
of phonological segments or features. These may involve reciprocal
metathesis of two elements, as in irrevelant, or simple metathesis
of one, as in BAGNÈRES-DE-LUCHON crabo < *cabro < LAT. capra
'goat.' Of course, the latter type may also be viewed as a special
case of the former involving transposition of nonnull and null segments or features. Further, in the case of reciprocal metathesis,
the two elements may be contiguous to one another, as in WEST
SAXON fixas (fíksas) 'fish' (pl.) vs. fisc (físk) 'fish,' or noncontiguous, as in irrevelant.

1.3 Hypotheses

Examination of the available data leads to a few empirically
based general hypotheses which will constitute the guidelines for
what follows:

1) Metathesis is a conservative process. That is, aside from
the change in order which constitutes the process, it serves to preserve phonological elements, or familiar patterns, that otherwise
might be lost, merged with other elements or changed in shape due
to the workings of other processes.[4] In this respect it differs fundamentally from most other processes: assimilation, dissimilation,
syncope, epenthesis, and so on. Thus in KOREAN, for example,
h is retained syllable-initially before a stressed vowel and lost
elsewhere. In h-final verb stems, however, when the following
suffix-initial is a voiceless stop, the resultant sequence h + stop >
aspirated stop, thus preserving an h (as aspiration) which would
otherwise be lost: jotha < joh-ta '(it) is good,' mantha < manh-ta
'(they) are many.' In this case, metathesis would appear to be
abetted (or induced?) by the analogical pressure of the existing
voiceless aspirates. In OLD ARMENIAN, vowels of final syllables
were subject to syncope but high vowels after penults containing
a metathesized with the preceding consonant, thus preserving the
original vowel as the offglide of the vowel of the preceding syllable:
artawsr < *artásur (< IE *drakur) 'tear' (note also earlier metathesis of *dr).

2) Metathesis is a recessive process. That is, it tends to be
inhibited or counteracted by other, more dominant processes. The
traditional relegation of metathesis to the "minor sound changes"
(along with dissimilation, epenthesis, apheresis, et al.) is a tacit
admission of its recessiveness. This characteristic also helps to
explain why instances of all-pervasive metathesis are so rare and
why, as noted above, some scholars look upon all or most cases of
metathesis as sporadic. However, a careful study of interference
from other processes may often lead to a more accurate picture of
metathesis as a regular process -- at least at some given period in
the history of the language. Thus in ATTIC and IONIC GREEK,

---

[4]Compare also in this connection Winter's characterization of
metathesis in ARMENIAN (1962: 260-1) "...a metathesis occurs
when the regular developments would lead to a deviation from the
established pattern."

the y of INDO-EUROPEAN presents in *-yo metathesized with the
preceding stem-final nasal (or stop + nasal), liquid, s or w, incidentally preserving it: phaínō < *phanyō 'I show,' phtheíro < *phther-
yō 'I destroy,' telō̂ (Homeric teleíō < *teleísō < *telesyō 'I complete,'
klaíō < *klaíwō < *klawyō 'I weep.' But stem-final voiced or voiceless stops followed by y resulted in occlusivization, assibilation or
assimilation of y. Intervocalically, y was lost and, following vowel
+s or w, it was lost with palatalization of the latter consonants. In
CLASSICAL GREEK, these developments result in a somewhat
flawed picture. Synchronically, metathesis is considerably limited
in scope, although evidently attributable to what must once have
been regular phonological causes.

3) The proneness of different phonetic classes to metathesis
tends to stand in direct correlation with a hierarchy of resonance.
Mutatis mutandis, the more resonant a sound, the more susceptible
it is to metathesis. In ARMENIAN, the evidence points to a chronological hierarchy in the introduction of metathesis of original clusters
of the type consonant + semivowel. The first to metathesize were
clusters containing semivowels, followed by the liquids, nasals,
spirants, stops and possibly the affricates, in that order. In the
EASTERN ESKIMO dialects, an earlier tendency toward uvulariza-
tion of stressed vowels coupled with a regressive shift of word
stress from the ultima to the antepenult with subsequent syncope
of the penult vowel produced metathesis in the resulting consonant
cluster when the second member was a voiced uvular spirant (r):
GREENLANDIC marLuk 'two' (cf. ALASKAN malruk and MACKEN-
ZIE RIVER maloerok). This occurred primarily when the first
member was a lateral or a nasal, more rarely when it was s or ɣ.
When the second member was a uvular stop (q), various kinds of
assimilation took place dependent upon the point and manner of
articulation of the first member. In TAGALOG, when the passive
suffixes -án ~ ín, presumably bearing obligatory stress, are added
to stems, the shift of stress to the ultima incurs syncope of the
penult vowel and metathesis in the resultant consonant cluster, as
in gikbán vs. gibík 'come with help.' While there is no specific
information as to the frequency of or restrictions on particular
classes of phonemes with regard to this metathesis, a simple count
of the distribution of various types in the examples cited by Blake
(1925: 54, 302-7) yields the following for the original first member
of the cluster: liquids 9, nasals 2, voiced stops 3, voiceless stops
1, h 1. The GREEK y-metathesis referred to above was unrestricted
as to the preceding vowel when the first consonant was w but limited
to a or o before liquids and nasals.

The disproportionately high (and widespread) frequency of occurrence of liquids in metathesis is proverbial.[5] A partial list of languages for which this is true includes:

Liquids: BRETON, CORNISH, EASTERN ESKIMO, MIDDLE and OLD FRENCH, GAELIC, ANCIENT GREEK, OLD ICELANDIC, ILOKO, INDO-EUROPEAN, INDONESIAN, OLD IRISH, LATIN, MANDAIC ARAMAIC, PERSIAN, SOUTH SLAVIC, OLD SPANISH, TAGALOG and ZOQUE.

r only: ANGLO-NORMAN, ARMENIAN, AVESTIC (and ZEND), BAGNÈRES-DE-LUCHON, MIDDLE ENGLISH, ITALIAN (SOPRA-SELVA), KAMHMUˀ, MAURITIAN CREOLE, VEDIC SANSKRIT, SARDINIAN and TOBA.

l only: AMUZGO and YOKUTS.

Excluding cases of liquid metathesis, the majority of which include vowels, metathesis of sequences composed of consonant and vowel or of two vowels is, in terms of the present sample, almost as frequent as metathesis involving liquids. Furthermore, if we subsume in the same context metatheses involving semivowels, vocalic metathesis is considerably more common than liquid metathesis (or, for that matter, any other consonantal type). Thus in OLD FRENCH the loss of an intervocalic stop sometimes resulted in an unfamiliar or inadmissible sequence of two vowels, a difficulty which was resolved by metathesis: tiule (< LAT. tēgula)> tuile 'tile.' In COMMON SLAVIC the strong tendency toward the conversion of closed to open syllables (which also triggered liquid metathesis in OLD CHURCH SLAVIC) produced syllabic metathesis of the sequence e + semivowel within the same syllable, *ey and *ew becoming *ji and *ju respectively. See also the developments of consonant + semivowel in OLD ARMENIAN and GREEK mentioned above.

While the limited size of the sample precludes any absolute reliance on statistical data, it is interesting to note that the frequency of occurrence of the various classes of sounds as initial and final members of sequences subject to metathesis generally supports the

---

[5]In connection with this kind of instability it is interesting to note Leopold's claim (1953-4: 8) that liquids are among the last sounds to be mastered by children during the learning process.

resonance-hierarchy hypothesis, the only major exceptions being
the sibilants (principally s) and stops. However, in all but three
of the cases involving sibilants the other member of the sequence
is a stop. Furthermore, 47 of the 53 formal types representative
of instances of contiguous metathesis that did not appear to be
purely sporadic consisted of sequences containing one or two resonants.

2. Formal Types

In this section, we will examine a sampling of formal types of
metathesis encountered in the present study. Rather than give an
exhaustive account, which would be in part repetitive, I have chosen
enough cases to be fairly representative of the whole, extending
preference to those with higher general frequency of occurrence
but also to others of low frequency yet of interest for typological
reasons. The general order of presentation follows as closely as
possible the resonance-hierarchy noted above, in descending order
of resonance. (V = vowel, W = semivowel, L = liquid, F = spirant,
S = sibilant, N = nasal, P stop, C = unrestricted consonant).

2.1 Types with one or two resonants

$V_1 + V_2 > V_2 V_1$. The only examples of this type were found in
OLD FRENCH (see Sec. 1.3) and PORTUGUESE: doesto 'affront'
< deosto < *denosto on the analogy of the more familiar sequence
oe. Metathesis, however, did not occur as a result of d-syncope.
Compare miolo [myolo]'pith' (LAT. medulla).

$V_1 + W_2 > W_1 V_2$ or syllabic metathesis. This type has already
been cited for COMMON SLAVIC (Sec. 1.3); it is also found in
OLD FRENCH: angoisse ~ anguisse (angóis < LAT. angustia becomes angwɛs, MODERN ãgwas) 'anguish' or paroisse (paróis <
LAT. parochia becomes parwɛs, MODERN parwas) 'parish.' Note
also in both these examples earlier metathesis of consonant (st,k)+
i following or concomitant with the weakening of unstressed final
vowels.

V + L > LV. OLD IRISH túaslucud < earlier túasulcud 'opening'
or OLD CHURCH SLAVIC prasę 'suckling pig' (cf. LAT. porcus,
LITH. par̃szas, RUSS. porošá).

L + V > VL. In SOPRASELVA ITALIAN rV > Vr in unstressed
syllables: carstiaun < christianu. Note also metathesis of final CV.
In late MIDDLE ENGLISH ri > ər before dentals: brid > bird.

C + V > VC. In ROTUMAN most words have two different forms corresponding to the grammatical contrast completive-incompletive. When the final vowel of the completive phase is more sonorous than the vowel of the preceding syllable, metathesis of the final CV in the incompletive occurs: <u>leka</u> (comp.) vs. <u>leak</u> or <u>lyak</u> (incomp.) 'go.' This type of metathesis appears to be fairly common in AUS-TRONESIAN. Among others it is also found in KWARA'AE, ROWA and KUPANGESE. Similar to this is the type C + V (high) > WC found in ARMENIAN (see example in Sec. 1.3), GREEK (see 1.3), MAN-DAIC ARAMAIC, and OLD SPANISH and PORTUGUESE. While this occurred in ARMENIAN when the vowel of the preceding syllable was <u>a</u>, in SPANISH and PORTUGUESE the range was extended to include all nonhigh vowels. Compare PORT. <u>coube</u> < LAT. <u>capuĩ</u> 'I took' and <u>caibo</u> < LAT. <u>capio</u> 'I take' (PORT. <u>i</u> and <u>u</u> represent semivowels here).

W + C > CW. Aside from <u>wr</u> > <u>rw</u> or <u>ru</u>, which constitutes a sub-type of VL > LV above, the only observed examples of this type show <u>y</u> as the semivowel. Thus in ZOQUE an original sequence <u>y + C</u> is morphophonemically subject to metathesis as follows: <u>y + t</u> > <u>t^y</u> initially and <u>yt^y</u> elsewhere; <u>y + T</u> (any other dental) > <u>T^y</u> every-where; <u>y + C</u> (any other C) > <u>Cy</u> initially, after nasals and vowels other than <u>e</u>. Metathesis also takes place across intervening <u>h</u>. Examples: <u>t^yatah</u> 'his father' < <u>y-tatah</u>, <u>poču?kumu</u> 'he went out running' < <u>poy-cu?kum-</u>, <u>nwyihtu</u> 'you walked' < <u>Ny-wiht-</u>, <u>kamah-čowa</u> 'oak-cotton gall' < <u>kamayh-cowa</u>. This type also appears in MIXE and YAGUA. In CASTILIAN SPANISH the earlier sequence *<u>yt</u> (< <u>kt</u>) yielded <u>č</u>: <u>fecho</u> ~ <u>hecho</u> vs. ARAGONESE and PORTU-GUESE <u>feito</u> 'done, fact.'

F + L > LF. In CORNISH <u>θl</u> in final position following a vowel was subject to metathesis: <u>whelth</u> 'narration' vs. <u>whethlow</u> (pl.). Compare GALLIC <u>chwedl</u>. In OLD ICELANDIC we find: <u>bílda</u> 'ax' < *<u>bídla</u>, <u>alfe</u> 'force' < *<u>afle</u>, et al. Additional examples may be found in GAELIC, SPANISH, PORTUGUESE, PERSIAN and OLD ENGLISH.

P + L > LP. In CAMPIDANIAN SARDINIAN the original sequence PL metathesized intervocalically: <u>arbili</u> < <u>aprile</u> 'April,' <u>sorgu</u> < <u>socru</u> 'mother-in-law.' In OLD ENGLISH this occurred in word-final position: <u>seld</u> < <u>setl</u> 'seat.' In OLD ARMENIAN this was a systematic device for eliminating initial and medial clusters with liquids by redistribution of their members: <u>ełbayr</u> 'brother' (with prothetic vowel and <u>r</u>-dissimilation, cf. LAT. <u>fráter</u> and example in Sec. 1.3), <u>k'irtn</u> 'sweat' (cf. GREEK <u>hidrós</u>). Further examples

of this type may be found in ILOKO, some INDONESIAN languages
(e.g. TOBA), OLD FRENCH and SPANISH, and as a recurrent
drift throughout the history of IRISH from the OLD IRISH period up
to the present.

P + N > NP. Many of the examples of this type appear in some
of the older INDO-EUROPEAN languages or groups, especially
SANSKRIT, GREEK, LATIN and BALTIC, in connection with the
nasal presents and nouns derived from them: SKT. limpámi, LITH.
limpù vs. OCS prilǐ(p)nǫ (from *leip- 'smear, stick'); LAT. fundus,
GREEK púndaks vs. SKT. budhnás 'bottom' (note also ENGLISH
bottom, GERMAN Boden). Examples of this type may also be found
in ILOKO and OLD SPANISH.

2.2 Types without resonants

P + S > SP. Extremely common in the present sample, this type
is particularly well represented in many INDO-EUROPEAN and
SEMITIC languages. In BIBLICAL HEBREW when the 3rd sg. perf.
refl. prefix hit- was added to stems with initial sibilants, metathesis took place: hištammer 'he watched himself' < *hit-šammer,
hizdakkex 'he purified himself' < *hit-zakkex. Loan words beginning with ps- in LOW LATIN were regularly subject to metathesis:
spyche (GREEK psykhḗ), spitacus (GREEK psittakós). Similarly,
in VULGAR FRENCH word-final -ks, largely in learned terms, is
transposed: tasque vs. STANDARD FRENCH taxe, lusque vs. luxe.

S + P > PS. The inverse of the immediately preceding this type
does not appear to be as common as the former nor as regular.
However, in LITHUANIAN verbs descended from INDO-EUROPEAN
presents in *-sko, metathesis regularly occurs before the dentals
of the infinitive (-ti) and future (-s) suffixes: drěks 'tear (fut.)'
vs. drěskia (3rd pres.), réikšti 'to mean' vs. reiškė (3rd pret.).
While examples of metathesis of an original sequence composed of
dental (or alveolar) stop + sibilant are fairly abundant: SAVOYARD
initial st < *ts < LAT. c[k] as in stanta 'sing' < cantare, MANDAIC
estar vs. SYRIAC ette' sar (Macuch 1965: 90, no glosses) as a result of syncope of the vowel and glottal stop due to shift of stress to
the suffix vowel, OCS meštǫ 'I throw' < *metšǫ < *metyǫ , I find no
examples of the converse. Thus there seems to be a general preference for clusters of the type sibilant + dental stop over those with
the inverse order. This observation leads to a tentative universal:
clusters with the order dental (or alveolar) stop + sibilant (i.e.
spirant) may metathesize but those with the inverse order do not.
The more interesting generalization to the effect that dental + sibilant

implies the presence of sibilant + dental may prove to be valid for phonological (as opposed to phonetic) clusters if dental, alveolar and palatal affricates are viewed as unit phonemes.

h + P   Ph.   This type has already been cited for KOREAN (see Sec. 1. 3). According to Cho (1967), the analogous metathesis of ? + voiceless plain stop or s̲ also occurs in KOREAN in certain verb forms and in substantival compounds: na:tk̓ari 'haystack'< na:t-?-kari, is̓ol 'toothbrush' i-?-sor. However, this analysis rests on the positing of a suffix -? "...whose morphological meaning is emphatic compounding..." (p. 150), a view that differs from that of other KOREAN scholars. Of course, what is of immediate interest to us in the present context is the possibility that such metatheses may on occasion be the sources of or at least contributing factors to the origins of aspirated and glottalized consonants. Compare also Bartholomae's Law in SANSKRIT and GREEK (see Sec. 2.4).

C + h > hC.   In MANDAIC ARAMAIC many class III verbs originally had h̲ (< ẖ) as third radical. Some of these lost h, some tended to retain it in "protected" position before t̲ or n̲ of the verbal suffix, and still others retained it by metathesis with the second radical: pāhra 'he flies' (cf. SYRIAC pāraḥ), mehš̓ī 'he measured it' (cf. SYRIAC mašḥēh). Particularly noteworthy is the fact that, although there appear to be no restrictions on the nature of the second radical, liquids are most often involved. With the exception of poholθa 'worship' (cf. also pihla and SYRIAC plaḥ),[6] all forms cited by Macuch (1965: especially pp. 85, 86, 88) show contiguous metathesis. Kiparsky (1967: 621) proposes an earlier, indirectly attested metathesis of this kind for PROTO-GREEK: LESBIAN ékrinna ~ ATTIC, et al. ékrīna 'judged' < *ekrihna < *ekrinha < *ekrinsa, LESBIAN and THESSALIAN krínnō ~ ATTIC, et al. krīnō 'judge' < *krihnō < *krinhō < *krinyō, which exactly parallels the y̲-metathesis in that language (see Sec. 1. 3).

2.3 Quantitative metathesis

This type differs in substance from those just described but not in principle. There are undoubtedly a number of formally distinct subtypes but only two of these appear in the present sample. In ATTIC and IONIC GREEK the earlier sequence ēo > eō as a result of the regular shortening of vowels before vowels (and semi-

---

[6]Malone (1971), however, refers to this root as "exceptionally nonmetathesizing" citing Classical polhā́nā 'worship.'

vowels): IONIC teθneótes 'the dead' < teθnḗ(w)ótes, ATTIC hippéōs
'horseman (gen. sg.)' < hippḗ(w)os. In this case, metathesis served
to preserve the overall quantity of the original vocalic sequence
following operation of the earlier vowel-shortening rule. In SIERRA
MIWOK simple, regular verb stems have three or four different
allomorphs depending in part on the syllabic shape of the basic
present form and otherwise determined by occurrence with the future or recent past suffixes, the habitual or iterative suffixes, or
in the syntactically identifiable environments of infinitive, denomi-
native verb or deverbative noun (the latter three morphologically
marked by stem-internal metathesis). Disyllabic present stems,
regardless of their internal sequential arrangements of consonants,
vowels and length, thus assume the same distinct canonical shapes
in each of the three relevant environments, e.g. tuya·ŋ- (pres.) ~
tuyaŋ· - (fut./past) ~ tuy·aŋ - (hab./iter.) ~ tuyŋa- (inf./deverb. or
denom.) 'jump.' Aside from the VC > CV metathesis in the second
syllable of the fourth form, there are rather complex metatheses
of syllable quantity that serve to distinguish one form from another.
CV or stem-final CVC constitute short syllables; all other sequences
are long (length is construed as a consonant). Thus the first (base)
form is composed of a short + a long syllable (CV·C), the second
short + long (CVC·), the third long (CVC) + short (·VC) and the last
long (CVC) + short (CV). This kind of metathesis depends on a
quantitative interplay between alternating long and short stem syllables, each of which may be represented by one of two (short) or
more (long) forms. The system is in part morphophonemic (with
accompanying suffixes), in part morphological (without suffixes).
In the latter instance, the formal differences between two or more
stem allomorphs serve to mark a grammatical contrast: ?umču
'winter' (stem 4) < ?umu·č 'approach winter' (stem 1). Although
the causes may differ, quantitative and syllabic metathesis are
formally but slightly different aspects of the same phenomenon.
Thus the OLD FRENCH syllabic metathesis (Sec. 1.3) involved
shortening and desonorization of o̲ simultaneously with lengthening
and sonorization of i̲.

2.4 Noncontiguous types

Up to this point, we have limited the discussion to contiguous
metathesis. The remainder of this section will be devoted to cases
of noncontiguous metathesis. Generally speaking, the latter appear
to be less systematic than the former, although there are still many
examples of systematic noncontiguous metathesis. If this observation should be validated by a larger sample than the present one,
it would point to a direct relationship between systematicity -- and

probably proneness to metathesis — and contiguity of the two elements involved in reciprocal metathesis. Following criteria of selection for noncontiguous types similar to those applied to contiguous ones, I will discuss here only those that are either frequent and systematic or are of additional typological interest.

$V_1 \ldots V_2 > V_2 \ldots V_1$. This type occurs frequently in INDONESIAN. Thus in some MADAGASCAN dialects, an original *ikur 'tail' (cf. also MALAYAN ikur) > uhi (< earlier ukir).

Simple metathesis of liquids. In BAGNÈRES-DE-LUCHON the liquid of a noninitial sequence of stop + liquid was regularly shifted to the corresponding postocclusive position in the originally initial syllable: trende 'tender' < *tendro < VULG.LAT. teneru, esplingo 'pin' < *espingla < spinula. While the noninitial cluster str was not affected by this metathesis, the analogous spr was: brespes 'vespers' < *bespras < vesperas. A similar instance of the same formal type reported by Grammont (p. 347), also systematically applied, is from the speech of an infant (from 20 to 22 months) based on STANDARD FRENCH. In this case the subject avoided cluster-final syllable-initial r, except word-initially, and syllable-final r: vrente 'belly' for ventre, proter 'carry' for porter.

Reciprocal metathesis of liquids. This kind is found in a number of different subtypes. In GAYO, for example, the widespread INDONESIAN type consisting of metathesis of the second and third consonants of the word affects all original sequences of $1V_2r$: INDONESIAN *tĕlur > GAYO tĕrul 'egg.' In LOWER LEONESE (BRETON) r...l > l...r due to the analogous product of a regressive r-dissimilation (i.e. r...r > l...r): melver 'to die' < mervel, teûler 'to throw' (cf. LEON. teûrel), blérim 'grindstone' < brélim. Similarly in SPANISH we find milagro 'miracle' < O.SPAN. miraglo, palabra < parabla, etc. The formally related type n...l > l...n is found in several languages, e.g. PROVENÇAL culugno 'distaff' (cf. LANGUEDOC, GASCON cunulho, FRENCH quenouille) or lèuno 'the void' ~ nèulo (< nebula).

Reciprocal metathesis of nasals. Throughout AUSTRONESIAN an active-passive contrast is marked by prefixes that alternate with infixes of the same or similar shape. Thus in TAGALOG the active um- and passive in- prefixes are infixed before stems with initial consonants: íbig vs. umíbig 'wish' but súlat vs. sumúlat 'write.' Some stems beginning with resonants (vowel, l or y) take ni-, an interverted variant of in-: niunáhan 'was preceded by' but ináral 'was taught.' This same alternation in the prefixal allomorphs of

the passive is also found in ILOKO and NGGELA while the mu-
allomorph of the active prefix occurs in NIAS and MENTAWAY.
In the BRETON spoken at Vannes combined contiguous metathesis
and subsequent (?) anaptyxis have produced forms like kanivet
'cobweb' (cf. LEON. kefniden 'spider') and kinivy 'moss' (O.LEON.
kifny).

Reciprocal metathesis of spirants. In the meridional FRENCH
spoken in the neighborhood of Agde and in the FRENCH-based
CARIBBEAN CREOLE spoken in Dominica when s and š of STAND-
ARD FRENCH occur in the same syllable in that order, metathesis
is the rule: AGDE šes for FRENCH sèche 'dries,' šus for souche
'stump;' DOMINICA šasfam for sage-femme 'midwife.' Parallel-
ing the contiguous type PS > SP noted above is a noncontiguous type
with the same formal characteristics. In the PORTUGUESE of the
Algarve, for instance, we find due to the analogical influence of the
common prefixes es and estra- forms like: espetola < pistola 'pis-
tol' and estrapôr < traspôr 'fade away, set (of the sun).'

Simple metathesis of aspiration. In MARATHI aspirated stops
in word-final position would normally lose the component of aspiration due to the relatively weak articulation characteristic of that
position. Instead, aspiration is preserved by a metathesis to word-
initial position: khāṃk 'armpit' < kāṃkh, homṭ < omṭh. This regular
process has produced a tendency to shift word-medial aspiration to
initial position as well: mhais 'buffalo' (SKT. mahiṣī), phattar
'stone'< earlier patthar.   Cases of apparent aspirate metathesis
are found in SANSKRIT and ANCIENT GREEK as a result of the
operation of two different phonological processes. Thus Bartholomae's Law accounts for a shift of aspiration due presumably to the
inadmissibility of a sequence of aspirated stop + obstruent. Briefly
stated, when such a cluster arises due to morphological juxtaposition, the aspirated release shifts to cluster-final position: IE
*kʷṇthskŏ > *kʷṇtskhŏ > PROTO-GREEK *pátskho > GREEK páskho
'I suffer' vs. páthos 'suffering, disease,' IE *lubhtós > SKT. lubdhás
'covetous' vs. SKT. lubhyāmi 'I yearn.' The other case is Grassmann's Law which describes a process of dissimilation: no syllable
may begin and end with aspirated stops, and when two successive
syllables begin with aspirated stops, the first of them to appear in
the string is deaspirated. However, this rule is subject to various
kinds of interference from other processes. For example, in the
SANSKRIT reduplicated present of a verb such as dhā- 'put, place,'
the first dual active indicative is dadhvás < *dhadhvas in accordance
with the rule but the third dual is dhattás < *dhadhtas rather than the
expected *daddhás which both Bartholomae's and Grassmann's Laws

would have yielded. Similarly the earlier mentioned GREEK thríks (nom. sg.) < *thríkhs vs. trikhós (gen. sg.) < *thrikhós shows apparent metathesis within the paradigm actually due to dissimilation.

Reciprocal metathesis of obstruents. Most of the examples of this type seem to be sporadic. However, there is the case of the FRENCH child already mentioned (see note 3) and the somewhat unique instance of mazaguin [maezaegɛ̃] independently evolved in popular, infant and dialectal (e.g. BEARNAIS and GASCON) FRENCH from magasin.[7]

3. Cause and Effect

As early as 1900, Wechssler (pp. 496-7) suggested that a more fruitful approach to the problem of determining the status of metathesis than a purely formal one would be a classification based on the effects of metathesis on syllabic structure.[8] With particular attention to the situation in WESTERN ROMANCE, he speculated that the ultimate causes of metathesis were to be discovered in the replacement of a rarer with a commoner pattern of ordering and in lingering substratum influence. I quite agree that both premises are valid although of course the second one can only be invoked where applicable. However, examination of the more immediate causes of metathesis can be expected to shed some light on the interrelations between that process and others while providing support for the underlying cause. Therefore in this section we will attempt to investigate as well as we can, given the available information, those conditions that have resulted in metathesis in some of the languages sampled.

3.1 Reduction

Of all the phonological, grammatical and lexico-semantic processes responsible for metathesis, various kinds of reduction phenomena figure as the most important in terms of the present sample. For our purposes, these may be divided into two

---

[7] As I was composing this paper, Karl Zimmer informed me that his son Paul (age 3.2 years at the time) said maezaegín for magazine.

[8] This led him to the general conclusion that: "Der Grund des Vorgangs [metathesis] ist stets, dass dem Sprechenden die Reihenfolge der Laute und die Silbentrennung ungewohnt sind und daher Mühe machen." (op. cit., p. 497).

categories: <u>imminent</u> and <u>actual</u> reduction. With the former, a process of or tendency toward reduction is arrested or prevented by metathesis of the reduction-prone segment or feature with another one; with the latter, the fait accompli of reduction triggers metathesis, usually simultaneously. Thus in the first instance, metathesis serves as a vaccine or preventive medicine and in the second as a therapeutic device.

3.1.1 <u>Imminent reduction</u>   The tendency toward apocope of un-accented final vowels frequently leads to metathesis with the pre-ceding consonant. ROTUMAN provides an excellent illustration of this kind of development, not only because of the metathesis involved but also because of related developments leading to umlaut and vowel syncope. Due to an original penult stress in most words which was shifted to the ultima before certain enclitics, completive (i.e. def-inite) phase forms retained final vowels whereas in the incompletive phase the unstressed final was subject to different developments depending on the nature of both the original (i.e. completive form) ultima and penult vowels. As noted earlier (Sec. 2.1) if the ultima was lower than the penult, the former metathesized with the pre-ceding consonant: <u>hoas</u>[9]< <u>hosa</u> 'flower,' <u>tiok</u>< <u>tiko</u> 'flesh.' If the ultima was a front or high vowel and nonidentical with the penult, an umlauted vowel was the result, in accordance with the following formulas: 1) back vowel + <u>i</u> > front rounded: <u>füt</u>< <u>futi</u> 'to pull,' <u>höt</u> < <u>hoti</u> 'to embark,' <u>marɜr</u>< <u>marari</u> 'smooth;' 2) unrounded non-high vowel + <u>u</u> > rounded: <u>ʔöf</u> < <u>ʔefu</u> 'bamboo,' <u>hɔg</u>< <u>hagu</u> 'to awaken;' 3) nonhigh back vowel + <u>e</u> > front: <u>mɜs</u>< <u>mose</u> 'to sleep,' <u>laej</u> < <u>laje</u> 'coral.' All remaining combinations resulted in syncope (or apocope?) of the ultima: 1) when both vowels were identical: <u>hag</u>< <u>haga</u> 'to feed,' <u>fuʔ</u> < <u>fuʔu</u> 'to stay;' 2) when the ultima was as high as or higher than the penult: <u>ʔaf</u>< <u>ʔafo</u> 'basket,' <u>fol</u>< <u>folu</u> 'three,' <u>heʔ</u>< <u>heʔo</u> 'to call.' All three processes are clearly relatable if for umlaut and syncope an earlier stage of metathesis is posited (see Biggs 1959: 25 and 1965: 388-9): <u>füt</u> < *<u>fuit</u>. Thus metathesis served to preserve most of those vowels that might otherwise have been lost in unstressed final position. Furthermore, the secondary umlauting produced five new vowel phonemes, doubling the original five-vowel system. The grammatical contrast completive-incom-pletive, earlier syntactically marked by enclitics or postposed de-terminers, is now marked by stem allomorphy. A very similar

---

[9]Vowel sequences resulting from metathesis are analyzed by Biggs (1959: 25) as semivowel + vowel: <u>hwas</u> for <u>hoas</u>, <u>tyok</u> for <u>tiok</u>, etc.

situation existed in GERMANIC with i̠-umlaut forms like OLD
ENGLISH f̠e̠t̠ < *f̠o̠t̠ < *f̠o̠i̠t̠ (?) < GMC. *f̠o̠ti̠(z). The threat of syncope in post-tonic position also produced metathesis and subsequent
umlaut in WESTERN ROMANCE. Developments in IBERIAN are
of particular interest since the PORTUGUESE forms often show
the products of metathesis vis-à-vis the equivalent SPANISH forms
which show the later stage of umlaut. The process is especially
noticeable in the descendants of LATIN -i̠o̠ presents and -u̠i̠ per-
fects: PORT. c̠a̠i̠b̠o̠, O. SPAN. q̠u̠e̠p̠o̠ (< *c̠a̠y̠p̠o̠) < LAT. c̠a̠p̠i̠o̠ 'I
take;' PORT. s̠o̠u̠b̠e̠, O. SPAN. s̠o̠p̠e̠ (< *s̠a̠w̠p̠i̠) < LAT. sapu̠ï 'I know.'
The tendency still exists; compare VULG. SPANISH n̠a̠i̠d̠e̠ for n̠a̠d̠i̠e̠
'no one.' See also the above-cited examples from OLD FRENCH
(Sec. 2.1). In IBERIAN metathesis was probably abetted by the
process of diphthongization and fracture of accented vowels that
was taking place at the same time. In any event, metathesis had
the effect of preserving unstressed high vowels that might not
otherwise have survived. Additional examples of this type of metathesis brought on by similar circumstances have been referred
to above in OLD ARMENIAN, ATTIC and IONIC GREEK (Sec. 1.3)
and MANDAIC ARAMAIC (cf. s̠e̠y̠n̠ā̠ < s̠a̠n̠y̠ā̠ 'ugly,' q̠e̠y̠n̠a̠ < q̠a̠n̠y̠a̠
'reed' — this occurred only with an original sequence of sonorant
+ y̠).

Another formal type that tends to be preserved by metathesis
is aspiration or h̠. In ANCIENT GREEK h̠ (< IE *s̠) was lost
intervocalically but retained initially before a vowel. When the
preterite augment e̠- was prefixed to an h̠- stem, metathesis
occurred: h̠e̠i̠p̠ómē̠n 'we followed' < *e̠h̠e̠p̠ōmā̠n, h̠e̠ĩr̠p̠o̠n 'they
crept' < *e̠h̠e̠r̠p̠o̠n. Compare also h̠i̠e̠r̠ós 'sacred' < *i̠h̠e̠r̠ós. Thus
the effect of the metathesis was to prevent the loss of intervocalic
h̠. In OLD ARMENIAN one of the sources of the voiceless aspirates in initial position was through metathesis. INDO-EUROPEAN
initial *s̠ before vowel was lost in ARMENIAN except in two instances where it became h̠: *s̠p̠ > p̠ʻ as in p̠ʻoit̠ʻ 'haste' (cf. GK.
s̠p̠o̠u̠d̠ḗ), apparently via *h̠p̠ > *p̠h̠, and *s̠w̠ > k̠ʻ as in k̠ʻoir 'sister'
< *s̠w̠e̠s̠ōr, via *h̠w̠ > *w̠h̠ > *g̠h̠ > *k̠h̠ (intervocalic *s̠ also lost).
In much the same way, imminent loss of syllable-final h̠ in KO-
REAN was avoided and additional voiceless aspirates produced
(see Sec. 1.3). In MARATHI threatened loss of word-final aspiration and subsequent metathesis to word-initial position, followed
by the analogical shift of word-medial aspiration (see Sec. 2.4),
have the ultimate effect of altering the distribution of h̠ and the
aspirated occlusives. The MANDAIC ARAMAIC example cited
in Sec. 2.2 appears to have been provoked in part by word-final
zeroing of h̠ and in part by vowel syncope between the second and
third radicals.

The alternating AUSTRONESIAN prefix and infix allomorphs referred to earlier (Sec. 2.4) should also be considered for possible inclusion in the present causal category. As Brandstetter (1916: 322) noted: "Most commonly a word is abbreviated at the beginning, less often at the end, and least frequently in its interior. ...In ACHINESE in consequence of the accentuation of the last syllable, the first syllable of many WB's [word bases] is dropped. ...In CHAM we meet with similar abbreviations..." [capitals mine]. Furthermore, the syllable preceding the accented syllable is weaker than the one following it. The accent is usually on the penult or ultima of the word base and when a prefix is appended, the accent remains on the appropriate word-base syllable. With few isolated exceptions, AUSTRONESIAN languages allow only one consonant word-initially. Some languages allow one, others two consonants intervocalically and these are limited to nasal + stop or stop + stop (due to reduplication). The general tendency toward word-initial apheresis appears to have triggered metathesis of the prefixes. Since initial consonant clusters are not permitted, the infixes could only assume the VC-form, which explains why the prefixes are found in some languages with both CV- and VC- allomorphs as opposed to -VC- for the infixes.

In CLASSICAL LATIN loan words with initial ps-, the inadmissible cluster was resolved by reduction: sabulum 'sand' < GREEK psámmos. However, as noted above (Sec. 2.2), the same difficulty was resolved in LOW LATIN by means of metathesis, thus preserving both phonemes of the original cluster.

The quantitative metathesis found in ATTIC and IONIC GREEK (Sec. 2.2) provides a slightly different example of the preventive function of metathesis. Here the dilemma created by the prior shortening of vowels before vowels vis-à-vis the tendency to preserve syllabic length was resolved by compensatory lengthening of the second vowel; in other words, first partial reduction, then increment, the combined effect being quantitative metathesis.

3.1.2 Actual reduction   Most of the instances of contiguous metathesis examined in the course of the present study were immediately caused by vowel syncope. The syncope itself was often brought on by accentual conditions. In CHOWCHILA YOKUTS, for example, with few isolated exceptions word stress is on the penult. Thus when either -haliy̆ consequent adjunctive or -ilin intensive possessor is suffixed to the absolutive stem (i.e. in word-final position) stress falls on the first syllable of the suffix. However, when the suffix precedes an oblique suffix (all examples show vocalic

forms) stress is retained on the original penult of the absolutive
and the new penult (the second vowel of the disyllabic suffix) is
syncopated with metathesis of the two resonants of the resultant
inadmissible cluster: xamithaliy̆ (abs.) vs. xamithay̆la (obj., glottalization lost postconsonantally) 'scythe,' pittilin (abs.) vs. pattinli
(obj.) 'one with many body lice.' In Sec. 1.3 we noted a metathesis
of the second and third consonants of the stem before -án ~ -ín in
TAGALOG. A similar case found in the VIGAN dialect of ILOKO,
another INDONESIAN language, shows metathesis of {t, k} + sonorant
and change of stop to ? before stressed final syllables: lim?út <
*likmút, lin?áw < *litnáw, daldal?ág < *datdatlág (cited without
glosses, Vanoverbergh 1955?:40). Stress may occur on either the
ultima or the penult. Since the sources of INDONESIAN medial
consonant clusters are either reduplication or syllable-final nasal +
syllable-initial stop, it seems likely that there was originally an
intervening vowel which was syncopated due to a shift of stress to
the final syllable. While in the TAGALOG and ILOKO examples
the ultimate cause of syncope and metathesis was a progressive
shift of word stress, in ESKIMO (Sec. 1.3) the motivating factor
behind the same processes was regressive stress. The metathesis
of t + sibilant noted above (Sec. 2.2) in HEBREW also occurred in
PROTO-ARAMAIC. Over a millenium after that metathesis, a
second one of precisely the same nature recurred in early MAN-
DAIC as a result of stress-induced syncope. In ARAMAIC word
stress shifts to the ultima in strong verbs and pretonic short vowels
in open syllables are lost. While other ARAMAIC dialects either
retained an original interconsonantal ?ə, vocalized it to e or assimilated ? to the preceding consonant, MANDAIC syncopated the entire
sequence with the shift of stress to the ultima thus recreating the
necessary condition (contiguity of the two consonants) for metathesis:
?esθár (later ésθar) < *?eθsár < PRE-MANDAIC *?eθ?əsár 'he was
bound.' Note that before unstressed inflectional suffixes, ? is lost
but the vowel is retained, hence no metathesis: metesrín (cf. SY-
RIAC mete'srín).

Metathesis in consonant clusters resulting from syncope that
does not stem from accentual shifts is found with a high degree of
systematicity in OLD SPANISH. In VULGAR LATIN posttonic
vowels other than a between liquids or s and occlusives or between
k and l disappeared. This syncope was later generalized to post-
tonic vowels between any two consonants (although the remaining
environments consisted largely of prevocalic occlusive and post-
vocalic liquid: letra < littera, pueblo < populu, etc.) in SPANISH
and most of WESTERN ROMANCE. Clusters of the general type
occlusive + liquid thus produced, many of which had no counterpart

in the pre-existing canons of the language, were subject to epenthesis, when the occlusive was a nasal: hombro 'shoulder' < humeru,
temblar 'to tremble' < tremulare, engendrar 'to engender' < in-
generare, fortition in the case of r: honr̃ar 'to honor' < honorare,
or metathesis: viernes 'Friday' < Veneris '[day] of Venus,' colmo
'limit (of one's patience, etc.)' < cumulu, cernada ~ cendrada 'ashes
(for soap)' < *cinerata, but also: cabildo 'municipal council' < capi-
tulu, molde 'mold' < modulu (cf. OLD FRENCH espalde 'shoulder'
< spatula) and the analogous candado 'padlock' < catenatu with a
nasal instead of a liquid. Another instance of metathesis caused by
simple syncope appears to be the treatment of sequences of the type
V_1 + $?V_2$ (where + represents morpheme boundary) in ZOQUE. Glottal stop cannot figure as the final member of a consonant cluster.
Reduction of V_1, either through loss or semivocalization, is sometimes optional, its occurrence being directly correlated with high
frequency of occurrence of the particular sequence of morphemes
(vowel quality does not seem to figure as a causal factor). Once
either degree of reduction has taken place, metathesis is obligatory:
?ʌ?wa?ɲi 'to that one' < ?ʌ?wa-?aɲi, mina? 'come now!' < *mina?? <
minʌ-?a?, ?upa?u 'it foamed' < ?upu-?ah.

Apocope of final vowels appears to have triggered metathesis of
an earlier spirant + liquid in PERSIAN: surx 'red' vs. ZEND suxra,
žarf 'deep' vs. ZEND jafra, ars 'tears' vs. ZEND asru. In MAN-
DAIC ARAMAIC borrowed ARABIC nouns of the general type
$FV^CL(un)$, especially those with liquid third radicals, were subject
to apheresis of the tanwīn (-un nom. indef.) thus producing an inadmissible final cluster which was usually resolved by inserting an
anaptyctic vowel between the two consonants: ꜥomer 'age' ꜥumr(un),
baɣal 'mule' < baġl(un), but some forms with liquid resolved the
cluster by metathesis: qolf 'lock' < qufl(un).

For examples of metathesis of two adjacent vowels induced by
prior syncope of an intervening occlusive, compare OLD FRENCH
tuile (Sec. 1. 3) and OLD PORTUGUESE doesto (Sec. 2.1).

3.2 Open syllable canon

In languages undergoing a change from a mixed or relatively free
syllable canon to a purely or largely open syllable type there are
bound to be rather far-reaching repercussions in sequential arrangements of phonemes. This general process sometimes engenders
metathesis. A particularly appropriate case in point is related to
the development of open syllables in SOUTH SLAVIC. The general
nature of the process is manifest in terms of a number of developments:

—Medial sequences consisting of stop + occlusive or s̲ across original syllable boundary lost the syllable-final stop. The remaining analogous sequences: stop + liquid or semivowel, g̲n̲ and s̲ + stop, which also occurred commonly in word-initial position, were retained as comparable syllable-initial clusters, hence giving rise to a certain amount of resyllabification. Probably in part related to this process is the metathesis of COMMON SLAVIC *t̲y̲ and *d̲y̲ to OCS š̲t̲ and ž̲d̲ respectively: OCS m̲e̲ž̲d̲a̲ 'boundary' < *m̲e̲d̲y̲ā̲ (cf. SKT. m̲á̲d̲h̲y̲ā̲), OCS m̲e̲š̲t̲ǫ̲ 'I throw' < *m̲e̲t̲y̲ą̲.

— Sequences of e̲ + semivowel in the same syllable were subjected to syllabic metathesis; a̲ + semivowel resulted in syncope of a̲ and vocalization of the semivowel. Thus falling diphthongs were eliminated.

— Sequences of vowel + liquid were eliminated in various ways. Thus high vowel (phonetically short) +liquid remained largely unchanged but mid vowel (phonetically long) + liquid, which exceeded the permitted syllabic quantity, developed in one of the following ways: 1) resyllabification, the liquid offglide becoming a syllable-initial consonant; 2) vowel syncope with syllabification and lengthening of the liquid (which could be construed as a special type of quantitative metathesis); 3) loss of the liquid; 4) metathesis of the two segments resulting in a nonsyllabic liquid + a (phonetically) long vowel: OCS p̲r̲a̲s̲ę̲ 'suckling pig' (cf. LAT. p̲o̲r̲c̲u̲s̲, LITH. pãr̲s̲z̲a̲s̲), OCS v̲l̲ě̲k̲ą̲ 'I draw' (cf. GK. h̲é̲l̲k̲ō̲ < *w̲é̲l̲k̲ō̲, LITH. v̲e̲ł̲k̲ù̲). Thus liquid metathesis as well as the earlier syllabic type are not merely isolated phenomena, rather two of the several links in the chain of developments that ultimately led to a uniform open syllable canon.

In many respects, the evolution of open syllables in FRENCH is strikingly similar to the corresponding processing in SLAVIC. Geminates were simplified, thus eliminating many syllable-final consonants; syllable-final s̲ was lost; postvocalic nasals were lost with accompanying nasalization of the preceding vowel (this was also the case with some VN-sequences in SOUTH SLAVIC); and falling diphthongs were removed by syllabic metathesis (see examples in Sec. 2.1). Probably connected with this chain of events was the tendency to metathesize syllable-final r̲ with the preceding vowel: b̲r̲e̲b̲i̲s̲ 'young lamb' < v̲e̲r̲v̲e̲c̲e̲m̲, t̲r̲o̲u̲b̲l̲e̲r̲ 'to disturb, worry' < t̲o̲r̲b̲l̲e̲r̲, f̲r̲o̲m̲a̲g̲e̲ 'cheese' < *f̲o̲r̲m̲a̲t̲i̲c̲u̲m̲, but compare also the counterexample: p̲o̲u̲r̲ 'for' < p̲r̲o̲. Compare also the structurally similar examples cited above (Sec. 2.4) from MODERN FRENCH infant speech.

The effects of an open syllable canon on CLASSICAL ARMENIAN were even further complicated by the fact that the only permitted consonant clusters were composed of sibilant + stop (post-vocalic preconsonantal resonants functioned as offglides). Some of the devices used to eliminate clusters were reduction of stops in original stop + liquid clusters, but also metathesis of the latter (see Sec. 2.2) and earlier *tθ (< IE *dt) which became wt via *θt: giwt 'find' < *widtim, various reductions and assimilations of occlusive + semivowel or s̰, metathesis of *k̂s (> *sk > c^h): vec^h 'six' < *wesk̂ (cf. GK. 'wéks, LAT. sex) vs. veš-tasan 'sixteen' *wek̂s-, prothesis before sibilants or liquids, anaptyxis between consonant and nasal, and metathesis of hw (see Sec. 3.1.1).

3.3 Phonotactic constraints

Many metatheses are automatically induced by morphological juxtaposition that results in phonotactically inadmissible sequences. That is, metathesis constitutes a regular morphophonemic process in such instances. Still other metatheses are brought about by the introduction of noncanonic sequences in loan words. The same, of course, applies to much of what has been discussed in 3.1 and 3.2. Thus the morphophonemic function of metathesis represents a superficial level, usually symptomatic of more general, underlying causes. Unfortunately, for many of the systematic cases of metathesis examined pertinent historical information as to the ultimate causes of the process was lacking and I can only attempt to relate some of these to probable causes in terms of formal and distributional resemblances to historically better attested cases of metathesis.

In SOPRASELVA ITALIAN and BAGNÈRES-DE-LUCHON cluster-final syllable-initial r metathesizes with a following unstressed vowel unless the preceding consonants are s + dental stop: SOP. fartont vs. ITAL. frattanto 'meanwhile,' SOP. parneit vs. ITAL. prendete 'you take,' SOP. parschun vs. ITAL. prigione 'prison;' B-D-L. pardyó 'meadow near a stable' < *pratina (cf. SPAN. prado), burdakin 'buskin' (cf. FRENCH brodequin). In BAGNÈRES-DE-LUCHON this metathesis is not only inhibited by a following continuant; the latter provokes an inverse metathesis: grumant 'gourmand,' presék < *persicu 'peach.' A closely related kind of metathesis is found in CAMPIDANIAN SARDINIAN (see examples in 2.1). In all three languages there is a preference for single-consonant initials in syllables. In most INDONESIAN languages clusters composed of stop + liquid are non-native. Thus when such sequences enter the language in loan words they are automatically metathesized: TOBA purti 'daughter'   SKT. putrī.

The noncontiguous metathesis r...l > l...r noted above in SPANISH may be in part due to the analogous product of r-dissim-ilation but is also attributable to the substitutionof the more fre-quently occurring gr for the disfavored gl. Thus word-initial gl > l and medial kl > x, tl and dl > ld (3.1.2), but initial bl remained intact (compare also O. SPAN. blago 'staff' < *baglo < *baculu). The formally similar case from BAGNÈRES-DE-LUCHON discussed in 2.4 seems to stem from different reasons -- anticipation of an awkward cluster which, especially because of its would-be occurrence in pretonic position, looms large in the awareness of the speaker. Presumably in an unconscious effort to deal with the difficulty as soon as possible, the original cluster is resolved by simple liquid metathesis to an initial postocclusive position. This, of course, does not resolve the problem; it merely prolongs the solution which, in BAGNÈRES-DE-LUCHON, was forthcoming at a later date in the form of a second metathesis (contiguous); Carbyewles ~Crabyewles 'Crabioules (name of a mountain)' < *capriolas. Anticipation may also explain in part forms like SPANISH blago.

Aside from cases of liquid metathesis produced by infrequent clusters, there are many instances where the phonotactics of the language in question absolutely rule out certain clusters containing liquids. For example, in ARMORICAN BRETON an initial cluster composed of gw + liquid was inadmissible, hence: gloan 'wool' vs. GALLIC gwlân, groac'h 'old women' vs. GALLIC gwrâch (o = w). In AMUZGO (Mexico) while lk may occur intervocalically, it does not initially. Furthermore, most initial sequences of l + C are reduced to single consonants through reduction and assimilation and initial clusters of more than two consonants are not tolerated. The plural of nouns is marked by a prefix l- (cf. l?a (pl.) vs. c?a (sg.) 'chile') which, when it precedes a k-initial noun stem,[10] trig-gers metathesis of the prefix to the nearest acceptable position, following the vowel of the stem-initial syllable: kalue? (pl.) vs. kacue? (sg.) 'dog' (lc > l), kalhɔ (pl.) vs. kachɔ (sg.) 'scorpion.' Thus the plural marker is preserved in the form of an infix. The above-noted ZOQUE restriction on the occurrence of ? as final member of clusters which, subsequent to vowel syncope, was re-sponsible for metathesis of ? +vowel also accounts for the trans-position of nasals or liquids followed by ?: pʌ?nis 'of the man'< pʌn-?is, luga?royh 'at the place'< lugar-?oyh (< SPAN.).

10
   I have no information as to the participation of other stops in this metathesis.

The cause of metathesis of root-final consonant + n-suffix that took place in INDO-EUROPEAN (cf. 2.2) probably lies in a phonological analogy based on the fairly common nasal + stop type of cluster as opposed to the relatively infrequent inverse. This impression is supported by the fact that only root-final stops or spirants are found in the metathesized nasal-infix class while the corresponding nasal-suffix class has finals in liquids, nasals or vowels but none in stops or spirants. Also a few related roots have a voiceless root-final corresponding to the voiced stop appearing in the nasal-infix present: LAT. pangō 'I fasten' but pāx, pācis 'cord,' pandere 'to extend' but patēre 'to be open, exposed.'

One of the effects of the phonotactically determined metathesis of yC sequences in ZOQUE and MIXE (2.1) is the creation of additional occurrences of the palatalized consonants. In these languages palatalization constitutes an important process and the phonemic system is richly endowed with a full complement of palatals. One wonders whether this sort of metathesis might not have originally given rise to these consonants or at least have been partially responsible. Alternatively, the existence of the palatals could have supplied added impetus to the metathesis. The latter explanation seems to be appropriate to the development of CASTILIAN č < *yt < LAT. kt (2.1).

Analogous to the ZOQUE situation is the KOREAN metathesis of ʔ + occlusive (2.2) which theoretically could have been a factor in the origin of the glottalized series or, conversely, could have been favored by the presence of glottalized consonants.

Most of the examples of PS > SP encountered in this study appear to be attributable to inadmissible or unfamiliar clusters. This is also true of some instances of the converse SP > PS but others may be due to other causes. Thus in WEST SAXON this metathesis generally occurred between stressed vowel and back vowel or between stressed back vowel and consonant or word juncture: dixas (pl.) vs. disc (nom. sg.), disces (gen.sg.) 'dish,' tūx < tūsc 'tusk,' hūxlic 'scornful' (cf. OLD ENGLISH hūsc, MIDDLE HIGH GERMAN hosche 'scorn'). However, considerable intraparadigmatic leveling eventually nullified the original phonological conditions.

3.4 Miscellaneous causes

The motivating factors discussed in this section, while just as different from one another as any of them are from those already discussed, are lumped together here simply because they are either uniquely or infrequently represented in the present sample.

3.4.1 Attraction and repulsion   In late MIDDLE ENGLISH the sequence ri of stressed syllables tended to metathesize to ər before dentals: bird, dirt, third < brid, drit, þridde, and also: burn, burst < brennen, bresten.   Similarly, in LATIN ri in initial syllables before dentals was often metathesized: tertius < *tritios 'third,' cernō < *crinō 'I separate,' while lu underwent the same process before labials and velars: pulmō < *plumō 'lung,' dulcis < *dlukwis 'sweet.' Such cases illustrate the contributory effect of a process which may be called attraction. Thus while in both ENG-LISH and LATIN initial clusters of the type Cr- were admissible, a postvocalic dental apparently exerted a strong attraction on the phonetically similar prevocalic r. This may have been strengthened by the general preference for simpler initial consonantal margins and the availability of a common CVC syllable type. On the other hand, an inverse metathesis occurred in ENGLISH when Vr was followed by a velar spirant + t: wright, wrought vs. WEST SAXON wyrhta, worhte, and fright < fyrʒt, bright vs. OLD ENGLISH berht. Here the dissimilarity of articulation between r and h[x] evidently produced a repulsion of r in spite of the other pressures to retain r in postvocalic position. Another case in point is found in the FRENCH spoken in the suburbs of Le Havre when rV > Vr before dentals: kɛrsõ < cresson 'watercress,' gɛrlote < grelotter 'to shiver,' but Vr > rV before m and v: pruvie < épervier 'hawk.'

3.4.2 Anticipation   When a sound that would normally occur later in a given string is shifted to a prior position due to an ex-pected (subconsciously so) difficulty of articulation inherent in the original sequence, the metathesis is anticipatory. This essentially psychological explanation has been applied to cases of noncontiguous metathesis like the one cited from BAGNÈRES-DE-LUCHON (2.4) but also by many scholars to the C + V > VC (where V may be either vowel or semivowel) type noted in ROTUMAN and IBERIAN (2.1; 3.1.1) among others, the P + L > LP of ARMENIAN (2.1) or the P + N > NP type found, for instance, in INDO-EUROPEAN (2.2; 3.3). Wherever possible I have preferred to seek a phonologically based explanation for such phenomena; however, anticipation cannot be entirely ruled out as a contributing factor in many cases. This is perhaps more obvious in certain kinds of slips and spoonerisms. All the types that have been dubbed anticipatory are of necessity closely analogous to regressive assimilations or dissimilations. Thus the ultimate development of the C + V > VC type is umlaut.

3.4.3 <u>Diphthongization</u>   When metathesis incidentally results
in the formation of a diphthong or diphthongs that are not only current in the language but are themselves in process of spreading,
the analogical pressure of diphthongization may be a contributing
factor in some cases of metathesis. While I cannot state with
certainty that this was so in SPANISH (3.1.1), PORTUGUESE (2.1;
3.1.1), FRENCH (2.1) and GREEK (1.3), it does seem likely in all
of them. It may also have been true of MANDAIC ARAMAIC (3.1.1)
but I have no information on the relative chronology of metathesis
and monophthongization which apparently began rather early in the
history of that language.

3.4.4 <u>Dissimilation</u>   Another kind of phonological analogy which
may induce or at least contribute to metathesis is the presence in
the language of a strong dissimilatory pattern as was suggested for
SPANISH <u>milagro</u> < *<u>miraglo</u> above. In MANDAIC ARAMAIC qua-
driliteral roots containing two <u>l</u>'s generally dissimilate the first to
<u>r</u>: <u>garg(ə)la</u> 'wheel' vs. HEBREW <u>galgal</u>. A number of loan words
show metathesis of the type <u>l...r</u> > <u>r...l</u>: <u>šarwāla</u> (~<u>šalwāra</u>) <
PERS. <u>šalwār</u> 'trousers,' <u>raškal</u> (~<u>laškar</u>) < PERS. <u>laškær</u> 'army.'
Thus the products of metathesis and dissimilation (the more regular
process of the two in this instance) converge, the former modeled
after the latter.

3.4.5 <u>Quantitative equilibrium</u>   The preservation of syllable-
or word-internal quantity may be a factor in some cases of metathesis. Thus in the SLAVIC liquid metathesis (3.2), in addition to
the pressure of the open-syllable tendency, syllabic quantity could
not exceed the length of a long vowel. The syllabic nucleus mid
vowel (phonetically long or half-long) + liquid (offglide) hence constituted an untenable sequence, resolved in part by metathesis.
The ATTIC and IONIC metathesis $\bar{e}o$ > $e\bar{o}$ is another case in point
involving a shift of vowel length instead of transposition of syllabic
segments. The "length mobile," to coin a phrase, of MIWOK, along
with the VC > CV metathesis characteristic of fourth base forms
is indicative of a system which tends to preserve a balance of alternating long and short syllables within the word.

4. <u>Summary</u>

In the course of the present paper, we have proposed and offered
evidence in support of the following theses:

1. Metathesis preserves segments or features that would other-
    wise have been subject to loss or mutation through: syncope,

apocope or apheresis; assimilation; epenthesis or anaptyxis;
consonantization; fortition; palatalization; or monophthongization.

2. Since metathesis is usually recessive in comparison with
   most other processes, it is prone to greater interference
   from more dominant ones like: reduction, assimilation,
   dissimilation, and epenthesis or anaptyxis.

3. Generally speaking, the more resonant a segment is the
   greater the likelihood it will be affected by metathesis given
   the necessary conditions therefor. The sole exception
   involves an original sequence of voiceless stop + sibilant,
   metathesis of which was found to be fairly common and
   widespread.

Examination of causes and effects showed that, while the superficial cause of most metatheses is conversion of a phonologically
inadmissible or disfavored sequence into an acceptable one, the
underlying causes that produce such sequences fall into a number
of different types:

1. The threatened or imminent reduction of a segment or feature
   (by apocope, syncope, or apheresis) due to accentual shift
   or other ultimate causes.

2. The actual reduction of a segment or feature, also due to
   accentual shift, grammatical process (e.g. the elimination
   of the tanwīn in ARABIC loans in MANDAIC ARAMAIC, see
   3.1.2), lenition (of intervocalic occlusives in OLD FRENCH
   and OLD PORTUGUESE, see 2.1) or other causes.

3. A change from a mixed to a predominantly open syllable
   canon produced by several processes, one of which is metathesis. The ultimate cause of such a change would seem
   to stem from unusually weak articulation of syllable-final
   consonants.

4. The necessity for maintaining a specific syllable or word
   quantity.

5. Phonological constraints of a morphophonemic nature violated by accidents of morphological juxtaposition, introduction of noncanonical sequences in loan words, etc.

6. Analogical processes reflecting existing models of dissimilation, palatalization, glottalization, diphthongization, favored
sequences, and the like.

7. Attraction and repulsion of phonetically similar and dissimilar,
respectively, segments or features.

8. Anticipation of disfavored sequences.

BIBLIOGRAPHY

General

Bawden, H . Heath.   1900.   A study of lapses. Psychological
Review, Monograph Supplements 3, No. 4. New York.

Bolinger, D.L.   1968.   Aspects of language. Harcourt, Brace and
World.

Chao, Y.R. 1968.   Language and symbolic systems. Cambridge.

Curtius, Georg and K. Brugmann.   1876.   Studien zur griechischen
und lateinischen Grammatik. Leipzig.

Goldstein, Kurt. 1948.   Language and language disturbances.
New York.

Greenberg, J.H. 1965.   Some generalizations concerning initial
and final consonant sequences. Linguistics 18. 5-34.

Hale, H.E.   1846.   Ethnography and philology. U.S. Exploring
Expedition, v. 6. Philadelphia.

Jakobson, R. 1941.   Kindersprache, Aphasie und allgemeine Lautgesetze. Språkvetenskapliga Sällskapets i Uppsala, Förhandlingar,
1-83.

Koutsoudas, A. 1966.   Writing transformational grammars: an
introduction. New York.

Lehmann, W.P. 1962.   Historical linguistics: an introduction.
New York.

Leopold, W. F. 1953-4. Patterning in children's language learning. Language Learning 5. 1-14.

Malkiel, Y. 1968. Essays on linguistic themes. Berkeley/Los Angeles.

Martinet, A. 1955. L'économie des changements phonétiques. Berne.

Meringer, R. 1908. Aus dem Leben der Sprache: Versprechen, Kindersprache, Nachahmungstrieb. Berlin.

_____, and K. Mayer. 1895. Versprechen und Verlesen. Stuttgart.

Merrifield, W.R., Naish, Rensch and Story. 1967. Laboratory manual for morphology and syntax (revised). Santa Ana.

Nandris, O. 1953. Compensation, quantité et attention. Orbis 2. 501-17.

Passy, P. 1890. Etudes sur les changements phonétiques et leurs caractères généraux. Paris.

Paul, H. 1888. Principles of the history of language [Prinzipien der Sprachgeschichte], tr. from 2nd ed. London.

Sievers, E. 1901. Grundzüge der Phonetik zur Einführung in das Studium der Lautlehre der indogermanischen Sprachen. Leipzig.

Sommerfelt, A. 1962. Diachronic and synchronic aspects of language. Janua Linguarum, series maior 7.

Sturtevant, E.H. 1947. An introduction to linguistic science. New Haven.

Trnka, B. 1936. General laws of phonemic combinations. TCLP 6. 57-62.

Trubetzkoy, N.S. 1969. Principles of phonology [Grundzüge der Phonologie]. Berkeley/Los Angeles.

Wechssler, E. 1900. Giebt es Lautgesetze? In: Forschungen zur romanischen Philologie, Festgabe für Hermann Suchier, 349-538. Halle.

Weinreich, U. 1957. On the description of phonic interference.
Word 13. 1-11.

Select

Biggs, B. 1959. Rotuman vowels and their history. Te Reo 2.
24-6.

Grammont, M. 1950. Traité de phonétique (4th ed.). Paris.

Haudricourt, A.G. 1957-8. La phonologie des voyelles en rotumien.
Bulletin de la Société de Linguistique de Paris 53. 268-72.

Kiparsky, P. 1967. Sonorant clusters in Greek. Lg 43. 619-35.

Malone, J.L. 1971. Systematic metathesis in Mandaic. Lg 47.
394-415.

Merzdorf, R. 1876. Vocalverkürzung vor Vocalen und quantitative
Metathesis im Ionischen. Studien zur griechischen und lateinischen Grammatik (ed. by Curtius and Brugmann) 9. 201-44.

Michels, V. 1894. Metathesis im Indogermanischen. Indogermanische Forschungen 4. 58-65.

Sørensen, H.C. 1952. Die sogenannte Liquidmetathese im Slav-
ischen. Acta Linguistica 7. 40-61.

Thompson, L.C. and M.T. 1969. Metathesis as a grammatical
device. IJAL 35. 213-19.

Žuravlev, V. 1967. Pererazloženie differencijal'nix priznakov kak
osnovoj istočnik fonologičeskix izmenenij. Linguistic Studies
Presented to André Martinet: Part One, General linguistics,
ed. by A. Juilland. Word 23. 588-91.

Specific Languages and Groups

Abaev, V.I. 1964. A grammatical sketch of Ossetic. IJAL Pub. 35.

Andersen, H. 1969. Lenition in Common Slavic. Lg 45. 553-74.

Barker, M.A.R. 1964. Klamath grammar. University of California
Publication in Linguistics [UCPL] 32.

Bennett, W.H. 1966. The Germanic evidence for Bartholomae's Law. Lg 42. 733-7.

Bergmann, H-G. 1963. Vergleichende Untersuchungen über die Sprache der Osterinsel. Doctoral dissertation, Universität Hamburg.

Biggs, B. 1965. Direct and indirect inheritance in Rotuman. Lingua 14. 383-415.

Blake, F. 1925. A grammar of the Tagalog language. New Haven.

Bloomfield, L. 1962. The Menomini language. New Haven.

Brandstetter, R. 1916. An introduction to Indonesian linguistics. Asiatic Society Monograph 15. London.

Broadbent, S. 1964. The Southern Sierra Miwok language. UCPL 38.

_____, and C. Callaghan. 1960. Comparative Miwok: a preliminary survey. IJAL 26. 301-16.

Brook, G.L. 1958. A history of the English language. New York.

Broussard, J.F. 1942. Louisiana Creole dialect. Baton Rouge.

Brugmann, K. 1888. Elements of the comparative grammar of the Indo-Germanic languages. New York.

Buck, C.D. 1955. The Greek dialects. Chicago.

Bunzel, R.L. 1933-8. Zuni. Handbook of American Indian Languages, Part 3. 385-514. Hamburg/New York.

Cho, S-B. 1967. A phonological study of Korean. Uppsala.

Crawford, J.C. 1963. Totontepec Mixe phonotagmemics. Norman, Okla.

Churchward, C.M. 1940. Rotuman grammar and dictionary. Sydney.

Deck, N.C. 1933-4. Grammar of the language spoken by the Kwara'ae people of Mala, British Solomon Islands. Journal of the Polynesian Society [JPS] 42. 33-48, 133-44, 241-56 and 43. 1-16.

Dobson, E.J. 1957. English pronunciation 1500-1700. Oxford.

Faine, J. 1937. Philologie créole (2nd ed.). Port-au-Prince.

_____. 1939. Le créole dans l'univers: I, le mauricien. Port-au-Prince.

Fox, C.E. 1950. Some notes on Nggela grammar. JPS 59. 135-69.

Frachtenberg, L.J. 1922. Siuslawan (Lower Umpqua). Handbook of American Indian Languages, Part 2. 431-630. Washington, D.C.

Freeland, L.S. 1951. Language of the Sierra Miwok. Indiana University Publications in Anthropology and Linguistics Mem. 6.

Grace, G.W. 1959. The position of the Polynesian languages within the Austronesian (Malayo-Polynesian) language family. Indiana University Publications in Anthropology and Linguistics Mem. 16.

Grammont, M. 1916. Notes de phonétique générale [on Armenian]. Mémoire de la Société de Linguistique de Paris 20. 213-59.

Haas, M.R. 1941. The classification of the Muskogean languages. Language, culture and personality, ed. by L. Spier, 41-56. Menasha, Wisconsin.

_____. 1945. Dialects of the Muskogee language. IJAL 11. 69-74.

Hale, W.G. and C.D. Buck. 1966. A Latin grammar. University, Alabama.

Hirt, H. 1927. Indogermanische Grammatik. Heidelberg.

Householder, F., A. Koutsoudas, and K. Kazazis. 1964. Reference grammar of Literary Dhimotiki. IJAL Pub. 31.

Hymes, D.H. 1964. Evidence for Penutian in lexical sets with initial *c- and *s-. IJAL 30. 213-42.

Jakobson, R. 1929. Remarques sur l'évolution phonologique du russe comparée à celle des autres langues slaves. Travaux du Cercle Linguistique de Prague 2.

Jespersen, O. 1961. A modern English grammar on historical principles. London.

Kent, R.G. 1946. The forms of Latin, a descriptive and historical morphology. Baltimore.

Lehmann, W.P. 1952. Proto-Indo-European phonology. Austin.

Lehnert, M. 1965. Altenglisches Elementarbuch (6th ed.). Berlin.

MacDonald, D. 1907. The Oceanic languages: their grammatical structure, vocabulary and origin. London.

Macuch, R. 1965. Handbook of Classical and Modern Mandaic. Berlin.

Marr, N. and M. Brière. 1931. La langue géorgienne. Paris.

Meillet, A. 1936. Esquisse d'une grammaire comparée de l'arménien classique (2nd ed.). Vienne.

_____. 1964. Introduction à l'étude comparative des langues indo-européennes. University, Alabama.

Menéndez Pidal, R. 1949. Manual de gramática histórica española (8th ed.). Madrid.

Menger, L.E. 1904. The Anglo-Norman dialect. New York.

Newman, S. 1944. Yokuts language of California. Viking Fund Publications in Anthropology 2. New York.

Partridge, E. 1934. Slang today and yesterday. New York.

Pischel, R. 1965. Comparative grammar of the Prākrit languages (2nd ed.). Delhi/Varanasi/Patna.

Pope, M.K. 1934. From Latin to modern French with especial consideration of Anglo-Norman. Manchester.

Posner, R. 1961. Consonantal dissimilation in the Romance languages. Oxford.

Powlison, Paul S. 1962. Palatalization portmanteaus in Yagua (Peba-Yaguan). Word 18. 280-99.

Pratt, G. 1862. A Samoan dictionary. Samoa.

Ramstedt, G.J. 1939. A Korean grammar. Helsinki.

Senn, A. 1966. Handbuch der litauischen Sprache, I. Heidelberg.

Shipley, W. F. 1966. The relation of Klamath to California Penutian. Lg 42. 489-98.

Skeats, W. W. 1958. An etymological dictionary of the English language (4th ed.). Oxford.

Tanquerey, F. J. 1915. L'évolution du verbe en anglo-français. Paris.

Taylor, F. W. 1959. A practical Hausa grammar (2nd ed.). Oxford.

Thalbitzer, W. 1911. Eskimo. Handbook of American Indian Languages, Part 1. 967-1069. Washington, D. C.

Thumb, A. 1964. A handbook of the Modern Greek language. Chicago.

Thurneysen, R. 1961. A grammar of Old Irish. Dublin.

Till, W. C. 1961. Koptische Grammatik. Leipzig.

Vanoverbergh, M. 1955? Iloko grammar. Bauko, Philippines.

Voegelin, C. F. 1935. Tübatulabal grammar. University of California Publications in American Archeology and Ethnology 34.

_____, and F. M. 1962. Typological and comparative grammar of Uto-Aztecan: I. IJAL Mem. 17.

Weyhe, H. 1908. Zur Palatalisierung von in- und auslautendem sk im Altenglischen. Englische Studien 39. 161-88.

Whitney, W. D. 1960. Sanskrit grammar (2nd ed.). Cambridge, Mass.

Winter, W. 1962. Problems of Armenian phonology III. Lg 38. 254-62.

Wonderly, W. L. 1951. Zoque II: phonemes and morphophonemes. IJAL 17. 105-36.

Phonological Processes

CHARLES A. FERGUSON

ABSTRACT

Two phonological processes, (1) d →ð and (2) ð → d, are
examined in some detail in SPANISH, GREEK, ENGLISH, ARABIC,
ARAMAIC, and DANISH in order to see the kinds of universals which
extensive cross-linguistic investigation of phonological processes
might yield. For each language, attention is paid to directionality
of the process(es), degree of inclusiveness in larger schemata,
favoring conditions for operation of the process(es), genetic vs.
areal diffusion, and evidence from language acquisition and pidginization. Process (1) tends to be highly context-sensitive (assimilatory), part of a larger schema of spirantization, and readily
diffusable. Process (2) tends to be relatively context-free (simplifying), restricted or isolated, and frequent in language acquisition
and pidginization. In both, the stop is favored initially and after
nasal, the spirant postvocalically. Exceptions to the proposed
'universals' are noted. The research strategy is found productive,
but requires reliable, comparable processual data (including diachronic changes) from many languages.

CONTENTS

O. One of the great merits of the approach of generative phonology
has been its recognition of the importance of processes and its
development of a convenient notation for representing them. The
notion of 'phonological process' will be understood in this paper in
the very broad sense of any relation between two sounds (or
stretches of sound, or components of sound) which may be regarded
as the one sound 'becoming' the other under specifiable (or conjec-
turable) conditions, in other words any relation which may be
represented by the formula

$$X \rightarrow Y / Z$$

read X becomes Y under conditions Z, where X and Y represent
sounds of human language.[1]

The explicit use of process formulations in the study of the sound
systems of human language goes back at least as far as the Sanskrit
grammarian Panini several centuries B.C.E., and the period of
great growth of the discipline of linguistics in the latter half of the
nineteenth century was largely focussed on diachronic processes in
language. More recently, however, the period dominated by structuralism c. 1930-1960, with its emphasis on synchronic description,
made less use of processual analyses of language. The period of
generative grammar has not only turned attention back to processes
but also, by its notations and formal models, has made possible a
much broader, more precise, and in a number of ways more sophisticated, consideration of processes.

In the broad sense of phonological process which is used here, a
relation of the type $X \rightarrow Y/Z$ may refer to a diachronic process,
i.e. an overt behavioral change in real time, whether in a whole
language community, the language development of a particular child,
or in a pathological change which takes place in an individual; it
may refer to any of a variety of synchronic processes which reflect
mental processes of the language user or simply descriptive conventions of the analyst. A process may be within a single language
system, as in the examples just given, or it may be between systems,

---

[1]This paper was written in part with support from grants of the
National Science Foundation for the Phonology Archiving Project
and the Child Phonology Project at Stanford University (NSF grants
BNS76-16825 and BNS76-08968). The thoughts in it obviously owe
much to Greenberg's state-and-process model and his views of language universals, but the sense of process used here is broader
than he usually deals with and the sample of languages is smaller
than he would be satisfied with.

as when the relation is between the source of a borrowing and the
borrowed form, between the target of a language learner and the
actual production, or between a systematic error and its correction. This list of types is not meant to suggest a classification but
merely to illustrate the range of possibilities.

The approach which will be taken in this paper is to examine in
some detail two well-known processes in a number of languages.
The two processes are:

(1)   d → ǧ / P   (2)   ð → d / Q

These are equally examples of phonological processes, and the
specified conditions P and Q vary by language, period of history,
phonological environment, grammatical environment, dialect,
register, speed of speech, and other dimensions. Also, both processes can be found in language interference, child language acquisition, aphasia, and other special conditions. A detailed examination of these two related processes will lead us to some general
points about phonological processes from the perspective of language universals.[2]

The languages to be examined are SPANISH and GREEK, which
exemplify d →ǧ; ARABIC and ENGLISH, which exemplify ð → d;
and ARAMAIC and DANISH, which exemplify both. These languages
are limited to two families, INDO-EUROPEAN and SEMITIC, and
certainly do not constitute an adequate sample for establishing universals, but they will be sufficient to suggest the kinds of universals
which such study can lead to.

Before proceeding to the study of our example processes, it is
useful to clarify some of the basic notions involved in the concept
of phonological process. First, there is the basic question of
directionality: Which way should the arrow point? In many cases
the phenomena identified as exemplifying a particular process
X → Y/Z can also be represented as Y → X/Z'. For example,

---

[2]Conventions followed here in naming and discussing processes
include: ⌜X → Y⌝is identified as a process without regard to considerations of time, X > Y is a diachronic (or developmental)
change, X → Y is a synchronic alternation, and X ⇸ Y is a transfer from one language system to another (e.g. 'realization rule,'
interference, or adaptation). Changes 'take place,' alternations
'exist,' processes 'operate.'

if in a particular language every stem ends in a short vowel when it has no suffix and in a long vowel when it has a suffix, the state of affairs may be regarded as vowel shortening before word boundary or vowel lengthening before suffix. Typically the linguistic analyst prefers one formulation to the other and the preferred direction is held to be 'true' or 'correct.' The criteria for deciding on direc- tionality are varied and are often not made explicit. If the process is a diachronic one, the 'true' direction is determined by whether X or Y existed earlier in time. Thus, if the stems at an earlier stage in the language ended everywhere in long vowels and later on final vowels were shortened, the diachronic process is shortening. The same criterion of real-time congruence holds for other dia- chronic cases, such as child language development if analyzed as development of the child's own phonological system and not as pro- gressive approximation to the adult model. Similarly, if a process represents a matching between target and source or filter, as when the speaker of one language attempts to acquire another, the target is typically regarded as the input and the substitution or 'error' as the output of the process. Thus, if a speaker of German substitutes [z] for English [ð] under certain conditions, this is usually inter- preted as $\eth \rightarrow z$ rather than the reverse.

In most processes, however, the directionality is more problem- atic, and arguments as to which is the basic allophone or underlying segment or input feature are in terms of generality of statement, 'markedness,' 'naturalness,' relative frequency, systemic centrality, or rule ordering. As sound changes take place in a language the synchronic directionality of a process may change. For example, a particular language at Stage I has a lateral phoneme /l/ with relatively little allophonic variation, then at Stage II has velarized variants in post-vocalic tautosyllabic positions, and finally at Stage III the velarized variants have spread to all positions but non- velarized values appear in careful speech and singing. In that case the synchronic process might well be identified as $l \rightarrow ł$ at Stage II but as $ł \rightarrow l$ at Stage III. In the examination of our sample processes in different languages the issue of directionality will be discussed in each case.

A second basic question is how inclusive a process is, i.e. where it fits in a scale ranging from a highly restricted, isolated phono- logical phenomenon in a particular individual at a particular time to a pervasive phenomenon affecting many sounds in a number of languages and recurrent in their historical development over long periods of time. Given the broad definition of process that we are using here, a process may fit anywhere on such a scale, and the

investigator is obligated to specify the degree of inclusiveness as
part of the characterization of the process, since facts of this sort
must enter into any productive general classification or explanation
of phonological processes. A process may be seen as part of a
larger process (or set of processes) in at least three ways. It may
be one of a set of similar processes with sufficient similarities in
input, output, and conditions that they may be regarded as a single
larger process, a 'schema.' Or, it may be one of a set of dissimilar processes which lead to the same outcome, a 'conspiracy.'
Or, it may have a 'feeding' or 'bleeding' relation to another process
such that the output of one is the input of the other or some similar
sequential dependency. The question of inclusiveness cannot be
elaborated here, but in the examination of our sample processes
in different languages, the question of inclusiveness in a larger
schema will be discussed in each case. One particular possibility,
the parallel with $\ulcorner$t → θ$\urcorner$ and $\ulcorner$θ → t$\urcorner$ will always be taken into
account.

A third basic question about processes is the locus, i.e. what
is the time period and the language (or idiolect, register, group of
languages, slip of the tongue ...) in which a process is operative.
As with the question of inclusiveness, the range of possible answers
is wide. For example, the process $\ulcorner$s → tʃ$\urcorner$ is well attested in
Spanish baby talk and Japanese baby talk (Ferguson 1977) but is
relatively rare in languages and does not seem to occur either as
a recurrent feature of 'drift' in related languages or as an areal
trait, whereas the merger of x̱ and ħ̱ is a characteristic of Semitic
languages, having occurred at various times in different Semitic
languages, sometimes more than once in the same language (e.g.
x̱ > ħ̱, totally merging with ħ̱ in Hebrew, then ħ̱ > x̱, merging with
a new x̱ < ḵ). In each case here the genetic and areal incidence of
the process will be noted.

Finally, the notion of a hierarchy of conditions must be clarified.
Although processes are usually represented as X → Y/Z where Z
is stated in absolute terms, it is typically the case that Z is variable. If the process in question is a diachronic change, it may
happen that it takes place first under the set of conditions Z_1, then
under another, Z_2, and so on until Z_n. If the process is a synchronic alternation it may be implemented under condition Z_1 only
in allegro speech, Z_2 in ordinary conversation, and Z_3 only in very
careful lento speech. Conditions may vary in many ways so that a
hierarchy is evident, and one of the important approaches to the
understanding of phonological processes is the specification of
'favoring conditions' (cf. Labov's variable rules in which the Z's

may be quantified either relatively or in absolute percentages, e.g. Labov 1969). Conditions for a process may be in terms of social context, grammatical categories, phonetic conditions, or even the physical state of the speaker; in this paper only three types of conditions will be mentioned in connection with the processes studied: phonetic (only immediate phonetic environment in the stream of speech), lexical (types of words most favorable to the process), and social (only in terms of user evaluations such as 'better,' more correct,' etc.).

Since a full range of data for each language and each process cannot be available, generally the only phenomena reported here besides diachronic change and synchronic alternation of the usual kinds will be language acquisition and pidginization.

SPANISH

1. SPANISH offers a well-known and well-documented example of the process ⌜d → ð⌝, which may be examined from several perspectives. It is a diachronic change which began centuries ago and is still continuing, appearing at the present time (i) as an allophonic positional alternation in which, roughly speaking, [ð] is postvocalic within the same phonological phrase and [d] occurs elsewhere, and (ii) as fluctuations in pronunciation ('free variation') [d] ~ [ð] ~ ∅ in which [d] represents the most careful and ∅ the least careful pronunciation; regional dialect differences and lexical conditions are evident both in the details of positional variation and in the 'free variation.'

Since the early centuries of the present era, speakers of LATIN/SPANISH on the Iberian peninsula (and wherever SPANISH has spread) have tended to fluctuate between [d] and [ð] post-vocalically in pronouncing words of their language, and the tendency has been for the fluctuation to move from [d] to [ð] (and ultimately to ∅) so that words earlier pronounced predominantly with [d] come to be pronounced later with [ð] or ∅. This has happened with words which had [d] in LATIN (e.g. Lat audire 'to hear' > Sp oir); it has happened with words in which LATIN [t] had changed to [d] (e.g. Lat vita 'life' > Sp vida [ð]; it has happened with words in which Latin [d] had been lost and was restored by dialect borrowing or learned classicization (e.g. Lat nidu- 'nest' > OSp nio ModSp nido [ð]). Over and over again post-vocalic [d] has become [ð] or even ∅ in the Spanish-speaking world, and at the present time, as probably at any time for a long way in the past and for some indeterminate period in the future, an orderly allophonic alternation

with regional and lexical variability exists which etymological
study would show reflects successive operations of the process.
Harris (1969, 37-46) offers a convenient description of the present
synchronic alternation; the diachronic changes are given in traditional sources such as Menéndez Pidal (1962, 129-130, 171), which
also provides some additional details about the modern regional
and lexical fluctuations (99-103). A number of characteristics of
the Spanish case are of interest.

1.1 <u>Directionality</u>. In modern Spanish the phone [ð] is a little
more than twice as frequent as the phone [d] in text occurrence
(Delattre 1965, 95), which runs counter to some notions of markedness since many phonologists would regard [ð] as more marked
than [d], less common in the world's languages, acquired by
children later than [d], less stable, etc. In spite of the high frequency of [ð], the stop is usually regarded as the 'principal'
allophone or 'underlying' specification (i.e. the directionality is
from <u>d</u> to <u>ð̤</u>), perhaps partly for diachronic reasons, perhaps also
because it is the more careful pronunciation in cases of fluctuation
and because word-initial [d] is spirantized in close juncture with a
preceding vowel (e.g. <u>dama</u> 'lady' [d]: <u>la dama</u> 'the lady' [ð] more
often than an intervocalic [ð] is occluded in clarifying pronunciations (e.g. <u>lado</u> 'side' [ð]: <u>la-do</u> emphatic pronunciation with [d]).
Some arguments are of course in terms of descriptive simplicity,
i.e. number and complexity of rules required in the grammar. In
some dialectal varieties of Spanish the spirant value has been
extended to all positions and the stop value remains only as a 'free'
variant in positions where other variants have [d] regularly.
Analysts of such dialects have argued for a reversal in directionality (Hammond 1976, Timm 1976).

1.2 <u>Inclusiveness</u>. The process ⌜d → ð⌝ in Spanish is part of a
schema, a set of interrelated processes. Specifically it is one
item within one of three related general processes operating on
intervocalic consonants in LATIN/SPANISH:

(a) Voiceless stops become voiced.

(b) Geminates are simplified.

(c) Voiced stops are spirantized.

The details of these three processes are found in the handbooks.
It may be noted here that all Latin geminate consonants (obstruents
and sonorants) were simplified in SPANISH except for <u>ll</u> and <u>nn</u>

(which became the palatal [λ] and [ɲ] and <u>rr</u> (which has remained in contrast with <u>r</u> to the present time, with various phonetic values). Also, it is generally accepted that from Latin to present-day Spanish the voiceless stops have remained unaspirated (or 'short-lag' in voice-onset time) and the voiced stops in initial position pre-voiced, as in the other Romance languages today. It is generally assumed that (a) took place first, allowing 'space' for the output of change (b), and that (c) operated on the output of both (a) and (b). Learned classicisms in SPANISH have restored earlier voiceless stops in some instances so that pairs such as <u>natación</u> 'swimming' : <u>nadar</u> 'to swim' offer a synchronic reenactment of <u>t</u> > (<u>d</u> >)<u>ð̮</u>.

The process ⌐d →ð̮⌐in SPANISH is not paralleled by a process *⌐t → θ⌐, and in the larger schema of post-vocalic voicing and spirantization there is no trace of a process of spirantization operating directly on voiceless stops. The /θ/ of SPANISH is the outcome of a desibilation process from earlier /ts/ from LATIN /k/ before front vowels, and the two phones /θ/ and [ð] are not parallel in distribution, frequency of occurrence, or positional allophony. The devoicing process which operates on [ð] in final position and in clusters with following voiceless obstruent yields a devoiced [ð̥] which in some regions, styles of speech, or particular lexical items may be pronounced identically to /θ/ but often remains distinct from /θ/ or disappears altogether whereas /θ/ remains. In many varieties of Spanish /θ/ has fallen together completely with /s/.

It must also be noted that in the Middle Ages a set of voiced affricates and fricatives emerged in SPANISH only to become devoiced and merge together with their voiceless counterparts.

1.3 <u>Favoring conditions</u>. Like any other phonological process, SPANISH ⌐d →ð̮⌐is more likely to operate under some phonetic, lexical, and social conditions than under others, [3] and in characterizing the operation of a process in a language or in language in general, it is important to specify conditions which favor or inhibit it.

---

[3]Evidence that a given condition 'favors' the operation of a process may be of many kinds, e.g. the process operates first or more frequently under that condition or operates to completion rather than partially, or obligatorily rather than optionally.

(a) Phonetic. The process is most likely to operate intervocalically and least likely to operate after the nasal /n/ and lateral /l/.
It is more likely after a vowel and before a consonant or boundary
than in initial position. Thus 11 varieties of SPANISH have instances
of [d] after /n/ and /l/. All varieties of modern SPANISH show
some [ð] ~ ɣ alternation intervocalically, and initial [ð] as in some
Cuban and Mexican varieties (Hammond 1976) is relatively rare.

(b) Lexical. The process is most likely to occur in certain
high-frequency words (e.g. lado 'side,' usted 'you'), certain grammatical formatives (esp. the participial suffix -ado), and formulaic
expressions (e.g. verdad? 'right?'). In these words or morphemes the [ð] is pronounced very lightly or disappears altogether
in the ordinary conversational Spanish of educated speakers. Part
of the explanation for the lexical preferences may lie in the phonetic conditions (e.g. a-o, _#), but it must be noted that the weakening is less common in cases where ado is not the participial ending
and that in verdad used as the noun 'truth' the final [ð] is less
likely to be lost. For details cf. Menéndez Pidal (1962, 99-102).

(c) Social. Throughout the Spanish-speaking world whenever
there is alternation between [d] ~ [ð] or between [ð] ~ ɣ the weaker
alternant ([ð] and ɣ respectively) is interpreted as more casual,
less educated, and lower in social stratification, and vice versa.
If, for example, in a particular community the norm for a particular word in a particular style of speech is [ð], a weaker [ᵈ] or ɣ
may be regarded as substandard and a pronunciation with [d] may
be felt to be pedantic, affected, or foreign. (For a discussion of
this kind of scale cf. Ferguson 1972; Labov 1972.) If the operation
of the ⌜d → ð⌝ process in Spanish is seen as an ongoing diachronic
change, then it is change 'from below' in the Labov sense (Labov
1972).

1.4 Genetic vs. areal spread. Part of the total schema of
which ⌜d → ð⌝ is a part in LATIN/SPANISH, namely the voicing
of intervocalic voiceless obstruents and the simplification of geminates, is to some extent shared with other Romance languages,
but the spirantizing of voiced stops, which includes ⌜d → ð⌝, is
almost completely limited to certain areas of IBERO-ROMANCE,
and it is only there that voiced fricatives are in allophonic alternation with voiced stops rather than functioning as a phonologically
distinct series (cf. FRENCH v z ʒ : f s ʃ /. On the other hand,
spirantization of voiced stops is a process operative at various
periods in BASQUE and the CELTIC languages, and it seems
unlikely that this similarity is purely coincidental. Scholars do

not agree on the fact or direction of the influence or on the possibility of some other pre-Latin language(s) now extinct being the
ultimate source of the process in the area. Martinet in a series of
articles on gemination and spirantization (cf. esp. Martinet 1952)
makes a good case for areal diffusion even if his hypotheses are
not accepted in full. Even if the process of spirantization of voiced
stops should operate some day in a similar manner in other Romance
languages, it still seems likely that the incidence of spirantization
in IBERO-LATIN was triggered or reinforced by areal influence
('substratum') rather than being a natural continuation of processes
inherent in the structure of a related set of languages ('drift').

1.5 Acquisition and Pidginization. In spite of the meager amount
of published research on child phonology development in SPANISH,
the data available from studies of monolingual Mexican-American
and Mexican children made by the Child Phonology Project at Stanford allow some preliminary generalizations (for some of the relevant data and interpretations cf. Stoel 1974, Macken 1976). In
acquiring the intervocalic voiced fricatives of SPANISH, children
tend at an early stage, at least in production, to identify them with
liquids and semivowels /l r j w /. The [β] and [γ] are typically
represented by [w] and the others by [j], although there may be
considerable variation. In acquiring the initial voiced stops, which
are in general less frequent than the initial voiceless (unaspirated)
stops, the children at an early age tend to produce them also as
voiceless unaspirated stops. The point of greatest interest is that
as [β] and [γ] develop toward their adult models, [ð] tends to be
classed with the liquids. Typically [ð l ɾ r] of the adult model
are represented in some children's speech by lateral substitutions
and in other children's speech by voiced stop substitutions, and as
the sounds are differentiated the [ð] may go either with l or with the
r's before it is finally mastered. Recent studies of voice onset
time (VOT) in the acquisition of stops in ENGLISH and SPANISH
indicate that the principal difference between production of adult
/ptk/ and /bdg/ in initial position is not VOT as with English-
learning children but is the occurrence of spirantal variants for
the voiced series (Macken and Barton 1977a, 1977b).

Although there are not as many attested instances of the pidginization of SPANISH as there are of PORTUGUESE, FRENCH, and
ENGLISH, those pidgins or creoles which have been described show
the operation of ⌜ð → d⌝. The Spanish-based creoles in the
Philippines show [d] throughout for SPANISH [d] ~ [ð] (Frake 1962,
15), and Papiamentu also has stops for /bdg/ even in intervocalic
position (Baum 1976, 90).

GREEK

2. GREEK offers a well-known example of $\ulcorner d \rightarrow \eth \urcorner$ in the form of
a diachronic change which began long ago and has proceeded in
some respects farther than the change described above for SPANISH.
ANCIENT GREEK, as represented in particular by the 'CLASSICAL
ATTIC' spoken in Athens about 400 B.C.E., had three sets of stops,
voiceless unaspirated / p t k /, voiced / b d g /, and voiceless
aspirated / pʻ tʻ kʻ / (Allen 1968, Sommerstein 1972). In the
course of the history of the language, the voiceless unaspirated
remained largely intact whereas the other two sets spirantized.
Thus the Ancient dental series / t d tʻ / appears in MODERN GREEK
as / t ð θ / respectively (Warburton 1970, Newton 1972b). The
change d > ð has been almost complete in that the only position
in which [d] has remained is after n. Ancient nt has also become
nd, however, so that the Modern cluster nd represents a merger
of earlier nt and nd, and since nt was more common than nd in
ANCIENT GREEK, in fact most of the MODERN instances of nd
go back to nt. The voicing of t after n appears also as a synchronic
alternation t → d / n___ at certain boundaries, notably between
the accusative definite article to(n), ti(n), and a word beginning
with t- (ton 'the' + tópo ' place' → tondópo).

In words of GREEK origin [t] and [d] are thus in full complemen-
tation and the instances of [d] could be regarded as the output of
the voicing process operating on /t/. GREEK has, however, borrowed words from Turkish, Italian, and other languages, which
contain instances of d, and most dialects of MODERN GREEK have
instances of a /d/ from this source. Also, a process of nasal
loss before obstruent which is very widespread in the case of
(voiceless) fricatives and fairly common before (voiced) stops
results in examples of medial /d/ which are sometimes in free
variation with /nd/ but are in some instances regularly pronounced
without the nasal, depending on the dialect, the lexical item, and
the presence of a boundary (for detailed discussion cf. Newton
1972b, 93-99).

Thus, in MODERN GREEK /ð/ is a well-attested phoneme
occurring initially, intervocalically, and in some clusters, whereas
/d/ is a phoneme of limited distribution occurring chiefly in foreign loanwords, in the cluster /nd/, or as a singleton in variation
with /nd/; the frequency of /ð/ is close to three times that of /d/
(Householder et al. 1964, 7). There is almost no trace of the
diachronic change d > ð left in a synchronic alternation between
the two, and even in a style of generative phonology which posits

underlying phonemes as abstract as synchronic alternation will
allow, "It is doubtful, though, whether there is much point in
setting up a rule '[d] goes to [ð] except after a nasal'" (Newton
1972b, 3).

As mentioned, /ð/ is nearly three times as frequent as /d/
in MODERN GREEK. In this rather unusual phonological system
the voiced spirants / v ð z γ/ are all more frequent than any of
the voiced stops / b d g / and in each place of articulation the
spirant is more frequent than the corresponding stop, the /ð/
being more frequent than / d / by a larger factor than the other
pairs. The voiceless consonants present the mirror image: the
stops are more frequent than the spirants, and /t/ is more frequent than / θ / by a larger factor than the other pairs (Householder
et al. 1964, 4-8).[4] The most striking fact from the perspective of
this study is the asymmetry of θ : t and ð : d.

2.1 Directionality. The diachronic change d > ð has no converse
counterpart in GREEK, and as already noted there is little reason
for recognizing a synchronic process in either direction. The
next stage of the d > ð change is apparently ð > Ø, and the Southeastern dialects (Chios, Cyprus, the Dodecanese Islands including
Rhodes) show this process in full operation, not only as a diachronic
change (e.g. póði 'foot' > pói) but also as a synchronic alternation
at boundaries (e.g. na modal particle + ðóki 'he gives' → naóki
'let him give'). This process of voiced fricative deletion has been
complicated by additional processes of nasal contraction, glide
formation, etc. (e.g. súða 'sewer'→ sfa). For full discussion
cf. Newton 1972b, 60-72. Interestingly, though probably an accidental coincidence, this Southeastern area which seems to have
carried the process ⌐d → ð¬ furthest in MODERN GREEK is also
where the first ancient indication of spirantization of /d/ appeared,
in inscriptions on Rhodes which sometimes used the letter zeta in
place of delta in the 5th century B.C.E. (Schwyzer 1959, 233).

2.2 Inclusiveness. The process ⌐d → ð¬ in GREEK is part of
a schema, a set of interrelated diachronic changes. Specifically
it is one item within one of three related general processes operating on consonants in GREEK.

(a) Voiceless aspirated stops become spirants.

---

[4]The spirant /s/ does not fit this picture; it is highly frequent,
tying with /t/ as the most frequent of all the consonants.

(b) Voiced stops become spirants.

(c) Geminates are simplified.

The first of these is part of a larger process of psilosis or loss of aspiration. For pre-Greek times, i.e. before the attested Greek of inscriptions, linguists have reconstructed with confidence the widespread change of s > h so that the /h/ of ANCIENT GREEK is mostly a reflex of earlier /s/. This aspiration in turn was universally lost in MIDDLE GREEK times, as the change h > ʘ spread from East Ionian dialects to the rest of the Greek-speaking world. The aspiration (or voicelessness) which occurred with r (often earlier sr) and the aspiration in the series /pʻ tʻ kʻ /, which was often spelled with the same letter in early inscriptions, also was lost, and in the latter case the outcome was voiceless spirants. For details cf. Schwyzer 1959, 218-222.

It is interesting to note that the changes s > h and h > ʘ also took place in the history of Spanish, but in different order and at widely separated times. In the LATIN/SPANISH of the Iberian peninsula the changes f > h and h > ʘ took place very early and their outcomes are universal in SPANISH, but the changes s > h and again h > ʘ are now taking place in certain SPANISH dialects. The remarkably parallel changes of s > h and h > ʘ in SPANISH and GREEK are instructive. On the one hand, they suggest universal processes or possibilities of change in a particular configuration of changes (or 'drift') which includes loss of final consonants, spirantization of stops, and simplification of geminates. On the other hand, they show language specific details which in many instances do not seem to follow from the phonological structure of the respective languages. Thus, for example, in GREEK the s > h took place initially and intervocalically but not finally, whereas in SPANISH it is taking place first finally and then preconsonantally and only slowly spreading to intervocalic and initial positions.[5] For

---

[5]The few faint evidences of a new s > h > ʘ change in MODERN GREEK seem quite different in origin although perhaps uptimately similar in outcome. In a number of dialects s is lost by dissimilation in sequences with other sibilants, and the loss is sometimes generalized in particular verb paradigms (Newton 1972b, 83-87). Only in one isolated instance, a variety of GREEK spoken on Corsica, is there evidence of the SPANISH pattern of change where final -s is lost (Newton 1972b, 102).

comparable differences in the GREEK-SPANISH parallel loss of
final -n cf. Ferguson 1975.

In ANCIENT GREEK the simplification of geminates probably
began about 300 B.C.E. and was carried to completion over most
of the Greek-speaking world. This change in GREEK seems less
closely related to the spirantization processes than in SPANISH.
Geminate voiced stops were rare and in general / p t k / have not
been subject to intervocalic voicing in the history of Greek. The
Southeastern dialects, although farthest advanced in spirantization
as noted above, have been conservative in degemination, preserving earlier GREEK geminates and even extending gemination by
nasal assimilation, foreign loanwords and 'spontaneous gemination'
(Newton 1972b, 89-93). Perhaps the most fascinating aspect of the
new gemination is that it seems to be bringing Greek phonology
full circle by introducing voiceless aspirates. The new geminate
voiceless stops in CYPRIOT GREEK, for example, are aspirated,
and in initial position they have been shortened, thus restoring the
Ancient Greek three-way contrast: CYPRIOT GREEK tíxos 'wall':
dínno "I dress': t'éli 'wire.'[6] In this kind of modern GREEK,
however, only initial /t/ is common, the other obstruents of the
same series / t' d θ ð / all being in some way marginal, whereas
in ANCIENT GREEK /t/ was more frequent than /t' d/ but the
latter were both in the 'core' phonology and there were no fricatives
in the series.

2.3 Favoring conditions. The evidence for the operation of the
spirantization process in GREEK comes from variant spellings,
foreign transcriptions, and other difficult sources, and the evidence
is so fragmentary that it does not seem possible to decide which
phonetic, lexical, or social conditions were favorable to the change,
although such judgments can sometimes be made for other diachronic
changes in GREEK. One fact that stands out is the total resistance
to spirantization of d after n in every period of the history of
GREEK and in every dialect area. The only example of the chain
of processes ⌐d → ð → ₭⌐ which is now in operation and hence
offers data for analysis is the process ⌐ð → ₭⌐ in Southeastern

---

[6]The initial aspirates could be regarded as phonologically geminate, but this seems a little forced in view of the foreign loanwords (e.g. t'eli 'wire' < TURKISH tel) which have never been
geminate and the lack of morphophonemic alternations indicating
initial gemination.

dialects. From Newton's description of the local and stylistic
variation (Newton 1972a, 96-97, 105-107, 109-118) it is possible to
list the following conditions, which may have implications for the
process ⌜d → ð⌝ as well.

(a) Phonetic. Loss of ð̠ is more likely intervocalically than
initially, and loss of ð̠ is less likely than loss of v̠ and y̠ .

(b) Lexical. There is great lexical variation ranging from
nearly universal loss in y̠áð̠aros 'donkey' (y̠áros) and póð̠in
'foot' (póin) to nearly universal retention in poð̠ílaton 'bicycle.'
This variation is clearly related to the social factor of standardization.

(c) Social. The influence of the STANDARD DEMOTIC GREEK
of the mainland and the Katharevusa of the schools is an inhibiting
condition to the spirant loss in CYPRIOT GREEK. Since many of
the differences between STANDARD GREEK and CYPRIOT result
from recent diachronic changes in the latter, they may be regarded
as non-operation of the relevant processes, or in Newton's words
'standardization often takes the form of rule suspension' (Newton
1972a, 116).

2.4 <u>Genetic vs. areal spread</u>. The phonological changes in
GREEK, including d̠ > ð̠ , generally seem unconnected with changes
in the surrounding languages, but the presence of interdental
spirants in ALBANIAN (otherwise rare in EUROPEAN languages)
and the appearance of z̠ for d̠ in remnants of ancient INDO-
EUROPEAN languages in the area have led several authors to suggest an areal or substratal origin but this seems highly speculative.

2.5 <u>Acquisition and pidginization</u>. The substitutions for /ð/ in
the speech of young children have not been a topic for discussion as
such in treatments of GREEK language acquisition, but examples
occur in the literature and deserve mention. Hinofotis 1977 docu-
ments the late development of the interdentals: "/θ/ and /ð/ do
not appear as part of his speech at seventeen months" and "Theodore
was consistently producing all of the stop phonemes, voiced and
voiceless, with the exception of ... /g/" (91). Drachman and
Malikouti-Drachman 1973 and Drachman 1973a have only one clear
example of ⌜ð → d⌝, : ð̠éka 'ten' ⇸ d̠éka (102) but no examples
at all of ⌜d → ð⌝, and to this extent offer evidence about the operation of ⌜ð → d⌝ in acquisition. The process of substituting the stop
for the adult fricative is the converse of the spirantization process
which operated as a diachronic change in GREEK; the latter process

could be assumed to occur developmentally in the child as the early substitute [d] is replaced by the normal adult [ð], but this seems quite different from the 'natural' intervocalic spirantization of history. It must be noted also that a number of other substitutions for /ð/ occur in Greek acquisition, exemplifying other processes. The commonest seems to be lateralization ⌜ð → l⌝ as in epíði 'because' ⇁ epíli (102), although most of the examples involve possible consonant harmony with other instances of /l/ in the word, e.g. kliðí 'key' ⇁ lilí (148), luluðáki 'flower' ⇁ lululáki (105). Cf. also examples from Hinofotis 1977: θoðoráki 'little Theodore' ⇁ lololáki, róða 'wheel' ⇁ lóla (91).

Another source to be examined for the operation of the process is the phonology of adult 'baby talk' addressed to Greek children, which exhibits simplifying and clarifying process (Ferguson, this book, vol. I). Among the GREEK baby talk lexical items examined in Drachman 1973b there are no words containing /ð/ although there are several with /d/. Among the hypocoristic nicknames analyzed in the same study, two which have /ð/ in the full adult form have variants with /d/ in Drachman's 'Stage II' forms: afroð íti ⇁ díti, ðéspina ⇁ dépi. Thus the baby talk forms illustrate even better than the available child language data the operation of 'fortition' or fricative stopping in GREEK.

ARABIC

3. ARABIC offers one of the clearest and best-documented examples of the process ⌜ð → d⌝. The language is known from as early as inscriptions of the fourth century C.E. and up to the present time. It is sometimes described in three stages, the OLD ARABIC of pre-Islamic poetry and the Quran, the MIDDLE ARABIC known less directly from such evidence as 'errors' in written ARABIC during the Middle Ages in particular by Christian and Jewish authors, and the MODERN ARABIC dialects which constitute the mother tongue of the millions of Arabs today. CLASSICAL ARABIC, which in most essentials in equivalent to OLD ARABIC, has remained the normal literary language of the Arabs for a millennium and a half while the spoken language has gradually changed.

It is universally accepted that CLASSICAL ARABIC has a voiced interdental /ð/ as a phoneme distinct from / d z θ / and that in most of the modern dialects /ð/ has merged with /d/ and disappeared as in independent phoneme. There are, however, dialect areas in which the /ð / has been preserved, as in many parts of the Arabian peninsula and Iraq, in most BEDUIN or

nomadic dialects throughout the Arab world, and in some non-
Beduin areas outside Arabia and Iraq (Cantineau's S_2 dialects,
Cantineau 1939). In fact, the existence of /ð/, along with several
other phonological characteristics, constitutes a principal criterion in ARABIC dialect classification.

The existence of a voiced interdental phoneme *ḏ̣ in PROTO-
SEMITIC is generally accepted on the basis of unequivocal correspondences among the Semitic languages; its phonetic value is generally reconstructed on the basis of the facts (a) that in those SEMITIC
languages which have preserved an independent phoneme (ARABIC
dialects and two SOUTH ARABIAN languages, MEHRI and SHKHAURI)
it is voiced interdental, and in all the other SEMITIC languages it
has merged either with the voiced apical stop /d/ or the voiced
alvolar spirant /z/, either of which is a plausible outcome from
*ḏ̣. A few Semitists are more cautious, e.g. Cantineau 1951-52
refers to the reconstructed phoneme as an 'apicale à pointe basse'
which could have been either an interdental or an affricate, but
there seems to be no evidence for any pronunciation other than
interdental.

Of particular interest for our discussion is the pronunciation
of Classical /ð/ which is used by speakers of dialects which do
not have it. The sound is generally recognized to be an interdental
spirant and is so pronounced in discussions about correctness in
pronunciation and by careful speakers, but it is very commonly
pronounced [z] in oral use of CLASSICAL ARABIC even by educated
speakers. This leads further to loanwords from Classical with
/z/ for /ð/ and in some cases to phonological doublets in which
the ordinary colloquial word has /d/ whereas the Classicism has
/z/. (For discussion cf. Brockelmann 1961, Ferguson 1957.)

3.1 **Directionality.** There seems to be no question that the
diachronic order has been ḏ̣ > d̲, and that the z̲ of modern Classicisms is not an intermediate step but a separate process ḏ̣ ⇢ z̲
which is observed in many instances of second-language acquisition
when the speaker of a language without /ð/ attempts to pronounce
the /ð/ of the target language.

3.2 **Inclusiveness.** The process ⌜ð → d⌝ in ARABIC is part
of a schema by which all interdental obstruents become dental
stops. PROTO-SEMITIC apparently had four interdental consonants *θ *ḏ̣ *θ̱ *ḏ̱ of which the first two were voiceless and voiced
interdental spirants and the third was an 'emphatic' interdental
neutral as to voicing, thus constituting a typical voiceless-voiced-

emphatic triad (cf. also */t d ṭ/; */s z ṣ/, etc. of the protolanguage; Cantineau 1951-52, Moscati 1964, 24). These three
interdentals constitute a group which either appears as a / θ ð ẓ /
or as / t d ḍ / in the modern dialects. The phonetic value of the
fourth consonant is problematic; it was apparently a lateral interdental emphatic of some kind but has merged with the reflexes of
*θ̱ in the modern dialects to be either [ẓ] or [ḍ] depending on the
dialect. Corresponding to the /z/ pronunciation of /ð/ in Classicisms in dialects which have lost the interdentals there are / s z̧ /
pronunciations for Classical / θ θ̱ /. In some instances the /z̧/
in such words is not a direct Classical borrowing but has come
back into colloquial ARABIC from a TURKISH word originally borrowed from Arabic. (CLASSICAL ARABIC / ð θ ḏ z / all appear
as [z] in TURKISH and PERSIAN loanwords and in other languages
which have borrowed from Persian.)

   None of the other fricatives in CLASSICAL ARABIC give any
indication of becoming stops. The schema of fricative stopping is
limited to the interdentals; other consonant changes which have
taken place in ARABIC, such as q > ? or palatalization of k to tʃ,
are apparently unrelated.

   3.3 <u>Favoring conditions</u>. There is no evidence to show that
⌈ð → d⌉ is more likely under one set of conditions than another.

   3.4 <u>Acquisition and pidginization</u>. The only substantial publication on child language development in Arabic deals with a dialect
which has no interdentals (Omar 1973) and so offers no evidence.
The same problem arises with studies of Arabic baby talk (Ferguson 1956) and pidginized varieties of Arabic (Nhial 1975). My
expectation is that ⌈ð → d⌉ evidence will be found when some
other studies of dialects with interdentals appear (cf. Bakalla 1975).

ENGLISH

4. ENGLISH provides an interesting case of the process ⌈ð → d⌉,
which apparently operated as a diachronic change very early in the
history of the language and then again centuries later. The two
occurrences of the change seem, however, to be part of the same
'drift' seen in other GERMANIC languages. The first operation of
⌈ð → d⌉ occurred in pre-OLD ENGLISH, i.e. in the period between
PROTO-GERMANIC and attested OLD ENGLISH. During this period, according to the consensus of GERMANIC specialists, medial
and final *ð̱ of PROTO-GERMANIC became OLD ENGLISH d
(*beuð̱an > beodan). The voiced obstruents of PROTO-GERMANIC

are commonly reconstructed as having had both stop and spirant allophones (Moulton 1972) of the sort [b ~ v], [d ~ ð], [g ~ γ], and in OLD ENGLISH this [ð] > [d], preserving the phonemic identity. (The labial and velar allophonic pairs each split, [v] merging with /f/, and [γ] merging with /x/ except where it was lost intervocalically.) It is usually assumed that the change ð > d took place before the voicing of intervocalic / θ f s x / since original medial ð did not merge with the new medial ð < θ (cf. cweþan with [ð] and beodan with [d]), Moulton 1972, 153.

The interdental spirant /ð / which came from earlier voiced allophones of /θ/ and from the voicing of initial θ- in pronominal and demonstrative forms (modern the, this, that, then, there, etc.) remained stable in ENGLISH for centuries, whereas in other GERMANIC languages, except for Icelandic, the interdental spirants became stops fairly early. The first sign of the second operation of ⌐ ð → d⌐ in English is the Middle English change ð > d /_r as in Modern English burden, afford. The earliest clear attestation of widespread operation is from the 19th century lower-class pronunciations in New York City (for references cf. Cofer 1972, 216).

The incidence of ⌐ ð → d⌐ in present-day English has been described in some detail in the studies of social dialect variation in New York (Labov 1964), Detroit (Wolfram 1969), and Philadelphia (Cofer 1972). Of these, Cofer offers the best data for our purposes, although unfortunately he did not count the occurrences in non-initial position, since "impressions had indicated that non-standard variants of (dh) [i.e. stop pronunciation CAF] occurred primarily at the beginning of words, rather than in the middle or at the end" (Cofer 1972, 217-218). All these studies show widespread use of [d][7] for [ð] in the casual speech of working-class informants, somewhat more prevalent among black speakers than whites of a similar socio-economic status. Thus these studies give strong indications that ð > d is a diachronic change 'from below' which

---

[7] The question of the phonetic identity of this d < ð and the original d will not be discussed here. It has been claimed on the one hand that the d's are identical and on the other hand that the d is more dental or more lenis than the original d and so remains phonologically distinct. It is likely that there is variation in the phonetic facts and that the phonological interpretation is correspondingly complicated.

may be spreading from New York outward and spreading as a
group identification marker for blacks.   The spread of ð̲ > d̲ is
complicated by several factors.   First, the stop pronunciation has
become heavily stigmatized; it is widely cited as a major 'error'
to be corrected in uneducated speech and even those who frequently
use it may criticize others for doing so.   Second, the fortition
process interacts with a different process which affects the same
words, namely the assimilation of ð̲ to the preceding consonant.
This assimilation process is particularly common after / s z n l /
and may result in a gemination of the preceding consonant, or in
gemination and simplification which gives the effect of deletion of
the /ð̲/, e.g. <u>in this house</u> → <u>in nis house</u> → <u>in 'is house</u>.   This
kind of assimilation of word-initial ð̲- is widespread in the casual
speech of all classes and seems to have relatively little stigmatization.

4.1 <u>Directionality</u>.   The diachronic process ð̲ > d̲ reconstructed for pre-OLD ENGLISH and operating at the present time in
MODERN ENGLISH has no converse counterpart d̲ > ð̲ in English. [8]
In addition, ð̲ →̵ d̲ operates in various synchronic 'simplification'
processes, as in the acquisition and pidginization phenomena described in 4.5.   Instances of the converse process may be found
only in such phenomena as the d̲ →̵ ð̲ of corrections or in the development of a child's phonology toward the adult norm.

4.2 <u>Inclusiveness</u>.   The process ⌜ð̲ → d̲⌝ in ENGLISH is related
to the corresponding process with its voiceless counterpart ⌜θ → t⌝.
In the modern change the processes seem to operate together as a
schema, but in the earlier change they were separate.

In the general drift of GERMANIC phonological systems throughout their history, the interdentals have become stops, and usually
ð̲ > d̲ is the first step, followed by a sequence of steps θ > d̲,
either by the route θ̲ > ð̲ > d̲ or by the route θ̲ > t̲ > d̲.   The
operation of these processes was completed the earliest in OLD
HIGH GERMAN (8th to 12 centuries), but in ENGLISH, after the
early change of ð̲ > d̲ and a later split of θ̲ > θ, ð̲ , only now are
the final steps in the sequence (θ > t̲ > d̲; ð̲ > d) under way.

---

[8]The converse process ⌜d → ð⌝ operated in early MIDDLE
ENGLISH with a small set of words CV́__r, as represented by
modern <u>gather</u>, <u>weather</u>, <u>wither</u>, etc., but there seems to be no
trace of such a process before or after that period or in any other
phonetic environment.

(Other GERMANIC languages represent different rates and phasing
of the changes.) The historical asymmetry in treatment of θ and ð̠
in GERMANIC languages may be related to the fact that they were
not both independent phonemes at the start: the voiced ð̠ when it
occurs in GERMANIC languages is typically a positional allophone
of a / θ / or / d / phoneme, whereas a θ in GERMANIC languages
is typically an independent phoneme (or its 'principal member' or
underlying phonetic value). In any case, the operation of ⌐θ → t⌐
and ⌐ð̠ → d⌐ is symmetrical in contemporary ENGLISH where /θ/
and /ð/ are independent phonemes. This rather formal taxonomic
explanation seems more plausible if the larger picture is kept in
mind, namely that in PROTO-GERMANIC /θ/ was one of a set of
voiceless fricatives contrasting with voiceless stops whereas [ð]
was part of a set of voiced obstruents all of which had stop ~
spirant allophonic alternation.

It is interesting to note that the core of the reconstructed
PROTO-GERMANIC obstruent system is identical with that of
MODERN SPANISH. If this reconstruction is valid, the subsequent
changes are surprisingly different from the continuing changes in
Spanish. It is as though the direction of change was suddenly reversed in Germanic languages at an early period but has continued
unchecked in SPANISH. It is this kind of difference in direction
and outcome from similar starting points that has posed the most
difficult problem in phonological theory from the days of the 19th
century doctrine of exceptionless sound laws to the current versions of 'natural' phonology.

4.3 _Favoring conditions._ By the time of recorded OLD ENGLISH
the early fortition of [ð] was complete so that there is no direct
evidence for the favoring conditions, but they are generally assumed
to be those of comparable processes in other Germanic languages
on which the reconstruction of the allophonics of PROTO-GERMANIC
is based: "All the oldest GERMANIC languages agree in sharing
the stop [d] initially, in gemination, after nasal, and after /l/, /z/,
and /g/" (Moulton 1952, 173).

In the modern fortition the formulation of the favoring conditions
is complicated by the assimilation process which intersects with
it, but the following phonetic, lexical, and social conditions are
well documented.

(a) Phonetic. The stop variant is more likely to occur after r̠,
b̠, or a vowel preceded in turn by t̠ or d̠. The likelihood after n̠ or
l̠ cannot be estimated because there are conditions favoring the

assimilation process. The stop variant is also more likely to
occur in unstressed than stressed position and more likely in
word-initial position than elsewhere.[9]

(b) Lexical. The stop variant is more likely to occur in high
frequency, familiar words. The incidence of [d] in the pronouns
and demonstrative the, this, there, then, etc. is striking. This
set of words seems to undergo special changes throughout the
Germanic languages. In the Scandinavian languages the t < θ in
these words became voiced /d/ before other instances of initial t-
(see sec. 6 below). In English the θ in these words became voiced
/ð/ while other instances of initial θ-remained intact. This is
customarily explained by the fact that these words are often unstressed, but this must be only a partial explanation since some of
them are often stressed (e.g. this, that, then), and it seems likely
that the semantic value or communicative function of these words
is also a factor. It is interesting to note that when English speakers
nowadays refer stereotypically to the stigmatized ⌜θ → t,⌝ ⌜ð → d⌝
processes they typically accuse people of saying dese and dose and
dem tings, using (stressed!) examples of these words.

(c) Social. As has already been pointed out, the stop pronunciation is associated with more informal speech, lower socio-
economic status, and to some extent black rather than white
speakers. In the Philadelphia study Cofer (1972) found, however,
that working class blacks in careful speech corrected to spirants
much more than working class whites and reached the middle
class level of spirant use.

4.4 Genetic vs. areal spread. The change ð > d in ENGLISH,
as discussed above, seems to be part of a general 'drift' in
Germanic languages which involves a set of related fortition processes affecting almost all obstruents one way or another. Within
that general drift, however, the stopping of interdental spirants
seems to have taken place relatively independently at different
rates in different languages.

4.5 Acquisition and pidginization. There is a considerable
body of information on the acquisition of /ð/ in ENGLISH (summar-

---

[9]Although word-initial position favors [d], this does not mean
that utterance-initial position is even more favorable, since in the
latter there is a stronger tendency to correct pronunciation toward
the standard norm (Cofer 1972, 232).

ies and discussions in Ferguson 1975, Moskowitz 1976, Edwards
1977, Ingram 1977). The process ð̠ ⇢ d̠ yields by far the commonest substitution for /ð̠/ observed in children. Other common substitution processes are ð̠ ⇢ z̠ and ð⇢v̠; less common include
lateralization and complete deletion. Insofar as conditions tending
to favor these alternative processes have been identified, it seems
that stopping and deletion processes are earlier than the others,
ð̠ ⇢ v̠ is more common in imitation than spontaneous speech, and
ð̠⇢v̠ and ð̠ ⇢ z̠ are more common in non-initial position. Comparison with substitutions for /θ/ shows a striking asymmetry:
θ ⇢ f̠ is much commoner than θ ⇢ t̠ whereas ð̠⇢d is much commoner than ð̠ ⇢ v̠; also /θ/ substitutions are more variable than
/ð̠/ substitutions. For possible explanation of this asymmetry cf.
Moskowitz 1976, Edwards 1977.

English-based pidgins and creoles almost universally show the
operation of ð̠ ⇢ d̠ (Hall 1966, 30) and some of the dialect variation
in AMERICAN ENGLISH discussed above has been attributed to
creole origin (Cofer 1972). It is reasonable to guess that the change
has begun in several places in the English-speaking world and that
in some areas the presence of a creole-speaking or decreolizing
black population has both accelerated the change and contributed
to its stigmatization, but this remains a guess until careful studies
exploring this question have been carried out, perhaps along the
line of explanation in grammatical variation of a similar nature
(e.g. Nichols 1976).

ARAMAIC

5.   ARAMAIC offers one of the best examples of a language in
which both ⌐ð → d⌐ and ⌐d → ð⌐ have operated. ARAMAIC is attested
in a variety of scripts and in many local forms over a long period
of time, from inscriptions in the 9th century B.C.E. to present-
day spoken varieties, and both the loss of interdentals and the
spirantization of stops have been repeatedly discussed (cf. Kutscher
1970).

The earliest ARAMAIC texts indicate that the interdental spirants reconstructed for PROTO-SEMITIC / θ ð θ̣ / were preserved,
whereas in later texts they have merged with / t d ṭ / respectively.
In the early ARAMAIC inscriptions the letters used to represent
the interdentals are those also used for / ∫ z ṣ / respectively, and
beginning in the 7th century B.C.E. they are replaced by those for
/ t d t /. Thus the whole interdental series merged with the corresponding apical stops; this sound change apparently began in mesopo-
tamia and spread westward (Segert 1975, 93).

During some period in the history of ARAMAIC a general process of spirantization affected all the non-emphatic stops / p t k b d g /. This spirantization applied to all non-geminate stops following a vowel and was a positional allophonic process, a combinatory change which tended to become phonologized by reduction and loss of preceding vowels. This stop-spirant variation in ARAMAIC remained a pervasive characteristic of the language for centuries and is still evident in some varieties of modern ARAMAIC although it has disappeared from others. The dating of the spirantization is problematic since its consistent indication in writing became possible only with the use of the diacritic dot (dagesh) after the 8th century C.E. Sporadic spellings of foreign loanwords and the like suggest it may have started as early as the 6th century B.C.E. in some areas; scholars have argued over various dates between these two extremes.

The spirantization in ARAMAIC apparently applied to all the stops equally although the much later history of merger and losses as shown in the modern dialects does show variation. The spirantization did not apply after consonants (including a geminate) or juncture, but in some instances spirantization affected the initial stop of a word where it followed the vowel ending of the previous word in a closely joined phrase.

The recent history of the stop-spirant alternation is complex, but some indication of it will be valuable (the account here is based primarily on Cereteli 1961). The interdentals continue as separate phonemes in some varieties (e.g. MOSUL), have merged with / s z / in others (e.g. ZAKHO), and with / t d / in still others (various Eastern dialects). In several varieties there is a tendency for the change θ̱ > ð to take place; in one (SALAMA) the change has been completed, eliminating / θ / altogether while shifting / ð / back to /d/.[10] Stop-spirant alternation in the same morpheme, which was common in older ARAMAIC, is much reduced in the modern varieties, for example by one value being generalized in the verb paradigms for each root. The phonetic conditions for the occurrence of the alternants have also been obscured by foreign loanwords, simplification of geminates, and vowel loss without reten-

---

[10]The evidence suggests two routes of the loss of /θ/, one θ̱ > ẖ > ð, the other θ̱ > ḻ > ð; both occur in the same town apparently in different social groups, Christian and Jewish respectively (Cereteli 1961, 247).

tion of spirantization. In short, phonological descriptions of the
modern varieties typically do not need to identify synchronic spir-
antization processes such as $\underline{d} \rightarrow \underline{\delta}$, and the scattered lexical
residues are noted by scholars chiefly on the basis of historical
information.

    5.1 <u>Directionality</u>. The early operation of $\underline{\delta} > \underline{d}$ in ARAMAIC
was a diachronic sound change for which the directionality is clear.
The later spirantization, as long as it was an active process, was
clearly in the opposite direction $\ulcorner d \rightarrow \delta \urcorner$ and both diachronically and
synchronically /d/ was the input. Evidence for the process work-
ing in both directions in the competence of ARAMAIC speakers
would have to come from such unlikely sources as foreign loan-
words with [ð] being incorporated into a $\underline{d} \sim \underline{\delta}$ alternation.[11] In the
modern varieties when the $\underline{d} \rightarrow \underline{\delta}$ has become marginal or non-
existent, the direction of the arrow presumably varies depending
on particular cases in particular varieties.

    5.2 <u>Inclusiveness</u>. The process $\ulcorner \delta \rightarrow d \urcorner$ in ARAMAIC was part
of a limited schema by which the three interdentals of PROTO-
SEMITIC * / θ ð θ̣ / became stops. The fourth * / d̦ / went a different path, eventually merging with the voiced pharygeal /ʕ/. On
the other hand, the process $\ulcorner d \rightarrow \delta \urcorner$ which operated centuries later
was part of a pervasive schema of spirantization affecting all non-
emphatic stops in the language. This schema differs from that of
SPANISH in that it applied to voiceless and voiced stops alike and
was not connected with processes of degemination or voicing of
voiceless stops intervocalically. It differs from that of GREEK in
that the latter began with a 3-way distinction in stops in which the
voiceless aspirated and the voiced stop were spirantized while the
voiceless unaspirated stops were largely unaffected.

    5.3 <u>Favoring conditions</u>. The early diachronic change $\underline{\delta} > \underline{d}$
was a context-free change and total phonemic merger, and there is
no evidence for favoring conditions. The later change of $\underline{d} > \underline{\delta}$ was
limited to post-vocalic position (including intervocalic, preconson-
antal, and final), which thus constituted the most favoring condition.
As mentioned in 5.1 above, spirantization appeared post-consonan-

---

[11]MODERN HEBREW is a fruitful area for psycholinguistic
research of this kind with the morphophonemic alternations
$\underline{p} \sim \underline{f}$, $\underline{b} \sim \underline{v}$, and $\underline{k} \sim \underline{x}$, but the other stop ~ spirant alternations
have disappeared and even the three remaining ones seem increas-
ingly not applied in loanwords or even in words of Hebrew origin.

tally as a result of syncope and word-initially in close juncture with a preceding word ending in a vowel. Fluctuation after a semi-vowel (i.e. after a diphthong) is shown by evidence of spirantiza-tion in some modern varieties and not in others. Absolute word-initial seems to be the least favored position for spirantization, although one of the modern varieties (Maʿ lula) has initial spirants.[12]

5.4 <u>Areal vs. genetic spread.</u> The early change $\check{\delta} > \underline{d}$ is not obviously either areal or genetic in origin and spread. Aramaic shares this change with later Arabic, but more closely related Semitic languages have / ʃ z / or / s z / for Proto-Semitic *$/\theta\,\check{\delta}/$. The change $\underline{\check{\delta}} > \underline{d}$ is part of a genetic drift only insofar as the interdentals have tended to be eliminated by merger in one way or another in almost all the Semitic languages.

The later spirantization of stops is found in almost identical form in Biblical Hebrew and is claimed for AKKADIAN (Knudsen 1969), and for the unrelated HURRIAN of the second millennium B.C.E. Accordingly, a number of scholars have suggested the areal nature of the phenomenon, and almost every direction of spread has been proposed (Heb to Aram, Akk to Aram, Aram to Akk, Hu to Akk). The prevalent opinion seems to be that spiranti-zation in the Semitic languages started with Aramaic (possibly from some other source) and spread to Hebrew, and that Akkadian exam-ples mostly come from ARAMAIC-speaking scribes writing after AKKADIAN was no longer a spoken language.

5.5 <u>Acquisition and pidginization.</u> No evidence is available. The only study I know which examines child language in ARAMAIC (Sabar 1974) is based on the ZAKHO variety which has lost spiranti-zation. Braine's (1974) comments on his child's acquisition of MODERN HEBREW include discussion of the acquisition of the stop-spirant morphophonemic alternation, but the situation is not fully comparable and in any case MODERN HEBREW does not have spirantal alternants of / t d g / but only of / p b k /.

DANISH

6. DANISH is unique among the GERMANIC languages as a lan-guage which has shared in the general fortition drift, including

---

[12]In MA'LULA ARAMAIC all stops in initial position have become spirants except <u>b</u> which remains; modern initial stops other than <u>b</u>-

ð̄ > d̲, and also has had a pervasive spirantization which includes
d̲ > ð̄ .

In all the Scandinavian languages except Icelandic, PROTO-
GERMANIC [ð] either became [d] or was lost, and the former
process began to operate already in the period of Common Scandinavian in that ð̄ > d̲ after l̲ and n̲ (OLD ICELANDIC aldr 'age, '
hond 'hand'). The loss of [ð] took place generally after vowels and
after r̲, although the exact details vary from one language/dialect
to another, and in the modern languages d̲'s have in a number of
cases been restored in the spelling and then in the pronunciation
(summary in Haugen, 266). Similarly [θ] > [t] in the SCANDINAVIAN
languages, in DANISH by 1300 and somewhat later in Swedish and
Norwegian. As in ENGLISH, the initial consonant of such pronouns
and demonstratives as þū̲'you, ' þat 'that, ' þā̲ 'then, ' etc. followed
a different path. In most of these words the t̲ < θ was voiced to d̲.

In present-day DANISH the process ⌜d→ð⌝is evident in the
allophonics of the dental stops. In initial position there is a contrast
between voiceless aspirate and voiceless non-aspirate (e.g. tale
'speak' : dale 'dales'), intervocalically there is a contrast between
voiceless non-aspirate and voiced interdental fricative (e.g. fødte
'bore' : føde 'bear') and in final position a contrast between voiceless, freely unreleased or aspirated, and the voiced interdental
fricative (e.g. kat 'cat' : mad 'food'); cf. Diderichsen (1972).
Phonologists have generally analyzed these contrasts in terms of
two phonemes / t d / of which the /t/ is stronger (more fortis) in
every position than /d/, and the phonetic equivalence of initial /d/
and medial /t/ has often been cited as an example of partial overlap in phonological analysis (e.g. Jakobson et al. 1952).

The overall phonological organization is more complex than this
solution suggests. For one thing, the parallel contrasts of labials
and velars are complicated by the existence of phonemically distinct fricatives / f v R /. For another, vowel-length contrasts
before final consonants may be interpreted as still marking the
contrasts in the consonants which were their diachronic origin.
Finally, the contrasts in at least some positions may be interpreted
as contrasts between single and geminate consonants, which were
their diachronic origin in part. The "correct" phonological analysis

---

(ftnt. 12 cont.)
are mostly in ARABIC loanwords. Non-initial stops are more complex in origin (e.g. /p/ is often devoiced earlier /b/).

depends on the theoretical assumptions of the analyst (e.g. degree of abstractness, role of morphophonemic alternations, and relation to dialect differences and diachrony), and no attempt will be made here to resolve these questions. From the point of view of this paper, the most important point is that earlier [d] (of whatever origin) has become modern [ð] in many positions and that synchronic alternations between the two exist, as illustrated by the [fø:d̯ə] : [fø:ð̯ə] pair given above.

6.1 <u>Directionality.</u> The directionality of the two diachronic changes is clear: the early one was ð̱ > ḏ and the later one ḏ > ð̱. It is much less clear which direction the synchronic process in modern DANISH goes, since this depends on the kind of phonological analysis adopted. If, for example a (systematic) phoneme /d/ which is [-tns, -cnt] is posited, then the [ð] phones can be derived by a spirantizing rule [-cnt]→[+cnt] and the stop of <u>fødte</u> will be derived by a degemination rule, since it is stem <u>fød-</u> + past marker <u>-de</u>. In this analysis the direction is ḏ → ð̱. Other analyses, which find a distinction between ḏ and ð̱ by virtue of possible contrast before unstressed <u>-i-</u> depending on morpheme boundary, vowel-length contrast preceding final <u>-ð̱</u>, and the presence of [d] in proper names and loanwords, might interpret ð̱ as the input and ḏ the outcome of the process.

6.2 <u>Inclusiveness.</u> The process ⌜d →ð̱⌝ in DANISH is part of a schema. It is one item within one of a set of three interrelated processes:

(a) Spirants are weakened, i.e. they become frictionless continuants or semivowels or are lost completely.

(b) Stops are weakened, i.e. they become more lenis or are spirantized.

(c) Geminates are simplified.

The details of these processes are quite complex if the developments of the various local dialects are included in the analysis. The four-way contrast of OLD DANISH (± voice, ± geminate) has ended in a striking variety of phonological systems in the different dialect areas of DANISH. Almost all the changes can be explained in terms of the three general processes, but differences in phasing and the outcome of phonemic mergers and splits have led to different modern systems (cf. Ringgard 1971 for a treatment of the dialect diachrony of DANISH obstruents).

In certain respects MODERN DANISH phonology seems to be
changing in the same direction as contemporary AMERICAN
ENGLISH, notably that the earlier voicing contrast initially and
before stressed vowel has become an aspiration contrast and that
the earlier voicing contrast finally and after stressed vowel has
been shifted to a length contrast in the preceding vowel. In DANISH
also the dental stops or spirants tend to develop differently than
their labial and velar counterparts, and the dialectal changes of
the unaspirated intervocalic stop [ḍ] (< dd or t) > jt or jr are reminiscent of the flapping of intervocalic d and t in AMERICAN ENGLISH.

6.3 Favoring conditions. In all periods of DANISH the position
most favoring the stop pronunciation has been word-initial before
stressed vowel and the position most favoring the spirant pronunciation has been intervocalic. The positions after / n l r / which
might be expected to favor [d] as opposed to [ð] (as in SPANISH
and GREEK) favor instead the assimilation and disappearance of
the dental obstruent, as in the ENGLISH assimilation of initial [ð]
after apical obstruents. Thus in the modern language there is no
trace of [d] or [ð] in such words as holde 'hold,' sende 'send,' and
ord 'word.'

There is great lexical variation among d ~ ð̠ ~ ð̠ in the dialects,
but the only general observation that can be made is that the spelling with ⟨d⟩ in proper names and obvious loanwords tends to call
forth stop pronunciation, even if the spelling ⟨d⟩ in comparable
native words represents [ð] or ð̠. As noted above for SPANISH
and GREEK, there are numerous examples of a dropped d or ð̠
which is reinstated in the language by learned borrowings, restored spellings, or spelling pronunciations.

6.4 Genetic vs. areal spread. The spirantization process in
DANISH is generally regarded as specific to DANISH, but it is
worth noting that voiced spirants occur in LOW GERMAN and regional varieties of GERMAN spoken in the German-speaking areas
near Denmark which correspond to stops in other German-speaking
areas. This possible areal convergence is, however, less well
attested for d ~ð̠ than for b ~ v ~ w and g ~ ɣ and is not a clear-cut
case of areal spread of d > ð̠.

6.5 Acquisition and pidginization. The acquisition of DANISH
has been studied repeatedly since Jespersen's little book of 1916,
but examination of three recent books in DANISH on child language
development yielded no references to the acquisition of [ð]. Similarly, no evidence could be found on DANISH 'foreigner talk' or
pidginization.

UNIVERSALS

7. On the basis of data from only six languages it is next to impossible to hazard any hypotheses about generalizations that hold true
for all languages, yet there are some striking indications of common properties of the processes we have examined, and they may
be presented under the same headings used in the treatment of the
individual languages.

7.1 <u>Directionality</u>. The processes ⌐d →ð⌐and ⌐ð →d⌐are both
fairly widely operative in languages. Out of its world sample of
225 languages the Stanford Phonology Archive identifies 22 languages which show an interdental fricative alternation of some
kind. The two processes are closely related in the sense that they
share certain favoring conditions for the recurrence of the stop
and spirant values, regardless of the direction of the process.
They are, however, quite different in other respects. The stop →
spirant process is essentially assimilating in nature and strongly
context-sensitive, while the spirant → stop process is essentially
a context-free, segment-simplifying process. These fundamental
phonetic characteristics may, of course, be modified by strong
social factors.

As an example of the different social functions of the ⌐ð→d⌐ we
may cite ENGLISH and FINNISH. In the former, as described
above, the diachronic change (or at least dialectal variation) is
spreading 'from below,' i.e. from lower socio-economic levels
and low-ranking ethnic groups toward higher levels and groups and
from more casual speech styles toward more formal styles. The
stop value is stigmatized and spreads in opposition to lines of
overt prestige. In FINNISH the diachronic change (or dialect variation) is spreading 'from above,' i.e. from the educated, urban,
standardizing sectors of the population toward the less educated,
rural, local-dialect-using sectors; it is spreading also from the
influence of orthography and the pronunciation of d in prestige languages used by Finns from which FINNISH is absorbing loanwords.
The [ð] of PROTO-FINNIC or BALTIC FINNIC was the product of
consonant gradation or lenition of the initial /t/ of a closed syllable
(Ultan 1977 and references). This [ð] developed in various ways
in FINNISH dialects (e.g. to r, l, d, v, j, h, or ∅). The Southwestern dialects on which STANDARD FINNISH was based had [r]
or [d] as a reflex of earlier [ð], and the [d] pronunciation became
established in the Standard language in part by the influence of the
spelling with ⟨d⟩ which dates back to the 17th century, replacing
earlier fluctuation between ⟨d⟩ and ⟨dh⟩. The pronunciation of
SWEDISH and GERMAN was a strong influence in this process, and

in modern times loanwords from English are spreading the distribution of /d/ to positions where it formerly did not occur. This
brief contrastive description illustrates the difficulty of comparing
phonological processes across languages.

A more general point must be raised in this connection. The
specification of a phone or phoneme by a set of phonetic features
may not in itself be sufficient for optimal characterization no
matter how well chosen the phonetic features may be. Phonetically
similar segments in different languages may behave differently
synchronically and may be expected to have different future outcomes if they are the result of different diachronic processes. To
illustrate from ⌐d↔ð⌐ processes, [ð] which comes from earlier
[d] may be expected to move toward ɑ unless counter processes
intervene, but [ð] which comes from earlier [θ] may be expected
to move toward [d] unless counter processes intervene. Examples
of the former are GREEK and SPANISH; examples of the latter are
the SCANDINAVIAN languages (except for modern DANISH). It may
be that more careful phonetic study will reveal consistent phonetic
differences between examples of [ð] of different origins (thus requiring additional phonetic features in the framework[13]) or it may be
that differences in phonotactic constraints and the nature of synchronic alternations will be sufficient to account for the 'memory'
of the phonological system. Such phenomena are well attested in
other parts of phonological systems. For example, voiced labio-
dental fricatives /v/ are known to behave differently depending on
whether they come from earlier /f/ by intervocalic voicing, etc.
or from earlier /w/ by strengthening in particular environments
(cf. Tiersma 1975). The best way to incorporate such facts into a
synchronic description is not clear.

Another implication of this study of processes is that notions of
'marking' and 'naturalness' must be much more sophisticated than
present models suggest. A model which has [ð] as more marked
or less natural than [d] on the basis of general considerations of
difficulty of perception and articulation, frequency of occurrence in
the word's languages, etc. will have a hard time accommodating a
phonology like MODERN GREEK in which the [d] is marginal,
functioning to a considerable extent as a variant of [nd].

---

[13]Martinet's distinction between spirant and fricative or the
presence/absence of stridency come to mind as possibilities here,
but the list should be kept open for what the experimental phone-
ticians find.

7.2 <u>Inclusiveness</u>. The processes ⌜d →ð⌝ and ⌜ð → d⌝differ considerably in the degree to which they constitute parts of larger schemata. The stop → spirant process seems always to be part of a more general spirantization in the language, either the spirantization of voiced stops or the spirantization of all stops. In the well-attested modern cases such as GREEK, SPANISH, and DANISH, the <u>d</u> >ð̠ change is generally less advanced than the spirantization of /b/ and /g/ and in dialect variation may go in other directions (e.g. to [j] or a liquid). This suggests that across-the-board spirantization processes tend to start with labials and velars and then spread to dentals. Spirantization is in some languages connected with voicing processes, but in other languages occurs without any evidence of voicing processes.

The process⌜ð →d⌝is sometimes part of a more general fortition in the language (as seen in the GERMANIC languages), but more typically it seems to be either isolated or associated with a parallel process⌜θ → t⌝. Characteristically these processes when operating diachronically end by merger of the original fricatives with other consonants. Although the <u>θ</u> and <u>ð̠</u> changes tend to be parallel, it may happen that the two part company (e.g. θ ⇢ <u>f</u>, ð̠ ⇢ <u>d</u> in ENGLISH acquisition; <u>θ</u> >ʃ, <u>ð̠</u> > <u>z</u> in pre-Hebrew); the end result in any case is the elimination of the (highly marked?) interdental fricatives.

7.3 <u>Favoring conditions</u>. Whenever it is possible to determine the favoring conditions for either end of the⌜d ↔ð⌝processes, certain major conditioning environments stand out, although there may be great differences in detail from one language (and time period and social setting) to another. No matter which direction the process is going, the stop outcome is favored by word-initial, post-nasal or post-liquid, and stressed positions. Similarly, no matter which direction the process is going, the spirant outcome is favored by post-vocalic positions, including intervocalic, pre-consonantal, and pre-junctural. These favoring conditions clearly reflect physiological constraints and are phonetic 'universals' of one kind. Nevertheless even these strong constraints can be modified or overridden by other processes. For example, when the process⌜ð → d⌝ is operating but is stigmatized, absolute utterance-initial position is so salient that the appearance of stops may be inhibited there. Another example is the conflict with assimilating processes after nasal or liquid. Diachronically in many languages and in child language acquisition, sequences of homorganic nasal + voiced stop may be assimilated to geminate nasals, and then degeminated to single nasal segments. In such cases there may be little or no

evidence of the post-nasal position favoring d̠ over δ̠. Also, in
this paper little attention has been paid to distant assimilation or
consonant harmony (cf. Vihman, this volume), but that is clearly
a factor in ⌜d↔δ⌝ processes in the vicinity of r̠. The study of
favoring conditions for phonological processes is fundamental to
our understanding of phonological systems, but it requires not only
the availability of comparable synchronic data from a large number
of languages, as in the Stanford Phonology Archive, but also
reliable, detailed diachronic information which is hard to come by.

In principle, lexical and social favoring conditions are more
difficult to generalize about in relation to ⌜d→δ⌝ versus ⌜δ→d⌝
since they tend to correlate with the manner of innovation or extension of a process rather than with phonetic inputs or outcomes:
they are more relevant to the direction of the arrow than to the
phonetics of the X, Y, and Z. Thus, in a diachronic change 'from
below' it is high-frequency, common words which will favor the
change, regardless of whether the outcome is d̠ or δ̠, whereas in
a change 'from above' it is more likely to be the names of new
cultural items or words marked as appropriate for public or formal
use which form the change. It is not impossible that there is a
direct tie between lexical semantics or interpersonal attitudes and
certain phonetic phenomena, but this will be hard to establish.[14]

Any general model of phonological processes which somehow
specifies universal favoring conditions must cope with the exceptions (cf. 7.1 above). For example, the favoring of stops in initial
position is a striking 'universal' which crops up under a variety of
phonological conditions, but MAʿLULA ARAMAIC does exactly the
opposite (cf. footnote 12).

7.4 Genetic vs. areal spread. The data on the spread across
languages of the ⌜d↔δ⌝ processes are tantalizing. The general
impression is that ⌜d→δ⌝ diffuses relatively easily across languages
and that ⌜δ→d⌝ tends to appear as a response to characteristics
within a phonological system rather than by diffusion, yet there
are enough counterexamples to cast doubt on this impression. Per-

---

[14]A speculation about the initial consonant of the this, that,
there, then words in the GERMANIC languages might be that strong
deixis favors stops as against spirants. This seems unconfirmable
in the present state of psycholinguistic research, but about as
likely as the usual explanation of unstressed position which ignores
the frequent stressing of demonstrative elements.

haps the best that can be said is that ⌐d→ð⌐tends to be part of a larger schema of spirantization (cf. 7.2) which spreads across related or unrelated languages in a given language area, and that in those instances when ⌐ ð → d⌐is part of a larger fortition schema it may also diffuse in that way, but it is more usually a restricted or isolated process.

Striking evidence of the diffusability of ⌐d→ð⌐appears in a number of American Indian languages in North and South America which have borrowed extensively from SPANISH and in doing so have incorporated a d̲ ~ð̲ alternation which is quite at variance with their core phonology (e.g. Tarascan, Foster 1969).

7.5 Acquisition and pidginization. The data here are spotty, since even well-described languages often have no published accounts of acquisition or pidginization. On the basis of the evidence so far, however, the conclusion is clear. Children tend to acquire stops before fricatives and to make stop substitutions for fricatives, as pointed out by Jakobson 1941/1968 and confirmed in subsequent investigations. Similarly, pidginization processes tend to replace fricatives other than s̲ by stops, and in particular replace interdental fricatives with dental stops. In SPANISH, where spirantization of voiced stops is a pervasive phonological phenomenon, however, children seem to acquire the spirant values of / b d g / long before they master the adult phonetic differences between the voiced and voiceless stop segments.

CONCLUSION

8. Process (1) ⌐d→ð⌐seems to be a highly context-sensitive assimilatory process which is typically part of a larger schema of spirantization (of voiced stops or all stops) which is relatively easily diffused across languages. Process (2) ⌐ ð → d⌐ seems to be a relatively context-free, simplifying process which eliminates highly marked consonants, often co-occurs with ⌐θ → t⌐, and is particularly characteristic of language acquisition and pidginization. In both processes, the stop value tends to be favored in word-initial and post-nasal or post-liquid positions, the spirant in post-vocalic (including intervocalic, pre-consonantal, and pre-juncture) positions. All these hypothesized 'universals' may be modified or overridden by conflicting processes, particularly those involving social factors, and some exceptions are unexplained.

This very limited study suggests that more extensive investigation utilizing the same strategy could contribute significantly to the characterization of phonological processes and conditions of their operation. Such investigations would, however, require reliable, comparable data on phonological processes (including diachronic changes) from a large number of languages.

BIBLIOGRAPHY

Allen, W.S. 1968. Vox Graeca. Cambridge: University Press.

Altheim, Franz and Ruth Stiehl. 1961. Geschichte der Hunnen. Vol. III. Kampf der Religionen. Berlin: Walter de Gruyter.

Bakalla, M.H. 1975. An account of the phonology of a two-year-old Saudi child. Paper read at the Third International Child Language Symposium, London.

Baum, Paul. 1976. The question of decreolization in Papiamentu phonology. International Journal of the Sociology of Language 7. 83-93.

Braine, Martin D.S. 1974. On what might constitute learnable phonology. Language 50. 270-299.

Brockelmann, Carl. 1961. Grundriss der vergleichenden Grammatik der semitischen Sprachen. Hildesheim: Georg Olsons Verlagsbuchhandlung. [Reprint of the 1908 edition.]

Cantineau, Jean. 1939. Remarques sur les parlers de sídentaires syro-libano-palestiniens. Bulletin de la Société de Linguistique de Paris 40. 80-88.

_____. 1951-1952. Le consonantisme du sémitique. Semitica 4. 79-94.

Cereteli, Konstantin G. 1961. Abriss der vergleichende Phonetik der modernen assyrischen Dialekte. [Translation of the Russian résumé of the original Georgian work, published in 1958.] In F. Altheim, Geschichte der Hunnen III, 218-266.

Coetsem, Franz van and Herbert L. Kufner (eds.). 1972. Toward a grammar of Proto-Germanic. Tübingen: Max Niemeyer Verlag.

Cofer, T. 1972. Linguistic variability in a Philadelphia speech community. Chapter Four (DH) 215-251. Unpubl. Ph.D. dissertation, University of Pennsylvania.

Degen, Rainer. 1969. Altaramäische Grammatik der Inschriften des 10.-8. Jh. v. Chr. [= Abhandlungen für die Kunde des Morgenlandes 38, 3.] Wiesbaden: Deutsche Morgenländische Gesellschaft, Kommissionsverlag Franz Steiner.

Delattre, Pierre. 1965. Comparing the phonetic features of English, French, German, and Spanish. Philadelphia: Chilton Books.

Diderichsen, Paul. 1972. Essentials of Danish grammar. Copenhagen: Akademisk Forlag.

Drachman, Gaberell. 1973a. Generative phonology and child language acquisition. Ohio State University Working Papers in Linguistics 15. 146-160.

_____. 1973b. Baby talk in Greek. Ohio State University Working Papers in Linguistics 15. 174-189.

Drachman, Gaberell and Angeliki Malikouti-Drachman. 1973. Studies in the acquisition of Greek as a native language I. Some preliminary findings on phonology. Ohio State University Working Papers in Linguistics 15. 99-114.

Edwards, Mary Louise. 1976. The interdental fricatives in language acquisition and language change. MS, Stanford University.

Ekwall, E. 1906. Zur Geschichte der stimmhaften interdentalen Spirans im Englischen. (Lunds Univ. Årsskrift n. s. Vol. 40, Afd. 1, No. 5.) Lund: Gleerup.

Ferguson, Charles A. 1956. Arabic baby talk. In M. Halle (ed.), For Roman Jakobson. The Hague: Mouton. 121-128.

_____. 1957. Two problems in Arabic phonology. Word 13, 460-478.

_____. 1972. Short a in Philadelphia English. In M. E. Smith (ed.), Studies in linguistics in honor of George L. Trager. The Hague: Mouton.

Ferguson, Charles A. 1975. Universal tendencies and 'normal' nasality. In C.A. Ferguson, L.M. Hyman, and J.J. Ohala (eds.), Nasálfest. Stanford University Language Universals Project.

Foster, Mary L. 1969. The Tarascan language. Berkeley: University of California Press.

Frake, Charles O. 1962. Zamboangueño: Creole Spanish in the Philippines. Report to NIMH. MS.

Hall, Robert A., Jr. 1966. Pidgin and creole languages. Ithaca: Cornell University Press.

Hammond, Robert M. 1976. Phonemic restructuring of voiced obstruents in Miani-Cuban Spanish. Paper read at the Spanish and Portuguese Symposium at the State University of New York, Oswego.

Harris, James W. 1969. Spanish phonology. Cambridge, Mass.: MIT Press.

Haugen, Einar. 1976. The Scandinavian languages; an introduction to their history. London: Faber and Faber.

Honofotis, Frances Butler. 1977. An initial stage in a child's acquisition of Greek as his native language. UCLA Workpapers in Teaching English as a Second Language 11. 85-96.

Householder, Fred W., Kostas Kazazis, and Andreas Koutsoudas. 1964. Reference grammar of literary Dhimotiki. Bloomington, Ind.: Indiana University Press.

Ingram, David. 1977. The production of word initial fricatives and affricates by normal and linguistically deviant children. In A. Caramazza and E. Zurif (eds.), The acquisition and breakdown of language. Baltimore: Johns Hopkins University Press.

Jakobson, Roman. 1968. Child language, aphasia and phonological universals. (Tr. from original edition of 1941.) The Hague:Mouton

Jakobson, Roman, C. Gunnar M. Fant, and Morris Halle. 1952. Preliminaries to speech analysis. [Cambridge, Mass.] Acoustics Laboratory, M.I.T.

Jespersen, Otto. 1916. Nutidssprog hos børn og voxne. 2nd ed. 1923 under title Børnesprog [Children's language]. Copenhagen: Gyldendal.

Knudson, Ebbe E. 1969. Spirantization of velars in Akkadian. In W. Röllig and M. Dietrich, eds., Festschrift von Soden,147-55. Kevela

Kutscher, E.Y. 1970. Aramaic. In T.A. Sebeok (ed.), Current trends in linguistics, Vol. 6. 347-412. The Hague: Mouton.

Labov, William. 1972. Sociolinguistic patterns. Philadelphia: University of Pennsylvania Press.

_____. 1969. Contraction, deletion and inherent variability of the English copula. Language 45. 715-762.

Macken, Marlys A. 1976. Permitted complexity in phonological development: one child's acquisition of Spanish consonants. Papers and Reports on Child Language Development 11. 28-60. To appear in Lingua.

Macken, Marlys A. and David Barton. 1977a. A longitudinal study of the acquisition of the voicing contrast in American English word-initial stops, as measured by VOT. Paper presented at the 2nd Annual Conference on Child Language Development, Boston. To appear in Papers and Reports on Child Language Development 14.

_____. 1977b. The acquisition of voicing contrasts in English and Spanish. Paper presented at the Linguistic Society of America meeting, Chicago.

Martinet, A. 1952. Function, structure and sound change. Word 8.1-32.

Menéndez Pidal, R. 1962. Manual de gramática histórica española. Madrid: Espasa-Calpe.

Moscati, Sabatino. 1964. An introduction to the comparative grammar of the Semitic languages phonology and morphology. Wiesbaden: Otto Harrassowitz. (= Porta Linguarum Orientalium, New Series 6.)

Moskowitz, B.A. 1975. The acquisition of fricatives. Journal of Phonetics 3. 141-50.

Moulton, William G. 1972. The Proto-Germanic non-syllabics (consonants). In F.V. Coetsein and H.L. Kufner (eds.), Toward a grammar of Proto-Germanic. Tütingen: Max Niemeyer. 141-73.

Newton, Brian. 1972a. Cyprist Greek, its phonology and inflections. The Hague: Mouton. (= Janua Linguarum Series Practica 121.)

Newton, Brian. 1972b. The generative interpretation of dialect; a study of Modern Greek phonology. Cambridge: University Press.

Nhial, Abdou A. 1975. Ki-Nubi and Juba Arabic: a comparative study. In S. Hurreiz and H. Bell (eds.), Directions in Sudanese linguistics and folklore. Khartoum: Khartoum University Press.

Nichols, Patricia. 1976. Linguistic change in Gullah: sex, age. and mobility. Unpubl. Ph.D. dissertation, Stanford University.

Omar, Margaret K. 1973. The acquisition of Egyptian Arabic as a native language. The Hague: Mouton.

Ringgard, K. 1971. bb-dd-gg. In K. Hald et al. (eds.), Studier i dansk dialektologi og sproghistorie, 305-11. Copenhagen.

Sabar, Yona. 1974. Nursery rhymes and baby words in the Jewish Neo-Aramaic dialect of Zakho.

Schwyzer, Eduard. 1953. Griechische Grammatik. Vol. I. 3rd ed. Munich: Beck. 204-211.

Segert, Stanislav. 1975. Altaramäische Grammatik. Leipzig: VEB Verlag Enzyklopädie. Die Vereinfachung des protosemitis- chen Konsonantismus 88-96 Spirantisation der Konsonanten 117-118.

Sommerstein, Alan H. 1972. The sound pattern of Ancient Greek. Oxford: Blackwell. (= Publications of the Philological Society 23.)

Stoel, Caroline M. 1974. The acquisition of liquids in Spanish. Unpublished Ph.D. dissertation, Stanford University.

Tiersma, Peter Meijes. 1975. The nature of f and v in Frisian and Marathi. Journal of Phonetics 3. 17-23.

Timm, L. 1976. Three consonants in Chicago Spanish. Bilingual Review 3. 153-162.

Ultan, Russell. 1977. Finnish d and ts. Unpublished paper.

Warburton, Irene P. 1970. On the verb in Modern Greek. Part II, Phonology of Modern Greek 15-47. Bloomington: Indiana University Press.

Wolfram, Walter A. 1969. A sociolinguistic description of Detroit speech. Washington, D.C.

Word Demarcation

LARRY M. HYMAN

ABSTRACT

The word plays an important role in phonology. It is the single
most important grammatical unit for the statement of distributional
constraints and boundary phenomena. It is the primary accentual
unit used by languages characterized by stress. It is the most widespread grammatical unit characterized by phonological prosodies.
After surveying all of these phonological correlates of the word, a
close look is taken at how the word relates to other grammatical
and phonological units and their boundaries (pause, phrase, syllable, morpheme, and internal word). In the course of this study a
constraint limiting the number and specifying the nature of word-
internal grammatical boundaries is proposed and justified. The
weakening of internal word to morpheme boundaries as the result
of lexicalization and grammaticalization is also discussed, and
illustrated from a number of languages.

Parts of this paper are based on research jointly carried out
with Kong-On Kim, to whom I owe a special debt. In this earlier
research, reported in Kim and Hyman (1973), the present author
was supported by a postdoctoral fellowship from the Miller Institute for Basic Research in Science at the University of California,
Berkeley. Subsequent research has been supported in part by a
National Science Foundation Grant No. SOC 75-16487. I would also
like to thank William R. Leben, whose many comments on earlier
drafts and presentations of the ideas contained in this work have
been extremely helpful.

CONTENTS

1. Introduction

Although elusive, and barely definable at best, the word plays an important role in the phonologies of many of world's languages. For whatever reason, language users tend to build utterances out of grammatical/semantic units known as words, which in turn have effects on the sound structures of languages. In this paper an attempt is made to survey the phonological effects of word units, their demarcation within larger units, and their relationship to other phonological and grammatical units used in structuring utterances. It will be demonstrated that phonological properties are extended to the word-unit both from above (e.g. from the utterance level) and from below (e.g. from the syllable level). The term 'word demarcation' will refer to any phonological consequence of the word, whether or not it can be demonstrated that this consequence serves the function of demarcation in the Prague School conception.

2. The Word in Phonology

The word as a linguistic unit has a long, and at times distinguished history in the field. It has been approached in a number of different ways, with definitions always falling somewhat short of perfection. It nonetheless maintains great intuitive appeal, and provides the starting point for several models of grammar, as well as models of phonology. It is not possible here to summarize the different views and definitions represented in the vast literature existing on the subject. Several studies already provide historical statements on the study of the word. A comprehensive bibliography is available in Krámský 1969. For our purposes, it is sufficient to acknowledge that the word has been defined as a grammatical unit, as a semantic unit, as a phonological unit — or any combination of these. It has been dealt with as a concrete reality, as well as an abstract idealization. Needless to say, there is only partial agreement on how to incorporate it into a linguistic framework.

We will address ourselves in this section to the various phono-logical approaches to the word. Phonological definitions of the word are basically of two kinds. The first definition attempts to relate the word to pauses or to potential pauses, e.g. "...it may be proposed that the presence of potential pause be employed as an independent definition of the word-unit" (Greenberg 1965: 70). This definition is compatible, if not identical, to the notion of the "isolatability" of words. That is, a word within a larger utterance could have conceivably been an utterances of its own, without affecting its relationship to the grammatical and semantic subsystems.   As an example, the FRENCH utterance <u>je te le donne</u> 'I give it to you' (Žirmunskij 1966: 68) consists of four orthographic words. However, since <u>je</u>, <u>te</u> and <u>le</u> are the reduced or cliticized forms of these pronoun, only one of the four candidates for wordhood can appear in isolation. Consequently, one might argue in this framework that this sequence represents one single word. Of course, the corresponding ENGLISH gloss would be analyzed as consisting of four (if not five) words, since each can occur in isolation.

The second definition attempts to formalize the word unit as having a phonological coherency, whence the term "phonological word," which may or may not coincide with the notion "grammatical word," depending on the language, and depending on the example. This approach is characteristic of Firth's prosodic analysis (Firth 1948) and Pike's hierarchical approach to language (Pike 1967), although it is not limited to them. To take the Pikean model, which is the most attractive for our purposes, a word is a unit within a <u>grammatical</u> hierarchy, which, however, sometimes interacts with, or penetrates the phonological hierarchy. The overlap which results is sometimes perfect, sometimes only approximate. Thus, in a given utterance, a phonological word (a unit of phonology, but having at least some grammatical basis) can in some cases include parts of a preceding, and parts of a following grammatical word or words.

The phonological coherency of words in at least some languages is demonstrated in the following ways:

1. A word can function as a unit in the statement of distributional constraints.

2. A word can function as a unit in the statement of boundary phenomena.

3. A word can function as a unit in the statement of accentual phenomena.

4. A word can function as a unit in the statement of phonological prosodies.

We take up each of these in turn.

2.1 Distributional constraints

The term 'distributional constraints' is used to cover constraints
on sequences, normally contiguous, as well as the timing characteristics found to characterize grammatical units (Lehiste 1964/73,
1970). It also seems to be appropriate to cover the kind of constraints reported for ̧IJQ by Williamson (in press), who noted a
statistical bias of certain consonants occurring in the first vs.
second vs. third syllable of polysyllabic words. It is a well-known
fact that languages exhibit constraints in the distribution and combination of their various sound segments. These constraints occur
on both underlying or phonemic representations, as well as on the
surface or phonetic level. They are stateable in terms of surrounding segments, but also in terms of grammatical units and their
boundaries. In Kim and Hyman 1973, we addressed ourselves to
the questions of whether distributional constraints of both the underlying and surface variety are needed (answered in the positive),
as well as the question of what grammatical unit they are best
stated in terms of. The answer to the second question was that
distributional constraints likely to have any consequence for language users (i.e. likely to be "psychologically real" in generative
terminology) are properties of the word, as well as the syllable,
a phonological unit (cf. also Vennemann 1974; Hyman 1975:194-5;
Hooper, in press). A well-known example which can be stated only
in terms of the word is the fact that the sound [ž] can not occur at
the beginning of an ENGLISH word. Similarly, in BAMILEKE, a
glottal stop cannot occur at the beginning of a word, while fricatives can only occur at the beginning of a word (Hyman 1972). Thus,
there are at least two reasons why the sequence [yū? fùu] 'hear the
chief' must be divided into the two words [yū?] 'hear' and [fùu]
'chief.' A third reason is that no word allows a consonant cluster
(with the exception of consonant-final verbs having the -si suffix).
Thus, the sequence [?f] would, as any other CC sequence, indicate
that a word boundary intervenes.

It is often the case that such constraints characterize syllables
as well as words, and in some languages such as BURMESE (Sprigg
1957, Okell 1969), where words tend to be monosyllabic, it may be
difficult to determine how such constraints should be stated. Since
syllables and words do not always line up (e.g. ENGLISH can have
a syllable beginning with [ž], e.g. he sees you [hiy.siy.žə]), we
know that there is a need to distinguish the two units for phonological purposes. There is, however, some question as to whether
any distributional constraints should be stated in terms of morphemes. The case against morpheme structure conditions has been

accelerated over the past few years (Shibatani 1973; Kim and
Hyman 1973; Vennemann 1974; Clayton 1976; Hooper 1976 —
but see also Kaye 1973, 1974; and the discussion in section 3.2).

2.2 Boundary phenomena

In addition to distributional constraints, languages often exhibit
phonological processes (or "rules") which occur at word boundaries.
These processes, together with the "static" distributional constraints,
constitute the class of boundary signals of Trubetzkoy (1939/69),
which were said to have a "demarcative" function. The languages
which devoice final consonants and/or vowels fall into this category,
as do the languages which, for example, insert a glottal stop before
a word-initial vowel. Again, it is not always easy to determine
whether such processes are to be attributed to the syllable or to
the word. Examples such as in 1.,

1. Jagd   [ya:kt] 'hunt'   cf. Jäger 'hunter,' jagen 'to
   Jagden [ya:kdən] 'hunts'   'hunt,' with [g]

where the /g/ of Jagden becomes devoiced word-internally (and
even before a voiced consonant) suggest that final-devoicing is a
syllable property in STANDARD GERMAN. As we shall see below,
many such processes have their roots in pre-and post-pausal phenomena which become "narrowed" to either word or syllable boundaries.

2.3 Accentual phenomena

Many languages have a regular stress placement rule of the type:
place primary stress on the first syllable, or the penultimate syllable, or the final syllable of a given accentual unit. Often that
unit is the word. Accent (of which stress-accent is a particular
instance) is so strongly identified with the notion of the word that
Garde (1968:18), for one, suggests that languages which do not have
accentual phenomena do not have words (i.e. they do not have any
unit intermediate between morphemes and phrases). Pulgram
(1970), on the other hand, shows that what may be a word in one
language might correspond to some other unit, e.g. the phonological phrase or phonological word in another language, and proposes
the dichotomy between "nexus" (where words in junction keep their
word properties) and "cursus" (where words in junction give up
their word properties, e.g. accent, to form a larger unit). FRENCH,
with its "groupes rythmiques" is an example of a cursus language.

Having word-final accent is, of course, quite similar to having word-final devoicing, since both are conditioned by the same boundary. Unlike accent, word-final devoicing, say, of consonants, may not be a reliable demarcator of words. Since in many languages when /b, d, g, etc. / become [p, t, k, etc.] word-finally, they actually merge with /p, t, k, etc. /, it is not the case that the presence of voiceless consonants necessarily means that we are at the end of a word — nor can we phonologically determine that devoicing as a <u>process</u> has occurred. If voiceless <u>vowels</u> are found only word-finally, this is much more reliable, since the likelihood of an underlying contrast between voiced and voiceless vowels is slight.

Even accent, however, is not entirely perfect as a demarcator. Martinet (1954) wishes to call penultimate accent an imperfect demarcation, since the demarcating property does not occur adjacent to the demarcated boundary. This may or may not be a relevant distinction to make. But far more serious is his demonstration (Martinet 1960/64: 87) that those languages which have syllable-weight phenomena, such as LATIN, do not always allow one to unambiguously determine where the word boundary lies. The example Martinet cites is [bónacalígula], which according to the LATIN stress placement rule could be, on the basis of the accent alone, segmented either as [bónaca] plus [lígula] or as [bóna] plus [calígula]. It is the meaning of the sequence which tells us that the second segmentation is the correct one. Thus, in such examples, one can assign accent on the basis of word boundaries (and some segmental information), but one cannot assign word boundaries on the basis of accent alone.

In many languages accent is not used demarcatively, since there is no general rule always assigning the accent to the same syllable within a word. Rather, a number of languages have systematic phonemic or "lexical" stress, where the placement of stress must be indicated in the lexicon. A language can also have contrasting surface (phonemic) stresses because of grammatical processes, e.g. the ENGLISH distinction between pérvert, a noun, and pervért, a verb. In either case we cannot unambiguously determine where a word boundary is on the basis of the accent alone. One can, however, determine how many word units are present in an utterance, if the principle of one stress per word is maintained throughout. In this sense the stress maintains a <u>culminative</u> function: we know how many word units there are, but not where they are divided. In Hyman 1977 it was suggested

that nondemarcative stress normally derives from demarcative
stress as a natural historical process. The one complicating
factor is the possibility of developing phonemic stress from the
stem-affix dichotomy. Thus, in a language with stem-initial stress,
pátu would receive initial stress, while pa=tú (where =tú is the
stem) would receive second-syllable stress. If the second instance
of pa- were to cease to be a prefix, we could derive the contrast
between pátu and patú with no synchronic basis for predicting the
accent.

2.4 Prosodies

The London School, whose approach to phonology emphasizes
the syntagmatic or prosodic aspect of sound systems, has noted
that a given phonological stretch can require an agreement with
respect to some phonetic property. The most common instances
are vowel harmony, nasalization and "flatness" (glottalization or
pharyngealization). These prosodies do not always coincide with
the word, but to the extent that they do, they demonstrate the coherency of that grammatical unit. And there is no denying that
such a tendency exists.

In IGBO, for instance, there is a harmony between the following
vowel sets in most dialects (Welmers and Welmers 1968):

2. Advanced tongue root   Retracted tongue root

           i   u   i̩   u̩

           e   o   a   o̩

It is normally the case that all of the vowels occurring within the
same word will be chosen from the same set, either the advanced
tongue (or "clear") vowels on the left, or the retracted tongue (or
"pharyngealized") vowels on the right. This produces a number of
common alternations, for example, the verbal noun prefix /A/ which
has two realizations, as seen in 3.

3. /sí/ 'cook'   ⟶ [èsí] 'cooking'
    /sí̩/ 'say'   ⟶ [àsí̩] 'saying'

However, sometimes when verb stems are compounded, no vowel
harmony takes place, e.g. /gá/ 'go' plus /fè/ 'cross' becomes
[gáfè] 'go across,' not *[géfè]. This compound does represent one
word, however, since it takes only one set of verbal suffixes, as
in [gáfèrè] 'go across for (someone).' We propose an internal word

boundary (#) to capture this fact, i.e. /gá#fè/, so that vowel harmony is blocked. What this means is that whatever occurs to the
left of # will have the same harmony properties, as will whatever
occurs to the right -- but the two will not necessarily agree. The
boundary in [èsí] and [àsí] is a simple morpheme boundary (+),
which does not have the ability to block harmony. To the extent
that speakers maintain the independent lexical status of each of the
components of /gá#fè/, harmony will not creep across the boundary.
If we look at another suffix, however, /tá/ 'towards the speaker,'
we find differences among individuals. For the verb /bú/ 'carry on
head,' some will say [bútá] 'bring,' and some will say [búté]. The
reason is that the historical # of /bú#tá/ is becoming weakened to
a + boundary, the reason for this being that /tá/, formerly an independent verb, has become grammaticalized. Thus, /bú#tá/ is
coming to be treated with /tá/ phonologically subordinated to /bú/.

One final prosody of increasing importance in phonological studies
is tone. Leben (1971, 1973) has attempted to argue for tone as a suprasegmental feature characterizing grammatical units, e.g. morphemes
and words. One argument which he gives is that words are sometimes
characterized in a language by a limited number of tonal patterns,
which occur independently of the number of syllables in the word.
While Leben has based much of his argument on MENDE, an equally
impressive case is built up for KUKUYA by Paulian (1975). In this
language high and low tones form sequences which can be stated without reference to the length of a word: "Ces deux tonèmes se combinent
pour former cinq schèmes, unités de même niveau que ce que nous
avons appelé 'mot phonologique' et qui peuvent tous se superposer à
ce dernier, quel que soit son nombre de voyelles..."(Paulian 1975:
138, our emphasis).

The second argument for treating tone as a prosody of some grammatical unit, perhaps the word, is that tonal alternations sometimes
affect whole grammatical units. Leben (1973:133-4) gives a convincing
example from HAUSA. Similarly, Elimelech (1976) has shown for
ETSAKO that when two nouns are joined in a genitive construction,
X of Y, when X consists solely of low tones, all of these are raised
to high, no matter how long the word is. In certain tenses, a verb
consisting entirely of high tones may go down to all low tones, regardless of its length. Such examples illustrate that words may be
undergoing tonal processes as units.

3. The Word and Higher Units

Having demonstrated the ways in which the word can have phonological consequences, we now turn to the question of how the word

relates to other, larger units. It has often been pointed out that
the word constitutes a unit bounded by potential pause. It is therefore not surprising to find that at least some of the phonological
properties of words — in particular, those which have their effect
at a word boundary — are also characteristic of the pause environment. In this section we shall first address ourselves to the origin
of word demarcation as a "narrowing" from pause position, and
then deal briefly with the combination of words into phrases and
the differences that are found in how "word junction" is treated in
various languages.

3.1 Words and pauses

In this section we would like to illustrate how distributional constraints, boundary phenomena, and accentual phenomena may have
their origin in pause-related phenomena, and that the word is thus,
phonologically speaking, a grammatical unit for which pause phenomena are embedded into a nonpause environment.

3.1.1 Distributional constraints   The distributional or sequential
constraints which are known to characterize the corresponding pause
environment.   Thus, if a word cannot begin with a glottal stop, then
an utterance also cannot begin with a glottal stop.   If a word cannot
end in a fricative, then an utterance also cannot end in a fricative.
An utterance (pause) boundary is necessarily also a word boundary,
though the converse is not the case: many word boundaries do not
coincide with utterance boundaries. Since there is a one-way implication only, and since pause provides a phonetic context for
phonetic and phonological statements, it is tempting to see the
origin of word-determined distributional constraints in the constraints imposed on pre- and post-pause position (cf. below).

3.1.2 Boundary phenomena   The relationship between pause and
word boundary is much clearer in the case of boundary-induced
processes. Vennemann (1974: 364) has noted Schuchardt's (1885/72:
46, 56) explanation of word-final devoicing as having its origin in
devoicing before pause. A corresponding hypothesis is also included
from Chafe (1959: fn. 23). This process of "boundary narrowing" is
quite common. Thus, consider a language which has the phonetically
motivated process of devoicing before pause. In this language, a
word in isolation will be realized with a final voiceless sound. The
same word may, however, be realized with the corresponding final
voiced sound when in utterance-internal position. Final-devoicing
may then become generalized to new environments, as when a speaker
wishes to clearly identify the word boundaries for his listener (or,

conceivably, demarcate a difficult utterance for himself). The result is that devoicing now characterizes voiced segments preceding any <u>word</u> boundary, whether that word boundary coincides with a pause boundary or not. The important point is that the resulting modified rule is <u>not</u> phonetically motivated, since there is no necessary phonetic pause between word boundaries. In fact, word-final devoicing can occur even when the following word begins with a voiced sound, as in GERMAN <u>das Kind geht</u> [das kInt ge:t] 'the child goes.' (The role of the syllable as another way of generalizing pause-related phenomena will be discussed below.)

3.1.3 <u>Accentual phenomena</u> In Hyman 1977 it was argued that word-accent comes from intonation in exactly the same way that word-boundary phenomena come from utterance-boundary phenomena. First, in the case of stress, it was noted that there are no clear phonetic distinctions between those features said to characterize (primary) stress, and those said to characterize intonation. The pitch, duration and intensity variations correlating with stress also correlate with the high points of intonation -- which, as often noted, has a tendency to superimpose itself on places of strong stresses.

Just as it is not always possible to draw a distinct line between pause- and word-conditioned phenomena (indeed, there is a continuum between all such units, as well as individual variation), it is not always clear whether we are dealing with stress or intonation in a given language. Applegate states for SHILḤA, for instance: "...primary or heavy stress occurs on the last vowel of the stem, provided that the word has no affixes after the stem" (1958: 9). But he later adds in a footnote: "It should be noted that the stress patterns referred to here apply only to utterances consisting of a single word. If the utterance contains more than one word, the stress is reduced slightly on all vowels except those in the final word. It can be said, therefore, that primary stress occurs only at the end of an utterance."

In a language such as SHILḤA, where primary stress is realized only in utterance-final position, it is hard to understand why one should speak of stress, rather than of intonation. Why should one consider such a language to have a word-accent at all? Words are first combined into utterances, and then a strong <u>intonational</u> pitch prominence is placed finally on the last word of that utterance. Applegate's statements represent a confusion which underlines the point being made here: stress not only is intricately intertwined with intonation, but it actually comes from it. We can hypothesize that a stress-accent comes into being when an intonational feature becomes associated with a grammatical unit smaller than a clause

(where a pause and intonation are normally attested). In other
words intonation becomes grammaticalized as a word-stress when
the suprasegmental features of pitch, duration and intensity that
would have characterized a word in isolation (where it gets prominent intonation) are encoded with the word, and thus come to function
in words not in isolation. The exact parallel involved when utterance-
final devoicing is generalized to word-final devoicing cannot be missed.

In summary, then, there is a strong tendency for utterance-
phenomena to narrow their domain to the word unit. If there is a
preponderance of word-final phenomena, as opposed to word-initial
phenomena (Javkin 1975), it is because much more goes on at the
ends of utterances than at the beginnings.

3.2 Words and phrases

The alternative to deriving word properties from utterance properties is to leave utterance properties where they belong. That is,
a language can simply choose not to generalize pre- and post-pause
phenomena to the word. Such an example is FRENCH, and there
are numerous other languages (perhaps including SHILHA) which
build on the "phonological phrase" unit. One key to determining
what kind of language we are dealing with has to do with syllabification: what does a language do when a word ending in a single consonant is followed by a word beginning in a vowel? The most natural
syllabification process would be for that consonant to go onto the
following word, as when FRENCH fils unique 'only son' is syllabified
[fi.sü.nik]. However, there is an opposing force, namely the coherency of the word, which may block the syllabification of a final
consonant onto the initial vowel of a following word. This is most
efficiently done by inserting a glottal stop before a word initial vowel,
as in the GERMAN das Kind ißt [das kInt ?Ist] 'the child eats.' Not
only do we observe the insertion of a glottal stop before ißt, so as
to block syllabification, but also the final devoicing said to characterize syllable-final position. If the glottal stop had not been inserted,
the final consonant of Kind would have syllabified onto the following
vowel-initial syllable ißt. (One can ask whether it would have been
a [d] or a [t].) Since the glottal stop characterizes utterance-initial
vowels, we can argue that here too the process has been one of generalizing from pause to word boundary.

As was mentioned, languages differ in how they deal with word
junction, and part of this difference at least is due to the different
concerns languages seem to have for preserving the word as a
phonological unit. Thus, in dealing with "internal junctures" as

involved in phrases such as <u>stay out, die Uhr, là aussi</u> and <u>una isla,</u> where two vowels come together across a word boundary, Delattre (1963: 210) points out the differences between ENGLISH, GERMAN, FRENCH and SPANISH: "In English, the second vowel may have a sharp onset or a smooth one. In German the sharp onset, with glottal stop, is much more frequent than in English, but the smooth onset is also heard. In French the smooth onset of the second vowel is the rule. There is no voice interruption between the two vowels, only a reduction of intensity. In Spanish the smooth onset is also the rule; but in addition, <u>the first vowel, if unstressed and not closer than the second, tends to fall</u>" (his emphasis). See also Gårding (1967) for SWEDISH, and Lehiste (1965), who compares FINNISH, SERBO-CROATIAN and CZECH.

4. The Word and Lower Units

In this section we will consider the relationship between words and syllables, on the one hand, and words and morphemes, on the other. We will then turn to the consideration of "words within words."

4.1 Words and syllables

We have already pointed out that there is an intimate relationship between words and syllables. In some languages words are mono-syllabic, in which case it is difficult to determine whether a given phenomenon is a property of the word or the syllable. In addition, distributional constraints and boundary phenomena that occur at word boundaries often occur at syllable boundaries as well. Here too, it is sometimes hard to tell whether the phenomenon in question is best stated in terms of the word or the syllable.

An even greater indication of the relationship between the two units is the generalizing of syllable properties to word properties. This is exactly what happens when a language develops a "word prosody." Consider nasalization, which has been treated as a prosody in several languages of the world, e.g. SUNDANESE (Robins 1957), TERENA (Bendor-Samuel 1966), DESANO (Kaye 1971), GUARANÍ (Lunt 1973). Although the exact statement may differ in detail, in general, a given stretch will agree in nasality, either being completely nasal or completely oral. In some cases nasalization may be stopped or ignored by phonological considerations (e.g. no penetration through a supraglottal obstruent), but in other cases nasalization is only checked by a boundary — e.g. a word boundary. Since nasalization is a phonologically motivated process, it is best treated as a property of segments which first spreads to characterize neighboring segments, and then full syllables. As it spreads from syllable to syllable, it may be checked only by grammatical considerations. Thus, speakers may control the spreading nasalization from one word to another. This is true not only in the languages which have been described with nasal prosodies, but also in phonetic studies. Lehiste (1965:177) thus states for FINNISH: "When the nasal consonant started the word, progressive nasalization of the vowel following the nasal consonant was always present... When a word boundary occurred between a word ending in a nasal and one beginning with a vowel, progressive nasalization was not observed." Thus, in certain cases, prosodies may not only demonstrate the phonological coherency of a word, but also, a change in prosody may signal a word boundary. Since two words in succession may have the same value for a prosody such as nasalization or vowel harmony, this means that the demarcation is not entirely perfect.

The most convincing cases of where a phonological prosody has been reinterpreted as a grammatical feature (or words) occurs when segments undergo processes which, when applied to them, are not phonetically motivated. Two clear examples come from BURMESE and AGBO. In BURMESE (Okell 1969:12), when two monosyllabic words are joined to form a compound, the initial consonant of the second syllable may undergo voicing; thus, compare [tè] 'hut' and [boudè] 'rest house.' Okell further points out that "when voicing occurs in the initial consonant of a syllable following a weakened syllable... and when the initial consonant of the weakened syllable is also voiceable, then the voicing may be extended to that consonant as well" (1969:16). Thus, [pà] 'cheek' plus [sa?] 'join' may be pronounced [păza?] (with intervocalic voicing) or [băza?] 'mouth.' In the latter realization, there is no phonetic explanation — the word-initial consonant has simply decided to undergo voicing as a process applying to the entire word.

In AGBO (Bendor-Samuel and Spreda 1969: 21) a similar observation can be made with respect to a "fortis prosody": "The fortis articulation of a particular consonant in the word is marked by several phonetic features, particularly, the lengthening of the consonant concerned and the shortening of the following vowel. The vowel of the preceding syllable is also shortened. For these reasons this feature is treated as a prosody which has implications for the word as a whole, with a complex of phonetic exponents, focusing on a specific consonant." What is interesting in AGBO is that when a consonant undergoing the above fortis prosody is preceded

by a syllable beginning with a fricative, that fricative will become
voiceless. Thus, compare /zoo/ 'find' vs. /esoki̱/ 'he is finding.'
In the latter form, the fortis prosody focusing on the /k/ has also
caused the /z/ of the preceding syllable to become voiceless. Again,
a prosody is seen to have its affect on an entire word, even when
there is no apparent phonetic motivation.

4.2 Words and morphemes

Although there are differences between American and European
approaches, the morpheme has been emphasized in phonology in
part because it is more tangible and more easily defined than the
word. However, many of the uses of the morpheme, as in the
statement of distributional constraints, have proven to be inadequate and are better approached within the framework of syllables
and words (including stems and "words within words," etc., as
will be seen below). Chomsky and Halle (1968: 364) have pointed
out that the morpheme boundary (+) never blocks any phonological
process. It has, however, been used to <u>condition</u> a process, e.g.
in an early analysis (Chomsky 1964/ 72: 404; cf. Schane 1973: 95),
the velar softening rule changing /k/ to [s] (<u>electric-electricity</u>)
was said to be conditioned by +, since an internal word boundary
(#) will block the process (<u>pick-picking</u>). In Kim and Hyman (1973)
and Hyman (1975: 197-8), this use of the + boundary to condition a
phonological rule was questioned. In order to evaluate this use of
the morpheme boundary, it is necessary to consider, briefly, the
relationship between words and morphemes.

Shibatani (1973) has pointed out that distributional constraints
on morphemes often differ from those constraints characterizing
the word. His example comes from JAPANESE, where a morpheme
can end in any of a number of consonants, but a word must end either
in a vowel or in a syllabic nasal. When faced with the problem of
borrowing ENGLISH words into JAPANESE, it is always the word
structure constraints which have the last say: if a morpheme can
permit a sequence, but a word cannot, the word wins out (but cf.
Kaye 1973).

No one doubts the need for some kind of morpheme unit in linguistic analysis, and few linguists would assert that the morpheme
has no reality of any kind for language users. However, its relevance
for phonology is open to question. In order to demonstrate the relevance of the morpheme to phonology (and we will only be interested
in this aspect of the question, since language users can be aware
of morphological structure without using it for phonological purposes), we will need evidence of one of two types. 1) We will need

to demonstrate the reality of some distributional constraint characterizing morphemes, but not words; or 2) we will need some process
to be conditioned by a + boundary, which could not have been conditioned by a ## (full word) or # (internal word/stem) boundary.

Kaye (1974) attempts to show the reality of the morpheme for the
statement of at least one distributional constraint (the nasal prosody
in DESANO) by showing that a DESANO word can have an internal
change in nasality, and that each unit having its own nasal prosody
is to be identified as a morpheme. Kaye's demonstration proceeds
as follows. First, he demonstrates that although a syllable must
be either completely nasal or completely oral, there are no morphemes which have one oral syllable and one nasal one. A bisyllabic morpheme will have both syllables either oral or nasal. Thus,
the syllable is too small a unit to capture the nasal prosody. On
the other hand, the word, he claims, is too large, because there
are cases such as [peamĩ] 'he breaks,' consisting of [pea] plus [mĩ],
where there is a word-internal change of nasality. Kaye then proposes that the correct unit is the morpheme, with 'he breaks' presumably analyzed as /pea+mĩ/, or conceivably, in a prosodic approach,
/pea+biᴺ/ with the nasal prosody (N) being assigned to the complete
morpheme.

Kaye's example fails to be conclusive, since it is not the case
that the "morpheme" has a property unknown to the word. In fact
it would be entirely possible to claim that 'he breaks' and other such
examples actually consist of two "words" within the same word (see
section 4.3), in which case we would represent the above example
as /pea#mĩ/ or /pea#biᴺ/. The nasal prosody would be blocked
by the internal word boundary, much like the vowel harmony rule
in IGBO was blocked in the example /gá#fè/ in section 2.4. Kaye's
argument depends crucially on there being a simple + boundary.
However, at least one problem with this analysis is that Kaye points
out in his earlier work (1971: 38) that there are certain suffixes such
as the question particle /di/ (cf. Kaye 1974: fn.8), which assimilate
in nasality to an adjacent morpheme or stem, e.g. [ãhsũ-nĩ] 'do you
buy?' vs. [waʔa-ri] 'do you go?' (/d/ becomes [r] intervocalically).
At least one analysis would recognize underlying /di/, separated
from the preceding verb form by a + boundary, i.e. /ãhsũ+di/ and
/waʔa+di/, with the appropriate rules changing /di/ to [nĩ] after a
nasal form, and to [ri] after an oral form. In this analysis the nasal
assimilation rule will not apply across a # boundary, the boundary
which we claim to be present in forms such as /pea#mĩ/. The result would therefore be that nasality is a prosody characterizing
the environment #...#. But what is this environment? The question

morpheme proves that it is larger than the morpheme, but the
example 'he breaks' shows that it is smaller than the full word
(# #). This might be a case for the "phonological word," which
would be smaller than the grammatical word. But the important
point is that this unit is <u>not</u> identical to the morpheme. Hence,
this fails to be an airtight argument for morpheme structure conditions.

The second kind of argument for the morpheme in phonology
consists of postulated phonological rules which must refer to the
+ boundary in order to apply. All such cases we have investigated
have either used the + boundary when the # boundary would have
done as well, or have used the + boundary diacritically, and could
just as well have used ad hoc boundaries such as $, % or ¢ or
referred directly to the morphemes involved. The velar softening
rule (later revised in Chomsky and Halle 1968, who recognize the
segment /k$_1$/, thereby marking the process diacritically) is a good
example, since the only truly productive use of the rule involves
words which contain (or seem to contain) the suffix -<u>ic</u>. More
important, however, is the absolute need of constraining grammatical boundaries in phonology so that the abuses seen in such
works as Stanley (1973), where boundaries are unnecessarily pro-
liferated (cf. Kari 1975 for a more acceptable reformulation of
NAVAHO prefix phonology), are controlled. To this end we would
like to propose the following constraint: within the word (# #) unit.
there can be recognized at most <u>two</u> internal grammatical boundaries.
One of these, #, can have phonological consequences, the other, +,
cannot. The # boundary, which plays a frequent role in phonology,
and is labelled "internal word boundary" (and perhaps is identical
to the "stem" boundary in some languages) is justified in one of two
ways. 1) In some languages we may have only one word-internal
grammatical boundary which is known to have phonological effect;
in such a language we do not hesitate to assign the # boundary to
it; or 2) in languages known to have more than one word-internal
boundary (where both are claimed to have phonological effects), the
one which bears a relationship to the full word boundary # # is the
one which is recognized as #. The other boundary is either specious,
or the phonological effects are better treated as conditioned by specific morphemes.

The above constraint is stated slightly differently from the position
taken by Kim and Hyman (1973) that morphemes and morpheme boundaries have no role to play in phonology. This latter claim was mis-
construed to signify that there would be no phonologically-relevant
word-internal boundaries. This is clearly not the case, as was shown

with respect to several examples, among which the following
KOREAN one. As seen in the derivation in 4.:

4. /kut # i/ ——→ kuči ——→ [kuǰi] 'firmly'
   "firm" "ly"

palatalization of /t/ to [č] before /i/ takes place across an internal
word boundary. However, as seen in 5,:

5. /tətita/ ——→ [tədida] 'to be slow'
   /əti/   ——→ [ədi]   'where'

palatalization does not take place where there is no boundary.
Thus, the rule can be written as in 6.:

6. t ——→ č / ___ # i

It is interesting to note, however, that 6. is the result of a restructuring which took place in the history of KOREAN (Kong-On Kim,
personal communication). As seen in 7.:

7. *ti > /či/   'earth'
   *ətɨy > /əti/ 'where' (pronounced [ədi])

*t did palatalize to č even when there was no boundary. However,
a second sound change converting *ɨy to i has produced new instances of synchronic underlying /ti/ sequences which do not
palatalize. Since 'earth' in 7. has been rephonemicized with an
underlying /č/, it is only across a boundary that rule 6. will apply.
Since the internal word boundary in 6. is independently motivated
on the basis of the rules of word formation in KOREAN, we feel
that this is the proper use of boundaries in phonological rules.

The strength of the above proposal is that it thus places a necessary second requirement on boundaries in phonology. The first
was stated clearly by Chomsky, Halle and Lukoff (1956) as Condition
III, cited in Lehiste (1964/74: fn. 6): "Junctures should be distributed in a manner that is significant on higher levels. Specifically,
junctures [read: boundaries] should appear only at morpheme
boundaries, and different junctures should correspond, by and
large, to different morphological and syntactical processes." Our
constraint places the requirement that boundaries be necessarily
hierarchized with respect to one another. They must bear a consistent relationship to each other which is not language-specific,
but rather which is universal. Thus, the very formalization of the
internal word boundary as # implies that a rule of the form in 8.:

8. A ⟶ B / __ #

will also apply to a full word boundary. On the other hand, a rule
of the form in 9.:

9. A ⟶ B / __ ##

will not apply to an internal word boundary, but only to a full one.
There are several implications of this approach, not all of which
have been investigated as carefully as would seem necessary. The
one which we would like to suggest here is that the strengths or
"ranks" (McCawley 1968, Stanley 1973) assigned to # #, # and +
cannot be violated. Thus, it should not be allowed either that
boundaries lower on a hierarchy condition processes not conditioned
by boundaries higher on the hierarchy; nor should it be allowed
that ad hoc boundaries be treated as part of the system (including
the = boundary said to account for a number of word-level processes
in Chomsky and Halle 1968). With this in mind we may eventually
consider reinterpreting even the KOREAN rule given in 6. above,
since the + boundary is too low, and the ## too high on the hierarchy to join in conditioning the palatalization in question. Since
only a limited number of suffixes condition the change from /t/ to
[č], we might consider the alternative of making specific mention
to those morphemes. At the very least the universal boundary
hierarchy must be in effect at the initiation of new boundary phenomena.

4.3 Words within words

In the DESANO and IGBO cases discussed above we have already
referred to the notion of a word within a word. This is, of course,
what is implied by the single # boundary. Either both sides of the
boundary are a word, or one side of the boundary is a word, and
the other side a loosely attached affix or "disjunct" in the terms of
Kari (1975). The problem of treating stem-boundaries is one which
we will not be able to resolve here, except by noting that although
they resemble our # boundary, they may at times involve a directionality, i.e. you have to know which side of the stem you are on
(see Langdon 1975 for a discussion of the need of a stem boundary
in YUMAN languages).

Nowhere is the notion of "words within words" clearer than in
compounding. This process has been studied in great phonetic
detail by Lehiste (1964/73: 305-6), who states for ESTONIAN: "A
tendency may be observed in the language to assimilate compounds
to the canonical phonological shape of noncompound words. In the

course of this assimilation, the word-initial allophone of the initial
consonant of the second constituent of a disyllabic compound is
replaced by an allophone in one of the three degrees of segmental
quantity, and the syllabic quantity of the second syllable is reduced
until it resembles that of the second syllable of a noncompound
disyllabic word with overlong first syllable." Thus, one of the
things which happens in ESTONIAN is that as a compound word
tends to become treated as a noncompound, the 9 vowels and 22
diphthongs possible in monosyllables and first syllables of words
become reduced to only 4 of the vowels and 3 of the diphthongs
in the nonfirst syllable of the emerging noncompound.

In the above process whereby a word consisting of two words
comes to be treated exactly the same as a word consisting only of
one (multisyllabic) word, we observe a change formalizable as
CV#CV becoming CV+CV and eventually CVCV. At the CV#CV
stage, the second monosyllabic word has all or nearly all of the
properties of a monosyllabic word in isolation. In the second
stage these properties gradually fade away (though language users
may retain awareness of the bimorphemic structure of the word).
Finally, in stage three, even this awareness which had lost its
phonological effects is lost, and we no longer speak of any internal
structure on any level.

We therefore propose that the boundary changes observed represent a natural, recurring phenomenon in language, summarized as
follows:

  10. $\parallel$ > $\#\#$ > $\#$ > $+$ > $\emptyset$

This represents the historical origin of many boundaries, as well
as their relative strength. We have said that pause boundaries
($\parallel$) include word boundaries — they also contain all of the boundaries to the right of $\#\#$ in (10). A word boundary contains an
internal boundary which in turn contains a + boundary. Qualita-
tively, when one passes from $\#$ to +, one enters into the realm of
a morphological boundary which has no phonological effect. Thus,
phonologically, CV+CV is equivalent to CVCV.

The narrowing of pause to word boundary is thus similar to the
narrowing of full to internal word boundary which is frequently
attested. Unfortunately, the natural history of boundaries represented in 10. is often not as transparent as one would wish. One
suffix may require a $\#$ boundary while another takes a +. Aronoff
(1975, 1976) presents a number of convincing arguments suggesting

that the same -able suffix in ENGLISH is sometimes bounded by
+, sometimes by #. Pronunciations such as cómparable and préf-
erable indicate an internal + boundary which has no phonological
effect and allows these words to appear as if they had no internal
structure. Pronunciations such as compárable and preférable be-
tray an internal # boundary, which indicates that these words are
not only stressed differently but also that to the left of the # boundary
are full words pronounced as they are pronounced in isolation (e.g.
with a full vowel in the case of compárable). Aronoff would like to
see some semantic consistency in assigning + vs. #, for example,
that words with + are lexicalized with special meanings not equivalent
to the sum of the parts (morphemes), but is forced to simply say that
if there is a meaning difference between two forms A+B and A#B,
A+B will tend to wander more from the underlying meaning of the
parts than will A#B. An illustration from Aronoff (1976:128) is
seen in 11.:

11. This is the cómparable model in our line.
     *This is the compárable model in our line.

The second sentence is starred because it cannot have the "lexicalized" meaning of 'equivalent' but only the literal meaning 'capable
of being compared.' In examples such as recollect 'remember' vs.
re-collect 'to collect again,' which have the same historical source,
we might propose that the former has gone all the way to losing its
internal structure. The latter must be represented as re#collect,
with its meaning consisting of the sum of the two parts re 'again'
and collect.

The historical weakening of boundaries, as when words are joined,
or affixes are more closely fused with their stems or neighboring
affixes, is summed up as follows by Žirmunskij (1966: 83): "Word
combination, in narrow sense of being more or less 'bound up,'
arises as a result of a closer grammatical or lexical unification
of the group of words as the new meaning of the whole develops
(grammatically or lexically) and becomes distinct from the aggregate meaning of its parts. Two trends are possible: 1) towards
the grammaticalization (morphologization) of the word combination;
that is to say, the group of words is transformed into a specific new
analytical form of the word; 2) towards the lexicalization of the word
combination; that is to say, the group of words is transformed into
a more or less solid phraseological entity constituting a phraseological equivalent of the word in the semantic sense."

It may be necessary to add, however, that a boundary may not
only weaken as the result of lexicalization or grammaticalization.

Also, a new combination of the same morphemes may be introduced
to contrast with an older, more fused one. Jan Kooij has discussed
the differences between DUTCH vruchteloos 'fruitless' and vruchtloo
'fruit-less.' The first has a lexicalized meaning of 'in vain,' while
the second is literal and means 'without fruit.' The first pattern is
older, carrying the genitive linker, while the second is newer, and
for some examples, can be created on the spot. Thus, the word
harteloos means 'heartless, without feeling,' while a body found
lacking a heart might be described as hartloos. The words with
-eloos tend to be lexicalized with special meanings and are formalized with +, while those with plain -loos tend to be more literal and
are formalized with #.

In concluding this section let us consider the famous problem
of /g/-deletion after the velar nasal in ENGLISH. As seen in the
forms in 12.:

12. /sɪng # #/   ⟶ [sɪŋ]   'sing'
     /sɪng # ər/ ⟶ [sɪŋər]   'singer'
     /long + ər/ ⟶ [lɔŋgər]   'longer'
     /fɪngər/   ⟶ [fɪŋgər]   'finger'

the /g/ of 'singer' has been deleted before an internal word boundary
just as it is deleted before a full word boundary in 'sing.' In 'longer,'
on the other hand, although we can establish an internal morphologic
structure, the word behaves phonologically as if there were no bound
ary, since the /g/ is not deleted (cf. 'finger,' which has no internal
structure). The /g/-deletion rule is stated in 13.:

13. g   ⟶   Ø / ŋ ___ #

Since there are dialects of ENGLISH which pronounce 'singer' with
an internal [g], it seems reasonable to propose that the generalizing
of /g/-deletion from word-final to word-internal position represents
an innovation. But why should it hit the agentive -er of 'singer' but
not the comparative -er of 'longer?'

While we cannot always provide proof for the explanations of such
problems, an argument can be made that words with the comparative
-er are more lexicalized-like than are words with the agentive -er.
For one thing the comparative suffix is constrained phonologically
while the agentive suffix is not. The comparative -er is normally
added onto monosyllables and adjectives ending in -ly, though even
some monosyllabic adjectives hardly can take -er (e.g. juster?
perter? coyer?). It is almost as though one has to know the list

of words taking -er rather than the productive counterpart employ-
ing more. The agentive -er suffix can be added onto any verb
no matter what the length is, and is constrained primarily by the
semantic content of the verb (e.g. be-er is odd). Even though in
a few cases an existing lexical agentive may preempt the -er form
(e.g. cook instead of cooker), it is almost always possible to produce agentive -er forms (e.g. disambiguater). The comparative
-er even has some suppletive forms (worse, better, instead of
*badder and *gooder), requiring the consulting of one's lexicon.
Finally, the agentive -er seems to be semantically so transparent
that a corresponding but nonexistent verb derived from cases
where a false analysis is made is easily understood -- e.g. burgle
from burglar, haberdash from haberdasher, agress from agressor.
Thus, if the ## were to generalize into words with internal structure, it would in most likelihood hit the agentive -er before the
comparative -er suffix.

5. Summary and Conclusion

In the above sections we have surveyed the various phonological
evidences for the word as a linguistic unit. We have seen that distributional constraints, boundary phenomena, accentual phenomena
and prosodies all make reference to the word. In addition we have
seen that there is a tremendous tendency to narrow down from the
pause to the word environment, and, in the case of prosodies, to
build up from the segmental and syllable level to the word. Finally,
we have seen the tendency for the word to impose its structure
within another word, creating the necessity for the internal word
boundary.

At a number of points it was necessary to point out that a continuum exists such that it is not always possible to determine
whether something is clearly a word (or word boundary) phenomenon
or something else. Also, since we have seen the tendency for a
distribution or process to change its realm of application (e.g. from
pause to word, from syllable to word, from word to internal word),
it is not always possible to make a clean statement concerning the
appropriate conditioning factor (e.g. final devoicing in terms of
words? syllables? words within words?). As a final illustration
let us consider some TURKISH data provided by Karl Zimmer
(personal communication), where the interplay between all of these
units is particularly revealing.

Consider the realization of /b/ in the following forms:

14. a. /kitab # #/   ⟶   [kitap]   'book'
     b. /kitab # lar/   ⟶   [kitaplar]   'books'
     c. /kitab # im/   ⟶   [kitabim]   'my book'
     d. /abla/   ⟶   [abla]   'older sister'

In 14.a devoicing takes place before a full word boundary. In 14.b
devoicing takes place before an internal word boundary followed by
a consonant. In 14.c where the internal word boundary is followed
by a vowel, no devoicing takes place. Finally, since /b/ is followed
by a consonant but without an intervening # boundary, no devoicing
takes place in 14.d. The appropriate rule is formalized in 15.:

15. [-son] ⟶ [-voice] / ____ # $\left\{ \begin{array}{l} \# \\ C \end{array} \right.$

That devoicing does not simply take place syllable-finally is seen
in 14.d which is syllabified [ab.la] (cf. [ib.ne] 'passive homosexual')
However, since the internal word boundary is the same in 14.b and
14.c, it appears that syllabification does have a role to play here.
In particular it appears that devoicing has spread from 14.a to 14.b,
and since syllable-final devoicing is not a general property of TURK-
ISH, it must be assumed that devoicing in 14.b signals the integrity
of the word /kitab/ in /kitab#lar/. The reason why /kitab/ cannot
be as readily isolated in 14.c is that the syllabification rules of
TURKISH place the /b/ with the following syllable, i.e. [ki.ta.bim].
That is, while there has been "analogy" in 14.b on the basis of the
[p] in 14.a, this analogical spreading of devoicing to internal word
boundaries has been hindered by syllabification processes.

Just how the word fits into the whole picture of syllables, affixes,
stems and whatnot is something which we have only made initial
stabs at in this study. In particular it will now be necessary to
look at some of the phenomena presented in the preceding sections
with an eye open to the so-called demarcative function. Do language users choose to mark words phonologically to generalize on
pause phenomena and to move word characteristics to within the
word so as to help the listener process utterances? Or do language
users accomplish these things so as to help themselves (e.g. to
keep things straight in their own minds)? Or do people just get
confused and make mistakes? It is tempting to see purpose in all
that we have said, but the theoretical apparatus is regrettably
lacking.

BIBLIOGRAPHY

Applegate, J.R. 1958. An outline of the structure of Shilḥa. New
York: A.C.L.S.

Aronoff, M. 1975. -able. NELS 5. 183-191.

_____. 1976. Word formation in generative grammar. Lin-
guistic Inquiry Monograph 1. Cambridge: M.I.T. Press.

Bendor-Samuel, J.T. 1966. Some prosodic features in Terena.
In memory of J.R. Firth, ed. by C.E. Bazell et al., 30-39.
London: Longmans.

_____ and K.W. Spreda. 1969. Fortis articulation: a feature
of the present continuous verb in Agbo. Linguistics 52. 20-26.

Chafe, W.L. 1959. Internal reconstruction in Seneca. Language
35. 477-95.

Chomsky, N. 1964. Current issues in linguistic theory. The
Hague: Mouton. Parts reprinted in Phonological theory:
evolution and current practice, ed. by V.B. Makkai, 401-23.
New York: Holt, Rinehart and Winston (1972).

_____ and M. Halle. 1968. The sound pattern of English.
New York: Harper and Row.

_____, M. Halle and F. Lukoff. 1956. For Roman Jakobson,
ed. by M. Halle et al., 65-80. The Hague: Mouton.

Clayton, M.L. 1976. The redundancy of underlying morpheme-
structure conditions. Language 52. 295-313.

Delattre, P. 1963. Comparing the prosodic features of English,
German, Spanish and French. IRAL 1. 193-210.

Elimelech, B. 1976. Tonal grammar of Etsako. Working Papers
in Phonetics 35. University of California, Los Angeles.

Firth, J.R. 1948. Sounds and prosodies. Transactions of the
philological society for the year 1948, 127-52.

Garde, P. 1968. L'accent. Paris: Presses universitaires de France.

468 Larry M. Hyman

Gårding, E. 1967. Internal juncture in Swedish. Travaux de l'Institut de Phonétique de Lund VI.

Greenberg, J.H. 1965. The word as a linguistic unit. Psycholinguistics: a survey of theory and research problems, ed. by C.E. Osgood and T. Sebeok, 67-70. Bloomington: Indiana University Press.

Hooper, J.B. 1976. Aspects of natural generative grammar. New York: Academic Press.

Hyman, L.M. 1972. A phonological study of Fe?fe? -Bamileke. Studies in African Linguistics, Supplement 4.

_____. 1975. Phonology: theory and analysis. New York: Holt, Rinehart and Winston.

_____. 1977. On the nature of linguistic stress. Studies in stress and accent, ed. by L.M. Hyman. Southern California Occasional Papers in Linguistics No. 4. U. of Southern California.

Javkin, H. 1975. Phonological rules influenced by boundaries: a search through the Stanford Phonology Archive. Ms., University of California, Berkeley.

Kari, J. 1975. The disjunct boundary in Navajo and Tanaina verb prefix complexes. IJAL 41. 330-45.

Kaye, J.D. 1971. Nasal harmony in Desano. Linguistic Inquiry 2. 37-56.

_____. 1973. On deep constraints in phonology: loan words. Paper presented at the Winter Meeting of the Linguistic Society of America, San Diego. (Published in French translation under the title "Contraintes profondes en phonologie: les emprunts," Cahier de Linguistique 5, University of Quebec at Montreal, 1974).

_____. 1974. Morpheme structure constraints live! Paper presented at the Winter Meeting of the Linguistic Society of America, New York. Ms., McGill University and University of Toronto.

Kim, K-O. and L.M. Hyman. 1973. On the non-status of morpheme boundaries in phonology. Paper presented at the Winter Meeting of the Linguistic Society of America, San Diego.

Krámský, J. 1969. The word as a linguistic unit. The Hague: Mouton.

Leben, W.R. 1971. Suprasegmental and segmental representation of tone. Studies in African Linguistics, Supplement 2. 183-200.

_____. 1973. The role of tone in segmental phonology. Consonant types and tone, ed. by L.M. Hyman, 115-49. Southern California Occasional Papers in Linguistics 1. University of Southern California.

Lehiste, I. 1964. Compounding as a phonological process. Proceedings of the Ninth International Contress of Linguists, ed. by H.G. Lunt, 331-36. The Hague: Mouton. Reprinted in Phonology, ed. by E.C. Fudge, 302-8. Penguin (1973).

_____. 1965. Juncture. Proceedings of the Fifth International Congress of Linguists, 172-200. Basel: S. Karger.

_____. 1970. Suprasegmentals. Cambridge: M.I.T. Press.

Lunt, H.G. 1973. Remarks on nasality: the case of Guaraní. A Festschrift for Morris Halle, ed. by S.R. Anderson and P. Kiparsky, 131-39. New York: Holt, Rinehart and Winston.

Martinet, A. 1954. Accents et tons. Miscellanea Phonetica 2. 13-24.

_____. 1960. Elements of general linguistics. Translated by E. Palmer. Chicago: University Press (1964). Originally published in French, Paris: Librairie Armand Colin.

McCawley, J.D. 1968. The phonological component of a grammar of Japanese. Monographs on Linguistic Analysis 2. The Hague: Mouton.

Okell, J. 1969. A reference grammar of colloquial Burmese. London: Oxford University Press.

Paulian, C. 1975. Le kukuya: langue teke du Congo. Paris: Bibliothèque de la S.E.L.A.F. 49-50.

Pike, K.L. 1967. Language in relation to a unified theory of the structure of human behavior. The Hague: Mouton.

Pulgram, E. 1970. Syllable, word, nexus, cursus. The Hague: Mouton.

Robins, R.H. 1957. Vowel nasality in Sundanese: a phonological and grammatical study. Studies in linguistic analysis, 87-103. Oxford: Basil Blackwell.

Schane, S.A. 1973. Generative phonology. Englewood Cliffs, N.J.: Prentice-Hall.

Schuchardt, H. 1885. Über die Lautgesetze: gegen die Jung-grammatiker. Translated as "On sound laws: against the Neo-grammarians," Schuchardt, the Neogrammarians, and the transformational theory of phonological change: four essays, by T. Vennemann and T.H. Wilbur, 39-72. Frankfurt am Main: Athenäum (1972).

Shibatani, M. 1973. The role of surface phonetic constraints in generative phonology. Language 49. 87-106.

Sprigg, R.K. 1957. Junction in spoken Burmese. Studies in linguistic analysis, 104-38. Oxford: Basil Blackwell.

Stanley, R. 1973. Boundaries in phonology. A festschrift for Morris Halle, ed. by S.R. Anderson and P. Kiparsky, 185-206. New York: Holt, Rinehart and Winston.

Trubetzkoy, N. 1939. Principles of phonology. Translated by C.A.M. Baltaxe. Berkeley and Los Angeles: University of California Press (1969). Originally published in German, Grundzüge der Phonologie, Travaux du Cercle Linguistique de Praque 7.

Vennemann, T. 1974. Words and syllables in natural generative phonology. Papers from the parasession on natural phonology, 346-74. Chicago Linguistic Society.

Welmers, B.F. and W.E. Welmers. 1968. Igbo, a learner's manual. Private publication by the authors, University of California, Los Angeles.

Williamson, K. In press. Consonant distribution in Ịjọ. Ms., University of Ibadan (1972).

Žirmunskij, V.M. 1966. The word and its boundaries. Linguistics 27. 65-91.

Intonation Across Languages

DWIGHT BOLINGER

ABSTRACT

The traits of intonation shared by the majority of languages, not excepting tone languages, are both formal and semantic, and cover the two main non-tonal uses of pitch variation: to form closures (descending lines, clause-final falls and non-falls) and to form accents (obtrusions for prominence, mainly upward). Terminals are almost universally low or falling for finality and assertion, and high or rising for the opposite, including yes-no questions. Accents are generally set off by contrasting pitch levels, and their position in the sentence indicates both focus and climax. Most deviations from the central tendencies can be explained in reference to those tendencies. The convergence between language A and language B, and the divergence between dialect a and dialect b, are potentially so striking that intonational typology has to be assigned a special basis, tied to inherent reactions of the human organism. Studies of child language support this view.

For want of a better form of thanks, I list the persons who by conversation or correspondence have helped to dispel some of my ignorance (and bear no responsibility for the rest of it): Isamu Abe, John T. Bendor-Samuel, Elizabeth L. Camp, Curtis Cook, George M. Cowan, Alan Cruttenden, María Beatriz Fontanella de Weinberg, Charles A. Ferguson, Mary LeCron Foster, Olga Garnica, Joseph E. Grimes, Mohamed Hassan, Harold Key, Bh. Krishnamurti, Karen Kvavik, Donald Macaulay, Joy McCarthy, J.D. McClure, Lise Menn, Ravinda Mistri, Stanley Newman, Laurie Reece, Lawrence A. Reid, Naomi B. Schiff, Robert B. Shilkret, Lynn Snyder, Susan Steele, Jeff Titon, Donald M. Topping, E.M. Uhlenbeck, Kullo Vende, Ethel Wallis, Viola Waterhouse, Thelma Weeks, John David West, Darryl Wilson.

CONTENTS

1. Introduction

1.1 Universality in extent and depth

The tentative yes that I gave in 1964 to the question "Is intonation
a universal trait of language?" can be affirmed with more confidence today, but also with a keener appreciation of the ability of any
given language to play variations on a central theme. Not only do
all languages probably have intonation (that claim is becoming almost as uninteresting as "all languages have phonology"), but there
are tendencies that go far beyond the resemblance in terms of "typologically similar systems" that Greenberg cautiously admitted
in 1959 (Greenberg 1959: 383). Clearly more than typology would
be involved if we found the majority of languages not only having
the same phonemes but using them to form the same words. I hypothesized that of the parts of the human vocal system that are used
linguistically, intonation responds more closely than any other to
states of the organism. There is now more reason than ever to
believe this and to look at the early stages of language acquisition,
and at manifestations of emotion at all stages and ages, for the key
to certain almost exceptionless tendencies and the repetition of intonational forms in the most widely separated languages.

1.2 The uses of pitch

Pitch has many uses, and it is not easy to decide how many of
them to include as "intonation." A rough but workable definition
can be inferred from Woo 1972. Intonation covers those significant
uses of fundamental pitch that are not associated in any way with
particular formatives, whether of lexical tone (the lexicon specifies
pitch features on every vowel) or of tone harmony (the pitch contour
of a formative can be predicted by some rule)(Woo 1972: 21). These
significant uses are mainly of two kinds, which have the physical
aspect of horizontal and vertical breaks. Vertical breaks are the
prominences of accent: certain syllables are obtruded upward or
downward, generally for some purpose related to focus on a particular constituent or on a whole sentence. Horizontal breaks are the
discontinuities in the melodic line that bear some relation to pause,
and generally correspond to grouping into constituents. ("Juncture,"
"separation," "continuation," and "suspension" are related terms.)
Intonation and pause are the chief phonological cues to constituent
organization. To some extent they are balanced against each other,
with intonation revealing, by means of integral melodic patterns,
the words and phrases that belong together, and pause marking the
divisions. But to the extent that a tune is recognized, the listener

knows when it comes to an end, and pause can be dispensed with.
This is especially true in that the end of an intonational tune is the
part with the most definite features.

1.2.1 <u>Intonational breaks, horizontal and vertical</u>   Intonational
breaks, whether sidewise or up-and-down, are either-or phenomena.
A syllable is either heard or not heard as accented. A separation
is either heard or not heard to occur. But once a plus has been
assigned to either of these features, the strength of the plus is entirely gradient. If a single accent occurs in a sentence, the speaker
can signal the degree of its importance or the force of his emphasis
by widening the pitch interval. In <u>His name is John. -- No, his name
is Henry</u>. -- <u>His name is John, I tell you!</u> the second <u>John</u> makes a
wider sweep than the first. If a sentence contains two accents, the
relation of higher to lower may be an all-or-none question, but how
much higher and how much lower -- as signals of relative importance
-- is again gradient. Similarly with separations. There is no absolute difference between the end of a sentence and the end of a
paragraph, but paragraphs (or discourses) regularly end lower than
non-final sentences. And when, to convey an attitude of finality (as
in argument), a "terminal fall" is brought inside a sentence, the
depth of the fall can signal how positive the speaker feels. Pitch
range and pitch height are clearly tied to emotional states. Angry
speakers everywhere use the same flights of pitch. Languages described as having "no intonation" (e.g. AMAHUACA: Russell 1958)
or "no contrastive pitch patterns" (e.g. KAIWA: Bridgeman 1961)
are still admitted to have changes in pitch corresponding to the
fluctuations of emotion. Intonation is a half-tamed savage. To
understand the tamed or linguistically harnessed half of him one
has to make friends with the wild half.

1.3 <u>Other prosodic elements</u>

    There are other prosodic elements that conjugate with fundamental
pitch, the three most important being voice register, intensity, and
rhythm. I shall have little to say about them, but at this point they
need at least to be identified.

1.3.1 <u>Registers</u>   There are three registers, loft (falsetto), modal ("normal"), and pulse (vocal fry) (Hollien 1974: 125-43). The
loft register has definite uses in intonation, and one or more of them
may well be universal. For example, in HUICHOL there is a scheme
whereby "voiced sounds are spoken with falsetto voicing...[with] a
meaning 'excitement, extreme involvement of the speaker'" (Grimes
1955: 31-35). This would seem to be a controlled use of the same

falsetto that appears in CHUAVE as a symptom of anger or panic
(Swick 1966: 42). On the other hand there is a way of expressing
politeness in EASTERN POPOLOCA which consists in a slow, lenis
upglide on the prepause syllable to well above the lexically highest
tone. "The height of the glide is the measure of the degree of politeness" (Kalstrom and Pike 1968). It would be natural for a rise
of this sort to fade into falsetto. The difference between the two
modes — one for shades of excitement and the other for shades of
politeness -- is a function of intensity, and both modes are commonplace in ENGLISH. Words such as shriek and scream describe the
first. As for the second, an incredulous So? with a short rise in
pitch can easily be curt; with a slow rise into falsetto at low intensity, it is sweetly reasonable.

The pulse register — more often referred to by linguists as lar-
yngealization or creaky voice -- also has its functions, mostly related to terminal fall. The deeper the fall, the greater the tendency
to fade into pulse, so that pulse register takes on a significance
related to low terminal pitch. Since pulse is also possible at a
fairly high pitch, one sometimes finds an illusory fall without a fall
-- pulse substituting for a final low pitch. Interwoven with this is
glottalization. To end an utterance, a speaker may let it drift away,
especially down; or he may check it. In ENGLISH either a glottal
stop or a labial closure may be used to check the words yes and no,
pronunciations that show up in the eye-dialect spellings yeh, yep,
and nope. The normal POPOLOCA utterance ends in a sharp glottal stop (Kalstrom and Pike 1968). Questions in JAPANESE and
MIKASUKI (West 1962: 89) are regularly ended with a glottal stop.
It is easy to appreciate the usefulness of glottalization as a substitute for intonation in a tone language. The affective use of exaggerated pulse as a mark of assurance (finality reinterpreted as
nothing-more-to-be-said certainty) and masculinity is found in some
languages and dialects; among male speakers it distinguishes the
SPANISH of Spain from that of Mexico (Olsen 1975).

1.3.2 Intensity   Intensity has been the most overrated of the
three major correlates of prominence, of which the two others are
pitch and duration. Brown and McGlone (1974) conclude from their
experiment that "vocal intensity was not a significantly used parameter by the speakers to denote stress" whereas "fundamental frequency was most significantly related to stress" (that is, accent).
Non-experimental linguists continue to speak of intensity as if it
were an important variable, permitting their inner sensations of
force and effort to color their judgment. In most if not all instances
statements like "an increase in loudness conditions a rise in pitch"

should be turned around. In the case of reverse accents (as on wor-
and hurt in Don't worry; he won't hurt you spoken reassuringly)
there may actually be a decrease in loudness. The only thing that
can distort a frequency or duration signal (so long as it is audible
at all) is relative motion -- as train passengers notice when they
approach a ringing bell at a crossing and then move away from it.
Intensity is affected by wind, intervening objects, position of speaker's head, etc., and is not very reliable.

Though intensity as an automatic correlate of pitch change for
accent can be pretty much discounted, it does contribute in its own
way to the prosody. For example, a person repeatedly urged to
eat spaghetti but who dislikes the stuff intensely might express his
disgust by means of intensity without pitch change (but inevitably
with some added duration) as follows:

>   want
>   don't
> I
>   to
>   eat spaGHETti !

-- the intensity is made more noticeable by strong closure of the [g]
and abrupt, heavy release. The low terminal pitch expresses topic --
the only new thing in this sentence is want; but the intensity enables
the speaker to express an emotional reaction to the topic. Intensity
is thus good for expressing 'pent-up emotion.' In a context such as
the following,

When you get a successful cross between two strains of sweet
corn, that's a hybrid, but the same people who confuse hybrid
with high-bred will tell you that a cross between black and white
is MONgrelization!

the speaker can mock the Bunker attitude by increasing the volume
and backing the vowel (an effect of the mocking gesture). The uses
of intensity need a study of their own, but do not concern this one.

1.3.3 Rhythm   Rhythm is of course the system of repeating or
alternating durations and their rate of succession. It appears to
play a secondary role, supporting (and sometimes replacing) other
parts of the prosody. A slowing down is part of the decrescendo
that occurs before pause, and may therefore -- alone or in concert
with pitch terminals and pause -- mark the end of a constituent.
Extra length is also more often than not a part of accent, accompanying a vertical break in the pitch line; it may serve alone under
some conditions as the signal of accent. One problem in any discussion

of rhythm based on secondary sources is the persistence of the ill-
defined notion of "stress." There is supposed to be a basic distinction between "stress-timing" and "syllable-timing," and stress-timing
is always exemplified by a supposed tendency to isochrony between
accentual peaks. But since accents respond to the meanings that
the speaker wishes to highlight, unless meaning is somehow adjusted
to rhythm the result can hardly be a succession of equal intervals.
ENGLISH is claimed to be a stress-timed language, but in a phrase
such as the quite unnécessary incomprehensibílity of his wórds the
central interval is substantially longer than the flanking ones (cf.
Bolinger 1965:164-71). What ENGLISH does have is a striking near-
isochrony based on vowel quality. Syllables with reduced vowels
"borrow time" from preceding syllables with full vowels, so that two
such sentences as John drank beer and Johnny drank a beer are of
nearly equal length (Bolinger 1963, 1976; Lehiste 1972). Much more
needs to be known about rhythm before it can be discussed in the
context of linguistic universals.

2. Accent and Tone

2.1 Relevance of tone

Accents -- the vertical breaks alluded to earlier -- are part and
parcel of intonation. Tone is irrelevant, except as a nuisance, or
as something perhaps historically related to intonation. This last
point deserves a few lines.

2.1.1 Intonational influences on tone   The segmental origin of
lexical tone is an established historical fact -- the loss, for example,
of a pitch-raising syllable-final consonant resulting in tonal contrast.
It is harder to determine whether intonation might also have contributed, especially in tone-harmony languages. In YORUBA, high tone
may signal the grammatical relationship that the "nominal piece"
bears to the "verbal piece" (Carnochan 1964: 404). This may have
involved, to begin with, some such imagery as Kirsner 1976 uses
for the human arguments in a sentence, namely "high participant,"
high pitch signaling highly important. Again in YORUBA, one form
of negation consists in a lowered pitch associated with "the prolon-
gation of the vowel sound of the last syllable of the nominal subject
piece" (Carnochan 1964: 398); there is a similar phenomenon in
SARAMACCAN, though it occurs along with an explicit negative
morpheme initially in the sentence at high pitch (Rountree 1972: 310).
How this could happen intonationally is documented in the speech of
three-year-old Leslie, who used a falling intonation to replace a
negative morpheme, for example in E gerd 'I'm not scared' (Weeks

1974:101-5). Leslie also lowered her head as a sign of negation.
Negative sentences favor lowered pitches intonationally, and Leslie's
discovery was a "tonal" reinterpretation. A similar tonal reinterpretation could be made for the two senses of funny, as in the following — the first is 'odd,' the second 'laughable':

That's   That's fun
       funny!   ny!

YORUBA has other indications too of an intonational basis for its
tone (Siertsema 1959). The line between tone and intonation is not
a sharp one.

2.1.2 Tone vs. accent So it is hard to make a clear distinction
between tone and accent. If accent is primarily a matter of pitch,
it might seem to differ only quantitatively from tone — one tonal
distinction per word, for example, instead of several; or grammatically — the word rather than a syllable (or a vowel) carrying
the change in pitch. An accent language then would be a tone language with just two pitch levels (high versus low or obtruded versus
unobtruded). The pitch accent systems of FORE (K. Pike 1963),
CHEYENNE (Frantz 1972a), and PENOBSCOT, ABNAKI, and ARA-
PAHO (Frantz 1972b: 223) behave very much like ordinary accent-
for-prominence. Similarly with the "stress" system of LUCUMI,
known to stem from the tones of YORUBA (Olmsted 1953). But
Eunice Pike proposes (1974) a way to decide, given a language in
which there is a high tone contrasted with other tones, whether the
high tone is a tone and not an accent. The difference is that high
pitch for accent affects its environment, whereas high tone is affected by its environment. For example, high tone may be (in fact
tends to be) shorter than low tone, whereas high accent tends to be
longer; accented syllables tend to have full vowels and unaccented
ones reduced vowels, but tone does not affect vowel quality; accent
affects quality of a consonant, but quality of a consonant may well
affect tone; etc. It is logical that accent and tone should differ in
this way, simply because of the function of accent, which is generally to highlight an element for focus. It has to be able to override the opposition, and accordingly calls upon other acoustic means
besides pitch, especially duration. Lexical tone is only one of the
phonemes making up a word, and context can easily make it redundant. Accent is directly meaningful, tone is only distinctive. Here
we have a special case of what Powlison (1971) calls perturbation
from the top down: discourse on paragraph, paragraph on sentence,
sentence (intonation) on segmental tone, etc. (Powlison 1971: 47).

2.2 Accent

As tone is not, by definition, intonational, we lay it aside and concentrate on accent, which is one of the two main manifestations of intonation.

2.3 Accent and stress

It has not always been seen in this light. Earlier discussion of "stress" have emphasized its demarcative function and overlooked its place in the melodic line. This was mainly a result of restricting the discussion to citation forms, which instead of being recognized as one-word sentences and hence as bearing a sentence accent, were regarded as morphologically basic, in some cases with distinctive stress (ENGLISH úndertaking 'funeral directing,' undertáking 'enter-prise'), in others merely demarcative (first syllable of a word regularly stressed in BENGALI). Given this assumption, it was then necessary, in a description of longer stretches, to provide for the "suppression" of all "stresses" except particular ones -- a suppression of something that was never there in the first place as a component of a word as such, but only as a manifestation of a sentence with a sentence accent. The most that can be said is that in the majority of languages when a given word is accented a given syllable (which I shall call the stressed syllable, reserving stress for this purpose) is marked to receive the accent. The occurrence of the accent is an intonational matter.

2.4 Intonational basis of stress

The intonational basis is best seen in the favored position of stress within a word or phrase. Assuming that any word can occur utter-ance-finally (not quite true, but true enough for a rough generaliza-tion), if we find that there is a widespread tendency to put the word stress at the point that will be most advantageous for the terminal sentence intonation, we may hypothesize that the needs of intonation are what determine, in the long run, the position of stress.

2.4.1 Favored stress position   Terminal intonations are univer-sally the most important and they require two things: an accentual prominence and a tail — the latter to point the direction of the final pitch (rising, falling, level, or a combination). This argues for an optimal minimum of two syllables, the first stressed, the other not. One then expects that the favored stress position in words should be the penult. As far as the intonation is concerned, the antepenult would be just as good — there would merely be one extra unstressed syllable to add to the tail; but in a language with an abundance of both bisyllabic and trisyllabic (or multisyllabic) words, there would then have to be at least two patterns, one for the bisyllables and another (or several others) for longer words. To the extent that stress is demarcative as well as a support to accent, a more regular position would have the advantage.

2.4.2 <u>Why certain positions are favored</u> In his survey of stress systems, Hyman 1975 observes both the advantage of non-final position for stress and the favoring of the next-to-last syllable: "a number of language-specific facts reveal that [the penultimate position] is in some sense preferred over final position" (Hyman 1975: 9); "languages often have mechanisms whose function is to remove stress from final position (often putting it into penultimate position)" (p. 10); "the cooccurrence of an initial primary and a penultimate secondary stress, or of a primary penultimate and an initial secondary stress is not fortuitous. Rather, it would appear that the intrinsic variations which give rise to stress accent are always present, and can become grammaticalized at any time. These intrinsic variations are ... intonational ..., and are ultimately derived from the articulatory and perceptual universals which characterize human speech" (p.19). The observation regarding secondary stress reflects the general tendency in longer utterances (including polysyllabic words) to have two accentual prominences, one toward the beginning and the other toward the end, each with its need to dominate other syllables.

2.4.3 <u>Preferences in twenty-three languages</u> Table 1 shows the preferences in 23 languages (not selected for any connection with stress) that do not already appear in Hyman's much larger sample. It confirms his conclusions, except that the penult here appears to be a much heavier favorite. (In JAVANESE, too, according to E.M. Uhlenbeck.)

Table 1

	variable	unfixed	1st	2nd	ante-penult	penult	last	tied to length
ABAU		x						
BALANGAO						x	x	
BONTOC				x		x	x	
BORORO						x		
CHAMA						x		
GEORGIAN (mt.dialects)						x		
IGNACIANO			x			(x)		

(Table 1 continued)

	variable	unfixed	1st	2nd	ante-penult	penult	last	tied to length
MARINAHUA			x					
PANJABI			x					x
SIANE			x					
SONSOROL						x		
SUENA						x		
SUNDANESE		x						
TAMAZIGHT							x	
TELEFOL		x						
TEPEHUA						x	x	
TERENA	x							
TIBETAN						x		x
WALTMANJARI			+	x				
WANTOAT	x							
WOGAMUSIN							x	
YAGUA	x							
ZOQUE						x		
	3	2	5	2	1	11	5	2

variable= stress on any given word is fixed, but no general rule
unfixed = stress may occur on different syllables in same word
( )   = secondary stress
+   = favored alternative

2.5 Syntactic adjustments that achieve favored positions

The intrinsic variations of which Hyman speaks can be seen in
languages with variable stress under conditions that leave speakers
free to adopt the most advantageous position. In ENGLISH a stress
can occur on any syllable, yet binomials, which theoretically can
put either word first, tend to have in final position the one with the
more favored stress type: paroxytones are favored over oxytones,
sonorous oxytones — open syllables or syllables closed with a voiced
consonant -- over non-sonorous ones, more open over less open
vowels, etc. (Malkiel 1959, Bolinger 1965:129-38). The same tendency can be found in GERMAN, SPANISH, FRENCH, PORTUGUESE,
RUSSIAN, and POLISH (Malkiel 1959:151). Examples: rags and
tatters, big and hefty, dirt and grime, pork and beans, hates and
fears, sick and tired. Semantic and other forces often override the
tendency, but it is unmistakable nevertheless. Terminal intonation
attracts words that give it latitude. And when a stress on the last
syllable does occur finally, the intonation makes do by adding length.
In:
What did you $^{fi}nd?$ What did you dis$^{cov}er?$
the vowel nucleus in find is, in effect, geminated.

2.5.1 Inherent nature of preferences   There is some evidence
from experiments on production and perception to suggest an inherent preference for the favored stress patterns. In one experiment (Oller and Rydland 1974), children aged 18 to 42 months were
asked "to pronounce bisyllabic words, both ENGLISH and nonsense
words, where stress is either on the first syllable (trochaic) or the
second (iambic). Especially with nonsense words, the children
have thus far tended to pronounce iambics as trochaics and to pronounce trochaics correctly" (Oller and Rydland 1974: 211) — that is, they tend
to level them all to a penultimate stress pattern. (But it is hard to
avoid circularity. ENGLISH has end-stressed words, but they are
fewer than penultimate-stressed ones, and the children may be
regularizing a system they have already learned.) Another experiment, this time with adult speakers of ENGLISH, BENGALI, POL-
ISH, FRENCH, and PERSIAN (Bell 1976), presented the subjects
with pulses that were regular except that every third pulse was
higher, stronger, or longer than the two others, which were equal.
Subjects were directed to report how they perceived the repetitions
of the three pulses, whether / − −, −/−, or − − / (/ = prominent).
Terminal prominence turned out to be least favored, initial prominence most, and medial prominence next most. There was no
significant correlation between the choices and the favored stress
pattern in the subject's language.

2.6 Functions of accent

Of the various kinds of stress systems, the most advantageous
of all, for intonation, is the rarest: that in which there are no
stresses -- that is, no particular syllable of a word is marked to
carry the accent. To appreciate the effect, we need to look at the
principal functions that accent performs. I distinguish four: demarcative, distinctive, contrastive, and attitudinal.

2.6.1 Demarcative   The demarcative function is important only
in the early stages of language-learning. The general question of
ontogeny will be looked at later, but for the moment we can say that
adults exaggerate the prosodic features of words (probably for the
most part unconsciously) as a way of helping children to learn them.
A fixed stress on a word is a handy peg on which to hang the syllables; its predictable position becomes as integral to the word as the
segmental phonemes themselves. But it is not essential, and it
becomes redundant after the vocabulary is learned: adults do not
require more information than is supplied by the segmentals (including vowel quality, of course, which is often a historic residue
of accent) in order to distinguish the words in a stream of speech.
In fact, more words probably lack accentual prominence than have

it, or have it in such a vestigial form that it serves no purpose. If a speaker knows the identity of a word, he can accent any syllable in it for contrastive or attitudinal purposes.

2.6.2 <u>Distinctive</u>   The distinctive function is simply one more way, in addition to the choice of different segmentals, of increasing the lexicon (<u>I'm not inclíned to accept</u>; <u>The plane is ínclined</u>). Like the demarcative function, it is abated whenever the word is not in accent position; we rely on context for the difference, as with any other homonymous pair.

2.6.3 <u>Contrastive</u>   The contrastive function is the most pervasive, setting off a given constituent within a sentence, or a sentence within a series of sentences:

I sent for them to come to the méeting, not the cóncert.
I sent for them to come to the méeting, not to take me hóme.
I sent for them to come to the méeting, nobody said anything
     about looking for a hóuse.

The phenomenon is general, occurring in tonal as well as nontonal languages.   Examples of tone languages having contrastive accent are THAI (Abramson 1962: 39) and HUICHOL (Grimes 1959: 229-30).

2.6.4 <u>Attitudinal</u>   The attitudinal function is illocutionary. It is the running commentary that intonation adds to the propositional content of sentences.   Terminals have this function all the time. Accents have it when they are not contrastive (and even then, in the sense that they signal the speaker's feeling of what is important and what is not).   Since attitudes are many, there are many ways in which accent signals them: by position, by relative height between one accent and another, and by phonetic shape.   Where position is concerned I do not refer to the possibility of accenting for contrast at any desired point in a sentence and de-accenting for the opposite -- that can always be done to the extent that the syntax of the language allows it, and the accent then belongs to a constituent:

Who did it? -- Jóhn was the one who did it.
              It was Jóhn.
              It was Jóhn who did it.

The more purely attitudinal uses of accent relate them to the utterance as a whole.   As Smalley writes of emphatic accent in COMAN-CHE, it "is used to give extra intensity to a situation, and not...to emphasize one word as against another" (1953: 299).

I take up first a use that is very likely to interfere with the demarcative function.   It conveys an attitude by its position in the utterance.

2.6.4.1 <u>Climax</u> I refer to this as <u>climax</u>. It is the principal means (along with widening the range) whereby the speaker imposes on the listener and marks the degree of thrust, power, positiveness, and zing of the utterance. To some extent the climactic is inseparable from the contrastive -- sentence-final intonations would not be as important as they are if a more dramatic effect could not be achieved by putting the new information and its intonational swing as close as possible to the end. Syntax cooperates by providing means for maneuvering the item with contrastive accent into end position: <u>John I like</u>; chiasmus in such things as <u>A superman in physique but in intellect a fool</u>; the passive to highlight the agent, etc. Alternative forms sometimes provide the means, e.g. <u>What on earth for?</u> instead of <u>Why on earth?</u> And some forms admit more than one treatment; a terminal vocative, for example, is normally at low pitch, but can be given an accent for emphasis: <u>No sir</u> instead of <u>No, sir</u>. Similarly for "empty words" or words not in contrast because they have already been mentioned; climax may shift the accent onto them. Sandmann (1954: 239) compares GERMAN and ENGLISH: "If somebody alleges that we have said something which in fact we did not say, it is quite natural for us to answer in GERMAN, <u>Ja, das hab' ich aber nicht gesagt!</u> ... The cognitionally important word <u>nicht</u> is almost swallowed up... Good ENGLISH examples seem ... to be <u>That is the very thing!</u> or <u>Such is not the case!</u>"

In a language without stress, there should be no phonological impediment to climax. The speaker could simply put the accent on the last syllable of any word that happened to be final. Unfortunately I have no actual reports of this. The closest is Van Syoc (1959: 61-67) on SUNDANESE. He found that it was impossible for him to mispronounce a word by shifting the accent from one syllable to another -- his informants would correct him on segmentals, but never on stress. The speaker is apparently free to accent any syllable he likes, and it is tempting to say that the one informant whom Van Syoc describes as almost always using a heavy accent on the last syllable of a pause group was simply being emphatic. SUNDANESE has contrastive accent and it is reasonable to suppose that it has climactic accent as well. Other "stress-free" languages where climax should meet no resistance include TELEFOL, ULITHIAN, and YUROK. In fact, what appears to be a climactic terminal accent is reported for YUROK, especially but not exclusively on imperatives (Robins 1958: 10).

But climax -- achieved phonologically rather than syntactically or lexically -- is not limited to stress-free languages. It may override stress. In some languages this happens regularly; it is reported

in the following, among others: CHONTAL (Waterhouse 1962: 44),
KUNIMAIPA (Pence 1964), MANTJILTJARA (Marsh 1969:148),
MARINAHUA (Pike and Scott 1962), SERI (Moser 1965), TAGALOG
(Dacanay 1963: 223), WALTMANJARI (Hudson and Richards 1969:184),
ZUNI (Cook). Of MARINAHUA we read that "when the speaker is
extremely irritated, the last consonant of the clause is lengthened,
and the intensity which is usually on the nuclear syllable [generally
the first in a word] is put instead on the clause-final syllable" (Pike
and Scott 1962: 4). Presumably the "anticipation tentative pause"
described for CHUAVE (Swick 1966) is this same phenomenon. In
WESTERN DESERT the shift may not only occur under conditions
of excitement, but the final vowel may also be distorted, or an
extra syllable, pu, may be attached at the end to carry the accent
(Douglas 1964: 22). In JAVANESE there are morphological processes that shift stress to the end, e.g. ábang 'red,' abíng 'very red'
(Uhlenbeck).

Probably most languages -- assuming that climax turns out to be
a universal -- permit the rightward shift of accent only sporadically,
or with particular classes of words or sentence types. One likely
type is the imperative, and we find the shift there in CALABRESE
(Southern ITALIAN), where it does not succeed in shifting the accent all the way, but one step rightward in such forms as lassàle,
calatìnne (Cooper 1972); SPANISH carries it all the way to the end,
at least in some dialects (sientaté for siéntate), and in Buenos Aires
SPANISH the vos form of the imperative, with its terminal stress,
is felt as more emphatic than the tú form (Fontanella and Lavandera
1975). In TELUGU the shift to the last syllable "is largely restricted
to the informal imperative and to the infinitive in its optative use"
(Lisker 1963: xxiv). The same shift occurs in the imperative in
CAYUVAVA (Key 1961: 148-9). I have found only one statement that
implicitly denies rightshift: in COMANCHE, Smalley says (1953:
299), emphatic stress always coincides with lexical stress.

In PERSIAN, Ferguson reports what he calls a "quasi-citation
stress" in which there is "a normally barytone word pronounced
with final stress...when used hypostatically," i.e., just before
being talked about as a word (1957:132). It is perhaps significant
that in the one example cited the word is not merely being talked
about but exclaimed at. One person says némiduninæm 'I don't
know;' the other responds nemidunináem čiye? 'What do you mean,
you don't know?'

Climactic rightshift is also reported for tone languages. It is
probably the basis for the "radical descriptive" words in CHICHEWA,

which include forms similar to such words as kersplash in ENGLISH (Watkins 1937). It provides one of two alternate forms of negation in MIXTEC (Pankratz and Pike 1967: 299). In OTOMÍ it occurs with low pitch on rhetorical questions used for scolding, and on high pitch for "strong final emphasis" — the illustrative examples are commands (Wallis 1968: 87) and emphatic questions in a story (Wallis 1970: 172-3).

In ENGLISH the rightward shift often overpowers the normal stress on a phrase-final word when the speaker is aroused or emphatic. As a rule it moves to the rightmost full vowel:

> ... a person whose full-time job was [slight pause] being a secretáry... (in a context of strong appeal)[1]
> ... necessáry, but not too kind.... [2]

The word maybe is regularly pronounced maybé when speakers are emphatically skeptical. Kenyon and Knott point out (1953: xxv) that in some cases a rightward shift for emphasis has become a fixture, at least for some speakers, and they cite ordinárily and necessárily. Bronstein cites justifíable and inflúence (1960: 246). We should probably add elsewhére. I have twice heard enthusiásm. The highest degree of emphasis can shift the accent to a reduced vowel, which then usually becomes full: golly goes to gollée, with two successive rise-fall accents.

2.6.4.2 Anticlimax Since no contrast operates in a vacuum, if there is climax one expects that there will also be anticlimax, an avoidance of what might seem to be excessive emphasis. The only evidence I have is from ENGLISH. For example, we have our choice between It may not be tíme yet and It may not yet be tíme. One is relaxed, the other dramatic. The empty word place gives us a choice between The signs are all over the pláce and The signs are all óver the place; we will pick the latter if we wish not to sound too concerned about the matter. The normal stress on the lexical phrase after all is on all, but anticlimax can backshift the accent to after: He didn't do it áfter all — a calmly assured way of asserting the fact. (See Bolinger 1955: 198-201 for additional examples.)

The fairly abundant evidence for climax and the rightward push of stress to accommodate it, plus the hint, at least, of a similar

---

[1] J. R. Ross, at LSA Executive Committee Meeting, 1 June 1973.

[2] Paul Benzaquin, Radio Station WEEI, Boston, 19 March 1973.

effect of anticlimax, suggests that if there are mechanisms, as
Hyman says, for moving the stress onto the penultimate syllable to
accommodate the prominence feature of intonation, there are also
mechanisms to move stress rightward and leftward to highlight or
downplay the whole utterance. It is a different kind of mechanism,
for instead of fixing the stress on one syllable, it makes for optional positions.

2.6.4.3 <u>Emotional backshift</u>   The backshifting that expresses
anticlimax does not carry the accent very far.   There is another
attitudinal use of accent that carries it farther, as often as not to
the first stressed syllable of the utterance. The following, with
italics in the original, illustrates:

"Did you write that 'Luck of Roaring Camp'? "
Harte confessed again.
"Sure? "
"Yes" — in a whisper.
The miner burst out, fervently and affectionately,
"<u>Son</u> of a — ! Put it there!" and he gripped Harte's hand in
his mighty talons and mashed it. [3]

The effect is that of an emotion too great to be contained, which
bursts out and then leaves the rest of the utterance deflated. It is
the FRENCH accent d'insistance, as in <u>Il m'a terríblement effrayée</u>.
It does not necessarily go back all the way — which is one indication
that it is a controlled and systemic part of intonation, and not merely
an overflow of adrenalin.   The same accent with the same voice
qualifiers — high pitch, tight closure (by a glottal stop if there is
no prior consonant) with forced release, added length, breathy
voice — can be found medially:

He   stared at them ó-o-o
                           pen-eyed.

We   stood there d-ú-m-b
                           founded!

For   G-ó-d's   watch what you're   do
               sake, man;   ing!

The discounting of "mere emotion" in practically all references
to intonation makes it impossible to tell how widespread the

---

[3] Mark Twain, <u>Mark Twain in eruption</u> (New York: Grosset and
Dunlap, 1940), p.272.

emotional backshift is. HUNGARIAN has what Varga calls (1975: 13) an "emotional sentence form" with accent at the beginning, defined as the reverse of the "rational sentence form" which, in its arrangement of topic first and comment last, puts the main accent at the end. His examples are A 'könyvet "olvastam (rational) and "Olvastam a 'könyvet (emotional). Matching the latter we might have, presumably, the ENGLISH sentence I've réad that stupid book (compare the oddity of ? That stupid book I've réad -- the emotional form is more hospitable to an emotional modifier). HUNGARIAN also has a rule of adverb position that looks suspiciously like a generalized emotional backshift. Degree adverbs that express 'completeness' backshift the accent in their phrases: "borzasztóan ,unalmas 'awfully dull' (the lowered tick is a tertiary) versus 'enyhén "viseletes 'slightly worn' (Varga 1975: 35-6). But the 'completeness' adverbs are precisely those intensifiers which even in ENGLISH can quite readily take an emotional accent. In answer to How do you like it? the backshifted accent on very in

It's $^{\text{v-é-r}}$ y good.

is perfectly normal. It would be unusual to do this with slightly, somewhat, a little, etc., unless they were contrastive.

2.6.4.4 Topic and comment The intonational treatment of topic and comment, old and new, is probably a diluted and grammaticized form of both the emotional and the climactic. What is newest in a situation hits us hardest, and if the impression is sufficiently overpowering, we come out with it first. But the tie-in of topic with context, which makes it more convenient to put the old stuff closer to what it refers to, plus the advantage of climax, makes the other arrangement more usual in ordinary discourse.

2.7 Two main accents and their relationships

Sentences with more than one accent invoke relationships not only between each accent and the sentence as a whole, but among the accents themselves. One of these relationships, that between a prominence toward the beginning of an utterance and another prominence at or near the end, is encountered so often that it can be hypothesized as a universal tendency. Cohen and 't Hart refer to it as a "hat pattern" (1967:183), which is regarded as basic for DUTCH ('t Hart and Collier 1975: 239). It is rather a slouch hat, when seen in its general possibilities, because the two peaks are usually not of the same height. But they tend to outrank intermediate accents, so that while there may be dips in the middle, the pillars at either end stand as the accentual framework of the sentence

-- rather than a hat, I prefer the analogy of a suspension bridge.
It is unquestionably the prevailing intonational shape for non-ellip-
tical declarative sentences and wh questions in European languages,
and is quite common with yes-no questions as well. How extensive
it may be elsewhere will have to be decided when we have descriptions that do not concentrate exclusively on sentence-final intonations. The two main accents correspond to theme and rheme, and
when the theme is omitted (or appears only in de-accented pronominal form), the rheme accent is all that is left. This is the basis
of the one-word and one-phrase utterances that are so common
among illustrative examples of intonations.

The effects of varying heights of initial and final accents will
remain a mystery till more descriptions are recorded. Our information even on ENGLISH is deficient. It is commonly said that
AMERICAN ENGLISH tends to make the terminal peak higher than
the initial one, and this is cited as an important difference between
AMERICAN ENGLISH and other varieties and other languages,
where the evidence for "down-drift" seems overwhelming. The
fact is that low-to-high characterizes sentences that make an emphatic appeal for acceptance, and are very common in answers to
questions. High-to-low is self-confident. It is the only intonation
that can be used in starting a story:

$$\text{On}^{\text{c}\,\text{e}} \qquad\qquad \text{be} \qquad\qquad \text{n}^{\text{am}\,\text{e}} \qquad \text{Smo}$$
$$\text{there was a} \qquad\quad _{\text{a}\,\text{r.}} \qquad \text{His} \qquad\qquad \text{was} \qquad\qquad {}_{\text{k}_{\text{e}_{\text{y.}}}}$$

It is also the usual intonation of commands:

$$\text{Hand} \qquad\qquad\qquad\qquad\qquad \text{shut} \qquad \text{win}$$
$$\quad _{\text{me}} \quad _{\text{those}} \text{pli}_{\text{e}_{\text{r}_{\text{s.}}}} \qquad \text{Would you} \qquad\quad \text{the} \quad {}_{\text{d}_{\text{o}_{\text{w, Please?}}}}$$

Example of an answer to a question, e.g. <u>Why do you do that?</u> --

$$\text{Be}^{\text{cause}}\,{}_{\text{I}} \quad^{\text{want}}_{\,\text{t}_{\text{o.}}}$$

If the relative heights were reversed, the answer would be rude in
its self-confidence. The only other language in which I have found
a description of precisely this difference between statements that
are answers to questions and statements that are not, is SWAHILI
(see section 4.5 below). My impression is that the contrast obtains for at least some European languages besides ENGLISH. As
for the "story-telling" high-to-low, it would be interesting to

discover how many descriptions of intonation are based on narratives
where a single speaker holds the floor and imposes himself on his
audience.

2.7.1 Resulting favored stress positions The initial accent
probably influences stress forms in the same way as that seen by
Hyman for the final accent, though its influence is not quite so
strong. The suspension-bridge pattern fits the over-all possibilities of stress: where the penultimate or ultimate carries the primary, we can detect the final accent; when the first or second
syllable carries it, the initial accent has probably been at work.
We need at this point a study of word classes, showing their favored
position in the phrase or sentence and their favored stress patterns.
A language that puts qualifiers before qualified might be expected
to favor some kind of forestress (probably first or second syllable)
for the qualifiers, which are most apt to come under the influence
of the initial accent. This at least appears to be true of adjectives
in ENGLISH -- and verbs, coming toward the end of the sentence,
show the contrary tendency. In any case, that the great majority
of languages stress the first, second, next-to-last, and last syllables is not only a reflection of how the words are spoken in one-
word utterances but of how the accents are assorted in a sentence.

2.7.2 Other specialized effects of relative height There are
specialized uses of relative height that will have to be passed over
here. One, for example, is its use in alternative questions. The
peaks in the following,

Are you go^{ing} or stay $_{i}n_{g}$?   Are you going or stay $_{i}n_{g}$?

are high-low and low-high respectively. The second is more insistent. It would sound misplaced in a polite offer such as Would
you like an apple or an orange? (unless the speaker wanted to suggest that 'orange' is a bright new idea and his guest would like an
orange even more than an apple). But it is reportedly the norm in
GUJARATI (Ravindra Mistri).

2.8 Accentual shapes

We come now to the shape of the contour on and around the accents. In ENGLISH, initial, medial, and terminal accents can
take any of three shapes, each manifested in gradient ways, though
there are strong preferences for one or another depending on position in the sentence. At least two of the three types are probably
general.

2.8.1 <u>Accent A</u> One of the two matches the description most commonly given for utterance-final accents: nuclear syllable at relatively high pitch and either a downglide within that syllable (especially if it is utterance final) or a downskip to the immediately following syllable. The assertiveness that we find in ENGLISH is probably also a general trait -- it is the most usual utterance-final accent in statements, commands, and wh questions. In ENGLISH it can be repeated for downright positiveness:

Do$_{n't}$ yo$_u$ da$_{re}$ move a ^{mus}$_{cle!}$

and it can distort the syntax to get its way:

Be^{lie}$_{v}$$_e$ yo$_u$ ^{m}$_e!$

(Compare *<u>Hit you him!</u>) The nuclear syllable may be approached from above or from below:

Don't you dare$_{move}$ $_{a mus}$$_{cle!}$ Don't $_{you}$ dare move a ^{mus}$_{cle!}$

And there are variations of height, level of approach, etc. I refer to this accent as Accent A.

2.8.2 <u>Accent B</u> The second, or Accent B, is risen to or risen on, but lacks the subsequent immediate fall. The pitch may level off or continue to rise or even descend slightly, but without a jump. Examples, showing a contrast in the two directions:

Was it ^{rain}^{ing} when ^{you} got here yesterday?

Was it ^{rain}$_{ing}$ when you got here yesterday?

(The first might be asked in making an inference from something that has gone before; the ice is already broken, and the speaker can afford to give his curiosity free rein; a possible addition, following a <u>no</u> answer, might be <u>Then how come your clothes are still wet?</u> The second might easily follow a <u>Hey, Joe!</u>; it can initiate a conversational exchange.) The B accent is neutral as regards assertiveness. How general it may be I am unable to say; it is almost never discussed, though given diagrams or tracings, we can generally see it. Non-final-clause terminals carry it as a rule, and also yes-no questions. (But A accents can occur in both places, A-rises especially in the former -- an A-rise is an A, as described above, plus a rise.)

2.8.3 <u>Accent C</u>   The third accent is a kind of inversion of A,
in both shape and implications. I call it Accent C. Instead of an
upward obtrusion it has a downward one. The nuclear syllable is
at the lowest pitch of a down-up excursion. In ENGLISH it is found
in all types of utterances:

Don't be   to him!   Why did you   that?
      mean   say

He isn't going to   D'you think I'm
         hurt you.   crazy?

The effect is anti-assertive, downtoning. Both the low pitch of the
nuclear syllable (with intensity generally low as well) and the terminal rise (suggesting inconclusiveness) contribute to this. The C
accent is common in Western languages: RUSSIAN, POLISH, ENG-
LISH, GERMAN, FRENCH, ITALIAN, SPANISH -- very likely all
of them. It is found in WESTERN DESERT, where "it reveals the
speaker's recognition of the standing of the person addressed,"
showing an attitude of deference (Douglas 1964: 22), and in KUNI-
MAIPA, where it "has meanings of polite request, or nonemphatic
call" (Pence 1964: 334). It is the usual pattern for yes-no questions
in Hawaiian ENGLISH (Vanderslice and Pierson 1967: 445-6), which
suggests that it probably holds for HAWAIIAN. It is reported for
wh questions in BENGALI, where it is said to show "greater interest and less formality" (Hai and Ball 1961: 62-63). It is the most
regular sentence-final accent in HINDI-URDU (Bailey 1956: xxxvi)
and in CHAMORRO (Topping 1969: 71). It is possible but infrequent
in TERENA (Bendor-Samuel 1962). In HUNGARIAN it is the usual
accent in yes-no questions (Varga 1975: 18-19, 104). It occurs on
statements in TURKISH (Nash 1973: 149), on exclamations (at least)
in JEBERO (Bendor-Samuel), and apparently on both yes-no and wh
questions in BORORO (Huestis 1963: 233).

What hints there are point to a common core of anti-assertive
meaning, so that it is probably fair to class these manifestations
together as one and the same thing. With HINDI-URDU and CHA-
MORRO there remains a doubt; one would have to assume a kind
of habitual attitude of deference in all conversational exchanges
(no more impossible than that conversations should begin with any
other deferential sign). I am assured that there is nothing in the
CHAMORRO manner to indicate anything like this; but still, in
scolding or arguing, a CHAMORRO speaker might well end a sentence with an A accent (Topping). The best evidence for C accents

outside Western languages comes from SWAHILI, where they occur
with exactly the same meaning as in ENGLISH (see section 4.5 below).

In three cases there is some evidence that C accents are excluded.
ILOCANO is one (Reid). WALBIRI is another, where C's are excluded even at the spot where most languages having them admit
them most freely, namely yes-no questions — instead of having a
level or a drop before the final rise, as in possible in ENGLISH
and is commonplace in many languages, WALBIRI yes-no questions
rise steadily from beginning to end (Reece). The third is JAPA-
NESE, of which it is stated that "sentence intonation can never
cause an inherent high-pitch to become lower than a neighboring
lower pitch, or vice versa" (Abe 1955: quoting Kaku Jimbo). A
C accent would face definite obstacles in any tone language.

3. Terminals and Drift; Questions and Nonquestions

3.1 Going down at the end

The most widely diffused intonational phenomenon seems to be
the tendency to "go down at the end." It is manifested in two ways,
often coinciding but sometimes contrasting: 1) a downward drift
from a high beginning, and 2) a rapid downmotion at the very end,
usually if not always associated with a terminal accent. There
seem to be favorite shapes from language to language, though generally, and perhaps always, more than one possibility exists. Instead of a high beginning and a more or less steady fall, there may
be a low beginning (a relatively low accent in the case of the suspension - bridge pattern) with a rise to the terminal accent and then
an abrupt fall. The effect of relative height has already been discussed — a downward tangent is itself a form of downmotion.

3.1.1 Downmotion in tone languages Despite certain complica-
tions, tone languages too manifest the general downmotion. Hyman
and Schuh argue that the descending line in the twin phenomena of
downdrift and downstep in tone languages is basically the same as
what is found in an accent language such as FINNISH, where "it
should be expected that the stress with the highest pitch will (bar-
ring contrastive stress) be ordinarily the first in the sentence and
each subsequent stress will be on a slightly lower pitch" (1972: 11).
The descriptions of tone languages are on the whole more faithful
in reporting downdrift than those of non-tone languages, as can be
seen in Table 2. (The blanks in the column do not indicate that the
phenomenon is absent, only that the source used does not mention it.)

Table 2

Languages	A Downdrift or Downstep	B.a Terminal at least on statements	B.b Fall statements and wh-Q's	C Internal open juncture with mid or high pitch	D Extra low at paragraph end
Angaataha					x
Balangao		x		x	
Bengali	x		x	x	
Bororo		x			
Campa	(1)	x			
Cayuvava		x		x	
Chamorro					x
Chontal			x (3)		
Chuave		x		x	x
Cora			x	x	
Daga			x	x	x
Danish	x				
Dutch	x			x	
French			x	x	
Gaelic	x			x	
Georgian	x			x	
Gunwinggu	(2)				
Hawaiian			x	x	
Hindi			(4)	x	
Huastec			x		
Iatmul	x		x	x	
Itonama		x			
Iwam		x			
Javanese				x	
Jebero	x			x	
Kunimaipa		x		x	
Maidu		x		x	
Mantjiltjara		x		x	
Mapuche		x		x	
Maya				x	
Pampango		x			
Papago		x			
Paresí	x			x	
Pintupi	x		x	x	
Pocomchi		x			
Polish			x	x	
Russian	x		x	x	
Saho		x			

Table 2   cont.

Languages	A Downdrift or Downstep	B.a Terminal Fall at least on statements	B.b Terminal Fall statements and wh-Q's	C Internal open juncture with mid or high pitch	D Extra low at paragraph end
Seri	x		x		
Sierra Popoluca			x	x	
Suena				x	
Sundanese			x	x	
Tamil		x		x	
Telugu		x	(5)	x	x
Tepehua	x	x			
Turkish	x			x	
Ulithian			x	x	
Waltmanjari		x		x	
Western Desert			x	x	
Wiyot	x				
Yagua		x		x	(7)
Yiddish				x	
Yokuts		(6)			
Yurok	x	x		x	
Zoque		x		x	
Zuni	x		x	(9)	x

Tone Languages	A	B.a	B.b	C	D	E Intonation modifies tone at end of pause group	F Intonation obscures tone at end of pause group
Bariba						x	
Chichewa		x		x		x	
Chinantec	x						
Chinese (Lungtu)							x
Etung	x						
Gadsup		x (8)					
Hausa	x						
Huichol					x		x
Japanese	x		x	x			
Kewa	x						
Mazahua		x		x		x	x
Mikasuki	x	x		x		x	
Mixtec	x	x					
Otomi	x	x					x
Panjabi		x		x		x	
Pawaia		x				x	

Table 2 cont.

Tone Languages	A	B.a	B.b	C	D	E	F
Saramaccan	x		x				x
Serbo-Croatian		x		x			x
Siane	x					x	
Suena	x	x					
Telefol		x			x		
Thai		x		x		x	
Tibetan							x
Vietnamese		x				x	
Weri		x					
Yoruba	(10)						
Zulu	x						

(1) Downdrift after nucleus
(2) Rise to nucleus, then sharp fall
(3) "Not even" assertions and wh-questions
(4) Terminal rise, also on commands
(5) Terminal rise for wh-questions
(6) Rise at end
(7) Extra low at mid paragraph
(8) Manifested by level replacing rise
(9) A leveling off that is higher than the terminal pitch
(10) Linked answer ends in lower tone

3.1.2 Physical basis of downmotion   The falling tendency is so widespread that one is prone to assign it a physical basis. That is the hypothesis of Lieberman 1967: "the infant's hypothetical innate referential breath group" results automatically from an initial build-up of subglottal air pressure, which gradually decreases up to the end of expiration, and then abruptly falls (1967: 42-3). It becomes "the phonetic marker of complete sentences" (p. 47).

3.1.3 Gradience of downmotion: paragraphs and discourses The tendency is not only present in an absolute sense; it is also graded: the steeper the fall, the greater the finality. Nearly all reports of distinctive intonation for paragraphs or discourses stress the fact that at their end they overlay a deeper fall on the already normal fall at the end of a sentence. The case of CHA-MORRO is especially interesting: a sentence is not quite final enough, as a rule, to call for a terminal fall (as we noted earlier, it might be used for the metaphorical finality of arguing or scolding); but discourse-final sentences do end with a fall (Topping 1969: 71). Very low pitch tends to fade into pulse register, and Lehiste's experiments (1976) with clues to paragraph endings show pulse to be the most reliable. In tone languages one may find what Grimes

describes for HUICHOL: "paragraph-size pitch patterns that involve a long-term downdrift with ordinary intonation and tone super-
imposed." Grimes adds that the terrace-tone patterns of many
WEST AFRICAN languages "reset the high tone level after quite
a stretch" in a sort of paragraph-size chunk. In TELEFOL there
is a "discourse terminal" particle, kwa, which has "a characteristic 'winding down' intonation" (Healey 1966). Akhmanova regards
"the last terminal contour being so much more 'terminal' than the
medial ones" as the basis of "supraphrasal unity" (1974: 830).

3.1.4 Non-falls, medial and final Looking in the other direction,
we find almost as often that falls medial within an utterance do not
go down quite as far as falls at the end. But sentence-medial position is just as often characterized by no fall at all, whereas in sentence-final position a non-fall is widely associated with yes-no or
complementary questions (e.g. And John?). Not that this, really,
makes much difference. A question awaits its completion in the
form of an answer. And just as often a non-paragraph-final sentence may lack a terminal fall simply because the speaker intends
to go on -- the same intention, obviously, as with a suspensive intonation of some kind sentence-medially. There are certain half-
grammaticizations of non-fall, in the main not very firmly fixed.
(For example, an initial conditional clause is probably more apt
to end higher than an initial temporal clause. This in turn may
reflect some underlying kinship between conditions and questions,
a kinship that shows up syntactically as well. Or it may simply be
the "unreality" of conditions by comparison with the greater "fac-
tuality" of other subordinate clauses that makes them want to end
in the air.)

3.2 A accents in various languages

The terminal accent with its abrupt fall has already been identified as Accent A. In descriptions of this fall that are detailed
enough to tell, it is apparent that some variety of A is being described. Of the languages checked in double column B of Table 2,
the following clearly have A accents: CAYUVAVA, CHUAVE, CORA,
FRENCH, HAWAIIAN, PAPAGO, RUSSIAN, SERI, TAMIL, WALT-
MANJARI, YUROK. In a few instances the description suggests
that the nuclear syllable is not above but at the lowest terminal
pitch -- this would mean that it is fallen to rather than from. But
such an option is perfectly good in ENGLISH as well. The terminal
low pitch is the one place where there need not be a fall after the
nuclear syllable for a contrast to be heard. In both

simply _{hate}
I   and
      it.

simply
I
          hate it.

the nuclear A is on <u>hate</u>. To get the intonational effect desired
(maximum finality), the speaker "uses up" all of the fall before
hitting the nuclear target, and the listener allows for this.

3.3 Wh-questions: A accents

Column B of the table also shows another tendency that appears
to be universal: wh-questions have the same kind of terminal fall
as statements. Of the 17 cases where wh-questions are mentioned,
all but three are named as having this tendency. In one of the three,
CHONTAL, ordinary statements are said to have a rise, but wh-
questions and statements meaning 'not even' have a fall (Waterhouse
1962); it would not be surprising for there to be a connection between
'not even' and greater positiveness. HINDI presumably has a rise
for statements, commands, and wh-questions; but the diagrams for
URDU in Bailey 1956 make one wonder, for they show a terminal
fall. For the third, TELUGU, there are diagrams for wh-questions
showing more terminal rises than falls (Lisker 1963); but this does
not necessarily go against the basic tendency. In ENGLISH a slightly
formal

And how are you today?

and surprised questions like

What's this?

are commonplace instances of rising wh-questions; yet ENGLISH
is described as normally having a fall.

3.3.1 Wh-questions: C accents In Western languages, Accent
C is about as common as A on wh-questions, and the difference in
implications tells us one possible reason for both intonations. Consider the following:

What's your name?   Tell me your name.

What's your name?   Tell me your name.

The A accent makes the question an order to tell; the C accent makes it a request. In fact, it is not unusual to find the fourth example above punctuated <u>Tell me your name</u>? Commands are at least as likely as statements to have a terminal fall.

3.4 Varieties of non-fall

A "suspensive" terminal, with pitch which if it falls at all falls only slightly, is as regularly reported as the terminal fall. There are commonly three shapes: a continuation of the previous level, a rise, or a slight fall. Some languages -- PARESÍ, JAPANESE, and FRENCH, for example -- are described as having all three. So is DAGA, which sometimes has a rise after its slight fall (Murane 1972: 26), and likewise RUSSIAN and YIDDISH (Weinreich 1956), with a slight rise before the fall. There is one suspensive terminal which is of special interest because it has been said to be taboo in certain languages, namely the fall-rise of DAGA, which also appears in WESTERN DESERT, and is a very common intonation in ENGLISH, e.g.

If a ^{person} believes $^{th}a^{t,}$ she'll believe $^{an}y_{th_{i_{n_g}}}$.

(The alternate

If a ^{person} believes $_{t}ha^{t,}$ she'll believe $^{an}y_{th_{i_{n_g}}}$.

is the more usual shape at the end of an <u>if</u> clause in most languages.) The fall-rise is of course an A accent -- for focus -- with a rise; the speaker is implying a contrast on <u>that</u>, not merely assuming that both he and his interlocutor know what the referent of <u>that</u> is. The focus may be logically unnecessary and used mostly for emphasis; in AMERICAN ENGLISH, not using it in an example such as the one above has a 'taken for granted' ring -- we find it, accordingly, on sayings,

Easy ^{come,} easy $_{go.}$ Give him an ^{inch} and he $^{takes\ a}$ $_{mi_{l_e}}$.

and in instances where the speaker "doesn't care":

If you don't $_{li}ke\ it,$ you know where you can $_{go.}$

ENGLISH-speaking learners of several languages are warned in textbooks not to use the A-rise (Varga 1975: 120-21 for HUNGARIAN; Hai and Ball 1961: 90 for BENGALI; Leed 1965: 69-70 for RUSSIAN).

The unacceptability of the A-rise is probably a matter of frequency
rather than of strict non-occurrence (at least this is true of SPANISH
vis-à-vis ENGLISH); as Varga notes, it is a dialectal preference of
AMERICAN ENGLISH, no doubt one more sign of our somewhat un-
subdued interpersonal relations. It is a fair guess that all varieties
of non-fall are found pretty generally, with varying preferences and
with gradience as regards degree of incompletion.

3.4.1 <u>Major and minor separations</u> One of the functions of gradience is to signal the rank of subordination. In

If I make it home ok^{ay} some time before 10 $o'cl^{ock}$ I'll ^{call} yo$_u$.

If I make it home ok^{ay} some time before 10 $o'cl^{oc^k}$ I'll ^{call} yo$_u$.

the higher pitch signals the major "separation" — in the first, the
<u>some time</u> modifies the final clause; in the second it modifies the
initial clause. These are the "major and minor separations" described for FRENCH, SPANISH, and ENGLISH (Delattre 1961,
Delattre <u>et al</u>. 1962) and for JAVANESE (Uhlenbeck 1965). The
essential identity of intonational grouping in JAVANESE, PACÓH
(Watson 1966), and all Western languages strongly suggests that
intonation as an utterance-binder is a universal phenomenon.

3.5 <u>Terminal non-falls: yes-no questions</u>

The other usual spot for "incompletion" is at the end of an utterance, and we find most (in some languages all) of the suspensive
intonations used internally repeated at the end, most often on yes-
no questions. This is the intonation universal that has been most
thoroughly studied. In his survey of 175 languages, Hermann 1942
found without exception a tendency to higher pitch somewhere in
the utterance. Ultan 1969 repeated the performance with 53 languages
and got almost the same result. In Table 3, I add 41 more. The
near-unanimity is such that one must view with suspicion any claim
that a language has absolutely no pitch-marking of questions — the
most reliable reports of its absence concern ZUNI, which appears
to have an invariable terminal fall (Newman, Cook). Only if "marking" is defined in the strictest way as a rise at some particular point
that can be assigned a phonemic or a morphemic value, can over-all
higher pitch be put down as merely some emotive side-effect.

3.5.1 <u>Tendency toward rising pitch in yes-no questions</u> Rising
terminal is clearly the dominant strain. This shows not only in the

Table 3

Terminal intonations in 41 languages, supplementing Ultan 1969: 58-9

r = rise; h = high

Balangao	r	Pintupi	r/h
Bororo	r	Polish	r
Campa	r	Quechua	(3)
Cayuvava	r	Seri	h
Cora	r/h	Sierra Popoluca	r/h
Czech	r	Suena	r + h
Daga	r	Sundanese	r
Hawaiian	r/h	Tamil	h
Hindi	h	Tepehua	r (6)
Huastec	r	Ulithian	r
Iatmul	r	Walbiri	r
Italian	r	Yiddish	r/h
Itonama	(1)	Yurok	h
Kunimaipa	r	Zuni	(4)
Manobo	r		
Mantjiltjara	r	Tone languages	
Mapuche	r	Mazahua	h (5)
Maya	r/h	Mikasuki	h (5)
Moré	h	Mixtec	h
Pampango	r	Serbo-Croatian	h
Papago	(2)	Telefol	h
Persian	h		

(1) no rise; high not reported
(2) no rise; high not reported
(3) same as declarative, though Spanish rise sometimes used
(4) no pitch marking of questions
(5) high on final syllable
(6) three recorded examples in Cowan 1971

proportion of terminal rises, 71.7% in Ultan's sample, but also in certain tendencies where other shapes are used. In CZECH, the rising rather than rising-falling terminal has come to be felt as the neutral one (Daneš 1957: 7). Russians who live abroad easily replace their rise - fall with a simple rise (Leed 1965: 72-3). Younger speakers of JAPANESE replace the fall-rise with a simple rise (Abe). It is often found that the "more questioning" a question is, as happens with surprised questions and echo questions, the greater the tendency is toward terminal rise. This can easily be appreciated in ENGLISH,

Did you lose it?   Did you lose it?

and the same is reported in GAELIC, HINDI, HUNGARIAN, and
TAMIL. The terminal fall may well be in some sense a "controlled" intonation. The upward flight is characteristic of excited
speech regardless of sentence type:

I said no such thing!   And why didn't you tell me?

3.5.2 <u>Complementary questions</u> Complementary questions are
a type that has been almost universally neglected, and yet offers --
because of its uncomplicated syntax -- the best proving ground for
the untrammeled effect of intonation. Probably all Western languages (definitely including HUNGARIAN) use the simple rise:

A Kátja?   (Leed 1965: 72)   Y usted?   His reason being?

It is purely the intonation here that makes us punctuate as we do.
With a terminal fall, the utterance is felt to be a command or a
command-like request:

Your name, please?   Your name, please.

I have found no reference to complementary questions in my sample
of non-European languages.

3.5.3 <u>Relevance of intonation to the category "question"</u> But
the greatest need, for comparative purposes, is for fuller descriptions of how and when particular intonations of yes-no questions are
used. The practice has been to lump all cases together, discrimi-
nating them only statistically: Language X may have a dozen ways
of intoning a yes-no question, but it comes out having "normally a
terminal rise." This is supposed to be true of ENGLISH, yet virtually anything can be done with a yes-no question:

And you believe that?   And you believe that?   And you believe that?

And you believe that?   And you believe that?   And you believe that?

These are some of the possibilities with accent on <u>believe</u>. It is
not by any means certain that "question" is a grammatical category
at all to the extent that it is marked only by intonation. And if it is

not, then we need to ask what the intonations mean, independently
of any grammatical type. An utterance such as

And ^{he} $^{be}l_{i}e_{v}e_{s}$ that.

can be a question, a statement, or an exclamation, depending on
context and gesture. But the intonation is just as conclusive one
way as another. As a question the sentence is incurious; it probably calls for confirmation of what is already assumed. With fuller
descriptions, we may find the same variety prevailing everywhere.

4. Some Detailed Comparisons

4.1 Similarities, with ENGLISH as point of comparison

It is the exceptional description that contains anything about
intonation that would not be just as true of ENGLISH. (The reader
often gets the impression that the analyst is not aware of the possibilities in his native language — pedagogical grammars are full of
explanations of points that offer no interference and need not be
taught.) Of course we can't be sure that a deeper description will
not turn up some radical divergences. So it is useful to exploit a
few of the fuller descriptions to see how close the analogy between
ENGLISH and other languages can be.

4.2 PINTUPI

In 18 non-European languages of my sample, either intonation is
dealt with in some detail and (except as noted) the descriptions
would be equally true of ENGLISH, or the author claims a high degree of similarity: CHUAVE, DAGA, HAWAIIAN (differences in
frequencies and in accent placement), HUASTEC, HUICHOL (except
for tone), IATMUL, JEBERO, KUNIMAIPA, MAIDU, PARESÍ (except for functional stutter at utterance end), PINTUPI, POCOMCHI,
SAHO, SARAMACCAN (except for tone), SERI, SIERRA POPOLOCA,
SUNDANESE (except for free stress), ULITHIAN. I omit SWAHILI
and BENGALI in this count, but will revert to them later. Following is the case for PINTUPI (Hansen and Hansen 1969:164-7):

1. Contrastive accent may occur on any word of the clause.
2. The clause-final word is the most frequent place for a
    "contrastive contour."
3. "Termination" puts falling pitch and decrescendo on the
    clause-final word. (Terminal voicelessness and terminal
    inhalation differ from ENGLISH.)

4. A non-final terminal has a rise.
5. Yes-no questions have a terminal rise.
6. Wh-questions start high   end with "termination."
7. In commands the last syllable does not glide down but levels off and ends voiceless. (Except for the voicelessness, this is normal with a very insistent command in ENGLISH.)
8. In expressions of doubt and hesitation the last syllable has a slow high-low glide. (Compare <u>Could be,</u> said musingly.)
9. To express strong agreement, each syllable starts high and glides to low. (Compare <u>áb-so-lúte-ly.</u>)
10. Boredom is shown by a monotone.
11. Excitement increases speed, raises pitch, and adds breathiness.
12. A quotation is raised in pitch.
13. Distaste is shown by deliberation and nasality.

This of course is a mixture of grammaticized and ungrammaticized phenomena (or would be criticized as such by those who believe that the distinction is possible), but the point is that in every important respect, as far as it goes it describes the situation in ENGLISH.

4.3 KUNIMAIPA

KUNIMAIPA is equally impressive. The terminal rises and falls (including varieties of Accent A), the presence of a C accent with meanings of politeness, the climactic rightshift of accent, all dovetail, in both form and meaning. There is even a fall-rise-fall for 'deep feeling' -- a C-fall, that is, a C accent followed by a fall. Compare the sentence meaning 'Those ones had pain' (Pence 1964: 334):

Po^{ri} ka ^{k}a$_{\text{m}}$ tó$^{\text{o}}_{\text{h!}}$ Was ^{it} pá^{i}^{n} ful!

4.4 HUASTEC

HUASTEC, besides having terminals that as far as the description goes are identical to those of ENGLISH (Larsen and Pike 1949), has a multiple A accent for 'superemphasis;' compare the following, in which the gloss has the identical intonation:

$^{?}$i$_{\searrow}$ba$_{\searrow}$ Ab$_{\text{so}}$lute$_{\text{ly}}$ no$_{\text{t!}}$

And also a "contempt contour" starting high and gradually stepping down to low:

$$hí_{ta?} \; kin \; k'a_{puw} \; am\text{-}bi\check{c}\grave{i}m \qquad Who \; e_{at_s} \; hor_{s_{e?!}}$$

4.5 SWAHILI

For comparison of the potential for detailed similarity the best
available study of which I am aware is contained in E.O. Ashton's
pedagogical grammar of SWAHILI (1947). Intonation contours are
delineated in great variety and with careful attention to meaning
and context. With almost no exceptions, the shapes described —
and their uses -- are identical to the semantically equivalent forms
in ENGLISH. There is of course the predictability of SWAHILI
stress -- penultimate -- against the unpredictability of stress position in ENGLISH. But concurrences of stress and intonation are
the same, as are the physical manifestations (added length on the
accented syllable, and pitch obtrusion, both up and down). Not all
of Ashton's contours can be transferred perfectly to ENGLISH. The
noteworthy exception is the yes-no question, for which she writes
only a terminal fall. But this appears to be either an oversight or
a case of the linguist's interference with his data. The point is
worth dwelling on, for given the attitudinal function of intonation,
it is certain to be more subject to distortion through the very act
of being inquired about than any other system in a language. Ashton
herself confesses to having been fooled by an overly explicit way of
asking a question with which her first informants regaled her to
make sure she understood (Ashton 1947: 27). A terminal rise on yes-
no questions is normal. This and a few other modifications of Ashton's description are based on productions supplied by Mr. Mohamed
Hassan (identified MH). Following are the points of contact (page
references are to Ashton):

1. Answers to questions tend to have their highest pitch on the
   terminal accent (20); other statements start relatively high
   and move down (16). This identical contrast was noted above
   for ENGLISH, section 2.7.
2. Wh-questions have a high level followed by a terminal fall
   (20, 33). SWAHILI syntax puts the wh word at the end; ENG-
   LISH intonation is the same when it uses this form, e.g.
   They're going where? (as an original, not a reclamatory,
   question). There is an optional terminal rise, which seems
   to be a C accent, also normal in ENGLISH.
3. Yes-no questions may use a simple rise (MH) or a slightly
   rising penultimate with final syllable low (27); the latter is
   reminiscent of SCOTTISH ENGLISH.

4. The imperative has a terminal fall (26).
5. Vocatives and other non-focused elements (such as resumptives and temporal adverbs), when terminal, form part of the low-pitched tail (17, 75-6). ENGLISH handles postnuclear low-information items identically.
6. Postposed typics similarly go at low pitch (94). ENGLISH may have to distort the syntax to get the same effect that SWAHILI gets by simple inversion:

Ninyi $_{(m)}$ wav   You're l_a
                iv_u. l_a ^{zy}.
(M) wa $^{vi}\diagdown$ You're $\diagdown$
            $\diagdown_{vu\ ninyi.}$ $_{zy,}$ you are.

7. Accent C may be used as in ENGLISH, for toning down and reassuring on expressions like <u>Haidhúru</u> 'No matter,' <u>Usijáli</u> 'Never mind,' <u>Nisáwa</u> 'It's OK' (MH).
8. Non-final clause terminals have a high level or a rise (115, 135-6, 138, 170), or even the "forbidden" A-rise (191-2). The suspensive intonations also apply to topicalized initial adverbs (129). Both syntactic types and intonations are identical to those in ENGLISH.
9. There is the climactic rightshift noted above (193).
10. The same "call" contours are found as in ENGLISH: two levels, high-to-low or low-to-high (194), or three, low-to-high-to-mid (MH). Likewise the same low-to-high response to a call, <u>Naam? Ye-es?</u> (194)

4.6 <u>BENGALI: interdialectal and interlingual differences</u>

The contrastive study of BENGALI (Hai and Ball 1961) is less extensive than that of SWAHILI, but tells us more about the possibilities of interdialectal as well as interlingual differences. British learners of BENGALI are warned against doing a number of things that they would avoid normally if they were speakers of AMERICAN ENGLISH, which in some respects resembles BENGALI more than it does Southern BRITISH. A similar closeness has been noted between DANISH and AMERICAN ENGLISH as against Southern BRITISH (Chatman 1966). BENGALI and AMERICAN ENGLISH align themselves together as follows (page numbers refer to Hai and Ball):
1. Avoidance of wide downskips before the nucleus (67, 75, 77).
2. Avoidance of a rise-fall tag in invitations (73). But BENGALI avoids it in all situations, whereas both dialects of ENGLISH do use it, on proper occasions. As far as I know, it is unique to ENGLISH, e.g.

You for^{got}
     ^{a}gain,   didn't
                   yo$_u$?

3. Avoidance of terraced downskips in exclamations (81).
4. Avoidance of repeated C accents in surprised exclamations (82).
5. Avoidance of utterance-final terminal rises except on questions (76, 91, 94-6). For AMERICAN ENGLISH we should
   perhaps say "used less" rather than "avoided."

The two main differences between BENGALI and Southern BRIT-
ISH are the fact that BENGALI tends to hug the lower registers and
shuns inconclusive endings. AMERICAN ENGLISH stands about
midway.

4.7 Extent of interdialectal differences

These similarities and dissimilarities suggest that two dialects
of a single language can be as different intonationally as if they were
two different languages. In segmental phonology this would be impossible by definition for two natural languages. It could happen
with intonation only under two conditions. Either intonation does
not count for much and can be ignored, or it is everywhere pretty
much the same. The first is true to the extent that monotone speech
is intelligible, and people can read most passages without benefit
of punctuation marks. The second has to be true in a very broad
sense, given the universality of the fundamental meanings assigned
to falling and rising pitches. If intonation were simply phonemic,
a fall ought to occur about as easily as a rise in marking a sentence-
medial clause separation.

4.7.1 Stylization: the Vas dialect of HUNGARIAN

So why the
variety, such as it is? The nature and the occasion of its manifestations point to cultural differences more than to narrowly linguistic
ones. In her careful comparison of the County Vas dialect of HUN-
GARIAN with the acrolect, Magdics found no great difference in
sentence intonation (1964: 19-20), but a great deal of dramatic styl-
ization in the Vas dialect. The standard seems to be much closer
to a kind of generalized urban European intonation, and one wonders
what the extent of diffusion may have been. In the alternation of
pitch levels in narration the Vas dialect resembles the rhythmic
alternation described in narrations told by BLACK ENGLISH child
speakers (Key et al. 1976). The powerful stylizations in BLACK
sermons (as in those of C.L. Franklin as recorded by Titon 1975)
make it clear that intonation at some points is not far from music,
and is perhaps both consciously and unconsciously cultivated as such.

4.7.2 Linguistic versus cultural contrast: BLACK ENGLISH
Even in ordinary conversation the differences may be social rather
than linguistic. How easily the investigator may be led astray is
shown by Tarone 1973, commenting on an earlier study by Loman
(1967). Loman reported a tendency among Black speakers to use a
terminal fall in yes-no questions, and Tarone replicated this. But
latter, "in the final Seattle study, where recordings were made in
an informal, non-threatening situation, the falling final contour
was not used for yes-no questions" (Tarone 1973: 34) -- the questions
had their usual terminal rise. In the first investigations, the Black
youngsters were reacting in a defensive way to the white investigator
or to the formality of the situation. Tarone adds (pp. 29-30) a news
report of a white policeman who arrested several Black youths because he thought they were in an altercation approaching violence --
not aware that they were playing "the dozens." Tarone's conclusion
epitomizes the dilemma that faces the student of intonation who would
separate the linguistic and universal from the pragmatic and cultural:
"The majority of the intonational characteristics found in the Black
English corpus could be traced directly to systematic differences
between black street culture and white 'mainstream' culture, with
regard to the function of the speech event within the two speech communities, rather than to differences in phonology (different rules of
intonation). Speech events occurring in black street culture seem
to call for specialized use of intonation patterns that are themselves
entirely consistent with standard English rules for intonation" (p.35).
(For a contrary statement see Winkler 1973.) It is not always rude
to be rude. Nor is it cordial to be cordial out of turn. Two things
may mean the same, yet it need not mean the same to use them.

4.7.3 Fixation of cultural contrasts How far this conclusion
can be extended across linguistic frontiers is of course the problem.
When the Spanish-speakers of Córdoba, Argentina lengthen the pretonic syllable (Fontanella 1971: 7) in a way that seems identical to
such things as ENGLISH

It's $^{p\,r\,e}$ Poste$_{r_{ou_{s!}}}$

have they, for effect, adopted an emphatic intonation and then for-
gotten all about what they meant by it?[4] Is the seemingly overheated

---

[4] Fontanella informs me that this was probably emphatic to begin
with, since markedly neutral sentences would still not receive it —
the markedness has shifted, with non-emphasis now the marked pole
of the opposition.

cordiality of Southern BRITISH really what it seems to be (to an
American), an affectation -- though now, certainly, an unconscious
one? (Of a kind with the facial expression that one critic has described as a perpetual question mark.) When CHAMORRO speakers
end most of their statements with a rise, are they being intention-
ally inconclusive? The fact that they use a fall on discourse-final
sentences proves that they are operating on the same gradient of
finality, only much closer to the "really final, final-final" end.
What of the identical phenomenon in Tyneside ENGLISH reported
by Barbara Strang(Bolinger 1964: 845) as being perfectly regular
and with no special value, and the same in Belfast ENGLISH (Jarman
and Cruttenden n.d.) -- did it have a value at one time, now lost?
(Like CHAMORRO, Belfast ENGLISH may represent not a break
with the system but a shift within it, low rises replacing falls and
rises being heightened [Cruttenden] -- this could happen if the entire
system is viewed as gradient, with no all-or-none break between
fall and rise, so that a low rise is only a graduated step away from
a fall.) Many speakers of American ENGLISH in giving a running
account of something will use exactly this kind of terminal rise at
the end of practically every sentence -- clearly a channel-clearing
device that says, in effect, 'Are you listening?,' for unless one
gives a sign of attention, the monolog comes to a halt. It would not
be hard to imagine such a habit becoming a contagion, after which,
with interlocutors weary of giving the countersign, the language
could be said to have a rising intonation as a mark of clause terminals in general.

4.7.4 Relative importance of differences   The differences between languages and between dialects are undeniable, but the question is how important they are and how stable in the long run. The
Mexican male speaker does not end a statement as low as a Spanish
male (Olsen 1975); similarly with Leipzigers saying the word Laute,
as against speakers of Hochdeutsch (Gericke 1963: 363). The BEN-
GALI speaker would not use an equivalent of the ENGLISH exclamation No! with rapid downmotion (Hai and Ball 1961: 83) -- but the voice
qualifiers and movements that accompany that exclamation expose
it as a put-on anyway: the husky voice and sudden drop of the head
show that it is a gesture of feigned collapse; much that we view as
intonational embodies kinesic and other paralinguistic features,
which have to be discounted. Probably the majority of intonational
differences from language to language are instances of doing the
same things but doing them in different degrees -- either more often
or less often, or to a greater or lesser extreme. If this is the case,
then we can think of an intonational core, an innate pattern of the
sort envisioned by Lieberman, from which speakers and cultures
may depart, but to which some force is always pushing them back.

5. Ontogenesis

5.1 Reinduction

To rephrase the question at the end of the last section, when does a mannerism become a manner? Assuming that cultures from time to time deviate from inherent tendencies, what makes the deviation become the norm? Presumably a new generation is at work, imitating the mannerism with no awareness of the now rare or defunct contrastive behavior. This is orthodox linguistic change by reinduction. How it may happen can be illustrated by an imaginary case that may be close to reality for some speakers — the reinterpretation of Accent C. As a sign of courtesy, the emphatic A accent is turned upside down. (This much appears to be a fact.) Speakers adopt a general pose of courtesy and use a C accent in all controlled situations where the thing they are communicating is clearly something they mean to be emphatic about. Young speakers encounter only that intonation under those conditions, and end by taking it as the norm for emphasis. (See, e.g., the descriptions of C accents in Jones 1956: ⟩⟩ 1057, 1065.)

5.2 Regeneration from below

If that were the end of the story, we would expect intonation long since to have developed connections between meaning and form as unpredictable as those found with segmental phonemes. That it has not argues for some kind of regeneration from below, a tendency perhaps for an inherent drive to reassert itself whenever dialect mixture or any other iconoclastic force opens the way. What do we know about the genesis of intonation in young children?

5.3 Innate tendencies toward similar intonations

I have already quoted Lieberman concerning the child's innate referential breath group. All the recent studies of child language that I have consulted are agreed that there is something innate about intonation — even that it may, unlike most of the rest of language, be controlled by the minor hemisphere of the brain (Weeks 1974:136, Peters 1976). Rhythms are the first to be detected — Delack (1974:13) cites Condon and Sander 1974 to the effect that "As early as the first day of life, the human neonate moves in precise and sustained segments of movement that are synchronous with the articulated structure of adult speech." Speaking of the relation between crying and non-crying vocalizations, he says that "such sound-meaning correspondences may begin as non-volitional responses to endogenous as well as exogenous stimuli. It would thus seem that

this ability arises very early in an infant's existence and is to a
large degree non-arbitrary" (Delack 1974: 16). By the babbling
stage, "seemingly adult intonation patterns are heard" (Kaplan
and Kaplan 1971: 362-3, Menn 1976: 182). In Nakazima's experiment,
the earliest that any difference in vocalizations between infants in
an AMERICAN-ENGLISH-speaking and infants in a JAPANESE-
speaking environment could be detected was at about one year of
age, and that difference was in intonation (Kaplan and Kaplan 1971:
374). Since intonation begins to become recognizable before that
(at seven or eight months -- Peters 1974: 212, Lenneberg 1967: 128-
30), this means a period during which future speakers of JAPANESE
and future speakers of ENGLISH are using identical intonations.
When we read that "by about eight months, he [Fred] had developed
English intonation patterns to go with his babbling" (Weeks 1974: 9),
can we assume that the "English" patterns are really universal ones?
A point on which all investigators appear to be agreed is that intonation is the first linguistic subsystem that the child is able to control. It is not till the beginning of the second year that supralaryngeal
mechanisms and cortical integration have developed to the point of
enabling the child to articulate (Delack 1974: 17). It may be that the
earliest intonations figure among the unlearned vocalizations of
infancy; or it may be that children are programmed to imitate
speech melodies before anything else, with those coming closest
to the "innate referential breath group" being the easiest to learn.
It is the only contour that increases its frequency radically during
the first year of life (Delack 1975: 6), despite the fact that adults
do their best to teach a terminal rise with all the questions and
terminal-rising commands they issue when speaking to children
(Garnica says that 85% of commands given to two-year-olds have
rising terminals; 1974: 68). Li and Thompson 1976 corroborate the
ease of learning a terminal fall. They found that CHINESE infants
have more trouble learning rising tones than falling ones; and they
point out that falling tones in the tone languages of Africa and Asia
are more frequent than rising ones, and also cite experiments showing that falls can be perceived and performed more easily. Appeal-
ing to the learning of linguistic tone has both the disadvantage that
the phenomenon is not the same as intonation (assuming this makes
any difference at that stage[5]) and the advantage that the contrasts
can be studied with greater precision.

---

[5] Children exposed to intonation languages rather than tone languages evidently learn some patterns as if they involved lexical
tone. Peters 1974 reports a 14-month-old learning What's that?
and Oh-oh with definite tunes. Probably the same is true of the
What's that? in Menn 1976: 195-6. But at least as early as the one-

5.3.1 <u>Teaching of falls vs. teaching of rises</u> The superior ease of learning a falling intonation casts some doubt on the anti-innateness inference that one might draw from Evelyn Pike 1949. The Pikes had observed their first daughter, Judith, using rising intonations from her very first words, in situations that in adult speech would call for falls. The reason seemed clear — this was the intonation always used <u>to</u> the child in naming things, as if to say "Can you say...?" "Can you name...?" "Do you want...?" Mrs. Pike decided to use only falling intonations with her second daughter, Barbara, and as the family was living away from an ENGLISH-speaking environment the daughter heard very little ENGLISH except from her mother. Barbara used a falling intonation on her first word, <u>baby</u>, and used no rising intonations at all until later, when she was left for a time with another family. What we need is a repetition of this experiment with the parent using only rising intonations! It would prove nothing if the result were only rises, but might suggest something if the child refused to eliminate falls altogether.

5.3.2 <u>Primitive basis of rises</u> But rises too seem to have a primitive basis, if we are to follow Menn's association of rises with whines: "The use of a rising-to-high contour when one wants something is probably indeed a primitive and natural use of intonation" (1976:193). At a year and three months of age the infant she was studying used a request (rising) vocalization that failed to get a response, and reacted by raising the pitch from 560 cps to 820 (p. 193). There is less reason to suppose that a learned vocalization would have the graded characteristic that this shows -- the kinds of things that an infant does "more of" when frustrated are likely to be emotional. (But even this idea is suspect, in view of what chimpanzees do with their artificially learned signs -- they grade them spontaneously. Washoe learned <u>more</u> and <u>sweet</u> and <u>drink</u>, but it was her idea to say <u>More more more sweet drink</u>. See Premack 1976: 73.) Menn surmises that there is "probably some innate component of the association of high pitch with weakness and low pitch with power" (1976: 220). For what it may be

---

(ftnt. 5 cont.)
word stage, children are matching words and intonation independently (Menyuk 1969), and independent uses of intonation antedate control of words -- Key (1975: 6) tells of a one-year-old who on hearing a siren go by produced a three-constituent sentence:

<u>da-da-da</u>   iiiiiii   <u>da-da-da</u>
--'Listen! The siren made a noise!'

worth, the well known phonesthematic tie between size and second-formant pitch shows a similar relationship, high with smallness, low with bigness (see Ultan 1970).

5.4 Importance of early acquisition of intonation

There is no proof, as yet, that intonation, or a strong predisposition to it, comes packed in our genes; but all indications are that it does. The child reacts to it first and controls it first. Its semantic domain is that of meanings that are most important to very young children: attention-getters, requests, inquiries, complaints — which function alone at first and then become an illocutionary counterpoint to words ("primitive illocutionary force" — Dore 1975: 31). The forms used resemble vocalizations that infants -- even deaf ones -- use in their first months. The most natural intonation, from the standpoint of speech production, is the one learned most easily. And there is a point that our adult casualness about the importance of intonation makes us apt to overlook: it is essential to the learning of the rest of language. Parents and others use exaggerated prosodic features with very young children (Garnica 1974: 28-9). Pause assists in the fixing of intonation patterns. Intonation patterns and pause in turn assist in the learning of words, then syntax: without the intonational segmentation of constituents it would be enormously difficult for the child to induce a syntactic pattern. But once the repertory of words and syntactic patterns has been mastered, intonation is free to embrace larger stretches of speech, up to paragraphs, carrying on both an organizing and an illocutionary role. What the child has learned with words in isolation now becomes the prime cue to the utterance. If it is distorted, intelligibility suffers. This can be seen in experiments in which words spoken in isolation — and hence presumably as intelligible as they can be made -- are strung together to form sentences; the resulting sentences are less intelligible than sentences spoken at normal speed. And when words from the latter sentences are excised and listened to in isolation, they are less intelligible than words spoken originally in isolation (Darwin 1975: 103). The common denominator in the intelligible utterances is, of course, the intonation contour. Children make the transfer of intonation from short to long segments. In the experiment by Shilkret and Wiener (1972), children were found to understand the most complex sentences just as well as the least complex ones when normal intonation was present; at a monotone, syntactic complexity made a difference.

6. Conclusion

6.1 Intonation as an essential human trait

Intonational shapes with predictable meanings are too widely shared not to lead to the conclusion that they come from some "essentially human trait" (Ultan 1969: 45). The exception is the language that appears to lack them, and this needs to be explained: our data may be incomplete, or there may have occurred some actual shift (as in Belfast ENGLISH) that maintains the larger features but subverts the smaller ones. Whether to account for the uniformities one should look to some still active physiological mechanism, such as expiration and drop in subglottal air pressure, or relaxation and untensing of the vocal cords, or whether that is past history and we now carry traces in our genetic makeup that compel us to adopt certain definite patterns, the fact is that human speakers everywhere do essentially the same things with fundamental pitch.

6.2 Difficulties of establishing a basic uniformity

The picture is clouded in a number of ways. The meanings conveyed by pitch are attitudinal, and attitudes are notoriously subject to distortion and inhibition: it isn't polite to yell, women should not sound too positive, it is unmanly to beseech. The competition is fierce -- much that intonation does is also done by gesture, and the two may be used in different proportions, or in different combinations, from one language to another. Other parts of the prosody -- pause, rhythm, range -- are as much part of certain patterns as pitch movement, and "intonation" is generally considered to include them. Pitch movement itself is symphonic: even discounting tone, as many as three things may be happening at once: an over-all wide range for a main sentence, an included narrow range for a parenthesis, and further included peaks and scoops for accent. The very integrity of intonation may lead to apparent differences between languages: given the same intonational rule for focus, if focus is partly controlled by syntax, the interaction may produce utterances that are superficially quite different. Yet despite these complications the evidence for a basic uniformity is impressive, and if they can some day be disentangled, it will probably be overwhelming.

6.3 Predictability of exceptions

To some extent, even what is absent or rare becomes compelling if we can predict it on the basis of what is most commonly present. The two intonational shapes that are found everywhere are fall and rise, with their targets, low and high. The meanings are as uniform as the shapes: falls for 'being through,' rises for 'not being through.' Spreading from each is a net of metaphor. 'Not being through' is akin to 'being aroused,' and since we are most aroused

by what is most important, a high pitch becomes the normal sign
of importance. One would predict that doing the opposite ought to
be less usual and might not appear in some languages at all, and
also that when it did occur it would represent some kind of downtoning. Both predictions appear to be true, with Accent C. Our
ability to predict the commonplace is also persuasive. If a fall is
'being through,' and coming to the end of a discourse is 'being more
through' than coming to the end of a sentence in the middle of a discourse, then discourse-final falls ought to be deeper than sentence
falls. This too is confirmed.

6.4 Need for corroboration from two sources

Two things are lacking for us to feel entirely comfortable as yet
with the hypothesis that intonation is "essentially human" both in
its presence and in the forms that it takes.

6.4.1 Further comparative work in child intonation   One is a
better understanding of the genesis of intonation in very young children. Most of the research has been done with children learning
ENGLISH and a very few other languages. To discover what is
inherent it is necessary to discount the influence of any one linguistic environment, and that can be done only when we have many more
comparisons like Nakazima's.

6.4.2 Research on basic units   The other lack is our unsureness
of the basic units of intonation. If pitch makes a contribution entirely
its own, independently of the rest of prosody, we should be able to
define it. The distinctive feature approach of Allerton and Cruttenden 1976 is promising. A rise has a particular meaning, and so
does a fall; patterns of falls and rises mean what they do by virtue
of how low or high they are and which comes first. Such a theory
needs the illumination that comes from more comparative studies,
for if we can find the true common denominators from language to
language, we may well discover that we have found the basic units.

BIBLIOGRAPHY

Abe, Isamu. 1955. Intonational patterns of English and Japanese.
Word 11. 386-98.

Abramson, Arthur S. 1962. The vowels and tones of standard
Thai: acoustical measurements and experiments. IJAL 28,
Pub. 20 of Indiana Univ. Research Center in Anthropology,

Folklore, and Linguistics.

Akhmanova, Olga. 1974. Approaches to the formatting of supraphrasal entities. Proceedings of the 11th International Congress
of Linguists, Bologna 1972, ed. by Luigi Heilmann, 829-31.
Bologna: Il Mulino.

Allerton, D.J. and Alan Cruttenden. 1976. Syntactic, illocutionary, thematic and attitudinal factors in the intonation of adverbials.
Preprint.

Ashton, E.O. 1947. Swahili grammar. London: Longman.

Bailey, T. Grahame. 1956. Teach yourself Urdu. London:
English Universities Press.

Bell, Alan. 1976. Accent placement and perception of prominence
in rhythmic structures. Preprint.

Bendor-Samuel, J.T. 1962. Stress in Terena. Transactions of
the Philological Society, 105-23.

Bloomfield, Leonard. 1941. Language. New York: Holt.

Bolinger, Dwight. 1955. Intersections of stress and intonation.
Word 2. 195-203.

_____. 1963,1976. Length, vowel, juncture. Linguistics 1.5-29.
(Revised, Bilingual Review 3.1. 43-61)

_____. 1964. Intonation as a universal. Proceedings of the 9th
International Congress of Linguists, 1962, ed. by Horace G.
Lunt. The Hague: Mouton.

_____. 1965. Forms of English. Cambridge, Mass.: Harvard.

_____. 1972. (ed.) Intonation. Harmondsworth: Penguins.

Bridgeman, Loraine I. 1961. Kaiwá (Guaraní) phonology. IJAL
27. 329-34.

Bronstein, Arthur J. 1960. The pronunciation of American English.
New York: Appleton Century Crofts.

Brown, W.S. Jr. and Robert E. McGlone. 1974. Aerodynamic and
acoustic study of stress in sentence productions. JASA 56. 971-4.

Carnochan, J. 1964. Pitch, tone, and intonation in Yoruba. In honour of Daniel Jones, ed. by David Abercrombie et al. London: Longman.

Chatman, Seymour. 1966. Some intonational crosscurrents: English and Danish. Linguistics 21. 24-44.

Cohen, A. and J. 't Hart. 1970. Comparison of Dutch and English intonation contours in spoken news bulletins. IPO Annual Progress Report (Univ. of Utrecht) 5. 78-82.

Condon, Wm. S. and Louis W. Sander. 1974. Neonate movement is synchronized with adult speech: interactional participation and language acquisition. Science 183. 99-101.

Cooper, Jonathan E. 1972. Linguistic remarks on a literary variety of Calabrese. Senior thesis, Harvard Univ.

Cowan, G.M. 1971. Whistled Tepehua. Paper at 7th International Congress of Phonetic Sciences, Montreal 1971.

Dacanay, Fe R. 1963. Techniques and procedures in second language teaching. Quezon City, Philippines: Phoenix.

Daneš, František. 1957. Sentence intonation in present-day Standard Czech. In his Intonace a věta spisovné češtině. Prague: Nakladetelství ČSAV.

Delack, John B. 1974. Prosodic analysis of infant vocalizations and the ontogenesis of sound-meaning correlations. Papers and reports on child language development 8. 16-18.

_____ and Patricia J. Fowlow. 1975. The ontogenesis of differential vocalization: development of prosodic contrastivity during the first year of life. Preprint.

Darwin, C.J. 1975. On the dynamic use of prosody in speech perception. Haskins Labs Status report on speech research 42/43. 103-16.

Delattre, Pierre. 1961. La leçon d'intonation de Simone de Beauvoir: étude d'intonation déclarative comparée. French Review 35. 59-67.

_____, Carroll Olsen, and Elmer Poenack. 1962. A comparative study of declarative intonation in American English and Spanish. Hispania 45. 233-41.

Dore, John. 1975. Holophrases, speech acts and language universals. Journal of Child Language 2. 21-40.

Douglas, W.H. 1964. An introduction to the Western Desert Language. Oceania Linguistics Monograph No. 4, rev. ed. Sydney: Univ. of Sydney.

Ferguson, Charles A. 1957. Word stress in Persian. Lg. 33. 123-35.

Fontanella de Weinberg, M.B. 1971. La entonación del español de Córdoba (Argentina). Thesaurus 26. 10-21.

_____ and Beatriz R. Lavandera. 1975. Variant or morpheme? Negative commands in Buenos Aires Spanish. NWave (Georgetown Univ.) 1-17.

Frantz, Donald G. 1972a. Cheyenne distinctive features and phonological rules. IJAL 38. 6-13.

_____. 1972b. The origin of Cheyenne pitch accent. IJAL 38. 223-5.

Garnica, Olga. 1974. Some prosodic characteristics of speech to young children. Stanford Univ. thesis.

Gericke, Ingeborg. 1963. Die Intonation der leipziger Umgangsprache. ZPSK 16. 337-69.

Greenberg, Joseph H. 1959. Review of Douglas 1964 (in its original version). Lg 35. 382-5.

Grimes, Joseph E. 1955. Style in Huichol structure. Lg. 31. 31-5.

_____. 1959. Huichol tone and intonation. IJAL 25. 221-32.

Hai, Muhammud Abdul, and W.J. Ball. 1961. The sound structure of English and Bengali. Dacca: Dept. of English, Univ. of Dacca.

Hansen, K.C. and L.E. 1969. Pintupi phonology. Oceanic Linguistics 8. 153-70.

't Hart, J. and R. Collier. 1975. Integrating different levels of intonation analysis. Journal of Phonetics 3. 235-55.

Healey, Phyllis M. 1966. Levels and chaining in Telefol sentences. Linguistic Circle of Canberra Pubs., Series B, No. 4.

Hermann, Eduard. 1942. Probleme der Frage. Nachrichten von der Akademie der Wissenschaften in Göttingen. Philologisch-Historische Klasse, Nr. 3, 4.

Hollien, Harry. 1974. On vocal registers. Journal of Phonetics 2.125-43.

Hudson, Joyce, and Eirlys Richards. 1969. The phonology of Waltmanjari. Oceanic Linguistics 8.171-89.

Huestis, George. 1963. Bororo clause structure. IJAL 29.230-8.

Hyman, Larry M. 1975. On the nature of linguistic stress. Preprint.

_____ and Russell G. Schuh. 1972. Universals of tone rules. WPLU 10.1-50.

Jarman, Eric and Alan Cruttenden. n.d. Belfast intonation and the myth of the fall. Preprint.

Jones, Daniel. 1956. An outline of English phonetics. New York: Dutton.

Kalstrom, Marjorie R. and Eunice V. Pike. 1968. Stress in the phonological system of Eastern Popoloca. Phonetica 18.16-30.

Kaplan, Elenor and G. 1971. The prelinguistic child. Human development and cognitive processes, ed. by John Eliot. New York: Holt, Rinehart and Winston.

Kenyon, John S. and Thomas A. Knott. 1953. A pronouncing dictionary of American English. Springfield, Mass.: Merriam.

Key, Harold. 1961. Phonotactics of Cayuvava. IJAL 27.143-50.

Key, Mary Ritchie. 1975. Paralanguage and kinesics (nonverbal communication). Metuchen, N.J.: Scarecrow Press.

_____ et al. 1976. Some linguistic and stylistic features of child black English. Preprint.

Kirsner, Robert. 1976. On the subjectless "pseudo-passive" in standard Dutch and the semantics of background agents. Subject and topic, ed. by Charles N. Li. New York: Academic Press.

Larsen, Raymond S. and E.V. Pike. 1949. Huasteco intonations and phonemes. Lg. 25. 268-77.

Leed, Richard L. 1965. A contrastive analysis of Russian and English intonation contours. Slavic and East European Journal 9. 62-75.

Lehiste, Ilse. 1972. The timing of utterances and linguistic boundaries. JASA 51. 2018-24.

_____. 1976. Some phonological aspects of paragraph structure. Stanford Colloquium, April 29.

Lenneberg, Eric H. 1967. Biological foundations of language. New York: Wiley.

Li, Charles N. and Sandra Thompson. 1976. Tone perception and production: evidence from tone acquisition. Paper at Child Language Research Forum, April 3.

Lieberman, Philip. 1967. Intonation, perception, and language. Cambridge, Mass.: M.I.T. Press.

Lisker, Leigh. 1963. Introduction to spoken Telugu. New York: ACLS.

Loman, Bengt. 1967. Conversations in a Negro American dialect. Washington, D.C.: Center for Applied Linguistics.

Magdics, Klara. 1964. First findings in the comparative study of intonation of Hungarian dialects. Phonetica 11. 19-38.

Malkiel, Yakov. 1959. Studies in irreversible binomials. Lingua 8. 113-60.

Marsh, James. 1969. Mantjiltjara phonology, Oceanic Linguistics 8. 131-52.

Menn, Lise. 1976. Pattern, control, and contrast in beginning speech: a case study in the development of word form and word function. Univ. of Illinois thesis.

Menyuk, Paula, and Nancy Bernholz. 1969. Prosodic features and children's language production. MIT Research Laboratory of Electronics Quarterly Progress Report 93. 216-9.

Moser, Edward W. and Mary B. 1965. Consonant vowel balance in Seri syllables. Linguistics 16. 56-57.

Murane, John and Elizabeth. 1972. Vocalic syllabicity in Daga. Phonetica 25. 19-26.

Nakazima, S. 1966. A comparative study of the speech developments of Japanese and American English in childhood (2) — the acquisition of speech. Studia Phonologica 4. 38-55.

Nash, Rose. 1973. Turkish intonation: an instrumental study. The Hague: Mouton.

Oller, John W. and James Rydland. 1974. Progress report in Papers and Reports on Child Language Development 8. 211.

Olmsted, David L. 1953. Comparative notes on Yoruba and Lucumí. Lg. 29. 157-64.

Olsen, Carroll L. 1975. Grave vs. agudo in two dialects of Spanish: a study in voice register and intonation. Journal of the International Phonetic Association 5. 84-91.

Pankratz, Leo, and E.V. Pike. 1967. Phonology and morphotonemics of Ayutla Mixtec. IJAL 33. 287-99.

Pence, Alan. 1964, 1972. Intonation in Kunimaipa. In Bolinger 1972, 325-36.

Peters, Ann M. 1974. Progress report in Papers and Reports on Child Language Development 8. 212.

_____. 1976. Paper at Child Language Research Forum, Stanford Univ., April 4.

Pike, Eunice V. 1974. A multiple stress system versus a tone system. IJAL 40. 169-75.

_____, and Eugene Scott. 1962. The phonological hierarchy of Marinahua. Phonetica 8. 1-8.

Pike, Evelyn. 1949. Controlled infant intonation. Language Learning 2. 21-24.

Pike, K.L. 1963. Pitch accent and non-accented phrases in Fore (New Guinea). ZPSK 16. 179-89.

Powlison, Esther. 1971. The suprahierarchical and hierarchical structures of Yagua phonology. Linguistics 75. 43-73.

Premack, Ann J. 1976. Why chimps can read. New York: Harper and Row.

Robins, R.H. 1958. The Yurok language: grammar, texts, lexicon. Berkeley and Los Angeles: Univ. of California.

Rountree, S. Catherine. 1972. Saramaccan tone in relation to intonation and grammar. Lingua 29. 308-25.

Russell, Robert. 1958. Algunos morfemas de amahuaca (pano) que equivalen a la entonación del castellano. Perú Indígena 8. 29-33.

Sandmann, Manfred. 1954. Subject and predicate. Edinburgh: University Press.

Shilkret, Robert, and Morton Wiener. 1972. The contribution of syntactic and para-syntactic cues in the comprehension of spoken and written language. Final Report, Project 0-A-019, Grant OEG-1-70-0009 (509) U.S. Department of Health, Education, and Welfare.

Siertsema, B. 1959. Stress and tone in Yoruba word composition. Lingua 8. 385-402.

Smalley, William. 1953. Phonemic rhythm in Comanche. IJAL 19. 297-301.

Swick, Joyce. 1966. Chuave phonological hierarchy. Linguistic Circle of Canberra, Occasional Papers, Series A No. 7, 33-48.

Tarone, Elaine E. 1973. Aspects of intonation in Black English. American Speech 48. 29-36.

Titon, Jeff. 1975. Tonal system in the chanted oral sermons of the Rev. C.L. Franklin. Preprint.

Topping, D.M. 1969. A restatement of Chamorro phonology. Anthopological Linguistics. 2. 62-78.

Uhlenbeck, E.M. 1965. Some preliminary remarks on Javanese syntax. Lingua 15. 53-70.

Ultan, Russell. 1969. Some general characteristics of interrogative systems. WPLU 1. 41-63.

_____. 1970. Size-sound symbolism. WPLU 3. S1-31.

Vanderslice, Ralph and Laura Shun Pierson. 1967, 1972. Prosodic features of Hawaiian English. In Bolinger 1972, 439-50.

Van Syoc, Wayland Bryce. 1959. The phonology and morphology of the Sundanese language. Univ. of Michigan thesis.

Varga, László. 1975. A contrastive analysis of English and Hungarian sentence prosody. Budapest: Linguistics Institute of the Hungarian Academy of Sciences and Center for Applied Linguistics.

Wallis, Ethel E. 1968. The word and the phonological hierarchy of Mezquital Otomí. Lg. 44. 76-90.

_____. 1970. The trimodal structure of a folk poem. Word 26. 170-93.

Waterhouse, Viola. 1962. The grammatical structure of Oaxaca Chontal. IJAL 28, Pub. 19 of Indiana Univ. Research Center in Anthropology, Folklore, and Linguistics.

Watkins, Mark Hanna. 1937. A grammar of Chichewa. Language Dissertation No. 24, Apr.-June Supplement.

Watson, Richard. 1966. Clause to sentence gradations in Pacóh. Lingua 16. 166-89.

Weeks, Thelma E. 1974. The slow speech development of a bright child. Lexington, Mass.: Lexington Books (Heath).

Weinreich, Uriel. 1956. Notes on the Yiddish rise-fall intonation contour. In For Roman Jakobson 1956, 633-43.

West, John David. 1962. The phonology of Mikasuki. Studies in Linguistics 16. 77-91.

Winkler, Henry J. 1973. A comparison of the intonation patterns of Black English and Standard English. Paper at Acoustical Society of America, Los Angeles, Oct. 30 - Nov. 2.

Woo, Nancy. 1972. Prosody and phonology. MIT thesis, 1969. Bloomington: Indiana University Linguistics Club.

Size-Sound Symbolism

RUSSELL ULTAN

ABSTRACT

Originally designed as a cross-language test of three related
hypotheses (diminutive sound symbolism is associated with marked
phonological features, high and/or front vowels, and palatal or
fronted consonants), this study was expanded to include a number
of size-related categories represented by the same kinds of symbolism found among diminutives. The most important of these is
distance symbolism, proximal demonstratives generally being analogous to diminutives in terms of sound symbolism.

Diminutive is most often symbolized by high or high front vowels,
high tone, or various kinds of consonantal ablaut (which is restricted in distribution mainly to western North American languages).
Proximal distance is symbolized overwhelmingly by front or high
vowels. For most of the remaining associated categories, the number of examples was too small to permit generalization.

Of the marked phonological categories, glottalized and nasalized
consonants as well as nasalized and long vowels conform to the
hypothesis; voicing of consonants does not. Both remaining hypotheses were confirmed.

The evidence for sound symbolism in diminutive and augmentative
affixes is negative.

Reprinted from Working Papers on Language Universals 3,
June 1970, S1-S30.

Russell Ultan

CONTENTS

CONTENTS

1. Introduction

1.1 Approach

Although the subject of sound symbolism has been discussed from time to time in the literature, it is usually approached in one of three ways:

a. A rather unstructured listing of examples, principally from the lexicons of European languages (compare e.g. Chastaing 1958, Fonagy 1963, and Jespersen 1922).

b. A more or less structured analysis of the grammatical function(s) of sound symbolism in a particular language (compare e.g. Sapir 1922 WISHRAM, Martin 1962 KOREAN, and Innes 1966 GREBO.

c. A psycholinguistic experiment, generally based on subjective responses to artificial data by linguistically homogeneous or heterogeneous subject groups (compare e.g. Sapir 1958a). Newman 1933, and Wissemann 1954).

If we are to determine whether there are any truly universal types of sound symbolism, it seems that an examination and a comparison of patterned instances in a large number of randomly selected natural languages would be in order. While the findings resulting from any of the approaches cited above may ultimately coincide wholly or in part with those obtained from more or less global comparisons of actual languages, not one of them enables us to make definitive statements about the universality of symbolic types. The purpose of this paper therefore is to make a modest attempt at comparing and evaluating data from a number of languages with a view to confirming, modifying, or rejecting several experientially (and intuitively?) derived hypotheses, and perhaps discovering additional constants.

Some of the most prevalent hypotheses concerning size-sound symbolism, in languages with diminutive symbolism, associate the following with diminutive size:

a. Marked phonological features

b. High and/or front vowels

c. Palatal or fronted consonants

1.2 Associated categories

Although my intention at the outset was to limit this study to size symbolism, it soon became apparent that a number of other semantic categories represented by the same kinds of ablaut systems were often interrelated, sometimes inextricably so, with the category of size. In fact, viewed in terms of semantic field theory, these may be said to constitute a few recurrent nexuses formally represented by symbolic processes. Some of these categories are directly associated with size, others only implicitly so.

Thus, for example, feminine in DAKOTA is marked by a front root vowel in the imperative particles yé (sing.) and pé (pl.) vs. the corresponding masculine forms yó and pó. A front vowel is also used to mark feminine in ARABIC, GREEK, HEBREW, et al. or diminutive in, for example, DIOLA-FOGNY, KHASI, and ROTU-MAN. GREBO has a front vowel for diminutive-feminine, and a great many languages have a diminutive-feminine category marked by either affixes or ablaut (cf. for example, PANJABI, SWAHILI, TILLAMOOK). The likelihood of finding diminutive-feminine represented by a front vowel is much greater than that of finding diminutive masculine with a front vowel — for that matter, of finding diminutive-masculine at all — or, conversely, diminutive-feminine with a back vowel; thus we may consider feminine ablaut in DAKOTA to be implicitly related to diminutive ablaut. It seems relevant to include this and certain other non-size ablaut types in the present study. Admission of such data not only allows us to make some interesting observations on the widespread diffusion of certain metaphorical types, but also indirectly adds to the data offered in support of the general characteristics of size-ablaut systems. For a complete list of these associated categories, see Sec. 2.5, 4.B, items 20 through 124.

2. Method

2.1 Generalities

A total of 136 languages[1] were examined in order to obtain a reasonably representative global sample. However, due to the relative abundance and availability of descriptions of AMERICAN INDIAN languages, the sample is weighted in favor of them (48 languages) and somewhat less so for DRAVIDIAN (11 languages); 77 others are more or less evenly distributed geographically.

---

[1]Plus additional data from SOUTHERN BANTU, INDO-EUROPEAN and SINO-TIBETAN.

Most of the sources chosen were fairly comprehensive grammars, descriptive wherever possible, but pedagogical or normative in a few instances. Others were partial treatments, descriptions of particular grammatical features, sketches, and comparative studies. The great diversity in individual coverage, focus of interest, and analytic approach do not make for the descriptive homogeneity which would be ideally suited to a study of this kind. These differences must often be taken into consideration in evaluating the data as presented.

Since a certain amount of sound symbolism is sporadic or onomatopoeic, it is well to define, at least operationally, the object of investigation. Thus we are interested primarily in all patterned occurrences of size and distance symbolism (principally vis-à-vis demonstratives), secondarily in size-related symbolism. In many instances (particularly in typically small subsystems such as demonstratives), the patterns may be limited to a small set of forms and/or may be nonproductive, but if there is any possibility of segmenting the suspect morphs, they are accepted as valid examples.

2.2 Degree of contrast

Size-ablauting systems are most commonly found among roots, but occasionally among affixes. They appear typically in noun derivation by root alternation, more rarely in verb derivation and elsewhere. The degree of morphemic contrast varies from overt, in which the semantic contrast between two or more forms is represented solely by ablaut (e.g. WISHRAM ikəč 'nose,' ik̓əč 'small nose'),[2] to semi-overt, in which the contrast is represented by an affix or a process (e.g. reduplication) plus an ablauted root allomorph restricted to obligatory co-occurrence with the affix (e.g. KAROK súruvara 'hole,' súnuvanač 'little hole'), to covert, in which an affix or a process is the primary contrast marker, optionally accompanied by a particular ablauted root allomorph (e.g. WISHRAM waskhán 'box,' wáck̓un 'cup' as against iškálkʰal 'hip joints,' isk̓alkʰal 'little hip joints,' where the primary diminutive marker in both pairs is the presence of a glottalized stop and the covert marker in the first pair is the presence of a high vowel). The degree of overtness must be taken into account in evaluating the data.

---

[2] Pre-phonemic and older transcriptions using now obsolete symbols or symbol values have been converted to currently accepted symbols.

2.3 Productivity

Another important factor to be considered is the degree of productivity of a given symbolic system. Does it constitute a major
pattern of derivation? Is it only mildly productive? Is it unproductive or limited to a small, closed subsystem? If unproductive,
is the frequency of occurrence high or low?

2.4 Historical considerations

The fact that a given symbolic process may have evolved from
forms which were nonsymbolic or even diametrically opposed to
what one might expect in terms of the hypotheses (see Section 1.1)
does not negate the validity of the example. An arbitrary representation which has developed into one which may be viewed as
sound symbolic and subsequently become productive through analogy is, at the later stage, no less an instance of sound symbolism
than one which may have remained unchanged over the same period
of time. Therefore, it would seem that historical considerations,
while of interest for other reasons, should not be permitted to influence our judgment too much in evaluating cases of sound symbolism.

2.5 Codes

After the data had been collected and compared, certain predominant formal and semantic types, more or less in accord with
the hypotheses at various points, came to light. These were further analyzed for shared features in an attempt to come up with a
small number of comprehensive generalizations and then assigned
codes to facilitate mass comparison of phonosemantic types. For
each language, the following kinds of information were considered
relevant and coded as necessary:

1. Language (no code)
2. Morph type, including ablauting forms and size affixes:
   prefix (p); suffix (s); reduplicative (r); root (unmarked)
3. Basic ablaut types: consonant (C); vowel (V); tone (T)
4. Symbolic types, broken down into:

A.	a	apex or peripheral	hf	high front
	cd	close (degree of closure)	l	long
	cm	manner of closure	n	nasalized
	f	front or fronted	t	lenis
	g	glottalized	v	voiced
	h	high		

These characteristics of ablaut systems are the ones most commonly equated with small size or associated categories. All but one of them imply a binary contrast with an opposing feature equated with normal or large size.

The symbol a refers to apex as opposed to central and mid vowels, as in the SHONA proximal demonstratives uyu, aya, and iyi vs. their distal correlates uyo, ayo, and iyo.

Degree of closure (cd) refers to a contrast between stops or affricates (close: small) and the corresponding spirants (open: large), e.g. KAROK č ~ θ in ičáni·pič 'small fir' vs. iθári·p 'fir.'

Manner of closure (cm) involves a contrast between a lateral (or y in RUMANIAN) and either a nasal (most commonly) or an alveolar or palatal stop, affricate, vibrant, or sibilant. Superficially, the evidence indicates no consistent patterning for the lateral-nasal alternations (e.g. nasals are as often as not associated with diminutive as with normal size or augmentative). If, however, we consider diminutive and the associated categories as marked versus their unmarked counterparts, lateral-nasal alternations which appear with a nasal representing diminutive, etc. may be analyzed as instances of nasalization (Cn) rather than manner of closure, i.e. the alternation is regarded as processual and unidirectional (oral becomes nasal concomitant with the appropriate semantic shift). Thus interpreted, a general pattern emerges: stops, affricates, vibrants, or sibilants represent diminutive, etc. when opposed to laterals (or y), and laterals represent diminutive, etc. when opposed to nasals. Compare for example: CHINOOK iáqoai ƛ 'large,' iáqoaicʰ 'small;' YUROK mo?ohkeloy- 'be large and round,' mo-?ohkeroy- 'be small and round;' TOTONAC ɬkuyuy 'burns it,' skuyuy 'smokes it;' NORTHERN SAHAPTIN tú·n 'thing,' tú·l 'little thing;' RUMANIAN -elj diminutive suffix, -anj augmentative suffix.

The feature front (f) refers to relative fronting of vowels and consonants or palatalization of the latter. In GREBO the third person pronouns ɛ (sing.) and e (pl.) are used to refer to small, unimportant worthless things while ɔ (sing.) and o (pl.) refer to large, important, valuable things or humans. WISHRAM shows fronting of consonants in iɬkáškaš 'child' vis-à-vis iɬkáskas 'little child.'

The feature glottalized (g) occurs only with consonants in the present sample. Compare COEUR D'ALENE marmarímantamɪɬš 'they were treated one by one' vs. mʼmaɬʼmaɬʼímahtamɪɬš 'they (little ones) were treated one by one.'

High (h) refers to high vowels or pitch as opposed to low. An
example of the vocalic contrast is BENGALI <u>bacca</u> 'baby,' <u>baccu</u>
'small baby.' For a tonal contrast, note the adjective <u>goli</u> in
EWE àtĭgo lè gòlĭĭ 'the barrel is cylindrical' and kpéví lè gólí
'the little stone is rounded.'

High front (hf) refers to vowels only, as in KONKOW wòċoṭin
'notch (with an ax),' wíċiṭin 'split a very small object.'

Length (l) appears only in conjunction with vowels, e.g. UPPER
CHEHALIS spatáln 'rock,' spatá·ln 'little rock.'

Nasalized (n) may be concomitant with vowels as in KOASATI
lakawwą̇· (female speaker) vs. lakawwá·s (male speaker) 'he will
lift it' or with consonants as in YANA lal foot,' nanṗa 'small foot.'

Lenis (t) represents a factor of tension, lenis vs. fortis with
consonants, lax vs. tense with vowels. An example of the vocalic
contrast is found in the GREBO demonstratives nɔno~nɛno (sing.)
vs. nono~neno (pl.) 'this' or third person pronouns ɔ and ɛ (sing.)
vs. o and e (pl.). Consonantal tension is contrasted in this KO-
REAN paradigm: <u>taeŋtaeŋ</u> 'ding dong,' ṭaeŋṭaeŋ 'jangle,' tʰaeŋtʰaeŋ
'clang.'

The feature voiced (v) occurs only with consonants, e.g DIE-
GUEÑO (IPAI) cəkuɬk 'large hole through something,' cəkulk 'small
hole through something.'

B. <u>Semantic categories</u>

These fall into two groups: size and size-related. The latter
may be further subdivided into two groups: actual or physical extension (20-50) and figurative or synesthetic extension (60-120).
Each category is viewed as containing a contrastive set, one pole of
which is indicated in parentheses. These poles represent semantic
components often found to be associated with small size. Some of
these categories have been included, even though they were uniquely
or rarely represented, because they were formally related to symbolic processes which were otherwise relevant to the main topic,
e.g. mode, age, duration, et al. Whether or not any or all of these
are ultimately to be included is a question which cannot be answered
on the basis of the present data.

        10.   size (diminutive)
        20.   distance from speaker (proximal)

30. quantification
    31. number (singular, dual)
    32. distribution (individual, collective unit)
40. magnitude
    41. force (weak)
    42. intensity (low)
50. weight (light)
60. affect or attitude
    61. hypocoristic, good
    62. pejorative
70. definition (definite, particular)
80. grammatical distance
    81. case (direct, absolute)
    82. form class (noun, pronoun)
    83. mode (nontentative, nonpotential)
    84. voice (intransitive, passive, introverted, subject-oriented)
90. person
    91. addressee status (consanguineal, familiar)
    92. person (first)
100. sensation
    101. sweet, good
    102. smooth
    103. high pitch
110. sex
    111. gender (feminine, neuter, inanimate, nonhuman)
    112. sex (female)
120. time
    121. age (young)
    122. aspect (completive, momentary)
    123. tense (present, recent)
    124. duration (short, fast)

5. Morphemic contrast: covert (-); semi-overt ($\pm$); overt (unmarked)
6. Productivity: unproductive (-); mildly productive ($\pm$); productive (unmarked)
7. Associated semantic categories (additional categories associated with the primary one, see Sec. 1.2 and 4.B above for code).

3. Data Analysis

3.1 Language data synopsis

In the synopsis, all languages examined in the course of this study are listed. This includes a number of languages for which

the source shows no systematically marked size category (e.g.
ACOMA). They are included to give the reader a complete picture
of the scope of investigation and to enable him to make negative
comparisons. The fact that a marked size category is not indicated
does not necessarily mean that the language in question lacks one,
merely that the source used does not mention one. This may be due
to incomplete description, sketchiness, focal preferences, etc.
The column heading numbers correspond to the identically numbered information types detailed above:

1. Language
2. Morph type
3. Basic ablaut type
4. Symbolic type
    A. Formal features
    B. Semantic categories (primary)
5. Morphemic contrast
6. Productivity
7. Associated semantic categories (secondary)

A question mark in columns 5 or 6 indicates lack of information;
elsewhere, it expresses doubt as to proper interpretation of a
given item. A hyphen immediately following a semantic code indicates an example that runs counter to the hypotheses proposed
in this paper.

3.1.1 Symbols used in data synopsis

C	consonant	10	size (diminutive)
V	vowel	20	distance (proximal)
T	tone	30	quantification
		31	number (singular, dual)
a	apex	32	distribution (individual)
cd	close (degree of closure)	40	magnitude
cm	manner of closure	41	force (weak)
f	front	42	intensity (low)
g	glottalized	50	weight (light)
h	high	60	affect or attitude
hf	high front	61	hypocoristic, good
l	long	62	pejorative
n	nasalized	70	definition
p	prefix	80	grammatical distance
r	reduplicative	81	case (direct)
s	suffix	82	form class (noun, pronoun)
t	lenis	84	voice (intransitive, passive,
v	voiced		introverted, subject-oriented)

90   person
91   addressee status
     (consanguineal, familiar)
92   person (first)
100 sensation
101 sweet, good
102 smooth
103 high pitch
110 sex
111 gender (feminine, neuter, inanimate, nonhuman)
112 sex (female)

120 time
121 age (young)
122 aspect (completive, momentary)
123 tense (present, recent)
124 duration (short, fast)

±   semi-overt contrast (col. 5), mildly productive (col. 6)

−   covert contrast (col. 5), unproductive (col. 6), counterexample (following a number code in col. 4B or 7)

Language	2	3	4A	4B	5	6	7
Acoma							
Agta	p, r			10		?	
Albanian	s			10			
Amharic	s			10			41, 61, 62, 91, 112
Annamese		T	h	20 −		−	
Arabic, Syrian	pattern			10			61
	V		f, h	111	±		
	V		l	20	−	−	
Aranda							
Armenian	s			10			61
		V	a	31	−		32, 81, 82
Asmat	s			10			20, 32, 123
		V	f	112			
		V	hf	20 −	−		
Assiniboine	s			10		?	
Azerbaijani							
Bantu, Southern[3]	p, s, r			10			
Bashkir	s			10			
Basque	s			10			
Bengali	s	V	h	10			112
		V	f	20		±	123
Berber							
Buriat	s			10			62
Canarese		C	t	84			81, 123
		V	l	82	±	±	
		V	h	20	±		
Carayan							

---

[3] Includes examples from Nguni, Shona, Tsonga, and Venda.

Language	2	3	4 A	B	5	6	7
Carib, Island							
Chehalis, Upper		V	l	10		±	31-, 123-
		V	f	20		±	
		C	cd	111-		±	
Cheremis, Eastern		V	f	20		–	
Chichewa							
Chinese	s			10			
Chinook		C	cd,cm,f,g	10			(cf. Wishram)
Chontal, Oaxaca	s			10, 62			
Chukchi	s			10			61
		C	cd	112-			
		C	cm	122			32, 70
Chuvash							
Cocopa	p			10			61
		C	cd	10		±	61
		V	l	31-			
		V	f	20		–	
Cœur d'Alene		C	f,g	10			
Dakota		C	f	42		?	10
	s			10		?	
		V	f	111		–	
Diegueno		C	v	10			
		C	cm	10		–	
Diola-Fogny	p	V	f	10			
		V	t	82-			
	s	V	f	20		–	
Dongolese	s			10			32, 82
Eskimo	s			10			
		C	n	112		?	
		C	f[4]	112		?	10
Estonian	s			10			
		V	f	20		–	
Ewe	s	T	h	10			
		T	h	10			50, 62, 101-3
		T	h	82			
Fula	s			10		–	
		C	cd	111	±		
Gafat	s			10			62
		V	f	20		–	

[4] From Sapir 1915: 190, fn. reference to W. Thalbitzer, A phonetical study of the Eskimo language, Meddelelser om Grønland, v. 31, 178-80, 1904. Source was not available to me.

Language	2	3	4 A	4 B	5	6	7
Gbeya							
Goajiro							
Gola		T	h	10		?	20,32,42-,101,124
Grebo		V	f	10			32,62,111
		V	t	31		±	
		T	h	20		?	
Greek, Lit. Dhimotiki	s	V	f	10			111
Gujarati							
Gunwinggu							
Haitian Creole	p,s			10			
Hawaiian							
Hebrew, Modern	s	V	f	111		–	
Hupa		C	f	122,123			
		C	v	122-,123-			
		C	cd		?		
Indo-European[5]		V	t	84		±	82,92,123
Japanese							
Kabardian		V	t	84		?	82
Kannada		C	t	84		±	81,123
		V	h	20		±	
Karen							
Karok	s	C	cd/f(?)	10			
		C	cd, n	10	±		
Kashaya	p	V	hf	10?		–	?
Khasi		V	f	10		?	50,61,62,91-,121
		V	f	10-		?	41
		V	hf	20		–	
Kikuyu	p			10			
Klamath	s			10			61,124
Koasati		V	n	112	+		
Kolami		V	ʔ	20		±	
Kolh							
Konda		C	n	84			
		V	h	20		±	
Konkow		V	hf	10			
		V	f	20		–	
Korean		V	t	10			62,101
		C	t	42			
Kota		C	t	84			
		V	h	20		±	
Kraho	s			10			

[5] Examples principally from Classical Greek.

Language	2	3	4 A	4 B	5	6	7
Kui		C	t	84			
		V	h	20		±	
Kurdish	s			10			
Kurku							
Kwakiutl	s			10		−	
		C	g, t	10	−		
		C	g	83-	−		
Lamut	s			10			62
Logbara	s	V	n	10		−	
		T	h	31			82,122
		V	h	20			
		V	f	20-		−	
Lutuami							
Maidu	s			10		−	
		V	h	20		−	
Malay							
Malayalam		C	t	84			81,123
		V	l	82	±	±	81
		V	h	20		±	
Maori		V	hf	20		−	
		C	n	20		−	
Marathi							
Mende							
Miwok, So. Sierra	s	C	cd	10			
		C	cd	10		−	
Mongolian, Classical	s			10			
Mongolian, Dagur							
Mongolian, Khalkha	s			10			
Muskogee							
Navaho	s			10			
		V	l	20-		−	
Nez Perce		C	cd, cm	10		?	62, 91(?), 92
		C	f	10-		?	
		V	f	10-		?	
		V	f	20	±	−	
Nimboran							
Nootka	s	C	f	10			61
Ossetic		V	h	20-		−	
Ostyak, Northern	s			10		?	
		V	f	20		−	
Panjabi	s	V	h	111			10, 32
		V	f	20		±	
Pashto	s			10			61, 62

Language	2	3	4 A	4 B	5	6	7
Persian	s			10			61, 62
		V	h	20		±	
Piro	s?	V	f	111-		-	
		V	t	111		±	
Pomo							
Quileute	p	C	f	10			
		C	n	112		±	
Rotuman	s			10			
		V	f	10			31, 70, 122
Rumanian	s	C	cm	10	±		
	s	V	h	10	±		
Russian	s	V	t	111			
	s			10			61, 62
Sahaptin, Northern		C	f, cm	10			
		V	l	10-			
		C	f	20		-	
Salish							
Shona	p, s			10			62, 121
		C	v	10-			
		C	cd	84		±	
		V	a	20		±	
		V	h	20		-	
		V	l	20-		-	
Sino-Tibetan[6]		V	t	84		?	82, 123-
Sotho							
Swahili	p, s			10			62, 111
Tagalog							
Tajik	s			10			41, 61, 62, 82
		V	f	20		±	
Takelma		V	f	84		±	92
		C	g	123, 123-		-	
Tamil		C	t	84			81, 123
		V	l	82	±	±	81
		V	h	20		±	
		C	cm	111		±	
Taos							
Tarascan	s			10		±	61
Tatar	s			10			61
Telugu		C	t	84			81
		V	l	82		±	
		V	h	20		±	

[6] Examples principally from Burmese, Tibetan and Chinese.

Language	2	3	4 A	4 B	5	6	7
Thai		V	f	20		—	
		T	h	82		—	
Tillamook		C	f	10	—	?	111
	r			10		—	
		C	cd	111	±	—	
		V	h	20	±	—	
Toda		C	t	84			
		V	h	20		±	
Tongan		V	f	84			31,70,81,92
		V	h	20		±	92
Totonac	p	C	f, cm	10			
	s	C	f	10			
		C	f	10			
Tsou		V	a	84			
Tswana							
Tulu		C	t	84			81,123
		V	l	82	±	±	81
		V	h	20		±	
Tunica	s			10		?	
Vietnamese							
Vogul	s			10			
		V	h	20		—	
Wappo		C	f, g	10		—	
		C	f	10-		—	
Washo	s			10		—	
Wintu	s			10		—	
		V	f	20		—	
Wishram		C	f, g	10			61,111
		V	h	10	—	—	
	p	C	f	31			10
Wiyot	s	C	cm	10			
		C	f, cm	10			
Wolio	r			10			41
		C	t	84(?)	—	?	122-
Yakut	s			10			61
Yana	s			10		?	
		V	a	84		—	82
		C	n	10		?	
		C	t	112-			
Yokuts							
Yoruba		T	h	42-	±	?	
Yuchi	p	C	n	20		—	123
		C	g	112		—	
		V	n	123-			
		V	f, n	112		—	

Language	2	3	A 4	B	5	6	7
Yurok		C	cm	10		±	
		C	g	20	±	−	
		V	f	20	±	−	
		V	a +1	31-		±	42-, 122
Zapotec, Mitla	s			10	±		61
		T	h	10	±		61
		T	h	20-			
		C	f, t	83(?)		±	
		V	f	84(?)	−	−	

3.2 Semantic distribution of symbolic types

Patterns of distribution are highlighted if we reexamine the symbolic processes in terms of the semantic categories further broken down into formal types. In the following chart, column A contains the semantic code, column B the total number of languages exemplifying the category, and column C the basic ablaut type and formal feature used to express it. Under the heading Languages the first column lists those which are exemplary of the formal feature norms (see Sec. 2.5); the second column lists counterexamples. Languages underlined are those which possess the category only in associated form.

			Languages	
A	B	C	Exemplary	Counterexemplary
10	38	Vf	Diola-Fogny, Grebo, Khasi, Rotuman	Khasi, Nez Perce
		h	Bengali, Panjabi, Rumanian, Wishram	
		hf	Kashaya, Konkow	
		l	Chehalis	Sahaptin
		n	Logbara	
		t	Korean	
		Ccd	Chinook, Cocopa, Karok, Miwok, Nez Perce	
		cm	Chinook, Diegueno, Nez Perce, Rumanian, Sahaptin, Totonac, Wiyot, Yurok	
		f	Chinook, Cœur d'Alene, Dakota, Eskimo, Karok, Nootka, Quileute, Sahaptin, Tillamook, Totonac, Wappo, Wishram, Wiyot	Nez Perce, Wappo

A	B	C	Exemplary	Counterexemplary
10	38	g	Chinook, Cœur d'Alene, Kwakiutl, Wappo, Wishram	
		n	Karok, Yana	
		t	Kwakiutl	
		v	Diegueno	Shona
		Th	Ewe, Gola, Zapotec	
20	46	Va	Shona	
		f	Bengali, Chehalis, Cheremis, Cocopa, Diola-Fogny, Estonian, Gafat, Konkow, Nez Perce, Ostyak, Panjabi, Rotuman, Tajik, Thai, Wintu, Yurok	Logbara
		h	Canarese, Kannada, Kolami, Konda, Kota, Kui, Logbara, Maidu, Malayalam, Persian, Shona, Tamil, Telugu, Tillamook, Toda, Tongan, Tulu, Vogul	Ossetic
		hf	Khasi, Maori	Asmat
		l	Arabic	Navaho, Shona
		Cf	Sahaptin	
		g	Yurok	
		n	Maori	
		Th	Grebo	Annamese, Zapotec
31	9	Va	Armenian	
		a +1		Yurok
		f	Rotuman, Tongan	
		l		Chehalis, Cocopa
		t	Grebo	
		Cf	Wishram	
		Th	Logbara	
32	5	Vf	Grebo	
		a	Armenian	
		h	Panjabi	
		Ccm	Chukchi	
		Th	Gola	
41	1	Vf	Khasi	
42	5	Va+1		Yurok
		Cf	Dakota	
		t	Korean	
		Th		Gola, Yoruba
50	2	Vf	Khasi	
		Th	Ewe	

A	B	C	Exemplary	Counterexemplary
61	6	Vf	Khasi	
		Ccd	Cocopa	
		cm	Nootka	
		f	Nootka, Wishram	
		g	Wishram	
		Th	Zapotec	
62	4	Vf	Grebo, Khasi	
		Ccd	Nez Perce	
		cm	Nez Perce	
		Th	Ewe	

A	B	C	Exemplary	Counterexemplary
70	3	Vf	Rotuman, Tongan	
		Ccm	Chukchi	

A	B	C	Exemplary	Counterexemplary
81	8	Va	Armenian	
		f	Tongan	
		l	Canarese, Malayalam, Tamil, Tulu	
		Ct	Canarese, Kannada, Malayalam, Tamil, Telugu, Tulu	
82	14	Va	Armenian, Yana	
		l	Canarese, Malayalam, Tamil, Telugu, Tulu	
		t	Indo-European, Kabardian, Sino-Tibetan	Diola-Fogny
		Th	Ewe, Logbara, Thai	
83	2	Cf	Zapotec	
		g		Kwakiutl
		t	Zapotec	
84	21	Va	Tsou, Yana	
		f	Takelma, Tongan, Zapotec	
		t	Indo-European, Kabardian, Sino-Tibetan	
		Ccd	Shona	
		f	Zapotec	
		n	Konda	
		t	Canarese, Kannada, Kota, Kui, Malayalam, Tamil, Telugu, Toda, Tulu, Wolio, Zapotec	
91	2	Vf		Khasi
		Ccd	Nez Perce	
92	5	Vf	Rotuman, Takelma, Tongan	
		h	Tongan	

A	B	C	Exemplary	Counterexemplary
92	5	t	Indo-European	
		Ccd	Nez Perce	
		cm	Nez Perce	
101	3	Vt	Korean	
		Th	Ewe, Gola	
102	1	Th	Ewe	
103	1	Th	Ewe	
111	13	Vf	Arabic, Dakota, Grebo, Greek, Hebrew	Piro
		h	Arabic, Panjabi	
		t	Piro, Russian	
		Ccd	Fula, Tillamook	Chehalis
		cm	Tamil	
		f	Tillamook, Wishram	
		g	Wishram	
112	8	Vf	Asmat, Yuchi	
		h	Bengali	
		n	Koasati, Yuchi	
		Ccd		Chukchi
		f	Eskimo	
		g	Yuchi	
		n	Eskimo, Quileute	
		t		Yana
121	1	Vf	Khasi	
122	6	Va+l	Yurok	
		f	Rotuman	
		Ccd	Hupa	
		cm	Chukchi	
		f	Hupa	
		t		Wolio
		v		Hupa
		Th	Logbara	
123	12	Vf	Bengali	
		l		Chehalis
		n		Yuchi
		t	Indo-European	Sino-Tibetan
		Cf	Hupa	
		g	Takelma	Takelma
		n	Yuchi	
		t	Canarese, Kannada, Malayalam, Tamil, Tulu	
		v		Hupa
124	1	Th	Gola	

3.3 Interpretation of data

From the above, it will be noted that size symbolism (10) occurs in 27.3%[7] of the languages sampled, and although AMERICAN INDIAN languages account for 34.5% of the sample, they represent 65.8% of the size-ablauting languages. The peak distribution is in the area of consonant ablaut, particularly fronting and manner of closure. However, with the exception of RUMANIAN and SHONA, the striking fact is that all instances of consonant ablaut are from AMERICAN INDIAN languages, most of them located in the West and Northwest coastal areas of North America. Hence, it would seem that this type of size symbolism is to be explained principally in terms of areal diffusion (see also Haas 1968 and Langdon 1968), rather than as a universal, or even a widespread type. The case for RUMANIAN is somewhat weak. The predominant sibilants, vibrants, and laterals which occur in the numerous diminutive suffixes, as opposed to a recurrence of n and y in the augmentative suffixes, while fitting the American type, do not appear to lend themselves to segmentation in RUMANIAN.

For the remaining types, the distribution is rather thin, but the favored ones are clearly high or high front vowels and high tone. Here there is at least the suggestion of a possible constant. Since high front vowels reflect proportionately higher second formant frequencies, and the higher the tone the higher the natural frequency, there appears to be a correspondence between a feature of high frequency (= short wavelength in physical terms) and the category of small size. It may be argued that this proposal entirely ignores first formant frequencies which, being inversely related to tongue height, would seem to partially negate the second formant effect. As Hockett has pointed out (1955: 200), distinctions of vowel color may be detected, if necessary, on the basis of second formant frequencies alone (but not, presumably, on first formant frequencies only), which perhaps indicates the primary importance of the former. Regarding the apparent discrepancy between high back vowels with second formants lower than low (back) vowels, and the correspondence of the former with diminutive and associated categories, only four of the 27 examples oppose high back to low, the remainder opposing high front to low. Of corollary interest is the importance of consonant fronting or palatalization already noted above for

---

[7] For statistical purposes, BANTU, INDO-EUROPEAN and SINO-TIBETAN are counted as one language each. Any discrepancy which this practice might engender is negligible, affecting only categories of lesser importance.

AMERICAN INDIAN languages. In terms of distinctive feature
analysis, this type could be viewed as an acute-grave contrast,
the acute representing acoustically higher frequency and articulatorily medial position. The limited number of examples, and especially the presence of two counterexamples, unfortunately obscure
the case for fronting of vowels. KHASI presents a bit of a para-
dox in the following pattern: i̲ 'small, light, young,' u̲ 'big, heavy,
old,' a̲ 'ungainly, stout,' but e̲ 'tall, big, grown-up' and o̲ 'small,
feeble,' i.e. a complete reversal of size values for the mid vowels
as opposed to the remaining vowels.

The evidence for more widespread symbolic patterns in dis-
tance-ablauting systems (20) is considerably more satisfactory
than for size. Languages with distance symbolism constitute 33.1%
of the sample. AMERICAN INDIAN and DRAVIDIAN languages
account for a more proportionate 24.1% each of the 46 distance-
ablauting languages. An overwhelming preference is shown for
front or high vowels corresponding to proximity to the speaker.
Typological distribution for front vowels is quite random and the
sole counterexample, LOGBARA, is a dubious one. The demonstratives occur in two paradigms:

	proximal	median	distal
pronouns	dɔ̀	dɪ̀	dà
locative adverbs	dɔ́	dɛ́	dá

From the description (see Crazzolara 1960), the value of ɪ is not
clear; it appears to be somewhere between [ɪ] and [ɨ], but this is
not certain. Comparing the proximal and median sets, LOGBARA
constitutes a counterexample to vowel fronting. But if we contrast
the proximal and median with the distal set, this may be interpreted
as an instance of high vowel symbolism. The case for high vowels
is somewhat impaired by the preponderance of Dravidian (11 of a
total 18). Nevertheless, the remaining languages are randomly
distributed and, compared with formal types other than fronting,
reflect a relatively high frequency of occurrence. OSSETIC remains an exception to this type.

Although examples are few, the general category of quantification (30) appears to be valid. For number symbolism (31) the three
counterexamples are formally represented by vowel-quantity ablaut,
one of the less strongly substantiated types, i.e. there is a reasonable possibility that the marked feature in terms of association
with diminutive symbolism should be short rather than long (cf.

chart, Sec. 3.4). In any event, the sample shows a correlation between singular (or dual-diminutive in WISHRAM) and diminutive. In distributive symbolism (32), diminutive-ablaut types are associated with the following distributional categories in the five languages samples: small quantity of uncountable items (vs. large quantity, see Innes 1966), collectives (Westermann 1921), partitives or special forms of objects (vs. wholes, see Bogoras 1922), accessory elements (vs. main elements of set, see Gill 1963), and particular items (vs. collectives, see Johnson 1954).

From the standpoint of formal patterning, a number of different ablaut types are used to represent affect symbolism (60), but semantically at least two things are worth noting: first, all occurrences come under the heading of associated categories; second, although hypocoristic contrasts with pejorative, both categories are found with the same formal features. Semantically this is not surprising; a small person or thing may readily be regarded in either an affectionate manner (e.g. the conventional attitude of adults toward the young of a species) or a derogatory manner (as small, hence unimportant, petty, worthless, contemptible). Considering these factors, it is obvious that both components, hypocoristic and pejorative, are common metaphorical extensions of diminutives. Indeed, in several languages (e.g. AMHARIC, KHASI, PASHTO, RUSSIAN), the same form may have either hypocoristic or pejorative connotations, depending on context. Augmentatives also may have pejorative, but never hypocoristic, connotations. The sole counterexample to this statement is LAMUT, which has several diminutive and three augmentative suffixes; one of the latter is cited as occurring occasionally with hypocoristic connotations, but the examples seem more diminutive than anything else.

The category of grammatical distance (80) is a sort of potpourri of loosely linked semantic categories, all of which pertain essentially to sentence-internal relationships, more particularly to those which hold between topic and comment. The general formal patterns which correspond to diminutive are often associated with topic or agent focus. Thus, in languages with case systems, the subject or direct case may show diminutive symbolism. In TONGAN the subject of a transitive verb is marked by the particle ʔe, whereas the subject of an intransitive verb or object of a transitive verb, i.e. ergative, is marked by ʔa. Where a change of form class is involved, a noun or pronoun may show diminutive symbolism vis-à-vis a verb or adverb. Compare, for example, one class of substantives derived from adjectives, adverbs, or picture words by a shift of word tone to the high register in EWE: lèbèlèbè 'long, stretched

out' vs. lèbélèbé 'a long part of a cut vegetable.' With the category
of voice, subject orientation (i.e. intransitive, passive) tends to be
associated with diminutive symbolism[8] as in TELUGU aḍaku 'to
press (tr.)' vs. aḍagu ~ aḍaŋgu 'to be contained (intr.).' Modal
symbolism (83) is extremely doubtful, the evidence being contradictory and from only two languages. The argument for case symbolism (81) is better documented but not very convincing in view of
the preponderance of DRAVIDIAN examples. Both form class (82)
and voice (84) symbolism offer more positive evidence, although
they too are weighted in favor of DRAVIDIAN.

The category of person (92), while not particularly well represented, is of interest as an associated category and because of the
regularity with which first person is equated with diminutive (as
in NEZ PERCE) or with intransitive or subject-oriented symbolism.

Gender symbolism (111) appears to be fairly well validated, with
a broad random distribution. Of the two exceptions, CHEHALIS
contrasts masculine t with feminine c in articles and demonstratives. This might be interpreted as a regular instance of palatalization rather than closure. PIRO shows the distinction between
masculine front vowel and feminine back vowel only in the third
singular pronoun. Sex symbolism (112) comprises special female
vs. male speech or agent markers. Since five of the seven languages possessing this category in conjunction with ablaut types are
AMERICAN INDIAN, it can hardly be presumed to be of universal
significance as a grammatical device.

The general category of time (120) constitutes another mixed bag
of related semantic features. Aspect (122) may appear somewhat
anomalous, but since it is often closely associated with tense it has
been included here. Although the particular aspectual categories
associated with symbolic types differ somewhat from language to
language (completive in LOGBARA and ROTUMAN, punctual in HUPA,
momentary in CHUKCHI, and simple vs. interative in YUROK), they
all share the common semantic feature of single action of short
duration as opposed to extended or repeated action. Whereas
there is only one counterexample, three of the five remaining

---

[8] For an interesting theory concerning "introverb-extrovert"
symbolism in KABARDIAN, see A.H. Kuipers 1965; in INDO-
EUROPEAN and SINO-TIBETAN, see Pulleyblank 1965a and b.

languages are AMERINDIAN. The category of tense (123), while
represented by a larger number of languages, is rather unevenly
weighted in favor of DRAVIDIAN (five) and AMERINDIAN (four)
from a total of twelve languages; additional doubt is cast on the
validity of this category by the presence of four counterexamples.

Of the remaining associated categories (41, 42, 50, 70, 91, 101,
102, 103, 121, 124), little can be said due to the paucity of examples.

3.4 Summary distribution of symbolic types

The frequency of occurrence of the various formal types can now
be reduced to summary form as in the chart on the following page.
Counterexamples of individual categories are preceded by a hyphen.

3.5 Distribution of basic ablaut types

The distribution of the Basic Ablaut Types corroborates some
of our earlier findings. Thus, statistics including all semantic
categories show the following distribution:

Basic Ablaut Type	Number of Languages			Total Number of Languages	Percentage of Total Occurrence
	Amer-indian	Dravidian	Other		
V	19	11	31	61	50.2
C	26	10	6	42	41.2
T	1		7	8	8.6

Note: The Percentage of Total Occurrence is based on all specific
instances of symbolic process observed in the sample, or 261 (see
chart below). It is not based on the total number of languages.

Formal Feature	Basic Ablaut Type	Number of Languages/Semantic Category												TOTALS	
		10	20	30	40	50	60	70	80	90	100	110	120	Ex.	-
a	V		1	2					5					8	
a+l	V			-1	-1								1	1	2
cd	C	5					2		1	2		2 -2	1	13	2
cm	C	8					2	1	1	1		1	1	15	0
f	V	4 -2	16 -1	3	1	1	3	2	4	3 -1		7 -1	3	47	5
	C	13 -2	1	1	1	1	2		2	1		3	2	25	2
g	C	5	1				1		-1			2	1 -1	10	2
h	V	4	18 -1	1						1		3		27	1
	T	3	1 -2	2	-2		2		3		4		2	18	4
hf	V	2	2 -1											4	1
l	V	1 -1	1 -2	-2					9				-1	11	6
n	V	1	1									2	-1	3	1
	C	2							1			2		7	0
t	V	1							6 -1	1	1	2	1 -1	13	2
	C	1			1				18			-1	5 -1	25	2
v	C	1 -1											-2	1	3
TOTALS		51 -6	42 -7	11 -3	3 -3	2	12	3	49 -2	8 -1	5	24 -4	18 -7	228	33

4. Conclusions

It is easy to see why any kind of sound symbolism must always
be of a peripheral nature. If it were not, the extremely limited
number of contrastive phonological features available in any language would hardly suffice to represent the enormous complexity
of all the semantic distinctions necessary in human communication.
Nevertheless, the basic and inescapable principle of the arbitrariness of language symbols is neither absolute nor inviolable. A
glance at the totals in the Summary Distribution chart will show
that only 14.5% of all recorded instances of patterned symbolism
run counter to the basic hypotheses (see Sec. 1.2). Even if we consider only the two most important categories, we come up with the
comparable figures of 11.8% for size and 16.7% for distance-sym-
bolism, neither of which can be regarded as a purely arbitrary use
of symbols.

However, a number of formal ablaut types and associated semantic categories are of doubtful validity with regard to sound symbolism.
Some are simply rare or represented so inadequately in the sample
that their value is indeterminate, e.g. nasalization of vowels (Vn)
or weak force (41); others may be sufficiently well exemplified but
have a typologically skewed distribution, e.g. close consonantism
(Ccd), for which 12 or 13 positive examples are from North AMERI-
CAN INDIAN languages, or direct case (81) with 10 or 12 examples
from DRAVIDIAN languages; still other formal ablaut types represent solely the associated categories, e.g. apex vocalism (Va), or
include only one case of diminutive symbolism, e.g. voicing of consonants (Cv).

Insufficient examples force us to suspend judgment on the relevance of the formal types: nasalization of vowels (Vn) and voicing
of consonants (Cv), and of the semantic categories: weak voice (41),
low intensity (42), light weight (50), definite (70), nontentative mode
(83), consanguineal relation (91), sweet or good (101), smooth (102),
high pitch (103), young (121), short duration (124).

Of dubious relevance for sound symbolism on a global scale, but
not necessarily on a local scale, are the distributionally skewed
features and categories. Perhaps these should be viewed as falling
into two different source types: genetically related and areally related. Hence the formal features of vowel length (Vl) and lenis consonantism (Ct), and the semantic category of direct case (81) are
suspect because most of the examples cited to support them are
from DRAVIDIAN. Similarly, half the examples of apex vocalism

(Va) are from ARMENIAN. Those which are suspect because the
bulk of examples come from North AMERICAN INDIAN languages
are the formal features: close consonantism (Ccd), manner of closure (Ccm), fronting of consonants (Cf), and glottalization of consonants (Cg), and the semantic categories: hypocoristic (61) and
completive aspect (122). Suspect because of a combination of genetic
and areal overweighting are nasalization of consonants (Cn) and the
semantic categories female (112) and present tense (123). Formal
features not used for diminutive symbolism, or restricted to one
example, are: apex vocalism, lenis consonantism, and voicing of
consonants.

Since the last-named features are also suspect either through
paucity of examples or skewed distribution, they must be regarded
as very doubtful indeed, as must also the semantic categories for
which there are too few examples. Discounting these, we are left
with two classes each of formal features and semantic categories
based upon the criteria for validity noted above: those which appear
to be valid but limited in global distribution (at least in terms of the
present sample) and therefore of little if any value in predicating
universal or general statements on diminutive symbolism, and those
which do not appear to be so limited, hence useful in generalizing.
The latter are the formal features: vowel fronting (Vf), vowel raising (Vh), both fronting and raising (Vhf), lax vocalism (Vt), and
raising of tone (Th), and the semantic categories: diminutive (10),
proximal (20), singular (31), individual distribution (32), pejorative
(62), nominal/pronominal (82), intransitive/passive (84), first person (92), and feminine gender (111). Of these, lax vocalism and
intransitive/passive are very nearly distributionally skewed.

Reverting now to the original hypotheses proposed in Sec. 1.1,
does the evidence support them? Ablaut types which figure as
marked features representing diminutive (hypothesis 1) are glottalization of consonants, voicing of consonants, nasalization of both
consonants and vowels, and vowel lengthening. The remaining phonological features associated with diminutivism -- fronting of vowels
or consonants, high or high front vowels, vocalic or consonantal
tension (and, associated with the latter, degree of closure), high
tone, and manner of closure -- could not for the most part be evaluated in terms of markedness due to lack of descriptive data on
such factors as distributional range and frequency of occurrence,
which are important criteria for determining markedness. However, in the case of two very important symbolic types, fronting
and raising of vowels, it is notable that most languages have more
front vowels than back and, similarly, many languages have a

greater number of high vowels than low. Since one of the characteristics distinguishing a marked feature is the fact that it belongs to
a class with membership less than or equal to that containing the
opposing unmarked feature (cf. Greenberg 1966: 70), vocalic frontness and height would generally appear to be unmarked, in which
case we have unmarked phonological features representing the
marked morphological category of diminutive. Of course, viewed
on the subphonemic level, the actual total of allophonic variants
may be greater for the set of low vowels, for example, than for
high, thus indicating that the latter are to be regarded as marked
(at least on the basis of the class-membership criterion.)

Glottalization conforms to the hypothesis but, as noted, is confined to AMERINDIAN languages. The evidence for voicing is extremely limited and negative. Vowel length is characteristized by
skewed distribution and a disproportionate number of contradictory
cases. As for nasalization: of vowels, the examples are few; of
consonants, the distribution is skewed. Thus the relevance of
marked phonological features for diminutive symbolism remains
inconclusive.

For hypothesis 2, both front and high vowels, also high front,
do represent diminutive, but the examples are few.

Hypothesis 3 is substantially confirmed, fronting of consonants
being statistically the most important type of diminutive symbolism
but, since it is evinced solely by AMERINDIAN languages, it does
not appear to be a general type.

Of the remaining features employed in size symbolism, but not
included in the original hypotheses, the consonantal features of
manner and degree of closure are moderately and consistently
represented, but only in AMERINDIAN languages. Lenis consonantism, i.e. voiced or lenis stops and/or nasals corresponding
to diminutive, and lax or open vocalism, are uniquely represented;
apex vocalism does not occur at all in diminutive symbolism. High
tone corresponds regularly to diminutive, but examples are few.

Thus, although the actual number of languages exhibiting size
symbolism is low in terms of the total number sampled (38 or 136),
formal agreement with the earlier-stated hypotheses is high (88.2%).
Furthermore, when we admit some of the better-substantiated associated categories, particularly distance symbolism, the evidence
permits us to make a few general statements on the validity of patterned symbolic processes:

1. Vowel ablaut has the highest frequency of occurrence and
    the most random language distribution both geographically
    and genetically.

2. Front vowels predominantly correspond to diminutive and
    associated categories, high vowels are next in importance,
    and the remaining vocalic types encountered in this study --
    long, lax, apex, high front, and nasalized -- are of indeter-
    minate relevance as universal tendencies due to nonrandom
    distribution and/or low frequency of occurrence.

3. High or rising tone corresponding to diminutive et al. may
    prove to be a general type of diminutive symbolism but this
    remains inconclusive, due to low frequency of occurrence.
    This is probably a natural consequence of the proportion-
    ately smaller number of languages which make any extensive
    use of tone for derivational purposes.

4. Consonant ablaut in general must be discounted as a complex
    of universal types due to its extremely localized distribution,
    although certain types, notably fronting, lenition, manner
    and degree of closure, and glottalization, are fairly frequent
    in the sample.

Some interesting comparisons may be made between Greenberg's
marked grammatical and semantic categories (Greenberg, 1966: 74-
103) and the relationship of the associated categories to diminutive:

Diminutive and associated categories	Greenberg's marked categories
diminutive	diminutive
feminine, neuter	feminine, neuter (more marked of two)
nonhuman, inanimate	inanimate
first person	first, second (more marked)
intransitive, passive	passive, medio-passive
young	young (kin)

but:

singular, dual (rare)	plural, dual (more marked)
direct case	oblique case
present	past, future (more marked)
consanguineal	affinal

All the examples of direct case except ARMENIAN and TONGAN
are from DRAVIDIAN.   Present tense is subject to a   similar

distributional limitation: five examples from DRAVIDIAN, seven from AMERINDIAN, and three others. Consanguineal is supported by examples from KHASI and NEZ PERCE only, and there is some doubt as to inclusion of the latter. Thus the only important disagreement lies in the area of number. If diminutive and the valid associated categories can all be viewed as marked, then we have another reason for admitting the associated categories.

5. Appendix on Size Affixes

In the course of research for this study, a large number and variety of diminutive and augmentative affixes were also noted. Although in general clearly peripheral to the purpose of this paper, some of these affixes show traces (perhaps submorphemic) of sound symbolism and many of them lend additional support to the acceptability of the associated categories, inasmuch as they show the same or similar semantic fields. Of general interest is the fact that 65 languages, 46% of the sample, were described as having size affixes, 64 with diminutives and 28 with augmentatives.

The chart below gives an approximate idea of the incidence of various vocalic and consonantal types in size affixes. The only occurrences of rounded vowels were back, and these were always rounded. The geographical distribution for all types except the most infrequent (hence indeterminate) was reasonably random. The formal types are given in descending order from the highest frequency of occurrence in diminutive affixes to the lowest. The figures represent the total number of languages which illustrate a particular combination of formal and semantic features.

	Diminutive	Augmentative
Vowels		
low central	25	13
high front	19	8
low front	17	2
high back	13	7
low back	7	5
mid central	3	1
Consonants		
velars (including h)	29	14
sibilants	23	7
dentals (or alveolars)	15	8
nasals	15	8
laterals	7	1
labials	6	2
vibrants	5	2
y	3	3

Generally speaking, the figures in the two columns are proportionate to one another, given the discrepancy in frequency of occurrence between the two kinds of affixes. For the vowels, with the
exception of low front, the distributions are roughly parallel; for
the consonants, the sibilants constitute the major exception, the
laterals a lesser exception, and possibly y. The disproportionate
frequency of low front in diminutives may conceivably be related
to the predominance of front vowels (sometimes low) in diminutive
symbolism. On the other hand, the preponderance of low central
vowels in both diminutive and augmentative affixes is quite unrelated to diminutive symbolism and appears to reflect the generally
higher frequency of occurrence of such vowels in most languages.
For the consonants, the disproportion in sibilant frequencies may
be related to consonant fronting, and is noteworthy because its
random distribution among the affixes may possibly indicate more
widespread distribution of fronting than shown by diminutive symbolism. The same may be said of the laterals, but to a lesser
degree. With the exceptions noted, there seems to be no reason
to suppose that the size affixes sampled are formally other than
arbitrary.

BIBLIOGRAPHY

Abaev, V.I. 1964. A grammatical sketch of Ossetic. IJAL Pub. 35.

Agard, F.B. 1958. Structural sketch of Rumanian. Language
    Monograph 26.

Aginsky, Ethel. 1935. Mende grammar. Language Dissertation 20.

Anceaux, J.C. 1952. The Wolio language. Verhandelingen van het
    Koninklijk Instituut voor Taal-, Land-, en Volkenkunde 11.
    s'Gravenhage: Nijhoff.

_____. 1965. The Nimboran language. Verhandelingen van het
    Kon. Inst. voor Taal-, Land-, en Volkenkunde 44. s'Graven-
    hage: Nijhoff.

Aoki, Haruo. 1965. Nez Perce grammar. Doctoral dissertation,
    University of California, Berkeley.

Armbruster, Charles Hubert. 1960. Dongolese Nubian, a gram-
    mar. London: Cambridge University Press.

Ashton, E.O. 1964. Swahili grammar. 2nd ed. London.

Bamgboṣe, A. 1966. A grammar of Yoruba. (West African Language Monographs 5) London: Cambridge University Press.

Barker, M.A.R. 1964. Klamath grammar. University of California Publication in Linguistics 32. Berkeley and Los Angeles.

Barlow, A.R. 1960. Studies in Kikuyu grammar and idiom. Edinburgh.

Basset, André. 1952. La langue berbère. Handbook of African Languages. London: Oxford University Press.

Benzing, Johannes. 1955. Lamutische Grammatik. Akad. der Wissenschaften und der Literatur, Veröffentlichungen der Orientalischen Kommission 6. Wiesbaden: Steiner.

Berlin, Brent. 1960. Sketch of Totonac. MS.

Boas, Franz. 1900. Sketch of the Kwakiutl language. American Anthropologist 2. 708-21.

_____. 1911. Introduction; Kwakiutl; Chinook. Handbook of American Indian languages. Bureau of American Ethnology Bulletin 40, Part 1. 79, 423-558, 559-677. Washington, D.C.

_____ and John R. Swanton. 1922. Siouan (Dakota). Handbook of American Indian languages. BAE Bulletin 40, Part 1. 875-966. Washington, D.C.

_____ and Ella Deloria. 1933. Notes on the Dakota, Teton dialect. IJAL 7. 97-121.

Bogoras, W. 1922. Chukchee. Handbook of American Indian languages. BAE Bulletin 40, Part 2. 631-903. Washington, D.C.

Böhtlingk, O. 1964. Über die Sprache der Jakuten. Indiana University Publications, Uralic and Altaic Series 35. Bloomington, Ind.

Bowen, J. Donald (ed.) 1965. Beginning Tagalog. Berkeley: University of California Press.

Briggs, Elinor. 1961. Mitla Zapotec grammar. Instituto Lingüístico de Verano. Mexico.

Bright, William. 1957. The Karok language. University of
California Publication in Linguistics 13. Berkeley and Los
Angeles.

Broadbent, Sylvia. 1964. The Southern Sierra Miwok language.
University of California Publication in Linguistics 38. Berkeley
and Los Angeles.

Brown, Roger. 1963. Words and things. New York: Free Press,
3rd ed.

Caldwell, R. 1875. A comparative grammar of the Dravidian or
South-Indian family of languages. London.

Cardona, George. 1965. A Gujarati reference grammar. Philadelphia: University of Pennsylvania Press.

Chamberlain, A.F. 1912. Women's languages. American Anthropologist 14. 579-81.

Chao, Y.R. 1965. A grammar of spoken Chinese. Berkeley:
University of California Press.

Chastaing, Maxime. 1958. Le symbolisme des voyelles. Signif-
ications des 'i.' I. Symboles de cris et de mouvements. II.
Symboles d'acuité et de petitesse. J. de Psychologie 55. 403-
23, 461-81.

Churchward, C. Maxwell. 1940. Rotuman grammar and dictionary.
Sydney: Australasian Medical Publishing Company.

Cohen, Marcel. 1936. Traité de la langue amharique. Travaux et
Mémoires de l'Institut d'Ethnologie 24. Paris.

Cole, Desmond T. 1955. Introduction to Tswana grammar.
London: Longmans, Green.

Conklin, Harold C. 1956. Tagalog speech disguise. Language 32.
136-9.

Cowell, Mark W. 1964. A reference grammar of Syrian Arabic
(Damascus dialect). Washington, D.C.: Georgetown University
Press.

Crawford, James M. 1966. The Cocopa language. Doctoral dissertation, University of California, Berkeley.

Crazzolara, J.P. 1960. A study of the Logbara (Ma'adi) language. London: Oxford.

De Angulo, Jaime and L.S. Freeland. 1931. The Lutuami language. J. de la Société des Américanistes de Paris 23. 1-45.

Doke, C.M. 1954. The Southern Bantu languages. Handbook of African Languages. London: Oxford University Press.

Drake, J. 1903. A grammar of the Kurku language. Calcutta.

Dyk, Walter. 1938. A grammar of Wishram. Doctoral dissertation, Yale University.

Eberhardt, M. 1940. A study of phonetic symbolism of deaf children. Psychological Monographs 52. 23-42.

Edel, May M. 1939. The Tillamook language. IJAL 10. 1-57.

Elbert, Samuel H. 1963. Conversational Hawaiian. Honolulu.

Emeneau, Murray B. 1944. Kota texts, part 1. University of California Publication in Linguistics 2, no. 1.

_____. 1951. Studies in Vietnamese grammar (Annamese). University of California Publication in Linguistics 8.

_____. 1955. Kolami: A Dravidian language. University of California Publication in Linguistics 12.

Fónagy, Ivan. 1961. Communication in poetry. Word 17. 194-218.

_____. 1963. Die Metaphern in der Phonetik. Janua Linguarum, ser. minor 25. The Hague: Mouton.

Forbes, Nevill. 1964. Russian grammar. Oxford, 3rd ed.

Fortune, G. 1955. An analytical grammar of Shona. London: Longmans, Green.

Foster, Mary. 1965. The Tarascan language. Doctoral dissertation, University of California, Berkeley.

Frachtenberg, Leo J. 1917. Abnormal types of speech in Quileute. IJAL 1. 295-9.

Gill, Harjeet Singh and H.A. Gleason, Jr. 1963. A reference
grammar of Panjabi. Hartford Studies in Linguistics 3. Hartford: Hartford Seminary Foundation.

Goddard, Pliny E. 1911. Athabascan (Hupa). Handbook of American
Indian languages, BAE Bulletin 40, Part 1. 85-158. Washington,
D.C.

Greenberg, Joseph H. 1966. Language universals. Current trends
in linguistics, III, Theoretical foundations, ed. by T.A. Sebeok,
61-112. The Hague: Mouton.

Grønbech, Kaare and John R. Krueger. 1955. An introduction to
Classical (Literary) Mongolian. Wiesbaden: Harrassowitz.

Haas, Mary R. 1940. Ablaut and its function in Muskogee. IJAL
16. 141-50.

_____. 1941. Tunica. Handbook of American Indian languages,
Part 4. 1-143. New York: J.J. Augustin.

_____. 1944. Men's and women's speech in Koasati. Lg. 20.
142-9.

_____. 1957. Thai word games. J. of American Folklore 70.17

_____. 1968. Consonant symbolism in northwestern California:
A problem in diffusion. University of California, Berkeley, MS.

Haeberlin, Hermann K. 1917. Types of reduplication in the Salish
dialects. IJAL 1. 154-74.

Haguenauer, Charles. 1951. Morphologie du japonais moderne.
Paris: Klincksieck.

Hall, Robert A. Jr., with the collaboration of Suzanne Comhaire-
Sylvain, H. Ormonde McConnell and Alfred Métraux. 1953.
Haitian Creole: Grammar, texts, vocabulary. American An-
thropological Association Memoir 74.

Harms, Robert T. 1962. Estonian grammar. Indiana University
Publications, Uralic and Altaic Series 12. Bloomington, Ind.

Harper, W.R. 1959. Elements of Hebrew by an inductive method.
Chicago: University of Chicago Press.

Healey, Phyllis M. 1960. An Agta grammar. Summer Institute of Linguistics. Manila: Republic of the Philippines Burea of Printing.

Hockett, C.F. 1955. A manual of phonology. Baltimore.

Hohepa, Patrick W. 1967. A profile generative grammar of Maori. IJAL 28.2, Pub. 20.

Householder, Fred W. Jr. 1962. Azerbaijani onomatopes. American Studies in Linguistics, ed. by Nicholas Poppe. Indiana University Publications, Uralic and Altaic Series 13. 115. Bloomington, Ind.

_____. Kostas Kazazis and Andreas Koutsoudas. 1964. Reference grammar of Literary Dhimotiki. IJAL 30.2, Pub. 31.

Innes, Gordon. 1966. An introduction to Grebo. School of Oriental and African Studies, University of London. The Hague.

Jacobs, M. 1931. A sketch of Northern Sahaptin grammar. University of Washington Publications in Anthropology 4. 85-292. Seattle.

_____. 1954. The areal spread of sound features in the languages north of California. University of California Publication in Linguistics 10. Berkeley and Los Angeles.

Jacobsen, William. 1964. A grammar of the Washo language. Doctoral dissertation, University of California, Berkeley.

Jespersen, Otto. 1922 (reprinted 1934). Language: Its nature, development and origin. London.

Johnson, Emma. 1954. Studies in East Armenian grammar. Doctoral dissertation, University of California, Berkeley.

Jones, Robert B. Jr. 1961. Karen linguistic studies. University of California Publication in Linguistics 25. Berkeley and Los Angeles.

Kähler, Hans. 1965. Grammatik der Bahasa-Indonésia. Wiesbaden.

Kálmán, Béla. 1965. Vogul chrestomathy. Indiana University Publications, Uralic and Altaic Series 46. Bloomington, Ind.

Kaufman, Terrence. 1967. Totonac lexical sets involving consonant symbolism. MS.

Kavadi, Naresh B. and F.C. Southworth. 1965. Spoken Marathi.
Philadelphia.

Kim, Chin-W. 1965. On the autonomy of the tensity feature in
stop classification. Word 21. 339-59.

Kinkade, M. Dale. 1964. Phonology and morphology of Upper
Chehalis: IV. IJAL 30. 251-60.

_____. 1966. Vowel alternation in Upper Chehalis. IJAL 32.343-9.

Koutsoudas, Andreas. 1962. Verb morphology of Modern Greek.
IJAL 28.4, Pub. 24.

Krishnamurti, Bhadriraju. 1961. Telugu verbal bases. University
of California Publication in Linguistics 24. Berkeley.

Kroeber, A.L. 1907a. The Yokuts language of south central California. University of California Publications in Anthropology,
Archeology and Ethnology 2. 165-377. Berkeley and Los Angeles.

_____. 1907b. The Washo language. University of California
Publications in Anthropology, Archeology and Ethnology 4. 251-
318. Berkeley and Los Angeles.

Krueger, John R. 1961. Chuvash manual. Indiana University
Publications, Uralic and Altaic Series 7. Bloomington, Ind.

Kuiper, F.B.J. 1948. Proto-Munda words in Sanskrit. Verhandelingen der Koninklijke Nederlandsche Akademie van Wetenschap-
pen, afdeeling Letterkunde 51.3. Amsterdam: Noord-Hollandsche
Uitgevers Mij.

_____. 1965. Consonant variation in Munda. Lingua 14. 54-87.

Kuipers, Aert H. 1965. Phoneme and morpheme in Kabardian
(Eastern Adyghe). Janua Linguarum 8. 's-Gravenhage: Mouton.

Kunene, D.P. 1965. The ideophone in Southern Sotho. J. of African
Languages 4. 19-39.

Landar, Herbert Jay. 1963. Navaho syntax. Language Dissertation 57 (Lg. 39.3).

Langdon, Margaret. 1966. A grammar of Dieguéño: the Mesa Grande dialect. Doctoral dissertation, University of California, Berkeley.

_____. 1968. Sound symbolism in Yuman languages. University of California, San Diego, MS.

Lehmann, W.P. and Lloyd Faust. 1951. A grammar of formal written Japanese. Harvard-Yenching Institute Studies 5. Cambridge: Harvard University Press.

Leslau, Wolf. 1956. Etude descriptive et comparative du Gafat (éthiopien méridional). Collection linguistique de la Société de Linguistique de Paris 57. Paris: Klincksieck.

Le-van-ly. 1948. Le parler vietnamien. Huong Anh. Paris.

Levin, Norman Balfour. 1964. The Assiniboine language. IJAL 30.3, Pub. 32.

Lisker, Leigh. 1963. Introduction to spoken Telugu. American Council of Learned Societies. New York.

Martin, Samuel E. 1962. Phonetic symbolism in Korean. American studies in Altaic linguistics, ed. by Nicholas Poppe, 177-89. Indiana University Publications, Uralic and Altaic Series 13. Bloomington, Ind.

Matteson, Esther. 1965. The Piro (Arawakan) language. University of California Publication in Linguistics 42. Berkeley and Los Angeles.

McLendon, Sally. 1966. The Eastern Pomo language. Doctoral dissertation, University of California, Berkeley.

Miller, Wick R. 1965. Acoma grammar and texts. University of California Publication in Linguistics 40. Berkeley and Los Angeles.

Newman, Stanley. 1933. Further experiments on phonetic symbolism. American Journal of Psychology 45. 53-75.

_____. 1946. The Yawelmani dialect of Yokuts. Linguistic structures of native America, ed. by Cornelius Osgood.

Newmark, Leonard. 1957. Structural grammar of Albanian. IJAL 23.4, Pub. 4.

Noble, G. Kingsley. 1965. Sketch of Goajiro. Proto-Arawakan and its descendants, 14-20. IJAL 31.3, Pub. 38.

Noss, Richard B. 1964. Thai reference grammar. Washington, D.C.: Foreign Service Institute, Department of State.

Nottrott, A. 1882. Grammatik der Kolh-Sprache. Gütersloh.

Oates, Lynette Frances. 1964. A tentative description of the Gunwinggu language (of Western Arnhem Land). Oceania Linguistic Monograph 10. Sydney: University of Sydney.

Obolensky, Serge, Z. Debebow and M. Andualem. 1964. Amharic, basic course. Washington, D.C.: Foreign Service Institute, Department of State.

Oswalt, Robert Louis. 1961. A Kashaya grammar (Southwestern Pomo). Doctoral dissertation, Univ. of California, Berkeley.

Pekmezi, G. 1908. Grammatik der albanesischen Sprache, Laut- und Formenlehre. Wien.

Pitkin, Harvey. 1963. The Wintu language. Doctoral dissertation, Univ. of California, Berkeley.

Poppe, Nicholas. 1951. Khalkha-mongolische Grammatik. Akademie der Wissenschaften und der Literatur. Wiesbaden: Steiner.

_____. 1954. Grammar of written Mongolian. Wiesbaden: Harrassowitz.

_____. 1963. Tatar manual. Indiana University Publications, Uralic and Altaic Series 25. Bloomington, Ind.

_____. 1964. Bashkir manual. Indiana University Publications, Uralic and Altaic Series 36. Bloomington, Ind.

Pulleyblank, E.G. 1965a. The Indo-European vowel system and the qualitative ablaut. Word 21. 86-101.

_____. 1965b. Close/open ablaut in Sino-Tibetan. Lingua 14. 230-40.

Rabel, Lili. 1961. Khasi, a language of Assam. Louisiana State University Studies, Humanities Series 10. Baton Rouge: Louisiana State University Press.

Radin, P. 1929. Grammar of the Wappo language. Univ. of California Pub. in Anthropology, Archeology, and Ethnology 27. 1-194. Berkeley and Los Angeles.

Rastorgueva, V.S. 1963. A short sketch of Tajik grammar. IJAL 29.4, Pub. 28.

_____. 1964. A short sketch of the grammar of Persian. IJAL 30.1, Pub. 29.

Ray, P.S., M. Hai and L. Ray. 1966. Bengali language handbook. Center for Applied Linguistics. Washington, D.C.

Rédei, Károly. 1965. Northern Ostyak chrestomathy. Indiana Univ. Publications, Uralic and Altaic Series 47. Bloomington, Ind.

Reichard, Gladys A. 1938. Cœur d'Alene. Handbook of American Indian languages. BAE Bulletin 40, Part 3, 515-707. Washington, D.C.

_____. 1945. Composition and symbolism of Cœur d'Alene verb stems. IJAL 11. 47-63.

_____. 1951. Navaho grammar. American Ethnological Society 21. New York: Augustin.

_____. 1925. Wiyot grammar and texts. Univ. of California Pub. in Anthropology, Archeology, and Ethnology 22. Berkeley and Los Angeles.

Robins, R.H. 1958. The Yurok language. University of California Publication in Linguistics 15. Berkeley and Los Angeles.

Rosén, Haim B. 1962, 1966. A textbook of Israeli Hebrew. Chicago: University of Chicago Press.

Samarin, William J. 1966. The Gbeya language. Univ. of California Publication in Linguistics 44. Berkeley and Los Angeles.

Sapir, Edward. 1911a. Diminutive and augmentative consonant

symbolism in Wishram. Handbook of American Indian languages. BAE Bulletin 40, Part 1. 638-46. Washington, D.C.

_____. 1911 b. Some aspects of Nootka language and culture. American Anthropologist 13. 15-28.

_____. 1922. Takelma. Handbook of American Indian languages. BAE Bulletin 40, Part 2. 1-296. Washington, D.C.

_____. 1934. Nootka baby words. IJAL 5. 118-9.

_____. 1958a. Abnormal types of speech in Nootka; male and female forms of speech in Yana. Selected writing of Edward Sapir, ed. by David G. Mandelbaum, 179-96; 206-12.

_____. 1958b. A study in phonetic symbolism. Selected writings of Edward Sapir, ed. by David G. Mandelbaum, 61-72. Berkeley: University of California Press.

_____ and Morris Swadesh. 1960. Yana dictionary, ed. by Mary R. Haas. Univ. of California Publication in Linguistics 22. Berkeley and Los Angeles.

Sapir, J. David. 1965. A grammar of Diola-Fogny. West African Language Monograph Series 3. London: Cambridge Univ. Press.

Senn, Alfred. 1966. Handbuch der litauischen Sprache. Heidelberg.

Shafeev, D.A. 1964. A short grammatical outline of Pashto. IJAL 30. 3, Pub. 33.

Shell, Olive. 1952. Grammatical outline of Kraho (Ge family). IJAL 18. 115-29.

Shipley, William F. 1964. Maidu grammar. Univ. of California Publication in Linguistics 41. Berkeley and Los Angeles.

Sloane, E.B. 1913. Grammar of the Kurmanji or Kurdish language. London.

Steuernagel, Carl. 1962. Hebräische Grammatik. Lehrbücher für das Studium der orientalischen Sprachen 5. Leipzig: Verlag Enzyklopädie.

Strehlow, T.G.H. (Orig. pub. 1942-4) Aranda phonetics and grammar. Oceania Linguistic Monographs 7. Sydney: Univ. of Sydney.

Swadesh, Morris. 1944. South Greenlandic. Linguistic structures of native America, ed. by C. Osgood, 30-54. Viking Fund Publications in Anthropology 6. (New York: Johnson Reprint Co., 1963, 1965.)

Taylor, Douglas. 1952. The principal grammatical formatives of Island Carib. IJAL 18. 150-65.

_____. 1956. Island Carib, II: word-classes, affixes, nouns and verbs. IJAL 22. 1-44.

Teeter, Karl V. 1959. Consonant harmony in Wiyot. IJAL 25. 41-3.

_____. 1964. The Wiyot language. Univ. of California Publication in Linguistics 37. Berkeley and Los Angeles.

Thalbitzer, William. 1911. Eskimo. Handbook of American Indian languages. BAE Bulletin 40, Part 1. 967-1069. Washington, D.C.

Trager, George. 1960. Taos, III: paralanguage. Anthropological Linguistics 2. 24-30.

Tucker, A.N., Margaret A. Bryan and Wolf Leslau. 1966. Linguistic analyses of the non-Bantu languages of northeast Africa with a supplement on the Ethiopic languages. Handbook of African Languages. London: Oxford University Press.

Tung, T'ung-ho. 1964. A descriptive study of the Tsou language (Taiwan). Bulletin of the Institute of History and Philology, Academia Sinica 48. Taipei.

Ultan, Russell. 1967. Konkow grammar. Doctoral dissertation, University of California, Berkeley.

Voorhoeve, C.L. 1965. The Flamingo Bay dialect of the Asmat language. 's-Gravenhage.

Wagner, G. 1934. Yuchi. Handbook of American Indian languages, Part 3. 295-384. New York: Augustin.

Waterhouse, Viola. 1962. The grammatical structure of Oaxaca Chontal. IJAL 28.2, Pub. 19.

Watkins, Mark H. 1937. Chichewa grammar. Language Dissertation 24.

Westermann, Dietrich. 1921. Die Gola-Sprache in Liberia. Ham.-burgische Universität, Abhandlung aus dem Gebiet der Auslands-kunde 6. Hamburg.

————. 1930. A study of the Ewe language. London: Oxford Univ. Press.

Winstedt, R.O. 1927. Malay grammar. Oxford, 2nd ed.

Wissemann, Heinz. 1954. Untersuchungen zur Onomatopoiie. I. Die sprachpsychologischen Versuche. Heidelberg: Carl Winter.

Zamarripa y Uraga, P. 1955. Gramática Vasca. 7th ed. Bilbao.

Index of Languages

Index of Authors Cited